MUSLIMS IN THE ENLARGED EUROPE

MUSLIM MINORITIES

EDITORS

Jørgen S. Nielsen (University of Birmingham)
Felice Dassetto (University of Louvain-la-Neuve)
Amira Sonbol (Georgetown University, Washington, DC)

VOLUME 2

MUSLIMS IN THE ENLARGED EUROPE

Religion and Society

EDITED BY

BRIGITTE MARÉCHAL, STEFANO ALLIEVI
FELICE DASSETTO, JØRGEN NIELSEN

BRILL
LEIDEN · BOSTON
2003

This book is printed on acid-free paper.

Library of Congress Cataloging-in-Publication Data

Muslims in the enlarged Europe : religion and society / edited by Brigitte
   Maréchal … [et al.].
     p. cm. — (Muslim minorities, ISSN 1570-7571 ; v. 2)
   Includes bibliographical references and indexes.
   ISBN 90-04-13201-5
     1. Muslims—Europe. 2. Islam—Europe. 3. Muslims—Cultural assimilation—
   Europe. 4. Europe—Ethnic relations. 5. Culture conflict—Europe. I. Maréchal,
   Brigitte. II. Series.

D1056.2.M87M864 2003
305.6'97104'09049—dc21

                                                                    2003049569

ISSN   1570-7571
ISBN   90 04 13201 5

CONTENTS

PART TWO

THE STATE AND LEGAL SYSTEMS WITH REGARD TO ISLAM

PART THREE

ISLAM AND SOCIETY:
PUBLIC SPACE AND INTEGRATION

FOREWORD

The history of humanity and of civilisations has been shaped by exchanges—of symbols or of goods—which human beings have engaged in through commerce, voyages, and the diffusion of cultural products of all sorts. This history has been shaped equally through connections between human beings, created through exogamous marriages, armed conquests, and movements of populations trying to gain access to a better quality of life or other goods. Since the 19th century, one of the most important ways in which populations interpenetrate each other is through movements of people looking for work, movements which have come to be called 'migrations'.

The 19th century and the first half of the 20th saw the great movement of migrants to the Americas from Southeast Asia and Africa, as well as other migrations such as those which left China and Japan bound for the Americas, those which left the Indian peninsula for Africa, and migrations within Russia toward the eastern part of that country, beyond the Urals.

Europe in the second half of the 20th century saw that which the French demographer Alfred Sauvy has called "the great secular turning-point of migrations". During this period, Europe was no longer the space that people leave, in order to populate the rest of the world, but rather became a destination and a stopping place. Following the Second World War and the division of the world into the Western and communist camps, a relocation of populations toward Europe took place, first from the east toward Northern Europe, and later from Southern Europe—Italy, Spain, Portugal, Greece—toward the north.

Something quite new began to appear toward the end of the 1950s, following the post-war European economic recovery. This consisted in the arrival in Europe, in significant numbers, of non-European immigrants, the result of the European economy's need for workers, who had been recruited for this reason. These populations arrived from former colonial territories, and from countries within the sphere of influence of various European powers. A significant number of them came from Muslim countries in Africa or Asia.

Thus began, by means of migration of workers, an extraordinary series of changes. On one hand, Europe, for the first time in its modern history, became the destination of millions of people who were not of European origin. On the other hand, the Islamic world and the Western European world encountered each other as never before, in many ways. There had been contact throughout history, and this contact had had an influence on the history of both worlds. But quite often those contacts were simply conflictual, even if a high level of intellectual exchanges managed to take place, slipping past the barriers caused by wars and fighting.

The history of the second half of the 20th century saw peaceful encounters between Islam and Europe. These were woven into the daily lives of immigrants and their families, and the two worlds, until then external to each other, met in factories, on construction sites, in neighbourhoods, schools, hospitals, and other public institutions. The other novelty consisted in the fact that the Islamic world, once external to Europe, came to live within it. In this way, from the British Isles to Berlin, from Sicily or Andalusia to the Scandinavian countries, the presence in Europe of populations native to Muslim countries became a reality which was confirmed in each succeeding generation.

These populations consisted of people belonging to Muslim cultures, who carried with them certain values, lifestyles, and traditions, which were sometimes part and parcel simply of Mediterranean cultures, not specifically Muslim. A number of these people maintained their religious traditions in creating institutions such as mosques and prayer rooms, renewed their connection to associated rituals and produced meanings. Overall, this part of the immigrant population became visible through their religious adherence, not just through their generic belonging to Muslim culture and civilisation.

Their belonging to Islam was in this manner made explicit and manifest. It also acquired a certain autonomy with regard to its origins. Though Islam in this context was once primarily linked to the history of a migration, it became more and more a fact pertaining to people who in terms of nationality and often in terms of citizenship were Europeans. In other words, Islam became a religion no longer of immigrants, but of Europeans; Islam in Europe became more and more an Islam of Europe.

This European Islam thus linked up with an ancient history of the presence of Islam which had roots in Eastern Europe and in the

Balkans, a region which today is emerging from its more recent past under communism. Through Islam, new convergences were created in every part of the continent of Europe, just as new relationships were emerging between Europe itself and the nations of the Muslim world. Thanks to this new dimension of European culture and identity, through institutions and people, and through their movements and relationships, Europe today enjoys a new and deepened connection to the Muslim world. Europe's foreign relations are already influenced by this fact, and they will be influenced even more in the future.

The purpose of this book is to sketch out the main characteristics of this European Islam.

After an introduction which discusses the historical background of the presence of Islam in Europe, and which gives some statistical information relative to the presence of Muslims in Europe today, the book is divided into four parts.

The first part analyses the process of construction of Islam in Europe. To begin, we analyse the logic of relationships of belonging (Chapter 1), and those having to do with religious instruction and socialisation (Chapter 2). In Chapter 3, forms of organisation, networks, and leadership are discussed. Chapters 4 and 5 concern the forms of institutionalisation of Islam and the forms of political participation on the part of Muslims, respectively.

The second part analyses the relations between various European states and Islam. After establishing a general framework, we discuss the question in juridical terms, in the context of the general relationship between state and religions (Chapter 6). In Chapter 7, this general relationship is discussed with more specific reference to the status of persons in Western Europe.

The third part deals with the forms of Islam's inclusion in European society. Five aspects are identified. First, the place of Islam in the world of communication and the media is discussed (Chapter 8). Next, periods of tension linked to the new presence of Islam—particularly in Western Europe—are analysed (Chapter 9). This new presence is also studied insofar as it bears upon the relations between religions (Chapter 10). There follow analyses of economic practices (Chapter 11), of the international relationships in which the new presence of Islam plays a role (Chapter 12) and of the manner in which the view on the future of European Islam has been changed after September 11 (Chapter 13).

The idea of Europe which informs this book goes beyond the institutional one of the Europe of Fifteen. More precisely, it extends to all the European nations in which a Muslim presence is observed. For this reason Bulgaria, Romania, and Hungary are within its scope—though, sole exceptions, Malta and Cyprus are omitted from consideration.

This book relies upon three principal sources of information. First, a wealth of bibliographical research has been accomplished. As of the date of its completion, the book is a comprehensive account of the state of such knowledge. The final bibliography lists all the sources consulted by the authors. Secondly, the book is based on field studies and interviews conducted *ad hoc* by S. Allievi and B. Maréchal.

Finally, the book has benefited from the contributions of scholars whose expertise concerns various countries, namely: S. Akgönül and G. de Rapper (Centre for Research on Central Asia, the Turkish world, and the Ottoman region, Strasbourg & Institut of comparative Mediterranean ethnology, Aix-en-Provence); S. Allievi (University of Padova); S. Amir-Moazami (European University Institute, Florence); J. Baeck Simonsen (The Carsten Niebuhr Institute for Near Eastern Studies, Copenhagen); S. Besch (SESOPI, Luxemburg); F. Frégosi (Robert Schuman University, Strasbourg; participated also in the conception and the settlement of this research); Z. Georgiev (BBSS Gallup, Bucharest); S. Grodz (Catholic University of Lublin); N. Landman (University of Utrecht); J. Nielsen (University of Birmingham); J. Otterbeck (University of Lund); T. Sakaranaho (University of Helsinki); A. Strobl (Karl-Franzens University, Graz); H. Mahnig († University of Neuchâtel); B. Maréchal (Centre for Interdisciplinary Research on Islam in Contemporary World, Catholic University of Louvain); A. Máté-Tóth (Documentary Centre of Denominations in Hungary, University of Szeged); J. Moreras (CIDOB, Barcelona); N.C. Tiesler (University of Hanover); A. Zhelyazkova (International Centre for Minority Studies and Intercultural Relations, Sofia).

This research has been made possible thanks to the support of the former 'Forward Studies Unit' of the European Commission, the Special Research endowment of the Catholic University of Louvain (FSR), and the National Endowment for Scientific Research of Belgium (FNRS).

The English translation of this work has been made possible thanks to a grant from the Special Research endowment of the Catholic

University of Louvain (FSR), and from the Al Tajir World of Islam Trust, London. The translation from Italian texts was carried out by Mr Joan Rundo and French texts by Mr Jeff Lewis.

We extend our warmest thanks to all those institutions and persons who in one way or another have worked on this project, and who made its realisation possible.

INTRODUCTION

FROM PAST TO PRESENT

1. THE PAST
BRIGITTE MARÉCHAL

Two types of Muslim presence coexist side by side in Europe, whose relative importance in quantitative terms tends to be equal. The first, reaching back a thousand years into history, belongs to more or less well-known periods, from *al-Andalus* and Sicily up to the Ottoman expansion into the Balkans and Central Europe. The other, much more recent, begins with the worker migrations of the 1960s, which took different forms in later years.

The stages of an ancient history

Three main phases of the millennium-long presence appear [Nielsen, 1999], which illustrate the constitution of Muslim communities on a large scale.

The first is that of Muslim Spain, Sicily, and the south of France. Muslim groups are noted in Sicily as early as the 7th century, though the real implantation occurs mainly from the 9th to the 11th centuries, ending only when Norman invasions reconquered territory once lost. In Spain, where the Muslim advances were the result of alliances and federations more than of armed struggle, the communities remained until the end of the *Reconquista* in Spain in 1492, which was legitimated after the fact by reference to religious differences. Still, a true Hispano-Arab culture had been created [Watt, 1972]: in addition to the considerable intellectual contribution of this culture, out of which the spirit of the Renaissance took wing, much visible evidence of its achievements remained in existence, and its memory remained quite alive.

The second period followed the Mongol invasions of the 13th century. The Khanate of the Golden Horde which passed across Bulgaria, Poland, and Hungary left behind permanent Muslim populations: groups of Tartars around the Black Sea region, extending from the

Volga to the Caucasus and the Crimean peninsula, were Islamised during the 13th and 14th centuries. Soon after the beginning of conflicts between the Mongols and the Ottoman Empire in the 14th century—an event which raised Western hopes of a Christian-Mongol alliance which would destroy the Muslim kingdoms—thousands of Tartars arrived in Poland, coming from Lithuania as prisoners, or in the wake of epidemics [Szajkowski, 1997]. During the next three centuries, more Tartars from the Crimean region came to join them, eventually obtaining rights equal to those of the Polish, though not the right to engage in political activities. Close to 100,000 Tartars were recorded there in a 1631 census, and though they continued to live in enclaves, they gradually became assimilated through marriages and a slow adoption of the values of the majority. In 1795, Tartars stood with the Polish in the fight for independence, swearing their allegiance on the Qur'an. They played a part in Bonaparte's campaigns against the Russians in 1812, and opposed the Russians again during the uprisings of 1830 and 1863, demonstrating a loyalty which earned them the admiration of all.

Ottoman expansion into the Balkans and Central Europe constitutes the third important and lasting wave of Muslim implantation. Following the conquest of Sofia in 1386 and the decisive victory at Kosovo in 1389, Turkish populations took up residence as far as Serbia and south-eastern Europe. Though the Ottoman Empire suffered defeat in the battle of Ankara in 1402 against the Mongol Empire, it succeeded in the crucial conquest of Constantinople in 1453. The Ottomans were thus present in Bulgaria, Romania, Yugoslavia (Montenegro and Herzegovina) and Greece from the middle of the 14th century, and Belgrade fell in 1520. In the course of large and systematic movements of populations which were part of a deliberate plan of demographic restructuring, the presence of Islam became 'indigenous' in these areas, and original non-Muslim populations acquired the status of *dhimmis*, that is, protected minorities [Nonneman, 1996]. Some groups were converted en masse to Islam— Albanians, Pomaks, and Slavic groups within Bosnia. Cultural diversity was nonetheless maintained within the Empire, and religious communities, which functioned as mediators in relation to the central governing power, retained their own leadership groups. Despite fear of the 'Turkish peril' which reached its height during the two sieges of Vienna in 1529 and 1683, groups of Muslim prisoners later decided to take up permanent residence in Germany.

The 20th century

The story of Muslim implantation in the 20th century has two main parts. On one hand, Muslim communities which had been settled in Eastern Europe after the Ottoman invasions suffered the consequences of the fall of that Empire. On another hand, there occurred migrations toward western countries which were connected to economic changes and to decolonisation.

Following the loss of territory once held by the Ottoman Empire in the 19th century, a number of nation-states emerged which counted Muslim minorities among their populations: this was the case in Bulgaria, Yugoslavia, and Albania, but there were also pockets of Muslim residents in Greece, Romania, Austria, Hungary, and Finland [Nielsen, 1981]. However, nationalism threatened their peaceful co-existence. The history of the Orthodox church became progressively associated with independence and a national political awakening, and finally acquired a mythical status. The struggle between Orthodoxy and Islam passed into the collective memory, a fact which certain groups would later take advantage of [Nonneman, 1996]. This may be seen in Serbia and Greece, where exchanges of populations left about 120,000 Turks in Western Thrace following the Treaty of Lausanne in 1923.

The situation became more difficult as the communist era approached. When the Second World War broke out in Poland, the Nazis massacred the majority of the Tartar intelligentsia. Close to 250,000 people were exterminated or scattered, and most of the rest of the Tartar groups were absorbed into the Soviet Union. Their organisational structures were not reconstituted until 1969, and not until the 1980s was it possible for them to re-establish close contact with the Islamic world. In general terms, this Soviet model was applied by the communist leaders who assumed power in Romania, Bulgaria, and Yugoslavia up to the end of the 1950s. These leaders tried to integrate the Muslim populations into the socialist order by giving them civil and cultural rights, while secularising them and suppressing the main Islamic institutions. Still, beginning in the 1960s and 1970s, variations began to appear from one country to another [Bougarel & Clayer, 2001:30 ff.]. In Romania, after independence, there were 300 mosques in Dobrudja, and although the instruction they provided in Islamic schools was given a secular emphasis, they remained religious schools, and employed the Arabic language until

1934. However, under communism all Turkish and Tartar schools were closed at the end of the 1950s, and persons connected with them were arrested. In 1976 there remained only 82 Muslim communities which operated about 70 mosques [Anghelescu, 1999], and the decline of the communities became more marked as training for religious leaders disappeared [Lederer, 1996]. Religious institutions did still receive subsidies and recognition as pillars of the Muslim community, usually in order to improve the image of the regime in the eyes of certain Arab or Muslim nations, and to obtain various types of financial assistance [Popovic, 1997]. In Bulgaria, two hard-line moves, results of a state policy of secularisation and 'Bulgarisation', greatly affected Muslim populations [Popovic, 1997]. At the accession of communists to power in 1950–51, most Muslim institutions were not only closed; religious freedom was extinguished, and religious instruction made illegal. And despite peaceful relations between existing communities, a policy of forced assimilation to Slavic norms (including mandatory name changes, repression, for example, of Turkish-language literature in schools, mandatory use of the Bulgarian language in all media, and a prohibition on certain types of clothing) motivated the flight of 370,000 people to Turkey in 1985 [Ilchev & Perry, 1996]. But after having maintained that a Christian state from before the Ottoman invasion was the true ancestor of the Bulgarian state [Peev, 1997], Bulgarian leaders later switched to a conciliatory tone. The persistence of such attitudes in Eastern Europe and in the Balkans can be explained by the fact that a certain ethno-religious awakening occurred when the communist regime fell. In the face of the evident destruction of political, economic, social, and cultural structures, religions assumed greater and greater importance, being the only independent institutions left standing: the church, Orthodox in the East and Catholic in the West. This could not occur in Muslim communities because of the lack of institutions, even if some families still felt that they belonged to mosques [Nonneman, 1996]. In the region, the case of Greece presents this difference: not having lived under a communist government, this country is "the only Balkan country in which Islamic religious institutions were never suppressed, and in which traditional Muslim elites were not eradicated" [Bougarel & Clayer, 2001]. Still, though the Muslim minority of Western Thrace underwent a kind of modernisation, including access to schooling or emigration to Western Europe, that process was also accompanied by a renewal of the adherence of this population to a Turkish national identity [Bougarel & Clayer, 2001]. The national policy of Hellenisation adopted by the Greek state, maintained until quite recently, was undoubtedly a factor [Küçükcan, 1999].

As concerns the establishment of Muslim populations in Western Europe in the 20th century, a few preliminary observations are in order. Since the time of Frederick II, when fairly close diplomatic and economic ties with the Ottoman Empire had been attempted, a Muslim community had existed in Berlin, remaining there until about 1914 [Nielsen, 1999]. In France, Muslims were recruited into the army beginning with the war in Crimea of 1854, but the official line was that their first entry into the army dated from 1870, when Muslim colonial troops participated in the conflict with Germany. The migrations in search of work began afterward, and 200,000 Algerians were involved during the First World War. Beginning in 1910, Russian Tartars emigrated to Finland, and received official status in 1925; this community has already produced a fourth generation! In Great Britain, Indians, Yemenis, and Somalians were recruited in port cities. Later there was an Indo-Pakistani presence which began slowly in the 1950s, almost unnoticed, coming more from traditional zones of emigration than from very poor areas [Lewis P., 1994:16].

Still, from a quantitative point of view, the bulk of emigration is associated above all with the worker migrations arranged when bilateral agreements were signed beginning in 1961 with Germany, followed by Austria, the Netherlands, Belgium, France, Sweden, Switzerland, and Denmark. These accords were not identical and several phases can be distinguished, more or less organised or chaotic, temporary owing to economic conditions or the product of longer-term planning. Typical immigration, chiefly by males, fairly heavily regulated and perceived as temporary, rapidly became important and turned into rather a chaotic flood of immigrants at the end of the 1960s. Later, after the oil crisis of 1972–74, immigrants established themselves progressively in their new countries. Since they were unable to go home and retain the right to re-enter Europe, they made the most of existing possibilities regarding marriages and bringing family members to join them.

From that point on, immigrants arrived in countries such as Greece, Italy, Spain and finally Portugal as tourists or as illegals; these became favoured destinations for immigrants, and a process of family reunifications began, which was almost completed elsewhere. Beginning in the 1980s, Islam emerged almost everywhere as a collective religious reality, no longer confined to its practice within families and homes. At the same time another process, the conversion to Islam of people born in Europe, grew in importance.

At present, immigration of Muslims takes place in various ways: through bringing family members to the new country, through schools and colleges, through illegal entry, and through claims to political refugee status. Among those in the latter category we find those who sought refuge from radical Islamic regimes in the Middle East, and those who were displaced in the break-up of the former socialist bloc, especially the victims of ethnic cleansing in the former Yugoslavia [Vertovec & Peach, 1997]. A high number of refugees are found in Scandinavian countries and in Austria, where since 1992 more than 90,000 Bosnians have been accepted.

All these histories converge from this point upon an unprecedented diversity in which Muslim populations themselves carry forward a plurality of traditions and varieties of worship, a plurality which remains in constant ferment as contacts with the host society multiply and deepen.

2. THE MUSLIM POPULATIONS OF EUROPE
FELICE DASSETTO

For several reasons, the question of the demographic makeup of Muslim populations in Europe is fairly delicate. First, there is the meaning to be assigned to the word 'Muslim'. This book will analyse the practices of Muslims who are counted as religious. But from this angle, there is no way of estimating the number of people who adhere to Islam as a religion.

Thus for practical reasons, but also for ideological ones, estimates of Muslim populations can only be based on national statistics, themselves the result of censuses or other counting methods. In Western Europe, since the presence of Islam is largely the result of the great currents of immigration over the last forty years, it has been the custom to count Muslims according to their country of origin.

This gives rise to problems of two types. The first is just statistical, caused by the fact that an increasing number of persons, especially those of the second or third generations, acquire or adopt the nationality of the countries where they live. These people are hidden in the statistics concerning people of 'foreign' origin, in the category of citizens in general. That is why attempts to count the number of naturalisations and correct the statistics have been made. The second range of problems is linked to something mentioned above, namely that this whole procedure assumes that if someone comes from a certain country where Islam is the majority religion, one belongs to Muslim culture, even more, one actively believes in that religion. These statistics based on nationality involve assumptions by researchers, but they correspond to the reality of only a part of the population.

The British census developed the category of ethnic self-identification or belonging in order to remedy this problem. A rather bitter debate ensued recently in France over the question of including such a category in the census. The project of including such a question should be discussed in terms of its political effect, and also in terms of the invasion of privacy the question represents. And even then we have not decided whether self-identification as 'Muslim' refers to a culture, a civilisation, or a religion. For the Balkans and Eastern Europe things are still more complicated. Ethnic and religious identification are interwoven, and the various countries pose different and considerable demographic problems.

As things stand, only an estimate can be offered of the number of people directly or indirectly counted as coming from a Muslim country—whom we could call 'attributed Muslims' for short. These figures do not indicate the actual number of believers. Some authors, based on opinion polls or limited inquiries into different practices, estimate that active religious Muslims represent something between a fourth and a third of attributed Muslims. At present this is all that can be said. As for the countries of Eastern Europe and the Balkans, the data are based on 'ethnic' statistics used in the different countries. The tables below offer a few demographic indications for the countries of Western Europe and for those of the Eastern Europe/Balkan region, including those that are candidates for European Union membership.

TABLE 1. ESTIMATES OF POPULATION IDENTIFIED AS MUSLIM,
EUROPEAN UNION MEMBER STATES (END OF 1990s)

Country	Estimated Muslim population (×1000)	Origin or citizenship:	% of total population (estimated)
Austria	200	Turkey: 120 Bosnia-Herzegovina: 50	2.6
Belgium	370	Morocco: 165 Turkey: 100	3.8
Denmark	150	Turkey: 36 Iran: 6 Pakistan: 7	2.8
France	4,000–4,500	Algeria: 1,500 Morocco: 1,000 Tunisia: 350 Turkey: 350 Sub-Saharan Africa: 250	7
Finland	20	Tartars Turkey	0.4
Germany	3,040	Turkey: 2,300 Ex-Yugoslavia Maghreb	3
Greece	370	Albania: 250 Western Thrace: 120	3.7
Ireland	7		0.2
Italy	600	Morocco: 150 Albania: 92 Tunisia: 50 Senegal: 35 Egypt: 26	1
Luxembourg	5	Bosnia	0.8
Netherlands	696	Turkey: 284 Morocco: 247 Surinam: 36	4.6

TABLE 1 (*cont.*)

Country	Estimated Muslim population (x1000)	Origin or citizenship:	% of total population (estimated)
Norway	23	Iran: 7 Turkey: 6	0.5
Portugal	30–38	Former colonies	0.3
Spain	300	Morocco: 170	0.7
Sweden	300	Iran: n.a. Turkey: n.a. Bosnia-Herzegovina: n.a.	1.2
United Kingdom	1,591	Indian subcontinent: 770	2.7

Total, European Union	11,000–12,000	With at least:
		Maghreb & other
		    Arabs: 3,700
		Turkey: 3,100
		Pakistan/India/
		    Bangladesh: 800
			4

Source: Census figures and national experts

TABLE 2. ESTIMATES OF POPULATION IDENTIFIED AS MUSLIM, OTHER EUROPEAN COUNTRIES (END OF 1990s)

Country	Estimated Muslim population (×1000)	Origin or citizenship:	% of total population (estimated)
Bulgaria	1,100	Turks: a majority Gypsies Pomaks	13
Hungary	2–20	n.a.	
Norway	23	Turkey: n.a. Iran: n.a.	0.5
Poland	15	Tartars: 5	0.04

TABLE 2 (*cont.*)

Country	Estimated Muslim population (×1000)	Origin or citizenship:	% of total population (estimated)
Romania	50	Turks: 40% Tartars: 60%	0.3
Switzerland	250	Turkey: n.a. Ex-Yugoslavia: n.a.	3

Source: Census figures and national experts

On the basis of these figures, we can see that 11 or 12 million people whose country of origin is, directly or indirectly, identified as Muslim, live in the countries of Western Europe—including, according to some sources, as many as 100,000 converts to Islam. But this number is hard to estimate.

These people come from five geographical regions with different cultures: the Maghreb and other Arab countries, Turkey, the Indian subcontinent, Africa, and the Balkans. There are patterns to the way they are distributed within European space, following ancient connections between certain European countries and certain Muslim countries. In Germany, Austria and Switzerland, Turk and Balkan natives predominate. This is as it were a survival of the relations between Austria-Hungary and the Ottoman Empire. In Spain and France, we find mostly persons native to the Maghreb. In France, there are also populations from West Africa, from Senegal, Mali, and Ivory Coast. Along the Rhine valley, along the German border, many Turks reside. In Belgium and in the Netherlands, there are populations from Turkey and the Maghreb (especially Moroccans) in more or less equal number. In the United Kingdom, populations from former British colonies in Asia are the most numerous. There are fewer Muslims in Scandinavia, mostly Turks, and persons of various nationalities who are granted refugee status. In Finland, we note, there are a number of Muslims, Tartars, who arrived as merchants in the 19th century, travelling up the Volga and by way of St. Petersburg. Finally in Italy, Muslim populations of several origins are found. They come from the Maghreb and from West Africa, but also from Egypt, Somalia, and Ethiopia.

Overall about 4% of the population of Europe is directly or indirectly of Muslim origin. In some countries, for example France, the Netherlands, and the United Kingdom, the percentage is higher. The average age of this 4% is younger than the population of Europe as a whole.

TABLE 3. ESTIMATES OF THE PERCENTAGE OF PERSONS OF MUSLIM ORIGIN IN SEVERAL EUROPEAN CITIES (BEGINNING OF 1990s)

Cities	% of persons identified as of 'Muslim' origin
Aachen	4.1
Amsterdam	8.6
Berlin	10.8
Birmingham	8.7
Bradford	10.7
Brussels	12.6
Köln	8.0
Utrecht	9.6

But this overall percentage does not make clear the fact that the presence of Islam in Europe is primarily an urban presence, the result of the work assigned to the Muslim populations at the time of their first arrival as immigrants. At the beginning of the 1990s, it was estimated that the population of cities such as Brussels, Berlin or Bradford was more than 10% persons of Muslim origin, with Köln and Birmingham between 5 and 10%. And it is quite probable that the actual percentage is even higher.

At all events, it is from now on evident that the space of Europe is more or less included in that space which is traditionally Muslim. It is the variegated aspects of that presence which this book will explore.

PART ONE

PROCESSES OF THE SOCIAL CONSTRUCTION
OF ISLAM

The object of this first part is to describe various aspects of the different ways of structuring Islamic institutions which are at work in contemporary Europe.

After an opening chapter which illustrates the diversity of types of Islamic self-identification in a subjective sense, based on different patterns of faith and rituals and practices, viewed in a fluid context, the opportunities for acquiring knowledge about Islam are examined next. These concern mosque-based instruction as well as the many programmes which have been established within national educational systems, or programmes begun in response to deficiencies in state systems.

As for the intra-Muslim organisational forms which are analysed, these range from a description of basic organisations, mosques or the many local associations, to an account of international ideological and religious movements, and including a description of actors in the process who are given or manage to acquire privileges as individuals.

In the context of the emergence of these new actors on the national scene, more attention is being paid to the processes through which an Islamic representative body is constituted, such as is regularly pleaded for by state agencies who wish to institutionalise their relations with Muslim communities.

The general review of the manner in which Muslims are structurally integrated into European societies finishes with an attempt to describe this integrative process at the national, regional, and local levels of political action.

CHAPTER ONE

THE QUESTION OF BELONGING

Brigitte Maréchal

From an Islamic point of view, a Muslim is anyone whose father was a Muslim, or anyone who has converted to Islam. Membership in the religion "is based on a minimal definition of belonging" [Dassetto, 1996:85]; the profession of faith consists in affirming before two witnesses that "there is no God but God, and Muhammad is his prophet".

The concrete implications of these facts, which draw their force from their simplicity [Dassetto, 1996], appear in different ways and have a variety of effects, more and less important. There is the expression of deference with regard to leading figures of a shared history, foremost the Prophet Muhammad. There is also the varying intensity of the feeling of belonging to a group which sees itself and is seen as distinct [Sunier, 1992]. There is, too, the elaboration of a specific conception of time and space, related to the religious custom which divides the day according to different times for prayer, and which orients daily life toward the central point of Mecca. But it remains true that the appropriation by individuals of this belonging means, above all and most deeply, adhering to the sacred text of the Qur'an, and even the Sunna.

1. THE FOUNDATIONS OF BELIEF

Different perspectives

Looking at all forms of Islamic teaching, three aspects of the content of belief can be isolated [with reference to Oubrou, 1998].

First: doctrine is the object of faith. It presupposes belief in a range of metaphysical truths, having mostly to do with an invisible world: that God is One, the Last Judgment, heaven, hell, angels, resurrection, etc. This doctrinal system is a philosophy of existence which defines the meaning of existence. More precisely: "since Muslims are required to establish an equilibrium between this world and the principles of religion, they must live their lives here guided by religious principles, and by the idea of the Beyond" [Ahmed, 1993:29].

Second: the law, the Sharia, that is, the group of norms which determines practices, and establishes ritual, cultural, juridical and moral prescriptions, respect for which leads to the spiritual health of human beings. There are five 'pillars of Islam': profession of faith, prayer, pilgrimage, charity as specified in the Sharia, and fasting during Ramadan. These things are related to a specific view of time and space, since religious practice divides the day into times for prayer, and continually orients the believer toward Mecca. However, Islam also prescribes behaviour in every part of human life and action, including diet, sexual behaviour, usury and gambling, etc. Islam, in effect, is asserted to be a complete way of life designed to introduce the consciousness of the divine in every moment of daily life, and every Muslim is accountable for all his or her actions within it. The most serious sins are: association with other 'gods' (that is, a failure to recognize that God is One), disrespect for parents, and sexual crimes such as homosexuality or extramarital sex. These close the doors of Paradise.

Third: the way, the experience of a personal relationship with God, for the perfection of the created consists in actualising his or her servitude in relation to God. In experience, this means the interior and spiritual realisation of great revealed metaphysical truths, especially the Oneness of the Names and Attributes of God. This personal and unconditional surrender to God implies absolute confidence, though the meaning of this be wrapped in the Mystery of God. God only allows humans to know a part of what he intends.

From the common possession of these theological, teleological, juridico-ethical and mystical horizons there results for each believer a feeling of membership in the Islamic *Umma* or community of believers, who in accordance with religious dogma, consider themselves to be one and equal. The notion that Muslims should live as members of a 'properly guided' community of believers is in fact crucial to Islamic teaching. This solidarity is all the more pregnant with meaning, because conflicts in Palestine, Bosnia, Chechnya, Kashmir, India and Afghanistan are important events in the news. These conflicts favour the emergence of 'romantic' forms of world solidarity, and/or lead certain Muslims to conceive the *Umma* as a "worldwide com-

munity of victims" [Modood, 2000]. Finally, in relation to technological advances in communication, we may say that the Internet
has allowed Muslims to create a re-imagined *Umma*, for in the mind
of many of its members, it provides "an image of their communion"
[Anderson, 1991 cited by Mandaville, 2000].

General sociological observations

In Europe, the relation to Islamic points of reference continues despite
the variations observed in the succeeding generations. In a survey
taken in France in 1994, a little more than 85% of those questioned
from the first generation considered themselves Muslims, but this
number dropped to 70% for younger persons of the second generation (INED survey), and dropped still further for children of mixed
marriages.[1] Using slightly different criteria, similar figures were obtained
in Great Britain, where the religion of the family appears as the
most important source of identity for people of South Asia, especially for Muslims [Modood, 2000]: according to the Fourth National
Survey of Ethnic Minorities, 90% said that it was important to them
personally, and two-thirds of Pakistanis and Bengalis questioned who
were between the ages of 16 and 34 said that religion was a "very
important influence" in the way they lived their lives (the percentage for older persons is 80%) [Modood, 1997b, 2000].[2]

As for questions about faith properly speaking, the percentages are
still high. In a survey in France taken in 2001,[3] religious identity
was still strongly affirmed, even more than in the past: 42% of all
those questioned presented themselves as 'believers', up from 38%
in 1989.

---

[1] IFOP/Le Monde/RTL/La Vie joint survey, 11/20/1989; 1,464 persons over
16 living in France were surveyed; the INED survey data has been published by
M. Tribalat, 1995.
[2] For a quantitative approach to religious orientation in Belgium's Turkish and
Moroccan communities, see Lesthaeghe & Neels, 2000.
[3] IFOP/Le Monde/Le Point/Europe 1 survey, two sample groups were surveyed
on September 27–28, 2001. The first group contained 940 persons determined to
be representative of the French population over 18, matching its composition as
regards sex, age, occupation of head of household, and was balanced in terms of
residence by region of France (stratification by region), and residence in cities and
towns of different sizes (stratification by size). The second group of 548 persons
over 16 had all identified themselves as belonging to a family of Muslim origin,
residing in France [X. Ternisien, "L'islam apaisé des musulmans de France" in *Le
Monde*, 10/04/2001].

At the beginning of the 1990s, it was often observed how much reference to and/or belonging to Islam appeared to go without saying for Muslims, irrespective of the depth of their religious knowledge: in general, their belief was a fact and was apparently never called into question [Rooijackers, 1992]. At present, it is rather the changing nature of identities which is underlined, or even the pride which is taken in them [Modood, 2000]. But it is still necessary to emphasise the extent to which the notion of belonging can be understood in a wide sense, which can even come to represent a sort of background, a rather distant system of reference which does not really have much effect on ways of thinking or on daily life. Even so, the idea of belonging can play a pivotal role in people's personalities in a variety of ways.

2. Muslim Ways of Belonging

Over and above the question of multiple or hybrid identities, which has been examined by many authors [including Modood, 1994; Malik, 1996; Caglar, 1997; Werbner, 1997; Mirdal, 2000] as this relates to religion, the 'subjective variations of belonging' are tied to a diversity of ways of believing and of being Muslim in practice,[4] and this is expressed in a certain number of specific practices.

A few parameters

This plurality is a function of various personal, community, and social factors. It is related first of all to "sexual and family divisions" [Dassetto, 1996:90]. Religiosity may vary with age, or even more, in relation to the phases of one's life: many young European Muslims—males especially—say that they are not particularly religious, but would like to become good Muslims when they have children. In addition, though many women claim to be more committed Muslims than the men, many customs or practices probably influence their

---

[4] This concept of belonging is more clearly defined by E. Pace as being "quite as much the complex of attitudes which mark one as forming part of a group or institution as it is the sum of mechanisms of membership, joining, and formal participation in the activity of a more or less organized structure, always of a religious nature" [Pace, 1994 cited by Dassetto, 1996].

feeling of belonging. Perhaps because women's religious practice is often confined to family life, or because of their supposedly 'weaker nature' as the fair sex, women sometimes benefit from exceptions in religious practice, such as being excused from ritual prayer or from fasting during Ramadan if they are menstruating.

Other factors also play a role in the feeling of belonging to a community of origin, ethnic and family-based or even tribal, religious or historical [Dassetto, 1996:90]. This question of affiliation is directly related to doctrinal adherence, Sunni or Shiite, and that distinction is itself different depending on the region of origin and/or with reference to one or another more specific organisation or movement. In relation to belonging to a community, the religious aspect of belonging depends on a mix of religious observances and other elements which make up a heritage of pre-established meanings.

Religious belonging is also a function of the relationship with the society of the host country, or with a conception of society in general. There are large differences in this regard from one Muslim population to another. For example, in France, between 48 and 64% of male immigrants born in Algeria say that they have no religion or do not practice any [Tribalat, 1995], but the Turkish Muslim society of Western Thrace is much more attached to the Islamic faith. This attachment can be explained if we note that Thrace is an agricultural society which never went through the secularisation process that Turkish society experienced, and that the Muslims of Thrace had to affirm their own identity faced with a dominant Orthodox culture [Akgönül, 1999; Dalègre, 2001].

Moreover, residence within Europe means that a great number of different Muslim traditions coexist and compare each other daily at closer range. And over and above the simple co-existence of cultures, many people, especially the young, find themselves caught up in a process of change within the dominant culture. Obviously such changes will have an effect on ways of conceiving and practicing religion. In the final analysis this process, like many others, involves the interplay of multiple social and cultural identities.

Different kinds of belonging

The types of belonging to Islam which are found can be categorised in a preliminary way as cultural/ethnic or religious.

'Sociological Muslims' probably represent the statistical majority.

In general, these people see Islam as only part of a cultural system, and they adopt more or less completely the norms of conduct of secular European society. Whether they are agnostics, indifferent to religion, or simply respectful of it based on a cultural identification which is "affective in nature and detached from any doctrinal considerations" [Hargreaves, 1995], religious dogma means little to them and hardly influences their daily life. But these same people still follow Muslim ritual in life's rites of passage. Moreover, these rituals are often rearranged or modernised in meaning [Dassetto, 1996], as with circumcision and the prohibition on mixed marriages, which are justified on the basis of cultural arguments [Bensalah, 1994; Beishon, Modood & Virdee, 1998]. Thus the practice of circumcision continues unabated, since this practice has an important symbolic meaning as concerns the transmission of identity, and is also justified as a sanitary custom, being more a practice of Muslims than of Islam. As concerns marriage, even if this is no longer a religious obligation—marriage is, in a famous hadith, 'one-half of faith'—foregoing marriage is still seen as a 'kind of anomaly' [Cesari, 1997]. Despite important differences between ethnic groups, it has been observed that mixing is more common than formerly. In France, 50% of males of the second generation, but only 25% of the women, reported a non-Muslim partner [Tribalat, 1995]. By contrast, in Turkish or Indo-Pakistani communities, such mixing is still quite rare.

When belonging is qualified as 'religious', individuals explicitly affirm the meaning of their belonging, follow certain rules of life, and ritualise certain moments in their lives according to Islam. Beyond personal belief, in fact, such belonging is differentiated according to many forms and practices, performed collectively or in private. Different types coexist [Dassetto, 1996; van Koningsveld, 1996a], not counting the category of converted Muslims [Allievi, 1998; Köse, 1996]. These include pious Muslims, whether they are mystics following the doctrine of a particular teacher, or those who hold to a literal approach in the interpretation of sacred texts, ritualists, moralists, proselytisers perhaps involved in social activities which aim mostly at bringing Muslims back to Islam, or militants who engage in proselytising, whether or not they are politically engaged—indeed, some reject such engagement.

Beyond the feeling of belonging to the *Umma*, other different types of relations are found between 'sociological' Muslims and those who are more religious, and between the individual members of each category. These relations range from convergence to ignorance, with mutual respect somewhere in the middle. Some attitudes may be quite incompatible with others, such that a consensus between them is practically impossible, though there may be no overt dispute— and although Islamic dogma proclaims that 'everyone is responsible before God', the only Judge.

Two quite general observations can be made with regard to the notion of the *Umma* as it is conceived by Muslim populations living in Europe. First, there is a greater awareness of differences, even incompatibilities, which can exist between members, especially between those who by the mere fact of being born into Muslim families are potential adherents to Islam, and those who are believers really involved in their faith. Second, in a majority of situations, behaviours vary widely, but are still tolerated within the *Umma*. Within the limits of orthodoxy, this very multiplicity and many other differences are assumed by Islamic dogma itself, and divisions within the community are considered to be a gift from God.

3. Changes in Belonging

Despite the appearance of a certain formalisation with respect to these categories, some attention must be given to the rapid changes occurring among young people, even if these are only the result of a need to affirm their individuality relative to their parents. For the young, more involved in self-redefinition, the ways of belonging to Islam seem more changeable, and appear as part of a permanent process of restructuration. Changes in religious belonging are even more complex and various because they are related to social contexts in which individuals find themselves, and these normally have their greatest impact on the young. But while the young experience more directly the influence of the external society than their parents do, it must also be underlined that they continue to be influenced by cultures and traditions from their regions of origin because of the close interweaving of ethnic culture and religion [Jacobson, 1998:147]. Several trends of different types result from this tension.

The difference between religion and ethnic character

Despite the great diversity among communities, a tendency seems identifiable among the young, involving a gradual departure from the particular framework of ethnic identity. In fact, though many ethnic and religious elements are difficult to separate, and though ethnicity "remains one of the most fundamental beliefs" [Bastenier, 1998], religion may also become a criterion of choice as a source of identity.[5] Studies which show an increased importance of this particular attitude on the part of young Muslims in Western Europe usually associate it with a higher level of religious knowledge [Knott & Khoker, 1993; Jacobson, 1998].

What is more, even if a certain irreducible plurality within Islam appears to be maintained and valued, sometimes this distinction works to the benefit of a greater affirmation of the spiritual and universal character of Islam [Babès, 1997] and/or efforts to put down roots for Islam in European territory [Dassetto, 1996]. Today, for example, references to the four juridical rites of Islam tend to disappear within Sunni Islam [Allievi, 1998].

In Bulgaria, though ethnic differences tend to be more forcefully expressed today than formerly, there is also a tendency toward a certain universalization of Islam: distinctions "between the majority Sunni and the Alawis[6] are tending to diminish" [Peev, 1997]. It is quite probable that the many convergences between Eastern and Western Europe also work in favour of encounters between different groups of Muslims at the European level.[7]

Voluntarism and personalisation

Religious belonging to Islam can be seen from this point on as a question of decision, moral choice, and faith [Dassetto, 1996; Babès, 1997; Roy, 1999]. It is more and more common for young Muslims to agree that real involvement in Islam does not come only from the circumstances of one's birth, but also mainly from a conscious choice and individual reflection [Jacobson, 1998:153].

---

[5] These links between ethnicity and religion are studied in diverse geographical contexts by Knott & Kokher (1993), Oran (1994), Sunier (1994), Scantlebury (1995), Höpken (1997), Bastenier (1998), Bloul (1996 and 1999).

[6] See the chapter "Mosques, organisations and leadership".

[7] See the chapters "Media" and "Mosques, organisations and leadership".

This attitude is involved in two types of behaviour. At the end of the 1980s, Schiffauer had already written about an individualisation of religious practices among the first generation. Since their ritual observances no longer expressed a belonging to society as a whole, as in Islamic societies themselves, this author concluded that those who practiced their religion did so more from personal and "purely religious motives" [Schiffauer, 1988:151 ff.]. Beside the fact that religion has become more a part of a relatively autonomous sphere of life [Sunier, 1992], a number of researchers have observed that a growing minority of young Muslims were developing an interest in the study of religious texts, one which was motivated by critical questioning [Nielsen, 1987; Andrews, 1994; Lewis P., 1994; Joly, 1995; Cesari, 1998a].

This movement should not be overestimated, though, because it is not fundamental beliefs but rather traditional interpretations of religion which are criticised and called into question. Even in cases of personal re-appropriation of the discourse on Islam, a classical interpretation of texts is often the result [Roy, 2000]. In a study of the Indo-Pakistani community of Great Britain, one author went further, asserting that orthodox Islamic thought is accepted most often without question, though young people are quite aware that there are different and even contradictory interpretations of Islamic teachings, and that Muslims throughout history have solved different problems in different ways [Jacobson, 1998].

Conservatism and reformism

At present a certain conformism may be prevalent in Muslim communities, including as concerns young people and also those who are not very religious. If a certain tendency toward resistance to secularisation sometimes becomes manifest, this is not only the consequence of the psychological and social limits which some practicing Muslims construct and maintain between themselves and the rest of society, especially by avoiding social activities considered typical of the non-Muslim majority [Jacobson, 1998:133]. Nor is this really the result of some type of social control exercised by communities upon their members: the attitudes of young people, when these are relatively conservative, are related to the fact that some of them deliberately emphasize continuity over change.

In fact, in accordance with the fundamental axioms of Islamic thought, which hold that doctrines have been established in their perfect and unalterable form by the Qur'an, Islam continues to embody a group of ultimate eternal truths. It represents an unchanging doctrinal body, a framework of reference which precisely determines proper behaviour, while cultures are nowadays considered as part of continual changes. The persistence of young people's involvement in religion may thus be explained not so much by the fact that religion represents a common symbolic heritage, but by the fact that it is seen as a 'source of guidance', useful and positive in the conduct of daily life [Jacobson, 1998:101].

Still, when an individual has a real desire to construct his or her personal self-affirmation through adoption of a Muslim identity which is rooted beyond the cultures of origin, it may occur that such an affirmation "is linked to a certain reformist attitude relative to an 'authentic' version of Islam". In a context in which Islam is no longer reinforced by direct authority or by social pressure, the redefinition of individual belonging takes on either a 'liberal' aspect in which Islamic injunctions are relativised, or a 'fundamentalist' aspect in which ideas of what is licit and illicit are placed at the centre of daily life [Roy, 2000].

In fact, "some young people make a new place for Islam, compartmentalizing it, in order to ease the tensions which exist between one's identity as a member of a Muslim community, and Islamic identity" [Vertovec & Rogers, 1998]. Religion thus represents one part of a complex whole, which can be used, even manipulated by different people for different reasons at different times, and receive different meanings according to different contexts [J.B. Simonsen cited by Vertovec & Rogers, 1998:3]. Rearranging the meaning of what is licit and illicit, some young people think that, despite the fact that promiscuity between boys and girls is prohibited under Islam, it is "enough to purify oneself 'inside' in order to make encounters licit" [Khosrokhavar, 1997]. More rarely religion is worked into activities that seem quite secular such as rap music or sports [Kaya, 1997; Straßburger, 1999]. Here, Islam becomes thus "a mental component of any given activity" [Khosrokhavar, 1997]. In general, religion is inserted or even used as a tool in some given area, rather than as something which indistinctly encompasses daily life. And it is often thought that there is no contradiction in mixing various lifestyles or modes of thought in this way [Vertovec & Rogers, 1998], though for more conservative persons, these attitudes are quite debatable [Werbner, 1996a].

On the other hand, since the 1980s it has been observed that an increasing number of young people are turning to religion as an encompassing system of all the aspects of human existence. If the religious reference comes to the fore, it is because the question of grounding a reconstituted identity is focused on by certain people as part of an intense quest for meaning in a world which seems to lack meaning, or to suffer from some social malaise, and this can occur in relation to some Islamic currents or as the result of some ambient hostility. Such expressions in regard to Islam are nonetheless limited. According to some authors, they concern only about 10% of young people (figures for France, but which are probably applicable elsewhere) [Tribalat, 1995; Khosrokhavar, 1997]. Further, this phenomenon should not be exaggerated, since not everyone who affirms in a sustained fashion the importance of Islam is necessarily deeply involved in religious practice [Jacobson, 1998:33].

Even if it attests a certain conformism in regard to a shared community tradition, the appropriation of a self-proclaimed Muslim identity often represents an alternative means of self-affirmation, a protest or form of political or social action in the face of a great variety of situations. These may be external or internal to the Muslim communities. The fact of associating oneself with Islam can, first of all, represent the desire of a person to stand forth as someone responsible, respectable, or virtuous, in a context where anomie seems too often the rule. Whether social success is still given a high value or not, it is the quest for purity and the sacred which are taken into consideration. In other cases, a recourse to Islam signifies opposition to that which is perceived as Western political and sociocultural imperialism, wherever on the planet it may occur, or else it is a matter of resistance to a social context which is perceived as hostile to the person concerned. Islamic identities are in such cases "forged in reaction to negative or essentialist representations of Islam and immigrants" [Vertovec & Rogers, 1998]. In France, it has been observed that the more Islamic or Arab origin is stigmatised, the more identification with those elements is reinforced, even if that appears essentially symbolic [Cesari, 1998:30]. Moreover, faced with a system of traditional Islamic thought which is still largely patriarchal, some women decide consciously to present themselves as Muslims, getting involved in an Islamic activism which sometimes is subconsciously felt by them as a sort of modernist resistance [Göle, 1993; Petek-Salom, 1995; Weibel, 1996; Timmerman, 1999; Venel, 1999]. In cases in which these women are associating themselves with ideological reference points which are familiar to their families, this is a means of real emancipation, without any traumatic rupture [Knott & Khokher, 1993; Haw, 1995 cited by Vertovec & Rogers, 1998], and without their having to renounce their status as wives and mothers [Amiraux, 2000a]. They may decide to start wearing headscarves on their own, but this custom is not necessarily linked to an intense practice of Islam.[8] And this kind of affirmation of Islam may also go along with a tacit rupture with the country of origin. The affirmation of Islam is made in a context which is tied to the community more than to the country of origin, even though a "legitimate but deeply ambiguous connection" may be preserved [Leveau, 1997]. From that point, activity within the religious community is sometimes seen as facilitating integration into European society, to the extent that such activity calls for attention from the larger society [Leveau, 1997]. In other cases, in contrast, Islamic identity forms a 'critical instrument' of resistance to the process of inclusion or fusion with European societies [Amiraux, 1997].

However things may stand with these behaviours, one item stands out: there have been changes as concerns what counts as apostasy or heresy. These questions—very delicate in Muslim countries—have altered, though there has been no real reflection about the subject with regard to the position in which minorities live. Having a heterodox position with regard to the Islamic faith is viewed as morally more acceptable than a hypocritical attachment to orthodox opinion. In this connection, passages of the Qur'an are cited: "there is no compulsion in religion" [II, 256], and also "To you your religion, and mine to me" [CIX, 6]. Together, these passages could begin to establish a sort of "Islamic manifesto specifically addressing freedom of conscience and faith" [Lewis P., 1994]. Such principles appear to be widely accepted, even though the percentage of those saying they have 'no religion' is decreasing: in France, at the beginning of the 1990s, between a third and a fifth of young people con-

---

[8] Different ways of observing the custom have been distinguished; thus there is a veil of the female immigrant, that of the adolescent, and another, more often claimed and worn in any context [Khosrokhavar & Gaspard, 1995].

sistently said they did not believe in Islam [Hargreaves & Stenhouse, 1991], but in surveys from 2001,[9] only 6% chose that answer, or said they had a religion other than Islam. Still, in 1989, 72% of young Muslims in France said that they would accept the decision of someone close to them to abandon religion [Leveau, 1997].

Religious practices

Few studies on religious practices have been carried out up to now. Some indicators, to be examined in relation to the multiple aspects of the ritualisation of Muslim life, are explored such as daily prayer, Friday group prayer, and Ramadan.

As concerns the practice of daily prayer, we refer to the above-mentioned 2001 French survey, in which 33% of Muslims said they pray each day, as against 31% in 1994. In France, though young people sometimes appear very attached to Islam, it is estimated that 85% of them follow very few religious practices [Tribalat, 1995]. In general, if they follow any practice, it is especially the fasting at Ramadan, or to avoid pork, perhaps in favour of halal meat [Benkheira, 1995]; alcohol is also avoided, and they go to the mosque once a week.[10] The latter is a fact especially for males, though the other customs are practiced as often by young women. However, it should be remarked that the indicator of daily prayer—theoretically obligatory—has not been studied in depth as regards its meaning. One French study did observe that 35% of the first generation claim to practice daily prayer, but the percentage falls to 14% for the second generation [Tribalat, 1995]. In the Netherlands, only 4% of Turks claim to pray five times a day [Rooijackers, 1992].

Daily fasting during Ramadan, which consists in letting nothing enter the body, no food, no drink, no smoking, no perfume, and no sexual relations, is still widely followed. It is respected by 65% of Muslims in France [Tribalat, 1995], and about 55% of Turks in the Netherlands say they respect the fast during the entire month [Rooijackers, 1992]. On the other hand its meaning appears to be

---

[9] Survey IFOP/Le Monde/Le Point/Europe 1 [Le Monde, 04/10/2001].
[10] According to the Fourth National Survey of Ethnic Minorities [see Modood, 1997b], involvement in Islam remains relatively high among the youngest generation of Muslims in Great Britain: 65% of Muslim males aged 16–34 said they went to the mosque once a week (older persons: 80%).

changing, because its social aspect, involving meals in company after sundown, is now sometimes more important than the aspect of personal self-denial [Dassetto, 1996]. According to the 2001 survey in France,[11] this tendency to emphasise the outer aspects of observance, and to do this collectively, is on the rise.

The pilgrimage to Mecca is observed more and more frequently, including among young people, at least as far as intentions go.[12] Above all, the *'Id al-Adha*, the feast of the sacrifice, marks solidarity and harmony between Muslims worldwide, on the tenth day of the month of the pilgrimage to Mecca. Everyone follows the same ritual of solemn sacrifice within the family. This is in honour of Abraham, the founder of history's first monotheistic religion, and it commemorates the profound meaning of Islam as submission to the divine will. For this reason this sacrifice, though not part of the five pillars of Islam, still constitutes a 'recommended' act which all believers try to perform as well as they can [Dassetto, 1996; Brisebarre, 1998].

In Eastern Europe, and especially in Bulgaria, a decline in religious adherence was observed during the communist era, resulting from many factors including "the dismissal of most former religious leaders, the suppression of religious holy days, the absence of a Muslim press, the impossibility of making a pilgrimage to Mecca, and also the formation of many clubs which encouraged 'scientific atheism'" [Popovic, 1997]. Despite the emergence of types of mystical belonging that appeared in the first years after the fall of communism [Nonneman, 1996], it appears that things have fallen back into ignorance and syncretism as concerns doctrine and ritual [Lederer, 1996; Peev, 1996]. In Bulgaria, in the mid-1990s, it was found that only 15% of Muslims, mostly elderly, went to mosques frequently, while 30% of them said they prayed more or less regularly [Ilchev & Perry, 1996].

---

[11] Cf. supra.

[12] Survey IFOP/Le Monde/Le Point/Europe 1 [Le Monde, 10/04/2001]; this survey showed that 69% of young people aged 16–24 "say they intend to make a pilgrimage 'in the next few years'".

CHAPTER TWO

MODALITIES OF ISLAMIC INSTRUCTION

Brigitte Maréchal

This chapter deals with the places in which religious knowledge is disseminated, and the ways in which this is accomplished. Several different perspectives are taken into account.

The first of these, of an introductory and theoretical nature, attempts to estimate the importance given to religious education within European nations. In like manner, questions are posed regarding the recognition accorded to the Islamic religion, and its status regarding the ongoing process of constructing a European identity.

After the exposition of several aspects of the situation as this relates to the instruction given to children of families from Muslim nations, we take stock of the manner in which religious socialisation within families is carried on. This account is completed by another, relating to religious education as offered in mosques. These two forms of transmission of religion are found together everywhere in Europe.

The next section concerns religious education in state-run public schools. A transversal analysis arranges the types of instructional method in use in public schools as a function of their position regarding religious education. Four types of approach are distinguished, in order: secular education, pluralistic education, preferential education, and cultural education. Religious schools are then compared in a similar fashion, including schools of the religious majority—Catholic, Lutheran, Orthodox, Anglican, etc.—and Muslim schools which are recognised and subsidised. From country to country, within the two school network types (public and religious), and within their various divisions, differences in organisation are quite marked, as are the schools' different dynamics and different goals. And this is even without taking into account the significant effect of classes focused on instruction in a language of origin, which are useful for many different purposes, and which are accorded recognition by private individuals and families in a variety of ways; and we shall also have to consider the 'private' instructional types, including home study, which is gaining in importance.

This overview is completed by a consideration of group instruction as offered in private Islamic institutes at all levels, particularly as this relates to qualification for Islamic religious office. Institutions of higher learning (high schools, colleges and universities) are discussed, and the section closes with a consideration of the conditions of possibility of Islamic theological reflection in Europe.

1. THE STATUS OF RELIGIOUS EDUCATION IN EUROPE

Contradictions in Union-wide policies and global dispositions

Although Europe as a whole is often involved in debates concerning the area of education, it is essential to remember that education remains entirely controlled by individual countries. The European Union has no competence in the matter of education, and moreover is a priori inclined to refrain from all reference to religions— unless it finds itself torn by a degree of internal dissension, and is led to seek some new means of including religion in its programme, eventually centring its approach on an ethics which claims to be universalistic. Since the Treaty of Amsterdam, the European Union has exhibited a marked preoccupation with the acquisition of a better acquaintance with our cultural patrimony [Schreiner, 2000:10]. By means of exchange programmes for students and professors, such as the Socrates programme and the Leonardo programme, the European Union has tried to create an educational sector which promotes the concept of shared norms and common values in an effort to stimulate a consciousness of European citizenship. As for the project called "Give Europe a soul", it represents the desire to go beyond a merely functional and utilitarian idea of Europe, so that Europe may attain the symbolic status of an institution which has its own ethics, and even its own spirituality.

However, in the recommendations of the Council of Europe upon the theme of 'Religion and Democracy', a somewhat different position regarding religions, a more voluntaristic one, can be observed. In fact, the Council takes up the question of religion directly, calling religion a "valid partner within democratic societies". The 41 member states are encouraged to "promote the teaching of religions" and along the same lines, to "cooperate with religious educational institutions".

Over and above such contradictory positions, some confusion remains concerning the equivocal nature of European identity. It is true that the "Declaration of European identity"[1] of 1973 makes the existence of a European cultural space, conceived as a common patrimony inherited from history, the base of the legitimation of the construction of a European identity, though still emphasising the changing nature of that identity, and the changing dynamics of the construction. But European officials tend to lean toward an essentialist definition of European identity, refracted through a single prism, that of History. In fact, the question of a European political identity is often simply voided in European Union politics, largely because the Union as an institution pays more attention to mechanisms than to goals [Massart-Pierard, 1993:51].

A close watch is nonetheless recommended, if we are not to "make Europe a nation of the purest tradition, protected against the enemies it has chosen from among several candidates, and not at all open to real cultural plurality" [Ferry, 1992:49], in which case the religions recognised as full partners in that common heritage would have to be clearly indicated. With so much at stake, it is time for the question of Islam to be considered and for its global importance to be appreciated.

Particular considerations regarding Islam

While the European Union supports many initiatives aimed at preserving harmony between its constituent parts, it still feels, as if from a distance, the moral necessity of recognising the 'stranger within' [Poncelet, 1994:119], and one sign of this is the project called "Averroes European Day". Even if they are fairly superficial, such initiatives admit the debt the West owes to the world outside it, since the West itself is "constituted as much through exchanges and oppositions vis-à-vis the Orient which 'inhabits' it, as through its own structures" [Khader, 1994:80].

Islam does not constitute "the first priority for the Western world", certainly, but it remains that which is "always there in the background",

---

[1] Copenhagen, 12/14/1973.

that which is 'intimately' foreign in the West [Rodinson, 1993:185 ff.]. At all events, it is precisely because of this complementarity that the Muslim world remains veiled with a certain mystery: the Other must remain ambiguous so that the Self can appear as clearly defined [Laroui, 1986:165]. Such considerations also allow us to explain why reference is too often made to "that which is not mythologically European", in the absence of any real argumentation of that subject, or to a symbolically constructed fiction about Europe as the 'country of reason' whenever it comes to mentioning an eventual cultural conflict [Lourenço, 1991:65]. It is important to face up to these prejudices and to evaluate the present situation as well as the past. At a moment in history when modern societies are trying to redefine the unity and the identity of a collective entity, it is fundamental to consider certain themes related to the question of identity in plain language, in order to be able to take up one's positions for well-defined reasons, and to opt for policies which will prove most pertinent to the actual situation.

At the moment, though it is affirmed loud and clear that education represents an essential key in the combat against ignorance and stereotypes, we still hear that Islam is not well represented in the programmes of general courses of study. Or that the teaching of the Islamic religion is not yet really provided for in most of the countries of Europe, and that Islam is rarely recognised, in works of history and geography, as a religion which makes a positive contribution to the variety of European cultural traditions.

In order to take account of the place which has been reserved for this cultural tradition, we must take a look at the way in which instruction regarding it has been organised, by means of a description which cuts across various European educational systems.

2. Educational Situation of Children from Muslim Families

The topic of the instruction of immigrant children, among them Muslim children, has been the focus of several large-scale studies. The present analysis limits itself to the particular aspects which have been mentioned by the authors.

Statistical data and information

Muslim students are subjected to rather unequal treatment within school systems, especially as regards the higher levels of instruction. We note the proportional over-representation of Muslim students in primary schools, while at the same time they are under-represented at the secondary level [Shadid & van Koningsveld, 1995:106] and at post-secondary levels. For example, Pakistanis and Bengalis are proportionately under-represented in British private schools, which have the highest rate of students gaining admission to universities [Anwar, 1998:51]. Many other statistics bear out this low-end stratification: the larger number of Muslim students at the lowest levels of educational systems, and the high rate (and early age) at which they leave school altogether.

Here are some figures, led off by the situation in Greece, where the illiteracy rate among Muslims is close to 60%, while the rate for the non-Muslim population is 14% [Shadid & van Koningsveld, 1995:125 ff.]. And in 1991, in Belgium, barely 3% of Turks in the 20–24 age group were attending school at some higher-level institution, while the rates for Belgians and Moroccans were 15% and 10%, respectively [Manço A. & Manço, 1995:119]. In Austria, 78% of Turks and 65% of Bosnians had not finished school or had only finished primary school in 1993 [AT File]. In Spain, where students are obliged to stay in school until the age of 16, the transition to the secondary cycle of studies shows a steep drop-off in the number of students registered for school: 61% for the primary cycle, and only 13% for the secondary [ES File]. In Bulgaria, in a 1999 census concerning the over-18 age group, 25% of Turks and Pomaks had pursued secondary-level studies, 50% had finished primary school, and only 4.3% had pursued or were pursuing higher-level studies [BG File].

Educational attainments have noticeably improved, nonetheless, for some groups. In Great Britain, the "results for some Asian groups improved significantly over the last ten years due to a lengthening of periods of residence, but also partially due to greater economic mobility". Their numbers at higher levels of education "have increased steadily", though most of them attend professional schools for technical education, rather than traditional universities [Anwar, 1998:31 ff.].

Parental expectations and difficulties

Whatever may be the motives cited, parents normally have great expectations in regard to their children's schooling. There are considerations related to the ability to find a job, to the possibility of improved social status, or to a comfortable financial situation—and, notably for parents of South Asian girls, the considerable advantages which accrue to educated women in the marriage market.

At all events, parents seem to pay the closest attention to the progress of their children in school, and their educational careers are often quite obviously the subject of discussions at home. On the other hand, 71% of a group of teachers queried in Great Britain believed that Asian parents were less involved in extra-curricular activities than other parents, not only because of difficulties related to language but even more because of a feeling that they were out of place at such activities, many of which involve games of chance (even if this meant only tombolas), and consumption of alcohol or meat; some parents do not consider schools as having any specific responsibility for socialisation [Anwar, 1998:40 ff.].

The rates of failure in school are explained with reference to figures such as those related to the socio-economic level of families, and by taking into consideration the structural constraints linked to ethnicity, culture, and the interaction of the two [Lindo, 1995:144 ff.]. Beginning with quite interesting comparative research concerning Turkish and Portuguese families in the Netherlands, other factors were taken into account, such as the ambivalent attitude of parents confronted with an educational system which was strange to them and perhaps liable to menace their relationship with their children, or the dearth of information concerning the educational system because of an absence of contact between Turkish families and Dutch society, especially as seen in the attitude of mothers whose relationships were strictly limited to their own community, and who thus deprive themselves inadvertently of information which might enable them to defend, for example, the interests of their children in the face of a father's opposition.[2] These gaps in information shrink the

---

[2] Such an observation should be modified relative to individual situations. It seems most applicable to Turkish communities, and probably also to Southeast Asian families across Europe, these often being considered as the groups most centered upon their own communities.

range of possibilities considered regarding children's education, limit choices, and often lead to forms of segregation; the choice of a school is often made simply on the basis of geographical proximity to the home.[3] In the case of Pakistani students in Great Britain, their long absences from school are also a factor, when they spend their vacation periods in the home country. But other types of structural constraint, in this case external to family matters, also affect children's possibilities: blame is laid upon divisions in classes which separate 'good' and 'bad' students, strategies of mobility practised by teachers, policies which show negligence or a lack of concern, low expectations on the part of teachers in regard to these students, etc.

Diverse situations

Despite these large obstacles, let us remain focused on the very great differences which can occur in regard to school success rates. Several factors must be considered in this regard.

First of all, the enormous sociocultural differences which exist between families: there is no possible comparison between the immigrants for economic reasons of the 1950s and 1960s—often illiterate and/or having some training, coming from rural areas—and the political refugees who have arrived since the 1980s, often well educated, with origins in urban areas. As for the presence of students from Muslim countries, this is another category altogether. In Poland, for example, there is a significant number of highly educated persons among the Tartars, many of whom have residency permits, and who are trained in one of the liberal professions—doctors, engineers, etc. [PL File].

Secondly, the possibilities provided (or not) by the host country for the promotion of the development and successful education of students. Greece is an example of failure: this country only subsidises two secondary schools for the 11,800 students attending the 240 primary schools for the Turkish minority in western Thrace [Akgönül, 1999]!

Thirdly, the eventual positive presence of elder brothers and sisters

---

[3] As an illustration, we note that in the United Kingdom in 1992 there were 62 public schools whose percentage of Muslim students was between 90 and 100%, while in 230 other schools the percentage was around 75% [Parker-Jenkins & Haw, 1998:205].

who may be ambitious for their younger brothers and sisters, and may aid them in gaining a better grasp of the language and culture of the host country, not to mention a better understanding of what may be gained in school, and how to use the school system to get it [Crul, 1999:118].

Fourthly, apparent differences in success rates between boys and girls. Girls are more aware of the possibilities for mobility and broadening of self which education offers, while boys, often freer and less closely monitored than the girls, are more easily seduced by activities outside of school, often finishing by rejecting school. This division between genders is so menacing in terms of long-term effects, that Baroness Uddin of Bethnal Green[4] has not hesitated to predict, even in the medium term, the emergence of an enormous problem which she has called a 'huge time bomb'. For the baroness, girls in the future will no longer accept invitations to go out with just anyone, and will seek more recognition of their own personalities. Not so long ago, education was not considered as something which could bring about a real change in mores, since girls were destined in the main to be housewives, education being only a sort of extra which they had been able to benefit from.

3. Religious Socialisation by Families

The area of familial religious socialisation is little represented in the literature. Only a few general considerations will be presented under this heading.

The importance of family socialisation

The place given to religious education by families can take on varying degrees of importance. Some hold that this instruction in the basics of religion is essential; others think it less so. Nonetheless, whether parents openly represent themselves as believers or not, and whether they practice their religion or not, they speak of religion in terms of self-respect and as a mainstay of the child's identity. No one seems indifferent to this. Religion represents a fundamental key

---

[4] First Muslim woman of Bengali descent to sit in the Chamber of Lords. Interview conducted during March, 2000.

to the transmission of the roots of a cultural heritage, to which the child is introduced within the family unit, a process sometimes later continued by other intermediaries.

A variety of types

Researchers who have studied these matters, whether they make reference to Muslims of Maghrebin origin in France [Cesari, 1997] or to those of Pakistani or Bengali ancestry in Great Britain [Vertovec, 1998], agree in holding that this kind of education, especially during early childhood, goes well beyond the responsibility of father and mother alone, and in fact extends to the entire family. Cesari mentions the frequency of the absence of fathers, while Vertovec explains that in Pakistan, the job of transmitting religion is most often the responsibility of grandparents. For Turks in Germany, the phenomenon of families which are stretched between two countries is underlined: this situation lasts for varying periods of time, and it is not rare for some children to stay behind in Turkey or to return there [Yalçin-Heckmann, 1998:167–192]. A wide range of factors show how difficult it can be to make sure such education is provided, once families begin to live partly in Europe and partly in the country of origin.

In Eastern Europe this transmission seems as uncertain as in the West. Though the Muslims of the East had to endure a half-century under communism, it is commonly admitted that immigrants of the first generation who still maintain a scriptural knowledge are rare in the West [Babès, 1997:117]. It has been pointed out that often enough the second generation is just as ignorant in this regard. When these people, who are now between 25 and 34 years old, arrived in Western Europe, there were no real existing structures to provide education for them [Cesari, 1998:30]. The leading authors have reversed their opinions in this matter, since it is the "ignorance of the parents", and no longer that of the children, which has taken centre stage today [Babès, 1997:117]. This topic is easier to focus on, since traditional parental attitudes often amount to grasping things in a quite simple manner, the easiest and most practical possible, but this approach quickly proves insufficient when it comes to facing people who are radically other, and it can even be harmful for children, who may be extremely vulnerable if confronted by Muslim fundamentalists.[5]

---

[5] From an interview with F. Nahdi, editor of the Muslim newspaper *Q-News*, March, 2000.

Other authors place emphasis on the tacit character of this transmission, in which "continuity is assured in and through change"
across several generations, and through contact with other cultures
[Balandier, 1988, cited by Hervieu-Léger, 1997:131–143]. These
authors underline the great number of misconceptions which cloud
the relation between "religion and cultural or ethnic belonging".
Moreover, this belonging is sometimes accepted by men only with
difficulty, who experience at times a sort of "ethnicisation of Islam,
experienced as a stigma" in which Islam is equated with the religion of Arabs, or with a religion of the poor [Babès, 1997:127]. Add
to the foregoing an excessive importance sometimes attached to the
gaze and judgment of the others, and various fears and taboos, especially regarding daughters, whatever may be their origin.[6] But transformations do occur, to the benefit of a more liberal approach to
the religious education of the third generation, more particularly
among educated families [Cesari, 1998:31].

All in all, it is a matter of a kind of familial transmission which
is 'partial and fragmentary', full of discontinuities and compromises.
These descriptions should not be taken as disparaging, and just to
set things in their proper order, here are some apposite words:
". . . must transmission occur necessarily in the academic setting, and
based on canonical precepts? Beyond the mere fact that parents are
familiar with the observances of their religion and practice it, there
are numerous values inherent in Islam which are transmitted, even
if this transmission is rarely made explicit or objective". ". . . the fact
that the mute and humble labour of transmission of the first generation was expressed in the language of simple religious feeling in
a context which rather thwarted many of its aims did not prevent
it from making its point and producing at least some of its intended
effects. These values are simply those of ethics, which all but a few
young people recognize quite well" [Babès, 1997:117 ff.].

---

[6] See also the study by Küçükcan on Turkish families in London, which shows
how much the difference in parents' attitudes is based on cultural practices: ". . . parents cannot justify themselves with reference only to religion, because if that were
really the case, they ought to adopt without prompting the same attitude toward
boys that they adopt toward girls, since religious principles apply to boys and girls
alike" [Küçükcan, 1998:112–113].

4. Religious Education Offered within Mosques

Framework

This type of education, organised by communities themselves, takes the form of Qur'anic courses given after school or on weekends. Supervised by imams, by teachers of Arabic from the host country,[7] or by volunteers, these courses are usually offered to children between the ages of 6 and 12. The classes sometimes take place in private homes, but more often in Islamic centres or in mosques, in rooms adjacent to prayer rooms. Although these locations are today better adapted for this use than formerly, it is still too often the case that communities which lack proper funding must put up with musty, poorly lighted, and dilapidated halls and rooms. And some classes are quite overcrowded, reaching in some cases as many as 70 children, ages 5 to 16, in a single room [Lewis P., 1994:140].

The pedagogy employed in these traditional settings features an approach based above all on memorisation and recitation of the Qur'an,[8] and on learning Arabic. There is actually a blend of curricular and pedagogical models, which gives more importance to religion or to language within a course of instruction according to different situations [Bastenier & Dassetto, 1984], because the use of the Arabic language is linked not only to "practical considerations, but also to symbolic ones". This emerges more and more sharply, especially as concerns the sermon during group prayers, the Friday *khutba*, because of the increasing importance of second generation youths, the increasing number of mixed marriages and converts, and the "multiplicity of origins of Muslim immigrants" [Allievi, 1998:232].

Within this framework, new approaches do occur, including the

---

[7] Actual state-sponsored institutions from countries of origin are involved here, such as the Hassan II Foundation for Moroccans who live outside Morocco (MRE's), which furnishes instruction in Arabic language and Moroccan culture as a means of preserving a sense of nationality in children. The Foundation sends most of its teachers to France and Belgium (86% of its teachers, serving about 53,416 students during the 1998/99 school year; cf. "The Hassan II Foundation for MRE's" in *Al Bayane*, 04/14/2000). Other countries apply this system, for example Turkey, through the Diyanet.

[8] Some authors use the terms "mosque education" and "mosque-schools" to emphasise the extended nature of this course of instruction, which they also describe as concerned with questions of faith, rules for behaviour, and with ethics in general. [Shadid & van Koningsveld, 1995:107].

renewal of new teaching methods and changes related to new educational objectives which themselves reflect the appearance of new
goals for education. For example, a game called "Steps to Paradise"
is now available in Great Britain. The game tests one's knowledge
of Islam; correct answers win the player cards which illustrate 'religious merits', which in turn help him or her get closer to Paradise
(and to winning the game). And attention is sometimes focused on
new elements of daily life: one may hear it said that trading cards
depicting Batman or the game of marbles are inappropriate activities to engage in on the grounds of a mosque [Lewis P., 1994:118].

Various interests and their relative importance

For parents, such religious instruction offered by mosques always
seems to be viewed as the only education, apart from their own
efforts, which has any very important influence on the construction
of the (religious) identity of their children [Shadid & van Koningsveld,
1997:160]. In general, this instruction continues to enjoy the prior
approval of many as a source of Islamic religious "knowledge", in
addition to the transmission of religious feeling and familiarity with
ritual.

Nonetheless some children find all this mechanical and boring
[Vertovec & Rogers, 1998:99], often because such classes cut into
their free time so drastically that they feel they have no more free
time at all. Also, repetitive and authoritarian methods have in some
cases brought about lack of interest and numerous complaints, especially when the class material is presented in a dry and stiff manner. It appears that the cane is sometimes used, at least to threaten
[Lewis P., 1994:140], and some children have complained openly
about old-fashioned punishments [Telhine, 1998:26].

Today this type of instruction is offered in mosques in almost all
areas, including Eastern Europe, where the majority of mosques or
Qur'anic schools were closed during the communist era, with a few
exceptions for propaganda purposes [Eminov, 1997:52 ff.]. Still, the
weakening of these institutions has led to the fact that, in Bulgaria,
for example, instruction offered in mosques is restricted to small children [BG File]. Religious instruction provided by mosques obviously
is a more crying need in countries which do not take responsibility
for offering it in the public schools. An example: in Great Britain it
has been estimated, though the figure is probably at least slightly

exaggerated, that 90% of Muslim children between 5 and 12 attended classes in mosques in 1990.[9] Another example: Luxembourg, where the first classes ever organized by the *Centre Culturel Islamique du Grand-Duché de Luxembourg* began in 1996. About 300 children began to study the Islamic religion at locations in Mamer, Wiltz, and Rumelange: they were taught by five volunteers offering instruction in Bosnian, Turkish, French, and even (eventually) Urdu [LU File].

At any rate, even when state-sponsored schools offer classes in Islamic religion, instruction in mosques continues to be provided by parents who see it as complementary to school-based instruction.[10] These supplementary offerings are all the more worthwhile, inasmuch as the awakening and development of religious feeling in children are considered in some circles as factors beneficial to performance in regular school.[11]

In comparative terms, a study performed in the Netherlands in 1988 which surveyed 65 mosques found that a quarter of children between 5 and 14 had attended such classes [Landman, 1992:59 ff.], with some variations in different ethnic communities, having to do with their organisational capacities [Karagül, 1987, cited in Shadid & van Koningsveld, 1997:159]. According to the president of one of the two Islamic federations in Germany, the *Islamrat für die Bundesrepublik Deutschland,* the percentage involved for Turkish children in Germany is 10% [Spuler-Stegemann, 1998:93 ff.]. But such figures may be taken in a relative sense, because only a small number of children complete the entire course of instruction. The great majority of parents do not appear to want to place an extra burden on their children, over and above regular schoolwork [Shadid & van Koningsveld, 1997:160]. There also appears to be a certain disconnection between the large number of parents who express the desire to have such instruction be made available to their children, and the number which actually makes use of the possibility, as if it were more of a question of principle than anything else [Yalçin-Heckmann, 1998:171].[12] A similar proportion of immigrants (of all

---

[9] Hussein, 1990, cited by Parker-Jenkins & Haw, 1998:194.

[10] J. Moreras makes reference to the case of Spain [ES File].

[11] From an interview with A. Ishtiaq, spokesman for the Council of Mosques, Bradford, March 2000.

[12] This author speaks about Turks in Germany, and affirms that similar observations have been made in Great Britain and France.

origins, Muslim and non-Muslim) express a desire for courses of instruction in their native language, and say they want their children to attend such classes.

Among the factors which explain this gap may also be counted instances of going against the opinions of the dominant society, which continually criticises these schools and their methods. Over and above pedagogical methods which are judged inadequate and of little application to the conditions in which young Muslims find themselves, a further reproach is levelled (for example in Germany), that in such schools "obedience to God, respect for parents, and prevention of or protection from abuse of drugs and alcohol" are given the highest priority. Although education which inculcates respect for the law can certainly be viewed in a positive light, the particular reproach is that this method constitutes too defensive a stance, and one which is too little integrative, so that "the emphasis placed on the ideology of the community contradicts the reality of German society, in which more and more emphasis is placed on individualism" [Gabert, 2000:96]. Another element mentioned in this connection is fear of fundamentalism, or the risk of 'contamination' of young people by Islamist ideologies via the various organisations which subsidise the mosques [Karakasoglu & Nonneman, 1996:254]. It appears difficult, then, to find examples of a challenging education in this regard, especially since the society of the host countries is often unenthusiastic about any form of Islamic education.

Before ending this section, let us mention a more 'privatised' form of this kind of instruction. An example comes from Keighley, an enclave-town in the North of England which has a very high percentage of residents of Indo-Pakistani descent. Almost every child living there receives a religious education, not primarily in one of the four madrasas, but within private homes in which certain parents have taken responsibility for the education of the children of the neighbourhood. A great disparity as regards the length and comprehensiveness of the education made available to girls and to boys is also noticeable. Boys are made to study and retain the content of more texts, and receive more instructions concerning religious observances and expected behaviour [Vertovec, 1998:98]. A second example, relating probably less to the lack of infrastructure than to the desire to preserve various particularities in instruction, is given by the activity of some splinter groups such as the Ahmadi movement, which takes responsibility for the education of its members' children in an exclusive manner [Nielsen, 1996:56].

5. Religious Education in State Systems

Preferences and tensions

We have already shown how much the question of education is thought crucial by Muslim parents. Beyond any symbolic or strategic reason, the relative limits of the two modes of transmission mentioned above allow us to understand the importance some families attach to the availability of instruction in Islamic religion in the state school systems.

But though education is rated very high,[13] many still perceive a contradiction between the school, a fundamental value-instilling institution of the dominant culture, and Muslim values. Such a feeling leads some to challenge the school system because it is not considered in all quarters as a "place where a neutral knowledge is dispensed", but thought rather to accomplish "a kind of brain-washing intended to discredit Islam".[14] Some parents are afraid they are losing their children to the school [Morck, 1998:136]. More generally, the dissatisfactions felt can be summed up in this way: parents see that they do not know how to help their children to grow up in an environment in which they control neither the people nor the events, where their own authority may be questioned, where traditional gender roles are undermined, and where independent critical thinking progressively replaces traditional authority, or even the authority of the revelation itself [Nielsen, 1999:64 ff.].

However this may be, the specific expectations of Muslims regarding school have been summed up in an outline of theoretical and 'ideal' recommendations made by Muslim authors in the United

---

[13] According to the Prophet, "the ink of scholars is more precious than the blood of martyrs" [Kepel, 1994:317].

[14] Kepel refers here to individuals marked by the process of re-Islamization in France (this applies also to Muslims who have remained quite attached to their beliefs and their cultural heritage). He reminds us too that even lay status is perceived as "taking an anti-religious position, abandoning the foundations of belief" [Kepel, 1994:317].

Kingdom [Parker-Jenkins & Haw, 1998:199 ff.]. The assumed needs of Muslim children are brought under three heads: first there are 'religious and cultural needs', such as praying five times a day and performing one's ablutions (which makes a flexible schedule of activities necessary, especially at noon or on Friday), participating in religious holy days such as the *'Id al-Fitr* or the *'Id al-Adha*, eating halal meat or vegetarian meals in school lunchrooms, dressing decently, including allowing women to wear headscarves, and staging sports events without gender-mixing after the onset of puberty etc. Second: 'educational requirements', namely that instruction should be carried out in a spirit of respect for different languages and traditions, and should pay particular attention to the problem of racism. Courses in geography and history should also reflect an Islamic dimension, sex education should be adequate, and books about Islam should exist in the libraries. Finally, 'general needs' are those which have to do with relations between school and family. These are easier to establish and maintain if Muslim teachers are hired to teach; they serve as a common point of contact in the relationship, and even constitute an important role model for students. And it is further recommended that an Islamic representative be included in the school administration [Parker-Jenkins & Haw, 1998:199–203].

Generally, Muslims want a larger place given to references to Islam in the educational system. In practice, three ways of doing this exist. First, quite a rare case, the creation of private Islamic schools (found mostly in Great Britain). Second, we find institutional systems which allow for the establishment of Muslim schools, recognised and financed by the state, provided their programmes of instruction conform to national standards: this situation is found mostly in Denmark, the Netherlands, and Bulgaria. The third way, found with the second sometimes, also depends on the characteristics of the existing system, which may allow courses in Islamic religion in public school curricula. This is not possible in France, for example, but is common in Belgium.

The situation today

Overall, though Islamic instruction and Muslim schools are in early stages of development, and though very uneven solutions have so far been arrived at from country to country as regards means and methods, Muslims have nonetheless handled the beginnings of their entry into the institutional context fairly effectively [Dassetto, 1996:312], even in Eastern Europe. In all but a few countries, this process has been accomplished without major opposition from European state governments [Dassetto, 1996:312].

But despite these good results, we note that problems persist, such as those involving the status of teachers of Islamic religion, which are often underestimated. It is still often necessary to fall back on imams and on language teachers, who are sometimes subsidised by outside agencies, or even on volunteers in order to be able to provide teachers in this area [Shadid & van Koningsveld, 1997:173]. In 1993, among 432 Muslim teachers in Greece with Greek nationality, 115 were still hodjas coming out of madrasas, or had not finished their secondary studies, 98 were militant kemalist Turks (advocates of a strong Turkish identity) with diplomas from Turkish universities, who were educated before 1968, and the other 219 were young products of madrasas in very traditional mountain villages who then received diplomas from the *Selanik Özel Pedagoji Akademisi* (SÖPA) [Dalègre, 2001:307]. For the rest, there is almost no institutionalised Muslim influence within state school systems, either at the level of school administration or system administration, though a few efforts are progressing slowly, for example in the administration of kindergartens and schools in Denmark [DK File].

From country to country, Muslims are led to demand different things with different levels of intensity in the demand.[15] Something which appears absolutely necessary in one is unimportant in another. Aside from the United Kingdom, where most of the 'theoretical' claims have been debated, a few other instances: the debate over girls' headscarves in France, school trips, participation in sports, and biology in Germany[16] and the discomforting presence of a cross on the wall in classrooms used for courses of Islamic religion in Austria [Strobl, 1997:171] and Bavaria.

Another range of cases appears in the reactions of European states and societies to these demands. The Bavarian example shows to what

---

[15] In Greece and Bulgaria, exclusively religious demands are sometimes replaced by ethnic ones.

[16] Spuler-Stegemann, 1998:98–99. This author adds that some students obtained from the federal administrative Tribunal the right to skip mixed classes in sports, but the Tribunal's decision stated that no similar exception would be granted for classes in drawing (said to violate a prohibition on images of humans), chemistry (contact with alcohol), or music (charms of the female voice).

extent the debate on religious liberty can be turned topsy-turvy. The fact that at the request of a minority a religious icon (recognised by the vast majority of citizens) was removed, has been perceived in Germany as an attack on a religious identity—though in France such handling of symbols is the norm. Still, "while the Constitutional Court of Germany found that religious liberty stood opposed to the state's taking the initiative in imposing a religious icon, the principle did not appear to them to exclude the presence of such a sign at school, if it met with the wishes of the school community in general" [Woehrling, 1998:47–48].

Over and above these national variations, much of the complexity of the problem is related to the pluralism of tendencies within Islam,[17] the more so because splinter groups, even at the local level, can exacerbate differences, especially with Muslim parents who refuse to accept Muslim teachers from other versions of Islam than theirs [Strobl, 1997:171].[18] And we have not considered the influence of states of origin, most important of which is Turkey's Diyanet.[19] This bureau possesses a modern infrastructure and trained teachers, manuals of religious instruction for all levels, the levels in Turkish schools at least. The Diyanet also exerts pressure where it can on governments in order to have Islamic religious instruction introduced, and to claim the right to provide this instruction itself. Germany, Sweden, Switzerland and the Netherlands have dealt with it, but some Muslim circles refuse this power play, and react sharply, saying essentially that the Diyanet "presents the image of a unified religious culture which recognizes little of the diversity within Islam in general or even Turkish Islam" [Gabert, 1999:92]. This range of situations shows that "there is no consensus in Muslim circles" [Shadid & van Koningsveld, 1995:107], and that religious prescriptions in the area of education are perceived or interpreted differently by different individuals and groups.

Aside from these internecine disputes, we note elements which sometimes pose obstacles to any authentic recognition of Islam within

---

[17] For a general review of these tendencies, see "Diversity of ideological and religious currents" in chapter 3.

[18] This author mentions the case of Bosnian refugees or Alawis refugees who will not accept a Turkish or an Arab teacher.

[19] This is the Directorate of Religious Affairs set up by the Turkish state, in charge of matters of religion and Islamic morality in regard to Turkish people living abroad.

state school systems. First, ignorance of the Islamic religion by some teachers [van de Wetering, 1992:90 ff.]. Sometimes, too, access to multicultural education is perceived as a meaningless addition to education [Anwar, 1998:43 ff.]. Then there are the courses which present historical events such as the Crusades or colonisation in a unilateral manner. Finally there is the absence of sufficient numbers of Muslim teachers who are tenured within the system, indeed, a lack of teachers with adequate language skills, or who are fit to teach in any ethnic community at all [Shadid & van Koningsveld, 1997]. In Germany the situation is made worse by the fact that qualified teachers are not evenly distributed across the Länder [Arayci, 1999:57]. And as regards Qur'anic schools, sometimes the consensus among the citizens of the host country holds that it is better to allow accommodations in formalities such as headscarves or non-mixed gym classes, than to face the prospect of "Muslim schools which would prevent children from learning about other sorts of people, and from learning tolerance" [Basset cited in Tangram, 1999:20 ff.]. This basic attitude is reinforced by the fact that school sometimes represents the only place Muslim girls, whose movements are checked and sometimes even timed, are allowed to go.

6. Interplay of Language of Origin, Culture, and Religion

All immigrant communities encounter the question of the teaching of languages of origin. Some Muslim children experience extreme linguistic diversity. Here is an example concerning Indo-Pakistani children in Great Britain described by P. Lewis.[20] This author explained that the children sometimes use five languages, because they study classical Arabic with the imams, watch satellite television in Punjabi, watch videos in Hindi, while all the time their 'serious' language is Urdu, and they speak English only at school. The same is true for most non-Arabic-speaking Muslims in Europe who, without counting local dialects, are obliged to speak at least three languages.

For all that, the situation of Arabic speakers is not much easier, due to the existence of Arabic dialects. Even if there is a rounding-off due to schooling and television, dialects are usually not written

---

[20] P. Lewis, conversation in Bradford, March 2000.

down as such but are still the languages of daily use other than the language of the host country, which gains ground in every succeeding generation. But apart from this, in the case of the children of Arabic-speaking Muslims, instruction in Arabic is considered part of instruction in religion, to the extent that Arabic is the sacred language of the Revelation.

Two types of situations

As concerns education, a fundamental difference is noted between countries where Muslims try to find a place in existing structures, common to all, and countries like Greece—more precisely, Western Thrace. There, Muslim populations are considered as constituting a separate linguistic and religious minority. As such, they benefit from recognition and from a specific infrastructure, especially in the area of education, where "Turkish is taught in all Muslim schools, even to children for whom it is not the mother tongue": Turkish "takes up half of instructional hours" and is also used in religious instruction [Dalègre, 2001:298]. Thracian students, however, are forced to finish school in Greek schools even though most of them have only a limited knowledge of it [Küçükcan, 1999:61; Akgönül, 1999]. In consequence almost no Muslim student from Thrace passes the university entrance exams, and more than 60% of students who continue to the secondary level go to Turkey.[21] Another difficulty awaits them: since the early 1980s, the state agency in charge of accepting diplomas from foreign schools, the Dikatsa, has accepted Turkish diplomas only as an exception. Still, in the wake of negotiations between Greece and Turkey, and between Turkey and Europe, the Dikatsa has begun to show flexibility in regard to Turkish diplomas, and an experimental quota system for the Thracian minority is in place in the universities [Akgönül, 1999].

In Bulgaria, the normalisation of the status of the Turkish minority is quite recent. From 1985 to 1989, the government said there were no Turks there, and that Bulgaria was an homogeneous nation. No sense bothering to debate about Turkish language and culture,

---

[21] The effect was not long in coming. Students in significant numbers departed, mostly for Turkey, though many probably did so for linguistic or professional reasons, not religious. These young people end up settling in Turkey, and often their parents follow [Akgönül, 1999a:34].

then [Eminov, 1997:128]. A decisive step was taken in February 1999, when the national Assembly ratified the European convention on minority rights. Elsewhere, in January 2000, a demand was made for the addition of official recognition of the Turkish national minority to the Constitution [Bougarel & Clayer, 2001:69]. At the moment the implications of this recognition are still limited: four hours of Turkish instruction per week have been offered to students in the 1st through 8th grades in regions with mixed populations since the school year of 1994–95 [Ragaru, 2001:253].

There was a European resolution in 1976[22] which attracted attention by underlining the desirability of organizing language courses and courses about culture for foreign residents. The resolution referred not only to the cultures of the country of residence and the countries of origin for EU citizens, but also to communities of immigrants. The resolution was widely taken into account, and such courses were eventually organised in most countries [Obdeijn & de Ruiter, 1998]. Turkish, for example, is offered as a foreign language in many German schools, and is otherwise well recognised in the educational system. In the Netherlands, a dozen or so minority groups were offered instruction in their own languages in schools [van de Wetering, 1992:90]. In relation to mosque-based instruction, the state courses ended up drawing 70% of primary school students, which puts in perspective the importance of the instruction offered in mosques [Shadid & van Koningsveld, 1997:160]. In Sweden, there is sometimes cooperation between Islamic schools and public schools in the area of language teaching [SE File]. In France, several curricula which include Arabic language teaching exist, including the language plus study of the culture of origin, or Arabic in the framework of introductory foreign language courses, offered in primary and secondary school. The first format is not offered to all primary level students, and is often simply mixed in with general education. The second is almost invisible; the number of students following this format has been shrinking for ten years [Affes, 2000:66]. In fact, failure to continue from primary to secondary level, and (again) the lack of competent teachers[23] are problems observed in France, and

---

[22] 41976Y0219 (01)—Resolution of the Council and education ministers including a programme of action with regard to education (Official Journal n° C 038 du 19/02/1976).

[23] 25 fully qualified and 67 certified teachers for 70,000 students [Naba, 1999:12].

explain perhaps why Arabic language class attendance is up in cultural and religious associations [Affes, 2000:67]. The steady increase of the importance of associations in this regard is also found in Spain, where it is interesting to note that public authorities have officially recognised the *Asociación de trabajadores immigrantes marroquíes en España* (Association of Moroccan immigrant workers in Spain) as the provider of language and culture classes for Moroccan children [Obdeijn & de Ruiter, 1998]. In Romania, the Muslim community has lost its institutions, its private primary schools, and its Islamic traditions. Although the Tartar language is the most commonly spoken in the Muslim community, it was Turkish literary language which was offered to 2000 Turkish-speaking and Tartar-speaking students in Romanian schools [Anghelescu, 1999:135]. Despite the opening of about a dozen bilingual crèches in Drobudja [RO File] and efforts by the Department of Turkish studies of the University of Bucharest, the few hours of mother tongue instruction given in a few primary schools in Constanta, Medgidia, and Vale lui Traian are insufficient [Lederer, 1996:359]. As for the offering of a special primary level class for the 2000–01 school year, only a few students are actually involved, though the offering is supposed to expand to three class levels. Intensive courses in Islamic religion and Turkish language and culture are given during regular school hours [RO File] in some locations in Romania.

What is at stake

It is interesting to observe how the reasons for organising such courses have changed in political terms. In the spirit of the resolution of 1976, the emphasis was placed on preserving languages and cultures of origin of children, in order to make it possible for them to be able to return there eventually. Since the 1990s such ideas have had little to do with reality. Now it is their integration into European societies which is the focus. And this goal is seen as reachable by way of the construction of a strong personal identity, together with a respectful assimilation of the culture of origin [Obdeijn & de Ruiter, 1998].

If we compare countries, the organising of such courses gives rise to considerable variations as regards religion, partly due to the teachers [Dassetto, 1996:280]. Sometimes they are transformed into real alternative forms of religious instruction, as in certain German Länder[24] where there are no religion courses as such, but sometimes they keep religion rather distant, as in Great Britain.

The various functions and the significance attached to these courses have not failed to elicit comments from the families involved. So for example in the Netherlands, where Dutch law does not provide for religious education within language classes, a survey of Moroccan immigrant parents found a degree of ambivalence toward Arabic classes. Arabic is considered not only a spoken language, which may prove to be of economic value, but the instrument of transmission of cultural values, religious values, and the feeling of belonging. The story is told that many parents were surprised when, after having been asked their opinion about Arabic language classes, they were then asked for an opinion regarding Islamic education. Some answered, Weren't we just talking about that? [van de Wetering, 1992:90 ff.; Sakkouni, 1998:11]. As for young people, they often see these classes as a way of being able to speak with the other members of their family, when they come for a visit [Obdeijn & de Ruiter, 1998].

---

[24] The German debate is not fixed whether "this type of education is to transmit knowledge about religion or to transmit a faith although such a distinction is not even conceivable from an Islamic point of view" [Gabert, 1999:96]. But since the Muslim community does not enjoy the status of a 'corporation under public law' (Körperschaft öffentlichen Rechts) or benefit from an 'ecclesiastical tax', and since education is a matter controlled by the Länder, each Land has developed its own model for instruction in Islamic religion. Four types of solution have been tried. The states of Berlin and Bremen are the only ones to favour teaching Islamic courses in public schools, while still giving the communities responsibility for them. In Bavaria, instruction in Islamic religion is considered a 'current subject' in the state schools' programme of instruction [Sunier & Meyer, 1998:110]. But other states only grant the right to instruction in Islamic religion when this accompanies complementary education in a mother tongue—Muttersprachlicher Ergänzungsunterricht, MEU. In the state of Nordrhein-Westfalen, courses are given by teachers paid by the state, and in the others (Baden-Württemberg, Berlin, Saarland and Schleswig-Holstein) diplomatic representatives have the responsibility [Karakasoglu & Nonneman, 1996:253]. In that case, Islam is managed "from the outside, by diplomatic personnel, as if it were a case of cooperation between two countries" [Amiraux, 1999:38]. But the children do not benefit from any inter-religious dialogue. As for the states of Hamburg and Brandenburg, they claim to have a preference for the culturalist and historical approach to religions.

7. In the Public Schools

There are four basic modes of organisation of religious instruction in public schools in Europe. They are presented in order here: a secular approach which refuses religious instruction; a plural approach which allows teaching about several different religions; a preferential and restricted approach which offers and authorises instruction in a given religion, but privileges instruction in the dominant religion in that society; and a culturalist and historical approach to religion.

The secular or laïcist approach

This secular option consists in refusing instruction in a particular religion within the curriculum, which as state-sponsored is considered incompatible with any one religion. The choice of this secular concept is the result of the "predominance it has within the French debate", though the uncontested principle of the neutrality of the state in religious matters is 'rarely affirmed as such' in that debate. This situation is interpreted as probably related to the fact that the concept of lay education "may be understood by some as containing another aspect, that of the idea of the primacy of the state" [Woehrling, 1998].

This approach is not widespread in Western Europe. In fact, apart from a few Swiss cantons, it concerns only France, though we note an exception for Alsace-Moselle, where instruction in four recognised religions is an option for students, and the state is obliged to provide the option [Woehrling, 1998].

Within such a framework, no programme of studies in religion exists in the public schools, except for the partial and indirect exposure gained in courses of general history or geography, or in language of origin classes.[25] Consequently the responsibility for religious education, morally and financially, falls on religious communities and on parents, who are all the same able to get the use of classrooms for this purpose [Sunier & Meyer, 1998:113].

As for Eastern Europe, one might think that such an attitude would be common after years of communism. But one ought not to

---

[25] Since 1996, a certain 'inflection' of programmes of study attests to a greater sensitivity to the place of religion in general courses.

forget that before the coming of that system, Muslim communities in some Eastern European countries had fairly well organised educational structures. Since the fall of communism, these structures, though very weak, have opened their doors anew, or have signed agreements with the state. So it is in Bulgaria and Romania, as we shall see in the next section.

The plural approach

Starting from a principle of religious diversity, this neutral option tends to offer instruction in various faiths in public schools. Most of the time it is based on agreements signed between the state and representatives of various religions in order to provide students with general instruction about religion, which may eventually be funded by the state. But this alternative poses problems with regard to Islam, when the question arises concerning the legitimacy of the religious authority which designs and organises the course.

Belgium and Spain are the only countries who have accomplished this officially.[26] Two representative institutions in Germany are trying to see Islam placed on an equal footing with Catholic religious education, but in the meantime stopgap solutions have been found, sometimes with success as in the cases of the states of Berlin and Bremen.[27] Besides these two states, which have placed Islamic religious instruction under the responsibility of the religious or ideological communities themselves, two other countries can be placed in this second category, namely Finland (when parental requests are made)[28] and Austria.

These authorities have made a place for Islam in the public schools;

---

[26] In Spain the agreement has only been partly carried out, since the various pilot projects which resulted from the Unión de Comunidades Islámicas en España (UCIDE) initiative, particularly in some schools of Madrid and Ceuta, still remain outside the regular school day [ES File].

[27] The Berlin Senate originally concluded an agreement with the Turkish Consulate which gave Turkish students two hours a week of Islamic cultural and ethical instruction, over and above their Turkish language courses (cf. infra). But at the end of 1998 the administrative High Court of Berlin granted the Islamische Föderation (Islamic Federation) of Berlin—this time mainly influenced by the Milli Görüs and no longer by the Diyanet—the right to offer Islamic studies to 30,000 Muslim students within the city-state. The appeals are still going on [Gabert, 1999:95].

[28] The state has paid for a creche directed by Muslims and open to all who can accommodate themselves to certain Islamic features, such as following an Islamic holiday calendar [FI File].

two hours of Islamic religion have been added to the curriculum of regular classes in obligatory fashion in Belgium and Austria (since, respectively, 1978 and 1980), and by option in Spain and the two abovementioned German states. Often there is a minimum number of students which must be met, which creates problems for small and widely separated communities. Two examples: a minimum of three is required to organise a class in Finland, with a total of only 450 Muslim students attending such classes [FI File], while in Austria only one hour of instruction is available if there are fewer than ten students, unless students from several schools meet together on the weekend [Strobl, 1997:166 ff.]. In most such cases the state lays down formal conditions, assigns classrooms, pays teachers and even furnishes texts, while the religious communities see to the content of the course. They also must pay for the cost of hiring competent teachers, giving them competence tests and providing them adequate pedagogical material, which may have to be approved by the state.

In practical terms, disparate modes of application among these states should be noted. As regards the selection of teachers, though no official standard has been established for hiring religion teachers in Germany, most of them come from abroad. Belgium recruits its 650 teachers of Islamic religion mostly among people living there, many of whom are already over-qualified for the job.[29] Spanish representatives have not been able to agree on a unified list of teachers,[30] and Finland has recruited teachers from among converts and immigrants [FI File]. But while Austria pays a limited number of teachers of religious instruction, they do receive approval from an Austrian Council of Muslims.[31] With regard to pedagogical material, all par-

---

[29] Teachers of Islamic religion have suffered from uncertainties regarding their status and from low salaries in comparative terms, but improvement was expected from the election of an 'organe chef du culte' in December 1998.

[30] In April 1996, the Spanish government and the *Comisión Islámica de España* (CIE) signed an agreement concerning the development of Islamic religious education, beginning with the 1996–97 school year in Spanish state-sponsored schools. The teachers involved were to be paid by the state beginning the following school year (1997–98). However, problems of funding and disagreements among representatives of Islamic federations regarding the drawing up of a unified list of teachers have almost completely prevented this agreement from coming into effect up to the present time, although the curriculum for the proposed instruction in Islamic religion was approved in January 1966.

[31] About 150 teachers are available to teach this subject to 30,000 students, after having studied Islam under Muslim teachers, or completing a good private course, and following successful completion of an examination given by the *Zentrale der*

ties seem to allow this to be funded by outside, foreign sources, either by design as in Finland and Germany, or because of lack of time and/or logistical coordination, as in Belgium. These remarks are to be gradually attenuated, at least for primary school, where initiatives for the production of texts which match with the European context are being worked out. Again Austria stands out: its manuals are put together by religious organisations, and then published by the Ministry of Education and Cultural Affairs [Jung cited in Schreiner, 2000:13 ff.], which furnishes copies to students; 20,000 copies of the Qur'an were also distributed in this way [Nielsen, 1995:29]. The course is offered in German, Islamic sources are translated into Arabic and the latest editions seem more adapted and open to their environment [Strobl, 1997:166 ff.].

In this category we also find the unusual case of Bulgaria, where courses in Islamic religion had been banned form public schools since 1952, and where the stated aim of education was described as "to develop an atheist and scientific vision of the world through the application of Marxist-Leninist principles". Courses in religion were officially reintroduced ten years ago in the national education system [Eminov, 1997:130] and various projects have emerged. In 19 municipalities, children averaging seven years old, in the second grade of elementary school, began to receive a weekly hour of Islamic religious instruction as part of pilot projects whose programmes were approved by the Ministry of Education [BG File].

Finally we may observe that Orthodox religious instruction has been reintroduced into Romanian public schools. It is a regular, obligatory course, except where parents have asked that their children be excused from it, or where they have decided (which happens less often) to replace it with participation in weekend catechism classes, whose grades are counted by the public schools. As for Islamic courses, they are organised and paid for by the state, as soon as requests from enough students are received; Muslim students from different levels and schools are brought together twice a week for instruction in the Islamic religion and in Turkish language and culture, given equal emphasis.

Islamischen Glaubengemeinschaft (central committee of the Islamic faith community), whose president is the inspector for religion courses [Strobl, 1997:166 ff.].

The preferential approach

This approach involves a lower degree of recognition for Islamic instruction. In some cases, national authorities respect Islam within public schools, but give it only a formal position in the system. In other cases, they favour instruction in a particular religion, but do not assign any status or recognition to Islam.

The first of these two cases applies to Great Britain quite precisely. In fact, while the Education Act of 1944 is founded on the notion of 'religion', and refers implicitly to existing communities (all Christian), the law of 1988 on education reform explicitly refers to Christianity. It is stipulated that the only required religious instruction in public schools concerns Christianity, including common prayer and religious instruction based on an approved syllabus, though other religions practiced in the country are taken into account [Nielsen, 1999a:227–231]. Here we find the bonds between the state and the church of England confronted with the trend of policies from the 1980s, which favoured an ecumenical approach. [Nielsen, 1999:51]. Structural changes were made in order to eliminate forms of discrimination, and in response to demands made by Muslim civic organisations such as the Islamic Foundation of Leicester, the Muslim Educational Trust of London, and the Islamic Academy of Cambridge [Kelly, 1999:197]. These changes involved school clothes and uniforms, physical education classes, prayer rooms, school lunches, and school closing on Muslim holidays when the majority of students are Muslim, etc. Despite the appearance of a relative flexibility on the part of local authorities, their attitude is sometimes perceived as an unhappy compromise, because it only deals with the formal acceptance of Islam in the schools, avoiding all debate over the ideological foundations of that which is considered to represent integration into the larger society.

In cases which fall into this second category, Muslim children cannot receive Islamic instruction within the public school because only official religions can be taught. That is how things stand in Portugal, Poland, Italy, Luxembourg[32] and in Greece, where Orthodox religious instruction is obligatory [Dalègre, 2001:290] for 35,000 Albanian

---

[32] The Catholic church is party to a convention with the government which stipulates that in primary schools, the students can choose between instruction in religion and morals, or instruction in social studies and morals [LU File].

Muslim children aged 5 to 18, living in Greece, and also for Turkish children coming from Thrace who are obliged to finish school in Greece [GR File].[33] In Italy, for example, Catholic religious instruction is required unless parents obtain permission to exclude their children from it, based on their personal principles or their membership in another faith. Theoretically, it is possible to arrange alternative instruction, but this is rarely requested, and schools do not encourage it. The case cannot be litigated because there is no agreement 'intensa' regarding Islam within the state framework [IT File]. However, within these faith-based systems, at least in Greece, it appears that other religions are presented, insofar as possible, through their own texts, and that a certain ecumenism is emphasised [Tskalidis cited in Schreiner, 2000:75 ff.]. Moreover, exceptions have been made as regards "absenteeism of girls from physical education classes or school trips, or the wearing of headscarves as soon as girls reach puberty" [Dalègre, 2001:308].

The cultural and historical approach

This approach takes into account the establishment of new religious communities, as well as of the progressive secularisation of states, and the functional decline of traditional churches. It first appeared in countries where religious courses in a state religion were offered. Historically, England is the pioneer, though the first offerings were not systematic, and still depend on the initiative of over 100 existing educational authorities [Nielsen, 1999a:227 ff.]. The English model was studied closely by the Netherlands and Scandinavian countries such as Norway, which changed official syllabi as a result. Some German states, such as Hamburg and Brandenburg, also became interested. In those states courses entitled 'Religion for all' and "Life orientation-Ethics-Religious Knowledge" are taught, from an independent standpoint as regards religion and visions of the world [Schreiner, 2000:49 ff.].

---

[33] By contrast, almost all Muslim children in Thrace go to their own minority schools. These offer two hours of religious instruction a week for the first two years, then three hours a week from third through sixth grade. Schools can choose to have Wednesday or Sunday off, and vacation periods follow the calendar for Greek schoolchildren. Besides, Qur'anic instruction in Arabic has been available at Xanthi and in a few mountain villages for several years, offered in the afternoon by the imam at the mosque [Dalègre, 200:306].

In the Netherlands, where it was observed that the whole society was becoming multicultural and multi-confessional, a course called 'Geestelijke stromingen' (Spiritual Currents), was created [Spinder cited in Schreiner, 2000:117 ff.]. Alongside that, parents have the right to obtain religious education for their children in public schools according to the Dutch Education Act of 1984, but local authorities do not have to pay the teacher's salary, and they retain the right to determine which language the course will be taught in. This decision to require teaching in Dutch has slowed the development of Islamic religious instruction because of the lack of competent teachers [Dassetto, 1996:279]. The local authorities do not determine the content of instruction, nor the costs associated [NL File] with pedagogical method or material; all this must be paid for by parents, and as a result only 3% of municipalities went through the process [Shadid & van Koningsveld, 1997:149]: only four towns in 1993–94 [Sunier & Meyer, 1998:122]. During this period, Rotterdam decided to fund such activities itself [NL File].

Although the English model was the darling of the continent in the mid-1980s, it has lately shown signs of weakness. The multifaith RE courses are often badly taught and quite superficial. Parents refuse to send their children to schools with a majority of immigrant children, and Muslim organisations are sounding more and more unhappy. They do not understand the rationale or the purpose of the 'new' approach, and they think that to teach religion as a simple human and social phenomenon is to expose it to a dangerous secular examination, and that traditional institutions and concepts of religious authority are menaced by such a course. In addition, the emphasis placed on the central character of Christianity in the political debate on the public schools gives them the feeling of being marginalised. So although the place of Islam in the system is guaranteed, local mosques continue to follow traditional practices in religious instruction, taught by teachers without formal credentials, according to methods remembered from villages of origin [Nielsen, 1999a:227 ff.].

8. Religious Schools for Already Established Religions

In this section we look at cases of religious schools for established religions, especially majority religions. These are Orthodox, Catholic,

Anglican, and Lutheran schools, etc., which offer systematic instruction in the religion they belong to.

Importance in quantitative terms

We do not have quantitative data in regard to the presence of Muslim students in schools run by the majority religions in European countries. In the Netherlands, it was announced that 41% of Muslim students were going to Catholic schools in the early 1990s, and that their numbers were important in maintaining the minimum number of students to keep some schools open [Versloot & van der Ploeg, 1992, cited by Shadid & van Koningsveld, 1995:118]. We cannot identify a significant number of such students in any other country, with the possible exceptions of Great Britain or Belgium. This type of school offers no Islamic instruction.

Interest on the part of Muslims and state administration

One should not, though, discount the attraction these parochial schools have for some Muslim parents. Beyond certain historical reasons, reasons of proximity, and the perception that these schools do a better job of disciplining students, some parents want above all to have their children educated by people who respect ethical and religious values, and so they sometimes have more confidence in religious than in public schools. On the other hand school authorities have adopted different policies with regard to the presence of Muslim students, some countries proving more liberal than others. In Belgium no definite policy regarding exemption from religion classes exists; things are worked out by those immediately concerned. In Austria students are not required to attend these classes [Nielsen, 1995:29]. In Great Britain, the system has shown itself flexible enough, and since 1985, Muslim students have been excused from religion classes and 'daily worship'.

This British policy is important for Muslim parents who see Roman Catholic and Anglican schools as the most disciplined and the best in terms of moral values. For them, these schools are the only means of getting their daughters a girls-only education [Parker-Jenkins & Haw, 1998:196]. We note also that in relation to other European countries Britain is the only one for which separating boys and girls in school is as much an issue for the majority society as for the Muslim minority.

A quite different problem occurs in countries in which Muslims are forced to resort to faith-based institutions. In Germany, 80% of crèches are related to a particular religion (non-Muslim). In this case parents' problems include the suitability of personnel for Muslim children, though in principle solutions to this have been found [Karakasoglu & Nonneman, 1996:248]. In the face of such a situation, Muslims have begun to organise: several kindergartens have opened, two run by the Turkish Milli Görüs in Berlin. Obviously the need for these is much greater [Amiraux, 2000a:125].

Mixed institutions

Before concluding this section, we should take note of an innovative experiment carried out at Ede in the Netherlands. In 1990, a school affiliated with the majority religion transformed itself into a place of meeting for all religions, called 'ontmoeting' or 'samenwerkingsschool' (working-together school). Apart from a vicar, not only are there three imams representing Islamic tendencies, each teaching a course, but beyond that, the Word of God is understood there as something which can come from other religions. Muslim parents can hold organisational posts on the school board. A programme of multi-faith instruction is offered to all students [van de Wetering, 1992:90 ff.].

For the moment this project continues, but it has not been able to keep any Christian students [NL File]. The National Union of Christian Schools has rejected the school, saying it should belong to the Union of Private Schools [Shadid & van Koningsveld, 1997:154].

9. Recognised and Subsidised Islamic Schools

Framework, specific types and importance

At the European level, there are about 90 institutions of this type, not counting the 250 schools in Western Thrace which are more a type of 'minority' school for Thracian Turks than an 'Islamic' type. Islamic schools are located in about half the countries of Europe, but not in France, Portugal, Italy, Spain or the countries like Finland, Poland, and Hungary that have very small Muslim populations. They are of various levels, but primary schools and pre-schools make up most of the total. Secondary schools are rare; fewer than ten operate in all Europe.

The legislation which concerns them has normally been written in order to "assure local communities and related organisations the right to design their own education", passing over any question about the designation of a single representative organism [Dassetto, 1996:281]. In this process of construction, local people, Muslim and non-Muslim, provide the impetus, apart from national legislative projects, which are important [Dwyer & Meyer, 1995].

These schools allow an education which puts more emphasis on religion, and on the spiritual dimensions of education, while remaining within a framework of administrative norms such as those which require a minimum number of students, impose conditions of operation on the school, or require compliance with state curricula (which are further reviewed by state officials) which take up the bulk of school hours, or which mandate that the language of the host country shall be the language of instruction, as in the Netherlands and Denmark [Hjarno, 1996:292]. They are generally open-admission to all who meet certain criteria: parents must respect the cultural background of the school, and children must attend the religion classes; but there are still no non-Muslim children regularly enrolled in an Islamic school in the Netherlands [Shadid & van Koningsveld, 1997:172].

Apart from analyses that concentrate on the Netherlands [Driessen, 1999:143 ff.], there are few ethnographic descriptions of Muslim schools in Europe—still fewer from private schools—and the differences between them are hard to identify. The purposes of an Islamic education go beyond the senses and the intellect, and offer a spiritual aim. But they also involve a grasp of Islamic values which generates a critical evaluation of society itself [Parker-Jenkins & Haw, 1998:196]. Still at bottom it is only a few hours of religion a week and daily life the rest of the time, from which the desired result must be produced. In general, aside from the programmes of study, this implies an effort on the part of the schools to develop students' Muslim identity starting with positive self-esteem; they are off on Friday afternoon, not Wednesday, and their vacations occur according to the Muslim calendar; girls and boys sit in separate rows; female teachers wear headscarves and somewhat voluminous clothing, and not one smokes [Shadid & van Koningsveld, 1992:107 ff.].

We note finally the practices of regular prayers, in which older children, aged 10–11, learn to make their ablutions and their noon prayer [Shadid & van Koningsveld, 1997:175].

Difficulties, advantages, inconveniences

Depending on the country involved, a variety of obstacles to organisation persist, mostly structural in nature. For example, the lack of Muslim teachers qualified to teach in national educational systems,[34] lack of funding for their positions, a lack of appropriate educational material [Shadid & van Koningsveld, 1992:107 ff.][35] or sometimes even ambiguity by the school concerning the content of Islamic education [Shadid & van Koningsveld, 1997:174]. Those who are simply opposed to Islamic schools also have their say, as in the Netherlands or in Great Britain, where debates on the nature of 'integration' frequently occur [Dwyer & Meyer, 1995:37 ff.], unless the opponents raise the spectre of "an Islamic school which criticizes or rejects Western modernity" [Jung cited in Tangram, 1999:18].

The advantages of this type of school are these: they offer an appropriate style of religious and moral education, and cultural traditions are maintained, in order to develop an Islamic identity and a positive self-image, which are believed to be indispensable for the emancipation of Muslim children in European society [Shadid & van Koningsveld, 1995:121]. At the collective level, there is also the increased interest of parents in their children's education, and the important role this kind of self-organisation can play in the emancipation of ethnic groups [Shadid & van Koningsveld, 1997:164 ff.].

As for disadvantages, it is a question of the expense for parents (public schools are much cheaper), the relative isolation and lack of contact with the 'multicultural society', and the possible concentration of children from poorer families. It is difficult to say anything about the academic results these schools have produced so far, in view of the absence of studies on this subject. As for the problems

---

[34] In the Netherlands, most of the teachers in these schools are non-Muslim (78.7%). A certain number of foreign teachers are hired, in preference to Dutch teachers who are perceived as less well prepared to handle schoolchildren with a Muslim background and experience [Shadid & van Koningsveld, 1997:173].

[35] In most Islamic schools in the Netherlands the materials used for religion courses come from a variety of sources, in which Dutch, Turkish and Arabic language are mixed together [Shadid & van Koningsveld, 1997:174].

related to the cost of providing a quality education, they are assumed to be resolved as soon as the state agrees to pay part or all of the costs of the school.

European comparisons

Before embarking on a country-by-country review, an important observation must be made concerning the conditions under which these schools are established. Two situations must be distinguished. In one group, there are schools which have had the right to exist for a long time, as in Thrace, Denmark, the Netherlands, Sweden, Bulgaria, and perhaps even in Austria. In the other group, the right to have such schools may exist, but their establishment depends more on particular and exceptional circumstances. Three countries are in this situation. First, Belgium, which has only one Islamic school, called Al Ghazali, founded in Brussels in 1989. It was created following two Brussels communes' refusal to arrange for a course on Islamic religion in their public primary schools [Shadid & van Koningsveld, 1995:123]. Second, Germany, where a private primary school, the *Berlin Islami Ilimler Okulu*, opened since 1989, was recognized as an official Muslim school in 1995, which involved the assumption of its costs by the Senate of Berlin[36] [Spuler-Stegemann, 1998:236]. Third, the United Kingdom, where the question of public financing of Muslim schools has been a source of dissatisfaction for some time, although surveys found that only 50% of Muslims who favoured public financing "declared that they would prefer to send their children to such a school if they had the choice" [Modood, 2000:50]. In principle, any religious community can open a school and demand public financing, either through voluntary contributions (financing through local organisations) or through subsidies (state financing), but the decision is made by the Minister on a case by case basis, after studying the circumstances of each [Nielsen, 1995:47]. In practical terms, only three Islamic schools have been recognized since 1998 that operate thanks to public financing. These had existed for a number of years, and obtained the 'privilege' of subsidies

---

[36] Legislation regarding Qur'anic schools is different depending on the Land involved. In Berlin, a waiting period of six years is imposed, intended to test the viability of the school [Sunier & Meyer, 1998:111].

because their students had produced good academic results, even exceeding those of public schools.[37] We note finally that a Muslim school was created in Dublin in 1990 with state help, and that the Irish Ministry of Education also pays the teachers' salaries.[38]

The countries in which schools have the right to operate will now be reviewed in a more detailed fashion, so that organisational and contextual differences can be shown. Regarding Denmark, first, which has 'the oldest legislation' in Western Europe concerning academic freedom: since 1986, 18 schools have been created for children of Muslim background, for a total of about 2,000 students [Simonsen, 2000:182]. These schools can be distinguished in two ways. Some put the accent on ethnic group membership—Arab, Palestinian, Lebanese, etc.—rather than on religious matters. All are supervised by representatives of the Ministry of Education, which verifies their instructional level, which must correspond to that of the public schools. In consequence, they must agree to teach biology according to a non-religious approach to the human being as such! In other respects, these schools do not place equal emphasis on learning the language of the country of origin and the language of the host country [Simonsen, 1998]. Most are located near Copenhagen and operate with state funds that cover up to 60% of costs, the rest being paid as monthly fees by parents [DK File]. These developments have been made possible because of the relatively high number of Muslim political refugees with a certain level of education, who were able to "take over teaching duties and administrative tasks related to this kind of initiative" [Dassetto, 1996:282]. One author remarked that "many parents seemed troubled by the possibilities offered, as if they had been defied on the existential level" [Simonsen, 1998].

In Sweden [SE File] the creation of the first subsidised Muslim school, at Malmö, came rather late because the process had only been begun in 1993. But other similar schools quickly appeared: in late 1998 about twenty schools with Islamic/Arabic emphasis had opened. They enjoy the status of 'free' schools, as opposed to 'pri-

---

[37] Conversation with H. Saad, of the office of equal opportunity in Birmingham, March 2000.

[38] J. Casey (1995), "Staat und Kirche in Irland" in S.C. van Bijsterfeld, *Staat und kirche in der Europäischen Union*, Gerhard Robbers (ed.), Baden-Baden, Nomos-Verlag; cited by Messner, 1996:198.

vate' (non-subsidised) schools. This status guarantees state support for about 85% of costs, a level of support slightly lower than that provided to public schools, with a few conditions, including adherence to the national curriculum.

In the Netherlands, next, there are 32 Islamic primary schools recognised and financed by the state since 1988, which educate about 5% of the Muslim children of the country, that is 7,000 students [Driessen, 1999:143]. This number has been growing by about 500 students per year [Shadid & van Koningsveld, 1997:168], and a secondary school opened in Rotterdam in August 2000 [Entziger, 2000; NL File]. Most of these schools have been founded through the efforts of religious organisations belonging to specific ethnic groups. Most are classed as 'autonomous' Islamic primary schools, but three of them (at least) are under the authority of the Diyanet [Shadid & van Koningsveld, 1995:121]. Judging by inspection reports, these schools use Dutch pedagogical material, but the material is vetted by competent Muslims, especially as concerns books of biology and history, which are checked for compatibility with Muslim norms, and for the possible presence of 'indecent photographs' [NL File]. At the national level, 29 schools are members of a coordinating body, the *Islamitische Scholen Besturen Organisatie* (ISBO). This organism's purpose is to guard the interests of the schools' personnel and administration, and to promote a favourable climate for Islamic instruction in accordance with the Qur'an and the Sunna, while instituting collective conventions on working conditions. Since 1994, the ISBO has operated under a model set of regulations which must be followed by Muslim and non-Muslim teachers.[39] In 1995, the ISBO established the *Islamitisch Pedagogisch Centrum* (IPC). Starting with the task of analysis and information, this centre is intended to contribute to the formation of an identity for the Islamic schools. It points out prejudicial and racist material in school texts, and has developed its own reference manual for the promotion of an image of Muslim education, used by teachers to help them weed out negative images which are always present to some degree in the textbooks [Shadid

---

[39] Covering such topics as: the necessity of knowing Islam and observing Islamic prescriptions; a rule forbidding teaching children anything contrary to the material in religion classes, avoidance of physical contact with parents, colleagues, and the students; a rule against decorative images of humans or animals in the school building, etc.

& van Koningsveld, 1997:179 ff.]. The centre also establishes statements of expectations for schools, and studies the situation of Muslim students at school and in their family groups from the standpoint of existing literature. It maintains a repertoire of new pedagogies as these appear, and attempts to develop new instructional methods for Muslim and non-Muslim students, especially as regards intercultural aspects, in order to be able to counsel not only schools but also individual teachers. The ISBO proceeds as if it were responsible for setting forth not only a code of conduct, but also the ideal profile for orthodox Islamic instruction. Still, it must be admitted that this gives rise to disagreements, due to the differences between the individual schools which at present are served by the centre [Shadid & van Koningsveld, 1997:176 ff.].

In Thrace, the situation is completely different though the Muslim presence is of much longer date, because the Greek state grants only a limited autonomy. There are no pre-schools which use Turkish as the main language, and despite the existence of 245 primary schools in which the courses offered are more or less equally divided as to language, there are only two secondary schools, one at Komotini and one at Xanthi [Akgönül, 1999]. These schools "have scarcely more than 400 students in all, for want of financing, classrooms, and political will" [Dalègre, 2001:306]. As for the freedom to develop their own syllabi [Tskalidis cited in Schreiner, 2000:75–82], this is probably more symbolic than anything else since teachers are paid by the state, and since the number of Turkish instructors has been progressively reduced, while students who graduated from Turkish colleges are not authorised to teach because their diplomas are not recognised. It is also illegal for these schools to accept funding from any Islamic organisation or foundation. One step forward was taken with the opening of the special teachers' college in Thessalonika in 1968, for the training of instructors for minority primary schools [Küçükcan, 1999:61; Akgönül, 1999].

In Bulgaria [BG File], in contrast, there is no recognised Muslim primary school which is granted funds as such. The state's position is that Muslim children are integrated into the national educational system. However, financing has been made available for the creation of secondary schools and even one college. There are three Muslim schools, in Rousse, Shumen, and Momchilgrad, each with about 130 students, which are financed jointly by the state and the Office of the Grand Mufti.[40] As elsewhere, students follow the programme of courses which is required in all schools, and also have access to courses in Islamic religion. They have the right to become imams, but in order to become teachers of religion, they must obtain a university diploma including a certificate of pedagogical training. As for the Higher Institute for Islamic Studies (HIIS) established and approved in accordance with article 11 of the "Law concerning religions in the republic of Bulgaria", it is indirectly supported by the state working through the Office of the Grand Mufti, and funding may have been obtained from other foreign sources, such as the Diyanet. The Ministry of Education maintains control over educational programmes proposed by the Office of the Grand Mufti. The faculty is composed of Bulgarian Turks, Turks from Turkey, and Christian Bulgarians who have served at various universities. There are 60 Muslim students who are regularly following this programme of study in person, and 30 others who are doing so by correspondence.

In Austria, the situation is of a different type, but just as important symbolically: an Islamic secondary school was begun at Rudolfheim-Fünfhaus, in Vienna, in September 1999, the first in the German language area. German is the language of instruction, but courses in Arabic and Turkish are offered in the afternoon. Apart from two hours of Islamic instruction, the programme is the same as that followed in other Austrian schools, and Austrian secondary school teachers paid by the federation teach the classes [AT File].

10. Increased Importance of Other Forms of Instruction

Self-instruction

There is little available data for Eastern Europe in regard to this area, and it seems that self-instruction hardly exists there. But acquiring religious knowledge on one's own is something more and more people are doing in Western Europe, where "many young people today are deeply engaged in their own learning of Islam through

---

[40] These religious schools may have been subsidised by Turkish private foundations [Poulton, 1997:211]; it could be a matter of cooperative financing.

study of the Qur'an, Sunnah, and various texts both classical and modern. They are often doing this without help or guidance. They organize and structure their own programmes of reading, and discussions with their peers and others" [Nielsen, 1999:77]. There may also be a high-volume use of media—magazines, audio and video tapes, parables and stories, the Internet, etc. (see the chapter 'Media').

These young people "have usually given up on the mosques schools and their traditional forms of Islamic instruction in their early teens. Their motivation to return to learning about their faith comes from the rejection which they have experienced in the wider European environment, the lack of understanding and often downright enmity towards religion. Their motivation has not usually come from the traditional system and its methods (. . .). They have a need to understand why (things are as they are)" [Nielsen, 1999:77].

Associations and preaching

Most authors agree that knowledge is being acquired more often by individual persons working by themselves. But a complementary pattern may also be discerned, different from the idea according to which "there is a lack of competent teachers, and young people have no choice other than to go directly to sources and basic texts because fourteen centuries of religious education and intellectual discipline are today inaccessible or not pertinent" [Nielsen, 1999:22]. This complementary pattern involves a variety of associations which place the highest importance on religion.

Regarding the situation in France, it has been said: "the intellectualisation of Islam takes place outside the family, through self-instruction when it is practicable, and even more through meetings and conferences organized by associations" [Babès, 1997:137]. This observation holds good in Germany: "the connection between parents and associations has to do with the difficulty of passing on codes, practices, rites and symbols, beyond simple imitation" [Amiraux, 2000a:125]. Elsewhere "young people fall away and distance themselves from the religion of their parents, the transmission of which has been distorted by gaps and silences (. . .); they prefer more intellectual forms of expression, and by the same token forms which are more objective. (. . .) Even the mosque, which is too close to the religious sociability of Islam, more spiritual and moral than intellectual, does not attract them much, and has been replaced by freer forms of social-

ization, though they are still related to the community around them"
[Babès, 1997:119].

Though the accent is on the individual nature of this self-socialisation
process, there can be seen a trend toward a relative transfer of authority in favour of theologians, conference speakers or preachers.[41] In
French-speaking countries, such a movement has formed around
Tareq Ramadan and Hassan Iquioussen, who offer a comprehensive and intellectualised perspective on the world which is attractive
to young people.

11. Private Islamic Institutes

Nature and importance

Private Islamic institutions exist in Europe for the secondary and
higher levels of education. Individual initiatives are the source of
their organisation and creation—often grounded in ideological tendencies that have an agenda of sorts. Many of these connections are
not advertised, but it has been observed that there is an increasing
number of informal convergences between several such tendencies
(cf. the chapter "Mosques, organisations and leadership").

These institutions do not receive public money. What is most
important to them is recognition within the community. Sometimes
one such institution will seek symbolic recognition from the European
state where it is located, even some financial help; but that is sometimes viewed as a necessary evil.

Officially there are no private Islamic schools in Finland, Sweden,
Denmark, Austria, Luxembourg or Switzerland. There are many in
the United Kingdom. Most countries have at least a few—Germany,
Italy, the Netherlands—or very few as in Belgium, France, Spain or
Portugal. As for the 'private' institutions in Bulgaria or Romania,
this concerns only a few Islamic foundations who have almost no
contact with the local population as such. That is the case with the
International Mathematics High School of Bucharest, which offers
instruction in English and Turkish, the Lebanese School, the Iranian

---

[41] This emergent phenomenon is dealt with at greater length in the point 2,
chapter 3: "Internal organisation of mosques and figures of authority", more especially under the title "New leaders".

School, etc., which are attended only by the children of Muslims coming from outside the country. In the case of open madrasas, the situation is different. They receive support, even partial, from the state, for reasons that will be explored in the next chapter.

As the case of Great Britain, France, and even Germany illustrates (Denmark is an opposite case), such private institutes emerge in response to a lack of facilities. This is the case where the Muslim communities have been in place for a long time, and even where they have not, as in Italy and Portugal (here the Netherlands offers a counter-example). There are other causal factors, such as the desire to educate in new ways, even if many ways exist already. Muslim organisations have to feel themselves to be pretty strong to embark on the creation of a private school, because the process is difficult, long, and acrimonious, a fighter's gauntlet, because of the scarcity of money, the lack of official recognition, and even, at times, distrust or hostility in their social environment.

Diversity on the European scene

Our grand tour begins with the United Kingdom, the most pronounced case, where the absence of an overall solution has pushed worried parents into taking the plunge to establish private Islamic schools. No fewer than 52 full-time schools were open there in the late 1990s [Kelly, 1999:199] despite the financial difficulties which have forced some schools to close. There are eleven boarding schools among this number, and the whole group has enrolled 2% of Muslim students. Seminaries were created in Bury and Dewsbury in 1975 and 1982 through the Deobandi movement which operates a dozen schools in the country as a whole.[42] Dewsbury, with 300 students in 1994, is also the European centre for the *Jama'at al-Tabligh* movement: the programme of study is divided between traditional Islamic studies in Urdu in the morning, based on a canon of books strictly linked to the Deobandis tradition and to be learned by heart, followed by secular classes in the afternoon in English. The two remain isolated from each other, which can lead to contradictions. After finishing at Bury, many of the students go on to complete their education in a Muslim country—at Al-Azhar in Egypt, or at Medina

---

[42] Lewis, conversation, March 2000.

University in Saudi Arabia. Dewsbury graduates often begin to preach, and to finish their studies in Pakistan or India [Lewis P., 1994]. We note the presence of another boarding school which has been opened for the Brelwis in Retford [Landman, 1996:37], and another new institute in Wales, near Lampeter, which had 20 students in 2000. This institution is connected also to *L'Institut Européen des Sciences Humaines* (LIESH) of Bouteloin (see below). And finally, we should mention the Islamic Foundation of Leicester, which with its boarding school, its library and its organised seminars, appears more as an academic research institute that also functions as a lobbying organisation and coordinator, trying to network with other, mostly British institutions.[43]

In France global solutions are also lacking for the problems of Islamic primary schools, public or open, and indeed also lacking at higher levels of education.[44] Only two Muslim institutes are open at present. The *Institut d'Etudes Islamiques* of Paris operates as an 'open university', offering a complete university curriculum open to all Muslims, in the hopes of attracting persons with leadership potential, that they might be educated and trained to be of value to Islam, and in the hopes of giving foreign imams living in France an opportunity to receive additional training [Frégosi, 1998a:113 ff.]. And the European Institute of Human Sciences of Bouteloin, commonly referred to as Château Chinon, represents a sort of Islamic seminary whose stated aim is to promote the intelligent and positive integration of Muslim communities; but the Arabic text inscribed near the front entrance criticises secular education, and calls for Muslim interests in Europe to promote the propagation of Islam [Frégosi, 1998a:110 ff.]. This institute has a European as well as a French national presence, and operates examination centres in a number of cities worldwide (London, Frankfurt, Geneva, Copenhagen, Istanbul and Chicago). Its students come from all of Europe [Frégosi, 1999: 53 ff.]. A comparative analysis concludes that both these institutions are philosophically based on Arabisation and re-Islamisation. They

---

[43] Conversation with D. Hussein, Islamic Foundation, March 2000.

[44] This negligence related to educational matters may appear to be the fault of the large Islamic organisations of France, too preoccupied with "the search for outside political and financial help and with lobbying in order to be granted an administrative baraka, which they think they can obtain from the Minister of the Interior in charge of religion" [Sellam, 1998:17].

are more centres of religious instruction than seminaries for producing imams. The latter do not take the society around them into account to any great degree, and their 'theology of 'ijtihad'—the task of research—is unfinished, while the theological project of the second, related to the ideology of the Muslim Brotherhood, is more or less decided on" [Frégosi, 1998a:118 ff.].

In Germany several organisations provide full-time education. The *Verband Islamischer Kulturzentren* (VIKZ), operated by the Süleymancis, has educational institutions open in Munich, where one school has attracted 500 students [Spuler-Stegemann, 1998:236]. Colleges for young women have also been created, often upon the initiative of a movement such as the Milli Görüs. Such schools operate in Nuremburg, Rotgau, Mannheim, Duisberg, Berlin, and Hamburg [Spuler-Stegemann, 1998:241]. In Bonn-Bad Godesberg, the King Fahd Academy opened in 1995. It has close to 600 students, and defines itself officially as a secular school, as opposed to the Islamic schools of Berlin and Munich, even though religion classes are mandatory in all three [Spuler-Stegemann, 1998:237 ff.]. As regards the training of hodjas, this is essentially the work of several independent organisations, such as the *Theologische Fakultäten* [DE File], but also through the activities of the Süleymancis. In the 1990s the VIKZ opened a centre for the education of hodjas in Köln, which gave them the opportunity to recruit persons who knew German society and who spoke German well enough to teach in mosques [DE File; Amiraux, 1999a]. In 1997 the VIKZ began a project for the creation of an Islamic Academy of higher learning in order to train imams. At present, a secondary level of Islamic education for teachers is available in Essen and in Mannheim [Landman, 1998:12], and there is a Shiite centre in Hamburg which trains theologians [Spuler-Stegemann, 1998:245].

In the Netherlands, alongside facilities arranged by the Boyazi school in Turkey, which were funded by the *Stichting Turks-Islamitische Culturele Federatie*, with close ties to the Diyanet,[45] there are only a few small training institutes, operated for example through the

---

[45] This is the Anadolu Imam-Hatip Lisesi College, created in 1992–93, located near the town of Anamur. It trains mainly students who grew up in the Netherlands and who want to serve as imams there [Landman, 1998:12 ff. & 24 ff.], offering them a bi-cultural education still under the single control of the Turkish state [Landman, 1997a:229].

Süleymancis,[46] working through the *Stichting Islamitisch Centrum Nederland*, whose objective is to improve opportunities for young people. There are also a few avenues for the training of imams: the Süleymancis, who transplanted their training programmes without ever asking for recognised status or money from the Dutch government, and two other organisations which are attempting to obtain recognition and subsidies. The Islamic University of Rotterdam (IUR) began in 1998 with private but limited funding. Up to this point the Dutch authorities know very little about it and no study of the institution has been carried out. Then there is the *Stichting voor Islamitisch Hoger Onderwijs* (Foundation for Higher Islamic Studies) of Utrecht, which plans to build a theological university, which will operate autonomously but in cooperation with the University of Utrecht. The government appears to have obtained what it sought: an academic-quality training programme in Islamic theology, but in a form it had not wanted— an independent institution [Landman, 1999:5].

In the Scandinavian countries, few such institutions are noteworthy, because of the very liberal education legislation in these countries, which often funds Islamic schools even if they have been created through private initiatives. There are no private Islamic schools in Finland or Denmark. In Sweden there are at least two Qur'anic schools, one at Fittja, and the other, mixed, at Västerås [Nielsen, 1995:60]. A Council of Swedish Imams has been set up to try to arrange facilities for the training of imams [Nielsen, 1995:60].

The situation of private Islamic schools in the Mediterranean area: four are mentioned in Portugal, in Lisbon, Pamela, Laranjeiro and Odivelas [PT File]. In Italy, thirty existing schools operate out of the main Islamic centres [IT File]. Two schools in Spain, at Madrid [ES File]. They follow the official curriculum plus specific courses in Arabic language and history, and Islamic religion, and are recognised by the Ministry of Education. One is operated by the Iraqi government, as a service for the children of consular staff, and the other, Umm al-Kura, offers primary classes in the Islamic Cultural Centre of Madrid [ES File]. And then there is the *Universidad Islamica Averroes*, established under a 1992 agreement, opened in 1995 in

---

[46] On a pilot basis, the city of Rotterdam subsidizes a boarding school for boys who are registered for school. It was created in 1989 by the Islamic sociocultural foundation Akyazili, connected with the Nursis movement [Landman, 1998:24].

Cordoba. Its four-year programme uses a credit-hour system compatible with the Spanish education system, and while the languages of instruction are Arabic and Spanish, Persian and Turkish are also taught. This school offers an Islamic education to all who apply, Muslim or non-Muslim, for courses in Arabic language and literature, Islamic studies, and Andalusian studies.

On its own, the question of training of imams, preachers, and other teachers of Islamic religion is now the subject of lively debates in several countries. This occurs in countries where the Muslim community is large, and has been present for at least several decades, even if in Germany, for example, the debate has remained internal to various Muslim organisations, not reaching the national level [DE File]. In other countries, such as Spain, Belgium, Austria, Switzerland, Denmark, Finland, or those where the immigrant community arrived more recently, like Italy or Portugal, the terms of such debates have not been established, but neither is there any organisation of higher level instruction. Even the leaders of national Muslim communities themselves have only recently come to feel any urgency about such problems [Frégosi, 1998a:12].

12. HIGHER EDUCATION IN THE PUBLIC SYSTEM

There are programmes featuring the acquisition of knowledge about Islamic culture and religion, which grant diplomas that are officially recognised. Traditionally in this matter only institutions in Eastern Europe are concerned with the training of Muslim cadres, while this question is not a current issue for public school systems in Western Europe.

But changes are in the offing, perceptible from the perspective of the Continent, involving a network of connections in the process of being established between two very different universes, which must eventually have a great influence on European societies. A few recent initiatives of note have occurred in the West, including research groups created within universities, not focusing on religious training, the result most often of initiatives by non-Muslim authorities. Such doctoral and post-doctoral programmes specialise in the advanced study of Islam, as does the Netherlands Institute for the Study of Islam in the Modern World (ISIM), at Leiden. It is financed by two ministries and several Dutch universities as a centre of excellence.

Its mission is to produce and organise scientific knowledge relative to developments in history, politics, society, culture, and economics in the contemporary period, which are linked to Islam and Muslim societies. Publicly financed also is the Institute of Islamic Studies and Muslim Societies in France, an institution of higher learning created in 1999. It concentrates on social sciences, and as regards regions in which Islam is present, it has a mission "to open a space of collaboration and exchange for scholars specializing in studies of the Muslim world, in cooperation with the scientific community, national and international". In the early stages, such instruction gave rise to criticism because it taught knowledge about Islam, but not Islamic knowledge [Frégosi, 1998a:203 ff.]. At the European level, there are many projects on the drawing board, witness the increased number of conferences and collective research projects that have sprung up concerning Islam.

Subsidized universities

There is another way of acquiring knowledge of the Muslim religion, other than in private institutions, some of which offer educational programmes at the post-secondary level: it is possible within public institutions of higher learning, state-financed and independent of any Muslim initiative. In almost all European countries, in fact, the university system allows programmes in Islamic studies to be pursued, by Muslims and non-Muslims [Waardenburg, 2000:74]. Universities furnish programmes in Oriental studies, Turkish studies, Arabic studies or Central Asian studies, often under the aegis of the History Department or the Department of Philosophy and Literature.

These offerings do come in for criticism, because of the relative emphasis on learning Middle Eastern languages and the concentration on either the history or the contemporary position of Muslim societies. This is considered to ignore all matters of theological or juridical Islamic thought. In view of this detachment from religion as such, these programmes represent only optional studies for Islamic cadres, whose training is thus limited to a diploma for teachers, without any relation to expectations for taking on certain functions in the Muslim community, official or otherwise.

In Eastern European universities, such programmes also exist, as in the Universities of Constanta and Bucharest in Romania, or the University of Sofia in Bulgaria. But it has already happened, that such programmes can get caught up in political debates which exceed their scope. When the communist government wanted to suppress the use of Turkish in Bulgaria, the Department of Turkish philology was closed in 1974, even though, or more precisely because, it was the last institution of higher learning in operation which could train advanced linguists [Ragaru, 2001:269]. After having been replaced by a Department of Arabic philology [Eminov, 1997:135], the original department was reopened in 1993 in Sofia, and another such department, newly created, was opened at the university in Shumen [Eminov, 1997:141]. Other factors sometimes play a role, connected with outside interests. In Romania, the influence of the Turkish state can be seen, if only in the choice of names such as the Atatürk section at the International Centre for Turkish-Romanian Studies at the University of Ovidius in Constanta [Fiche RO].

Official religious studies in Greece and Eastern Europe

In Greece and in the East, in contrast with what takes place in the west, public institutions accept responsibility for the training of religious leaders. This task is assumed traditionally by the entire community, especially as organised through the Mufti and other religious foundations, while the state pays all or part of the cost, and sometimes collaborates with foreign agencies.

In Western Thrace, there are two madrasas financed by the *waqfs*, the religious foundations, in Komotini and Ehinos. Maintaining close relations with the minority schools, these madrasas "offer an archaic religious education for five years after primary school" [Akgönül, 1999a:33] for about 200 students, 80% of whom are of mountain origin, and who receive free lodging [Dalègre, 2001:306]. Alongside future imams, there are many Pomak children who take classes in Greek and Turkish, and also study the precepts of Islam and the Qur'an [GR File], eight hours of study of religious discipline, in Arabic [Dalègre, 2001:306]. For a more secular programme, future Pomak teachers of religion coming from madrasas go to the Pedagogical Academy of Thessalonika, in principle the only school which can certify primary school teachers for the minority schools [Küçükcan, 1999:61; Akgönül, 1999:135], while Turkish-speaking candidates, though of Greek nationality, often take teachers' courses in Turkey [GR File].

In Romania, the Medgidia seminary was closed in 1967 [Popovic,

1997:61], but reopened in 1993 for 20 students from all parts of Dobrudja, an accomplishment in which the community took great pride. The classes offered are like those elsewhere: two-thirds are in Romanian and the rest consist of three weekly instruction periods of Turkish language and literature, and one instruction period a week of Arabic language, Islamic history, music, and ethics. The programme of studies is established and supervised by the Mufti of Romania in cooperation with the Ministry of Culture, in accordance with a protocol signed with his Turkish counterpart in April 1994 [Lederer 1996:359]. Two years after the signing of this document, which praises the role of the minority as a cultural bridge between two countries, this seminary has been renamed the Kemal Atatürk Muslim Pedagogical School. This probably indicates the presence of aid from Turkey in the region to support the reaffirmation the Muslim identity of Turks and Tartars in Dobrudja [Anghelescu, 1999:135]. Another author confirms that "the fastest, the cheapest, and the best way for members of the new generation of Muslim intellectuals to get an education is for them to accept the scholarships offered by Arab countries, by Turkey, and by certain private Turkish foundations" [Lederer, 1996:359].

In Bulgaria, the situation is formally similar. There are three Muslim secondary schools financed by the state, plus the Higher Institute for Islamic Studies in Sofia. In addition to receiving funds from the state dispensed through the office of the Mufti, this school also receives money from the Turkish Diyanet.[47] As for credentials for teachers of religion, the programme connects this to getting a university diploma, in pedagogy, for example, or some other related field.

State initiatives in the West

Generally, these countries do not invest in the very particular area of training for ecclesiastical personnel, leaving this up to Muslim

---

[47] We note that deficiencies in religious education have allowed the Nursis-Fethullahci Gülen movement to gain a foothold [Peev, 1997:186]; it has furnished teachers and financial help to these four religious schools since 1995. But this "cooperation came to an end in 1997 following the signature of an agreement between the Bulgarian and Turkish directorates for religious affairs, which gave them responsiblity for the appointments of Turkish teachers" [Ragaru, 2001:269].

communities, that is, to their private organisations and agencies. Only the Dutch authorities have tried to resolve certain problematics by intervening at several levels, though this raises a question of state interference for some [Shadid & van Koningsveld, 1997:150].

Though they do not subsidise Islamic institutions, the Netherlands have initiated programmes intended to familiarise arriving imams with the character of the nation and the host society. These became obligatory for new imams seeking residence permits in the summer of 2000 [NL File]. The idea of organising refresher courses for imams who have been trained abroad is currently attracting interest. And certain dispositions have been made which favour imams trained in the Netherlands; they will upon completion of their studies receive preference over candidates coming from outside the country [Landman, 1998:22].[48]

As for the higher level training of professors of religion, this is provided by the Hogeschool Holland, once located at Diemen but now part of the 'Faculty of Education of Amsterdam', whose four-year programme trains imams in pedagogical methods. The various institutes under the *Stichting Islamitisch Centrum Nederland* also appear to be about to adopt this programme of studies [Landman, 1998:21].

We also note the existence of a new project begun by the Faculty of Theology of the University of Helsinki which aims at organising a one-year programme, financed by the National Education Board, for teachers of Islamic religion. The courses will be given by the Faculty of Education of the University of Helsinki, in collaboration with the Department of Comparative Religion [FI File].

New personal and institutional connections

Mention is often made of the individual initiatives of persons who often go abroad to study at traditional institutions such as the Al-Azhar University in Cairo, or who enter European public universities in order to complete their studies in Islamic theology. The Centre

---

[48] This author also mentions a pilot project located in Zuid-Holland under the Ministry of Justice, in collaboration with an Islamic umbrella organisation. This project offers refresher courses for imams as regards spiritual counseling skills, based on Islamic principles, within prisons and jails, and also aims at regularising the status of imams. A similar project was overseen by the Public Health Ministry, for imams working in health care institutions in Utrecht.

for the Study of Islam and Christian-Muslim Relations (CSIC), since August 1, 1999 part of the Theology Department of the University of Birmingham, has signed formal agreements concerning exchanges of students and professors with the University of Kuwait and with Al-Azhar. Eighty percent of the CSIC students are Muslim, two-thirds coming from Africa or Asia, including Malaysia, Iran, Turkey, Saudi Arabia, Kuwait, Jordan, and Lebanon. Under a different status, the Oxford Centre for Islamic Studies has signed agreements with Al-Azhar, permitting participants who have knowledge of English to spend time studying to improve their English and to accustom themselves to modern disciplines.

Some developments, however, are produced at the level of institutions, over and above exchanges between European and foreign institutions. It now happens that other types of relationships are formed between European institutions both private and public. These bring about various degrees of more or less active cooperation, including shared requirements between many different related programmes of study, modifications in pedagogical methods or courses of study, going as far as actual additions to the value of certain diplomas as credentials. In this area, Great Britain appears to be at the centre of many developments.

We first note two educational institutions associated with British universities. The Hijaz college in Nuneaton, near Birmingham, teaches juridical studies, including Islamic law, during a four-year course leading to a law degree plus a diploma in Islamic law accredited by the University of London. As for the Muslim College of London,[49] it has organised its programme in relation with Birkbeck College of the University of London. Its post-doctoral programme of Islamic studies (three years) covers Islamic law, but in the context of Western concepts, methodology, and culture [Landman, 1996:37 ff.]. Through the creation of bridges and connections between different courses of study, there is no doubt that these institutions have increased the value of their diplomas and the reputation of their programmes.

Other pioneering developments have been produced by cooperation

---

[49] We recall that this institution tried to train Islamic officials in Europe during the 1980s: it insisted on teaching imams about Islamic preaching during the early period of the religion, and about the modern rhetorical disciplines connected with public speaking [Reeber, 2000:238].

between private schools, which indicates a certain openness. For example, Westhill College of Birmingham had a relationship with Dar al-ʿUlum, a respected institution in Bury which offers an abbreviated programme of studies. Westhill benefited by participating in a Christian religious tradition, and its Muslim teachers have been trained in Western universities [Lewis P., 1998:53].

Finally at quite another level it has been observed that a first group of imams has entered institutions of the majority culture to pursue 'B.A. programmes' for the training of primary school teachers in Birmingham in 1990. Such a commitment implies a certain familiarity with the pedagogical methods used by majority-culture institutions. The programme will probably lead the imams to change the way they teach the courses they will be assigned in private and even public schools, "filling in this way the gap that exists between school and mosque" [Lewis P., 1999:28].

In Eastern European countries, the fall of communism has meant the re-establishment of ties between Muslim populations in the Balkans and the rest of the Muslim world, first of all Turkey, but also the Arab world. In these countries, it is the restoration of these external relations which counts the most. Many posts have been created by the Turkish authorities to be given to students from Bosnia-Herzegovina, Greece, Bulgaria, Macedonia, and Yugoslavia, in order to employ them at different levels of the Turkish educational system. In concrete terms, from 1993 to 1996, 300 students have entered religious schools, 250 have entered secondary schools, and 12,000 have entered universities [Poulton, 1997:211]. In Bulgaria, bilateral cooperation agreements have been reached between the Turkish studies department of the University of Sofia and the University of Istanbul [Ragaru, 2001:271 ff.]. As for the restoration of contacts with Saudi Arabia and Egypt, educational trips are offered through representatives of religious foundations or other private agencies, or even through the Office of the Grand Mufti, who each year awards several dozen scholarships to students who have a diploma from the Higher Institute for Islamic Studies of Sofia. Coming from Romania, a few young Muslims study in Syria, Egypt, or the Sudan, and it was reported in 1992 that 16 students returned from the *Madrasa Ghazi Husrevbeg* in Sarajevo, while most students were transferred to Turkey [Lederer, 1996:359]. But these exchanges do produce a little friction at times. Along with the restoration of religious liberty and the resumption of religious instruction, this "reinsertion into a Muslim world crisscrossed by deep political and religious divisions has given rise to a confrontation with new models" [Ragaru, 2001:267 ff.].

A faculty of Islamic theology in Europe?

This possibility is the aim of a project begun in 1996 by E. Trocmé, professor emeritus of New Testament exegesis and former President of the University of Human Sciences, who wanted to create a faculty of Islamic theology at Strasbourg. But the project seems unable to bring about any authentic introduction of the Islamic religion in its programmes. In fact, administrators of publicly-funded universities generally refuse any responsibility for the establishment of schools or programmes teaching a scholarly Islam. This is a dimension of the presence of Muslim populations in Europe we have not yet considered. Here it is not a matter of transmission of culture, or of training of Islamic cadres or imams, social workers or professors of religion, but of the emergence of a theological philosophy, one moreover appropriate to a European context.

This question seems all the more important since such philosophical reflection is still limited today, with the exception (itself uncertain) of a few individuals and a few private institutions such as the European Institute of Human Sciences of Bouteloin,[50] and perhaps the Islamic University of Rotterdam or the *Universidad Islamica Averroes*. This lack is caused by the absence of scholars, or more precisely, the lack of intellectual connections between such scholars and the mass of Muslim populations [Roy, 2000:89].

The French case thus represents the current debates in a quite revealing manner. It illustrates, in fact, the serious nature of the tension which exists between knowledge of Islam and Muslim societies, and theological knowledge in the strict sense, questions about the latter having been avoided up to now. Besides, public authorities have completely neglected this particular project.

---

[50] An institute whose scientific council "is made up of well-known Arab 'ulamâ', noted for their connections with the Muslim Brotherhood", like the Egyptian sheikh Y. al-Qaradawi, the Lebanese sheikh F. Mawlawi, founder and spiritual leader of the *Groupement Islamique en France* (GIF), or other intellectuals linked to Islamist movements in the Maghreb like the Algerian M. Nahnah [Frégosi, 1998a:110 ff.].

But even now some people believe that, in the short term, "the creation of an institution of higher learning of Muslim theology is a necessity and a prior condition for the integration of Islam" in Europe [Messner, 1998:152 ff.]. Such a need has even been felt in a country like Poland, despite the small size of its Muslim community: nothing has been set in stone yet, but in 1998 a group of Muslims contacted the authorities of the Catholic University of Lublin, and then the Catholic theological academy of Warsaw, in order to explore the possibility of setting up a section devoted to Islamic theology [PL File].

On one side, there are numerous critiques of the rapidly vanishing traditional Orientalism or Islamology in the Western sense, because these patterns of study are supposed to constitute a form of 'essentialism'. On another side there are more and more insistent demands for the setting forth of an authentic and intelligible form of the Islamic faith, such that it can be adapted to judgments of jurisprudence in the European context. This requires not only a good understanding of customs, literature, and proper manners (ʿurf and adab),[51] but in addition this matter must be studied scientifically in the context of theology, exegesis, and Islamic philosophy.

These requirements are set forth in detailed fashion in a manifesto issued by the Centre for Islam in Europe (C.I.E.): ". . . it is necessary that in our universities, Islam as a subject of research and training should receive more emphasis, in a manner which is culturally, intellectually, and socially pertinent. In a university department, and in the context of a complete programme of studies, including necessary courses in social and cultural sciences, qualified graduates must be produced in the areas of Qur'anic studies (tafsîr and hadîth), Islamic law (fiqh) and theology (kalâm), Muslim languages, literature, and culture (Arabic, Turkish, Persian, etc.), the history, sociology, and philosophy of the Muslim world, etc.".[52] In terms of France, this would mean bringing about a merger of two projects previously mentioned, since "their reciprocal interactions could produce in the long term the establishment, outside the Muslim world, of a course of studies leading to qualified personnel and Muslim

---

[51] Conversation with A. Siddiqui, Islamic Foundation, Leicester, March 2000.
[52] http://allserv.rug.ac.be/~hdeley/CIE.htm, website text dating from November 5, 1999.

cadres, which would benefit Muslims in Europe and elsewhere. And that would enable the intellectual and spiritual foundations to be laid for an Islam in Europe" [Frégosi, 1998a:203 ff.].

While we wait for such pious wishes to be realised, outside forces remain active, and the Muslim 'doxa' is still being developed outside of Europe. Religious leaders are mainly drawn from the principal Islamic centres, from the Middle East (Cairo, Damascus, Riyadh, Mecca, Medina) or Western Asia (Peshawar), or even the Maghreb and Africa (Sudan, Mauritania). But the young Muslims born in Europe who want to get a quality religious education are almost forced to go abroad, whether they are operating on their own initiative or with the help of an organisation or network,[53] and whether they come from Eastern or Western Europe. The effects of this emigration are not well known, and have not been studied. The most common criticism heard today is that which is levelled at the dominant influence of Wahhabis (fundamentalist tendency based in Saudi Arabia). Sometimes emigration for the purpose of education works the other way, stimulating renewed interest in the host society in Europe.[54] However this may develop, and even if it is useless "to wait for European Islam to cut itself off from outside influences", the essential question remains to know how European Islam will seek autonomy, constructing its specific status as a minority religion, without cutting itself off from its roots [Cesari, 1999a:221]. In this context, we must realise that a generation of educated European Muslims is probably the most valuable resource shared by Muslim communities and by society as a whole, in the effort to integrate the whole into the multicultural society of the future [Nielsen 1999a:231].

---

[53] In a bulletin of the *Fédération Nationale des Musulmans de France* (FNMF) from 1997, it was stated that the federation had sent 22 imams to the Hassan II mosque in Casablanca for "a week long course of study, and was negotiating with Al-Azhar (Cairo) and Al-Qarawiyîn (Fèz) in order to arrive at durable agreements" [Islam de France, n° 2, 1998:147].

[54] Conversation with A. Siddiqui, Islamic Foundation, Leicester, March 2000, in which the case of young people who leave Great Britain for Pakistan is discussed.

A PICTURE OF THE SITUATION

	Spain	Belgium	Finland	Austria	Germany	Bulgaria	Nether.	Denmark	Sweden	Norway	U. Kingdom	France (Alsace-Moselle)	Switzerland (Several cantons)	Greece (Western Thrace)
PUBLIC — PLURAL APPROACH	×	×	×	×	× (Bavière, Berlin, Bremen)	×	~							
CULTURAL & HISTORICAL APPROACH					× (Hambourg Brandebourg)	×	×	×	×	×	× & no formal discrimi.			
LAÏCIST APPROACH												×	×	
PREFERENTIAL & RESTRICTIVE APPROACH														×
COURSES OF LANGUAGE OF ORIGIN	~	~	~	~	×	~	~	~	~	~	~	×	~	~
ISLAMIC SCHOOLS RECOGNISED & SUBSIDISED		1 prim.		1 sec.	1 prim.	3 sec.	35 prim. & 1 sec.	18 prim.	20 prim.		2 prim.			250 prim. & 2 sec. (Thrace)
TRAINING OF MUSLIM CADRES				~ (?)	?	×	×				?	?		×
PRIVATE — PRIVATE ISLAMIC SCHOOLS	~ (-)	~ (-)	~ (-)	~	~	~ (-)	~ (-)	~ (-)			52	~ (-)	?	2 madrasas
MOSQUES	~ (-)	~ (-)	~ (-)	~ (-)	~ (-)	~ (-)	~ (-)	~ (-)	~ (-)	~ (-)	×	~	~	~

NOTA BENE: 1. Public education considered out of religious schools and higher education
2. Private education considered out of higher education for the training of cadres

×   Majority approach/Important
~   Minority or partial approach/not important
~ (-)   Not very important
?   Debates on the agenda

13. BY WAY OF CONCLUSION . . .

Besides religious education in families, Qur'anic courses taught in mosques, and various forms of independent learning, four possibilities for organising Islamic religious instruction have been systematically analysed: Islamic religious classes in public schools; the creation of Islamic schools recognised and paid for by the state; the foundation of private Islamic schools; and the establishment of programmes at other types of higher-level institutions, including universities.

On this basis, we can determine that half the states reviewed have taken serious steps in order to give Islam a greater place within the educational system. Among these are the countries which have adopted a neutral and plural approach to religion which permits courses in Islamic religion to be offered in public schools—Belgium, Spain, the German states of Berlin and Bremen, Finland, Austria, Bulgaria and Romania—and also the countries which take a cultural and historical approach to religion, which also allow, subject to administrative norms, for the creation of state-supported Muslim schools, with limited but effective funding, as in Sweden and Denmark, or complete funding, as in the Netherlands. That country has generated the greatest number of creative initiatives in the matter, and tries always to think in terms of long-term integration, not assimilation. Certainly, problems persist, but re-evaluations are continuous, and there are now religious schools which are Dutch and Muslim at the same time. As for Denmark, despite similarities to the Dutch position, results are less satisfactory because of the lack of an adequate government policy [Nielsen, 1999a:231 ff.]. However things stand, in general, and though the modes of instruction vary greatly, they basically support the objective of real integration with respect for people's differences, as illustrated by the fact that these states see few private Islamic institutions created within their boundaries.

In states in which real overall solutions have not been found, the situation is becoming more and more unsatisfactory, complex, and obscure.

Great Britain is caught up in several types of change; its policies remain fairly superficial, though improvements are slowly appearing. Its generally culturalist and historical approach to religious instruction, which favours references to Christianity, is being gradually rethought, and exemptions have been granted in the matters of school clothing, physical education classes, and school lunches, in order to eliminate certain types of discrimination. Still, despite the appearance of relative flexibility of local British authorities, there are needs which are not met, and so about 50 private Islamic schools have been created within Great Britain, which are subject to minimal state control as regards the quality of the instruction offered, and such problems are the result of financial problems at these schools.

Things are different in Western Thrace (Greece), where Islam has a particular status in relation to a state that privileges the Orthodox religion. Despite the existence of 240 schools for minority Turks, the character of the Islamic instruction offered is only a symbolic formality, due to the many conditions on the training teachers must have received, and restrictions on the pedagogical material used, etc. Some positive change is slowly becoming perceptible.

In countries such as France and in most Swiss cantons, which retain a purely secular approach to education, or in countries which restrict religious education to teaching the state-recognised religion (Greece outside Western Thrace, Portugal, Poland, Italy, Luxembourg, most German states such as Nordrhein-Westfalen, Baden-Wurttemberg, Saarland and Schleswig-Holstein), the possibilities for getting an Islamic education are slim. This education is often condensed into a few references in general courses, or picked up in courses in languages of origin, which thanks to the good will and help of some teachers may deal with religious matters. For want of organisation, regardless of the long presence of the Muslim community in the country, there are only a few private initiatives which are noteworthy, except for the two private Islamic institutions of higher learning in France, and a few institutes in Germany, which still put too little emphasis on the relation between theological material and a reflection on its application to the society of the host country. The situation is unsatisfactory; many debates are underway, but there are many gaps to fill.

In relation to existing educational systems, it appears that the majority of Muslims do not wish to place emphasis on their differences from the society of the host country, but only to obtain some signs of recognition, in the absence of which separatist initiatives sometimes spring up. Overall, even if instruction in Islam and Muslim schools are still work in progress, having reached to date only fairly unequal solutions with regard to modes and methods of education, we note that Muslims have handled their entry into the system fairly adroitly. Except in a few countries, the process has gone on without major opposition from the authorities of European states [Dassetto, 1996], even including those in Eastern Europe.

Still, alongside the start of programmes of study and other concrete results obtained, it seems important not to forget a more global and perhaps more profound dimension: that regarding the system of education as a whole, whose need for multicultural emphasis is easy to see. This can be seen in small details, such as the need for a multicultural calendar, to be posted in schools, which marks the dates of holy days for all the principal religions. In turn, parents must also take responsibility for letting schools know about their particular sensitivities [Otterbeck, 1999:35]. There are some less obvious points to make about obstacles to an authentic recognition of Islam within state-run educational systems. First there is the general ignorance of teachers in regard to Muslim students and their religion [van de Wetering, 1992], and the unsuitability of courses which sometimes continue to present events such as the Crusades or colonisation in a unilateral manner, the lack of tenured Muslim teachers, the need to professionalise the status of teachers of religion [Shadid & van Koningsveld, 1997:150] or the fact that there is almost no Muslim representation on the administrative staff of state schools, either at the level of individual schools or that of the bureaucracy.

Finally, as concerns the various types of higher education, such institutions are less numerous than might be expected, and they are the subject of serious debates in countries which have a large Muslim population or one which has been established for at least several decades. In general, in fact, the construction of an instructional framework for the production of religious leaders has a long way to go, not only in quantitative terms or in terms of existing structures (the exception here is Britain), but also in qualitative terms, because except in Eastern Europe this instruction is left to private means. It is also often focused on the study of religious precepts alone, neglecting a wider analysis of the European context in which these schools exist. New initiatives do appear, and connections between different levels of instruction are multiplying. These attest not only to a bond between Islam in the Balkans with Islam worldwide, but also the beginning of the gradual autonomisation of a properly European instruction in Islam.

CHAPTER THREE

MOSQUES, ORGANISATIONS AND LEADERSHIP

Brigitte Maréchal

The organisational aspects of Muslim communities are described from two points of view, first as concerns the establishment of places of worship, including mosques under purely local leadership. From the second standpoint, connections and affiliations of these local formations with various larger-scale ideological movements are studied.

The process of construction, establishment, and growth of worship centres is described in the course of an historical account of these developments. After an examination of the internal management and functions of these mosques, we will examine authority figures. These are distinguished according to their training, their titles, the way they get their jobs, their responsibilities. A comparison between Eastern and Western European countries allows several different problems to be considered. After this basic framework has been delineated, some account of recent developments is given, concerning the functions of imams, the growth of associations, renewed interest on the part of young people, the slow but undeniable move of women into the public sphere, and the appearance of new leaders.

As for vertical organisations, these sometimes create local organisations, and sometimes work from within them. These organisations have various ethnic and national affiliations, relations (or lack of relations) with various states, and ideological and religious differences; we examine this in a variety of contexts of action. But the study of Islamic organisational networks must concentrate on determining their relative importance, and on the relationships of cooperation and/or competition which exist between them within European territory. It is in fact essential to understand that these movements are constantly changing, not fixed in place, and may support or oppose one another depending on particular problems and on the circumstances of the moment.

It is also essential to understand the extent to which the overall situation of Muslim populations is in a transitional phase. In Western

Europe, the transition passes from one generation to another, and another. These stages run parallel to another development, in which immigrant communities centered on the country of origin become centered on the host country, while remaining connected to the Muslim world as a whole. In the Balkans, on the other hand, the contemporary period is also filled with changes, and these are connected to the end of the communist era. Two of the most important are the re-establishment of Muslim institutions once suppressed, and the renewal of various ties to the rest of the world, whether this is with worldwide Islam or also, nowadays, with European Islam.

1. ESTABLISHMENT OF MOSQUES

Quantitative aspects of the implantation process

In order for a historical account of this line of development at the European level to be presented, two aspects must be considered. On one hand, there is the fact that implantation in Eastern Europe took place a very long time ago, and each country has established forms of religious institutions that differ to a fairly large degree. For example, in Bulgaria there are not only a number of mosques which were built during the Ottoman period, but several *tekkes* (convents) and *türbes* (mausoleums) which hold the remains of sheikhs and the founders of various fraternal orders or brotherhoods. These are maintained in good condition by the Muslim community [BG File]. On the other hand, recent times have seen remarkable growth in the construction of places of worship in Western Europe. At present, in all the countries we have studied here, there are approximately 8,900 mosques and prayer rooms.

Table 4. ESTIMATE OF THE NUMBER OF MOSQUES WHICH ARE BUILT IN MUSLIM STYLE, WITH MINARET AND/OR DOME, AND PRAYER ROOMS IN COUNTRIES IN WESTERN AND EASTERN EUROPE (AS OF END OF 1990s)

Country	Number of mosques and prayer rooms	Country	Number of mosques and prayer rooms
Austria	1 + 200	Luxembourg	0 + 3
Belgium	4 + 308	Netherlands	30 + 350
Bulgaria	1283	Norway	n.a.

Country	Number of mosques and prayer rooms	Country	Number of mosques and prayer rooms
Denmark	1 + 60	Poland	3 + 13
Finland	0 + 17	Portugal	4 + 14
France	8 + 2,150	Romania	62 + x
Germany	66 + 2,200	Spain	6 + 300
Greece	295	Sweden	6 + 100
Hungary	11	Switzerland	2 + 100
Ireland	n.a.	United Kingdom	80 (?) + 1,100
Italy	3 + 150	Total	1,865 + 7,065 = 8,930

Sources: authors' research and national experts

Reckoning from estimates which place 12 million Muslims in European territory, this works out to one mosque or prayer room for every 1,345 persons of Muslim origin. Other estimates from 1996 found 3,000 Muslims per mosque, concluding that "the infrastructure of mosques which spreads over European territory (has) a density which is comparable, in proportional terms, to that which exists in Muslim countries" [Dassetto, 1996:165]. Such general indications, counting by thousands, take in quite different situations from country to country, as regards the public profile of the mosque or the average size of its congregation. 'Prayer rooms' are local branches of larger organisations of various types. The locations themselves are not usually very visible at street level; some prayer rooms are visited by only a few people each day. And in Eastern countries, there are probably a number of places of worship which are maintained and counted in statistics, but which no longer have regular worshippers.

A single process

Despite differences between Western European countries as to the period in which Muslim immigrant communities were implanted and grew larger, the process at work is a single one. It began in Great Britain, where most large industrial cities saw the first mosques constructed during the 1950s. In France, Germany, Belgium, and the Netherlands, most constructions did not begin in earnest until the mid-1970s, occurring often in connection with the process of families re-uniting in Europe, a process which gathered momentum in the 1980s. In contrast, in countries such as Italy and Spain, whose immigrant communities had their growth spurt later, permanent implantation started at a much faster rate [Allievi & del Olmo Vicén, 1996c]. The Italian case is set apart to some degree by the fact that the first mosques were built by and for an intellectual elite composed of Middle Eastern students, not by immigrant workers [Allievi, 2001].

Authors in the field agree that such a pattern always occurs [Cesari, Dassetto, Kepel, Nielsen, Shadid & van Koningsveld among others]. The first stage consists in the creation of single prayer rooms for some definite area, as soon as the population is large enough. These rooms are the product of the initiatives of local believers, constructed with their resources: heads of families take responsibility for renting or buying buildings that can be remodelled to serve as places of worship. But soon this unity becomes divided, and a few worshippers sometimes establish another place of worship, so that eventually we get a number of small competing mosques. Several factors help explain this phenomenon, including increases in residential concentration, preferences for living within one's ethnic or linguistic group, or for persons who share the same juridical interpretation of the sacred texts, and finally influences from certain religious movements whose activities cross national boundaries. When these movements become associated with local mosques, the latter undergo changes, either in organisational terms or in terms of doctrine.

In general, except for large central mosques in major cities and mosques in towns which cannot afford more than one place of worship, mosques tend to be attended by people of a single ethnic group. Many of these are known to favour a particular interpretation, often under the authority of any person erudite in religious matters, but there are cases in which several tendencies co-exist in one mosque while still keeping their specific features. All Muslims are nevertheless welcome to worship at these mosques. This process illustrates the comment, that "the more Muslims there are, the more likely it is that the variety of religious organisations will become important" [Shadid & van Koningsveld, 1995:24]. But one fact must be borne in mind: as with the British case, the increase in the number of mosques built does not necessarily mean the expansion of Islam itself. The increase can also be interpreted as an effect of the rise of "sectarian differences which break out among various groups, (which) those who have hegemonic ambitions make use of to the prejudice of Islam" [M.S. Raza, Islam in Britain, Leicester, 1991, cited by Kepel, 1994:159].

Alongside this, there has been a gradual realization that many places of worship do not meet even minimal conditions of security and maintenance, and are too small to meet peoples' needs, especially as regards the number of attendees at Friday prayers. The desire to build real mosques thus increased rapidly; what was needed were more permanent arrangements, including purchases of buildings. These may originally have been private houses, businesses, stores, public baths or cinemas, or they may have been built new. These projects were often viewed with dismay in the host countries, but for their instigators they were "not (evidence of) a refusal to integrate, but to the contrary, an acceptance of exile and its consequences" [Cesari, 1997:33]. Until quite recently mosques have been confined to industrial or boundary areas in large cities, or to ethnic neighbourhoods, because of unwillingness in the host country to accept public expressions of Muslim worship.

The question of visibility

It is striking to notice the enormous contrasts found in various countries in this regard. There is a sort of antithesis between certain neighbourhoods in London or Birmingham and Kreutzberg, the Turkish quarter of Berlin. There is a very great difference between them as concerns the importance of exterior signs attached to the buildings, the presence of a minaret, signs written in Turkish, Arabic or Urdu to denote a place of worship, and also as concerns the general condition of the neighbourhood, the way people are dressed, the storefronts, etc.

Beside the reactions from host countries, sometimes quite positive,[1] other factors also bear on this disparity of situations, first of all the resources of the various communities, whether these come from host country sources or from foreign sources. Western European states, unlike those in the East, generally take the position that they have no duty to intervene in this area, or to provide funding, although

---

[1] We note the support of some local non-Muslim organisations, who have used their influence, and provided assistance in the name of inter-religious solidarity. Such groups provided aid in the beginning and continue to do so.

fairly substantial aid is sometimes provided. This policy is responsible for the modest overall condition of Muslim places of worship in Europe, although there are a few remarkable exceptions. As for this prestigious aspect of some buildings in some capital cities, it is not only the result of money from foreign countries, but is often linked to very specific authorisations often adopted in host countries as part of diplomatic arrangements, made in order to facilitate relationships between countries.

Since the mid-1990s, the building boom in mosques and prayer rooms has slowed in Western Europe. The pace of creation of such places of worship "appears to have reached a point where the curve of growth flattens out" [Dassetto, 1996:173], except, probably, in Italy, Spain, Portugal, and some Eastern countries. Since the early 1990s there, external influences have worked to revive the religious practices of Muslim populations by building mosques, as in Bulgaria, for example [Peev, 1997:184].

Before ending this section, we should mention the remodelling of former churches, buildings which have ceased to be used by them. The case has rarely come up in Great Britain, but some re-adaptations have been permitted. In Belgium the debate is joined, involving some well-known buildings located in neighbourhoods which today have large Muslim populations. This emerging issue will probably become more important in the near future, and provoke a number of reactions, because of its highly symbolic nature.

2. INTERNAL ORGANISATION OF MOSQUES AND FIGURES OF AUTHORITY

Autonomy of local mosques

In Western Europe, most mosques are local organisations with considerable if not total administrative autonomy. The fact that a mosque belongs to a religious movement does not necessarily mean that it is only a part of a large-scale organisation, even if some organisations do try to round up mosques in a federation-type structure [Shadid & van Koningsveld, 1995].

The leaders of mosques have up to now almost all been men, which illustrates the near-monopoly of the early generations over the structure of worship associations and over the choice of imams—

though change is visible in Great Britain, it has barely affected France or Germany. The naming of imams usually takes place as part of a sometimes adversarial process which should produce a consensus among the members of the community, although individual persons sometimes wield enough authority to determine certain aspects of mosque organisation in a more or less arbitrary fashion. Imams are chosen for their personal qualities, because of social or socio-political considerations such as the status of a particular family, because of credit and/or prestige acquired through participation in various projects in the host country, or fund-raising ability, etc.

The leadership is responsible for giving direction to the mosque's activities, especially in terms of choice of worship services and other activities offered. Prayer rooms and small mosques are concerned first of all with arranging a central place for worship, made more pleasant by social contacts and the growth of community feeling and solidarity between members. But as soon as the mosque gets a little bigger, it takes on other functions, sometimes quite numerous: offering courses in religion and Arabic language for children, putting together a library, arranging a special place for preparing bodies for burial, giving members information about jobs and/or occupational training, etc.

Recruitment of imams[2] and the networks which participate in it

One of the most important tasks of the leadership of a mosque is to "recruit and supervise religious personnel" needed by the mosque, the most important of whom is the imam [Landman, 1998:10]. This task is difficult because there are too few trained imams, and almost no facilities in Europe for training them. This means that the majority of imams of mosques in Europe are brought from abroad. Beyond the two reasons for this given above, this practice finds itself reinforced by the fact that these imams are cheaper to hire, and in general less demanding.[3] Some intend to come to Europe only for a while, but others' family survival may depend on their being able to come to Europe. Still others may simply be filled with zeal to spread the faith. It is estimated that out of the 500 to 1,000 imams

---

[2] Literally, "the one who stands in front", hence "the one who leads prayers".
[3] Conversation with Ph. Lewis, Bradford, March 2000.

on French soil, only 4% have French nationality; 40% are Moroccan, 25% Algerian, 13% Turkish, 5% Tunisian, and 13% come from sub-Saharan Africa, the Middle East, or elsewhere [Frégosi, 1998a:103].

The same shortage is found in Eastern Europe. It is difficult to find sheikhs who are qualified, and the leaders of various brotherhoods often have limited theological or intellectual competence [Chodkiewicz, 1996:534; Popovic, ibidem:386]. In the Balkans, "there are practically no sheikhs who can read Arabic or Ottoman (...) and rituals are often limited to a reduced or simplified dhikr [Popovic, 1996:386]. In Bulgaria, the number of imams has been 'drastically reduced', and the country has been without trained theologians since the end of the communist era [Ragaru, 2001:273]. Most of the imams, the hodjas, are self-taught, trained by their parents, whose religious knowledge was sometimes sketchy. But compensatory mechanisms have begun to operate, to make the authority of the hodja depend "on the memory of his predecessors, who were cultivated and pious men, and above all on the holy men, the saints who may have been his ancestors" [Peev, 1997].

In Western Europe, several methods of recruitment have been identified [Dassetto, 1996; Reeber, 2000:236 ff.]. Sometimes the mosque's selection committee decides to go it alone, and then there are two possibilities. First, an appeal may be made to someone "who has acquired a local reputation for real or supposed competence—young people, foreign students, self-proclaimed imams—or who is among the oldest or longest residing in the community, a store owner or a retired person" without rhetorical or theological training [Frégosi, 1998a:103]. Or, the committee may attempt to bring someone in from a foreign country at its own expense, and in a way at its own risk, even if the risk is reduced by the custom of bringing in someone from the region of origin.

In other cases it may seem easier, or somehow ideologically or financially advantageous, for local leaders to turn to larger organisations, which compete against each other, and only take part in the selection of imams when they are requested to. This can happen in three ways. The state of the country of origin can be appealed to; large-scale international Islamic federations can be consulted; and the assistance of particular ideological movements can be sought.

The first of these is handled in the framework of consular services, and appears to be especially related to the absence of religious training facilities in Europe; this increases the dependence of local communities on the country of origin [Frégosi, 1998a:203]. They are ethno-national structures, mosques and/or more or less official associations, which have responsibility for religious affairs in Europe, like the *Institut Musulman de la Mosquée de Paris* (IMMP), whose rector names a hundred imams, often paid for by Algeria [Sindonino, 1998:86]. The largest efforts are made by the Turkish state, whence the influence of Turkish imams organized since 1979 under the *Diyanet Isleri Türk Islam Birligi*, (DITIB, Directorate of Religious Affairs, called simply the Diyanet). The Diyanet is an important administrative apparatus which favours centralised structure and practices; it is connected to the highest levels of the Turkish government. The Diyanet controls half the Turkish mosques in Europe, about 1,100 mosques, including over 700 associations in Germany, 110 in the Netherlands, and 51 in Belgium, and it employed 760 imams in 1995. Each imam is assigned for a period of 4 to 6 years to European mosques, and has the status and salary of a Turkish state employee [Manço, 1997]. This policy of high turnover of imams is intended to insure that the languages used and the type of Islam practiced remain largely as they were for the first generation. Later generations are not taken into account, and the policy might eventually cause problems for the Diyanet [Landman, 1997a].

Aside from intervention by states on behalf of their citizens in Europe, it is also possible to seek help from large international Islamic federations with an international profile, which are themselves related to national political organisations in Muslim countries, and which uphold the positions of the countries where they originated. The most important is the Muslim World League, founded in 1962, which takes its lead mainly from the official Saudi line. The League itself founded the High Council of Mosques in Europe in 1974 in order to fund the construction or restoration of mosques, and to support their activities, as well as to provide for the training of preachers. As for the World Muslim Congress, it expressed the Islamic tendencies of Pakistan, and now complements the Saudis. Libya, Iran and Sudan also engage in activity of this type. But Libya's efforts seem to have been "relatively improvised and without much lasting result", Iran's effort is "limited to only a few organized groups", composed of students supervised by embassy personnel. The Sudan appears to have 'no specific strategy' in regard to European Muslims. Despite the geopolitical issues involved, we take no further notice of these efforts, because in most cases "Muslims in Europe watch this game play out without participating, and often without understanding" [Dassetto, 1996:25].

The third possibility, not the least, consists in recruiting imams through the networks of particular ideological Islamic movements. These provide imams trained in their ideological line, coming from their country of origin, unless they were trained at the movement's own private institutions, some in Europe, as sometimes happens. The Süleymancis movement, for example, has centres in Germany and the Netherlands [Landman, 1998:12]. These tendencies are not always as mutually antagonistic as it appears, though, even in relation to state authorities, and bridges exist which tie them together. As an example: imams who have or have had sympathy for the Milli Görüs movement may later work for the Diyanet [Nielsen, 1992:149]. And the Milli Görüs movement recruits imams who have worked for the Diyanet who want to stay in Europe after their Diyanet mission expires [Landman, 1998:12]. Such a transfer requires that the candidate undergo additional training which 'reforms' the imam according to the tendency he will now be called on to uphold.

The ways in which imams are trained

The majority of imams practicing in Europe have "received an initial classical training, obtained at an Islamic institution in the Maghreb, Middle East, or in Saudi Arabia. This consists in study of the text of the Qur'an, its psalmody, principles of exegesis and hadith, and fundamentals of Islamic law" [Reeber, 2000:239]. We do not question the truth of this statement, but it masks other real aspects of the situation. The idea that all imams are trained like this needs to be taken in a relative sense.

As concerns the countries mentioned, it is true that these historic regions of Islam, especially the last two, still enjoy a certain aura and prestige, even for younger people. But it should not be forgotten that other regions also have distinguished themselves. They may be on the periphery, their accomplishments of more recent date, or less famous; but they should not be neglected, if only because of the number of persons who have studied at their institutions in order to acquire this training, and even if the training itself has been quite neutral in design, and of a formal nature: Turkey, Pakistan, and India come to mind, among others.

In addition, beyond the course titles of curricula, often identical, very important variations occur in regard to interpretations offered, and the quality of Islamic teaching varies widely, according to the educational systems in operation in the various countries of origin. Take for example Turkey, for the imams of the Diyanet, and Morocco, Pakistan, and Surinam. It is undeniable that the characteristics of programmes in these places differ greatly. The various levels of imams working for the Diyanet are quite different from each other, but in all cases the imams have finished a programme of higher learning in theology, and a four-year professional training programme before arriving in Europe. On the other hand imams who come from Morocco or Surinam are usually alike: they come from villages and have a more modest level of training. But the Minister of Habous and Islamic affairs considers it part of his job to produce imams with the proper qualifications, a goal he hopes to accomplish by instituting examinations [Landman, 1998:12].

All these national distinctions should not cause us to overlook the great differences in what these various imams have experienced, and their paths in life influence the way they do their jobs. This is shown in the Spanish example: all Spanish imams do not have documents proving they have completed Islamic studies, but the majority have a good knowledge of the Qur'an and hadiths. Their religious attitude is more important than an official certificate [Moreras, 1996]. This observation quite probably explains the high number of Moroccan imams in Spain but it is probably not representative of the situation as a whole, since most major institutes now make sure that their programmes confer legal status on the students.

Expansion of imams' responsibilities

After completing such training, imams arrive in Europe to be faced with the needs of communities in Europe, for which they are often unprepared. Not only are they perceived as the only ones with any religious knowledge, but the tasks they are used to are added to and transformed [Shadid & van Koningsveld, 1996b:121].

Once they are hired, their responsibilities include numerous and diverse activities. In addition to traditional functions such as leading daily religious services or preaching sermons that can fill the mosque[4]

---

[4] For M. Reeber, "Islamic preaching in Europe is cast in a rigid mold, not to

for Friday prayers (they are usually given more latitude of expression than in the country of origin [Reeber, 2000:232 ff.]), they have
other functions to fulfil. They may have to direct the Qur'anic education of young people, be available for personal counselling, handle ritualised practices such as circumcision, marriages, and funerals,
and even play a role in the public eye outside the mosque itself.
Some, in more devout communities, are even responsible for organising the public procession on the Prophet's birthday, for making
amulets to ward off the evil eye, or for whispering the call to prayer
in a newborn baby's ear.[5]

It must be difficult to try to do all this. Only the strongest imams
come out of it stronger than before; that is why they are the most
striking figures from the 1980s, especially in the countries with Muslim
communities of longer standing in Western Europe.

Problematic situations

In general, when imams arrive from abroad, a number of problems
arise. Usually, the training they have followed does not provide the
level of knowledge or know-how necessary for them to be effective
within a European community.

These imams are often poorly adapted by reason of under- or
over-qualification, when related to an intellectualised approach to
religion or to a lack sensitivity in regard to human relations and
social action. Occasions for tension are not lacking when they find
themselves in local communities of immigrants, composed of adults
from rural backgrounds and of young people who have a more urban
outlook, and who have been exposed to a diversity of cultures
unknown to the new imam. Moreover, they usually arrive with no

---

gratify an elite, but simply because preaching in a Western European country is
first of all and essentially a ritual act. One must 'pronounce' a khutba. Whether
the message is received is secondary under certain conditions. What counts is the
intonation of the preacher's voice, and the atmosphere which is created when he
speaks in Arabic" [Reeber, 2000:232].
  [5] Regarding more serious problems, it is reported that in the Netherlands some
Muslims employ Islamic healers whose works or powers are inspired by the Qur'an,
and who use the Qur'anic verses which are supposed to bring the *baraka*. Even
among imams who support official doctrine, a majority accept such practices, and
some even practice techniques of healing themselves [Hoffer, 2000]. As regards
other countries, there are no systematic studies of this subject, but such practices
are probably widespread.

more than a minimum of information about the host country, which causes problems in the situations they may be called on to manage, which require good knowledge of the culture and the institutional framework of the host country.

Their plight is even more difficult, considering the fact that they often find themselves in a precarious situation in social or administrative terms. They must maintain good relations with the selection committee that hired them, and they must comply with policies of the host state, which issues their residence permits. A certain instability results from the fact that their acceptance of a position "does not necessarily come with a level of social protection adapted to the corresponding religious activity, although this is provided for ministers of other religions" [Frégosi, 1998a:203]. Considerations relating to the maintenance of public order or the security of the host country's territory can be invoked, and these may quickly suffice to bring about their expulsion from the host country. In this regard, the Netherlands, Belgium, Austria, and Spain have adopted relatively progressive legislation. The first three have granted imams a legal status equivalent to that of other ministers of recognised religions, though Spain requires the presentation of a document from their community which conforms to the CIE, the *Comisión Islámica de España*'s requirements [Shadid & van Koningsveld, 1995:41]. But difficulties continue to arise in Spain because most communities do not have much contact with the *Comisión*, hence the semi-irregular status of their imams [Moreras, 1996].

Visiting or itinerant preachers

Alongside relatively well-established imams, more or less attached to a place of worship, there are also preaching imams who appear occasionally. Some are itinerant, and others are invited [Reeber, 2000:237]. The first usually focus on the revival of Islam among Muslim populations, and are connected to ideological movements who may finance them: the *Jama'at al-Tabligh* movement has worked in this manner, as well as persons working for the Société pour l'appel islamique (Society for the Islamic Call, a Libyan organisation; in Arabic *Al-Da'wa al-Islamiyya*), and also the Muslim World League, affiliated with the Saudis. Such imams are usually received with hospitality in the mosques they visit, and are allowed to preach. Invited imams are "sometimes personalities in the Islamic world who are passing through, and who are invited to speak, and sometimes preaching imams asked to come for the month of Ramadan, with the task of increasing attendance" [Reeber, 2000:237].

Though these comings and goings are less frequent now than in the 1980s, they are still part of the scene, sometimes under various conditions, as in Greece, where they are forbidden to enter from Turkey during Ramadan [Dalègre, 2001:308]. Preachers from Arab countries, and sometimes from Iran and Sudan also enter Eastern Europe. They also visit Bulgaria, even though since 1994 reports of the activities of Islamic missionaries have been received less often [Ragaru, 2001:271]. Their appearance sometimes causes disquiet among people, who fear their country may become a breeding ground for Islamic fundamentalism in Europe [Ilchev & Perry, 1996:132]. But the results of such missionary activities are quite small, and for most Bulgarian Muslims, they are "foreigners who, despite their apparent religiousness, inspire little confidence" [Peev, 1997:186; BG File].

Jurists or ʿulamâ'

There are still other roles beyond those filled by the committees responsible for the day to day administration of mosques, the imams they employ, and the various "suitable persons who assist, at special times, in the performance of certain solemn acts only, especially during the holy days or when the psalmody of the Qur'an is presented by trained readers" [Frégosi, 1998a:14 ff.]. Within the body of religious professionals, there is also the role of the theological jurist, usually known as a ʿâlim or ʿulamâ'. At the head of this corps of scholars, we traditionally find a mufti, empowered to hand down official opinions, worthy of respect, on points of doctrine, and juridical opinions of a consultative nature concerning questions which have been presented to him.

Divisions between various kinds of religious practitioners exist in Europe, but these should not make us forget that at bottom there is no 'Muslim clergy'. In the Sunni Islamic doctrine, in fact, it is the direct relationship of the believer to God that is essential. The formal operations of a personnel which is "religious and civil at the same time" [M. Arkoun, cited by Frégosi, 1998a:17] are only supplementary, though these persons still exercise a 'certain degree of influence'.

In Eastern Europe, Islamic communities were often created in each Balkan country of the post-Ottoman period according to the Ottoman model of a centralised religious hierarchy controlled by the state. The institution of the mufti and the functions of counsellors on religious law, each with a regional jurisdiction, thus assumed an official character: they are recognised in Bulgaria, Romania, and Greece.[6] They receive subsidies from the state and play the role of interlocutor vis-a-vis the state, and have (at least in Greece) juris-dictional competence in matters of marriage, divorce, and even civil and criminal matters,[7] though the state supervises the latter power.[8] In Greece the other religious positions are fairly well defined. Among 420 persons so employed in 1995, the functions of imam, preacher, and muezzin were mentioned. These posts are filled by persons "named by the Mufti, but they receive no salary from the state or local groups" [Akgönül, 1999:136]. As for other 'ulamâ', we do not have much information. They would appear to be independent, but can consult the mufti if necessary.

In Western Europe the situation is quite different: much less hier-archical and homogeneous, and thus much more complex and uncer-tain except, apparently, for Austria. This country, in fact, possesses a traditional institution[9] under the title of a Council of the Shura[10] (*Schurarat*), a Council of Elders (*Der Oberster Rat*), and a Grand Mufti. The latter, elected by a simple majority of the Council of the Shura, is responsible for religious affairs, and supervises the work of imams and teachers of religion in accordance with the Council of Elders and inspectors of the national education ministry [AT File].

---

[6] In Greece, the interference of the state in the election and nomination of the Muftis of Komotini and Xanthi has given rise to parallel structures, which oppose. Thus there are "two legal Muftis, paid and recognized by Greece, whose juridical acts alone are valid, and two 'illegal' Muftis, directly elected by the faithful, often condemned by Greek authorities, but supported by Turkey" [Dalègre, 2001:302; GR File].

[7] Other details about the institution of the mufti are found in chapter 4 "Institutionalisation of Islam".

[8] The Greek law n° 1920 of February 4, 1991 "establishes that the decisions of the Mufti shall not be carried out and do not constitute a definitive judgment unless the appropriate and competent Court has declared them binding" (after an exam-ination for the purpose of deciding whether the Mufti acted within his powers, not basing his judgment on an interpretation of sacred Islamic law or on any particu-lar evaluation of the given case) [GR File].

[9] Concerning this institution, which is quite different from the administrative (and non-religious) body which was established following elections among Muslims in Belgium in 1998, see "Institutionalisation of Islam".

[10] Traditionally considered as a consultative body made up of doctors of the law.

In other countries it is the imam who appears to represent the highest authority [Landman, 1998:10], an observation which in fact corresponds with the theoretical position of the twelver Shiites, who recognise the imams as the keepers of the keys to the Kingdom, and who are infallible. A number of reasons explain the development in the conceptions of Sunnis since the abrogation of the caliphate in 1924 by Mustafa Kemal. The first has to do with the absence of any consensus which would recognize the present governments of Muslim countries as administrators of the divine authority, a negative opinion reinforced by the increasing number of Muslims who do not live in any of these countries anymore. The second concerns a generally agreed-to proposition, which tends to be elevated to the rank of a principle, namely, that there are no persons learned in fiqh, Islamic law, in Europe, and so there can be no consensus of scholars. And this position leads people to presuppose that the debates which are going on now have to do with practices only, and that authoritative exegesis appears to have been suspended. To be more precise we could say that in relation to many crucial questions linked to contemporary problems, no one has yet been found who is recognized widely enough as having the authority to answer them, no one equal to the task of establishing general rules which can aid the believers in the interpretation of the texts in the light of our times. The third reason has to do with the public profile and added responsibilities of imams in Europe, which can lead them to get involved in areas which are as varied as they are vast and influential.

For sometimes the imams, who have in principle no intellectual pretensions, and who are accessible and close to the daily life of the faithful, nonetheless are obliged to step into the spotlight. From the historical point of view, though, the status of the imam is not all that elevated, at least not in any systematic way, the more so as a form of retribution is agreed to. In the countries of origin, beyond leading prayers, the imam is not thought to have any additional status whatsoever; he gives counsel if he is asked. Even the Friday sermon is often not considered to be his prerogative, and is performed by more educated persons when possible. As for other regions, a description of Pakistani villages written in the mid 1980s made it apparent that their imams normally possessed only the barest knowledge of Islamic theology, and enjoyed no special social status at all. They were considered as low-level salaried workers, no higher than barbers or carpenters, men who might be consulted on questions, but who were not seen as leaders [A. Sved, cited by Lewis P., 1994:122].

A few reflections on the loss of status of 'ulamâ'

The overall development, in which the imam has apparently gained status and the 'ulamâ' have lost it, requires some explanations. In fact, the relative importance of savants does not seem strictly related to the European situation. On the contrary, their position varies as much with time as it does in principle, as a function of the origins and tendencies of Muslim communities to which they belong. And these distinctions have an influence on the range of traditional Islamic institutions in the European countries we are studying. A few observations will help illustrate the changes in the role of the 'ulamâ'.

The first has to do with territorial considerations. At present, in Muslim countries, some 'ulamâ' are connected with the legal exercise of justice. They operate in the context of tribunals, and are responsible for stating the law, although a larger and larger proportion of the population already says it relies on other authorities with regard to legal problems, including neo-'ulamâ' and lay persons, even women and young people [Masud, 2001]. In Europe, there is hardly any institution where to acquire a theologian training; that means that there is a limited number of 'ulamâ', most of whom studied abroad.[11] Their status is much more precarious, since they perform their official function either full-time or in combination with another function, such as that of teacher of religion. In addition, their decisions are binding only on members of the community who choose to recognise them, and the strictly consultative aspect of their decisions is often enough set at naught by the juridical systems of European countries. And lastly, after years of influence by mass education and the media, Muslims are more and more inclined to try to interpret religious prescriptions for themselves, in the privacy of their souls and consciences.

In respect of certain temporal aspects, we note the change which occurred during the Indian colonial period, when muftis began to

---

[11] The most famous 'ulamâ' are still established in Muslim countries but it is becoming more and more difficult for European Muslims to refer to them due to the different contexts and to the language difficulties (Arabic language, for example, is less and less known among the European Muslim youth).

pronounce fatwas concerning individuals, and not only as general advice. Such a practice seems to be followed in Europe, where many persons have questions, and eventually turn to some source of authority in a personal meeting, a telephone conversation, by mail, or through the Muslim press. So it is with the accountant who asks himself or herself questions about the compatibility of certain practices with Islamic doctrine, or the taxi driver who wonders if it is licit to drive people to bars, or another person who wonders if watching television is a prohibited activity or not, or the woman legally divorced in the courts of the host country who wants to know how to get her divorce recognised according to Islamic doctrine, so she can find another husband within the Muslim community. This trend toward personal questions, away from general advice to the community, is perhaps responsible for the fact that the function of the 'ulamâ' has lost much of its lustre, and much of its symbolic importance as well.

The importance given to 'ulamâ' also varies according to the different branches and tendencies which co-exist within Islam.[12] The Deobandi movement grants them a certain pre-eminence, which is related to developments in history: from the beginning of that movement, consultations with a mufti have always been considered very important. This priority took the form of the regular issuance and publication of the consultative decisions of the muftis—the fatwas— beginning at the end of the 19th century, which gained a measure of fame. For them, this was a means of spreading their reformist vision of Islam [Lewis P., 1994:118]. The *Jama'at al-Tabligh* movement maintains a certain respect for this function, despite its formality, but they insist on the role of the individual Muslim in working for the good and against evil. For other movements, including mystical ones, such juridical interpretations were less important than piety, which was the highest priority. Some Sufis sometimes treat 'ulamâ' as "pedants who are only concerned with the external part of Islam" [Lewis P., 1994:113]. This observation is probably connected to the increase of individualism as much as to the trend to discount the mediation of scholars in favour of a direct approach to sacred texts [Lewis P., 1994:80].

---

[12] A description of these will be found later in this chapter.

In general, even if we observe a relative absence of 'ulamâ' across Europe, some Muslims feel the need to have some authorities which European Muslims could refer to. Recently, certain names have emerged here and there, especially those surrounding the European Council for Fatwas and Research (CEFR) created around personalities such as Yusuf al-Qaradawi and F. Mawlawi in 1997. Such a Council illustrates the relative weakening of the role of 'ulamâ' although the situation is made complex by the contradictory movements which exist between struggles for influence and the trend among movements toward greater inter-Muslim unity on European territory. Consequently, it is quite difficult to predict how things will go in the future as regards the recognition, the role or the importance of theological jurists in Europe. It is possible that some of their prestige will be regained, but it is likely that this will occur within the context of wider debates, even theoretical ones, which concern for example the status of Muslim communities as minorities in a non-Islamic society. But all this is quite obscure, and depends above all on certain other contextual factors which may gain a certain pre-eminence.

New leaders

Together with the relative stabilisation of managers and entrepreneurs who are distinguished by their business acumen and their capacity to act on behalf of Islam in the realisation of projects [Sindonino, 1998:418], another significant change arises, which may or may not come into relation with the multiplication of organisations: that which has to do with the emergence and increasing number of new leaders, producers of discourses about Islamic action who try to gain position "in a market which is quite open and quite competitive" [Dassetto, 1996:152]. These new leaders acquire the status of role models for many young people who are asking themselves questions about their place in global society, and who are trying to harmonise their citizenship and their religion.

These leaders are most often former foreign students who may have received some training in Muslim countries, or young immigrants who may have attended courses in foreign countries—which appears more and more frequently and signifies a direct connection to the sheikhs—or, much more rarely, they are converted Muslims [Allievi, 1998]. Those who manage to distinguish themselves are often charismatic personalities whose authenticity and authority comes from the testimony they give to a personal experience [Hervieu-Léger, 1997:14]. But this category also includes persons who are admitted to have good knowledge of the current situation, or certain abilities. The latter group give evidence of a level of intellectual training [Dassetto, 1996:153], not necessarily restricted to Islamic disciplines, or of good knowledge of basic theological writings, which "tends to demonstrate a religious practice which is more rigorous and conforms more exactly to Islamic precepts than did that of their elders" [Sindonino, 1998: 419].

In fact, these are 'new mediators' who contest the position of the 'ulamâ', but not their knowledge, and who put forward a "pragmatic discourse, an exhortation, intellectualised and rationalised, which says what the hearer wants to hear" [Roy, 2000:90]. Moreover, in Great Britain, it appears that "the debate should concentrate more directly on the recognition and support of communities than on ecclesiastical or spiritual representation in political institutions" because "few of those who aspire to be the spokespersons or representatives for Muslims have any religious authority", something which "Muslims do not demand anyway" [Modood, 2000:52].

In addition, through increased use of vernacular languages in conferences and seminars which take place outside of places of worship, the new leaders are increasing their influence among Muslim populations, and thus reinforcing the process of re-Islamisation [Reeber, 2000:244 ff.].

Finally, their "absence of militant commitment does not keep Muslim organisations (. . .) from courting them" [Frégosi, 2000:247]. This sort of thing seems to confirm the fact that, in the medium term, these leaders will marginalise traditional authorities who draw their powers from 'bureaucratic' or 'popular traditional' sources [Dassetto, 1996].

As for their relative ability in dealing with public European authorities, which furnishes them with credibility even if they are non-Muslim [Dassetto, 1996:153], it would be a mistake to think that it will keep them from preserving a certain closure around the community, which itself allows them to continue to present themselves as necessary intermediaries [Kepel, 1994:172]. In the meantime, we must acknowledge the very limited presence of scholars of Islamic law, true Muslim intellectual leaders living permanently in Europe, who are concerned by the situation of Muslim minorities in Europe, and who would open debates on "the possibility of applying certain elements of the Sharia within the European system" [Waardenburg, 2000:64]. Several disparate versions of Islamic theology are in circulation, supported by persons who take the Muslim world as their point of reference; but the appearance of a true theology adapted to life in contemporary Europe still lies in the future.

3. RECENT DEVELOPMENTS

The points taken up here concern only Western Europe, and usually only those countries whose Muslim communities have been present longer; there is little information in this regard for Eastern Europe. It appears that these processes have not yet begun there, because of the weakening of Muslim communities suffered during the communist era. The various changes which have occurred involve the functions of the imam, the increasing influence of associations, the increasing commitment of young people, and the appearance of women on the public stage.

The role and status of the imam

At the same time as the figure of the imam was losing some of its symbolic importance for young educated people, partially due to the emergence of new figures other than that of the traditional 'ulamâ', several transformations have occurred in the makeup of the role. These are consequences of the many additions to the tasks of the imam which were requested or ordered during the 1970s and 1980s, and subsequently there were attempts to restructure all these new responsibilities, assigned to imams in Europe. Two terms describe these attempts: 'division' and 'specialisation'.

The area of the imam's responsibility has not ceased to be extended, and eventually has come to involve secular functions such as the role of educator or inter-cultural mediator. This diversification of tasks in time required more personnel, since no one person could do them all. Once this point is reached, the governing committees of mosques and their leaders, volunteers from the neighbourhood, assume greater responsibilities, such as hiring teachers to give courses in religion. And from that point imams and mullahs gradually became 'minor bureaucrats' [Modood, 2000:52]. It is not unthinkable that this trend toward overturning the traditional ecclesiastical pattern should win out in the long term, in which case the Muslim community itself would become the real guardian of the faith.

During the period in which these tasks were being redistributed, a process which has now been going on for some time, a kind of specialisation was observed which in some cases created new occupations. For quite specific tasks such as visiting the sick in hospital, or counselling people in prison or soldiers in the army, a number of people have, after the completion of a preparatory course, become chaplains. These are at present paid by the state for the job they do. This is a current practice in Belgium, where 12 people have been appointed to chaplain's posts, and in France, Great Britain, the Netherlands, Greece (through religious foundations), Sweden, and Bulgaria [cf. the respective files on these countries].

The increase in the number of associations and groups identified as Muslim

This phenomenon began in the mid 1980s and grew rapidly in Western Europe, especially in relation with an increase in the commitment of young people to such organisations. For comparison, we note that there are about 3,000 associations in France [Naba, 1999:12], and more than 2,000 regional organisations in Germany [Karakasoglu & Nonneman, 1996:255]. Young people who join existing associations or create their own represent about 12% of the total of young Muslims in Germany [Jonker, 2000:303], and a very rough estimate of 30,000 young people counted as active in Muslim associations is given for France. This figure is related to the number of young people who met at Bourget in 1997 [Khosrokhavar, 1997]. Similarly, in Great Britain, Muslims themselves estimate that about 10% of young people belong to Islamic organisations [Lewis P., 1999:28].

This involvement by young people is sometimes explained by the fact that dialogue with the older generation has become difficult. In Great Britain, in France [Bourg, 1998:76], and in the Netherlands [Sunier, 1998:49], the same context is reported everywhere. It has to do more with a 'cultural difference' than with a generation gap, since "most young people do not respect the capacities of the members of the first generation either as regards their ability to understand the difficulties of their daily lives, or to help them progress along their spiritual paths" [Bourg, 1998:76]. Thenceforward, the young people take their distance, act in other ways, and create other kinds of associations and/or groupings, while taking care not to let differences become open conflicts.

These Muslim associations are quite varied in scope [Shadid & van Koningsveld, 1995]. Beyond strictly religious or cultural groups, which have among other aims that of promoting improvement in Islamic knowledge or Arabic, some associations have social goals, working at the union-union level as in Germany, the political level (see Chapter 'Institutionalisation of Islam') or the educational, through awarding scholarships for particular studies. Associations are involved in sports and games as well: there are associations which play soccer or practice taekwondo (including the Milli Görüs), or which do calligraphy, and since the early 1990s Muslim Scouts troops have been organised in France and Belgium by persons connected to the 'Alawiyya movement. These Scouts are trained according to the Baden-Powell code, slightly modified, and summer camps have been organised. Beyond groups based on specific activities, other associations are created for people in certain categories: young people, children, parents, women, people who graduated from the same faculty at university and who belong to the same ethnic group, student groups, etc.

Several general characteristics are often found in these associations: they are interested in 'local' concerns, that is, focused on bettering daily life of the social situation in the neighbourhood or town, and they also focus on integration into the larger society, sometimes speaking out about the developments of Islam in Europe, while remaining interested in the spiritual needs of the young. The reference to 'young Muslims' in France illustrates this double interest in religious identity and the rights of citizenship and participation in political processes. This focus on the larger society is observed in Denmark, where a comparison of the attitudes of young members of an association of Muslim Students (*Foreningen af Studerende Muslimer*) and those of their parents showed that the parents avoided discussions with the larger Danish society, but the young people, who were members of this transnational and pan-Islamic group, felt differently, laying claim to equal recognition of a personal sort within the democratic society [Simonsen, 2000:184 ff.].

When Muslims organise, not because it is especially prescribed in Islamic doctrine but in order to accomplish specific goals [Nielsen, 1992:118], this process of organisation can be called a 'social movement' or even 'movements in search of identity'. This term refers to the transformation of individual demands into collective demands which are rational attempts to get a response from outside agencies, and to reach goals which sometimes go beyond the area of religion [Sunier, 1998:41 ff.]. In some countries, certain Muslim associations are already subsidised by states [Cesari, 1997:170]. Usually, the associations may have to be categorised as 'lay associations' in order to be eligible to receive funds.

In general, associations are local, but they are sometimes affiliated with specific Islamic movements or international organisations; a number of associations are related to the World Assembly of Muslim Youth (WAMY), headquartered in Saudi Arabia with an office in London, or to the International Islamic Federation of Student Organisations (IIFSO), headquartered in Kuwait with an office in Germany. With the help of such an organisation, the *Unione degli Studenti Musulmani in Italia* (USMI) played a leading role in the establishment of mosques and Islamic centres [Shadid & van Koningsveld, 1995:43].

In still other cases organisations go beyond local issues and take up regional or even national positions. In Great Britain, the UK Islamic Mission has focused its efforts on the development of young leaders, and on education and the production of appropriate literature in English since 1963 [Lewis P., 1994:102]. In Leicester, the Islamic Foundation attempts to carry on research and to publish translations of works such as those written by the intelligentsia of the Jama'at-i-Islami, as well as works on Islamic economics, Islam in Europe, and Muslim-Christian dialogue. The Young Muslims UK group begun in 1984: originally linked to the Jama'at-i-Islami, this main youth organisation publishes the magazine *Trends*. Its members participate in regular activities as well as in discussions of social problems of the day, which are more or less informal. The Muslim Association of Britain (MAB) is one the latest organisations which was created in UK, and one of the most active: beside Islamic *da'wa* work, numerous events and activities are created around the country to increase the Muslim youth awareness of their responsibilities and role towards the society. In France, Lyon stands out as a regional centre of activity. Located there are the *Groupement pour la Jeunesse et l'Entraide* (Group for Youth and Mutual Assistance), and the Union of Young Muslims (*Union de la Jeunesse Musulmane*—UJM), founded at the end of the 1980s around the bookstore/library *Al-Tawhid*. Following the beginnings of re-Islamization among the Beurs, the UJM tried to combine claims on behalf of the Islamic community with the exercise of rights as French citizens, as illustrated by their slogan, "French, yes, and Muslims too".

At the national level, the second organisation is ideologically closed to the influential *Union des Organisations Islamiques de France* (UOIF), while still competing with the youth branch of the latter, headed by Hassan Iquioussen, which is largely cantered in the northern part of France. We should also note the *Présence Musulmane* organisation, led by Tareq Ramadan, who since 1996 has enrolled many young people in France, Belgium, and Switzerland in conferences and courses on religious and philosophical reflection. Basically open to discussion, he has initiated a growing movement of young responsible Muslims toward cooperation and united action, especially in the framework of better relations with the European societies.

In a general way these associations tend in a sense to displace the mosque as the centre of social events, since they are able to affect social situations through sponsorship of many activities. But while the increase in the number of activities allows them to increase their own importance, it also increases the importance of the mosque in absolute terms. These areas of activity are of every kind. Those concerned consider it important to take responsibility for the needs of the second generation, in many ways: offering remedial classes for young people who have been deprived of education, obtaining space for sporting activities, opening bookstores or publishing companies, organizing conferences, helping families in need, sponsoring matchmaking activities in support of the extra-marital abstinence which is recommended by religious leaders, etc. [Kepel, 1994:342 ff.; Bourg, 1998:78; Babès, 1997].

Women's groups

Muslim women appear these days not only in the job market but in the public eye [Lewis P., 1994:177]. They have begun their self-affirmation, though the process is slow, still in its beginnings; for most women it goes no further than participation in informal groups although young women are becoming more and more visible and implicated within the various activities.

The testimony of some women attests to the uneasiness of the process, often in relation to cultural practices. The problem is partly women's real interiorisation of a conception of themselves as tied to a private and not a public world. In order to learn about Islamic culture, they much prefer to read up on it than to study it through organisations [Babès, 1997:134]. And when they do attend conferences, they appear content to see other women, without any apparent consciousness for the roles they might play.[13] Above all, "a certain reticence, an unwillingness on the part of the men to work in mixed groups" is still at work in many organisations [Babès, 1997:134]. In the Netherlands, it has been observed that women maintain "a fairly low profile" in public life, and that segregation between Moroccan men and women is still important [Strijp, 1999:68], a phenomenon which is echoed by the purdah custom, according to which South Asian women in Great Britain are supposed to associate only with women of their own family. Segregation still occurs in France, where it is alleged that "often within associations women remain restricted to specifically female issues" [Khosrokhavar, 1997], or end up creating separate associations [Bourg, 1998]. This separatist attitude is even more common when any kind of power is at stake. It has been observed that young girls and young women "are usually found at the local level or lowest levels in any Muslim or Islamist association", and "are noticeable by their absence at higher levels" [Khosrokhavar, 1997]. And it is not surprising to hear that in France, for example, "women are rather invisible in comparison to men, who have created a collective Muslim identity that is generically male", while even in a public controversy such as that over the wearing of headscarves, "men monopolised the debate" [Bloul, 1996:234].

Nevertheless, there are two currents at work, which aim at different objectives. One is based on the initiative of individual persons, and the other is linked to the actions of ideological and organisational networks, which in turn are seeking to rally women to their cause.

The first type is illustrated by women who decide, individually or in a group, to get involved not only in European society through participation in non-Muslim associations, but dare further to try to work on social problems which affect the community they live in. Such action is quite rare, but it is probable that it will become much more important in the near future, especially in Great Britain, though the Muslim feminist movement is weak there and only beginning to emerge in relation to labour issues. One quite exemplary organisa-

---

[13] L. Latrache cited by A. Sindonino, "Louisa Latrache, femme, musulmane, militante" in *Islam de France*, n° 5, 1999:125–133.

tion in Britain is the *Al-Nisa Society*, created in 1985, which has 50 active members, 10 very active, and 600 'friends'. It is headquartered in London but has contacts in Bradford and Birmingham. Its members speak of a desire to develop the identity of the Muslim community through providing a range of services that are not provided by the larger society. These occur at various levels. The association distributes information and furnishes counselling concerning the rights of women, e.g., the right to obtain an Islamic divorce, marriage contracts, dowries (*mahr*), etc. The association encourages them to develop as persons by organising self-esteem classes, and in partnership with several established schools provides courses in calligraphy or in English. In an effort to raise consciousness with regard to various issues, and to encourage women to learn to play a role within the community, even to influence certain positions taken by certain imams, the association facilitates contacts.[14] Women may spend an hour or so a week deciding what kind of Islam might help them grow, rather than limiting them. They speak openly and with passion about problems such as contraception, abortion, adoption, rape, and children's education. There are also questions about "how to get men to be better husbands and fathers, and discussions of geopolitical or ecological matters" [Alibhai-Brown, 1994 cited by Vertovec & Peach, 1997:40]. Finally, aside from offering information about the Islamic religion to certain public agencies, the association tries to help older people to organise themselves, or to establish safe places or crisis shelter for Muslim women who are experiencing family crises.[15]

On a smaller scale, but with the same apparent objectives are the women's group of the Islamic Information Centre at The Hague, and the Foundation for Muslim Women in the Netherlands, and an Al-Nisa group at Almere. These organisms have developed programmes which are useful for women, including courses in Arabic and ritual prayer, and also provide social assistance. There are groups like Al-Nisa in Zwolle, Venlo, Haarlem, and Arnhem [van Bommel, 1992].

Autonomous associations of women have appeared in France since the early 1990s, each for a quite particular purpose. The *Union des Sœurs Musulmanes* of Lyon was a support group for women who had

---

[14] Interview with Khalinda Khan, director of the association—Brent, March 2000.
[15] Idem.

been excluded from the educational system for insisting on wearing headscarves. The association *Femmes Actives et Sportives* has promoted participation in sports for women. The *Ligue Française de la Femme Musulmane* was created to encourage social contacts between Muslim women from different cities in France [Hawwa Magazine, 2000]. The Ecole Lamalif, created by Louisa Latrache, offers courses in classical Arabic, tutoring for school and literacy classes, and is working on opening the first Muslim female chaplaincy in France, in the women's prison at Nanterre [Sindonino, 1998:380 ff.].

As concerns ties to ideological organisational networks, some of these associations themselves change, creating sections for women, and encouraging them to get involved in the structure or to organise activities within the association. Beyond ideological or internal organisational reasons, such changes can sometimes be explained in part by a sort of pressure from the political environment, even a kind of demand from European governments that women be better represented in public life, a demand that can eventually be tied to the granting of various privileges. Here, the Turkish Milli Görüs federation leads the way. Among 791 local branches in Western Europe, 674 have a 'youth' section, and 445 have a 'women's' section [Manço, 1997]. These women's groups have proved successful, even though some young women have been greatly influenced by their family, before they get the idea themselves [Amiraux, 2000a:125]. These groups are a "frame of reference for religion" as well as a "place to make contacts, to exchange knowledge and experiences, concerning the areas of home economics, home hygiene, care and feeding and education of small children, sexuality, and contraception". All this training seems to take place in a more accessible way than if it was organised through 'public institutions'. Some of the precepts or principles upheld in the groups are "the formation of young couples and nuclear families", the "effort to find clothes that look good and still respect Islamic norms", "meetings with groups of Western women", and finally, "putting an end to traditional chauvinistic mentalities and practices" [Manço, 1997]. All this attention demonstrates how much girls, as future mothers, are seen as key to the transmission of ideas, Islamist or otherwise [Kandiyoti, 1995:318, cited by Timmerman, 1999:185]. The educational message is the easier to communicate, since participation in these activities has other advantages for these girls. They get opportunities to "meet outside their homes without their parents worrying", or husbands, and they taste a "freedom of movement". They may also be able to present these activities as an argument in favour of staying in school and completing programmes of study, in the case of "female students who want to postpone an eventual marriage", etc. [Manço, 1997].

As concerns other ideological networks, things are less clear. Procedures for including women appear more discreet, unless they are being done outside any given institutional framework. All things considered, the Sufi groups such as the 'Alawiyya brotherhood and some modernist Islamic movements appear the most open to women's groups and/or their participation. In France women's groups have been included in the large organisations claiming to be representative of all Muslims, such as the *Union des Organisations Islamiques de France* and the *Fédération Nationale des Musulmans de France* (FNMF), but at present women "are participating much more freely in all activities", such as members of the *Jeunes Musulmans de France* (JMF). The Deobandi reformists have probably made fewer changes, since they usually perceive women as "a bastion of superstition and non-Islamic or Hinduist traditions". A new approach to the Muslim woman is intended, but "only as playing a central role in the project to reform the family" [Sikand, 1999:42 ff.]. As for the *Jama'at al-Tabligh* movement which is popular with South Asians and Arabic speakers, even if it does "aim at reinforcing the traditional division of the sexes as concerns duties" [Sikand, 1999:48-49] and though debates on women's issues hardly appear in its teachings (in contrast with the Jama'at-i-Islami) [Metcalf, 2000:46], it does permit women to be active insofar as they are an "integral part of the reformist agenda of Islamization". It may be possible to discern a "light criticism of male supremacy" here [Sikand, 1999:50 ff.] or even a plea for better 'complementarity', since in their preaching activities there has been a "rapprochement of the sexes" such that "their roles are interchangeable" [Metcalf, 2000:49 ff.]. These considerations show again how complex are the relationships which must be grasped, and also that Muslim women still have a long way to go before wielding any decisive influence in the public sphere.

4. The Global Framework of Islamic
Organisational Networks

Aside from the matter of recruiting imams, who usually come from abroad, the account given up to now of the organisation of mosques may have given the impression that they and their organisational structures are quite homogeneous. But diversity is more typical, despite the fact that only a few mosques are completely autonomous, standing alone. And even these are usually local organisations of small to medium size, which are ethnically and/or theologically quite distinct. Examples are the mosques of Javanese Muslims of Surinam, that of the Moluccans (Indonesia) in the Netherlands, and that of Indian Muslims of France [Shadid & van Koningsveld, 1995:43 ff.].

Most of the time, different ideological currents or networks have relations with many mosques and even other Islamic organisations, though they operate relatively independently on a day to day basis. Before we try to explain the majority and/or typical tendencies which are present in Western Europe in the following, some general observations can be made as a preliminary. Certain factors which go beyond them, which influence their characteristics and their spread, are identified. This allows us to put their importance in perspective. We may mention questions of ethno-national belonging, intervention by states of origin in religious matters, which takes effect through organisational structures existing in the host country, and finally the impact of political structures which call forth reactions from some religious movements.

Ethnic and national belonging

Distinguishing between movements by origin is important, though more or less so depending on the ethnic group. In general, the tendency to cling to one's roots developed fairly rapidly among Pakistanis and Turks in the 1980s and 1990s, while Arab populations do not seem as interested.

This criterion still holds when we look at the history or the composition of movements, but is not as important for members of the second or even the third generation. For them, ethnic heritage may become obsolete; it is felt to be further and further from the composite identity of their daily lives, in which it is more common for them to befriend Muslims from other regions than their own.

Intervention by Muslim states

Over and above the operation of large Islamic federations on an international scale which are connected to political and state agencies in Muslim countries, and which defend the positions of the country they are from, especially the Muslim World League and the World Muslim Congress, briefly mentioned above, it sometimes happens that states operate real state structures in European countries which have influence over their former residents. The Diyanet, for example, has responsibility for Islamic morality and religious practice among Turks, and the '*Amicales*', associations connected to consular locations (or created by them), do the same for countries of the Maghreb. They are intended to preserve social ties between people from the same country of origin, either Morocco, Algeria, or Tunisia, thus preserving as well a degree of control over their former residents and their religious convictions, with the ultimate aims of maintaining some political allegiance, and perhaps even raising money. It may be easier for the Moroccan state to take on this task, inasmuch as the title of "commander of the faithful" is still a birthright of the King of Morocco, and gives him considerable authority in the area of religion.

At present the Diyanet seems quite strong. Starting with financial and organisational power, it has succeeded in "establishing a strong institutional position", but has never managed to control the entire Turkish population [Landman, 1997a:220]. At any rate, all Islamic movements of Turkish origin are reactionary above all. They want to escape from state control and must be understood in the light of this bureaucratic reality, which promotes a loyalist and quietist Islam [Landman, 1997a:222], to be observed in private, and which emphasizes ritual and moral obligation. The differences between one and the other have more to do with the role of Islam in society and ways of achieving political aims than any purely doctrinal matters [Sunier, 1992:151]. We should observe, in fact, that the Diyanet is officially responsible for "getting control of Islamic deviance, that is, ideological Islamic groups" [Amiraux, 1995:75]. In the future, the Diyanet may run into more difficulties because it favours Turkish national feeling, while Turkish populations are being gradually assimilated, and because competition from other movements is on the rise [Landman, 1997a].

As for other countries, they appear less influential, though Morocco did give evidence of effort in the creation, in 1986, of the *Communauté marocaine de Madrid al-Umma*, closely linked to the Moroccan Embassy in Madrid, and the installation, in 1989, of a delegation from the *Conseil Continental Européen des Mosquées* in that city [Moreras, 1996]. In fact, apart from Spain and Italy, where the '*Amicales*'—slowly replaced with the Foundation Hassan II—will probably gain some more importance in the future [Allievi, 1997:217], such structures are weak and getting weaker. They are everywhere perceived as instruments of ideological control on the part of governments abroad. This consciousness is the more decisive for many and becomes even more embarrassing, since new types of associations are being created [Sindonino, 1998:108 ff.], which open the range of possibilities of membership.

Imported political parties or trends

Although these spin-offs may have some autonomy in relation to their parent organisations in the countries of origin, they may try to continue to manoeuvre politically in terms of the situation in the country of origin, while still trying to have some influence over the character of religious movements. Without overestimating their importance, we should note that they indirectly affect these movements and even contribute to them.

In the typology of Turkish political movements found in Europe, all the divisions are reproduced [Bozarslan, 1990, cited by Amiraux, 1995]. The "dichotomous pluralism which makes up the Turkish political landscape reappears in immigrant associations: Turks/Kurds, Islamists/secularists, Sunni/Shiite, left/right, etc." [Manço, 1997]. Thus we find transnational organisations which have networks of local associations throughout the European Union: Kemalist social democrats, right wing and extreme right wing positions (such as an association which groups together 64 racist and nationalist associations, including the Grey Wolves), those in favour of Kurdish autonomy, and the Alawis, who claim to be secular Kemalists and democrats, although their identity poses a problem for many of their members. As for Islamic tendencies, three federations are competing ferociously (the Milli Görüs, the Süleymancis and the Diyanet), but "none has managed to establish itself as the indispensable representative of all", despite the ebb in the force of radical currents, relative to the early 1980s [Manço, 1997].

Although this kind of political structure is probably less obvious in the case of other ethnic and national groups among Muslim populations located in Europe, there is no doubt that they exist and divide their populations. For example, some are Moroccan royalists, and some are opposed. There is a traditional opposition between *Harkis* and other Algerians, although this is fading away. There is also conflict between different peoples of the Indian peninsula as regards Kashmir.

5. Diversity of Ideological and Religious Currents

Here we present a panorama which illustrates the variety of important Islamic movements present on European soil, though their importance must be put in perspective with regard to the equally important 'silent majority' of Muslims. This majority is as crucial to the construction and spread of Islam as the movements, but is barely organised, and exists not in wide networks but at the local level [Allievi, 2001]. However this may be, it is the characteristics of these movements that we now examine. We estimate their relative importance, and note their mutual relations and their geographic diversity, including the Arab world, the Indian subcontinent, and the Turkish world.

This review of movements concerns only the countries of Western Europe, because so little information is available in this regard on Eastern Europe, and this is especially true as regards Bulgaria and Romania. The impression remains that these currents exist, but invisibly, or seem to the people there to be quite negligible; they concern two distinct orders that are rather antagonistic.

Among the native Muslims of Bulgaria, Romania, and Greece, embedded in popular customs, are several mystical movements being shaped as (neo-) brotherhoods: Naqshbandis, Bektashis-Alawis, Nursis-Fethullahci, Süleymancis or Rifa'is (cf. infra) and also Qâdiris and Shâdhilis. Though the ancient Sufi networks were "almost completely wiped out in the 20th century, except for the Alawis-Kizilbash communities" [Clayer & Popovic, 1999:32], and though their organisational structures have sometimes disappeared, as in Dobrudja in Romania [Popovic, 1996:388], their influence has continued through history. Paradoxically, it appears that Soviet anti-religious policy "reinforced the importance of structures which had no official existence", up to the point of giving them a "monopoly on the representation of Islam, and the right to recruit new adherents" [Chodkiewicz, 1996:534].

These ancient brotherhoods or their modern avatars are more easily accepted by local people than members of other, reformist and Shiite currents, who are mainly thought of as outsiders. Shiite proselytisers have been particularly successful in Sufi regions of the western Balkans; they try to instil their doctrine in the same manner among Alawis groups in Turkey [Clayer & Popovic, 1999:32]. As for the reformist elements, they come from the Middle East and are connected primarily to the Salafi tendency which preaches a return to the purity of the first successors of the Prophet, that is, the four well-guided caliphs.[16] In this line we find the literalist Wahhabi movement [Peev, 1997].[17] This group spreads its influence through former students, Arabs, and through financial help or even by sending missionaries. These movements support authors such as Abu'l-A'la Mawdudi (cf. infra), apparently because he opposes popular religious practices, nationalism, and secularism [Lederer, 1994]. An examination of movement literature, in tracts which present the same arguments or are even translated from one original, "it appears that a general strategy for teaching has been worked out for all the Eastern countries". An "Islam in local dress or for 'Eastern European markets' is not even offered, because only the foundations of the faith seem important there; the past is idealized, and set against the deviations of modernity, and the extent of Islam's penetration in the Balkans during the pre-Ottoman period is exaggerated", etc. [Lederer, 1996]. The people of these countries, even the Muslims, often reject these notions, and they put up stiff resistance. They are concerned about the spread of extremist Islam, and perhaps fearful

---

[16] This ideological movement began in Cairo, in the middle of the 19th century, with men such as Muhammad 'Abduh, Jamal al-Din al-Afghani and Rashid Rida. Its objective was to reconcile Islam and modernity through a return to Islam's origins and to the faithfulness of the companions of the Prophet, coupled with severe criticism of theologians and a refusal of the distinction which had been established subsequently between Sufism and *fiqh*.

[17] A reformist movement, understood to include the tradition which followed it, instituted in the Hijaz by Muhammad ibn 'Abd al-Wahhab (died 1787). It aims at a return to the principles of the Qur'an, which from its standpoint had been compromised in the medieval period, and seeks to lessen the degree of veneration given to the saints of Islam. When Ibn Saud converted to Wahhabism in 1745, the tendency "became the religious ideology of tribal unification in central Arabia" [Lapidus, 1988:673, cited by Lewis, 1997a:127].

of finding themselves divided by doctrinal schism. At the same time attempts to preserve their traditional culture, language, and history are encouraged. At bottom, these movements are not considered there as to be feared, but the general impression is that they should not be ignored [RO and BG files].

Before beginning the review of the most important movements in Western Europe, we should observe that there are very few of Shiite origin,[18] even if there does seem to be a noticeable number of conversions to this ideological tendency. The converts are often former Sunni Muslims, and the phenomenon is often related to a political position which seeks to oppose Western imperialist models such as that of the United states. However at present few studies of the phenomenon exist, and we note only a few minority Shiite tendencies in Europe, essentially movements with a rather mystical character.

We note first in order of importance the Alawi, of Turkish or Kurdish origin, who are said (by the Federation of Alawi Communities in Europe) to have 700,000 members in Europe [Almanya Alevi Birlikleri Federasyonu, 2000]. This number may be exaggerated. The movement is mainly found in Germany, the Netherlands, and Belgium. The Alawis are connected to the Bektashi movement begun in Anatolia between the 13th and 16th centuries,[19] whose members are found

---

[18] Literally, Shi'at Ali, the partisans of 'Ali (fourth Caliph, cousin and son-in-law of the Prophet). These split from the Sunnis in 661, along with the Kharijites. There are several tendencies within Shi'ism: imamites, Ismailis, the Druzes, Zaydites, Alawis, etc., but the Shiites (who await the return of the twelve imam, who disappeared in 874) are the dominant one. This tendency exists in Iran, Iraq, Lebanon, Pakistan, Afghanistan, India, Turkey, and in the former Soviet Union, etc. One of Shi'ism's distinctive characteristics has to do with the *walâya* (power to guide and to initiate persons into the faith) which the Prophet had given to all imams. In this way "imams continue the tradition of prophecy" [Zarcone, 1996:319]. The Sunnis, on the other hand, hold that prophecy ended with Muhammad himself. They claim the mantle of Islamic orthodoxy, and insist on consensus (*ijmâ'*) within the community. More than 85% of Muslims worldwide belong to this tendency, though they are dividied into four juridical schools: Malikis, Shafiis, Hanafis, and Hanbalis.

[19] Bektashism is a "pantheist and syncretic doctrine based on a heterodox Turkmen version of the faith, inspired by Iranian and Indian mystics, and by the 'doctrine of blame'; it took on a Shiite and Sufist tint during the 16th century. Its principal beliefs concern the central place given to 'Ali, manifestation of God on earth, who represents the esoteric aspect of the divine while Muhammad represents the exoteric aspect [. . .]. Allah, Muhammad, and 'Ali form a sort of trinity which manifests a single truth. The members of this order also venerate the twelve imams (like the twelve imam Shiites) among others. [. . .] In moral terms, the Bektashis follow this precept: 'be the master of your hands, of your tongue, and of your loins,' which means do not steal, do not lie, do not speak idly, do not commit adultery" [Clayer, 1996:468 ff.].

in the countries just mentioned, in France, Sweden, Denmark, Switzerland, and (in very small numbers) in Romania and Bulgaria, and in Western Thrace among Pomak communities in the mountainous region. The question of the real identity of the Alawis is still a live problem, which concerns them and other Muslim communities as well, because it is not clear whether they constitute an ethnic group or a doctrinal tendency. Judging by the literature of their federation itself, one conflict has to do with the fact that the patron saint of the Alawis is Hâdjî Bektache, but since he is also the patron saint of Turkish nationalism, Kurds prefer to venerate the rebel poet Pîr Sultan Abdal. Then there are doctrinal dilemmas: the Alawis are inclined to revere 'Ali as the central figure in the Alawis faith, which explains their similarity to Shiite tendencies, but in a context of rivalry between Turks and Iranians, they give preference to the Sunni tendency nonetheless. Two even more important facts are their refusal to recognise the Sharia as divine law, and that they do not cling to the letter of the Qur'an: they consider the five pillars of Islam as only the outer part of divine knowledge. The Alawis do not build mosques, they do not make the pilgrimage to Mecca, and do not observe the Ramadan fast, but fast rather for 12 days during the month of Muharram. In essence they see themselves as a cultural religious group that has developed a distinct religious personality within the Islamic cultural zone. In a positive fashion, they try to draw nearer to God by rejecting violence, preaching the equality of men and women, preserving a matriarchal family structure, and carrying on the tradition of their culture through poetry and music [Almanya Alevi Birlikleri Federasyonu, 2000]. They mean to arrive at a sort of modernity, and have even attempted to set forth a scriptural theology beginning with discourses which were once common among the people, and that had up to a certain date had been part of an oral tradition [van Bruinessen, 2001a].

We come to the Ismailis, present in France, Britain, Portugal, Italy, and Switzerland. This is an originally Iranian group, Shiites who revere Ismâ'il as the seventh imam, and who attach great importance to their central religious authority, the Aga Khan. They take an esoteric stance, consider the Sharia as of only transitory value, and hold that the Qur'an takes on importance only by means of involved allegorical interpretation. They practice the *samâ'*, as do the Bektashis and the Alawis, a "tradition of spiritual attention to music" which constitute for them "a means of revelation of mystery, and of entry into higher knowledge" [During, 1996:157 ff.].

Then there is the order of the Ni'matullâhis, which constitutes the greatest Iranian Sufi order, since most of the Iranian Shiite mystical brotherhoods are connected to it. This movement combines elements of various Sufi traditions, especially those connected to the order of the Chistis, though this order is traditionally opposed to that of the Naqshbandi brotherhood (cf. infra), which instead of recognising 'Ali as one of the links of the apostolic chain (silsila) recognises Abu Bakr, the first caliph [Zarcone, 1996:312]. This order has members in Britain, France, Spain, Sweden, and the Netherlands, where it has acquired some converts [Landman, 1992a].

We also note the existence of Bhoras and Khojas, two communities which come from the Indian Ocean region, from Mauritius and Madagascar [Nielsen, 1992]. The former are seventh-imam Shiites only found in France, and the latter are twelfth-imam Shiites, a handful of which are found in Great Britain, France, and Belgium [Dassetto, 1996].

There are a number of groups on the fringes of Sunni orthodoxy who are considered deviant sects despite their ambitions for worldwide Islam. First, the Ahmadi movement. Founded in India in the 19th century by Mirza Ghulâm Ahmad (died 1908), its doctrine is strongly influenced by Sufism and a brand of Western modernism [Laoust, 1963:361]. Motivated by missionary zeal, this Muslim movement was the first to establish itself in Europe [Shadid & van Koningsveld, 1995:49; Metcalf, 1996:113]. An impressive number of Internet sites are devoted to it. It is found in Great Britain, Germany (50,000 members according to Spuler-Stegemann, 1998:56 ff.), France, the Netherlands, Sweden, Denmark, and Hungary [Dassetto, 1996; Popovic, 1997:60]. It is also present in countries such as Poland and Bulgaria, where it was the first to produce a translation of the Qur'an into Bulgarian, printed in London and made from an English version [Peev, 1997:192]. Since 1976, in the wake of doubts which its founder allowed to exist concerning his real identity, in contradiction of the dogma according to which Muhammad is the "seal of prophecy" [Kepel, 1994:38], the movement has been branded a heresy by the Pakistani government, a decision followed by other Muslim countries [Shadid & van Koningsveld, 1995:49], its disciples have been "obliged to move the centre of their activities to the

United Kingdom" [Kepel, 1994]. We place also in this category the Baha'i faith, which began in a messianic socio-religious revolt in Iran around 1850, and which now presents itself as a universal, peaceful, egalitarian religion for which differences between humans are thought of as an essential resource in the development of civilisation. Its adepts independently seek the truth, in which search they are enjoined to study only the holy writings, and to attain religious knowledge through reason alone. There are about 6 million Baha'is in the world, but few in Europe (only 5,000 in Germany [Yegane Arani, 1999]).

There are a number of aspects which, taken into account, can guide the understanding of Islamic currents in Europe. They have disparate geographical and historical origins, some quite ancient and some much more recent. Their relationship to their founding events or texts varies, according to outlooks which favour modernization, or are traditional, or which attempt a re-founding of Islam. Their programmes of religious action vary according to different visions of the world or ideological proclivities, and different practices, attitudes, or modalities of action (interventionist or isolationist). There are differences of organisational form as well, more or less institutionalised, but these also involve different conceptions of the relationship with the West [Dassetto, 1996:181].

A typology of Sunni movements can be presented, which categorises them in terms of those actions which are of significance only to Muslims, as occurring between groups of Muslims.[20] This typology pays special attention to the specificity and the importance of these movements and even their mutual relations in Europe today. Not every movement is categorised; those which are the largest in quantitative terms and those which are most important symbolically best illustrate the diversity of the phenomenon. The first category is that of associative sufism. In this category, emphasis is placed upon the Naqshbandis, the Brelwis, the Murids, the 'Alawiyyas, and the neo-Sufist groups. The second category, that of "movements of rationalization and preaching", includes descriptions of the Deobandis and Nursis movements. The third includes all the movements which claim a more specific responsibility for "preaching and missionary work": the *Jama'at al-Tabligh* (Foi et Pratique movement), the *Ahl-i-*

---

[20] This typology adds, to the three action-types established by F. Dassetto (1996), two supplemental divisions.

Hadith movement, and the Süleymancis. The fourth division includes movements which attempt to heighten awareness of certain political and religious considerations, for example the Milli Görüs organisation and the different associations which share allegiance to the ideology of the Muslim Brotherhood. The last category includes movements of a militant character which favour Islamic states and societies: Jama'at-i-Islami and other groups such as *Hizb al-Tahrir* or the Kaplan group.

Associational Sufism

Although the presence of members of certain brotherhoods is recorded as early as the 1920s, the spread of Sufism and the formation of brotherhoods in Europe have been largely the work of European converts;[21] René Guénon is one of the best known [Hamès, 1996]. Still, the arrival of the first immigrant workers caused such brotherhoods to flourish. Each one indicates a path to follow toward ecstasy and immediate contact with God, which is supposed to go together with forms of a personal inner perfection. Tracing their origins back to the Prophet (sometimes in an ad hoc manner), the brotherhoods' goal is to "preserve, transmit, and spread the mystical teachings of their founders, ways of access to God, through specific patterns of rituals, practices, and exercises, and through forms of esoteric knowledge" [Veinstein, 1996:12].

In historical terms, the definitive doctrinal insertion of Sufism into Sunnite orthodoxy was accomplished in the work of the celebrated Abu Hamid al-Ghazali[22] at the end of the 11th century. But despite this theoretical reconciliation, and "once past the period of lay and progressivist attacks in the mid-20th century, the religious, social, and political opposition to the brotherhoods comes from so called Islamist groups" [Hamès, 1996:523]. In the Maghreb, for example, where Sufism is "closely associated with the cult of saints, known under the name of maraboutism" [Andezian, 1996:389].

As we try to determine the nature of this opposition, and to verify whether the above observation really applies to the European

---

[21] The two are not necessarily coterminous since some Sufis, including those self-styled, consider themselves as standing outside any brotherhood of this kind.

[22] From that standpoint, orthodoxy accepts from Sufism that there are saints, that saintliness is an eminent perfection, reachable by privileged men, that 'revelation' is to be recognised as an intuitive mode of appreciating spiritual truths, and that saints can perform miracles through the grace of God [Gaboriau, 1996:196–7].

context, we shall only take note of the most numerically important brotherhoods, unless they are examples of a special type. We exclude brotherhoods whose membership in Europe is very small, or concerning which no studies exist: one hears tell of informal meetings in private homes of groups such as Shadhilis,[23] Darqawis,[24] Khalwatis,[25] Tijanis,[26] Qadiris,[27] Rifa'is,[28] Burhanis,[29] Chistis,[30] Mevlevis,[31] Bouchichis,[32] Isawis,[33] etc., often but not often enough. It must be said in general that there are "many more books on Sufism than on the brotherhoods, though they are the framework through which Sufism gains purchase in the real world" [Veinstein, 1996:23]. The

---

[23] This brotherhood is especially well-established in Great Britain. Other than by sobriety, total and serene acceptance of destiny and the high value placed on the relation of master to disciple, this movement "distinguishes itself by setting gnosticism (which sees God in everything) in opposition to devouts and ascetics (who give this base world too much importance by trying to renounce it); human beings must be convinced that one arrives at God only through God". In addition, the "Shadhilis act as filters for Sufi doctrine, which they present and conceal at the same time, depending on the level of the person they are speaking to", "which has permitted them to penetrate the world of 'ulamâ' as well as the widest range of social classes" [Geoffroy, 1996:509 ff.].

[24] A principal line of the Shadhilis is present in France, Belgium, Great Britain and Italy.

[25] This movement's members are found mostly in Turkish areas or among local converts. They practice solitary retreats in monkish cells, reciting a litany composed by Sâyyid Yahyâ Chirvânî, which glorifies the oneness of God, the Prophet, and his companions, while the *dhikr*, transmitted by 'Ali, is read in a loud voice. The Khalwati name has a certain prestige, partly linked to its quite undefined character which is quite typical and thus it has been used by some persons who wanted to adapt the path they had been following to a new historical and social context [Clayer, 1996:487 ff.].

[26] Derived from the Khalwatis, this movement was formed in the Maghreb in the last quarter of the 18th century. Its way is easy to follow, but its adepts are prohibited from joining any other brotherhoods. It has become one of the most important movements on the African continent while appearing as well in the Middle East, Turkey, Indonesia, and Albania [Popovic & Veinstein, 1996]. It appears in Europe in the countries of France, Italy, Belgium, and the Netherlands, sometimes in its particularist form, like the Hamalists, a branch from Mali.

[27] Present in limited numbers in Great Britain, France, and Belgium.

[28] The way of humility, contrition, and modesty, this brotherhood distinguishes itself by a very particular *dhikr* which includes physical trials and ritual mortification of the flesh [Popovic, 1996].

[29] Originally an Egyptian brotherhood, whose European site is in Munich and Hamburg, and which has some presence in Austria and Italy.

[30] Exists in Great Britain.

[31] Especially in Germany [Schlessmann, 1999].

[32] Found in Great Britain, Belgium and in France.

[33] Found in several areas, and among Moroccans of France. Berber folklore and African magic are influences on it [Geoffroy, 1996:514].

organisational forms of these groups, which normally are difficult to contact or observe, possess a "great capacity to adapt". This can be observed even before the modern forms of neo-Sufism are taken into account, such as the Sufi Movement and the Sufi Order in the West of Inayat Khan and Vilayat Khan, found in the Netherlands and in France, or the Society for Sufi Studies of Idries Shah in London [Keller, 1994], or new tendencies which are more and more congenial to New Age philosophies, to which they contribute certain doctrinal elements or variations of meditation techniques. Otherwise, in general, though "doctrinal content apparently does not play a dominant role within the brotherhoods, either with respect to their formation or their development" [Hamès, 1996:236], one may belong to more than one group, and so the various orders sometimes overlap to a considerable degree.

The Naqshbandis
Founded in Central Asia in the 14th century, this is one of the world's most important brotherhoods. It is present from Iraq to South Asia, and in between, in Iran, Afghanistan, and Turkey. One of its more activist branches, the Stamboul tendency, is directed by the former theology teacher and Sheikh Esat Coshan[34] and spreads his mystical teachings and doctrine to disciples through "his spiritual, educational, social and editorial activities" [Zarcone, 1996:374]. Even for the Turkish population of Europe, this movement's moral influence remains, and extends over other movements [Manço, 1997], such as Milli Görüs and Süleymancis [Hamès, 1996; Zarcone, 1996]. In general, it is characterised by its Sunnite orientation, emphasising the Sharia and the Sunna, and by a tradition of full political and social participation in the world [Damrel, 1999].

The Naqshbandis are found in Belgium, the Netherlands, France, Sweden, and Italy, but their influence is greatest in Germany and Great Britain. They had 55 mosques in Germany as of 1992 [Manço, 1997]: these are divided into two tendencies, the Mezilci (quite radical and anti-Christian, 750 members) and the followers of Sheikh Nazim al-Qubrusi al-Haqqani (born 1922), who shows greater openness [Spuler-Stegemann, 1997:69 ff.]. The number of his followers

---

[34] Son-in-law of the most important personality in contemporary Turkish Sufism, Mehmed Koktu.

has grown rapidly since the mid-1970s [Damrel, 1999]. This second group is the most significant in Great Britain, and the most popular, attracting young people and converts to Islam [Samad, 1998:66]. In Britain the Naqshbandis preach on mystical themes, on spiritual elevation, love, respect for the natural environment, religious tolerance, or on apocalyptic visions drawn from Sunni eschatology, which is made to apply to every daily event [Damrel, 1999]. Also in Great Britain we find the influence of Sufi Abdullah, the head of a regional Naqshbandis cult, which reveres Pîr Hazrat Shah, known under the name of 'Zindapir', the 'living Pîr' who was the most illustrious disciple of a famous saint of the Naqshbandis order who travelled from Afghanistan to Pakistan at the end of the 19th century [Werbner, 1996:167]. For the adepts, united in their loyalty to these two men, Darbar-e-Alia Ghamkol Sharif is the centre of the symbolic universe [Werbner, 1996:179].

These observations seem to confirm that the unity of the movement is largely theoretical [Werbner, 1996:179], and that it is more appropriate to describe this tendency as a "regional cult" rather than as one of a single Sufi 'order' [Richard Werbner, 1977, cited by Werbner, 1996:179], though they do use common mystical practices in order to reach oneness with God. In general, the rules of their doctrine show how to follow the way of contemplation while living in the world: human beings must "live in the world in appearance and in secret with God"; it is important to follow an interior path and to practice, as individuals, the dhikr (recollection, a form of prayer) in silence. They aim at a continual coming to consciousness of themselves, of their past and present acts, and at a "return to God" through techniques of meditative respiration [Zarcone, 1996:451 ff.]. The Naqshbandis rejects "all the external and worldly aspects of the mystical, such as dance or music, and only concentrates upon the practice of meditation" [Zarcone, 1996:378].

Turkish offshoots are quite distinctive, in that they defend conservative positions, especially related to the defence of Sunnite orthodoxy, and demonstrate a desire to oppose to Shi'ism; they are engaged in a struggle against Kemalism, especially its secularisation movement, and they support centrist political parties and Islamic parties.

Though they are considered a rather elitist movement, they appear to support religious education for all persons, especially in the Netherlands [Landman, 1992a:30]. But the ethics propounded in the discourses of the Naqshbandis (at least in this Turkish form) encounters at last the spirit of capitalism: the resultant morality sees religion triumphing through economic and social success [Manço, 2000; Zarcone, 1996:375].

The Brelwis—Ahl-i-sunnat wa jama'at
The founder of this popular pietist movement is Ahmad Raza Khan (died 1921), an Indian thinker in the neo-Sufi tradition, and member of the Qadiris brotherhood. He combined Hanafi theological and juridical thought with gnostic mysticism [Hamès, 1996:445] in order to counteract literal or modernist tendencies such as those represented by the *Ahl-i-Hadith* or the Deobandis, or even the Jama'at-i-Islami, all of whom Khan characterises as Wahhabis [Lewis P., 1994].

This movement remains tightly bound to its country of origin and is characterised by an intense devotion to the Prophet, to whom members attribute powers such as knowledge of the invisible, omnipresence and omniscience, and whose birthday is the most important holy day on their Islamic calendar. Another important aspect of their organisation is their penchant for grouping themselves around a spiritual leader (pîr, in Urdu), who is credited with the power to intercede with God on our behalf [Nielsen, 1992; Lewis P., 1994]. Loyalty to a pîr may be a real personal relationship of master to disciple [Landman, 1992:222], and it may signify something which unites several groups in one country, even worldwide. But the various networks jockey with each other for influence at times, which brings them into conflict [Landman, 1992a:36].

The Brelwi movement is most important in Great Britain, where it is, with the Deobandis, one of the largest Muslim movements [Metcalf, 1982; Lewis P., 1994]. It has been found to be 'consistently present' in the Netherlands [Landman, 1992:212 ff.], where the Muslim Hindustanis of Surinam operate about 30 mosques [NL File]. Sheikh Noorani, Abd al Wahhab Siddiqui, who lives in England, and Pîr Maroof Hussain Shah are the most influential Brelwis. Two mosques at The Hague are dedicated to the last named [Shadid & van Koningsveld, 1995:47 ff.]. He enjoys privileged status in Bradford, but keeps in touch with several Pakistani communities in Germany, Belgium, and France.

The Murids

This brotherhood sprang from the Senegalese branch of the Qâdiriyya, and has ties to the Tijanis. It reveres a founding saint, the Sheikh Amadu Bamba (died 1927) [Schmidt di Friedberg, 1994]. In history it appears as a 'wandering of Islam', and represented a peaceful resistance to colonial domination [Diop, 1985]. But it came to represent the economic power of Senegal, which had increased because of an important peanut crop; in this role the brotherhood acquired political power and a position in the government near the end of the 1920s. But the price of peanuts went down and that plus drought and loss of the soil's fertility caused many Murids to emigrate. At present they constitute a sort of commercial diaspora, whose networks extend from Dakar to Western Europe, to Jeddah and Hong Kong [Ebin, 1996:92].

Today, despite their being scattered across such distances, cooperation among members has been maintained, among travelling merchants as most of them are, among those who are students in European universities and other schools, and among the participants in a network for international commerce in electronic products [Ebin, 1996:96]. This solidarity, it should be observed, is in accordance with the doctrine established by the founder, which is based on a compact of allegiance between master and disciple (the *Bay'a*), on the will to seek God (the *irâda*), and above all on the importance of work (the *khidma*). This work has three aspects: the love and obedience owed by human beings to God, unceasing introspection and self-criticism on the part of the individual, and the importance of one's community [Diop, 1985:198]. Members help each other, and also meet together in small groups to read the Qur'an, to sing poems written in Arabic by Amadu Bamba, and to share a meal [Cruise O'Brien, 1971, cited by Ebin, 1996]. Through a sheikh to whom they pay a part of their incomes, they maintain a link with the sacred city of Touba where the Sheikh Amadu Bamba is buried.

The Murids are found in France (mostly in Marseilles, Paris, and Lyon) [Ebin, 1996:100], in Italy [Schmidt di Friedberg, 1994], in Spain and in Belgium. Since 1983, there has existed a *Mouvement Islamique des Murides en Europe*, or MIME [Hamès, 1996:446], which was the successor to an organisation started in 1977. It organises cultural events, and establishes contacts with a variety of Islamic associations, especially the 'Alawiyya [Diop, 1985:203]. At that same time another Murids association was established, the *Association*

Internationale d'Aide et de Diffusion du Muridisme (AIADM), which emphasises the international character of the community, not strictly limited to Senegalese people [Diop, 1985:203].

The ʿAlawiyyas

The Sheikh Ahmad al-ʿAlawi (died 1934) is the founder of this branch
of the Shadhili-Darqawi located in Mostaganem, Algeria. In 1949,
Sheikh al-ʿAlawi's successor, the Sheikh Adda Bentûnis, moved the
association to Paris, giving it the name "*Les Amis de l'Islam*". Members
include immigrants from the Maghreb and converts. The group is
"still active today in the form of a *zawia*, plus a publishing house
for the works of the founder", and the *dhikr*, now led by the grand-
son of Adda Bentûnis, takes place on Sunday, a sober gathering of
men and women [Hamès, 1996:444].

The movement extends to Germany, Belgium, Switzerland, the
Netherlands, Italy, and Great Britain. While the worldwide total of
the faithful is supposed to reach 120,000, its geographical breadth
belies the quite limited number of its adherents in Europe. However,
over the long term, in company with the development of other new
forms of spirituality, this "intimate form of spirituality" [Dassetto,
1996:194] could attract a fair number of people. In fact, beginning
with a modern language and a re-individualisation of Islamic mysticism which is expressed more through personal thought and the
intellectual relationship of master and disciple than through life in
a community or the emotion of collective rituals [Hamès, 1996:443],
this brotherhood emphasises religious experience within an Islam that
is tolerant, moderate, and open to dialogue with other religions. In
relation to daily or public life, it is maintained as an individual ethics,
and does not try to transform itself into a collective ethics [Dassetto,
1996:196]. The brotherhood hopes thus to show the modernity of
Islam, and attempts to demonstrate what Islam has to offer the
West.[35] Some associations have already taken the name '*Terres d'Europe*'
in order to "accentuate the Muslim dimension of European society,
and to promote Muslim integration according to the reality of republican government and concepts such as citizenship".[36]

---

[35] Interview with Mrs B. Fekkar-Lambiotte, president of the association in France
since 1996, in Paris, March 2000.
[36] Idem.

Movements of rationalization and preaching

Within this second category we find movements which, while they maintain to some extent their symbolic positions and their ties to certain brotherhoods, are better characterised by their actions which seek to provide information to Muslims, or to present to them the message of the Qur'an in a fairly methodical manner. These explanations allow them to make Islam easier to learn about, and easier to spread. Two such movements are the Deobandis and the Nursis.

The Deobandi movement

The founders of this movement, Muhammad Qasim Nanautawi and Rashid Ahmad Gangohi, were both pious Sufi reformers and religious scholars, preaching strict Sunni orthodoxy. They were members of several brotherhoods such as the Chistis, the Suhrawardis and the Naqshbandis, whose method of silent meditation is highly recommended to all their students [Nielsen, 1992:131]. However, they do not claim any power of intercession, seeking rather to function as examples for their students. They reject local practices such as the cult of saints (which is important for the Brelwis), in favour of universal beliefs and acts of worship.

With the creation of their Dar al-'Ulum seminary at Deoband near Delhi in 1867, the Deobandi 'ulamâ' had a means of affirming Islamic identity in the face of British colonial power, by providing a system of religious education which updated the traditional model of studies centred on the Qur'an and the Sunna [Lewis P., 1994]. Within the Hanafi tradition, they attempted to codify religious law, handing down thousands of juridical opinions concerning rules of conduct. These fatwas acquired a certain legitimacy, but the realisation of Islamic unity the 'ulamâ' sought was hindered by their own elitist nature.

This movement is one of the two most important in Great Britain. It maintains close ties to South Asia, and forms a network of personal relationships among imams and other religious officials, especially in connection with the seminaries at Bury and Dewsbury. These institutions receive students from 'popular' recruitment activities carried on by the informal networks of the *Jama'at al-Tabligh* [Nielsen, 1992:45], and represent important meeting places at the national and international level. At the annual Christmas meetings, between 8,000 and 15,000 members have gathered at Dewsbury, coming from every part of Europe [Faust, 2000:142].

The Nursis or Jama'at al-Nur movement
This 'Movement of Light' owes its existence to Saïd Nursi, a Kurd who died in 1960, and who was linked to the Naqshbandis-Qadiris, though he defined his organisation as a school rather than a brotherhood [Schiffauer, 1997:163]. He offered a neo-mystical approach based on personal piety, and on reflective and intellectual activity, beginning with his commentaries on the Qur'an, 130 essays gathered into a work entitled *Risale-i-Nur Kulliyati*. Considered by his disciples as a gift from God, this quasi-sacred text does not exemplify the personality of the leader as often happens among the brotherhoods, but the nature of the movement itself [Spuler, 1981, cited by Landman, 1992:135].

Some of its fairly conservative themes emphasise the family and traditional roles, while others explore the "harmony which exists between the faith in the Creator and the results of research in modern natural science" [Landman, 1992:135]. Thus the movement is able to join together Islam, science and religion, belief and freedom, tradition and modernity [Yavuv, 2000]. But divisions arose within this 'moderate' community [Manço, 1997], over the issue of whether support for Turkish conservative parties was in line with the doctrine or not. These resulted in a split between the Aczmendi group, who provided such support, and the Fethullahci group, who refused to do so. Since 1983, other, ethnic-based divisions have appeared, between Turks and Kurds [Yavuv, 2000]. As for the emphasis placed on religious instruction considered as a missionary activity, it is represented by many publications and by the establishment of madrasas, including a theological institute in Berkeley, California. Dialogue with non-Muslims is not neglected there [Shadid & van Koningsveld, 1995].

The movement's influence is weaker in Europe than in Turkey, and it appears relatively weak in comparison with other Turkish tendencies, possibly because of its elitist nature [Manço, 1997]. Nevertheless, in Germany in 1992 it controlled about 30 associations or bookstores serving around 800 adepts and close to 5,000 sympathizers [Manço, 1997; Shadid & van Koningsveld, 1995:48]. The movement is also present in Bulgaria, in the Netherlands where it operates two madrasas, in Belgium where there are two mosques dedicated to it, and in Switzerland [Manço, 1997].

Preaching and missionary work

This third category presents movements whose main goal is the revitalisation and propagation of a religious message. While maintaining a defensive or mistrustful attitude toward Western influences, these numerous movements aim at ritual and ethical regulation of conduct. They are proselytisers, and reach out to those who have fallen away from Islam among others. The three focused on here are the *Jama'at al-Tabligh*, the *Ahl-i-Hadith* movement, and the Süleymanci movement, though there are others with aspirations to influence in Europe, which may not possess organised structures. One example is the *Da'watul-Islam*, created in 1981 in Pakistan within the Brelwi tendency, whose members wear white clothing and green turbans. Wishing to promote the unity of Muslims, this movement's motto is "love for the Prophet and for the first community of Muslims of Medina", while its "main characteristic is to teach what is right and virtuous, and to set forth what is prohibited" [Ahmad, 1999:16]. The movement called the *Idarah-l Minhaj ul-Qur'an* (Institution for the Way of the Qur'an) is found in Denmark [DK File], and the *Tabligh ad-dawa* (Mission and Call) presents itself as one of Islamic renewal whose religious initiations are simple and demanding, emphasising the profession of faith and the interior path without abandoning ostentatious religious practices [Sindonino, 1998:71].

Jama'at al-Tabligh, Faith and Practice

This is a popular movement for the propagation of Islam, founded in India by Mawlânâ Muhammad Ilyas (died 1944). Though initiated into one of the branches of the Chisti brotherhood, he separated himself from it, though he retained certain practices such as the *dhikr* [Landman, 1992:33]. This movement's main goal is a reawakening of the religious life among Muslim communities, following the example of the Prophet at the beginning of Islam, and with reference to the Qur'an and the hadiths. Based on action and practice above all, it has passed gradually from a "general idea of religious duties [...] to that of a spiritual renewal of Islamic religious awareness" [Masud, 2000:79–80], which has certain political implications, even if only in the consciousness of its members of having a separate religious identity. The movement's possible political aims have drawn much attention from scholars, who hypothesise that even if "politics has always been kept in the background", it still figures in their long-range plans. It has been thought that the inter-nationalist character of the movement aims at Muslim solidarity, and at the creation of institutions "beyond (political) boundaries while ignoring nation-states", which "in time could exert a more lasting political influence" [Gaboriau, 1999].

In the meantime, the fundamental aims are to invite people to submit to God, to urge them to pray, to promote knowledge of the Qur'an and the hadiths, and to promote the *dhikr* (remembrance, hearing the call), the two latter priorities "symbolizing the move-ment's efforts to reduce the gap between 'ulamâ' and Sufis". Other priorities are Muslim solidarity, the sincerity of intentions, and abstain-ing from futile things [Masud, 2000:21 ff.]. As concerns methods, these put emphasis on ease of entry (novices are easily accepted), active participation, and a change in lifestyle, for the *da'wa* is not an affair of specialists but much rather the duty of every Muslim. Members are supposed to withdraw from their close environment on a regular basis, taking up preaching for at least three days a month, for a total of 40 days a year, and to do this once during their lives for four months straight [Tozy, 2000:167]. A self-financed sojourn among *Jama'at al-Tabligh* groups, in which "a mingling of social classes is mandatory" while "ideological and political contro-versy is prohibited" [Gaboriau, 1999], is considered the most effective means of bringing about personal life changes. Some adepts seem to take this method to be the message itself [Masud, 2000:30]. But in fact the message goes further, attaining a rather Puritanistic vision of Islam from the standpoint of certain practices which do not favour a particular form of religiosity [Masud, 2000:30-31], but whose obser-vance guarantees one's reception in Paradise.

The movement focuses on marginalised persons who wish to regain respectability (unemployed, former hooligans, drug users, etc.), and emphasises piety, humility, and simplicity. Considered by some as 'anti-intellectual' [Mumtaz Ahmad cited by Masud, 2000:102], it has an aversion to modernity and places emphasis on the transitory nature of life here below. It denounces corruption, and turns away from the power and pomp of the world, as being false and grotesque [Talib, 2000:71]. These positions lead this movement to "isolate its adepts in a cultural sense from any impious environment" [Kepel, 1994:139], and thus it takes no part in struggles over the right to represent the community vis-à-vis the state.

Its internationalism is a means of seeking legitimacy, for the further

the Jama'at extends worldwide, the more its ideology will be recognised in universal terms [Masud, 2000]. And this expansion is taking place: preaching began in 1933 in India [Masud, 2000:10], and
gradually gained the support of Deobandi 'ulamâ'. Then it reached
out toward Arab countries in 1946, beginning with pilgrimages to
Mecca and with teams which were sent to continental Europe
[Gaboriau, 2000:127]. Only in 1962, however, was the movement
permanently set up in Britain, and in Paris in 1972. Sometimes considered the most important Islamic group in the world [Kepel, 1987;
Sikand, 1999], especially because of several million members in South
Asia, the movement appears to be one of the most cosmopolitan in
its recruitment, since its activities extend to 90 countries [Masud,
2000:17 ff.], or 165 countries according to other sources [Farruqi,
1992 cited by Sikand, 1999].

Over and above this major expansion, the movement still has a
relatively informal structure. After a succession of three individual
leaders, the community is now led by an elected council (Shura),
while personal relationships, sometimes temporary, are most important, some having to do with shared regional origins or itineraries.
The movement is sometimes able to make use of the facilities of
various existing mosques, though the affiliation of these latter with
the movement may turn out to be quite temporary, based on sympathy
more than shared convictions—unless registration of effective participation of such movements in mosque administration is required as in
Belgium and France [Masud, 2000:28]. But the movement does exercise a high degree of control over those who become members, and
its internal organisation has remained secret [Gaboriau, 1999].

Although this movement claims to be situated at the heart of
Islamic orthodoxy [Dassetto, 1988, 2000b], movements of renewal
imply new ideologies which come to be challenged and debated
[Masud, 2000:79–80]. The *Jama'at al-Tabligh* thus is criticised, especially by the Jama'at-i-Islami, which faults its apolitical stance—
though such re-Islamisation would benefit Jama'at-i-Islami itself in
the quest for potential members. Certain Brelwi 'ulamâ' accuse the
Jama'at al-Tabligh of ties to Wahhabism. *Ahl-i-Hadith* attacks it as an
adherent of the Hanafi school, and condemns its indifference to the
jihad, which it interprets only in accordance with the expression
"nafar fi sabîl Allâh" (go out and preach on the road toward God).
Some Deobandi 'ulamâ' have expressed reservations about the calls
addressed to all Muslims to take part in preaching missions, having

observed a number of confusing public discourses [Masud, 2000:91 ff.]. The public discourses are in fact normally reserved for a certain category of persons, often distinguished by their education, some form of saintliness, or by belonging to prestigious families [Metcalf, 2000:46]. The connections between the Deobandis and the Tablighi are nonetheless facilitated by their co-existence in the diaspora, especially in Great Britain [Faust, 2000:143].

The *Jama'at al-Tabligh* is quite popular in Great Britain among Indo-Pakistani people, while in other countries such as France, Belgium, Spain, Italy, the Netherlands, Sweden, and Denmark, their support is drawn from the Maghreb population [Aguer, 1991; Allievi, 1996c; Dassetto, 1988; Landman, 1992; DK File]. Turkish people have not flocked to the movement, not even in Germany where it has a network in twenty cities. This is perhaps explained by the fact that the international aspect of this movement is based essentially upon national, regional, and ethnic group activities [Faust, 2000], as illustrated by the high number of Gujaratis within it [Lewis P., 1994; van der Veer, 1994 cited by Metcalf, 1996:112], which is in turn related to their shared mercantile activities.

Ahl-i-Hadith

The name of this movement, 'People of the Tradition of the Prophet', places at its centre the importance of hadiths in the interpretation of the Qur'an and the Sunna. Its existence dates back to the mid-19th century, part of the heritage of the reformist Indian Shah Waliullah (died 1762). In a drive to return to the sources of Islam, this tendency rejects not only the authority of various Sufi orders, but also that of many classical juridical schools and their interpretations [Ahmed, 1967, cited by Lewis P., 1994:219]. It does remain close to the Salafi tendency, which causes it be considered as Wahhabi, though its relations with Saudi Arabia are quite obscure [Gaboriau, 1996:200]. This movement attaches primary importance to the person of the Prophet, and its members even claim to maintain a direct link with him, which distinguishes them from the Deobandis. They also condemn the popular practices of the Brelwis involving the veneration of saints [Nielsen, 1992:131].

In Great Britain this movement controls about twenty mosques, plus a centre in Birmingham. It distributes books, tapes and videos which promote separatism with regard to non-Muslim society, and the ideas of Ahmad Deedat, a Gujarati preacher who lives in South

Africa [Nielsen, 1992:46]. The movement pays for the annual preaching tours of this anti-Christian polemicist, who says that any Muslim living outside the Muslim world must preach [Lewis P., 1994]. While the movement's tapes have certainly been circulated throughout Europe, particularly in Belgium and France, it remains fairly marginal across both the European continent and the Indian sub-continent.

Süleymancis or Süleymanli

This movement was founded by a Bulgarian-Romanian sheikh, Süleyman Hilmi Tunahan, who died in Istanbul in 1959, a member of the Naqshbandis [Algar, 1985], though this fact is not emphasized—rather the reverse [Landman, 1992a]. The group was heavily repressed after the 1971 coup d'état in Turkey, because of their opposition to the government and their ties to the Kurdish people, and some of its leaders have sought refuge in Europe.

The group's founder was known for his intense preaching style [Landman, 1992a], but this extremely hierarchised group now keeps a low profile and produces few documents [Manço, 1997:114]. This discreet stance is probably linked to their rejection of the Kemalist approach to Islam, and to their close ties with the right wing, and even the extremist right wing of Turkish politics [Landman 1992a; Manço, 1997]. They reject not only the authority of the Turkish Directorate of Religious Affairs, but also attendance at 'official mosques'. They find themselves in competition with the Milli Görüs in several respects. On one hand, the two share a militant view of history, one which is bent on establishing an Islamic state though not by radical means [Karakasoglu & Nonneman, 1996:258]. And they both appear to favour greater openness toward dialogue with the community at large, including dialogue with other religious groups [Svanberg, 1995; Landman, 1992a]. The movement has had contacts with certain churches in Germany [Manço, 1997]. It does retain a millenarian character [Manço, 1997], and the great stress laid upon personal piety [Shadid & van Koningsveld, 1995:47] has caused it to be called 'mystical' by the Milli Görüs [Amiraux, 1999:27].

Over and above its social and spiritual function, this movement can be considered as 'ideologically based' in its aim of "providing religious education for the masses" [Landman, 1992a]. It intends to bring about social change by following a line of 'pragmatic politics' [Schiffauer, 1997:169], directed toward its base of support. The movement establishes mosques and concentrates on educational activities, boarding schools, classes in Qur'anic studies and publishing companies. It also distributes videos [Landman, 1992a:29 ff.] and sponsors scholarships for students, including university students [Dassetto, 1996].

It is found across Europe, mainly in areas with high Turkish populations. In Germany, in 1992, it was estimated to have 20,000 members spread over 270 cultural centres, but operated only 20 of these in the Netherlands, 13 in Belgium, and 11 in Sweden, where the movement enjoys exceptional public recognition, equal to that of the Diyanet; this is the only case in which the Süleymancis are better established than the Milli Görüs [Manço, 1997]. It has a token presence in Switzerland, France, Austria, Norway, Bulgaria [BG File] and Denmark [Gür, 1993 cited by Svanberg, 1995; Manço, 1997]. Its national associations form a European federation, the *Avrupa Islam Kültür Merkezleri Birligi* (Union of Islamic Cultural Centres in Europe), located in Köln [Svanberg, 1995; Shadid & van Koningsveld, 1995:47; Landman, 1992a].

Movements for raising political and religious awareness

Because these are the most active movements within contemporary Islam, they are often called 'Islamist' movements, in view of their "desire to resolve through religion all social and political problems, and at the same time to restore the unity of dogma" [M. Rodinson cited by Etienne, 1987:168]. Since they believe they possess a complete vision of the world, they go beyond preaching and an interest in right conduct, in the formal sense. They go on to take positions concerning the values of the West and base their political aspirations on the original Islamic fact, as source of inspiration, or as a goal to be attained. For the time being, European Islamism does not look exclusively toward Muslim countries any longer. As it has put down roots in Europe, it has gained autonomy and has modified the forms of its action. At present it furnishes points of reference for Muslim populations in Europe, for whom the representatives of European Islam play a dominant if informal role in the circulation of ideas. Favouring an ethics of responsibility, these movements are willing to take up the question of minority status and its specific aspects. The two most important currents (the Milli Görüs and the Muslim Brotherhood) are commented on here, though similar minor groups exist elsewhere in Europe, such as the *Minhadj ul-Qur'an*, who appear in a significant position in Denmark.

Avrupa Milli Görüs Teskilâtleri (AMGT)—Union of the New Vision in Europe

The activities of this organisation are connected to the Turkish National Islamic party *Refah Partisi*, although it has an autonomous existence. Its implantation in Europe followed the 1971 military coup in Turkey which outlawed such parties, and forced the group's leader, Necmettin Erbakan, into temporary exile in Switzerland, then Germany, where he laid the foundations for the organisation [Dassetto, 1996; Manço, 1997]. The first associations appeared in 1973 in Berlin and in about 1978 in the region around Paris, but only in 1981 did it have a public presence in West Germany, and then in 1983 in France. Once the headquarters was located in Köln, expansion began: the first Milli Görüs mosques appeared in Belgium, and in the Netherlands two years later. In 1985, the formation of a German federation and a multi-national one was well underway, and the organisation as a whole has seen "rapid and sustained growth in the number of associations in its federation and the number of their affiliates" [Manço, 1997].

At present the movement is represented in 11 countries and 30 regions [Köln meeting, June 3, 2000], the regions being drawn on the basis of membership without regard to borders between countries. It is a large movement, and one deeply rooted in Western Europe. The number of its members is highest in Germany, most living in Berlin, North Rhineland, Westphalia and Hesse, then Austria, France, the Netherlands, Belgium, Switzerland, Denmark, Sweden, the United Kingdom, Italy, and Finland. The organisation appears to be "overrepresented in Austria but underrepresented in France and in the Netherlands" [Manço, 1997]. In all, the organisation maintains a relationship with 791 mosques, of which 520 were founded by the Milli Görüs, and 71 local associations which had formed independently but decided to join the federation [Manço, 1997; Nielsen, 1992; Allievi & Dassetto, 1993; Shadid & van Koningsveld, 1995].

A total of 112,323 has been put forward for the number of this group's members, including young people, women, students, and adult males, but the total number of people contacted by them has been put as high as 300,000. Such a figure would represent 10% of the Turkish immigrant population in Europe [Milliyet, August 2, 1996, Istanbul, cited by Manço, 1997], and while it is probably "a little overstated", "it is certainly not a fantasy" [Manço, 1997].[37]

---

[37] Important differences of size must be noted. It is thought that 480 out of 791

At the organisational level, a 'double structure' is noted [Pedersen, 1999:56–107]. On one side there is an international network, which is "relatively centralized" [Dassetto, 1996:215] under direction from Köln. This in turn is made up of a "modern technocratic counter-elite" [Dassetto, 1996:215] rather than of theologians, and operates using membership fees paid directly, as well as with financial contributions from local chapters estimated at 13 million DM per year [Manço, 1997]. Although "the decision-making process is fairly opaque", with 66 employees and two solidly controlled regional executive councils, one for the North of Europe and one for the South, administering and coordinating the activities of regional and local associations, the central network dominates the regional councils. It plays a role in the choice of their leaders [Manço, 1997] and sets the tone through an infrastructure which carries out in broad fashion its actions and recommendations. The central network fosters a common vision "which guarantees continuity of the ideological foundation of the movement", and acts more to shape the organisation than "to dictate policies, which allows sharing of experiences at the European level" [Pedersen, 1999:57 ff.]. Still, it should not be forgotten that "the cadres of the organisation make use of connections and opportunities in the community already existing to advance their strategy of expansion, which is to construct a working pressure group or Turkish-Islamic lobby in Europe" [Manço, 1997]. The other half of the double structure involves local associations, in which immigrants from the first generation predominate [Manço, 1997]. Operating on membership fees and donated services, these are locally rooted and provide, in a relatively autonomous manner, various activities or services. These are mostly religious, because "any local association affiliated with the Milli Görüs is first of all a mosque" [Manço, 1997]. Qur'anic classes, moral counselling, organisation of pilgrimage trips, marriages, confessional meetings, etc. are typical examples. In the area of social or cultural activities: juridical counselling, social assistance, translation services, educational and/or occupational training,

---

associations are found in Germany [Manço, 1997]; however, some authors view AMGT as the second largest group in Germany, but speak only of 262 member-associations [Karagasogly & Nonneman, 1996:257]! As for German membership, the figure of "30,000 militants" has been offered [Bilici, 1997:40–41], while others suggest that there are 13,600 members, the total for the Süleymancis, being only 12,000 [Karagasogly & Nonneman, 1996:259]. These estimates are difficult to pin down, and the figures put out by the Milli Görüs themselves have been accepted.

conferences, theatre or folklore workshops, and sports clubs, etc., are variously offered. There are profitable activities as well, but at present these are carried on only in Germany (see the chapter on Muslim economics) [Manço, 1997].

Historically opposed to the secular reforms of Mustafa Kemal, the movement has been trying to create a new Turko-Islamic synthesis since the mid-1980s, although nationalism and Islamism had tended to oppose each other. But despite modernist speeches, their ideology is rather a nationalist and traditionalist orthodox Islamist one; they "subordinate national identity to religious identity" [Landman, 1997a:219] and the organisation also promotes Turkish culture as remembered from its rural Anatolian origins, and harks back to an idealised Ottoman dynasty [Manço, 1997]. Turkish immigrants who do not support such a conception are considered as non-Islamic and thus "not authentically Turkish" [Timmerman, 1999:185].

In general, this group tries to keep harmony between its sociopolitical activism and its modernist aspirations, and the sociological composition of its base of membership. This effort coincides with the institution of an Islamic order within families, and as concerns personal conduct [Dassetto, 1996:214], all based on the notion that "adherence to Islamic principles is in perfect agreement with modern conditions" [Pedersen, 1999:105], and even in agreement, at the popular level, with science viewed as a "proof of the divine Creation and the revealed nature of the Qur'an". In other statements science appears as a favourite subject of 'allegorical interpretations' which evoke the great expansion of Islam during the period of the first Caliphs, or the superhuman powers of the Prophet who spoke in the cradle, cast no shadow under the sun, and who was circumcised by the angels [Dassetto, 1996:214].

On this basis, and in the face of a degree of social marginalisation, the organisation is able "to satisfy the demands for identity, self-esteem, and legitimacy of several categories of immigrants for whom belonging to Islam is primary" [Manço, 1997]. This attraction is reinforced by a certain critique of the West which is based on arguments concerning the 'feminine condition' [Dassetto, 1996:214] or on anti-Semitism, a political position held by some members of the movement [Pedersen, 1999:93].

Accepting the definitive settlement of Turkish immigrants in Europe, the Turkish-Islamic movement in exile is attempting to transform itself "to become a Turkish-European Islamic movement whose programme concerns the creation of an Islamic identity among Turkish minority immigrants in Europe" [Pedersen, 1999:105]. Like the Muslim Brotherhood movement, with which it sometimes collaborates [Manço, 1997], it is youth-oriented, with a view toward Islamisation of the young, in order to make them the primary vectors of the spread of Islam in Europe. Its members tend to define themselves as "Muslims of Turkish origin rather than as Turks" [Landman, 1997a:219], and many contacts with Muslims of other nationalities, especially from the Maghreb and the Balkans, have been established. But that is as far as things go for the moment, because the civic recommendations[38] which the leadership continue to issue, if only as a feature of the public image of the organisation, are not really followed by the membership [Manço, 1997]. A "large gap separates the vision of a future harmonious Islamic society from the actual initiatives of the movement, and for the members it is the relationship between the individual and God, between the here and now and the beyond, which fills that gap" [Pedersen, 1999:187].

The Muslim Brotherhood—al-Ikhwan al-Muslimun
Created in 1928 in Egypt by Hasan al-Banna, this movement began as an educational and religious charitable association, before entering political activities in 1938 because of the increasing influence of Western culture and secularism. In 1940, it began to develop as a secret military organisation and became financially independent, setting up its own businesses, industries, schools and hospitals. After having infiltrated the labour unions and the armed forces, it came into direct opposition to the Egyptian government, and Hasan al-Banna was murdered in 1949 [Mitchell, 1969].

Originally inspired by Sufism and its ideals, the movement has been strongly influenced by the thought of the Salafis, in particular that of Ibn Taymiyya, whose ideas were discussed around the famous reformist Rashid Rida [Carré & Michaud, 1983]. Its essential message is that Islam has a vocation to organise all aspects of human life. According to Hasan al-Banna: "Islam is dogma and worship,

---

[38] Examples: to devote oneself to the regular study of religion, to acquire double nationality, to begin higher education and to involve oneself in business, to stand with existing associations in the host country for the defense of immigrants and in the struggle against racism, to hold a dialogue with members of other religions, and to cooperate with the public authorities of the host country [Manço, 1997].

fatherland and nationality, religion and state, spirituality and action, Kuran and sword". Under the leadership of Sayyid Qutb (died 1966), the movement's early doctrine took on a more radical political colouration. It stood opposed not only to the dominant ideologies of the Arab world, including modernism and Westernisation, but embarked upon an ideological project of exegesis in which the Qur'anic word is held up in opposition to injustice. In Egypt, all political parties were dissolved in 1952, but the movement survives as an association. As the "unavoidable base of Islamist ideology" [Grignard, 1998], it has expanded very quickly throughout the Arab and Muslim world through associations connected with political parties, sometimes through parliamentary representation as in Egypt and Jordan, through political and armed groups as in Algeria, and even as a party in power, as in Sudan. It is accordingly divided into various currents and subtendencies. Nowadays, even if the Muslim Brotherhood officially rejects violence [Carré & Michaud, 1983; Etienne, 1987:210], it remains true that a fringe of the original group has created a radical ideology, which gave birth to the first armed Islamist movements in the world.

In Europe, some people linked to the Brotherhood came first independently as students or as asylum seekers. They rapidly expanded into Switzerland, France, Germany, the Netherlands, Belgium, Great Britain, Italy, and Spain (where they translate and publish many texts), and even into Poland. The first institution that was established by some of them was the *Centre Islamique de Genève* (CIG) in 1961, which enjoyed a certain representative status within the Muslim world [Dassetto, 1996:224]. Its objective was to "give Muslims living in Europe the opportunity to participate in a structure which allows them to preserve their identity" [Sindonino, 1998:372]. But only in the 1980s was there a "real beginning of political Islam in the religious life of immigrants" [Grignard, 1997:169]; some local organisations were created, that were closed to the main ideas defended by the Brotherhood even if many of them did not have any organisational link as such to the Egyptian matrix.

Nowadays, the Muslim Brotherhood is literally a 'movement', an ideological reference point, and not so much an organisational structure. Still, in schematic terms, it is traditionally seen as divided into several national tendencies such as the Egyptian or the Syrian branches. But this division between the two tendencies of the Brotherhood is not that well-marked, especially for the base of membership, and keeps on disappearing with the growing influence of local European organisations. This has to do with the change over time of the areas of action involved. The Muslim Brotherhood is involved in activities of education and preaching which are "focused on political affairs", but it does not really consider itself a missionary movement, rather one which aims at changing the way Muslims think [Masud, 2000:lix]. Today, in conferences and debates intended to stimulate thought, they speak of a "re-moralization of society" though individual effort, and they encourage "involvement in the society of the host country while preserving religious identity" [Grignard, 1997:170].[39]

The main impact of the Muslim Brotherhood is thus located in "the diffusion of a modernist discourse" which "explores the modalities of Muslim presence in European public space". The Brotherhood represents a source of spiritual and ideological inspiration from which networks for action spring up, and upon which numerous associative forms converge [Dassetto, 1996:223 ff.], such as youth and student movements. Within this framework, it is not so much their "holistic and political conceptions" [Babès, 1997] but rather their "intellectual vision of the world and their unitary, abstract and global concepts of Islam" which makes them attractive for Muslims who are already well integrated [Grignard, 1997:170].

This movement is also characterised by its propensity to inspire and/or act as a melting pot for the training of European Islamic leaders. Connections have been established already with the Milli Görüs and the *Jama'at-i-Islami*, mostly through the Islamic Foundation of Leicester, which produces translations of works by authors from both these ideological tendencies. At present the activities and positions of the Muslim Brotherhood appear to constitute a major point of reference, if not the primary reference for orthodoxy, and they are often presented or "present themselves as a tradition", though their reputation is historically linked to the fact that they have "put forward innovative ideas and practices" [Waardenburg, 2000:67].

---

[39] Though T. Ramadan does not admit to connection to the Brotherhood, he was in one way or another influenced by it. In his various media appearances, we may point that he puts forth "a pedagogical and methodological discussion, which tends in practical terms to present laicism status as reasonably acceptable for Muslims in Europe". He defines "the shape of what is Islamically acceptable in laicism, and what is not negotiable in the nature of Islam, all based on keeping up with or reinforcing the confessional connection"; he not only "indicates the shape of a global Muslim identity", but also "works to re-actualize Islamic thought" [Frégosi, 2000:250 ff.].

Militant social groups and groups favouring an Islamic state

This last category includes groups which have more radical ideological positions, sometimes not without a certain modernism. They favour and work for things like the installation of Islamic governments in the world or the restoration of the Caliphate, organising debates and collecting money, and even recruiting volunteers for the jihad. They are usually minority groups. In Germany, internal security data from 1995 indicates that only 1% of Muslims spread such extremist ideas.[40] But despite small numbers, such organisations are sometimes considered as a standard, or rather a reference point.

Whatever may be the factors giving rise to the creation of such movements within the various countries of origin (inequality, injustice, corruption, primacy accorded by some regimes to secular models of state operation, etc.), two phenomena have had a major impact on their process of formation. On one hand, there are some references and/or connections to the Pakistani *Jama'at-i-Islami*, and to the Egyptian experience of the Muslim Brotherhood. In symbolic terms, the latter hold a near-monopoly in the Machreq but also represent a major source of influence in the Maghreb, especially after Algeria's decision to bring in some Egyptian 'ulamâ' connected to this tendency to help with policies of Arabization and to defend the religious legitimacy of the state against opposition... from Islamists, since these dignitaries were precisely asked to attest the state's conformity to Islam. On another hand, certain hopes were encouraged by the Iranian revolution which while claiming to reconcile the temporal and spiritual worlds also furnished a model for generating enthusiasm in Muslim society.

The *Jama'at-i-Islami, Hizb al-Tahrir* movements and Kaplan group are commented on here, while some networks operated by Islamist exiles are simply noted. But other groups are present in Europe, which have some mutual relations. For example, the organisation *Supporters of Sharia* puts forth a hard-line critique of certain existing governments: it agitates in favour of the creation of Islamic states in the world and for the replacing of Arab leaders considered as 'apostate criminals' who no longer apply the laws of God. As for the *Al-*

---

[40] Bundesamt für Verfassungsschutz, *Islamischer Extremismus und seine Auswirkungen auf die Bundesrepublik Deutschland*, 2nd edition, 1995:6 cited by Karakasoglu & Nonneman, 1996:263.

Muhajiroun movement, this group has taken on the mission of establishing an Islamic state even in the West, and its "Internet sites host those of other movements such as *Hamas, Hizbullah*, the Algerian FIS and the Taliban of Afghanistan". This group's title is paradoxical, because the term Muhajiroun refers here not to those who emigrate from a country which is no longer Islamic toward the territory of Islam, but the reverse, another sign of the fact that confusion about what is and is not Islamic territory has become universal [Roy, 1999:75]. Whenever these small groups spring up, a careful vigilance is required, because their importance is often increased by media exposure, though they are not necessarily among the best organised of groups [Allievi, 2000].

Jama'at-i-Islami

This intellectual re-Islamisation movement which historically aims at political power was begun by Abu'l-A'la Mawdudi in 1941 and led by him until his death in 1979. It seeks to establish the conditions for an Islamic state and seeks to be the ideological binding force of Pakistan; it works to train leadership cadres within the state administration and infiltrates educational associations, student groups, general associations, labour unions, the bureaucracy, and the army [Masud, 2000]. Like Sayyid Qutb, Abu'l-A'la Mawdudi opposed Westernisation [Lewis P., 1994] and the movement offers a catastrophic interpretation of contemporary society. Mawdudi put forth a theocentric vision of God's absolute sovereignty, considered as the sole principle of authority and the only normative principle [Kepel, 1994:139]. Islam for this group is "an ideology, an activist credo, and a legal system which aims at regulating all aspects of life" [Lewis P., 1994:41].

Within the framework of practical politics and modern reformist Islam, Abu'l-A'la Mawdudi offers "a formal homage to Sufism while eliminating its content" completely, since he believes that "the disciple is completely obsessed with the guide's personality and authority" [cited by Lewis P., 1994:41]. This attitude separates him from religious movements such as the Brelwis or the Deobandis. He also maintains the "necessity of going beyond the *taqlîd* (conformity with the teachings of Islamic law, formulated during the Middle Ages), and favours a turn to the *ijtihâd*, an effort of scholarship which attempts to establish Islamic injunctions and their real intentions" [S. Saulat, 1979 cited by Lewis P., 1994:41]. Mawdudi's prolific output has gained him "a certain following among the Muslim Brotherhood", and he was "courted by the government of Saudi Arabia" [Lewis P., 1994:42]. Mawdudi maintains the necessity of a broad missionary strategy. In the end he influenced the modern movement toward preaching (da'wa) "in a more influential manner than Mawlana Muhammad Ilyas, since the latter did not leave behind a theory in written form" [Tozy, 2000:167].

In Europe, this movement has had 'little success' outside Muslim communities from the Indian sub-continent. Further, it possessed only a "weak social base until the Rushdie affair" [Kepel, 1994:197], even though "its sharp nose for political opportunity allowed it to keep a high profile politically in Great Britain, which exceeds its actual popular support" [Nielsen, 1992:136]. Its European activities are coordinated in Great Britain, essentially by means of two networks whose issues and goals seem to have modified over time: the UK Islamic Mission and the Islamic Foundation. The former, founded in 1963 by students and young professionals of Pakistani origin, has headquarters in London and a high degree of support in Birmingham. Its objective is "to promote an Islamic social order in the United Kingdom in order to please Allah", bringing individuals and whole societies back to Islam, which is "a complete way of life which must lead to action in every area of human activity". Beginning with a hard core of devoted militants, its programme aimed originally at "the propagation and the exposition of the true teachings of Islam, the denunciation of false concepts and innovations, the development and creation of mosques, the promotion of Islamic educational activity through the Muslim Educational Trust founded in 1966, and a permanent campaign for the establishment in the United Kingdom of the Islamic law of personal status". The Islamic Foundation, founded in 1973 and located near Leicester, is set up as a research institute and is one of the major sources for the spread of militant Sunni Islamist thought. It produces print and audio-visual publications, including the Personal Computer Islamic Quiz, a video game which "shows how new technology can lead to Islamic art" [Kepel, 1994:185]. Published works draw on basic texts such as the hadiths of Bukhari and Muslim. They are also steeped in the works of A. Mawdudi, S. Qutb, and contemporary Islamic thinkers [Dassetto, 1996:230]. They also produce popular works such as the *Muslim Guide*, intended for non-Muslim people such as teachers, employers, police, social workers, and administrators who come to take multicultural training at the Foundation [Kepel, 1994:184 ff.]. Though such initiatives, mostly published in English, can represent "a way of contesting Western cultural hegemony on its own territory" [Kepel, 1994:199], the positions which are put forward show a certain flexibility and a certain breadth of interests and activities. In fact, aside from particular attention paid to Islamic economics, there is even interest in relations with Christianity, and in the situation of minority Muslim populations in Europe.

Hizb al-Tahrir—Party of Islamic Liberation
Following the line of the radical wing of the Muslim Brotherhood, the PLI was created in 1948 in what is now Jordan by Sheikh Taqi al-Din al-Nabhani (died 1977). This Islamist splinter group operates in secret and favours the restoration of the caliphate, suspended in 1924 by Turkey. It looks forward to the overturning of local powers judged illegitimate and iniquitous, supposedly supported by the West, and favours the "setting up of an Islamic avant-garde" [Etienne, 1987:223]. It has been severely repressed in Tunisia and in Egypt.

In Europe, it strikes a certain chord, but constitutes more of a symbolic point of reference than a rallying cry. This "radical and very politicised" movement [Taji-Farouki, 1996:178] has its head-quarters in Germany [Etienne, 1987:223] and has a separate branch for the Turkish community [Grignard, 1998]. In Great Britain it has 300 members, and has had some success with South Asian young people in cities where unemployment is high; it has made efforts to recruit members among students and intellectuals on various college campuses since the 1980s [Vertovec & Peach, 1997; Lewis P., 1998:43]. It exists in France, and in Denmark it has about 80 male activists and 30 women [DK File]. Working in groups it has organised mostly on English university campuses, it has acquired a bad reputation: it commonly produces anti-Western, anti-Jewish, and anti-homosexual propaganda [*Times Higher Education Supplement*, February 25, 1994, cited by Vertovec & Peach, 1997:38].

Kaplan group (ICCB—Islami Camiler ve Cemaatler Birligi, also called the Union of Islamic Societies and Communities)
With about 50 associations, this tendency is mostly present in Germany [Karakasoglu & Nonneman, 1996:258] and has some influence in the Netherlands, where under the name of the Islamic Federation of Taw'hid Movements it operates eight mosques and receives support

from an estimated three to four thousand persons [Sunier, 1992:153 ff.].
But the organisation has never been able to gain solid footing outside Germany, and there is for example only one mosque of this
tendency in Belgium [Manço, 1997:114].

Created in 1983, the movement sometimes known as the Khomeinist
movement was formed out of a break within the Milli Görüs; its
founder, Cemalettin Kaplan, was won over by the success of the
Iranian Revolution, and favoured a political struggle which ignored
parliamentary forms of government in order to establish an Islamic
society on the pattern of that established by the Prophet at Medina.
One of the main affirmations of this scriptural movement is that the
true Islamic revolution can only come when the masses are mobilised
[Schiffauer, 1997:172]. In 1992, Cemalettin Kaplan, pursuing his
original reasoning, adopted a position in favour of the complete abo-
lition of Kemalism, and the establishment of an Islamic state in
Anatolia [Landman, 1997a:219].

As for the members, they are critical of other Turkish movements.
They are irritated by the organisation of the Süleymancis, who in
their view oversimplify the tasks of believers; but they are most
opposed to the Milli Görüs. They disapprove of their acceptance of
institutional frameworks, and their "compromise with the idolatrous
system", also observing that the "political thinking of an established
party does not allow much spirituality". Even more fundamentally,
it appears to this group that party organisation, always a little doubtful and suspect, is "incompatible with Islamic principles" [Schiffauer,
1997:171 ff.].

Although the members of this splinter group consider themselves
the last to defend the true banner of Islam, differences with other
groups are sometimes muted in favour of cooperation [Schiffauer,
1997:174]. We may observe that the organisation is suffering from
serious internal disputes in the wake of Kaplan's disappearance, and
that the total number of members is declining—estimated at 2,900
in 1996—a loss which has corresponded with a return toward the
banner of the Milli Görüs [Manço, 1997:114]. (As this book is being
prepared for publication, the events of September 11 have led to
this organisation being banned, and its places of worship closed.)

Networks established by Islamist exiles
Some references have been made to national Islamist movements,
networks "occupied above all in supporting resistance in various

countries of origin". These must be distinguished according to whether they generate simply a certain ideological support from a few Muslims in Europe or imply the "existence of real organized structures within which activists plan their return" to the country of origin. Examples are the Tunisian *Al-Nahda*, the Algerian *Front Islamique du Salut* (FIS) and the *Groupes Islamiques Armés* (GIA), the Kurdish Islamist Movement of Kurdistan and the Islamist Party of Kurdistan, the Palestinian *Hamas* movement for Islamic resistance, and certain opposition groups from Iraq or Syria. All are in general dependent on their countries of origin [Dassetto, 1996:226; Pedersen, 1999].

Al-Nahda (The Renaissance) developed out of the *Mouvement de la Tendance Islamique* (MTI) directed by Rached al-Ghannouchi and founded in the mid-1970s [Tamimi, 2001]. After having stood for the Islamisation of public life, the movement changed from being a revolutionary tendency to a movement with a properly political approach at the end of the 1980s, despite the refusal of the Tunisian state to recognise it as a legal party, followed by death sentences for its militants. In exile in England, its president has shown himself open to pluralism. While trying to reconcile Islamic norms with liberal democracy,[41] he has made overtures to the Tunisian nationalist forces, and is seeking other help against the despotism of the state. In France, the *Al-Nahda* continues on its militant path, through the less visible structure of the *Union Générale tunisienne des étudiants en France* [Sindonino, 1998].

Since the interruption of the elections of 1992 which deprived it of victory and the prospect of sole power over the entire country, most of the leaders of the FIS who were not arrested or shot by the Algerian military powers have gone into exile. They have developed networks of financial and logistical support needed in order to challenge a regime which was installed by a 'coup d'etat', and to foster opposition within civil society. This strategy took a dramatic turn toward armed resistance with the formation of the Islamic Salvation Army (AIS) and other autonomous groups [Sindonino, 1998:64].

---

[41] Interview, London, March 2000.

6. Observations and Perspectives

The four great zones of origin—Indo-Pakistani, sub-Saharan Africa, Turkish and Arab—have given birth to quite similar tendencies which find a place in each of the categories presented. Despite the variety of national contexts, similar modes of action have emerged in all parts of the Islamic world. They emphasise contradictory positions in alternation: mystical or ascetic, separatists or universalists, modernists or traditionalists, isolationists or interventionists, etc. Founded on different types of relationships—rational or charismatic, egalitarian or hierarchical, open or kept under watch—these tendencies stem from different goals, depending on whether they develop a ethics of conviction or one of responsibility [Schiffauer, 1997].

The various groups may hold each other in mutual disdain, which can also at times worsen into something more serious, but in most cases they are supportive of each other, at least as regards the groups from the Indian peninsula [Alavi, 1988 cited by King, 1997], and certainly elsewhere as well. But while the tendencies do recognise each other in accordance with the dogma which says that variations are a source of enrichment, and not a source of division or tension within the Umma, it remains true that in Europe they are placed "in direct competition with each other" [Dassetto, 1996; Waardenburg, 2000:67]. Sometimes a real struggle ensues, which may be the extension of an older rivalry, like the opposition between the pietist Brelwis movement, which particularly reveres the Prophet (a characteristic which is usually shared by all the Indian peninsula groups) and more literalist and scriptural tendencies such as Wahhabism. But in the European context, even if different Islamic traditions are all credited with an 'equal legitimacy', they do not all have the same "importance and force" [Dassetto, 1996:93].

Thus it is impossible to describe one particular organisation without making reference to the whole group, all subject to contradictory tensions. On one hand there are forces pushing them all toward "incessant divisions which may be as dramatic as they are momentary". On the other hand, there is a current which "affirms and seeks unity, inclining toward a convergence as utopian as it is real, which establishes an identity and unifying processes" [Dassetto, 1996:83] These movements are crisscrossed by relations of attraction and repulsion, possible alliances and conflicts over influence. And since the boundaries are never fixed, the overlaps and similarities between groups appear quite common, even between certain groups that appear opposed to each other. Looking at the spiritual character of certain organisations, it becomes possible to place on the same footing currents such as the Deobandis and Brelwis of Great Britain [Metcalf, 1982:157–164]. The main difference between the two schools is found in their style of devotion, such that the first "are frank and austere, while the second are more enthusiastic and more pleasant" [King, 1997:135].

Such overlaps are even more likely in Europe because of other forces, internal and external, acting on the movements. In fact, the global landscape for these organisations is moving in time, and changing with respect to different geographical contexts as well. These changes may eventually bring about developments in the two types. There may be changes in the form of membership and in the organisational form of the groups. On another hand these contextual modifications may eventually alter the ideological content of the movements, and variations in their programmes will have an effect on their practices and potential public audiences, their relations with other groups, and their relations with non-Muslim people. One example concerns membership in brotherhoods, which in Europe is usually the result of a choice by individuals. Membership may sometimes be the subject of an automatic decision by a community, related to considerations linked to heredity, but it is more often a personal and voluntary choice, as was the case in early Sufism. A second example is the Brelwi group, which in its country of origin was most popular among rural people from sparsely populated areas, while the Deobandis always addressed themselves to more educated urban dwellers. Now that the former have reached into cities [King, 1997:136], their organisational forms, their relations, and their respective importance have probably been altered. Third, dissimilar tendencies may claim a connection to the same movement, as is the case with the Naqshbandis which have several branches worldwide, and at least two different tendencies in Europe. Even if a historical connection exists, as for example between two different brotherhoods, sometimes the traditional relations are modified like those of the Tijanis and the Murids who have entered into competition in France, where "their confraternal differences have become much sharper", while "each order defends its spiritual castle" [Diop, 1985:199].

The range of these general observations shows to what extent the main trend is not toward secularism but toward a pluralism of tendencies, toward a differentiation of religious programmes or toward new forms which appear, as for example with the New Age Sufi groups.[42] Still, over and above the effect of these trends, there are others which in a more precise manner raise the question of the actual organisational situation, thus illustrating the degree to which the general complementarity of the various tendencies is being put to the test in Europe. They are situated within a general trend toward awareness of Islamisation, which in turn is affected by a tendency to de-traditionalise Islam in order to reinforce it, as seen in the tendency to emphasise the uncreated, non-temporal, and immutable character of the Qur'an. There exists most often, in fact, a predisposition which attempts to present the Qur'an as standing apart from any cultural tradition, which leads eventually to more emphasis on reflection.

In this context, the boundary between Islamist movements and preaching movements has been erased [Dassetto, 1996], though this convergence seems not to benefit some movements such as the *Jama'at al-Tabligh*. After rapid growth during the 1980s [Nielsen, 1992:19], this movement has apparently been declining since the mid-1990s [Dassetto, 2000b:187], and this is related to its critical and suspicious attitude toward Western education and its refusal of dialogue with the outside world [Sikand, 1998:185]. By limiting itself to recruiting persons who are disadvantaged and uneducated [Masud, 2000:30], it cuts itself off from more and more of the young Muslims who are choosing a modern higher education. They prefer to follow secular paths, or, the reverse, to ally themselves with 'cultural tendencies' which appear less organised, like that of the Salafis (even if this tendency is undoubtedly at the centre of an extensive international network quite visible in certain mosques) [Allievi, 2001], or to join more activist Islamic groups, whether these groups are in favour of greater integration into the society of the host country or not [Sikand, 1998:185]. For those young people, very few in number, who are attracted by groups promoting more extreme ideas, such as *Hizb al-Tahrir*, it is not their radical anti-Western rhetoric as much as the example of their leaders, sources of personal inspiration and imitation, which makes them attractive [Sikand, 1998:190; Lewis P., 1994:205].

---

[42] Conversation with Mustapha Draper, Birmingham, March 2000.

In fact, the main motives for their participation are often a resistance to a lack of autonomy and authority, and a loss of control over their interpersonal relations [Samad, 1998:84].

As for Islamism, it is seen as an instrument which attracts and mobilises, a "creative deviance" [Badie, 1992:221], which in time can construct a political project on a cultural and religious base, all while forming part of a relatively moderate vision. Radical tendencies are being transformed, except for a few made up of diehards, and whose organisational structures are completely different from those which aim only at a kind of ideological sympathy. At any rate, "theologians as reputable as Yusuf al-Qaradawi and Sayyid Muhammad Husayn Fadlallah long ago abandoned their traditional ideas about an exclusive Islamic state, and have begun to explore concepts such as human rights and democracy", though this debate has unfortunately not been given any publicity, except for a little in France where Muslims speak Arabic [Nielsen, 1998a].

Even if some re-Islamisation movements act in a social context to provide services which are not provided by public agencies, and though they stir up socio-political awareness in young people, their method does not consist only in political and social activism which attempts to put Islamic ideology into practice. Their organisations are quite flexible, and so are their activities, and it appears that the Islamist movements tend to respond to intellectual and spiritual developments related to the settlement of Muslims in Europe—unless their discussions are restricted to the type of discourse favoured by certain elites, or unless the movements only go as far as stating intentions. However this may be, even if they are still very limited, such initiatives are sometimes propelled onto the European stage, as happened in 1994 in France, where plans were made to provide an Islamic juridical framework for Muslims in Europe, or in London in March 1997, when the European Council for Fatwas and Research was created in order to unite Muslim scholars and to provide juridical opinions. Such reflective attitudes have emerged from people closed to the Muslim Brotherhood, but also closed to the *Jama'at-i-Islami*, and to the Milli Görüs. In this way, the movements can be seen to converge. From this point, as M. Ahsan (third director of the Islamic Foundation) confirms: "the Foundation belongs to an international Islamic movement, just as the Arab Muslim Brotherhood does, or the *Jama'at-i-Islami* of the sub-continent, or the Turkish *Refah Partisi*" [Kepel, 1994:199]. By coming closer together, these movements come closer to the aspirations for unity of the second generation, especially in Great Britain and France.

On another hand, though Sufism in the Balkans has today only a limited importance in relation to the size of the local Islamic communities [Clayer & Popovic, 1999:32], the brotherhoods attract many young men looking for spirituality and community in Western Europe. They are usually thought of as instruments of social resistance to the individualisation found in the larger society. They and others multiply "beginning with the very discreet emergence of limited groups who have no official or public recognition and are not looking for any" [Chodkiewicz, 1996:542 ff.]. But their importance is all the more unavoidable, seeing that some of them go through real modernist transformations. The Murids and the 'Alawiyyas, for example, have undergone an "evolution sui generis, and adapt themselves to individualistic and cosmopolitan European societies" [Hamès, 1996:446].

True agents of consolidation of Islam in Europe, the confraternal tendencies end up "representing more and more of a real challenge for Islamist groups" [Hamès, 1996:446], or even an openly declared opponent. For example, it appears that the *Fédération des Associations Islamiques d'Afrique, des Comores et des Antilles* (FAIACA) "strongly resembles an anti-Islamist, anti-*da'wa* movement. Paradoxically, the leaders of the federation accuse the Islamists of the *da'wa* of being ignorant of Islamic law, and ignorant as regards Islamic religious sciences" [Hamès, 1996:446]. In return, these "complex historical and doctrinal disputes between the Sufism of the brotherhoods and Sunnite orthodoxy, especially as orthopraxy" [Gaboriau, 1996:201] are carried on in new forms, as seen in the fact that the brotherhoods have come under attack from the new Muslim clergy produced by Islamic institutes in Saudi Arabia, Iran, or Pakistan, though at one time the clergy was mostly trained by persons from such brotherhoods [Hamès, 1996:444].

But in the ferment of European post-Islamism, an attitude of flexibility of moderate Islamist groups vis-à-vis Sufism is being observed, which makes a place for more suppleness, even for more openness. And this trend seems favoured by the fact that the traditional opposition between oral tradition and scriptural tradition, in which we see, set in opposition, the authority of the master and the drive towards the autonomy of the individual, is today being transcended by electronic media, which create what some have called a 'second orality' in which we find again the "inevitable plurality of voices"

[Lewis P., 1994:80]. An extreme example of this kind of mixing and matching is the Murabitun movement, which came out of the Darqawis brotherhood, which is headquartered in Granada, and led by a convert who is at present in Scotland. He claims descent from Sufism, adding to it a radical Islamic reading which couples anti-democratic and anti-capitalist polemics with strong anti-Semitism.

Beyond these various organisational convergences, it is possible to imagine their being transcended as well, based on several phenomena.

First, the importance of the criterion of membership in an ethnic group, as an element which is distinct from one's system of belief, has diminished. This is true for young people overall, though the importance of ethnic membership has grown within various movements. The fact of ethnic identification is thus no longer seen as the primary factor in mobilisation for action which seeks to have an effect in European reality. This universalist tendency, traditionally stronger in populations of Arab origin, is being taken into account by other ethnic groups, especially as a result of the establishment of cultural or religious associations which are relatively independent of mosques, and not explicitly affiliated with any movement [Landman, 1992, cited by Dassetto, 1996:215]. At the local level, young people from different origins and ideological tendencies work together, while their leaders jockey for influence. And those who have a conciliatory attitude find the same attitude at the national level, when that is the only way they can make themselves heard by the many state agencies in European countries.

It should also be mentioned that beyond the traditional respect given to orthodoxy (regarding the fact of proclaiming one's belief) and orthopraxy (in which primordial obedience to the revealed Law is expressed through external acts and also tied to certain distinctive cultural traditions), other things are valued. The questions of intentions, of motivations, and of interior sincerity, are beginning to predominate. Certainly the conformity of acts to the letter of the Law still counts, but in accordance with the importance placed on individual study within the original sources of Islam, respect for observance of the Law is becoming a strictly personal subject.

In company with that trend, comes another, this time one of disinterest among some young Muslims for the question of belonging to any ideological movement whatsoever. Many prefer to concentrate on solving problems and challenges in daily life such as racial discrimination, conflict between generations, or conflicts between different value systems and lifestyles. In this connection, we note the emergence of widely scattered groups who are linked by the circulation of ideas rather than by specific movements. An example is the association *Présence Musulmane*, which links dozens of leaders from Islamic associations in Belgium, France, and Switzerland. Its meetings attempt to "rise above the centrifugal logic which can arise from multiplying structures" and to "open up the experience of young Muslims, who are testifying to their faith, toward the society in which they have their roots" [*Islam de France*, n° 1, 1998:155].

From this point, though ideological and religious tensions persist, it seems they are being overtaken by the emergence of an Islamic identity, better grasped and more conscious of itself, and by a feeling that there are too many needs that must be met. For example, that of being able to live harmoniously as a member of a minority and in a "situation in which they lack power to affect a pluralist state" [Lewis P., 1994:110 ff.]. From the experience of coexistence of different organisations that appear to have contradictory principles, perhaps we can see the foundations of a reinforced intra-Muslim unity in which ideas of universal scope predominate. This tendency appears to have begun since the opening of Eastern Europe, whose Muslim communities already seem closer to the rest of the Umma than they once did.

CHAPTER FOUR

INSTITUTIONALISATION OF ISLAM AND REPRESENTATIVE ORGANISATIONS FOR DEALING WITH EUROPEAN STATES

Brigitte Maréchal

The question of the institutionalisation of Islam, that is, its official recognition by state agencies, depends mainly on particular national juridical frameworks in force in those states. After defining fairly precisely what kind of organisations we are referring to, we will present a quick typology of regulations on religion relative to the legislative frameworks just mentioned. That will re-orient our analysis of the institutionalisation of Islam to the European level. It will also allow us to explain and to some extent place in perspective the main subject of this chapter, namely, processes of constitution of organisations representing Muslim communities in their relations with various European states.

From country to country, these representative organisations are today at quite different stages of development. The effort to build these structures is seen by Muslim communities as vital to the recognition of Islam and/or the practical establishment of eventual legal dispositions which are favourable to Islam. These favourable dispositions are thought likely simply because states often seem to be requesting the structures, if only in an indirect way. We will examine the motivations behind this situation.

In order to estimate the importance of such organisations, especially with regard to another criterion, that of the general degree of effective institutional structuring of Muslim communities, each country will be reviewed, with emphasis on procedures which have begun to be put in practice, and the particular characteristics of the main actors. In arrangements within this highly symbolic area, there is no one dominant principle, and subjective factors are numerous. Only a case by case approach will shed light on the matter.

Before embarking on the topic, we should specify that only political organisations are considered here, those which have been established in a European country for the benefit of Muslims who live in that country. Two types of organisation are excluded from consideration. The first is any international Muslim lobby or advocacy group which, acting under outside influence, attempts to represent and promote Islam worldwide. Two examples are the World Muslim Congress, based in Pakistan, and the Muslim World League, under Saudi leadership. Second, as regards still nascent efforts aimed at creating representative organisations at the pan-European level, they are not considered as such. Little information, for example, is available regarding two competing efforts to organise a federation of Islamic communities in the Balkans which have begun, each related to a different current of influence: the Islamic Council of Eastern Europe, created in 1991 with support from the Muslim World League, and a Shura of Eurasian Muslims, called together in 1995 by the Turkish Diyanet. The latter met again in Sarajevo in August 2000, a fact which shows sustained interest on the part of Turkish authorities, despite the rapid changes affecting Islam in the Balkans [Bougarel & Clayer, 2001:46 ff.]. What is more, in 1992 it was reported that Bulgarian officials participated in a conference at Vienna which proclaimed the creation of a Council of Muslims in Europe. This organisation was supposed to "increase the role of Islam, to explain its true meaning, and to promote cooperation among Muslims" [Müslümanlar-Muslumani, N11/14 cited by Peev, 1997:194]. The leader of the 'ulamâ' of Yugoslavia was chosen to head the group, but given the enormous upheavals in the region, it seems likely that this initiative has either slowed to a crawl or simply come to an end. Later, in 1996, under the aegis of the European Parliament, fifteen Muslim associations with members from France, Belgium, Ireland, the Netherlands, Spain, Denmark and Germany joined to form a Coordinating Council of European Muslims (CCME). Without claiming to represent all the Muslims of Europe, the CCME was intended to defend the identity of European Muslims in general, by opening a dialogue between them at the European level, with reference to the ethical values of Islamic education [Spuler-Stegemann, 1998:110; Couvreur, 1998:65].

Whatever the status of these initiatives today, their existence shows to what extent the obstacles to the organisation of pan-European Muslim associations are already being cleared away. In the 1980s, these included the high degree of linguistic, cultural, ethnic, ideological, and political differences, the ignorance on both sides of the other's religion, and the lack of authority and leadership competent to establish procedures of consultation and negotiation—without counting the many pre-existing alliances with Muslim organisations in the countries of origin of Muslims, which have represented real stumbling blocks to the establishment of European-based organisations [van Bommel, 1992:141 ff.]. It is apparent today that other forces are at work, and that they are likely to multiply and grow in the near future. The success of such initiatives would carry considerable prestige, and this is another reason why they are not likely to diminish.

1. Legislative Regulations of Religion and Beyond

We have already noted that official recognition of Islam primarily depends on national juridical frameworks. Under many titles, all European countries have specific legislations applying to organized religions, whose modes of organisation differ, and whose scope of application differs according to which religion is concerned. The question of the eventual emergence of an agency representative of Muslim communities is thus reopened here.

Typology

A typology of existing legislation has been established, which is presented here because it will help us understand the overall framework of efforts by Muslim communities to build structures and obtain recognition. What is more, this information will be of help for an eventual understanding of the ways in which states react to the process of creation of representative organisations, and perhaps of the types of power states have, a priori, to affect such organisations and to enter into relations with them.

This typology distinguishes two or three broad types of religious regulation within the European Union [Messner, 1996]. First, there are 'universal' systems of regulation, "applicable to all religions", found in France, the Netherlands, Ireland, and Sweden.[1] These establish the equality of all religions, unless some religion becomes subject

---

[1] Sweden once clearly gave preference to the Lutheran church, but a separation of church and state was accomplished in January 2000. Legislation was modified such that all religions were thenceforward treated equally in principle [SE File].

to administrative or judicial sanction, usually for reasons having to do with the maintenance of public order. Second, there are "systems of recognition *lato sensu*, that is, systems which subject the granting of status to religions to prior procedures and/or inspections, applying the regulations to some religions and excluding all others", as in Belgium, Germany, Spain, Italy, Austria, Luxembourg, Switzerland, Poland, Hungary, Bulgaria, and Romania. Among legal advantages that may be obtained we find "large public subsidies such as paying the salaries of the ministers of a religion, religious instruction in public schools, and tax exemptions" [Frégosi, 2000b:96 ff.]. Finally, there are "systems with national or culturally entrenched churches" which, in a variation from the second type, limit public subsidies of various kinds to one single religion, while other religions are relegated to a secondary status: Great Britain, Denmark, Finland, Portugal and Greece, with the exception of Western Thrace, where the Muslim community has particular rights related to specific historical considerations.

In addition, it has been observed that the state powers with regard to the recognition of religions are drawn from several areas, that could eventually consolidate each other. All such regulations could be brought under the concept of public order, or be affected by various ways of defining which communities can be qualified as 'religious'. As concerns the second scheme above (and its variation), a variety of criteria may figure in the administration of the procedures and/or inspections mentioned before. These may be linked to demands for a certain minimum number of members and/or a certain longevity of the particular religious community in the given country, and/or the familiarity (even as being 'traditional' or 'European') of the religion concerned, etc. Taking these elements into account is a means of justifying or refusing possible privileges that the state grants to recognized religions.

Practical interests: what is at stake for Muslims

The importance of such religious legislation comes from the fact that the main principles of modes of application of regulations on religion, and principles of ecclesiastical law, are established in it. These principles cover many different areas, and give rise to many practical implications. In fact, legislation about religion covers principles of "the free organisation of churches and religions, the status *sui generis* of ministers of a religion, the right to work within the churches, the status of religious institutions (whether from the standpoint of private or public law), classes of religious instruction in public schools, spiritual guidance in prisons, hospitals, and in the armed forces, direct or indirect financing (tax exemptions) of religious activities and institutions, faculties of theology in state universities, and finally, recognition of the civil effects of a religious marriage" [Messner, 1996].

Aside from these general observations, certain domains are more directly concerned in certain countries. There is some sensitivity to Islamic holidays, and, on the part of administrations, to dietary prohibitions or questions about ritual slaughtering, which may sometimes require even the establishment of a halal label. Sometimes provision is made for women to be photographed in identity card pictures wearing scarves over their heads. Sometimes special access to national media is reserved, and in rare cases religious decision-making bodies are allowed to settle disputes between members which otherwise might have gone through the justice system. And a better awareness of particular requirements from local authorities as regards funeral arrangements may be assumed, sometimes going as far as the establishment of reserved areas in cemeteries, and/or concessions in perpetuity.

An additional demand

The institutionalisation of Islam is often taken to mean simply the formation of a representative organisation for Muslim communities. Dispositions adopted by a number of states seem to assume this. But in fact, beyond the attitudes feigned by the representatives of some states, who are content to make allusions or vague promises of good will and cooperation in this area, sometimes those state representatives really do have relative discretionary authority over certain matters. And processes which are aimed at producing and putting forward a designated spokesperson are actually expected or desired (quietly) by some states, whatever their relationship to a particular juridical system of regulation of religions. In exceptional cases, the existence of a spokesperson is a pre-condition for real recognition of the religion.

What must be underlined is the degree to which this sort of understanding between government and Islam is expected to come from the organisation of one central structure which is supposed to represent the interests of all the Muslims living in a given country. Some even expect, as is the case with some churches, that this organism should express the reality of Islam with a single voice.

Arguments made by state agencies

In Bulgaria, Romania, Greece, Austria, and Spain, the arguments in favour of the establishment of such an organism are often related to the desire for a harmonisation of the status of all religions which are recognised for historical reasons. Some other countries, that are also sensitive to the need for representation, argue in the sense of an extension of democratic values—an improvement in the representation, and thus a greater participation in the democratic process by Muslim communities. Behind these positive expressions, other reasons weigh in, especially the desire of policy-makers to resolve the question as quickly as possible, before it can become the object of larger partisan disputes. And there are some reasons which are less praiseworthy, or which cannot be stated openly: there could be a desire to place the communities in a state of relative dependence, if only financially, and by that means to exercise a form of control over them. More, it has been suggested that the establishment of this kind of tutelary relationship would probably allow the state to more easily silence or neutralise extremist groups by having the Muslim community itself see to the matter. In France in the early 1990s, important changes in the political landscape (including the appearance of the Islamic Salvation Front—FIS) led the socialist government to "encourage a central administration of this [Muslim] religion within the Hexagon in order to liberate it from Algerian influence" [Kepel, 1994:17].

Overall, if states attempt to create a certain manoeuvring space for themselves in such a manner, it is less for objective reasons than the result of a choice, a certain political will, even discretionary—unless it is related to some unconscious attachment to a religious tradition, such as the Roman Catholic model [Frégosi, 2000b]. In the area of religious administration, this model is the very type of a centralised and hierarchised organisation, which appears as the only one of its kind which is complete and effective, and some may think that all churches should be modelled after it. As for the structure adopted in certain Eastern European countries which have Muslim communities centuries old, in which the muftis represent political authority and spiritual authority, this also furnishes an example of successful organisation, but it is less likely to serve as a source of inspiration in Western European policy discussions.

General remarks regarding this demand

From a Muslim point of view, the establishment of such a centralised authority, even if wished by the state, is not so easily accomplished. People are classified as Muslims according to a minimum standard, and principles for the assumption and legitimation of such authority or power are not to be found in the sacred texts [Dassetto, 1996:84 ff.]. This organisational arrangement seems to many to be practically difficult and to come from outside Islam.

It is also the case that this demand is usually made in an informal manner. No juridical system mandates the existence of a representative organism for recognised religious communities (or those to be recognised), except for two types of country which are a priori capable of mandating such an arrangement—those which apply the second type of juridical regime under the condition that this element is precisely specified—or, more probably, countries which have a traditional representative authority led by a Mufti as in Greece (for Western Thrace), Bulgaria, Romania, and Austria. In other countries, considerations linked to the political situation determine the degree of attention paid to this problem by the state.

We note further that the expression of so singular a desire on the part of states, which implies a real influence over the administration of Muslim communities, is not only absent from most legal texts, but in general contrary to constitutional texts in the majority of European countries. These guarantee, in fact, the principle of religious liberty including free exercise of worship and freedom of self-organisation for religions, plus (usually) a separation between church and state and neutrality of the state in religious matters. And these principles themselves rest upon the European Convention on Human Rights, which guarantees individual and collective freedom of worship.

Over and above all that, the appearance of this wish of the state seems all the more paradoxical, because it happens just as "all sociologists of religion agree that the important phenomenon, currently, is the general de-institutionalisation of religion, and the crisis in the hierarchies which regulate and validate belief" [C. de Galembert

& D. Hervieu Léger[2] cited in Frégosi, 2000b]. The "loss of social influence by great religious institutions is a main feature of the European religious landscape today" [Frégosi, 2000b], also seen in Eastern Europe, where "the renewed activity of Islamic religious institutions in the Balkans" during the 1990s cannot be interpreted as equivalent to a "restoration of Islamic religious institutions" [Bougarel & Clayer, 2001:41 ff.]. The fact that Islam there is "suspected of having become the tool of careerists and converted communists" only furnishes "one more sign of secularisation" [Bougarel & Clayer, 2001:41 ff.].

2. National Situations

An exhaustive panorama of national situations is presented here, one which is aimed at judging the level of Islamic institutionalisation in Europe and the actual degree of state involvement in the process of creation of representative organisations. But first, at any rate, the distinction which exists between Western and Eastern Europe should be discussed. In the east, the institutionalisation of Islam was achieved long ago, and that religion also benefits from institutional representation in the form of secular organisations which have developed hierarchies, and are traditionally dominated by the leadership of the mufti. In the west, the question of recognition and representation for Islam are recent questions, drawing widely varying response from country to country. In some cases Muslims themselves come up with a host of attempts to create representative organisations, sometimes pushed in this direction by European states.

To say this more simply, it is the degree of the effective operation of some representative organisation which is taken as a standard, provided the standard is not taken to validate any particular agenda. Thus, schematically, it is possible to distinguish four situation-types existing in Europe. Beside the religious institution traditionally headed by the mufti in states which have had Muslim

---

[2] Galembert C. (1998), "Eglises chrétiennes, Etat et islam en Europe: entre institutionnalisation et dés-institutionnalisation" in R. Leveau (dir.), *Islam(s) en Europe. Approches d'un nouveau pluralisme culturel européen*, Berlin, Les travaux du centre Marc Bloch, p. 70 and Hervieu Léger D. (1999), *Le pèlerin et le converti. La religion en mouvement*, Paris, Flammarion, 290 p.

communities for centuries, representative authority is formally established in only three states, Spain, Austria, and Belgium. Elsewhere, initiatives exist at various stages of development, but in many countries whose immigrant communities are of more recent implantation, nothing has been done.

Countries with long-established Muslim communities

Bulgaria, Romania, and Greece are familiar with the institution of the mufti as titular head of the Islamic religion, though not always independent. Since the end of the communist era, however, the mufti's authority has been called into question, such that the interests of Muslims, though not necessarily Islam, seem better represented sometimes by other types of organisation, e.g., certain political parties or party leaders.

This phenomenon is to be explained by a number of factors, internal for the most part but external, too, as with the appearance, from outside, of religious currents which make the monopoly on the interpretation of Islamic texts of the traditional Islamic religious institutions easier to challenge [Bougarel & Clayer, 2001:41 ff.]. After the disappearance of communism, many new institutions appeared in most Balkan countries—political parties representing Muslims, newspapers, cultural associations, intellectual forums, etc. [Bougarel & Clayer, 2001:35]. Like the re-establishment of religious liberty, coming after the deep impression left by a once mandatory secularisation that ended up deeply ingrained in the public mind, the new organisations reveal gaps and weaknesses in Islamic religious institutions. To this we must add the fact that religious institutions "never received restitution of rights and possessions which had been taken from them in the period after the war; only a few of the administrative offices that were confiscated from them after 1945 have been given back, and religious education in the schools has not been resumed" [Bougarel & Clayer, 2001:41 ff.].

In **Greece**, the Muslim community of Western Thrace enjoys a special status in accordance with the 1923 peace treaty of Lausanne which provided for an exchange of populations between Greece and Turkey. Remaining from that time, there are vestiges of the old Islamic infrastructure which represented the community before national political authorities, mainly through endowments which benefit religious service organisations or the institution of the mufti. The latter officially possesses great authority, and is both a religious and a political leader. The mufti is also the only official in Balkan countries who has retained power to administer the law of Sharia in cases of personal or family law [Bougarel & Clayer, 2001:41 ff.]. He can decide cases of marriage disputes, divorce, alimentary pensions, adoption, and any other civil matter including inheritance cases [Ziakas, 1995:70], even if it is true that his decisions must be validated by a superior court in the jurisdiction in which the mufti has his seat. However, following the state intervention in the procedure of nomination of muftis, contrary to the Treaty of Lausanne, and which was condemned recently by the European Court of Human Rights [Bougarel & Calyer, 2001:75], a rift was created between the muftis paid by the state and those who are recognised by the Muslim community [Küçükcan, 1999:62; Dalègre, 2001]. Over and above its symbolic aspect, this competition between muftis, one located in Komotini and the other at Xanthi, has an economic aspect, since the control over community finances is at stake. What is more, having failed to get their own political party recognised, the leaders of the Turkish community have no choice but to participate in traditional parties in order to make their voices heard. Their political movement was broken up by the passing of a new law in 1990 which required a minimum of 3% of the votes in elections in order to secure representation in Parliament, and the elections of 1996 marginalised the political participation of ethnic Turks in Greece [Küçükcan, 1999:63]. In general, the minority still manages to unite in order to deal with community issues such as education [GR File]—and they must feel somewhat more confident in their rights since December 1999, when the European Court of Human Rights condemned the Greek state for its sanctioning of 'illegal' muftis elected by the Turkish minority [Bougarel & Clayer, 2001:75].

In **Bulgaria**, the traditional religions of the country, including Islam, enjoy the same level of recognition and status despite a certain privilege given to the Orthodox church. Traditional Islamic institutions are also maintained but remain quite weak because of a crisis of legitimacy which has affected them since 1989 [BG File]. During the communist era, a Muslim religious organism was propped up for propaganda purposes, naming a Grand Mufti and regional muftis. But because these religious leaders were named for political reasons and not because of their religious training, and to the extent that they remained loyal to the government, most of these regional muftis and imams backed the assimilationist and anti-Muslim policies of the regime. They stayed in their jobs until 1992 because they received support [Eminov, 1997:61 ff.; Ragaru, 2001:279]. Further, during a period of intense structural change, the country found itself "completely lacking trained theologians", so that "the only elites able to play a role in the restructuring of Muslim communities were those who had been enabled to do so by the communist government since the 1950s, lay Turks for the most part who had been converted to the ideals of the socialist revolution—if in name only" [Ragaru, 2001:279]. Later, an open conflict was declared between two camps identified as 'pro-Turk' and 'pro-Arab', which, some assert, "tore apart the Office of the Grand Mufti" [Ragaru, 2001:273], unless it was operating on a political level. Other analysts thought that the tension was situated rather between the 'party' of religious Muslims around the Grand Mufti, who maintained excellent relations with representatives of Muslim religious organisations from Arab countries [Popovic, 1997:66] and the *Dvizenie na Prava I Svobodi* (DPS—Movement for Right and Freedoms), which has representation in Parliament on behalf of Bulgarian Turks and, by extension, Pomaks and Muslim Gypsies. This party, secular, pro-Western [Lederer, 1994; BG File] and closer to official Turkish circles [Popovic, 1997:66], appears rather unusual since it manages to attract even Bulgarian Christians [BG File]. The party recognises only an 'extremely modest' place for religion [Ragaru, 2001:283]. Islam represents for it only a simple "community reference point, a symbolic resource bringing extra prestige to political leaders while legitimising their actions on behalf of a political clientele" [Bougarel & Clayer, 2001:43 ff.] However this may be, in October 1997, on the initiative of the Directorate of Religious Affairs, and thanks to DPS support, a "conference of national reconciliation" was organised to try to remedy the situation, which illustrates how close "personal ties between 'ulamâ' and political leaders" really were [Bougarel & Clayer, 2001:43 ff.]. This assembly officially elected as Grand Mufti Moustafa Alich Hadji, a 35-year-old Pomak who had pursued studies in theology in Jordan. However, his election provoked the resentment of Turks who maintained that the leadership of the community was theirs by right. Though the former Grand Mufti Gendjev appealed the results, the Turks' feeling of bitterness became even greater when the new Mufti named only Bulgarian-speaking Muslims who were (like the Mufti himself) from Western Rhodopes to key posts in the religious hierarchy

[Ragaru, 2001:280]. Even if the persistence of factional squabbles has prevented the Office of the Grand Mufti from taking control of the religious renewal [Ragaru, 2001], and though the power of the DPS in social and political life has seemed to fade since the beginning of the 1990s, it remains likely that Muslim communities will play a greater role in Bulgarian politics in the future [Küçükcan, 1999:58 ff.], thanks to a certain momentum in favour of autonomisation which draws strength from the fact that the Bulgarian state was also condemned by the European Court of Human Rights, in October 2000, for meddling in the naming of the Grand Mufti of Bulgaria in 1995 [Bougarel & Clayer, 2001:75].

In **Romania**, Islam is one of 15 religions currently recognised by the Constitution [RO File]. The Muslim minority is represented in Parliament through two political organisations which differ in ethnic origin, though their languages, traditions, and spiritual bent are quite similar: the Democratic Union of Tartar Turkish Muslims in Romania (UDTTMR) and the Democratic Union of Turks in Romania (UDTR) [RO File]. A democratic reform of Romanian Islamic institutions was favoured by the latter, with the aim of controlling the office of the mufti of Constanta, who had been an instrument of communist propaganda, and had poorly administered his office [Lederer, 1996]. As a result clergy lost respect due to their poor training, and the secularised Tartar intelligentsia gained prestige [RO File]. For the moment, Muslim institutions such as the mufti continue to receive state subsidies; the state pays for building and maintaining mosques and for the salaries of the imams.

Some recent institutions

The countries of Western Europe in this category, which all belong to the recognition-type system, have also all succeeded in establishing an organisation for the representation of Muslims. They "often appear as the most advanced" in this stage of institutionalisation of Islam, even in the eyes of "certain rising stars of the European Islamic intelligentsia" who consider these countries as "possible models for a successful integration of Islamic identity in a non-Muslim context" [Ramadan, 1994 cited by Frégosi, 2000b:101]. But a detailed view still shows great differences in the agents and emerging characteristics of these organisations in connection with the processes of institutionalisation.

First, in **Spain** the state recognised Islam as a 'well-established' religion in 1989. Problems of representation were legally resolved in 1992, with the establishment of a convention concerning internal law between the Spanish state and the *Comisión Islámica de España*. This organisation was created through the unification of the *Federación Española de Entidades Religiosas Islámicas* (FEERI), formed by converted Muslims, and based on an ideological profile of considerable complexity (they maintain relations with Morocco, Libya, and Iran), plus the *Unión de Comunidades Islámicas en España* (UCIDE), which includes Middle Eastern Muslims, connected to the Muslim Brotherhood, considered reasonably moderate [ES File]. This organisation was then considered the only fully representative one, and as the official interlocutor with the state, the one with responsibility for questions of day-to-day management. It is responsible for guaranteeing and overseeing the body of religious practices, places of worship, and organisational structures among Spanish Muslims, as well as for the preservation of the Islamic architectural and artistic patrimony [Moreras, 1996]. Benefits to the Islamic religion include Islamic religious instruction in public and private schools at state expense, recognition of the civil effects of religious marriage, the observing of six Islamic holidays, the recognition of the sacred character of places of worship, respect for particular forms of burial, and recognition of the right to confessional confidentiality for officials and ministers of the religion. In general, this option was considered the easiest for the Spanish state, which believed itself the main beneficiary of the agreement because it ended up with a valid interlocutor and avoided getting bogged down in lengthy negotiations with disparate structures [Moreras, 1996]. But the efficiency of the organisation is cause for worry, because it does not represent the diversity of Muslims, nor the immigrants who are the poorest and the most recently arrived, often illegally [Vertovec & Peach, 1997:34]. And there are still Islamic religious organisations which "are not in the federation, and situate themselves outside the institutional framework developed by the *Comisión Islámica de España* and its two federations" [ES File].

In **Belgium**, the process of Islamic institutionalisation has been marked by a number of contextual events of different types, including the problem of a 'representative organism' which is supposed to provide centralized management of public funds given to the Islamic religion and play the role of a "spiritual and hierarchical authority". This procedure has been affected by the strategies of various actors and by what they hoped to gain. First, the state authorities were trying to organise a representative for the Islamic religion in a manner contrary to their Constitution and its principle of state neutrality in matters of religion. These authorities not only participated in the selection and arrangement of the Muslim leadership, but attempted to determine the conditions under which it would act [Panafit, 1999]. The history of this process goes back to the early 1970s. Joining the already recognised Catholic, Protestant, Anglican and Jewish religions, the Islamic religion was recognised by a law of 19 July 1974 at the time of the oil crisis. Belgium then adopted juridical dispositions concerning two problems considered quite delicate. In 1978, instruction in Islamic religion was planned within the state educational system, and the Director of the *Centre Islamique et Culturel—Parc du Cinquantenaire* in Brussels, representing the Muslim World League, was recognised as the privileged interlocutor with the government. Because of ideological reasons and reasons having to do with spheres of influence, other Muslim organisations nonetheless rapidly appeared, evidence of a sectorial approach to questions having to do with the institutionalisation of Islam [Panafit, 1999:291]. These new bodies competed for leadership with the Centre Islamique et Culturel, which found itself left in a subordinate position by the mid-1980s as the idea of fundamentalism gained momentum. In 1990, the Intergovernmental Committee on Immigration Policy took a hand and instituted a *Conseil Provisoire des Sages*, composed of leading secular citizens, with the task of making proposals regarding the organisation of Islam in Belgium, and handling the nomination of teachers of the Islamic religion. Weakened by internal divisions, this Council soon met competition from a *Conseil Supérieur des Musulmans*, which was formed through consultation with Muslim populations, but not recognised by the authorities. In 1994, after discussions with the public authorities, who wished to come up with an effective set of rules for an organisation that they had helped to create, the *Conseil Supérieur des Musulmans* ceded its place to a transitional consultative body: the *Exécutif des Musulmans de Belgique* (EMB), made up of members of the *Conseil Supérieur des Musulmans* and of independent Muslims, often coming from various associations. In 1998, the government accepted electoral arrangements under the direction of the Centre pour l'Egalité des Chances (Centre for Equal Opportunity), and on December 13, 1998, 48,000 votes were cast. In accordance with the royal decree of 3 May 1999, the new *Exécutif des Musulmans de Belgique* was officially inaugurated and legally recognised. It defines itself not as "an organism for the regulation of a religion, but rather as a council of managers".[3] The makeup of this organisation has been the object of much discussion, especially as concerns the nationality of the electors, but not with regard to doctrinal tendencies within the religion. Its members represent the various Muslim communities as individuals. The 17 members are chosen by 68 persons who form the assembly of the 'Organe Chef du Culte' (the organism which regulates the religion), themselves elected or retained in order to assure continuity of work on various projects of the Executive. Some of the seats were reserved for women, young people, and certain minorities of the community, as well as certain persons with specific and valuable technical competence, without their having to be elected [Panafit, 1999]. In principle, the responsibilities of the Executive are divided among four departments: instruction, youth and social affairs, cultural affairs, and information/communication. At this time it would be premature to give an opinion about the organisation's effectiveness, especially since the technical nature of its structure has removed it from public debates in the media, confining it to relationships with governmental departments and ministerial offices, involving a limited number of actors [Panafit, 1999]. Problems have appeared related to the makeup of the Executive, raised by its own Assembly, but apart from that the activities of the Executive have seemed limited and rather superficial. In its defence, it must be said that the budget of the Executive has never been fully funded, and only its president is actually paid at the present time to accomplish his many tasks.

In **Austria** special laws regulate relations with the Muslim community. Starting in the mid-1960s, these communities lobbied the government to get the Imperial laws of 1874 and 1912, relating to the recognition of Islam, considered as still valid. In 1979, this was granted, but only as applying to the Hanafi rite. The next year, nonetheless, recognition was extended to all schools of Islamic jurisprudence following an opinion from the Austrian Constitutional Court which judged the restriction discriminatory [Frégosi, 2000b:98]. The Islamic community was recognised thenceforward through the organisation known as the 'Islamic Community of Austria'. This body

---

[3] Exécutif des Musulmans de Belgique, Rapport d'évaluation des activités, 1995 cited by Panafit, 1999:303.

represents the various doctrinal tendencies, and it is composed of three officially recognised organisations: *Schurarat*, *Der Oberste Rat*, and the mufti, who has the right to contest any decision of the *Der Oberste Rat*, half of whose ten members must possess a certain degree of religious education. Composed of 16 members elected for four years, the *Schurarat* is made up of elected representatives, a secretary-general, a treasurer, and the chief imam of all the Muslim congregations. It is considered as the most important organisation in the community. Its tasks include granting permits for the construction of mosques and naming imams, but also decisions about a budget and oversight of the activities of *Der Oberste Rat*, which for its part oversees certain religious and cultural matters, including the public relations of the Islamic community with the outside [Strobl, 1997:47 ff.]. At the local level, the community is organised in much the same way, with a *Gemeindeversammlung*, a *Gemeindeausschuß*, and the imam. Every four years, the members of the various Muslim congregations elect local councils. At least a third of members elected must have had a religious education, half must be Austrian citizens, more than half cannot belong to the same linguistic or ethnic group [Strobl, 1999:49]. Although recognition of such organisations does not guarantee their direct subsidisation, either on the national or the local level [AT File], recognition does bring numerous advantages for Muslim communities in the areas of taxation, public instruction, and access to public media facilities [Vertovec & Peach, 1997].

Other experiments

With varying levels of determination, a number of countries (including those which have the highest proportion of Muslims) have experimented with institutionalisation and/or the formation of representative organisations, and these experiments have met with varying degrees of success.

In **Great Britain**, although the established nature of the church of England originally represented a barrier to the recognition and equal treatment of Muslims and other minorities [Modood, 1994, cited in Vertovec & Peach, 1997:32], today hundreds of Islamic organisations operate under a variety of kinds of legal status [UK File]. What is more, attitudes have changed, and Muslims have succeeded progressively in uniting in order to change them further. Many attempts at federation have been made since the end of the

1970s in the hopes of building an identity and presenting a united front to national authorities. The constitution of the Union of Muslim Organisations, that of the United Kingdom Action Committee on Islamic Affairs, at the moment of the Rushdie affair, that of the Council of Imams and Mosques or that of the Council of Mosques—all bear witness to this. But the unity established around these entities was still founded on a search for the least common denominator between them. In terms of popular support, these experiments have usually been led by a few individuals, and their influence has been rather formal [Samad, 1998:68]. One unusual experiment in progress since 1997 is that of the Muslim Council of Britain (MCB), which aims at promoting consensus and cooperation within the community, expressing its opinion with regard to problems of common interest, and at the eradication of disadvantages and other discrimination which Muslims face, while encouraging better understanding of Muslim culture, and supporting all efforts to improve the society as a whole. Founded following many consultations with a majority of mosques, and with Islamic organisations belonging to a variety of Islamic traditions, this organisation includes a large spectrum of tendencies, although not yet Shiite, but excludes some minority groups considered as extremist, like *Hizb al-Tahrir* or *Al Muhajiroun*, and some groups considered as religiously too unorthodox, like the Baha'is. This group still is not officially recognised, and its results seem modest enough, judging by the establishment of committees for social affairs. But the process does seem to be moving forward, because the MCB has shown a certain facility in negotiations with the government and the media. Regular meetings are held with the Home Secretary and Foreign Office Ministers, in addition to various meetings with members of the other religious communities. Besides these events involving the Muslim community, we also note that a proposition has been made before the House of Lords, that the current number of religious representatives within that body should be modified, in order to have some representation for elite Muslims in addition to 26 bishops.[4]

In **Germany**, Muslim communities can organise according to private law and benefit from recognition as organisations in the public interest (i.e. religious communities) [Messner, 1996]. Requests for

---

[4] Interview with Professor M. Anwar, March 2000, UK.

official recognition have been regularly made since 1977, but each time rejected because "no organisation exists which groups together to a sufficient degree the interests of all Muslims, so as to be designated as representing all Muslims" [Amiraux, 1999:37]. Today most organisations are grouped in one of two platforms in which four federations appear most prominent: the AMGT (*Avrupa Milli Görüs Teskilâtleri*), the VIKZ (*Verband Islamischer Kulturzentren*, Süleymancis), the DITIB (Diyanet) and the ADÜTF (*Türkische Föderation*), an organisation once known as purely political but which developed a strong religious orientation, toward a interior religion—but in truth its concrete religious orientations are rather poorly defined. Other organisations, many of Sufi (Naqshbandis, Qadiris, Rifa'is, Mevlevis), have much less influence. One platform is called the *Islamrat für die Bundesrepublik Deutschland*, created in 1986, essentially under the aegis of the Milli Görüs. It unites 27 Muslim organisations, including the Milli Görüs, the Nursis, the *Avrupa Türk Islam Birligi* (ATIB) groups of German converts, and representatives of Bosnian and Arab Muslims. In general, this organisation tries to arrange courses for children, to help Muslims in their daily lives, and to see that a place is made for the Muslim contribution to German history [Spuler-Stegemann, 1998:115]. In 1993, this organisation asked the government to recognise it as the official representative of Islam in Germany, but this designation was refused due to counter-pressure from the Diyanet, which remains the sole official interlocutor in matters regarding Islam. The other platform is the *Zentralrat der Muslime in Deutschland*, created in 1991, which includes the Diyanet, the Süleymanci community, and some quite active student organisations. This organisation maintains a number of working groups on issues such as protection of environment and animals, media relations, kindergartens, and classes in religion, as well as the establishment of a Muslim calendar [Spuler-Stegemann, 1998:115]. These two have ideologically opposed orientations, but their interests with regard to the German state are the same. A union between them is thus not impossible, and joint actions and consultations have taken place [Karakasoglu & Nonneman, 1996:259 ff.]. It must be said that there is much at stake, for whenever an official representative of the Islamic religion is identified, that representative will be consulted on political matters involving immigrants, to be sure, but he or she will also have decision-making power in areas such as establishment of curricula in schools, the opening of religious schools, the designation of directors of conscience and the lead role in media relations [Amiraux, 1999:37]. With the help of the state, this organisation will enjoy the right to collect an ecclesiastical tax from German Muslims in the amount of 32 million DM per year [Cumhuriyet, 30/4/94].

Over and above the almost spontaneous recognition of the Islamic religion in **France**, several attempts have been made already to create a federation representative of Islam, such as the government's creation of a *Conseil de Réflexion sur l'Islam en France* (CORIF), which operated from 1990 to 1992, and the *Coordination Nationale des Musulmans de France* (CNMF), between 1993 and 1995. But the influence of the *Institut Musulman de la Mosquée de Paris* (IMMP) has cast a large shadow over negotiations, while other initiatives illustrate the difficulty the authorities have in "grasping the situation of the Muslim religion other than as a centralized entity, and outside a preconception which overestimates the objective reservations of Islam with regard to the secular community" [Motchane, 2000 cited by Frégosi, 2000b]. Thus the largest organisations are still squabbling. We name them in order of importance [FR File]: the *Union des Organisations Islamiques de France* (UOIF) (an association which claims to speak for 200 other associations, and which has close ties to the moderate Muslim Brotherhood); the network of the IMMP (representing the Algerian lobby); the Foi et Pratique movement and the *Fédération Nationale des Musulmans de France* (FNMF) (founded in order to unite the opposition to the IMMP, but now reduced to a group of Moroccan leaders linked to the Muslim World League); the *Fédération des Associations Islamiques d'Afrique, des Comores et des Antilles* (FAIACA); the *Tendance Nationale Union Islamique en France* (the French branch of Milli Görüs); the *Association des Etudiants Islamiques de France* (AEIF); the *Union de la Jeunesse Musulmane* (UJM) (mostly found in the Rhone-Alpine region); and there is also the increasing importance of a few large regional mosques, not affiliated with the abovementioned organisations [FR File; Branine & Renard, 1998:20 ff.]. In general, associations of young Muslims express a lack of interest in the question of official representation [Bourg, 1998:75] and a desire to cut free from state structures and mosques [Babès, 1997:132]; but their leaders are growing progressively more aware of the importance of such participation [Bourg, 1998:78]. Since November 1999, the Minister of the Interior and the national federations, regional mosques and various Muslim personalities have been engaged in a vast consultation in order to take stock of the overall situation [FR File]. This is supposed to conclude with the "ratification, by all Muslim groups, of a solemn declaration entitled, 'Fundamental juridical principles governing the relationship between the Muslim religion and public authorities', the opening of a search for solutions to practical problems of the organisation of the religion, and the creation of a federative organisation of national scope" [Frégosi, 2000a]. However, few things seem to have changed in the years since, when it was noted that "negotiations between public authorities and Muslim communities concentrate on organisation without providing for eventual mechanisms of support" [Messner, 1996].[5]

In **Sweden**, the state and the Lutheran church were separated in January 2000 [SE File] in favour of a policy of equality of religions. Efforts to organise Muslim communities had begun in 1974, with the establishment of the *Förenade Islamiska Församlingar i Sverige* (FIFS), which contained Shiites and Sunnis of different ethnic background, though not Ahmadis. In 1982, frictions within FIFS over economic matters led to the creation of the *Sveriges Förenade Muslimska Församlingar* (SMUF). The members of that group were mostly Arabic-speaking Sunni Muslims, so another schism led to the creation of the *Islamiska Kulturcenterunionen* (IKUS) in 1990. That was essentially made up of Süleymanci Turks and Somalis. Even if the FIFS and the SMUF now cooperate on a *Sveriges Muslimska Råd* (SMR), there is no unique representative federation because the three organisations are divided as to national origin. Despite this state of affairs, an effective recognition of Islam has been obtained, which is accompanied by subsidies for religious communities from a National Commission for subsidies to religious communities (Samarbetsnämnden för statsbidrag till trossamfund, SST). This commission divides up the subsidies for religious communities in proportion to their numbers. These subsidies often cover the cost of renting space, and supplements are available for special activities such as visits to prisons, women's groups, or adult education. There is also an ongoing dialogue with government representatives, including two official meetings per year [Nielsen, 1996:58]. At present only the three organisations

---

[5] Due to the strong impulse of the Minister of Interior, who fixed a previous (criticised) agreement with some national federations, some elections were organised in order to nominate the administrative council of the *Conseil Français de Culte Musulman* (CFCM) and of the regional councils. This is now organised since the 13th of April 2003.

mentioned above are recognized as valid intermediaries representing Muslim communities. This situation is supported by all three, and is all the more entrenched. It is probably true that other organisations are too new to flex their muscles, but one day the cultural centres will be heard from. They are in effect the best organized structures, especially the centres of the Süleymancis and the Milli Görüs: their leaders often act as spokespersons for the Muslim community in media debates, and maintain good contacts with the Swedish authorities [Svanberg, 1995].

The situation in **Finland** is quite unique [FI File]. Islam has had official status since 1925, but the question of representation only arises in the context of a decentralisation which is more or less assumed. The signatures of twelve persons suffice for an official request for recognition, and a few communities have obtained official status. At the beginning of the 1990s, only three had done so: an Islamic congregation of Tartars in Helsinki, one in Tampere, and a community of immigrant Muslims. At present, 14 Islamic communities have been recognised, mostly in Helsinki and in the south of Finland, but most of them are very small, and some may have ceased to exist. As for the formation of an organisation of national scope, no Muslim has shown an interest.

Nascent processes

In other countries the process of formation of organisations of wider scope is perhaps underway, but has not reached its destination in a real dialogue with the state. So it is in **Denmark**, where Islam is not recognised by the state, and Muslims associate quite freely. Previous unsuccessful attempts may yet succeed. At the end of 2000, a meeting was to be held by a certain number of Muslims, to decide about establishing an organisation which would represent Muslims in relations with the Danish state [DK File].

The **Netherlands** is the model for government accessibility for all religions; religious communities may organise under private law, and establish their own by-laws. As for financing, besides a series of tax exemptions, public support is sometimes available "as assistance toward an effective realization of the principle of equality in religious matters, and for Muslim communities, which are at present disadvantaged" [Messner, 1996:197]. As concerns representation, though efforts have been made since the 1980s [Sunier, 1998:47], and though Dutch authorities would like to have a Muslim liaison organisation to deal with, there have still been no formal consultations with the government, and no organisation has been created [Sunier & Meyer, 1997]. Several organisations are disputing the right to speak for Sunni Muslims [Landman, 1998:16], hopeful of obtaining official status and state subsidies for television time and the nomination of imams for hospitals and prisons. In 1991 the *Islamitische Raad Nederland* (IRN), an umbrella group for three large federations of mosques (including those connected to Turkish or Moroccan authorities), was created, as well as a *Nederlandse Moslimraad* (NMR), which contains small organisations of various tendencies. In 1997, hoping to settle the differences between the two councils, the *Raad voor Moskeën* entered into cooperation with the Diyanet. But instead of replacing the first two organisations, it simply added a third party, all while a small group of quite active Muslims established a fourth council with a name quite similar to the others, the *Nederlandse Islamitische Raad* (NIR) [Fiche NL]. There is also an interest group for imams, the *Vereniging Imams Nederland* [Landman, 1998:16–17]. Among these conflicts of interest, we should remember that the people who sit on these councils have usually no particular relevant experience, but are simply delegates from affiliated organisations. It remains true that the leading political parties have accepted the notion of equality between religions, and so the question of a representative body is considered as relatively insignificant.

In **Poland** the Muslim community is officially recognised, but Muslims do not wish to constitute a single representative entity, and are practically invisible on the national political stage. Only the Union of Tartars of the Republic of Poland (*Zwiazek Tatarow*) has appeared since 1992 [PL File]. Its programme, fairly extensive, consists in "commemorating and continuing the history of Tartar and Muslim ancestors who were established in the Republic six centuries ago" [Warminska cited by Szajkowski, 1997:97]. This union does not hold consultations with the state, but at the local level in Tartar neighbourhoods, they attempt to help people get their political rights [PL File]. Other associations exist, but there is hardly anything to distinguish the Muslim Religious Union of the Republic of Poland (*Muzulmanski Zwiazek Religijny*) from the Union of Muslim Students, or the Muslim Brotherhood Society [PL File].

None of the **Swiss cantons** [CH File] have publicly recognised Islam as an association under public law, though Muslims have asked for such recognition in several. Nonetheless some cooperation does seem to be in the process of becoming the rule, such as access to imams in hospitals, prisons, and refugee reception centres, and in matters of burial. In fact there has been no attempt to form a federation of Muslims of national scope. Groups of Arabic-speaking intellectuals, despite their not being quite representative, are treated as spokespersons for Islam, especially by the media [Mutlu & Tschannen, 1995]. By contrast, at cantonal level, federations connected to the Turkish community exist, such as the *Vereinigung der Islamischen Organisationen*, which has had a relationship with the Mayor of Zurich since 1996, or the *Basler Muslim Kommission* which groups 18 Islamic associations [Tangram, n° 7, 1999]. About 150 associations have united in an umbrella organisation called the *Coordination des Associations Turques de Suisse*, which is supposed to represent only the Turkish community of Switzerland in negotiations concerning immigration. It is still an organisation in the early stages of development.

In **Italy**, Islamic communities are not recognised; the social actors who are most important are just those who are involved in the effort to obtain representation for Islam before state institutions [Allievi, 2001]. The nature of this leadership seems not to have changed in the wake of the later arrival of immigrant workers, and it is still dominated by a certain elite group which arrived mostly from the Middle East in the 1970s [Allievi, 2001]. The most representative organisation is the *Unione delle Communitá e delle Organizazioni Islamiche in Italia* (UCOII). Founded in 1990 through the collaboration between the *Centro Islamico di Milano* and the network of the *Unione degli Studenti Musulmani in Italia* (USMI), it "attempts to consolidate a number of socio-religious realities, and to interact as much as possible with the media" [Allievi, 2001]. This group worked up the first 'intesa' project, involving a made-to-measure agreement proposed by the state in order to regularise the presence of Islam in Italy. Wishing to become the representative front of 'true' Islam, it is opposed to the official Islam of the Islamic Cultural Centre (*Centro Islamico Culturale d'Italia*), linked to the Muslim World League. The centre has operated since 1996, and does not conceal its ambition of representing Islam on political and organisational levels [Allievi, 2001]. In the meantime, it remains "the only Islamic religious institution which enjoys a juridical and moral personality" [Allievi, 1997:217]. Three small groups of converted Muslims are also present in this competitive situation: the *Comunitá Religiosa Islamica* (COREIS), which receives aid from Saudi Arabia; the *Associazione dei Musulmani Italiani* (AMI), and, even smaller, the *Unione dei Musulmani d'Italia*, which since its formation in 2001 has been trying to be heard [IT File]. In all, since the early 1990s [Allievi & Dassetto, 1993] and the signature of an agreement in Spain, which "certainly revived the question of institutionalisation of Islam in Italy" [Frégosi, 2000b:101], no fewer than three separate projects toward an agreement—*intesa*—have been proposed to public authorities in order to achieve a public recognition of Islam, which would offer economic and legal advantages. The terms of the competition are still not defined, and a solution is far off, despite one attempt at the creation of a federation (*Consiglio Islamico d'Italia*) led since 1999 by members of the Centro Islamico Culturale d'Italia and the UCOII [Allievi, 2001]. Discussions concerning the *intesa*, which constitutes "a bilateral agreement and not a state policy" [Allievi, 2001], have hardly begun, and the political climate seems rather hostile. As witness, the re-examination of the preliminary *intesa* signed with the Buddhists and the Jehovah's Witnesses, following the parliament's refusal to ratify the agreements signed by the government. These developments will probably not fail to influence future decisions to be taken with regard to Islam [IT File].

In **Luxembourg** [LU File], Islam is not recognised by the state, but the government received a request for official recognition in 1998. Actually, there were two requests, from two different organisations, namely, the *Centre Culturel Islamique du Grand-Duché de Luxembourg*, opened in 1984, and the association *Communauté musulmane du Grand-Duché de Luxembourg*, begun in 1994, with its headquarters at Wiltz. The first association claims to be politically neutral, and receives no foreign subsidies. Its founding members are Turkish, Pakistani, and Luxembourgeois, but its 300 active members have twenty-odd nationalities, including quite a few Bosnians. The second association defines itself as a religious community which is unique and independent, and which claims to represent all Muslims in Luxembourg, regardless of nationality, race, or language. Its founding members are almost all Bosnians, though, and they are distinguished by their desire to explain religious questions of various kinds and to administer the prescriptions of the Sharia as regards personal behaviour. Although these objectives were purged from their by-laws in 1998, they have made the government wary of recognising them. But the diversity of the Muslim community and such struggles for power are considered by some as holding back or preventing the emergence of a representative organisation which could serve as an official partner in negotiating a convention with government authorities.

In **Hungary** Islam is not recognised by the state, and no attempt has been made to form a representative body at the political level. The Hungarian Islamic Society is the most important organisation; it promotes Islamic culture and religion, but has no ambition to represent Muslims at the national level [HU File]. In **Portugal**,[6] it is not so much the political will lacking as a fear of attracting public attention. Despite satisfactory contacts between local and national authorities and some Ismailis, and also with some Sunni communities, especially as regards urgent questions, no demands have been made concerning their own interests. One form of exteriorisation was attempted, a fairly original one. In 1996, when the commission for the reform of the law on religious liberty (*Comissão de Reforma da Lei de Liberdade Religiosa*, CRLLR) invited religious associations to submit suggestions for changing the law. Portuguese Muslims and Jews allied to organise a coalition of non-Christian religions, and made several requests including observance of Muslim holy days, and formal acceptance of ritual slaughter, and observance of alimentary prescriptions in certain public places [PT File].

3. Concluding Remarks

The question of institutionalisation

Except in countries with long-standing Muslim communities, the recognition of Islam in relation to state structures goes back to the mid-1970s. This institutionalisation has now been realised in more than half of the countries involved, which have three kinds of juridical systems. Recognition has been granted in the countries which have the 'universal' system, "a universal character, accessible to all religions", including France, the Netherlands, and Sweden. Institutionalisation also occurs in countries that have established a 'system of recognition', like Belgium, Spain, Austria, Romania, Bulgaria, and Poland, and several countries that have a priori ties to a national

---

[6] In Portugal, Islam is not recognised by the state but we note that legislation is now under discussion with the goal of "placing all religions on equal footing" [Messner, 1999].

church. These countries have established, despite obstacles, special clauses recognising Islam—e.g., Finland and Greece (for Western Thrace).

As for those countries which have not moved to institutionalise Islam, they belong to the latter two regimes. On one hand, there are countries which have not yet applied existing procedures for recognition of Islam: Germany, Italy, Luxembourg, Switzerland, and Hungary. On another, there are countries in which a national church is dominant: Portugal, Great Britain and Denmark. In the first case, that non-recognition has to do with a relatively small Muslim population, with a recent growth of the community. In the case of Germany and Great Britain, however, we note the adoption of certain practical modes of de facto recognition of Islam, which make these regimes more flexible, despite the fact that a lack of official recognition of Islam means that the religion does not come under a standardised legal category.

In view of the powers which state authorities have, recognition depends on a unilateral political choice, possibly one which is pushed forward by Muslim communities themselves, as in Austria, Germany, and Great Britain. The motives of these actors vary widely. Most often, Muslim communities desire recognition because it may bring legal advantages, or considerable financial assistance, which also varies widely from country to country. As for the motivations of various states, they range from a disinterested willingness to provide for more equality between different religious groups and their members, to a desire simply to streamline or resolve certain external and/or internal questions.

The question of representation

The themes of institutionalisation and centralised representation of Islam are often associated and even identified. This is easy to do, since the importance given by some states to this supposedly useful additional demand, which is even presented as necessary to the real institutionalisation of the religion, often ends by derailing the debate on the institutionalisation of Islam or monopolising it. Polemics about the lack of a representative structure go even further. This idea rapidly stimulated interest, even involvement, but also imitation. It has spread to the majority of European states which, desiring to be seen as accepting their responsibilities toward a reality which is still sometimes quite new, want to have someone to negotiate with, an interlocutor who can adapt to the state's needs for mediation and conciliation. Sometimes it is expected that this procedure should also permit the systematic arrangement of effective management of a complex reality which is too often misunderstood.

This dynamic movement, which should preferably relate to the will of Muslim communities themselves, appears in most European countries, regardless of their legal system. It appears in varying degrees, but is most often present in the 'recognition' type of system, where it is regularly presupposed, and considered as an integral part of the procedure of institutionalisation. This is the case in Bulgaria, Romania, and Greece (Western Thrace), but also in Belgium, Spain, and Austria. In places where the recognition type system is in place and where Islam has been officially recognised, state authorities have helped the process along. What is more, they have usually intervened to a fairly great extent, except perhaps in Austria. In contrast, in countries which have the recognition-type system but have not recognised Islam, and under the two other legal system types, the attitudes of states and their level of participation in the process are more diverse. They may show active stimulation (France), passive encouragement (Germany, the Netherlands), or some lack of interest (Italy, Finland, Sweden, Luxembourg, Switzerland, Hungary).

Furthermore, whatever the attitudes of states or the possibility of such a centralising organisational conception becoming valid for Muslim communities (an unconscious inspiration caused by the hierarchical Roman Catholic model, or by supposedly positive experiments in Balkan or Eastern European countries), it is no less true that this is resented by some Muslim communities as requiring jumping through hoops. The interest shown by these communities in the question of representation has in fact grown greatly over the last twenty years. In some countries, it has soon appeared as a good way of getting rid of a lack of legitimacy, and as giving due credit to certain pretensions, in cases where it has not actually been made a condition for the official recognition of Islam, or the advantages which eventually accompany that power. More and more regularly, this question has been taken up by Muslim communities themselves, especially in Luxembourg, Switzerland, and Italy. But it is above all in the countries that do not formally recognise Islam, though the Muslim communities there are quite old and relatively important, that the phenomenon takes on its most important form, as in Germany and Great Britain. In this progressive self-organisation of Muslims, communities form different kinds of groups and try to increase their symbolic clout by mobilising associations which represent the widest possible ethnic and ideological spectrum. Sometimes it even happens that the theme of diversity in the Muslim community is invoked in order to demonstrate the democratic nature of the organisation itself.

But the road of consensus is a winding one. Once begun, the process of creating such a structure is far from easy, even with possible aid from the state as in France. Not only do Muslims not control the principles of creation and legitimation of authority and power, but the groups are from very different ethno-national, intellectual, ideological and social strata. Functional considerations also come into play. This produces defensive reflexes in the face of external interference, and/or a struggle for leadership between different groups for fear that a rival movement may obtain greater privileges [Waardenburg, 1991:33]. Still, beyond these divergences of opinion and contextual difficulties, the notion of a common good progresses, and thanks to this heightened awareness the gaps between the camps are narrowing.

Representative character

It has been mentioned that the governments of Eastern Europe and the systems of the recognition type appear often as the most advanced on the institutional level. The existence of recognition procedures appears to provide the most favourable environment for the institutionalisation of Islam, even if the 'most equitable' system appears a priori to be that in which "all religions must basically be treated on a basis of equality, and benefit from the same conditions of freedom of worship and support" [Frégosi, 2000b:97].

Some remarks and/or criticisms should nonetheless be formulated regarding systems of recognition, in order to make certain contrasts appear more easily.

Let us take first the case of Bulgaria, Romania, and Greece, where traditional religious institutions have been in place for centuries. Despite their longevity, they are at present very weak. This is partly for internal reasons, since they were turned into instruments of the policies of the communist era, especially as concerns procedures of nomination. That interference by the state has not only persisted, but in some cases, it has functioned again as a political tool. Muslim religious hierarchies have sometimes been supported against dissident factions in exchange for their low-key support of the most moderate Muslim political leaders [Bougarel & Clayer, 2001:43]. Such interference by the Bulgarian and Greek states was recently condemned by the European Court of Human Rights. It still happens that circumstances from outside weigh in to challenge the authority of religious institutions. Since the end of the communist era, the religious monopoly has been contested by ideological movements from outside the region, especially those which brandish variant interpretations of religious texts. We should also mention an increasing complexity of the relations between religion and ethnic self-identification, which pushes Muslim communities to consider themselves more as ethnic communities with a common culture. Elsewhere, since "political actors always win out over religious actors" [Bougarel & Clayer, 2001:43 ff.], it is necessary to complete the observation by noting that acceptance of and response to demands from Muslim minorities occur today in the course of dealings with more overtly political organisations, and these demands are therefore handled not on the basis of faith but of ethnicity. In this welter of regional circumstances, it can be affirmed that the power of representative religious authority is in decline, though it remains at the centre of many debates (symbolic and political at once), and these authorities still benefit from a great deal of support, including money, from states.

As for the countries of Western Europe who find themselves directly concerned by the question of single representation (Spain, Belgium, Austria, but also France), other types of considerations must be mentioned as regards the actual representative nature of certain authorities. On the face of it, the single representative organisation should simply be made up of a cross-section of organisations adhering to various religious forms and of diverse ethnic and national membership, in proportion to the composition of the communities. And yet it rarely seems to have this quality. One may note an elitist tint to these structures. One tendency is everywhere present: people who are educated and/or moved to act by specific ideological convictions try to position themselves in the debate on the institutionalisation of Islam, and especially as regards the question of single representation. Relative to state authorities, they try to monopolise the symbolic power of representation of Muslim communities, without really having any social constituency. This is the case in Spain and also in Italy, even if the process has stalled. As for Switzerland, its case shows how much local community representation is sometimes neglected in favour of a few charismatic personalities. Tareq Ramadan, an Egyptian, is often taken for a spokesperson by the media, though the Muslim community is majority Turkish. And in the event of a rare state intervention in the process of establishing such a body, beyond the establishment of some guarantees of democratic principle (especially as concerns representation of women), sometimes the elitist and/or non-representative side comes out stronger, somehow. This happened after the establishment of criteria as regards those eligible to serve within the representative body, including the requirement of a certain level of education. These were imposed in Belgium and Austria for the members of representative assemblies for Muslim communities. On another hand, sometimes different ideological tendencies in Muslim communities, likely to give rise to tensions or real antagonisms, end up not being taken into consideration in the formation of the representative body. It is a rare policy that is at first really conscious of that important diversity. And at times, in order to accelerate or facilitate the process, this pluralism is voluntarily sacrificed in favour of other criteria more easily measured, such as ethnicity or seniority, or some privilege given to a community because it was founded in the society long, long ago. This observation does not apply to the Austrian and French situations, where different ideological tendencies are formally considered, even if it is quite probable that moderate tendencies have some advantage. As for other countries, it is a safe bet that the dominant ideological background is always present informally, unless a splinter group succeeds in monopolising the representative body, profiting from its symbolic prestige to reinforce its own strength in the community.

In general, the diversity of Muslim communities owing to multiple ethno-national origins or various ideological tendencies is too often treated as a problem, as has happened in Germany, France, Luxembourg, and Belgium, even if this is not openly admitted. Islamic heterogeneity is sometimes used by political parties as a 'pseudoscientific argument' in order to "justify a particular attitude toward Islam by the public authorities" different from that adopted toward other religions (as in Germany) or, "in contrast, to win social legitimation for certain forced initiatives toward organisation from on high" as in France, with the establishment of CORIF [Frégosi, 2000b:111], or in Belgium.

The establishment of such single representative structures some-times causes an indirect form of bureaucratisation of Islam. When its sociological and organisational particularities are not really taken into account, certain authors affirm, the emphasis on the formation of a single body may slow down or even prevent any authentic recog-nition of Islam in principle, which is the true object of all these efforts [Frégosi, 2000b; Panafit, 1999].

Beyond any good intentions expressed or real steps taken, the emphasis placed on single representation allows questions about this religion to be avoided, which despite appearances to the contrary, may be quite a bit more 'modern' than it appears. And we are not counting the dangerous confusions which some also have fostered, insidiously, concerning the relations between the political and reli-gious aspects of the matter. The form of a single entity is debated in many places, but questions about the status this entity will acquire are not pursued, and thus misunderstandings in this regard persist, especially in Western Europe. There are still too many hesitations about whether it is a question of installing a hierarchical authority, a spiritual authority, or just a management structure for the busi-ness side of the religion. Misunderstandings of this type still exist in Belgium.

New advances

The idea of representation for Muslims in relation to states based on the formation of a single entity is not now accepted as a matter of course, either by the diverse Muslim communities, or by European societies or their politicians. This observation is valid for countries which have a tradition of religious plurality, well-structured laws regarding religion, or active and effective religious policy. But it may go further.

There are first of all situations in which the official recognition of Islam has been established without any thought of forming a single representative body, as in Poland, and even more in Sweden and Finland. As for Denmark, we note that though Islam is not recog-nised, the communities are quite freely organised without a central body. Elsewhere, the absence of such a body has not systematically blocked all other initiatives. For example, take the fact that instruc-tion in Islamic religion in Belgium has been organised since 1975, and that in Germany it is understood that the *Staatskirchenrecht*, applied 'flexibly and openly', allows "a framework to be given to all religions" [Messner, 1996].

The tide of opinion is swinging toward a questioning of the representative character of single bodies, and of the legitimacy of imposing, even indirectly, such a form. It is a question of whether the state has exceeded its powers when it meddles in this domain, as when Belgian authorities tried to determine "a proper Islamic orthodoxy, supported by certain Muslims, in so doing intervening directly in the definition of the Muslim religion, in a manner contrary to Constitutional principles" [Panafit, 1999]. As for the Balkans, one should not forget the possible impact of the decisions of the European Court of Human Rights that condemned the Greek and Bulgarian states for their interference in the internal management of Muslim communities. These decisions reopen the question of the usual conceptions of relations between the state and Islamic religious institutions [Bougarel & Clayer, 2001:75].

Sometimes, finally, other solutions to the problem of representation have begun to come into view since "a more pragmatic approach recentered on local affairs, favouring contact with more modest structures which still enjoy real local credibility, having earned respect at grass roots level" began to be employed [Frégosi, 2000b]. In Sweden, in the Netherlands, and in Finland, state authorities want to be able to designate interlocutors, but stay away from attempts to form organisations intended to be central authorities. They favour equality of religions, and they have been able to come up with diverse procedures for recognition, relatively flexible, suited to limited bodies. They have also instituted practical methods of granting aid to Islamic communities, including financial aid. A certain decentralisation is expected there, and this seems appropriate for Islam.

Such decentralised organisation will not fail to generate interest from the many Muslim communities present in Europe, often in search of solutions in order to arrive at some form of institutional autonomy. Even if a degree of state support from supranational agencies is not to be rejected out of hand, it remains probable that the Muslim communities will prove more and more independent in their relations with state agencies in European societies.

CHAPTER FIVE

MUSLIMS AND POLITICS

Stefano Allievi

1. THE POLITICAL SUPPLY AND DEMAND

Muslim minorities in Europe have faced the difficult problem of their relationship with the political dimension of their presence in highly different ways: depending on the country where they have settled, their country of origin and its situation, the relationship between their country of settlement and the country of origin (for example, whether it is a former colony or not), the period when they emigrated as well as on other factors such as the gender component, the prevailing age groups, and the conditions of urban settlement (concentrated or spread throughout the territory).

From some points of view, the development of the political dimension and, above all how this has been revealed, has been in response to an interrogation by the society of arrival and its demands; from others, it has been a process of independent and intrinsic development, in parallel with the social processes under way. In each case, a role has been played by both of these dimensions.

What we can call the 'demand effect' which apparently may seem less immediate and obvious, has been clearly visible in situations of confrontation or even conflict which have produced requests by the countries of immigration for 'explanations' on some fundamental problems: for example, questions of international politics such as the bombing of Libya, the Rushdie affair, the Gulf War and also, in some ways, the Palestinian, Algerian and Afghan questions and there are others. But this effect has also been created in the wake of domestic issues, differing according to the countries: for example the impact of the question of the *hijab* in French schools (and more in general, issues on the condition of women: mixed marriages, circumcision and infibulation, girls not attending school, etc.), episodes of racism and xenophobia directed towards the Muslim minorities in various countries, situations of urban violence involving immigrants, the building of mosques or a strong request for recognition and institutionalisation by the Muslim communities.

However, this 'demand effect' has also taken on even more substantial forms of organisation within a given political-institutional system, according to the forms it has taken on in each country, that is, according to the structures of political opportunity and the possibilities of institutional insertion present at a given time in a given territory, in turn dependent on the mechanisms of exclusion or inclusion implemented by the state or by the political system with respect to the minorities present there [Martiniello, 1998b]. Whether minorities are perceived as ethnic or religious, or only as 'social minorities' is also anything but secondary.

We will see below (in some of the forthcoming chapters) how the institutional system more as a whole, in particular at juridical level and specifically with regard to the ways in which religions are handled, has a decisive importance, including on political questions. However, we will begin with the most classic manifestation of political will in Western democracies: the vote.

2. VOTING

The question of the right to vote is one of the main aspects of political mobilisation, as well as the main 'sign' of the full enjoyment of political rights: this question, which is still open and has been solved in different ways in different countries but is the subject of discussion in others, requires immediate analysis due to its importance which is also of a symbolic nature.

The problem is obviously not posed for those who have acquired the citizenship of any European country: in virtue of this act, full political rights are automatically acquired, in the first place, the right to vote and to be elected, including in general political elections. In this case, it is a question at the most of seeing if and how new citizens make use of this right and if they do so in a different way from that adopted by those who have been nationals of the country since birth.

Immigrants from another member state of the Union (or from a third country, but who have acquired the citizenship of a European country other than that of residence) are not allowed to vote in political elections but, in virtue of the European citizenship introduced into the Treaty of Maastricht and confirmed in that of Amsterdam, today their right to vote and be elected in local and European elections is guaranteed: even those countries which showed some resistance in complying with these regulations have now adapted to the new rules, although with some delay. On the other hand, if an immigrant does not have the citizenship of the country of residence or of another European country, which is the most frequent case amongst Muslims, a fairly diversified range of possibilities opens up, depending on the country of residence.

Five member states of the European Union have for the time being granted the right to vote and to be elected in local elections, after a certain period of continuous residence in the country: they are Ireland, where this has been the case since 1963, Sweden (since 1975, where they can also vote in regional and religious elections, and in referendums), the Netherlands (1985), Denmark and Finland (both since 1991). Seven countries have not granted this right (Austria, Belgium, France, Germany, Greece, Italy and Luxembourg), although there are proposals in this direction in some of them. The other countries are in a situation that is, in a certain sense, intermediary: in the UK immigrants from Commonwealth countries, considered British subjects and not foreigners, acquire the right to vote, including in political elections once they are resident in the country; in Spain and Portugal foreigners can vote and be elected in local elections if they come from countries with which there is a situation of reciprocity at the same level [Martiniello, 1998a].

In some of the countries where this right exists, the experience is nevertheless recent and as yet little research has been carried out. It is also difficult at times to analyse this situation through official sources, in view of the fact that statistics may fail to record national or ethnic origins, let alone religious affiliation. The most remarkable exception to this is represented by Great Britain, where research has been done, focusing on the 'ethnic' aspect of the vote, and the Netherlands.

We can recall that, according to a definition acquired in political disciplines [quoted in Tillie, 1998], a vote 'characterised' and guided by ethnic, religious, social or other cleavages, presupposes a number of pre-conditions: the existence of a recognisable and recognised separation, in the first place; the fact that at least some of those belonging to a given specific group are aware of this difference and

act accordingly; that there is an organisational activation, namely
the difference and the specificity are expressed in organisational terms
and, in particular, for the purposes of voting, through the representation of a specific political grouping.

These conditions are not necessarily expressed univocally. Immigrants
can at times express themselves through specific representations in
order to achieve a specific objective with an ethnic or religious objective (as Turks, for example, or referring to a supranational identity,
as Arabs or as Muslims) or by acting through bodies that associate
them with other specific groups against the same objective (as an
immigrant, for example, regardless of ethnic origin and religious
affiliation, against exclusion, discrimination and racism); but they can
also take organised action in order to achieve an objective that asso-
ciates them with natives (as workers, for example) and lastly, simply, they may take action as residents and vote according to criteria
common to all other residents, whether nationals or not, natives or
non-natives, according to local interests or diversified ideological sym-
pathies and affiliations.

In the study on the electoral behaviour of Asian minorities in the
United Kingdom, the main ones in the country (over 1.5 million
people, about 2/3 of the minority electorate), we are far from being
able to demonstrate that *ethnicity counts*, and above all counts more
than anything else [Saggar, 1998]. Nor is there any proof of the
hypothesis that the political engagement of ethnic minorities passes
necessarily and as a priority through the manifestations of their own
ethnicity. This is also true when there has been a high turn-out in
elections: according to statistics of the BES (*British Elections Study*) on
1997, for example, some Asian groups (in particular the Indians, the
largest group) showed rates of inclusion in the election registers and
participation in the vote that were even higher than the white population (respectively 93.8 against 91.8, and 82.4 against 78.7%)
[Saggar, 1998]. Incidentally, at the same elections there were about
twenty constituencies where Pakistanis and Bangladeshis alone represented at least 8% of the electorate, a percentage that is largely
sufficient to determine the attribution of a seat in a constituency voting system such as the British one [Runnymede Trust, 1977].

In addition, voting does not necessarily mean voting for one's own
candidates, and even less so within one's own parties: indeed, many
immigrants and members of ethnic and religious minorities have preferred to vote for natives in 'traditional' parties who have greater

possibilities of access to the levers of power and therefore to the allocation of resources. Moreover, having one's own elected members does not always and not necessarily mean seeing a more effective representation of one's interests as a 'minority' population: differences and opportunities must always be assessed on a case by case basis.

In the last place, attention must be drawn to the importance of a variable which is not due either to the political will or engagement of immigrant populations and which can favour or, on the contrary, discourage them from voting. We are referring to the electoral system in any given country. The following example shows that it is not neutral in its consequences: in France, where the majority of immigrants, including the Muslims, are nationals of the country, and can therefore fully participate in the political process, in 1989, with the proportional system, two candidates of Algerian descent were elected to the European Parliament, one in the Socialist Party and one for the Greens. In 1993, with a majority system, none of the main parties, with the exception of the ecologists, supported candidates belonging to these minorities [Hargreaves & Wihtol de Wenden, 1993].

3. IMMIGRANTS, ETHNIC MINORITIES OR MUSLIMS?

There are many variables at play and the religious one is not the only one nor, probably, the main one. Even where we are in the presence of a collective vote which can be 'measured' to some extent, expressed in communities that are also concentrated from the point of view of urban settlement and 'visible' as such, as in some situations in Great Britain, it is not easy to isolate the variables. In particular, an attempt can be made to define this electorate in religious or ethnic terms, or as immigrant populations. Let us examine these three different aspects.

If we refer to the electorate of these communities as Muslims, the religious variable must prevail: but the success of specific lists characterised in this way has been inconsistent to date and the degree of identification poor. The basic illusion of these parties is that of the very existence of homogeneous religious communities: it does not take into account the fact that many presumed Muslims are often not Muslims and if they are, they are Muslims in a highly diversified way. In addition, there is often only an instrumental use of the

Muslim reasoning by leaders, with the aim of achieving some visibility, thus producing an Islamisation of a debate which, up to now, has only tenuous religious characteristics and which is often short-lived.

The *Islamic Party* in **Great Britain**, for example, founded in 1989 by some British converts to Islam and Asian Muslims, which had candidates at the general election in 1992 in four constituencies with a strong Muslim presence, in order to capitalise on the mobilisation following the Rushdie affair, failed to obtain more than 1% of votes; and Kalim Siddiqi's *Muslim Parliament*, given great exposure by the media after the deliberately explosive declarations of its founder and which was also launched in the 'post Rushdie' period with a highly publicised *Muslim Manifesto*, was not any the more successful and seems to have disappeared from the scene since the death of its leader.

In Bradford, to quote the English 'citadel of Islam' par excellence, in those elections, the *Islamic Party*, out of some 16,000 Muslim voters, obtained a ludicrous score of 471 votes; and of the local members of the *Muslim Parliament*, none belonged to the elite or at least were members of any influence in the Muslim community [Lewis P., 1997].

In **France**, there was an ephemeral attempt to create a *Parti des Musulmans de France* (PMF) in Alsace for the legislative elections in 1997. This party directed its efforts especially at the *harki* electorate, but without this political investment having any significant effect [FR File].

In **Belgium** there is a tiny Muslim party, with its own Internet site, *Parti Noor*, founded in Brussels in February 1999. "Noor is not fighting the Flemish or the Wallons, but injustice and corruption", was its slogan. But at the legislative elections in June 1999, it only obtained 1244 votes (out of an estimated Belgian Muslim community of 400,000 members . . .!) [Lambert, 2000], and following this failure it did not take part in the municipal and provincial elections of October 1999, inviting the electorate to abstain. Its existence today is probably doubtful [BE File]. Even less well known is another Muslim party, the *Islamitische Partijvrij* which stood for the 1999 elections in three of the municipalities of Brussels (Schaerbeek, Saint-Gilles and Saint-Josse), and which has officially existed since 1991 but its lack of renown is eloquent [BE File].

In **Germany** the attempt, dating back to 1989, to organise a Muslim party (*Die Islamische Partei Deutschland*), has been abandoned, for reasons mainly due to the electoral system which penalises small lists: the hurdle of 5% did not allow any hope of obtaining any concrete result [DE File].

The situation in **Greece** and in **East European countries** is different, where existing parties are not described on a religious basis but rather on an ethnic basis, even if these are clearly superimposed. The existing parties do not usually have an explicit religious reference, even in their name, but describe themselves as parties of the ethnic group of reference (mainly Turkish or Tatar) and they are perceived as such: the linguistic and cultural difference here seems to be at a premium compared to the religious one. Moreover, the positions expressed are often moderate and far from the Islamist political rhetoric, with which they have nothing in common [GR, BG, RO Files].

Going back to the analysis on Western Europe, it is too early to deduce any trends from these single facts—the failed attempts by Muslim parties. In particular it would be hasty to deduce from them the impossibility of giving rise to political experiences on a religious basis in Europe. There are too many variables that may have played in the failure of these first experiments: ahead of time, organisational incapacity, lack of roots and non-representativeness by the leaderships and excessive personalism. However, it must be noted that the religious variable does not come into play alone: it is not mutually exclusive, but on the contrary it can be superimposed on others. The presence of Islam in politics may therefore appear in indirect forms: for example, it has been noted how some non-Muslim MPs who have been elected in constituencies with a large ethnic presence in the United Kingdom had their electoral offices in the local mosques. However, this method reflects more the system of notables and favouritism on a traditional community basis than 'modern' forms of a presence in politics that Islamism often expresses.

If we refer to these electors as Pakistanis or Bangladeshis, as Algerians or Turks rather than as Muslims, it is obviously the ethnic-national origin that prevails, reinforced by the fact of coming, in some cases, from identifiable and relatively small regions and areas, such as to allow links of family, clan and notables connected to the countries of origin and to the relations of caste and local 'patronage' to come into play, giving rise to forms of 'ethnic—or tribal—favouritism' which have contributed in not a minor way to the deprivation of legitimacy of the ethnic vote. The fact remains that the parties which have taken advantage of this have contributed to reinforcing it, using the ethnic leadership and the community inter-mediaries as mediators to attract this type of 'community' vote ["they put an Abdallah or a Mohamed on the lists and then they say they are against communitarianism"; Tareq Ramadan, personal interview, May 2000]. Moreover, the community vote is often such only pre-sumably, to the extent that in relation to the role of the North African elites in the case of France, it has been possible to talk of 'projective communitarianism' [Geisser, 1997], to the advantage of the universalist parties. In the first place, the community of refer-ence is also presumed.

Probably however, the first Muslim MP elected in Great Britain, the businessman Muhammad Sarwar, elected in the constituency of Glasgow Govan, for the *Labour Party*, owes more to the ethnic vote than to the religious one, and to the type of ethnic vote just men-tioned, in particular, to the extent that his election, object of great controversy moreover (the MP was first suspended, following an accu-sation of electoral fraud and then reinstated to his seat once the accusations were dismissed), was accompanied by harsh discussion which also continued after the election. Moreover, the Muslims of Great Britain point out that if the level of representation were to be proportional to the (theoretical) numerical weight, there should be about twenty Muslim representatives in the Houses of Parliament.

We can however also refer to these electors, with a more general and wider category, as *Asians*, who, as such, according to some, express a common system of values, for Muslims, Hindus and Sikhs, and for Pakistanis, Bangladeshis and Indians, which would play a larger part than religion and even ethnic and national origin: some have attempted to identify it with specific conceptions, which for the sake of brevity we can define 'traditional', of the family, of the role of religion in social life, of the work ethic, of some community val-ues, and so on. The existence of these shared values is nevertheless difficult to identify and the relative observations take them as ascer-tained too easily. The fact remains that their translation into local politics continues to be problematic: it is no coincidence that the Conservative political class has maintained that these values are the same as its own [Saggar, 1998], which did not stop the majority of the votes of these sectors continuing to be for the Labour Party (about 4/5), and it has been so with remarkable continuity, even regardless of the national trend of the vote and its oscillations between Labour and Conservative, and even before *New Labour* brandished family values and a new civil morality as its own flag.

Lastly, we could refer to this electorate simply as immigrants, with common values to defend and above all with common interests to guarantee. The few electoral experiments in this direction have shown, however, the scarce political attraction of movements characterized in this way. For example *Merci*, the European movement for the recognition of citizens of immigrant origin, which stood in Belgium in the 1994 elections, obtained only 0.8% of votes, whilst in the same year 14 candidates of foreign origin were elected for the first time in the traditional parties [Martiniello, 1998b]. *Merci* did not survive its electoral fiasco. Experiments of the same kind promoted during the regional elections of 1999 were no more successful: *Mars* and *Gauche Plurielle* both gained less than 0.1% of votes [Lambert, 2000]. However, it is probable that considerations based on belonging to a disadvantaged group, such as that of immigrants, weigh, more than in the 'vote for', in the 'vote against', making problematic the support for parties that champion anti-immigrant policies and/or policies of 'white' superiority, as many conservative parties do; this is even truer for organisations and parties of the extreme right-wing, explicitly xenophobic and racist. However, these parties, both moderate and conservative and even if extremist and openly xenophobic, do not renounce presenting their candidates of immigrant origin, often only as tokens and without any real chance of victory: there have been examples in Le Pen's National Front [FR File], which in the regional elections of 1998 in the Ile-de-France even supported a candidate of North African origin from the anti-racist movement *France-Plus*, and in the Flemish *Vlaams Blok* and even in the *Alleanza Nazionale* in Italy, where there is no immigrant vote either at national or local level, as the immigrants do not have the right to vote and naturalised citizens represent an inconsistent and therefore politically unusable figure. More recently we have seen elected MPs in the party created by Pim Fortuyn, in the Netherlands, in the occasion of the political elections in May 2002.

4. PARTICIPATION AT LOCAL LEVEL

The examples of participation at local level are highly diversified.

In **the Netherlands**, after a period of experimentation in the consultative councils of immigrants, the municipal vote in elections was introduced for the first time in 1986. The rate of voting by immigrants was lower than that of the natives (48% against 61%).

All the main parties had immigrant candidates in their lists. The preferences of the immigrants, amongst whom those of Muslim origin cannot be distinguished, went mainly to the Social Democratic party (PVDA). The Christian Democrats (CDA), although having invested more than others in terms of having immigrant representatives in their lists, were not rewarded by votes. It is interesting to note that in the following elections, in 1990, there was a drop in the turn-out at the vote, the reason for which should be analysed: not excluding the simple weight of the factor of the novelty in the previous elections, and without wishing to deduce too much from possible dissatisfaction with the malfunctioning of the system or the pointlessness of voting, for example. Overall, however, about fifty municipal councillors were elected belonging to the minorities (but out of about 10,000), and one Member of Parliament (out of 150 in the Lower Chamber).

In more recent elections, a vote has been expressed that can be defined as ethnic, or perhaps more properly, national: in Utrecht, at the municipal elections of 1998, 59% of the Turks voted for *Isçi*, a 'Turkish' party, the leader of which (called Isçi) created his own party after a failed attempt to stand in the Christian Democrat list [Tillie, 1998]. However, local factors may come into play in this case: in the Hague, only 16% of the Turks voted for the Turkish party *Demir*, whilst 13% of the Turks voted for a Turkish candidate in a party of immigrants ('M '98', or Multicultural Party '98), and the others made different choices in the traditional parties (with preferences, at the national level, in order, for the Labour Party, PVDA, for the Christian Democrat Party, CDA, and for the Greens of GroenLinks). Elsewhere, there were no groupings present that could be distinguished as 'Turkish'.

There are also differences between the various immigrant communities, although all Muslims: for example, the great majority of Turks have opted for voting for an ethnic candidate, whichever the party of reference (83%), whilst only 47% of the Moroccans did the same, voting with a similar percentage for a Dutch candidate (42%), and lastly the Surinamese expressed themselves for the two options with identical percentages (47% in both cases) [Tillie, 1998]. It must also be specified that it is not automatic and, in any case, would have to be proven, that although the majority of Turks are Muslims, the expression of the ethnic (or national) vote is also based essentially on a factor and mobilisation of the religious type.

In **Belgium** the first candidates from Muslim countries were elected for the first time in the municipal elections of 1988, in Flanders. Some non-Europeans were elected for the first time in Brussels in the 1994 elections. In the 2000 elections, there was a real 'explosion' of the immigrant vote, which has made Brussels an advanced case compared to the rest of Europe. Ninety-one people (including 23 women) from Muslim countries were elected in the region, out of a total of 650: even in a percentage greater than that of the immigrants (13% and 10% respectively), to a great extent elected in the lists of the Socialist party (35) and Greens (32), mainly of North African origin, especially Moroccan, and only 9 Turks, mainly elected in the Liberal list (5) [BE File]. There were also at least 13 candidates elected from the Arab world and 8 of Turkish origin in French-speaking Belgium and in Flanders.

In **Great Britain**, the case of Bradford [Lewis P., 1994], is of particular interest. In 1992 it had 12 Asian councillors, 11 of whom were Muslims and 1 Sikh. But they never succeeded in electing, as they had hoped, the first Muslim MP in the history of Great Britain: in that safe constituency, Labour preferred seeing a Sikh elected. However, the internal struggles between local Muslims played a role, as did the factor of the caste of origin which was not the least in importance [Lewis P., 1997]: this factor is more properly ethnic or of the clan than religious.

In Great Britain, there are a total of about 150 Muslim municipal councillors [Anwar, 1999]: 13 in Birmingham and in Tower Hamlets, 10 in Bradford, 7 in Waltham Forest (where the first woman Muslim mayor was elected in a European city in 1996; Vertovec & Peach, 1997), 5 in Sheffield, etc. [Runnymede Trust, 1997] with the majority for the Labour Party.

It is interesting to point out a rather unexpected local variant in Birmingham: a strictly ethnic and political Kashmiri list was created, on the basis of a campaign to free young Pakistanis who, about twenty years ago, when they were just over 18, had killed an Indian diplomat in London, in relation to the question of Kashmir. The list was formed to protest against a presumed ethnic-political injustice: the prisoners would normally be released from prison after about fifteen years, on the condition of good conduct, but in their case, the sentence was stiffened during the period of detention. This *single issue* list, inspired by a factor of international politics linked to the country of origin, nevertheless succeeded, in local elections, to obtain first two councillors and then a third one at a by-election; this shows that it had not been a flash in the pan [Birmingham, personal interviews, May 2000]. The case is in itself unique in Great Britain, and elsewhere as well: but its most surprising characteristic is that this very strong interest for the country of origin (even if in reality putative: the votes for this list could be a simple protest vote relative to the conditions *here*) is manifested through a list organised and supported to a great extent by young people of the second generation, most of whom were born in Great Britain.

The complexity of the factors at play leads to a more complex reflection on the weight of the individual factors: which counts for more, the ethnic group, the country of origin, the religion or the social class and the living conditions? The answer cannot be unequivocal. Any generalisation is nevertheless suspicious, whether it refers to the 'Asian' vote or to the more than 150 'Muslim' councillors. But above all, the other factors at play cannot be forgotten. Even restricting ourselves to the ethnic vote, for example, an internal confrontation between the mobilisation on a religious basis of the Muslim Asians in Great Britain (above all Pakistanis and Bangladeshis), compared to that of Hindus and Sikhs (Indians), who on average enjoy a significantly superior level of insertion and per capital income, could in part, relativise the fact that it is a question purely of the right to cultural difference [Statham, 1999]. The comparison should however be widened to include the autochthonous populations with comparable standards of living and, where applicable, of exclusion.

Lastly, to quote a completely different case, in **Italy**, where the immigrants do not have the right of vote, for the first time there was an attempt to play the card of Muslim presence at a local level in the municipal elections of 2001. On that occasion the Left-Wing Democrats presented in their lists the spokesman of the very active *Centro Islamico di Milano*, a well-known convert in Muslim circles, but without obtaining any electoral success [IT File].

5. SOME CONSIDERATIONS ON ELECTED CANDIDATES

A different aspect of the analysis of the ethnic vote and of the possible expression of a religious vote, lies in the analysis of the elected candidates of immigrant origin. There are few cases and consequently few studies, also in view of how recent the phenomenon is. However, some conclusions can be reported.

On the one hand and in the first place, the fact of standing as a candidate presupposes a strategy and a desire for political integration in the society of insertion, even if this aspect, usually taken for granted, should be analysed and ascertained. On the other hand, it can be hypothesised that the fact of qualifying oneself with respect to the specificity of origin presupposes a 'use' of this and so, in a certain way, its restatement: in this way the (real, presumed and/or possible constructed) collective diversity acts as a starting point for a strategy of integration—a strategy that can be a group one but mostly appears as individual.

A survey of 29 candidates in Amsterdam in the municipal and district elections between 1990 and 1994 [Cadat & Fennema, 1998], as well as showing a preference, which can also be found elsewhere, for left-wing parties, allowed reconstructing a typical candidate whose characteristics include being between 40 and 45 years of age, having emigrated in the early 1970s at about 25 and that about ten years passed between arrival in the country and the start of political activity. Little attention seems to be shown to the religious factor: however, and this is valid as a general consideration, in some cases this under-representation can also be the effect of the scarce interest shown in this aspect by researchers, who are more interested in the ethnic factor. We also wish to underline that this data is greatly influenced by a factor that is usually overlooked, which we could call the 'cohort effect' and which tends in itself to underestimate the current importance of the religious factor: in many countries of origin, since the early 1970s, there has been a significant process of change and today, for example, students, but more generally the social and political context, are far more 'Islamically socialised' than they were in the 1970s, when an approach to non-religious, nationalist and left-wing parties could almost be a 'natural' choice—this could allow us to hypothesise that we will find different data in the future, in the elites formed more recently or currently being formed.

The situation does not appear to be the same in Great Britain, where the approximately 169 local councillors elected, often involved in initiatives supporting activities concerning their countries of origin (for example, the Kashmir question) seem, on the other hand, to show a somewhat marked 'sense of Islam' [Purdam, 1996].

In Belgium, where immigrants who are not Belgian nationals do not have the right to vote in local elections, there has been a presence and election of persons of immigrant origin: 14 councillors of non-European origin were elected in the towns making up the agglomeration of Brussels in 1994, 4 'new Belgians' were elected to Parliament in the region of Brussels-capital (one of the three regions that make up Belgium) in 1995, and in general there has been a widespread tendency to present candidates of immigrant origin in the main parties—which, incidentally, does not mean the same commitment or any moral obligation in having them elected [Martiniello, 1998b]. Amongst the 14 elected candidates in 1992, 12 were Moroccan, 1 Tunisian and 1 Algerian, mostly elected in left-wing parties (12 out of 14 in the ecologists' list and the PS, the Socialist Party), and 4 of them were women. Of the 4 candidates elected in 1995, 3 were Moroccan and one Tunisian, with three Socialists and one ecologist. The fact that there are no Turks, who nevertheless form an important component of Muslim immigration in Belgium, can probably be explained by the linguistic factor: the North Africans are Francophone and not by chance all the elected candidates belong to Francophone Walloon parties and none to Flemish parties; and the Turks do not belong to either linguistic area. Conversely, we should not be surprised that the linguistic factor has also played a role in the Netherlands, where we have seen in some cases Turkish ethnic lists (perhaps also due to the greater difficulty to enter the political world?). Mostly they state they are not Muslims, or 'militant' lay individuals. But the reasoning of a 'generational' type already made is also valid for Belgium—the 'cohort effect' mentioned earlier—as often these are former foreign students politically active in the 1970s; whilst amongst the workers and descendants of immigrants there are some practising Muslims. The fact of not feeling subjectively Muslim does not, however, exempt them from having to deal with 'Muslim' questions, such as the organisation of slaughtering for 'Id al-Adha, obtaining Muslim areas in cemeteries and even of more political questions, such as the election of the representative Council of Muslims of Belgium. However, we cannot speak of 'religious entryism' in politics, just as it is premature to speak of 'ethnic entryism', although some voices on the subject have begun to circulate [Lambert, 2000].

The problem of what they do and who they represent, once elected, is also raised in France. Often they are co-opted or elected along-

side personalities as representatives of sectors of the population considered as having specific problems and are given politically controversial and difficult cases concerning these same populations, for
whom they do not necessarily have, merely by the fact of their origin, a specific preparation: this seems to have led to situations of
political frustration and even of substantial failure [Geisser & Kelfaoui,
1998]. In short, there is the sensation that this emerging or potential political class is not fully inserted; as is often the case with women,
who deal with or are appointed to deal mainly with problems of
women or at the most of family and welfare problems, and confined
to these, this seems to be happening to these fragile elites of immigrant origin, who are given responsibility for the policies relative to
immigrants and, even more problematically, those relative to relations with the natives and social conflict in the territory.

The failure becomes even more burning on religious issues. Often
these leaders of immigrant origin, are not necessarily, as we have
seen—and in particular at this time in history, due to the 'cohort
effect' already seen—the bearers of a specific religious sensitivity, of
which they often have a fairly poor knowledge and also, visibly in
the French case and more subtly elsewhere, they are almost forced
to muffle any explicit religious reference (through professions of faith
in laïcité and in the bounty of the republican ideology) in order to
be accepted in the political club. The problem arises when there are
reasons of conflict or issues of a religious type, such as the building
of a mosque or even only the organisation of the ordinary aspects
of Muslim religious life: slaughtering, the 'Id, hijab, school and so on.
The use, due to their ethnic origin, of these immigrant leaders in
the role of intermediaries, far from making the solution of problems
easier, may represent, if not an obstacle, one more or one too many
an interlocutor or intermediary. These intermediaries, precisely due
to their scarce sensitivity (only one-quarter of them respect Ramadan,
mostly neglecting the other pillars of Islam), and probably also due
to the correct intuition that they are not the real holders of decision-making power, or that they owe too much, in terms of loyalty
to ideology and values, to the system they represent, are not accepted
as such by the Muslim leaders, who prefer to negotiate directly with
the mayors and local authorities [Geisser, 1997]. Moreover, in general they are generally little known or not known at all by the communities that they are supposed to represent, to the extent that in
their case there can be said to be 'communitarian invisibility' [ibidem].

Geisser's study also shows the social origin of elected candidates of North African origin, toning down in part the 'pitying' representation that is given to them (the poor that 'have made it'), usually accompanied by a meritocratic vision of their success. It is to be noted—and the fact could lend itself to further considerations—that about one-quarter of them come from a situation of a mixed couple and that as many as 64.5% have in turn established a mixed family. Furthermore, the female presence is conspicuous, around one-third of the total.

6. OTHER FORMS OF POLITICAL PARTICIPATION

So far we have concentrated on participation in elections and on adhesion to the party system: however, for reasons which in the first place are institutional and constitutional within the different countries, these are not the only or the main instruments of political participation that Muslims, especially if nationals, have at their disposal. Moreover, as is well known, not all politics are party-based, and not everything that is public is institutional. In addition to elections, there are also, in a broad sense, other forms of political participation.

That of *associations* is certainly the most immediate and main one. Forming an association is the first and essential way of organising the presence, often regardless of the real impetus of associations, that is, of participation and collaboration in order to achieve a common objective. Associations, in a certain sense, come first and are the necessary instrument and nevertheless are 'required' by the political-institutional panorama of the country of settlement. It is unlikely that an individual who, for example, wishes to give a neighbourhood its mosque, or intends carrying out activity of a religious nature, would be received and listened to by the local authorities. A major institutional fiction, which concerns not only Muslims but, in the first place, the natives, means that only associations and the representatives of these can be heard: this represents a very strong even if little remembered impetus towards associations including Muslim ones, and the officialisation of the association in structures which are, or at least tend to be, stable.

Mosques and Islamic centres therefore form associations but with names that recall specific forms in the countries of origin: many, not by chance, are called *waqf al-islam*, 'property of Islam', with an emphasis which is in itself a way of Islamically marking the territory. The *waqf* networks represent in fact, according to some Muslim thinkers [Ennaïfer, 1996], together with the mosques and the possibilities of religious transmission, therefore schools, one of the elements of transformation of a non-Muslim society into *dar al-islam*, into the house of Islam, incidentally also giving legitimacy to the political action within it.

The Sufi groups or those with a more political characterisation do the same. Not infrequently there are forms of links with the country of origin or rather, with its individual organisations, both in official and para-institutional forms, especially if they are government bodies such as the Turkish DITIB, and in more openly grassroots forms.

A more specific form of associations is inter-ethnic, for instance anti-racist, which has as examples some of the more well-known movements like France's *SOS Racisme*, founded in 1984 and *France-Plus*, established the following year. Often a stage for subsequent engagement, including at the political level, they have however seen a more ethnic, rather than religious, participation: with respect to the latter there has not been or hardly ever been a common language and objectives.

Another form of participation which has played an important role, especially in the past, was that of the *trade unions*: as work is the first real element of 'citizenship' and of legitimisation of the presence of immigrants. It cannot be denied, as has been noted, that the trade unions represented one of the few channels (if not the only one, in some cases) through which a certain 'air of equality' was made accessible for immigrants [Bastenier & Targosz, 1991]. For a certain period, the trade unions had a sort of quasi-monopoly of the process of integration of immigrants, as such often recognised, when not frankly given an incentive, even by institutions, national and local governments, continuing, it must also be said, the action done previously, since the years of post-war reconstruction and all the more so by the economic boom, in favour of immigrants, then from the south of Europe.

In this sphere, the appearance of some requests, already made in various countries, linked to the productive cycle but having as their origin religious motivations is interesting. For example, the particular negotiations implemented by Muslim workers: the right to *halal* food or even a prayer room in the firms where they are present in a conspicuous number, the possibility of changing working hours according to specific requirements (for example beginning earlier and finishing earlier, during the month of the fast of Ramadan—or directly taking the holidays at this time of the year, in order to spend the month in the home country—or in accordance with the Friday prayer). All these things which, in virtue of the flexibility allowed by new manufacturing technologies, are increasingly less problematic for employers, who are often willing to accept these requests in exchange for guaranteed social peace at, all things considered, a small price. Today, the 'Muslim' trade union struggles which nevertheless represented one of the first elements of visibility, for example, of French Islam [Mouriaux & Wihtol de Wenden, 1987] seem very distant. Moreover, Islam, even then, had shown it could be played both for the purposes of assimilation by its followers, in the form of individual integration and in a tactical interpretation of identity, through a collective negotiation of their presence [Barou, Subhi and Wihtol de Wenden, all 1985].

It is also interesting to note how the Muslim presence, where it has appeared in the trade union sphere, has caused a certain cultural revolution, as its bargaining power is for religious reasons that are culturally distant from the contents and sensitivity of contemporary trade unions, including those of—distant and usually, by choice, put in the background—Christian origin, for which the religious motivation was if anything the impetus for action, its ethic substratum and not the reason for negotiation, with some exceptions, soon to take second place, for work on Sundays. Phenomena such as the prayer in a public square by Muslim workers during the 1st May marches, as has been the case in Milan and elsewhere in Italy, or the fact that the *Comisiones Obreras*, heirs of the anti-Franco struggle and ideologically anti-religious, gave their premises for Muslim workers to pray in, as has been the case in Catalonia [Moreras, 1999], cannot pass unobserved.

A form of more specific participation is what has been offered to immigrants in various countries, subordinate to and sometimes 'in preparation for' genuine political participation. We find important expressions of these in the consultative bodies set up in Belgium, where they give rise to the creation of councils of immigrants, or in Great Britain, the Community Relations Council which then formed the Commission for Racial Equality Council (CRE) in 1981. These places of representation and mediation have played the role of training grounds or, as it has also been said, 'nurseries' for future Asian politicians, including Muslims, as was the case, for example, in Bradford [Lewis P., 1997]. Some members of the local *Council of Mosques* learnt here how to run and organise consent within their respective communities. However, the experiment, according to some, is to be considered superseded. Some have even spoken almost ironically of a *tribal approach* [Saad, 1997], to the anxious search for community representatives, underlining that there are no leaders for the majority of the white community, the natives, but there are only leaders of specific interests.

In Germany the councils of foreigners (*Ausländerbeiräte*), considered by some 'puppet bodies' have also actually been the starting point for subsequent political commitments at a higher level, a sort of area of transition to real political life, both in the country of origin and in the local, regional or even federal community, with cases of persons with a double or triple political affiliation (movements of ethnic reference, Turkish for example, bodies of religious affiliation and German political parties) [Bozarslan, 1990]. If in the past the lists for elections were on a national basis, meaning the nationality, there have recently been transversal, horizontal lists, based on a reference of a religious type, possibly also inter-ethnic. In some länder, such as Rhineland, from the 1990s, Muslim lists of various tendencies were the first to appear. In Germany there is also the particular experience of the works councils (*Betriebsräte*), which are also a possible first arena of investment, even if only informative and consultative, before moving on to commitment on a wider scale.

Experiences similar to the councils of foreigners have also taken place in other situations, including on a local basis, in various countries, through councils of immigrants, sometimes elective, where an organised presence with an explicitly religious reference has not always been well considered, either by the institutions or by other immigrant communities. Bodies resulting from co-optation on a local and in some cases, national, basis are more frequent than the elective committees.

However, Islam has represented a specific problem, which some countries have decided to approach as such, with *ad hoc* bodies. For example, the consultative Muslim councils promoted and proposed in France to achieve a representative body of the Muslim religion in the country have a long history but without a definitive solution having been reached to date. The Belgian experience is extremely complex, as the country recognised Islam as one of the state religions as early as 1974, without this recognition of principle being applied in practice a quarter of a century later [Panafit, 2000]. We refer to the later chapters on this and other experiences of Muslim representation, where they are dealt with at greater length. Here we are interested above all in recalling their function that also includes producing and making visible a potential political leadership, capable of being spent in other spheres of representation and political mobilisation.

7. THE POLITICAL PRESENCE: AN OVERVIEW

In order to give an idea of the complexity and articulation of the Muslim presence on the European political scene (and it is a presence that cannot be traced back to unity and coherence) we can summarise the forms of its political expression in some countries.

In **Great Britain**, mention has already been made of a Muslim Member of Parliament and of about one hundred and fifty Muslim town councillors. In addition to this presence there is a representation in the House of Lords of three or four Muslim representatives (the number is debatable because, in one case, the person comes from a mixed family and because the criterion is self-definition on a religious basis), all recently appointed in the Labour era (we can recall that some 500 life peers and about 90 hereditary peers make up the House of Lords; 26 bishops and archbishops are also entitled to a seat. The Lords mentioned all belong to the category of life peers). There is also a Conservative Muslim member of the European Parliament; at the European elections in 1999, there were five Muslim candidates in all: one Labour, three Conservatives and one Democratic Liberal. There is no Muslim member of the Scottish Assembly, although the region has a significant presence of Muslims: the first Muslim MP, elected to Westminster, comes from a Scottish city, Glasgow. On the local level, there is no shortage of examples of Muslim mayors, in Luton, some London boroughs and elsewhere. But the political weight of the Muslim electorate is 'heavier' than can be read through the number of elected candidates. It is calculated that about 35 seats depend on the Muslim vote. The newly-appointed Lords took the oath for the first time on the Qur'an and 'Id was once symbolically celebrated in Downing Street, in the presence of the Prime Minister Tony Blair [Lord Ahmed of Rotherham, personal interview, May 2000].

Much has already been said about the **Netherlands**, in particular regarding engagement at a local level. At a national level, there are five Muslim MPs, three of whom are of Moroccan extraction and two of Turkish origin [NL File]. For all the local and national representatives, it is possible to take the oath on the Qur'an. It is worthwhile underlining that the Netherlands is one of the countries where the political debate on integration is effectively present and it is possible to identify the different positions of the various parties [Fermin, 1999]. The debate on the presence of Muslims in the Christian Democratic party is interesting and it is probably the party most attentive to community rights and with the strongest link to the system of 'pillars', which today are no longer on the agenda. The party is the result of a coalition, created at the end of the 1980s, by three religious parties, one Catholic and two Protestant. The debate is cyclically brought up within the party, which includes a group, especially outside the large cities, very much against the Muslim presence in the party: however, this is not a debate on Islam, but on the Christian identity of the party itself. The solution adopted, with a pragmatic attitude, is that of leaving the ethical problem of deciding whether the individual, Muslim in this case, wishes to commit himself politically to a party which, in its founding documents, defines itself as Christian [Nico Landman and Jan Rath, personal interviews, 2000]. Moreover, the religious background of the Muslim representatives does not seem to be highlighted. It is to be noted that they also end up by assuming the role of specialists within the various parties on religious questions and ethnic issues [NL File].

In **Germany**, as emphasised, to date there have not been many—even if things have recently been changing, following the legislative changes on the matter—immigrants who have acquired citizenship and, with it, the right of vote. And the double path of commitment of Turkish immigrants in relation to their country of origin (where they can vote in the elections) and to that of settlement is clear, producing atypical careers, where political-religious activists in Germany, for example of the Milli Görüs, have used this consent as a springboard for politics in Turkey, becoming mayors or members of parliament of the then *Refah Partisi* [Amiraux, 2001].

The use of these 'structures of political opportunities' is also seen with some concern in the country of origin, in particular by the military, aware of the greater support for the religious movements and their greater freedom of action in Germany: it is not by chance that the National Security Council imposed on the *Refah Partisi*, when it came to power in a coalition government in 1997, a sort of Decalogue which including rules that prohibited Turkish parties from receiving funding from organisations in Europe [Amiraux, 1999]. There have also been cases of political careers that have been aborted in Germany, this time due to Muslim militancy, as was the case of a leading representative of the CDU of Berlin, involved in the AMGT in the Turkish neighbourhood of Kreuzberg, designated by his party as the delegate to the Landtag for the city of Berlin but who had to resign following the accusation of a colleague in a Turkish but 'secular' party who revealed his 'Islamist' past [Amiraux, 2001].

Two members of Turkish origin today sit in the Bundestag, Cem Özdemir and Leyla Onur. However, the commitment displayed is on immigration issues (the former, a Green member of parliament, is well-known for his self-definition as an *immigrün*, and for his auto-biography in which he defined himself as an *inländer*), and not on religious subjects. Özdemir has nevertheless promoted days of aware-ness on Islam and is currently the Green delegate in the Government.

In **Denmark** some Muslims stood for election to Parliament in 1998, but without success [DK File]. In November 2001 two were elected.

In **Sweden**, undue emphasis is not placed on the fact of being a Muslim, but there are some MPs of the Social Democratic party with a Muslim background, including a Kurdish MP. At a local level, there are also Muslims active in the Christian Democratic Party [SE File].

In **Spain**, as the Prime Minister Jose Maria Aznar has repeated on several occasions, Islam is not a political problem, and does not appear as such in politics. There is however the significant experi-ence of the participation of the Muslim populations in the elections in the enclaves of Ceuta and Melilla, the exact Muslim population of which is not well known, also due to a certain political determi-nation to maintain the fiction of the *españolidad* of these towns. The data from the National Institute of Statistics, relative to the mid 1980s, speak of 22.5 and 32.5% of the population in Ceuta and Melilla as Muslims. Caritas figures show significantly different num-bers: 38.3 and 51.6% respectively. It is interesting to note that at the last regional elections, held in 1999, in Melilla, thanks to the support of an atypical electoral coalition (the GIL, Liberal Independent

Group, of a populist-conservative tendency, the Pim, Independent Party for Melilla, and two Socialist MPs), Mustapha Aberchan, president of the aforementioned Coalition for Melilla, was elected as the first Muslim chairman of the city assembly. The news, in a certain sense, is not that this happened but that it had never happened before, as after all it is an enclave in Moroccan territory and with a significant Muslim electorate. Moreover, in July 2000, a motion of censor by the opposition succeeded in removing him from power; Aberchan accused the motion of being a xenophobic manoeuvre by the Spanish parties, which did not want a Muslim president [Planet, 1998; ES File].

A Muslim MP was elected to the European parliament in *Izquierda Unida*: this was Mohamed Abdelkader Ali, who spoke on the report on "Islam and Averroes European Day", presentated at the European Parliament on 16th September 1998 [ES File].

In **Portugal** there is no explicit Muslim presence, but Valy Mamede, president of the Muslim community of Lisbon for 17 years, was for a long time an active member of the Social Democratic Party, in which he was also the vice-president of the international relations department. Although the Islamic question is not on the agenda, the absence from the political game is all the more surprising if we think that the Muslim community consists of 70% of nationals and, as it is highly concentrated in the Lisbon area, it could have some electoral influence [PT File]. The virtual absence from the political arena, and the non-visibility of Muslims, can probably be explained by the good level of insertion of the local Muslim community and the lack of widespread feeling of marginalisation. The Muslim electorate does not seem to have specific battles to propose which cannot be channelled into the existing political picture.

France has already been discussed and it can only be recalled here that, after all, the country has already had a Muslim deputy in 'historic' times in 1897, represented by a convert, Dr. Grenier, deputy for Pontarlier [Etienne, 1989]. And as early as the period between the wars, there had been an electoral interest in the North African electorate, including with religious arguments. In Marseille, at the 1937 elections, the race to win over this electorate by all the parties led to the proposition of various projects to build a mosque for the use of the Muslim population [Renard, 1999]; incidentally, the city still does not have a purpose-built mosque.

In other countries, such as **Italy**, there is no visibility of the Muslim

question at electoral level, except of references to it with a xenophobic function by right-wing parties. Or, on the contrary, we have
the presence of candidates of foreign or 'ethnic' origin, but not necessarily in a religious key; even where there is not an ethnic electorate. For example, there has been the flag-carrying candidature
(that did not succeeded), as an anti-racist testimonial, of Tahar Ben
Jelloun for the European Parliament in 1999, for the Democrats,
the party of Romano Prodi [IT File].

The situation where it is not a case so much or only of immigrants, but mainly of religious minorities present with many centuries of history, especially if linked with a strong ethnic identity is
completely different from the political point of view. This is the case
both of member states of the European Union and of some candidate countries.

Amongst the former we can recall **Greece**. Here the 'historical'
Muslim component is that of the Turkish minorities in Western
Thrace and of the Pomaks, with the addition in more recent times
of a significant presence of Albanians who are, however, in a completely different situation: the former are nationals, the latter, especially since the collapse of the dictatorship of Enver Hoxha, recent
immigrants, often in an irregular situation and excluded from the
political rights connected with holding citizenship.

The Turkish minority has participated actively in political life,
both on the regional and national level, since 1923. Since then, there
has always been at least one, if not two or sometimes three Muslim
deputies. In the last elections, two were elected, one in Komotini
and the other in Xanthi, the two historical areas of the presence of
the Turkish minority in Thrace. They take their oath on the Qur'an,
according to Greek law, as do the dozens of Muslim mayors in the
villages of the area, which are wholly Muslim or mixed. In regard
to the latter, it should be noted that, since the 1950s, forms of coexistence have been created, with forms of division of the administration of the villages, where it is not rare for a Muslim list to have a
Christian at its head or, vice versa, there are Muslims in the Christian
lists. Moreover, the difference in votes between the Muslim ethnic
presences and the votes taken by the Muslim lists shows that there
are a certain number of Muslims who prefer to vote for Christian
parties. It is also to be noted that the governors or prefects in Greece
are elected: therefore in the areas with a Muslim majority there are
Muslim vice-governors [GR File].

At national level, a Muslim representative was elected for the first time in the Pasok, the Socialist Party, in 1980. In 1985 'independent' lists appeared in the departments of Xanthi and Rhodope, not connected with Greek parties. The election of independent deputies in 1989 led to the approval of a law which in 1990 ratified the obligation for each candidate to belong to a party that gained at least 3% of the votes at national scale, which is mathematically impossible for a Muslim party and which was to lead to revived presence of the Muslim presence in 'Greek' parties: in 1996, three Muslim candidates were elected, in the Pasok, in New Democracy and in the extreme left coalition of Synaspismos [Dalègre, 2001].

Since 1992 there has also existed a Turkish-Muslim party, the DEB (Party of Friendship, Equality and Peace), the representatives of which often act, however, as ethnic representatives more than religious ones [GR File].

In the whole of the **Balkans** the effects of a 'passage to the political' by the Muslim populations can be noted [Bougarel & Clayer, 2001]. Following the fall of the communist regimes, parties representing these populations have appeared in the majority of the Balkan countries. Some have adopted neutral names: such as the SDA, Party of democratic action in Bosnia-Herzegovina, the PPD, Party of Democratic Prosperity of the Albanians in Macedonia, LDK or Democratic League of Kosovo for the Albanians in that region, or the DPS, Movement for Rights and Freedoms, for the Turks in Bulgaria. Others have openly shown their ethnic nature, such as the Turkish Democratic Party and the Party for the Complete Emancipation of the Rom in Macedonia, the Turkish Democratic Union in Kosovo and in Romania, or the DEB in Greece. Albania is an exception, where there is no need for specific representation as the Muslims are a majority and not a minority looking for political space and recognition.

Ever since the first free elections in 1990 and 1991, these parties have won a large majority of votes in their respective communities. However, there is both a community and a non-community vote, as the communities are often divided internally, and in some countries, such as in Bulgaria and Montenegro, and also in Bosnia-Herzegovina, at the last elections there was a relative 'de-community allocation' of the Muslim vote. Profound 'de-secularisation' does not necessarily imply a re-Islamisation of customs: the classic sociological distinction between religion and faith is visible, where the former is an element of community recognition, but the latter tends to be increasingly individual. This means that political actors prevail over religious actors. It should also be noted that, in traditional and rural environments, the politicisation of Islam encourages favouritism of the notables, but represents an obstacle to the diffusion of the ideological and militant conceptions of Islam [Bougarel & Clayer, 2001].

To limit ourselves to the countries of our interest here, we can note that in **Bulgaria**, a country that is a candidate for entry into the European Union (incidentally, the Turkish-Islamic party, DPS, see below, considers entry into Europe its 'priority objective' [Ragaru, 2001]), Muslims represent 14% of the population and are mainly Turkish, although there are also Muslims who are ethnically Bulgarian, Roma, Tartars, Arabs and a small group of Circassians.

Political activity is mainly carried out by the Movement for Rights and Freedoms, a party of Turks and Muslims (but also supported by fringes of the Christian electorate), present in Parliament and with a significant sphere of influence at local level. In coalition with the Alliance for National Salvation in order to overcome the limit of 4%, it obtained 7.6% of votes at the last elections, with good results in the Turkish districts, although below expectations. Here too, as in Greece, it can be deduced that, on the one hand, the ethnic parties do not take all the votes of the ethnic group to which they refer and, on the other, they do not get other votes from elsewhere [Küçükcan, 1999]. There are currently also Muslims in the government coalition as well as in parliament and in local government. A political agreement between the DPS and the National Movement for Simeon II, the former king who triumphed in the elections in June 2001, was signed the month afterwards.

There are also a couple of minor Muslim formations, one of which promoted by the former Grand Mufti of Bulgaria, who has fallen into discredit due to his collaboration with the communist; however, they have no following [BG File].

In **Romania** the minorities are represented in Parliament, as decreed by article 59 of the Constitution. Muslim representatives are elected both locally and nationally, both in their own lists and in other Romanian parties. The Democratic Union of Turks in Romania, and the Democratic Union of Tatar Turkish-Muslim in Romania are both present with their own MPs in Parliament. The Cultural Union of the Albanian Community in Romania, although it is not a party, has its own president elected to parliament, as the representative of the Albanian community [RO File].

In Poland and Hungary, on the other hand, where the Muslim minority is very small, there are no signs of visibility in the national political system [PL and HU Files].

8. On the European Right of Vote: Some Considerations

The events described so far show how Islam, from being transplanted to the peripheries of Europe and becoming a peripheral Islam [to paraphrase two well known texts, referring to a period and a phase of migratory cycle previous to the present; cf. Kepel, 1987 and Dassetto & Bastenier, 1984], moves relatively quickly towards a progressive institutionalisation. Amongst the elements which show it and probably encourage and accelerate it, there is also the right of vote, even if it is extremely problematic to succeed in demonstrating to what extent and if the political vote really has an effect on the economic and social integration of Muslims. This remains more an assumption of principle, therefore, than a statement that can be proved, in the current state of research. As some countries grant the administrative right of vote and others do not, and as in some the Muslims, as nationals, have the right to vote in political elections and in others, as they are not nationals, they do not have this right, we have to examine the principle as such, before trying to answer the question on the opportunity of its possible extension.

Must the right of vote be granted? Is it possible and opportune to detach it from the concept of citizenship? Is the latter a historical form subject to revision or an undeniable constitutional right, such as it is, as a *raison d'être* of European democratic political systems? It is evident that an evolutionary principle is intrinsic to democratic systems; however, to what extent? Democracy is *embodied* in the nation-state, but must not be *petrified* in it [Carlier, 1998—our italics]. The right to nationality thus institutionally expresses the 'state prerogative of inclusion and exclusion' [Weil & Hansen, 1999]: which obviously passes through the right to vote, in particular the political vote, but also, to mention an aspect that is underestimated by political and social reflection but very present in the daily life of immigrant communities, through the guarantee against deportation. These factors remain at the centre of individual identification, from the definition of 'us' compared to the 'others', whoever they are, despite all the evolutions in the direction of post- and transnational citizenship [Soysal, 1994]. And at the same time they are subjected to what we could define 'institutional stress', precisely by the new presences, which are posed by their mere existence in friction with a mechanism that conceptually does not contemplate them. It is no coincidence that the laws on citizenship continue to change, and moreover in different directions: narrowing the criteria of its acquisition, in some countries, but also widening them, by decreasing for example the period of residence necessary in order to apply for it, in others. The British law was reformed in 1981 and in France in 1993, with a reduction of the criteria but, in these countries, they were extremely wide; the Belgian and Italian reforms date from 1992 and 1993 in Germany, widening the mesh. Dual citizenship, for example, is accepted by France, Italy, Great Britain and Ireland and tolerated in practice, even if formally rejected, by Germany and the Netherlands, and citizenship is accompanied by the right to vote.

Voting and participating in elections are, however, important symbolically and as an extension of democracy to the highest possible number of its potential beneficiaries: this represents a long-standing tendency of Western democracies which have gradually overcome the limit of property, education and gender, in favour of suffrage tending towards universality, which today only excludes the age group of people younger than a certain age (usually eighteen years old). The universe of today, however, has been further enlarged.

In addition, the extension of the rights correlated with political citizenship can be assumed as finalised for the administration of the common good, although starting off from an individualist point of view such as that of the members of ethnic and religious communities, but also local, etc. (moreover, as has been noted, forms of claiming particular rights, such as the right to wear a headscarf according to Muslim rules, increasingly take on the forms of a universalistic discourse, that of the protection of fundamental rights and freedoms; Soysal, 2000). Its aim is also that of defusing conflicts or, more properly, of channelling them towards forms of shared and non-destructive management.

But what type of representation? Direct political representation, through quotas corresponding to the percentages of presence, as is in fact the tendency of, for example, the Anglo-Saxon model (not only in political parties: therefore today statistics circulate on the

under-representation of the various minority ethnic components in
public administration, in schools or the BBC, with relative commitments to adjustment of the percentages)? This is what is happening,
moreover, with the female component and the quotas guaranteed
for women. But where does affirmative action, in some ways exemplary and by its very nature transitory, limited to the phase in which
there is effective substantial trampling of rights of a social group,
finish and where, on the other hand, does a consociative multicultural democracy begin? And further: what happens to the struggle
for the imperative mandate that is also at the origin of Western
democracy, which has brought about the principle of universal representation to prevail (at least in theory and as a hope, if not always
in the facts)? However, it is true that some conditions of the social
landscape have changed, on a global level as well, and the movements of men and woman are one of these decisive conditions from
the political point of view.

On the one hand, we have significant numbers of people who live
permanently in countries of which they do not hold the nationality,
for whom forms of trans- or post-national citizenship are beginning
to appear. On the other hand, some of these minorities, for example some groups of Turks in Germany, if on the one hand ask to
be able to vote in European elections, on the other activate forms
of pressure on the Turkish government to obtain facilitations to vote
in Turkish political elections [Soysal, 2000]. The extension of forms
of dual nationality only further complicates the picture, leading to
the possible constitution of multi-referential politics, according to the
occasional context of reference: local and regional, if there is the
right to vote in local elections, if citizenship is held or if there exist
bilateral agreements between states or forms of involvement of specific
populations; European, where there is possibility of exercising this
right, as is the case for intra-European immigrants; and lastly, that
of the country of origin.

This naturally poses the problem of possible double or triple loyalties or disloyalties, of plural forms of belonging, which include the
political formations of the countries of origin, in general of a different
vision of political involvement, in a certain sense more sectorialised.
The extension of the concept of European citizenship should encourage wider forms of political participation: but, precisely, limited to
those who have acquired a European citizenship. Furthermore, the
concept of European citizenship remains contradictory in itself, as

there is no competence of the European Union with respect to the attribution of nationality, which remains the competence of the individual states, nor is there any restriction as to the criteria used by the states in granting or refusing it: this means, in short, that the grounds of European citizenship are in themselves outside the competence of the Union [Crowley, 1999]. As for the European vote, it must be recalled that European elections are not elections of the individual states, although they take place according to national constituencies. This explains therefore that requests have been put forward in the direction of extending the right of the European vote to foreigners resident in Europe, for example by the Migrant Forum. We limit ourselves here to an exercise of prospects, without sponsoring a specific solution in this direction.

Probably less than one-quarter of European Muslims, holding citizenship, can also vote in European elections. If those who have been resident for a reasonable period of time could also vote, we could hypothesise, in a Europe with a population of some 365 million people, that to elect a member of the European Parliament some 500–750,000 votes are necessary [Brewin, 1997]. In theory, this could mean about 10–15 Muslim MPs, who however would not represent a unitary group, as they would presumably be divided not only by ethnic origin, as well as by national origin, but also on the ideological level, as there could be Socialists, Conservatives, Liberals... and Christian Democrats amongst them. Many Muslims, as they already do now, would continue to vote for parties and candidates that are not Muslims. And lastly, some would not vote, even if invitations in this direction *motivated on a religious basis* have been little followed (classic abstention is different), on the style of a sticker which appeared, for example, in Derby during the 1995 elections with the warning "Don't vote. It's *haram*" [Andrews, 1996]. In the perspective of an enlarged European Union, we should hypothesise the forms of interaction with Muslim minorities already fully inserted into the political game of the respective countries.

From some points of view, this type of vote could also encourage the birth of transnational Muslim parties, even if a movement in this direction is not to be taken for granted nor, in this case, destined to enjoy greater success than in other transnational initiatives (for instance, the Transnational Radical Party, which has remained a small although significant democratic lobby). Naturally there would be a problem of perception of this presence, at least in a first phase:

any religious Muslim involvement would risk being seen as funda-mentalist. But this is a problem that is already posed: "In Europe, an apolitical conservative is often preferred to a politicised progres-sive" [Tareq Ramadan, personal interview, May 2000]. Significantly, the Muslim groups, even the radical ones, urge exercising the right of vote, where they have it: "Why we need to vote", is the significant headline in a Muslim magazine [*Muslim Today*, May 1999], to quote only one example; the articles motivates the exercise of this right-duty with the fact that a Muslim is never a minority, because he belongs to the Muslim *Umma*.

Lastly, we can note that the Muslim presence and, more gener-ally the presence of immigrants, even where it appears, has less weight than the parallel growth of extreme right-wing and xeno-phobic movements and parties, of which there are certainly more elected candidates and perhaps more electors; where the immigrants exercise the right of vote, especially locally, they nevertheless elect a lower number of candidates with respect to those who stand on clearly anti-immigrant platforms; and in some countries, they seem to make Muslims the new Jews, salvaging much of the traditional anti-Semitic arsenal: theory of a conspiracy, a plan to invade Europe etc. [Bjørgo, 1997].

However, we underline that much of the (little) debate on the sub-ject reflects a static conception of social processes which are dynamic, condemning it to a short-term view. Only to give one example, but the most important, the debate laid out this way reflects a first-gen-eration image of immigration, which does not take into account that in many countries, even where there is not or there is no longer the *jus soli*, the forms of mixedness and other rights allow easier acqui-sition of citizenship, at least relative to some categories of immigrants with the relative political rights. And the transformations under way in some countries, both restrictive and facilitating, of the acquisition of citizenship for the second generations, mixed couples etc., repre-sent so to speak an 'upstream' solution of the problem raised here.

PART TWO

THE STATE AND LEGAL SYSTEMS WITH REGARD TO ISLAM

Up to this point we have dealt with analysing the processes of social construction within the Muslim world transplanted to Europe. From here onwards, in the following chapters, we will look at how European societies react to this presence, at various levels: starting from how the states and their respective legal systems stand with regard to Islam.

One of the fundamental elements of the institutionalisation and establishment of European Islam has been taken, on the one hand, by the cogent and rigid, so to say, force of the legal system receiving it, which in a certain way forms it in its image; and on the other, by its evolutionary dynamics which transforms this new presence, but is also transformed by it, expressed in the legal form as through a privileged and primary, founding language.

We see all the power of that effect of demand which we have started to analyse, in its political form, in the preceding chapter, expressed in the legal form characteristic of the state. We must not underestimate the logics within the legal system itself, which lead to a further legalisation of social problems: often they become such, in the public space and there is awareness of them only if and when they are posed as legal problems.

We have already seen, and we will see better in this chapter, the diversity of the structure of Islam in the different countries, depending on the legal system in place, its political traditions but also the system regulating state-religion relations, or between state and religions and its evolutionary mechanisms.

In particular, in the next chapter we will examine some problems concerning the process of integration of Islam. However, these problems cannot be understood without taking into consideration, as the decisive factor, state-religion relations, the various conceptions and practices of the idea of secular state, relations with the religions or rather, the dominant churches in the respective countries. The following chapter will highlight the variations on a general level, in the different European states, and not concerning Islam specifically: they are relevant to Islam, because it is to be inserted here, in a frame that pre-exists the arrival of Islam. The relations with and the role of religious minorities, but also the status of ethnic or other minorities, where taken into consideration, come into this sphere.

However, these conceptions and relations are less rigid than we normally imagine: they move, evolve, according to the tensions to which they are subjected, the impetus due to the social and political climate and the changes going through them. One of the privileged channels of this evolution is the jurisprudential dimension, namely the interpretation of the law in the face of a concrete case: this dimension is of special interest to us when the case in question is Islam. This aspect will be examined in the last chapter of this part of the report, with particular reference to those sensitive and crucial, from the juridical points of view, problems for both actors—Islam and the state—represented by personal status and family law. These issues include some of the most evident motives of conflict with Islam on which emphasis is placed, including by the mass media, and on which social debate is produced: polygamy, divorce and repudiation and connected rights, and other issues related to the status of women and the family law.

CHAPTER SIX

THE LEGAL DIMENSION

Silvio Ferrari

1. INTRODUCTION

Islam is a religion which has yet to find a stable place in state-religion relations in Western Europe. In this chapter of the report, we intend (a) to examine if, under the great variety of national systems, there are shared elements of such an importance as to justify the statement that there exists a common model of state-religion relations in the European Union (sections 2–5); (b) to survey and describe the problems which, in the field of state-religion relations, have been posed by the settlement in Europe of numerous and consistent Muslim communities, including an evaluation of the answers that have been and are being given to these problems in some countries of the European Union (section 6); (c) to formulate some observations on the scenarios that are appearing in relation to the insertion of Islam in the model of the relations between state and religions characteristic of Western Europe and, in a now not too distant perspective, of the whole of Europe (section 7).

2. THE TRADITIONAL CLASSIFICATION OF THE SYSTEMS OF STATE-CHURCH RELATIONS

The traditional approach to the subject of the relations between states and religious faiths starts off from the identification of three distinct models: a) systems based on the conclusion of concordats and agreements between states and religious faiths; b) systems characterised by a state church or a national church; c) systems where there is a separation between states and religious faiths.[1]

---

[1] For a synthetic introduction to the system of relations between state and religious faiths in force in the countries mentioned in this paragraph, cfr. European

Countries with a concordat

Portugal, Spain and Italy are the three 'concordat' countries, defined thus due to their relations with the Catholic church (which is the majority church) which are regulated by a concordat. This definition, exact in the past, today requires correction as both Italy and Spain (and, in the future Portugal as well, if the new law on religious freedom is put into effect)[2] have made agreements with other religious faiths alongside the concordats with the Catholic church.[3] The degree of autonomy enjoyed by the religious *faiths* in the state legal system and the extent of collaboration the state grants them depends on the stipulation of these concordats; the faiths that have concluded an agreement or a concordat enjoy more than the others, as will be seen in greater detail in the fourth section of this chapter.

Germany is another state with a 'concordat' where however (unlike the three countries mentioned above) there exists a substantial equilibrium of forces between Catholics and Protestants: therefore at the top of the pyramid we find not one but two churches. The relations with religious faiths are often regulated by concordats and agreements stipulated with the *Länder* (new agreements have recently been concluded with some *Länder* which used to be part of East Germany)[4] but the fundamental distinction, on the subject of relations between state and religious faiths, lies between the faiths that are considered corporations of public law and all the others. The former are given the right of collecting the ecclesiastical tax from their faithful; they also enjoy a particularly wide internal independence, also extended to the social institutions connected to them (consequently denomi-

---

Consortium for Church-State Research, 1994, 1995; Robbers, 1996. For the historical origins of this system see Basdevant Gaudemet & Messner, 1999.

[2] Cfr. Law 22nd June 2001 no. 16 "Lei da Liberdade Religiosa", in *Diario da Républica*, n. 143, 22 June 2001, in particular, articles 45–51.

[3] In Italy the churches represented by the Tavola Valdese (Valdensians), the Christian churches of the Seventh Day Adventists, the Assemblies of God in Italy, the Union of Italian Jewish Communities, the Christian Evangelical Baptist Union of Italy, the Lutheran Evangelist church in Italy, the Italian Buddhist Union and the Christian Congregation of Witnesses of Jehovah in Italy (the last two agreements have not yet been approved by Parliament); negotiations are under way for the stipulation of an agreement with the church of Jesus Christ of Latter-Day Saints, with the Orthodox Archdiocese of Italy and other religious groups. In Spain, agreements have been reached with the *Federación de Entitades Religiosas Evangélicas de España*, the *Federación de Comunidades Israelitas de España* and the *Comisión Islámica de España*.

[4] On these agreements cfr. A. Hollerbach, 1999.

national schools or hospitals can have an organisation other than that imposed by state law on the corresponding lay institutions).

Within the European Union, concordats are also in force in Austria and, in France, in the dioceses of Metz and Strasbourg, where the concordat stipulated between Pius VII and the French Republic in 1801 is still in force.

Looking beyond the borders of the European Union, concordats with the Catholic church (and sometimes agreements with other religious faiths) are in force in Estonia, Lithuania, Latvia, Poland, Hungary, Slovakia, Croatia, Yugoslavia, the Principality of Monaco, the Republic of San Marino, Malta, and in some Swiss cantons.[5] These are obviously agreements of different natures and scope but their number and growth in recent years lead us to believe that this model of relations between states and religious faiths is not only firmly established but also in a phase of expansion.

Of all the 'concordat' countries, Spain is the only one that has concluded an agreement of a general nature with the Muslim communities.

Countries with a state church

The countries of the European Union that feature the system of a state church or national church (Finland, Denmark and, with some peculiarities, England) are all concentrated in northern Europe. The constitutions of these countries recognise a specific church as the state church: on the one hand this implies a particularly penetrating control by the state over this church (in England for example, the head of state is also the head of the church and appoints its bishops), on the other it ensures the state church is in a position of privilege regarding public funds, religious education, religious assistance in public institutions and in other sectors of the legal system.[6]

It has been asked why these particularly close bonds between the

---

[5] On these agreement cfr. the contributions collected in the section of the *Quaderni di diritto e politica ecclesiastica* 1999/1 on "I concordati di Papa Woityla". For the relative texts cfr. Martin de Agar, 2000.

[6] This last statement is only partially apt for the church of England, the privileges of which are more formal than substantial. It should be recalled that the Church of England is not, strictly speaking, a state church but a church "established by law" and that the the United Kingdom does not have a written constitution (but there exist measures with a constitutional value: cfr. Lyall-David McClean, 1995).

state and the church have survived precisely in that part of Europe which is most exposed to the process of secularisation. The sociologists who have studied this phenomenon reply that the secularisation of society has reduced the push towards the secularisation of the institutions which is, on the other hand, a characteristic of other countries [Bauberot, 1995]: as the independence of the state and of politics is no longer put at stake by the church and religion, the system of the state church has been able to survive, even if the advantages connected with this qualification have progressively been reduced.

The difficulty of reconciling the privileges enjoyed by the state church with the principles of religious freedom and equality could well lead to significant changes in the near future. The Church of Sweden ceased to be the church of state in 2000, following a general reform of the system of the relations between the state and religions in force in that country;[7] the Church of Norway is on the way to follow the same path;[8] in England, the Prince of Wales has shown intentions that could lead to some form of disestablishment on the model of what has taken place in Wales and in Northern Ireland. More generally, it appears significant that none of the countries soon to enter the European Union (Estonia, Poland, Hungary, Czech Republic, Slovenia, Bulgaria, Cyprus) have a system of a state church, which on the contrary is explicitly excluded in the constitution of Estonia (art. 40); a similar clause also appears in the constitution of Lithuania (art. 43).

Greece, where the Orthodox religion is constitutionally defined as the dominant religion (art. 3), is often grouped amongst the countries with a state church. From a strictly legal point of view, this association is not without justification: the state exercises considerable control over ecclesiastical life (even if not to the extent of the countries in northern Europe) and the Orthodox church enjoys a position of privilege comparable to that of a church of state. But these points of contact must not let us forget that Greece has social, cultural, economic and religious characteristics that greatly distinguish it from the countries of northern Europe: the Greek model is

---

[7] On this reform cfr. the contributions by R. Schött, R. Persenius & L. Friedner in nos. 2–6 (1995–1999) of the *European Journal for Church and State Research*.

[8] Cfr. "Norvegia: Chiesa-Stato. Un nuovo ordinamento", in *Il Regno-attualità*, 15 aprile 2002, p. 234.

actually the typical model of Orthodox countries, where the church conceives of itself as a national institution and religion is understood as the synthesis of the whole history and culture of a people.[9] It is possible that precisely Greece will become the point of reference for many countries of central and eastern Europe which, in the next few years, will have to construct a system of state-church relations that is compatible with the rules of the European Convention on Human Rights and, at the same time, respects the Orthodox tradition which distinguishes them: for this reason the debates and conflicts which have arisen around the prohibition of religious proselytism in the Greek Constitution (the object of repeated sentences of condemnation by the European Court of Human Rights),[10] the elimination of the indication of religious affiliation from identity cards (established by the Greek government but firmly opposed by the Orthodox church)[11] and, more in general, the recognition of Orthodoxy as the dominant religion (contained in the Greek Constitution but absent from that of other countries with an Orthodox majority, such as Cyprus or Romania) must be carefully followed.

It is superfluous to note that in none of these countries is Islam qualified as a state religion, national religion or dominant religion.

Separatist countries

The other countries in the European Union are, technically speaking, separatist countries: France, the Netherlands, Belgium and Ireland have not stipulated agreements with the religious faiths nor have they recognised churches of state. But, from a strictly legal point of view, the 'separatist countries' category is a residual category, without an identity of its own: if it is true that the separatist countries are distinguished by the fact of regulating the legal position of religious faiths through unilateral state regulations, it is equally true that this feature is also present in those countries that recognise a state church. More in general, the separation of church and state has

---

[9] On this model cfr. Perenditis, 1994.

[10] Cfr. Anastase N. Marinos, 1994. More in general on the question of proselytism see Stahnke, 1999. On the sentences of the Court of Strasbourg which have condemned Greece in relation to the prohibition of proselytism cfr. Evans, 1997.

[11] On this issue, see the news contained in *Il Regno-attualità*, 14/2000, p. 450 and 16/2000, p. 558.

become a very wide notion which lends itself to extremely diversified applications: it is difficult to find many resemblances between the law of a country that opens its constitution with the invocation of the Holy Trinity, as is the case in Ireland, and that of a country (France) which has amongst its fundamental principles the secular status of the state. Similar differences can be easily found in all the sectors in which the discipline of relations between the state and religious faiths is articulated: the ministers of religion are paid with public funds in Belgium but not in the Netherlands; religion is taught in state schools in the Netherlands but not in France and so forth. In particular it is not possible to state that the separatist countries are more 'secular' than those with concordats or those with a state church: this statement could perhaps apply to France, but certainly not to Ireland and, on close examination, not even to Belgium.

Similar reservations on the usefulness of the notion of separation emerge in relation to the countries which, in a more or less near future, will join the European Union: the Hungarian (art. 60) and Croatian (art. 41) constitutions proclaim the separation of the state from the church but this has not prevented the Hungarian and Croatian states from stipulating agreements with the Catholic church; the same situation will be repeated in Slovenia if the talks currently under way reach a successful conclusion.[12]

The juridical discipline of Islam reflects the variety of forms and systems which is characteristic of these countries.

3. The Insufficiency of Traditional Classification

The reservations expressed regarding the utility of the category of 'separatist countries' lead to a more general question: is the traditional division into three of the European countries into concordat states, separatist states and states with a church of state still useful to analyse and explain the current evolution of relations between states and religions? The answer is negative: this triple division is culturally and legally obsolete.

From the first point of view, it appears subordinate to a concep-

---

[12] In Slovenia an agreement with the Evangelical church is already in force, signed on 25th January 2000.

tion of Western Europe divided, generally, into Protestant countries (with a church of state), Catholic countries (that is, with a concordat) and 'secular' countries (represented by separatist France). But it is not at all certain that these distinctions are still significant.[13] After the levelling caused by decades of secularisation and after the Second Vatican Council, is the border between Catholic and Protestant countries still a real watershed? Or, as the French historian François-Georges Dreyfus has maintained [Dreyfus, 1993], is Europe a cultural entity corresponding to peoples who have as their credo the symbol of Nicea-Constantinopole (which includes the *filioque* refused by the Orthodox)? If so, this Europe would bring together the Catholic and Protestant countries but would exclude the Orthodox ones (as well as the regions inhabited by Muslims). Or again, if we do not want to accept such an extreme interpretation (which would push Greece out of Europe), does the real line of demarcation not run today between secularised Europe and Europe where (old and new) religious traditions maintain a certain importance, at times fuelling identity tensions around which nationalistic and xenophobic impulses coagulate? And is the debate on the 'laicité' which has been under way in France for several years not a sign of the doubts and uncertainties that surround this notion in its own elective country?

From the more specifically legal point of view, the triple division into countries with a concordat/separatist countries/countries with a church of state attributes an excessive importance both to the source (bilateral or unilateral) of the law regulating the relations between the state and churches and to their formal qualification (presence/absence of a church of state). These elements had a certain significance in the second half of the 19th century, when the conclusion of a concordat or the emanation of a law of separation meant a clear choice of position and entailed a series of consequences in all sectors of the legal system. But this situation has been superseded for some time now. There is no concordat in Belgium but the juridical position of the Catholic church is not inferior to that of the same church in a country with a concordat such as Spain; and the Church of England, although the 'official' church of England, receives from the state much less than, for example, Protestant churches in Germany do. A classification based on the form assumed by state-church

---

[13] Cfr. in this sense Ferrari, 1996.

relations or on the tools adopted to regulate them appears unsuitable to reflect their real content and to constitute a reliable interpretative model.

Lastly, it is necessary to ask, after 1989, what the present borders of Western Europe are and if it does not already extend to some countries which were behind the 'iron curtain'. The examination of the constitutions, fundamental laws and decisions of the Constitutional Courts shows that in the countries of central and eastern Europe, relations between states and religions are being modelled along lines that are not dissimilar from those which have been prevalent in western Europe for the past few decades. It must not be taken for granted that this process is easy and painless: in countries with an Orthodox tradition, in particular, there prevails a conception of the state-church relations which in some points does not adapt well to the Western model. But the example of Greece, although with the elements of conflict that have been brought to the light, indicates that a reconciliation is possible.

4. The European Model of the Relations between the State and Religions

Beyond the epistemological limits that have been highlighted in the previous section, the uncritical insistence on the distinction between countries with a concordat/separatist countries/countries with a church of state raises another problem. It prevents the principal question being asked: does a European, or at least Western European model, of state-church relations exist?

The affirmative answer to this question is based on the observation that there are some common principles underlying the various national systems. More precisely, the existence of a European model of relations between states and religions is based on three principles which, in different forms and with different force, recur in the juridical systems of each country.

The protection of the individual rights of religious freedom

Many of the countries in Western and Eastern Europe have signed art. 18 of the Pact on Civil and Political Rights or art. 9 of the

European Convention on Human Rights; in addition, the member states of the European Union have signed a Charter of Fundamental Rights that contains a ruling of a similar content (art. 10). The wordings of art. 18 of the Pact, of art. 9 of the Convention and of art. 10 of the Charter are not identical, so that it is not indifferent that one state has signed one document rather than another. But at the level of the definition of theoretical models, the differences between these rules are not decisive: all contain a central nucleus aimed at guaranteeing the respect of the freedom of thought, conscience and religion and the recognition of the right to manifest, individually or together with others, in public or in private, one's religion or conviction, with the sole limits laid down by the law and necessary to protect some fundamental values, such as public order, health and public morals, the rights of others and fundamental liberties.

Going on to the examination of constitutional rules, the picture does not change. All the constitutions of Western countries contain at least one provision that protects the freedom of religion according to ways and within limits which, explicitly or in the interpretation by the different Constitutional Courts, replicate those outlined by the articles mentioned. The same is now valid for the countries of Central and Eastern Europe, the constitutions of which present similar rulings. The constitutions of Romania (art. 29), Hungary (art. 60) and the Czech Republic (art. 15 and 16 of the Charter of fundamental rights and liberties, which is part of the constitutional system), to restrict ourselves to only a few examples amongst the many that could be given, contain provisions that match those of Italy or Germany.

Going one step further down, to the level of ordinary laws, differences begin to emerge that are not negligible in the way religious freedom is protected (or not protected) in the individual national systems. If in Greece the opening of a place of worship of a minority faith is subject to the authorisation of the Orthodox Metropolitan (decr. 1369/1938, art. 41, par. 1), in France it is an offence to celebrate a religious marriage that has not been preceded by the civil one: at this level, each country has its skeletons in the cupboard and it is difficult to establish which are the most cumbersome. But these differences do not seem to be composed according to a precise model, except under one point: the tendency of some states to introduce by legislation a distinction between religious faiths and 'sects', subjecting the latter to an unfavourable juridical regime.[14] This distinction, which presupposes a definition of religion which is very difficult to formulate in legally correct terms, has been accepted in Belgium, France and Germany and tends to inspire legislative policy in other countries, causing choices which do not always appear coherent with the protection of religious freedom.

Drawing a first conclusion from the observations that have been made in this section, it is possible to state that a unitary notion of religious freedom has taken form in Western Europe and is spreading to other parts of the Old Continent. It is probably possible to go further and extend this consideration to the whole of the West. The Constitution of the United states, through the 'free exercise clause' in the First Amendment, protects religious freedom in equally full terms and the interpretation that this clause is given by the Supreme Court is not very dissimilar from that which has inspired the European Constitutional Courts. This is proven by the fact that in some particularly significant sectors—conscientious objection to military service and health treatment, the consideration of the religious element in fostering and adopting minors—the solutions which have been reached on both sides of the Atlantic are not different. The notion of religious freedom that has been sought to be identified— born from the encounter of Christian roots and the secular roots that form the historical and cultural identity of Europe—is an acquisition that probably defines today the whole of the West, even if its specific applications record differences which are not negligible both between Europe and the USA and between the individual European countries.

Underlying this notion of religious freedom lies the idea of the pre-eminence of the individual conscience, namely the right of each person to take the decision on religion that he/she deems in compliance with his/her own conscience in absolute freedom, without this choice entailing any negative consequences on juridical grounds. This conception is the origin of at least two consequences that it is opportune to specify for the reflections that they have on the legal status of Islam and other religious groups in Europe. In the first place, in both Western and Eastern Europe, amongst Catholics, Protestants and the Orthodox, the apostate, the atheist and the wor-

---

[14] Cfr. in this regard the contributions collected in Champion & Cohen, 1999.

shipper of a minority religion is not subject, due to their religious or conscience choice, to any decrease of the civil and political rights due to all citizens.[15] This implies that each individual not only has the right to adopt a religion, but also to leave it or change it: the person who leaves the religious group they belong to (even in the event of having belonged to it since birth) exercises a right that the state is obliged to guarantee for everyone, including the religious group that is abandoned.

In the second place, religious freedom must respect some fundamental values that art. 9 of the European Convention of Human Rights identifies in public order, health and public morals, in the rights and freedoms of others. The member of a religious community that violates these limits with his/her acts, writings or words, will be punished like any other individual and cannot invoke obedience to a precept of his/her religion as a cause for impunity. But these limitations of freedom only concern the manifestations of a religion and not belonging to a religion: no-one can be punished for the sole fact of belonging to a religious group.

The lack of competence of the state on religious matters and the independence of religious faiths

The idea that the state does not have the competence to intervene in religious matters also has its roots in Christian doctrine and, at the same time, in liberal thought. It corresponds to the conception—dating back to the theory of Gelasius of the two swords but *in nuce* already present in the Gospel text—that humanity is governed by two authorities, the religious and the secular, each of which has its own order and competence for regulating the relations within it.[16] At the same time, this idea reflects the secular character of the contemporary state, already expressed by Talleyrand in a famous speech

---

[15] This last statement is not fully valid in the countries—for example Denmark, Great Britain and Norway—where some authorities of the state have to profess a given religion: however these are measures which, whilst having a very great symbolic value, concern an extremely limited number of individuals.

[16] Even if, according to the traditional Christian concept, the order of spiritual matters precedes that of temporal matters. Cfr. in this regard the writings of Francesco Ruffini collected in *Relazioni tra Stato e Chiesa*, Bologna, il Mulino, 1974.

of 7th May 1791 with the affirmation that "religion is a private question over which the state cannot exercise its control".[17]

The lack of competence of the state on religious matters finds its most evident juridical acknowledgement in the recognition of independence and autonomy of the religious faiths: sometimes this recognition is included in the constitutions, as in Germany (art. 140), Italy (art. 8), Ireland (art. 44) and, amongst the countries soon to join the European Union, the Czech Republic (art. 16 of the Charter of fundamental rights and liberties), Bulgaria (art. 13) and Poland (art. 26); at times it is contained in the rulings of the Constitutional Courts, as in the case of Hungary (see decision 4/1993); it almost always recurs in the concordats and agreements stipulated between the states and some religious groups,[18] as in the case of Spain, and, outside the borders of the European Union, Poland and Croatia. But even in countries where a similar recognition is absent—the northern European countries in particular, where there is a system of national church or church of state—the autonomy of the religious faiths is increasingly considered a consequence of the principle of collective religious freedom and, therefore, a limit before which the authority of the state must stop.

The most important difference that, from the point of view of the autonomy of religious faiths (or the lack of competence of the state on religion), can be found in European countries concerns the extension of this independence: in many countries it concerns the doctrinal profile, that is, the capacity of freely defining the system of belief, as well as the organisational profile, the power of having its own juridical system and self-government; in others, it only covers the former of these profiles. But even in countries of the second group (mainly those of northern Europe), the public authorities appear increasingly less inclined, even when they have the juridical possibility, to interfere in the internal organisation of the religious faiths: thus in England the ordination of women to the clergy is first approved by the General Synod of the church of England and then becomes

---

[17] It is clear that, although converging in the affirmation of lack of state competence on religious matters, the liberal conception moves from presuppositions that are very different from the Christian conception. This is the origin of the instability of the synthesis between Christian and liberal values on which the current model of relations between states and religions is based in Europe.

[18] Cfr. supra par. 2.

law by British parliament and in Sweden the reform of church-state relations evolves in parallel steps taken by the action of Parliament and that of the Synod of the Church of Sweden. It would certainly be a mistake to overlook the fact that in some countries of the European Union the bishops are appointed by the head of state and the ministers are considered civil servants. But in general, it is possible to state that not only doctrinal but also organisational independence of the religious faiths tends to be asserted increasingly widely: the history of the Church of England or of the Church of Norway[19] throughout the twentieth century clearly shows the progress made in this direction even in countries that have kept closer links between state and church.

As will be seen shortly, the autonomy of religious faiths is graduated: some of them enjoy a more extensive and greater autonomy than others. But what it is important to underline now is that this principle of independence, while not exclusive to religious faiths, is not asserted to the same extent and intensity in relation to organisations of a secular nature. Evidence of this lies in the fact that the state's collaboration with secular organisations is often subordinate to the democratic structure of their internal system, whilst a similar requisite does not occur with reference to the organisations of a religious nature; or, the fact again that freedom of opinion is guaranteed by the state within many social formations but not religious communities, where the dissident has only the right of withdrawal. The contemporary secular state stops at the threshold of religious faiths and passes this limit only in cases of particular gravity (when an offence is committed within the community, for example): but in general the elaboration of the doctrinal heritage and (within the limits indicated above) the internal organisation of religious faiths is widely removed from the control of the public authorities. Confirmation has recently been given of this with the sentence of the European Court of Human Rights in the Hassan and Tchaouch case against Bulgaria, where it is stated that "the autonomous existence of religious communities is indispensable for pluralism in a democratic society and is thus an issue at the very heart of the protection which art. 9 [of the European Convention on Human Rights] affords".[20]

---

[19] Cfr. in this regard Rhodes, 1991 in particular pp. 317 ff.; Askeland, 2000.
[20] Hasan and Chaush v. Bulgaria, October 26, 2000, n. 62, in www.echr.coe.int/ Eng/Judgements.

This principle of lack of competence of the states is also the origin of some major consequences. The most important, in the context of this chapter, concerns the latitude of not only organisational but above all doctrinal autonomy of religious faiths, with the consequence that they cannot be placed outside the law only because their doctrine contains precepts that are in contrast with the laws of the state. To give some concrete examples straight away, this means that a Jehovah's Witness will be punished if he refuses to do military service (at least in those countries where this service is compulsory) but the Christian Congregation of Jehovah's Witnesses cannot be wound up because it advocates the refusal of military service, or it means that a Muslim will meet with penal sanctions if he contracts a polygamous marriage but the same sanction will not be applied to the whole of the Muslim community due to the sole fact of considering such a marriage licit according to its religious precepts. In a democratic society it must be possible to maintain ideals other than those professed by the majority of citizens and even in contrast with the laws currently in force.

This is a delicate point which requires precision in order to avoid dangerous misinterpretations. Preaching violence to reach an objective, even of a religious nature, lies outside the autonomy recognised to religious faiths because it violates the very rules of the democratic game which must be respected by everyone; the same would apply in the case that a fundamental right of the human person protected in absolute terms were at stake (for example if the inferiority of one race compared to another were advocated). But when we remain within the limits marked by the rules of democracy and the respect of fundamental rights and liberties, the affirmation of religious precepts that are in contrast with the laws of the state (punishable when translated into concrete behaviour) comes, in my opinion, within the sphere of the autonomy due to religious faiths.

The 'selective' collaboration between states and religious faiths

In the European Union—but I would say once again in the whole of Europe—collaboration between states and religions is the rule and not the exception. This collaboration may have a different scope, involve different subjects, become materialised in diversified juridical forms: but in the whole of Europe, with the conclusion of the Communist experience, a system of cooperation between the public authorities on the one hand and religious groups on the other is in force.

Sometimes this collaboration is contemplated and regulated in concordats, or agreements between states and religions; in other cases the forms of collaboration with religions are disciplined by unilateral state laws. On some occasions the two systems—pacticional and unilateral—coexist within a single state: in Italy for example, concordats and agreements regulate forms of collaboration between the state and the main religions, whilst unilateral laws regulate this collaboration (normally on a more reduced scale) with the less important religions.

This outline shows that the choice of pact-based or unilateral juridical instruments is scarcely indicative of the inclination of the state to cooperate with religions: countries where agreements do not exist between the state and churches, such as Belgium or Ireland, are distinguished from an equally wide collaboration as Spain or Italy, where concordats and agreements have been concluded. More generally it is correct to state that separatist countries, countries with a church of state or a national church and countries with a concordat all collaborate, to an extent and with an intensity that does not depend on this qualification, with the religious faiths. The explanation for this inclination is to be sought in the fundamental characteristics of the post-liberal state, the genetic code of which contains the tendency to cooperate with all social, religious and non-religious organisations.[21] Cooperation with social groups is the normal and at

---

[21] The contemporary state is a state with an increasingly limited sovereignty, both externally by supranational organisations and multinational companies and internally where, throughout the 20th century, the power of organised groups has grown. This is a process which began in the period between the 19th and 20th centuries and evolved in parallel with the access of increasingly wider masses to the political and social life through the gradual extension to all citizens of civil and political rights, education, the diffusion of means of communication, industrialisation and urbanisation. This path of introduction of the popular masses to public life was to a great extent organised by large-scale organisations—political parties, trade unions, the churches and later opinion and pressure groups—with which the state soon had to come to agreement, yielding to them a part of its sovereignty. The splendid isolation of the nineteenth-century state, which governed society from above under the leadership of an enlightened élite, gave way to the participation of these organisations in the government of public affairs through the mechanisms of consultation, negotiation, mediation, bargaining between the authorities and the most representative social groups. Around the First World War, the theorisation of the plurality of legal systems reflects in the world of law these transformations, giving juridical

the same time compulsory way of governing the contemporary state: religious faiths also fit into this context and the states appear willing to maintain a relationship of collaboration similar to that established with other social organisations.

If things were simply in these terms, the discourse could come to a halt at this stage: the state collaborates with the religions because it collaborates with all the organisations representing social interests. But things do not stand this way: the collaboration of the state with religions presents an element of peculiarity due to the fact that state is not competent to intervene in religious matters, in the sphere, that is, where the religious faiths operate.

From this lack of competence of the state on religion, it follows that the collaboration of the state cannot be subordinate to the adoption, by the religions, of doctrinal contents or juridical structures in compliance with the values on which the state is founded. This has always represented, in Europe, a reason for tension between states and the churches: but these difficulties have become more acute since religious groups—and in particular I am thinking of Islam[22] and some of the so-called 'new religious movements'[23]—distinguished by principles, structures and behaviour far from the values and rules shared by the majority of European citizens, have appeared in the

---

citizenship to the idea (that had already taken firm root at a social and political level) that the state was no longer the only *societas perfecta*. (Cfr. in this regard Ferrari, 1988). Since the times of Hauriou and Santi Romano many things have changed but this model of the state founded on the participation of social formations in the exercise of power has survived, overcoming the parenthesis of the totalitarianisms that had deformed (but not denied) its fundamental characteristics and re-emerging from the catastrophe of the Second World War as the surest support of democracy. The strategy followed in the past decades to govern the transformation in a multicultural sense of Western Europe confirms the vitality of this form of state: the difficulties experienced with groups of Muslim immigrants do not derive so much from the absence of the will of European governments to collaborate with these communities as from the fact that they are still lacking in sufficiently representative institutions to establish a solid relationship with the public authorities.

[22] On the legal problems raised by the growing Muslim presence in Europe cfr. Shadid & van Konigsveld, 1995. More recently, see number 1996/1 of the *Quaderni di diritto e politica ecclesiastica*, on "Lo statuto giuridico dell'islam in Europa"; part of the essays in this journal have been published, together with new contributions, in Ferrari & Bradney (eds.), 2000. For the latest development relative to the legal profiles of the Muslim presence in some European countries see Ferrari (ed.), 2000 (the second part of the volume brings together contributions on Belgium, France, Germany and Spain).

[23] Cfr. in this regard the contributions in European Consortium for Church-State Research, 1999.

European juridical space. The public authorities have had to face a difficult alternative: exclude these religious groups from every form of collaboration, risking the violation of the principle of equality and, indirectly, the very rights of religious freedom; collaborating with groups which, at the level of doctrinal statements and/or practical conduct, contradict in the name of their religious precepts the equality between men and women, the respect of the freedom of conscience and religion or other cornerstones of civil coexistence as elaborated within the Western legal tradition.

The answer to this dilemma has been extremely flexible and diversified. From the point of view of interest to us—the collaboration between states and religions—it is however possible to identify a basic line that has guided the action of the Member states of the European Union: the accentuation of the characteristics of selectivity and graduality that has already characterised the ways of collaboration between states and religions.

It has already been said that the European states tend to be willing to collaborate with all religious groups. However, this willingness has never been indiscriminate: it is wider where there is a harmony between the values underlying the religious society and those that form the foundations of civil society and narrower where this harmony does not exist.

Some examples will help to explain this statement better. In almost all European countries, the state collaborates with religions, supporting them financially directly or indirectly, but this economic support is not equal. In Belgium for example only the ministers of the six recognised faiths are paid by the state [Torfs, 1999]; in Spain only the faithful of the religious communities that have stipulated an agreement with the state can deduct the donations given to their religion from their taxes [Sanchez, 1992]; in Greece the Orthodox church receives financial support from the state which is far greater than that received by any of the other religious faiths existing in that country [Papastathis, 1992]. This is no coincidence: the same pattern is repeated whenever the collaboration between the state and religious faiths is at stake. On education, for example, some European states provide for the possibility of religious education in state schools: but not all religions can be taught nor are they all taught on an equal footing. Thus, in Italy only the religions of the six faiths that have stipulated an agreement with the state can be taught and of these, only Catholic teachers are paid by the state; in Portugal only

the teachings of Catholicism and, to a much lesser extent, Protestantism, have citizenship in state schools.[24]

More generally, it is possible to see the outlines of a pyramidal
model that is repeated, although with considerable variants, in many
countries of the European Union. At the base of the pyramid is a
group of religious faiths which have a very limited collaboration with
the state. Normally they can acquire juridical status through the
forms established for associations and then they can exercise the
essential acts necessary for their existence (for example purchase and
sell goods, receive donations, stipulate contracts): but they do not
obtain financial support from the state, they do not have access to
public means of communication, they cannot teach their doctrines
in schools. These religious groups are usually regulated by the general law, i.e. common law that regulates all associations.

A second group of religions occupies a higher position: they receive
support from the state in the form of tax exemptions or subsidies,
its ministers can carry out religious ceremonies with civil effects (for
example, celebrate marriages), contributions are foreseen to build
places of worship and so on. Usually these religions are regulated
by special rules, other than the general law for associations and the
passage from the first to the second group is subordinate to some
form of state control: in Spain and in Sweden this takes place on
the registration of these religions, in Italy through their recognition
according to the law on admitted religions.

Sometimes, but not always, there exists a third level of the pyramid where the religions that enjoy maximum collaboration with the
state are to be found. This is the level of national churches and
the state churches, the Catholic church in concordat countries, the
Orthodox church in Greece, religious communities with which agreements have been stipulated in countries that provide for this form
of regulation of the relations between state and religions: in all these
cases specific rules regulate the relations between the state and a
particular religion, cutting out, in the context of the collaboration
between these two institutions, a sort of made to measure dress which

---

[24] Cfr. de Sousa e Brito, 1994. Art. 24 of the new law on religious freedom (cfr.
above, note 2) extends the possibility of teaching religion in state schools to all the
registered religious faiths. For a picture of the rules regulating the teaching of religion in the countries of the European Union cfr. the volume quoted in the previous note and Messner (ed.), 1995.

can be fitted in the best way possible to the needs of the religious group.

What has been described here is only a paradigm or an ideal model that is not applied perfectly to any country in the European Union. In some cases, the legal system currently in force could be better described by distinguishing two or four steps of collaboration, rather than the three levels shown here; in other cases, the distinction between common law of the associations, special discipline for religions, a special law for one religion is not applicable; in addition, the rights and faculties corresponding to the various levels of the pyramid are not the same in all European countries. In any case, however, the collaboration of the state with religions is selective and graduated. On close examination, it can be seen that this selectivity and graduality also concerns the independence enjoyed by a religious group in the state legal system: its extension and depth varies according to the religions, even if this takes place according to criteria which do not always correspond with those that direct the choices in the field of collaboration between states and religions.

The question that must be asked is the following: what are the rules that guide this selection and graduation of the collaboration that the state gives to religions and the independence it guarantees to them? Are these criteria compatible with the principle of the state's lack of competence on religious matters? And are these criteria compatible with the principle of equality confirmed by all the constitutions of the Member states of the European Union?

5. Problems and Prospects of the European Model of the Relation between States and Religions

To answer these questions, the discourse must once again be taken back to a more general level, which concerns all social groups and not just religious ones.

The constitutions of all European states contain rules that guarantee the freedom of associations that pursue licit ends: within this area, each constitution lays down more specific provisions that oblige the state to collaborate with some institutions and associations, at times specifically identified (the political parties, the trade unions, religious faiths and so on), at times identified in more general terms (for example, social groups which foster the development of the human being). This means that once all licit associations are guaranteed a sphere of freedom, the state can graduate its collaboration according to the characteristics of the associations and their objectives: in many countries, for example, voluntary associations and associations which are non-profit-making enjoy a more favourable organisational discipline or tax system than other associations.

The public authorities can thus select and graduate their collaboration with the organisations of a secular nature according to their characteristics and objectives: is a similar criterion also applicable to collaboration with religions despite the state's lack of competence on religious matters?

An answer in the affirmative can be given to this question. The state's lack of competence precludes all interference and therefore all differentiation based on the doctrine or internal organisation of the religious faiths but does not exclude the power to appreciate the external effects of a religion, that is the behaviour that corresponds to the precepts of a religion but which concerns primarily civil coexistence. Even when this is in the context of lawfulness, this behaviour may present a different degree of deservedness from the point of view of the state: behaviour can contribute differently to the development of those values—the dignity of the human individual, democratic coexistence, freedom of conscience, equality and so on—which are the basis for political order and social peace. On this basis it is possible to graduate the collaboration between public authorities and religious faiths and the independence they enjoy in the state system without violating the principle of lack of competence of the state on religious matters.

This is once again a very general indication, translated into provisions which differ greatly from one state to another. Thus the problems connected to the refusal of blood transfusions or military service have kept Jehovah's Witnesses at the lowest level of the pyramid of religions in many European states: however, this is not the case in Italy, where this religion has recently concluded an agreement with the state putting it at the top of this pyramid.[25] A similar discourse can be repeated for the Muslim community: in Spain it has concluded an agreement with the state,[26] in many other European coun-

---

[25] On this agreement cfr. Colaianni, 2000.

[26] On this agreement and on other problems related with its application, cfr. Martínez Torrón, 1996; Motilla, 2000.

tries it continues to be regulated in forms common to groups with which the states have a more reduced collaboration. But, generally speaking, the religious faiths that encourage in their followers behaviour that complies with the principle on which civil coexistence is based enjoy a wider degree of autonomy and collaboration from the state than those religions based on a different constellation of values.

This selection and graduation of autonomy and collaboration (in which the European model of relations between states and religions is substantiated, together with the protection of individual religious freedom) has not been free of criticism: it would actually favour the most important religions from the point of view of the number of the faithful, historical presence in a country and social importance. This is an observation which is essentially accurate because usually a religion that has been present for many years in a country, with a large number of followers and well inserted into the social structures is a religion that has contributed to forming the cultural and social identity of a people and therefore is normally in tune with the rules and values to which it refers. But I do not think that this criticism, although correct in its actual profile, can be agreed with. Each society is in fact based on a nucleus of relatively stable values and principles that form its identity and represent the specific and characterizing contribution that it can offer in dialogue with other societies. The development and evolution of this identity forms the main path for a progress that is not cancelled in the levelling out the differences between the different civilisations.[27] This nucleus of shared values does not only form the point of reference, capable of orienting the development of the political and legal system (or, to use another term, the deposit 'of values' without which democracy runs the risk of becoming relativistic and absolutistic at the same time). It also represents the framework which cannot be eliminated within which the values of other groups (cultural, ethnic and religious) which have relations with the majority group and settle permanently within its geographic area, must also find a place. This implies a delicate work of reflection and selection aimed first at identifying values and principles (to a great extent deriving from the encounter between the Christian tradition and that of the Enlightenment, as already mentioned) which form the European identity; then

---

[27] Cfr. in this sense Torfs, 1998.

to distinguish inside this what belongs to the deeper nucleus of this identity (and which therefore is not negotiable without disfiguring it) and what appertains to the more superficial layer and is therefore negotiable; lastly to evaluate the ways (which normally are diversified and allow margins of adaptation) of translating these principles and values into the world of law.

In this perspective, the European model of relations between states and religions can be considered a useful tool of integration on condition that some conditions are respected. In the first place, the guarantee of a wide and well defended space of freedom for all religions, including the newest and farthest from the social values traditionally shared. Notwithstanding, obviously, the limit of lawfulness of individual and collective behaviour, this area must guarantee for all religions the possibility not only of surviving but also of developing, ensuring the availability of the legal instruments necessary to guarantee individual and collective religious freedom, as well as the respect of the internal autonomy of the religious group. In more recent years, this rule has not been applied, in my opinion, by all the states of the European Union which, in the face of the diffusion of Islam, and the so-called new religious movements, have at times had recourse to questionable instruments from the point of view of the respect of the rights of freedom.[28] This has cast a shadow not only over the action of individual states but, more generally, on the validity of the European model of church-state relations.

It is moreover indispensable to maintain a certain proportion between the collaboration and support that the states offer to the various religions: if the range between those placed at the lower levels and at the higher levels is too wide—as could be the case in Greece today—not only equality suffers, but also individual religious freedom, which is reduced. There exists in fact a relation between individual freedom and equality of religious groups: the greater the inequality between religions, the more limited the freedom of each member of the less favoured religious groups risks becoming.

The mobility of religious faiths along all the levels of the pyra-

---

[28] Concerning the situation of the new religious movements in France, Belgium and Germany cfr. the contributions published in *Conscience et liberté* nos. 57–59, 1999–2000; more specifically on Germany, cfr. Davis, 2000. In relation to Islam, cfr. Basdevant Gaudemet, 2000, pp. 108–10 for some jurisprudential and administrative action on the issue of the *foulard*.

mid in which they are distributed must also be guaranteed. The European model of state-church relations must be open to the transformations of history: a constant correspondence between social reality and legal reality is essential in order to avoid sudden and traumatic breakdowns which could take place if the system of relations between states and religions were not to reflect, without haste but also without delay, the changes that have already taken place and those under way in the religious panorama of contemporary Europe.

Lastly, it is necessary to reduce the degree of discretionary power enjoyed by the public authorities in establishing the level to which each religion can have access along the hierarchical pyramid mentioned in the previous paragraph, ensuring an effective system of claims against the decisions of the executive power.[29]

If these conditions are respected, the European model not only has good chances of surviving but also of emerging as a reasonable instrument of mediation between 'old' and 'new' Europeans, contributing towards ensuring the evolution of European society through the integration of communities of more recent immigration.

6. Islam and the European Model of Relations between the State and Religions

European Islam has yet to find a precise place within this model. The development of Muslim communities is a relatively recent fact in the majority of the countries of the European Union and only in the past two decades has a set of legal problems linked to their permanent settlement in Europe taken a definite form. The most frequently occurring of these problems are the following:[30]

– the building of mosques, prayer halls and other places of worship;
– the inclusion of spaces and times for prayer in workplaces and public institutions (schools, universities, hospitals etc.);

---

[29] Cfr. in this regard the ruling mentioned above of the European Court of Human Rights in the case of Hassan and Chausch v. Bulgaria, where a request is made for the registration or state recognition of religious communities to be regulated by clear and verifiable provisions and the absence of means of appeal against discretionary decisions of the executive power is condemned.

[30] For an indication of these problems cfr. Vertovec & Peach, 1997, pp. 24–28. Regarding how these problems are dealt with in the European legal systems cfr. Shadid & van Konigsveld (eds.), 2002.

- the recognition of Muslim religious holidays;
- the supply of *halal* food in schools, hospitals, prisons and in other public institutions;
- the possibility of slaughtering animals according to Muslim precepts;
- Muslim sections in cemeteries and the respect of Muslim religious obligations regarding burial;
- the creation and recognition of Muslim schools;
- the teaching of Islam in state schools;
- the separation of genders in physical education classes in schools;
- religious assistance in the armed forces, prisons, hospitals;
- the possibility of wearing the *hijab*;
- the application, in all or in part, of Muslim family law.[31]

Not all these problems will be dealt with in the following pages. They are aimed above all at identifying a methodology with which to evaluate the possibility of accepting the requests put forward by the Muslim community, bearing in mind the European model of relations between states and religions which we have attempted to define in the first part of this chapter.

It must be observed in the first place that the questions raised by the presence of increasingly large Muslim communities do not require a uniform solution in all the countries of the European Union: when they do not have an impact on the platform of common rights and duties which must be respected in all the Member states, they can be regulated in different terms in the individual national legal systems. This solution is coherent with the method with which the issue of coexistence of different religious groups in the European Union has been dealt with to date and which has to a great extent been left to the competence of the national legislations, and it appears perfectly in line with the Declaration on the status of churches and of non-confessional organisations signed by the Member states of the European Union at the Conference of Amsterdam in 1997, according to which "the European Union respects and does not prejudice the status under national law of churches and religious associations or communities in the Member states".[32]

---

[31] In this study the problems connected with Muslim Family Law are dealt with in the contribution by M.-C. Foblets in this volume.

[32] The complete text appears in the *Official Journal of the European Communities*, 10th November 1997, no. C 340. The declaration is dated 16th June 1997.

Bearing in mind these observation, a first set of problems can be approached.

In the first place, the *building of Muslim places of worship* must be examined. Although this is an issue which is full of symbolic and emotional values, the building of mosques or other places of Muslim worship does not raise new legal problems and does not require particular efforts of legislative imagination: the disputes raised, almost everywhere in Europe, by the building of mosques are disputes of a political nature or are connected to concerns of a practical nature (traffic management, parking difficulties, etc.: but these are not problems that are any different from those caused by the erection of any other building which is to house a large number of people) or they are caused by the use as places of worship of buildings that do not have the requisites required by the law for this purpose (and this problem should also be solved by the application of general rules, even if the courts of some countries appear reluctant to apply town planning regulations to these places of worship [van Bijsterveld, 1994]). From a more strictly legal point of view, the possibility for the worshippers of any religious group to establish and maintain places where they can meet to practise their faith and hold meetings of a religious nature is explicitly contemplated as an essential part of the right of religious freedom in art. 6 of the Declaration of the United Nations on the elimination of all forms of intolerance and discrimination based on religion or conviction and is recognised, as part of this same right, by all the legislations of the countries of the European Union. The building and maintenance of places of worship belong to those fundamental rights of religious freedom that are due to all people resident in Europe and which cannot be violated directly or indirectly: the provisions of Greek law which subordinate the opening of places of worship of other religious faiths to the opinion of one religious community (the Orthodox church) have been condemned by the European Court of Human Rights with the Manoussakis ruling of 26th September 1996.[33] In the same ruling, the attribution to the public authorities of excessively great discretionary

---

[33] Cfr. Konidaris, 1994. For the ruling cfr. European Court of Human Rights, Reports of Judgements and Decisions, 1996–IV, n. 17, p. 1346 ss. More in general on the building of mosques in Greece (where there is a difference in the situation between the areas where Greek Muslims live and those where Muslim immigrants live) cfr. Charalambos K. Papastathis, 1998.

power in the process of authorisation necessary for the opening of a place of worship was also declared illegitimate.

Naturally it is possible to discuss whether the public authorities can or even should financially support the building and maintenance of places of worship: but this is another question. Within the European Union there are different rules in force which in some cases (as in Italy and France)[34] privilege some religious faiths compared to others (the Muslim community is amongst the latter in both countries), in other cases (more infrequent) they have led to encouraging the building of mosques (as was the case for a certain period in the Netherlands),[35] in other cases they exclude every form of financing (this is the situation at present in the Netherlands and in Ireland).[36] These different choices come within the scope of the selectivity and gradualness which, within certain limits, can legally distinguish the collaboration of the state with the different religious faiths. As this is a right which directly affects the essential nucleus of religious freedom, this selection and gradualness of the economic support that the public authorities offer the religious faiths must however be based on criteria that are objective as far as possible, such as the numerical consistency of the community requesting financial support to build their place of worship or the non-availability of other places of this type: however, in actual fact these criteria are not always respected.

A similar methodology can be used to approach the problem of *religious assistance in the armed forces, prisons and hospitals.* In this case too there exist well established national rules that can be applied, without substantial modifications, to the Muslim communities. The central

---

[34] In Italy some regional laws lay down economic facilities for the building of places of worship of religions that have stipulated an agreement with the state: a limitation of this type, in the law of the Abruzzo region no. 29/1988 was declared illegitimate by the Constitutional Court with ruling 195/1993. However, not all the regions have adapted to the indications of the Court (cfr. Botta, 2000:117–18). In France, Catholic places of worship built before 1905 are owned by the state and granted for use free of charge to the Catholic church: the expenses for their upkeep are therefore paid by the state. To make up for this situation of inequality, at times the public authorities have supported the building of mosques or synagogues (cfr. Basdevant Gaudemet & Messner, 1994:128–29; Messner, 1999:102–03).

[35] Cfr. van Bijsterveld, 1994:136.

[36] For the Netherlands cfr. *ibidem* (but it is not impossible, in this country, to obtain economic support from the local authorities): in the volume of Ferrari & Bradney (eds.), 2000 there are indications on the current legislation in Belgium, France, Germany and Italy. For Ireland cfr. Casey, 1994:195.

nucleus of the right that must be guaranteed lies in the possibility for the Muslim (as for the member of any other religion) in hospital, prison or serving in the armed forces, to receive religious assistance from a representative of their religion: this possibility is generally acknowledged by the legislation of the countries of the European Union. The concrete methods of organising religious assistance vary from state to state and go from the recognition of the simple right of access to the hospital, prison or military structure for a minister, at the expense of the religious faith, to chaplains permanently resident in the public structure and paid by the state. More frequently there is a combination of the two systems mentioned here, the first applied to the minority religions, the second for the more important ones (this is the case of Portugal, Denmark and Italy, for example).[37] Once again—if the proportions between the support that the state offers to the different religions are respected and if this difference in support has a rational basis (for example in the different numerical consistency of the various religious groups)—these choices could come within a legitimate scope of the discretionary power of the public authorities.

The question of the *recognition of religious holidays*[38] is not as simple. This heading covers the request for absence from work or school on days declared holidays by the religion to which a person belongs. The right to have the time necessary for the activities prescribed by a religion or that of abstaining from work in the fulfilment of a religious obligation is certainly part of the right of religious freedom: but the exercise of this right may have effects that are not negligible on the rights of third parties, for example, when the systematic abstention from a work or school on one day creates problems for organisation of activity at work or school. The problem has been solved in different ways in the various European countries. In relation to the weekly day off some countries (France and Belgium for

---

[37] For Denmark cfr. Garde, 1994:112–114. For Portugal, at least as far as prisons are concerned, cfr. de Sousa e Brito, 1994:248 (but now see also art. 13 of the new law on religious freedom). For Italy cfr. Musselli & Tozzi (2000). On the more complex situation in Germany cfr. Guntau, 2000:285–87.

[38] For a general picture of the civil recognition of religious holidays in the countries of the European Union cfr. European Consortium for church-state Research, 1998. Where not otherwise mentioned, the information in the following lines comes from this volume.

example)[39] do not accept the request, put forward by various religious groups of being able to abstain from work or school on a day other than Sunday:[40] this has created some tension with members of the Adventist religion who refused to send their children to school on Saturdays. Other countries, such as Italy and, to a certain extent, Spain, have on the other hand, recognised the right for Jews and Adventists to abstain from work (except in order to ensure essential services) and school on Saturdays.[41] The Netherlands have generalised this right so that every worker has the right to abstain from work on the day they prefer, independently of religious affiliation and on the grounds of a simple written communication to be given to the employer [van Bijsterveld, 1994:132-33]; parents can have their children exempted from school attendance when this prevents them fulfilling religious obligations [van Bijsterveld, 1994].

In the first instance, the requests of the Muslim community should find a reply similar to that given in these countries to the claims of the same type put forward by other religious communities, in order to avoid unjustified differences of treatment. There could be deviation from this line only where differences emerge in the actual situation, linked for example to the type of request (in relation to the weekly holiday, the Muslims only request having the time necessary to fulfil their religious duties, unlike other religious groups that request abstention from work for the whole day: this is the case of Jews and Adventists), the number of people to whom this exemption should apply (higher in the case of Muslims than in that of Jews and Adventists) or the day on which it falls (Friday, which is a 'full' working day, rather than Saturday, when many productive and scholastic activities are suspended). It is easy to note that these elements play in the opposite direction: some facilitate, others complicate the acceptance of the Muslim requests. In this situation it could be opportune to encourage the implementation of some solutions of a compromise. The agreement between Spain and the *Comisión Islámica*

---

[39] For France cfr. Guimezanes, 1993:88–89: jurisprudence tends to apply this rule with a certain flexibility (cfr. *ibid.*, pp. 89–90). For Belgium cfr. Torfs, 1993:72–74.

[40] But each country has its particularities. In Greece, for example, this rule is applied: however, if the company works continuously throughout the week, the employee is entitled to ask for his day off to be fixed on the day that is a holiday according to his religion (cfr. Manitakis, 1993:153–54).

[41] The relative discipline is contained in the agreements stipulated by the Italian and Spanish states with these religions.

de España lays down (art. 12) the possibility for Muslims to suspend work from 1.30 p.m. to 4.30 p.m. every Friday, subject to agreement with the employer,[42] and to abstain from school during the same period. In England, the problem tends to be solved pragmatically: following the trend of U.S. jurisprudence (but applying it in more restrictive terms), the courts admit the possibility to abstain from work on the holiday laid down by one's religion (or at the times necessary to fulfil worshipping obligations) if, concretely, the organisation of work allows accepting this request without imposing additional obligations on the other workers or generating tension in the management of the company [Bradney, 1993; Slaughter & McClean, 1993:241].

A similar reasoning can be repeated in relation to the question *to abstain from work and school on the days on which other Muslim holidays fall.* In Italy, this right has been recognised, as well as to Jews, to Buddhists and Jehovah's Witnesses;[43] in Austria this possibility does not exist;[44] in the Netherlands the problem is dealt with in the context of the collective labour contracts; in Germany the legislation of some *Länder* allows, on some religious holidays, the members of that religion to abstain from work and school (this rule also applies to members of some non-Christian religions) [Hollerbach & de Frenne, 1998:135]. In this case, the request from the Muslim community does not present any particular features that differentiate it from that put forward by other religious groups: there seems to be all the more reason to put it into the context of the solutions already adopted in the individual countries of the European Union.

The request by Muslims to obtain *halal* meat in the canteens of public institutions raises a more complex problem. In this case something more than the introduction of an exception to a general rule (as in the case of the weekly day off) is being asked of the public authorities: they are being asked to take on a positive service (the supply of food that complies with a religious precept) to allow the

---

[42] The need for an agreement of this kind is also contemplated in the *acuerdos* that recognise the possibility for Jews and Adventists to abstain from work on Saturdays. On the provisions of these agreements, cfr. García Pardo, 2000:293–99.

[43] Cfr. the agreements mentioned *supra*, n. 3.

[44] But in Portugal the employee and the employer can agree to replace the optional holidays of the local patron saint and "Mardi Gras" by a different holiday: cfr. de Sousa e Brito & Teles Pereira, 1998:361. For Austria cfr. Potz, 1998:328.

fulfilment of a religious rule that could be respected even in the absence of that service (as it is sufficient not to consume religiously forbidden foods). In this case the respect of the religious freedom of Muslims (or of Jews, for example) requires that food that is not forbidden by religious rules is available in the canteens of public institutions: a fuller implementation of religious freedom could suggest the supply of food prepared in the respect of religious rules (for example *halal* or *kosher* meat).

As always, the situation is Europe is highly diversified. In some countries (France, for example) neither *halal* (for the Muslims) nor *kosher* (for the Jews) meat is provided in public canteens, but only food (for example eggs or fish) that are normally acceptable for the members of these religions.[45] In other countries (Italy, for example), the agreement with the Union of Jewish Communities lays down under art. 7 the possibility for Jews in hospital, prison and barracks to observe their food obligations with the assistance of their religious community and without costs for the public institution: this means that the institution does not provide *kosher* food but admits that it can be brought from outside and consumed in the canteen at the expense of the Jewish community. In the Netherlands, the law obliges the prison director to do everything possible to provide the prisoners with food that meets their religion or conviction (and the new Italian prison regulations establishes the same thing);[46] furthermore, again in the Netherlands, the food requirements of Jews, Muslims and Hindus serving in the armed forces must also be respected [van Bijsterveld, 1994:131]. In Spain, art. 14 of the agreement with the Islamic Commission establishes that, in schools and public institutions, the utmost must be done to adapt food to Muslim religious precepts.[47] Again there are different solutions, some dictated by concerns of an organisational type, and the fear of creating 'food ghettos' which slow down the process of integration, others more sensitive to the problems of religious freedom (even if formulated with a certain vagueness): however, both appear compatible with the basic

---

[45] Since 1991 it has been possible to obtain *halal* meat in the French Armed Forces (cfr. Basdevant-Gaudemet, 2000:113).

[46] Art. 11 of Presidential Decree no. 230 of 30th June 2000: "In the formulation of the food tables, the obligations of different religious faiths should be taken into consideration as far as possible".

[47] No similar provision is contained in the agreement with the *Federación de Comunidades Israelitas de España*.

principles on which the European model of relations between the states and religions are based, at least as long as the Jew or the Muslim can obtain food in a public canteen that does not go against their religious beliefs.

The questions connected with the request to introduce *the teaching of Islam into state schools* is far more complex. In order to fully understand the complexity of the problem, some general remarks must first be made that illustrate the legal discipline of the teaching of religion in state schools in force in the countries of the European Union. In some of them (for example in France) there is no teaching of this type. In secondary schools, the presence of chaplains, to teach religion, is contemplated and in fact these chaplains are active in 52% of French middle schools and in 62% of lycées:[48] however, none of them teaches Islam.[49]

In other countries, the teaching of religion is non-denominational. This is the case of Great Britain where the doctrine of a specific religion is not taught but a syllabus devised at local level by the representatives of the various religions, by teachers and by the community: under art. 8(3) of the *Education Reform Act* of 1988, this syllabus must attribute special importance to knowledge of the Christian faith, but also supply some notions of the other main religions practised in the United Kingdom, including Islam.[50] Something similar takes place in the Netherlands: religious education is a compulsory subject in primary schools and is taught in non-denominational terms, bearing in mind the various religious situations, including Islam.[51] However, these non-confessional forms of religious education are considered with mistrust by wide sectors of the Muslim community, which fear a certain relativistic drift [Pisci, 2000:17].

In other countries the teaching of religion in state schools is of the confessional type. In Italy the teaching of the Catholic religion is contemplated in all schools. The pupils can choose whether to

---

[48] Cfr. Swerry, 1998:101.

[49] Cfr. Basdevant-Gaudemet, 1994:110. In France (as in Germany and other European countries) Muslim religious teaching is often given in the courses on "Langues et Cultures d'origines": but this solution, juridically improper, has given rise to many controversies.

[50] For a detailed description of this system cfr. Ockelton, 1995.

[51] Cfr. van Bijsterveld, 1994:134. Schools can also offer (and support financially) denominational religious teaching, attendance of which is not compulsory for pupils: in this context in 1992, Islam was taught in four towns.

attend or not; the teachers (who are paid by the state), the textbooks
and the syllabi must be approved by the ecclesiastical authorities.
The religious communities that have stipulated an agreement with
the Italian state[52] can send their own teachers of religion to the
schools on the request of pupils, their parents or teachers: the costs
are at the expense of the religious group. As the Muslim community has not concluded an agreement with Italy, Islam is not taught.[53]
In Spain, where there is a partially similar system in force, the
Comisión Islámica de España concluded an agreement with the state
in 1992, followed in 1996 by an agreement on the appointment
and economic regime of the people appointed to teach Islam. On
the grounds of this rule, at the beginning of each school year the
parents can request that their children are given Muslim religious
teaching by the school; this request is forwarded to the territorially
competent Islamic community, which has the duty to propose teachers, who must have the requisites required by the Ministry for
Education, in turn they are subject to approval by the *Comisión Islámica
de España*. The system is modelled along the lines of that contemplated for the teaching of the Protestant religion in Spanish schools;
but whilst the latter system has worked reasonably well, the mechanism relative to the teaching of Islam has rapidly been hampered
by the contrasts which have arisen between the various Muslim
groups represented on the *Comisión Islámica de España* and for the latter's disagreement with the Ministry for Education regarding the requisites that the teachers of Islam must have. As a result, this religion
is taught only in the autonomous authority of Madrid and in the
town of Melilla, where there is a special discipline in force due to
the large number of Muslims who live there (35% of the total population).[54] The situation is more complex in Germany, where the
(compulsory) teaching of religion in state schools is regulated by the
laws of the various *Länder*:[55] an organic teaching of Islam does not

---

[52] Cfr. *supra*, note 3.

[53] For a presentation of the Italian system, cfr. Finocchiaro, 1995:404–22. In particular on the teaching of Islam cfr. Colaianni, 2000:157–73.

[54] For this information cfr. Mantecón Sancho, 1998:119–134. Note that, when
there are certain conditions, it is contemplated that the teaching of Islam is at the
expense of the Spanish state.

[55] For this reason special disciplines are in force in some *Länder*, such as those
of Brema, Brandeburg and Berlin. On these situations and on the German system
of religious education, with particular reference to Islam, cfr. Guntau, 2000:277–84;
Puza, 1998:129–34.

exist, even if a recent decision by the administrative court of Berlin has opened up this possibility [Puza, 1999:56].

At the end of this brief overview, two observations can be made. In the first place, it is important to note that in no state of the European Union is a Muslim (or a member of any other religion) obliged to receive religious education other than his own: this minimal requisite of religious freedom is respected everywhere.[56] If however we go on to examine the possibility of receiving instruction in one's own religion, it has to be acknowledged that, for one reason or another, the teaching of Islam finds little room in state schools in the countries of the European Union. The objection could be raised that this situation is common to other religions, which are marginalised or even excluded from the state educational system, but they are usually made up of small groups of members, who are not comparable numerically with the Muslim community. The absence of Muslim religious teaching in state schools therefore depends on other reasons and, in the first place, on the fact that in many European countries, the settlement of stable Muslim communities is relatively recent: therefore the conditions that can guarantee the good functioning of the complex mechanism that regulates the teaching of religion in schools are still lacking.

The first of these conditions is the presence of teachers with the necessary background to teach the Muslim religion and having the requisites essential for this function in state schools. In some countries the absence of qualified teachers has been remedied by 'importing' teachers from abroad: this was the case, for example, of Belgium (where the teaching of Islam became possible in 1974, after Islam had obtained state recognition) and Austria where the teaching of Islam in state schools was introduced in 1983. In this country, for about 30,000 pupils there were only 150 teachers, mostly from abroad and therefore not very familiar with German and with the lifestyle in a multi-faith country such as Austria (whereas many Muslim pupils of the second or third generation were now used to these conditions). This situation was incompatible with the objectives of an educational system which, out of respect for the culture and religion of origin of the Muslim immigrants, at the same time wanted to start

---

[56] In the countries where religious education is compulsory, there is always the possibility of exoneration or of opting for a "secular" moral teaching.

up integration in the country where they were going to live. In order
to remedy this difficulty, the *Islamische Religionspädagogische Akademie*
was founded in June 1998 with the task of training teachers of Islam
for state schools [Potz, 1999:72]. It is too early to assess the prospects
of this experiment (the first steps of which appear positive, however)
but it is certain that this road—although not an easy one and which
will take a long time to cover—seems to be the only one capable
of giving a permanent solution to the problem of the training of
teachers of Islam in European schools.[57]

A second condition is the presence of one or more institutions
with a sufficient degree of representation of the whole Muslim community. The need for a similar institutional structure is particularly
pressing in countries where the choice of teachers, syllabi and religious textbooks is the task of or must be approved by representatives of religious communities. The case of Spain is emblematic: the
possibility of teaching Islam is seriously limited by the contrasts that
separate the Muslim organisations belonging to the Spanish Islamic
Commission [Motilla, 2000: 257–59]. Similar difficulties have been
encountered in Belgium: it is hoped that the recent (December 1998)
election of a body named the Executive of Muslims in Belgium can
provide a solution to this problem [Lo Giacco, 2000]. In any case,
these experiences show that it is opportune to wait for a certain sed-
imentation, including organisational, of the Muslim communities
before proceeding with the definitive legal structuring of the teaching of Islam in state schools.

7. Conclusions

From the observations made in the previous paragraph, it is possible to draw some conclusions.

In the first place, the presence of the Muslim communities does
not pose legally unsoluble problems or, on close examination, particularly new ones. On the grounds of experience matured with other

---

[57] In this sense the project of establishing a Faculty of Muslim Theology at the
University of Strasbourg must be mentioned (cfr. Messner, 1997:72–77; Prelot,
1999:114–16). A training programme has also been developed for the leaders of
ethnic and religious minorities, including Islam, in the Netherlands: cfr. van Bijsterveld, 1999:58.

religions, the legal systems of the European countries have the necessary instruments to deal with and solve many of the questions that have been shown in the previous paragraph. The newness and the complexity of the 'Muslim question' does not depend on legal questions but on other factors: on the number of Muslims (much higher than that of the members of any other non-Christian religion), the rapidity with which the Muslim communities have grown up, the absence of stable organisational structures with a wide representation or (to mention elements which are not exclusive to the Muslim community) the radical nature and fundamentalism with which a part of Muslims experience their religious faith, applying the precepts to areas which Western culture is used to considering extraneous from the religious dimension.

In this situation, there are things that not only can but must be done immediately. These are reforms aimed at ensuring for Muslims those fundamental freedoms without which the inequality between the various religious communities inherent in the European system of the relation between state and religions becomes oppressive. In actual fact, the term reform is not exact: it is not a case of innovating but of applying rules that already exist. On the subject of building places of worship, the availability of separate sections in cemeteries, spiritual assistance, ritual slaughtering, the supply of food that does not go against religious obligations and freedom of dress, the legislation of European countries does not have to be modified (except in particular points) but to be applied with equity and far-sightedness.

The need to ensure from the present time these fundamental freedoms is all the more pressing as there are other sectors where a complete levelling of the Muslim community with the other religions, characterised by a longer presence in Europe, will take longer; the teaching of Islam in state schools is an example of this; questions connected with the personal status and family law could provide others. In these sectors, the phase of experimentation and research has not yet come to an end: it is opportune to encourage the attempts that are being made in some European countries in order to have a database allowing more meditated decisions to be taken.

This dynamic appears coherent with the European system of state-religion relations, distinguished by a base of rights and freedoms immediately available for all and by progressively more important facilitations available in correspondence with the process of integration

of the religious communities in the system of fundamental values of
the West. However, this dynamic is not neutral. It presupposes the
capacity and the will of the European Muslim communities to adapt
to the model of religious institution accepted in the West: this implies,
in particular, the construction of a centralised structure (for example, forming national federations of local Muslim communities) and
the acceptance of the distinction between spiritual and temporal, religion and politics introduced into the West by Christianity and revived
(exasperated to some extent) by liberal thought in the past two centuries. This is a long and complex process of transformation but not
devoid of precedents in European history of the past two centuries.

   For all these reasons, Islam represents a particularly significant test
bench for the European model which we have tried to outline in
the first part of this chapter: hence the importance of finding solutions which, without distorting the European identity and legal tradition, allow the 'new Europeans' of Muslim faith and culture to
make their contribution to the construction of a common house.

CHAPTER SEVEN

MUSLIM FAMILY LAWS BEFORE THE COURTS IN EUROPE: A CONDITIONAL RECOGNITION

Marie-Claire Foblets

1. Introduction: Putting Muslim Family Laws into Practice in European Countries. A Thorny Question

Islam in Europe is a new reality. In this paper we have a particular interest in Muslim family law. The way Muslim families organise their life in Europe raises questions that have occupied many lawyers for a number of years. How to take into account family institutions which are foreign to our legal traditions? What effect does the law produce when a Muslim family tradition turns out to involve values which infringe, for example, principles established under human rights conventions?

We will focus here exclusively on those aspects of the question, which have arisen since the 1960s and 1970s in connection with mainly labour immigration of Muslim communities in Europe. The analysis focuses on the way in which courts and tribunals have taken Muslim family law into account in later years.

When called to intervene in cases involving private persons who remained citizens of countries in which Muslim law is applies, judicial and administrative authorities in European states may sometimes be compelled to apply rules derived from Muslim law. In other cases they have to handle the question which effects to grant under local (*lex fori*) law to arrangements made in accordance with Muslim law. These institutions may be unknown in Europe, or significantly differ from corresponding institutions as they have developed in Western legal tradition [Bensalah, 1994; Rude-Antoine, 1997]. Overall, the question of putting family laws into practice in Europe which draw their inspiration from Islam—whether dowry, repudiation or consent to marriage—raises a number of questions that affect the position of an increasing number of families in Europe.[1]

---

[1] For several years many authors have taken an interest in the question of the

The experience of the last few years across Europe shows that the majority of the cases arises in matters relating to the personal status. Some compare the situation to a 'conflict of civilisations' [Mercier, 1972; Deprez, 1988]. In legal practice, the question of whether to take Muslim family laws into account in the regulation of everyday practices and behaviours is bound to the condition that these laws meet the criteria of protection prescribed by human rights and fundamental liberties. In some ways, the legal position of Muslims constitutes in Europe today, fifty years after the adoption of the Universal Declaration of Human Rights by the General Assembly of the United Nations, a new test-case of their application. Muslim family laws derive from a religion and involve institutions not always compatible with the principles which inspired the Declaration and the European Convention on Human Rights and Fundamental Liberties.[2] These principles are imperatives. For almost half a century they have guided both legislators and courts in Europe.

In this brief communication we will attempt to identify some of the arguments used by the courts when faced with questions about the applicability of Muslim family law in Europe. Either they refuse to recognise institutions of infringing the criteria of protection for human rights and fundamental liberties—citing perhaps the need to maintain public order—sometimes on the contrary they accept, allowing Muslims to remain subject to their own family laws in the name of those same criteria (for example, a child's best interest).

An examination of recent European jurisprudence shows similarities and differences. Solutions vary by country and also—as we will try to show—according to the objectives of judges in individual cases. In order to be convinced it may suffice to analyse the jurisprudence in cases of polygamy and repudiation, or to focus attention on cer-

---

application of Muslim family law in Europe. For France, see (among others): Bourdelois, 1993; Deprez, 1988; Deprez, 1989:17–92; Elgeddawy, 1971; Jahel, 1994:31–58; Monéger, 1994:344–374; Rude-Antoine, 1990. For Belgium, see: Carlier, 1996:20–32; Foblets, 1994; Foblets, 1998; Lardinois, 1996:605–629; Rommel, 1980:193–243; Rommel, 1986:604–620; Taverne, 1981; van den Eeckhout, 1996:317–340. For the Netherlands: Buskens, 1999:536–560; Jordens-Cotran, 2000; Rutten, 1988; Rutten, 1997. Austria: Schmied, 1999. For Italy: Mancini, 1998. For comparative approaches, see: Carlier & Verwilghen, 1992; Aldeeb & Bonomi, 1999; von Bar, 1998; Ferrari & Bradney, 2000. This list of available works is far from complete.

[2] For an in-depth study of this Convention and a systematic examination of related jurisprudence, see: Petiti, Decaux & Imbert, 1995.

tain particular rules, such as marriage rules, custody or inheritance. The difficulties are twofold. On the one hand the differences between Muslim family law and systems of family law in European countries confront the judges with a number of particular questions of international private law, such as how to identify and handle a situation correctly (see below, section 2, 'Qualification') as well as to which law applies (the question of applicability; see below, section 3, 'Reattachment to a legal system'), and most importantly the question as how to apply foreign law in a concrete case (see below, section 4, 'The maintenance of public order'). Courts follow different procedures—ending up sometimes with the same conclusions—in dealing with these questions. All this has created a situation of great uncertainty, both for litigants directly involved and for practitioners who must decide cases facing members of families who have migrated from countries where Muslim law applies.

To properly analyse these problems, we would have to scrutinise the bibliography and jurisprudence from the countries with the largest Muslim populations which also share a largely common or at least comparable tradition in the realm of international private law: France, Belgium, the Netherlands and Germany. The writings on this subject have multiplied in recent years.[3] For the purpose of this introductory article, we will limit ourselves to the formulation of a number of observations beginning with an analysis bearing principally on our own experience in doctrine and jurisprudence in Belgium and (to a lesser extent) in France.

We will successively deal with difficulties of qualification, of determination of the law to be applied and finally with the maintenance of public order. In the third section, we will deal briefly with the matrimonial rights of Muslim immigrant women, that today occupy European lawyers as their position is at the core of the question whether or not to recognise discriminatory aspects of some institutions in Muslim family law problem: it raises the question as to what extent the discrimination of women in the realm of family law clashes with local law and therefore is to be refused recognition.

---

[3] *Cf. supra*, note 1.

2. The Qualification: Difficulties Involved in Qualification in the Sense of International Law Concerning Private Persons

The problem of qualification, well-known in international private law, arises whenever it is necessary—either for the judge or a public officer—to determine which law is applicable to a concrete situation or relationship. In order to decide which law applies—in most cases, deciding between the *lex fori* (or local law) and Muslim family laws—the judge must first 'qualify' the case.[4] The question is not a formality. From this initial qualification may depend which law will eventually apply to the case. Consider a marriage between two Muslims. In Belgium procedural and administrative aspects of the marriage usually follow the *lex fori*. The question however may arise as to know what aspects relate to the procedure. Does the obligation under Islamic law for the wife to have the consent formulated by a male relative relate to procedure? Depending on the qualification of this particular obligation—whether form or basic condition—the public officer will require the wife or her representative to consent to the marriage. By conceiving of the matrimonial guardian or representative as a formal requisite, a formal aspect of the marriage ceremony so to say, the public officer may ignore this formality, as it is unknown in local law. Not so if he qualifies the matrimonial representative's intervention as being a basic condition of validity of marriages under Muslim law. In other words, the judge or a public officer must first decide how he identifies (in legal terms, qualification) a particular institution or aspect of family law that applies in the case that is submitted to him.

At times the basic characteristics of Muslim family laws raise difficulties simply because they are unknown in western law. Courts then are led or even forced to innovate: judges may in given cases attempt to treat situations involving Muslims correspondingly to local law, thus allowing the handling of their consequences for the parties. This is notably the case when courts have to settle disputes of

---

[4] For an analysis of questions which can be raised by the difficulty of 'qualification' under French law of an institution from Muslim family law, see: Hochart (1994), note sous Cour d'Appel Paris, 8 décembre 1992, Dalloz, II.272. The aim of the text is to give as correct a juridical interpretation as possible, in terms of French law, of the rights and privileges which accompany Muslim marriage.

polygamy or repudiation, or cases of (non-) payment of the dowry (*mahr*), of recognition of the legitimacy of a child (*iqrar*), or of *kafal'ah* (equality of status).

It is generally assumed that the requirement for a judge or a public officer to qualify a concrete situation involves a double obligation. First of all one has to consider the foreign rule that will perhaps apply in order to determine its characteristics and its function. This analysis must be carried out with reference to the particular foreign legal system involved.[5]

In the second phase, qualification proper, the foreign institution must be so to say 'identified' and thus placed in a category among those provided in international private law: marriage and its effects, matrimonial regimes, divorce, etc. In practice it is customary that judges or public officers show flexible in identifying rules or institutions that in foreign law appear to have similar functions. If this were not to be the case, it would be impossible to determine which law is applicable, each time a particular institution appears alien or unknown to the local law (*lex fori*).

Along these lines, for example, only a flexible interpretation of notions known in international private law in relation to the dissolution of marriage allows judges to apply conflict of law rules to cases of repudiation. The courts do not stick to the letter of the law, but apply the same conflict of law rule in all cases of voluntary dissolution of the marriage including repudiation. The act of repudiation is so to speak 'treated as' a divorce, for the reason that its effect is just the dissolution of a marital contract. And this is done even though repudiation under Muslim law is a private act which—in contrast to the provisions made in divorce laws throughout Europe—does not normally require the intervention of any judge or state authority.[6] But this does not mean that a judge is forced to recognise, as a 'fait accompli', the dissolution by repudiation of a Muslim marriage. In practice it often happens that a judge will refuse to recognise any effect to a repudiation by reference either to fair trial or to the principle of equality before the law of men and women, or even to both. We will return to this point.

---

[5] There is no other way to proceed, particularly when the law of the country of residence is silent regarding the foreign institution in question.

[6] It may occur, that in order to be contestable, repudiation must be pronounced before a judge. Such is the case, for example, in Moroccan law (art. 48 *Mudawwana*). *Cf.* Carlier, 1985.

Another commonly cited example in this context is that of polygamy, accepted under Muslim family law,[7] but prohibited in Europe. To the extent that polygamy fulfils the same function as marriage, courts have allowed that the conflict of law rules relating to the validity of the marriage may equally govern the question of the effects resulting from polygamous marriage[8] and that therefore some effects may be opposable.

Qualification becomes even more complicated when one and the same rule or institution under Muslim law fulfils (under various circumstances) various functions which in the European legal tradition belong to different institutions. In such cases it is necessary to carry out a detailed analysis of the institution under foreign law, and then to choose from among rules of conflict of law the one most appropriate to the given case. These two tasks are not always easy to accomplish. How should one qualify, taking a concrete example, an institution such as the *tanzil*, which under Muslim law has the object of assuring an heir for someone who has no descendants? The judge may hesitate between the rules of conflict of law applicable to adoption and those applied in cases of conflict over an inheritance. The result will vary according to the position the judge will take (that is, according to his qualification). Criteria of connection which apply in cases of adoption may not coincide with criteria applied in cases of inheritance and their settlement. However, to our knowledge this question has not yet come up in Belgian jurisprudence.

A particularly complex problem of qualification judges are regularly confronted with is that of dowry (*mahr*), an institution which may fulfil different functions in different cases [El Karouni, 1999: 85–108]. Usually considered under Muslim law as a condition of the validity of a marriage, its real function becomes apparent especially in case of dissolution of the marriage while it then may ensure some means of existence for the wife. From this point of view, it is most closely related to laws governing divorce and alimony. But the dowry can also be considered as an attribution of patrimony settled by the husband upon the wife; from this angle dowry relates to matrimonial property law. Thus different qualifications lead to the applica-

---

[7] Legally abolished in Tukey and Tunisia.

[8] The question whether a married person can legally marry again is traditionally considered in most European countries as a question of the validity of a marriage. See, among others: Bourdelois, 1993.

tion of different conflict of law rules and may therefore end up in different solutions.

One more particular example of qualification dealing with Muslim family law is the hypothesis when a judge or public officer has to consider a rule or an institution which is unknown under the *lex fori*, that is, the private law of a given state. It is for the court then to decide whether it handles the case as a problem of conflict of law or possibly as an issue of recognition of an act (or judgement) accomplished under foreign law (with its own consequences). This is the case with repudiations accomplished in Muslim countries. Though even Muslim family laws usually require that the wife be notified of her repudiation before a judge, that condition does not alter the fact that the repudiation *in se* is a private act, thus valid by the sole will of the husband and that the Muslim judge in such a case has no function except to *attest* the unilateral decision of the husband to dissolve the marriage [Carlier, 1985]. Jurisprudence on this question is not unanimous: some courts have refused to grant recognition to a repudiation accomplished in a foreign country, trumping the rules of recognition of foreign judgments by reference to the due process requirements that are not guaranteed in the case of repudiation. We will return to this point as well. Other courts have, by contrast, handled repudiations accomplished in foreign countries in terms of conflicts of law.[9]

3. The Connecting Factor: On the Role of Nationality versus Domicile

Once a situation has been properly qualified, it is possible that the connecting factor—which assigns a particular situation to one system of law or another—leads to application of Muslim law. This is frequently the case in countries where international private law techniques attach great importance to nationality as the connecting factor. Nationality so to say connects a person to a particular (national) law. It is the case particularly in France, Belgium, Spain, and Italy,

---

[9] But quite often these rules of conflict (of laws) only have divorce in view—repudiation does not exist in our legal tradition. In such cases, as we mentioned, courts depart from the letter of the law, and apply the rules of conflicts of law to any kind of voluntary dissolution of marriage.

where many Muslims have retained the nationality of their country of origin and to whom therefore Muslim law still applies in matters relating to their personal status.

On the incompatibility of Muslim family laws with public law and order

The question then is to know under what conditions this applicability in principle of Muslim family law will effectively be recognised within the jurisdiction of one of the above mentioned European countries. This question is not an easy one to answer. A particular problem which arises, linked to the status of Muslims in Europe, is the question of the compatibility of certain institutions and practices known under Muslim law with public order.

In order to lessen the risk of having to apply in Europe rules or institutions that fall under Muslim law, violating fundamental principles of the local law, there is a well-known technique in international private law that consists of simply setting aside the foreign law every time the application of that foreign law risks leading to situations of incompatibility with fundamental principles of an internal legal system. The foreign law is set aside whenever the court invokes public order as a reason. The court's openness toward foreign institutions is thus limited by the necessity of respecting certain principles, considered as ranking higher. The maintenance of public order has been cited more often in recent years whenever the connecting factor tips toward Muslim law [Meeusen, 1997]. It is a fact that a number of Islamic institutions are likely to generate a conflict with principles considered fundamental in European countries. The examples often cited in this context bear on the unequal treatment of Muslim women in the realm of family law, which conflicts with the principle of non-discrimination for reasons of gender (polygamy, repudiation, custody of children), or for reasons of religion (religious prohibitions regarding marriage, or in other cases, rules which prevent non-Muslims from inheriting from a Muslim).

In general, unequal treatment of Muslim women in the area of family law may have two reasons. One of them, which by definition cannot be remedied—at least in the short term—by legal means (that is, by the techniques of the law), involves traditions: within certain families, discriminatory practices persist. These mainly deal with education and culture. However, discriminatory practices which are the result of traditions and customs are not found only in Muslim families. They occur in all strata of society. One might mention, for example, the case of stricter education given to girls, of parents who claim the right to choose their children's marriage partners (particularly in the case of girls), or of husbands who claim the right to keep control over marital property.

The second reason is linked to the system, already mentioned, that connects a person to his or her national law, a system which is still valid in several European countries. This system may lead to the application within the country of residence of the parties of a discriminatory foreign law. This possibility results from the rule of conflicts of law in private international law (derived, in Belgian law, from line 3, article 3 of the Civil Code) which either declares the law of the nationality of the parties applicable, or may lead to granting recognition to the consequences of a judgment handed down in that country. We referred to this above.

Jurisprudence and doctrine are divided on the way(s) of countering the discriminatory effects of Muslim family laws. In practice, gender-based discrimination in the area of personal status due to the applicability of rules valid or judgements made under foreign law(s) often runs up against the *public order exception*:[10] both courts and public officers refuse to apply discriminatory regulations even if they are perfectly valid under foreign law.[11] Most European countries today are bound by various treaties and regulations which prohibit discrimination [Lemmens & Alen, 1991; Bossuyt, 1976; Velu, 1981; Rimanque, 1987; Theunis, 1997]. The prohibition against gender-based discrimination belongs to the domain of public order, which in principle suffers no exceptions.

However, the reference to public order does not eliminate the problem of unequal treatment of Muslim women. The maintenance of public order constitutes in practice a last line of defence which nonetheless cannot annul all the effects resulting from an actual situation which has been established in accordance with foreign law. Despite the protective function of public order, several specific forms of discrimination still persevere. This occurs either because (1) these

---

[10] On the public order exception and its use in international private law, see especially: Lagarde, 1993:263–282. For a very critical approach to the use of the public order exception in Belgian international private law, see: Heyvaert, 1981–1982; van Mensel, 1990:8–15; Carlier, 1991.

[11] For examples, see (among others): Sarolea, 1997:9–30.

forms of discrimination remain in fact recognised and maintained
under foreign law, which implies differences of treatment—in the
country of residence (in Europe) versus the country of origin—in
identical cases[12] (these situations are termed 'limping' in private international law), or because (2) courts and administrative bodies dis-
agree among one another on the way in which discrimination is to
be prevented: some magistrates eventually give preference to a partial recognition of discriminatory practices, arguing that by doing
otherwise they would not improve the situation, meaning there is no
better solution for the parties to the conflict.[13] In principle, courts
maintain the rule of conflicts of law declaring foreign law applicable, but without authorising the application—this holds good in
France, Germany, and the Netherlands as well as in Belgium—of
rules or institutions under foreign law which are themselves discriminatory. In other words: courts accept the consequences of non-
discriminatory foreign laws, but refuse to uphold discriminatory laws
or institutions. This solution is very flexible, but for that reason just
as uncertain: whether or not foreign law is discriminatory is a matter of case law, and courts decide such questions case by case.

This observation also holds for the (already mentioned) recourse
to the public law and order exception: in practice, courts' opinions
differ when it comes to the question which principles of law in par-

---

[12] This applies also in the case of bipatride women, i.e. who are naturalized
Belgian citizens and therefore have the double nationality.
[13] See for example: Tribunal de Première Instance (civil, 5ème chambre), Namur,
17 mai 1990. The court held that the *talaq* (unilateral repudiation on the husband's
initiative) is a private juridical act which draws its entire force from the sole will
of the husband, without any possibility of denial or sanction, since there is no
homologation of it. Therefore no assertion of the right to due process (for the
woman) can be made. The *talaq* cannot be held to be contrary to public order
under Belgian international law, simply because of a failure to respect the wife's
rights to due process. The court opined that it was necessary to understand and
accept the existence in other juridical systems of a different conception of divorce.
As for the notion of public order, a distinction must be drawn between the acquisition of a right in Belgium and the recognition of the consequences of a situation
legally acquired in a foreign country. The court recognized the validity of repudiation. But as concerned alimony, Moroccan law was set aside in the name of public order. Over and above the "gift of consolation", judged insufficient, the court
awarded the wife regular monetary support. The judge further opined that in conformity with Belgian law unilateral repudiation could be compared to divorce based
on mere separation (art. 232 of the Belgian Civil Code), and thus cause to weigh
upon the husband a presumption of responsibility for the separation of the parties
(Civ. Namur (5ème ch.), *Revue trimestrielle de droit familial*, 1990, 431, note Carlier
and *Revue du droit des étrangers*, 1991, n° 64, 225).

ticular might be threatened in cases of Muslim family laws. A quick review of jurisprudence shows that the kind of arguments related to threat to public order that are objected against the application of Muslim family laws differ from country to country, and according to the jurisprudence of various courts.[14] For example, religious objections to marriages have sometimes been seen as contrary to the principle of the freedom of marriage, sometimes contrary to the principle of the secular nature of marriage, and sometimes contrary to principles of non-discrimination for reasons of religion or gender (equality of men and women). As for repudiation, it has been considered to contradict the principle of the equality of partners in a marriage, the principle of the dignity of women, as well as the woman's right to due process (because of the unilateral character of repudiation).

All this obviously renders the recourse to the public order exception quite problematic. In order to limit the undesirable effects of making such recourse too easy, so that Muslim law should be set aside in a more or less systematic fashion but for different reasons, it is generally held that foreign law can only be set aside in cases in which its application, *according to the circumstances of the case*, would lead to an intolerable result. In other words, the examination (of the violation of certain principles held to be fundamental) must be made in the light of the concrete situation, and the aspect of public order cited must have a concrete character [Lagarde, 1993]. This means that the concrete examination of the situation must eventually allow, in the light of the particular circumstances in which the situation was produced, for the recognition of at least some of the effects of a foreign (e.g. Muslim) law, even if this law considered in an abstract fashion is in flagrant contradiction with a fundamental principle within the country of residence's legal system. Thus for example some courts have been led to recognise at least some of the effects produced by a polygamous marriage, considering that the interest of children, and their protection, would be better served by recognition—even partial—of the actual marital situation of the parents. Another example is that of repudiation: it is not rare to see a judge take into consideration the fact that repudiation may have been effected with the consent, or even at the request of the woman, and to allow her to obtain the dissolution of the marriage [Ballion,

---

[14] For a recent comparative analysis, see: Aldeeb & Bonomi, *op. cit.*, 1999.

1989:69–94]. In particular, this is the case when the recognition is requested by a woman who wants to remarry (another man). It is true that this opinion is not universally held. Some judges continue to refuse to recognise any effects of repudiation. The third example we will cite here concerns the automatic extension of parental authority to the father under Muslim law. Although this is fundamentally discriminatory against the mother, it may occur that this provision is recognised, in certain cases, as to be in accordance with the actual interest of the child involved. The examination of the actual situation of the parties then defeats the principle of non-discrimination. As a result a rule of Muslim family law will be applied.

There is another nuance which also allows lessening the undesirable effects of arbitrary recourse to the public order exception. A judge may namely decide not to take recourse to the public law and order exception with as much force when it comes down to recognise, locally, the effects of a situation which was established without fraud in a foreign country, and in conformity with the rules of international private law. This nuance borrows from the theory of the *diminished effect* of public order (*'l'effet atténué' de l'exception d'ordre public*). The application of this theory has for a number of years allowed a great flexibility in the jurisprudence—in France especially—as regards the recognition of the effects of repudiation and polygamous marriage [Bourdelois, 1993; Ancel, 1993], when those arrangements were effected in the country of origin of the parties. Though a repudiation might be without effect when carried out (for example) in France or Belgium, some effects of repudiations carried out in the country of origin in conformity with the national law of the parties (of that country of origin), have been recognised.[15] The same is true with regard to the effects of a polygamous marriage validly contracted in a foreign country [Taverne, 1983:237–248]. Still, apparently this approach, which had some success during the 1980s, is today put to doubt, to the point that some courts—French courts in particular—have reversed course, beginning to tilt toward the systematic *refusal* of recognition of any effect of repudiations carried out in a foreign country.[16] The critics have a point, it is true. Some have warned

---

[15] For an analysis of the jurisprudence on this question in the Netherlands, see: Jordens-Cotran, 1999:199–220; more recently, by the same author: *op cit.*, 2000:207–222.

[16] See on this question (among others): Lagarde, 1993:263–282; Monéger,

against possible abuses which might occur if citizens of a Muslim country were in some way 'authorised' to repudiate their wives in their country of origin, even if the marriage had been established in Europe. There is a great risk then that the interests of the repudiated woman will be neglected. How can a judge be assured of her free and full consent, in cases where repudiation has been pronounced in a foreign country? Accordingly, courts are more cautious today. Judges express their desire to protect the woman's interests, especially in cases where she has acquired the nationality of the host country (for example, France or Belgium). Courts also give priority to divorces initiated in Europe—that is, where the parties live—*before* any eventual repudiation in a foreign country. Such decisions have been based on fundamental principles recognised under the European Convention on Human Rights: equality of the partners in a marriage (article 14) and the right of the woman to a due divorce procedure (article 6). The hostility of the jurisprudence to the recognition of the effects of repudiation today is quite patent.

The examples could be multiplied. The various techniques used by the courts to moderate the recourse to the public order exception are evidence of the dilemma which confronts European judges when they are faced with Muslim family laws. Recourse to public order, based on a hierarchisation of interests, can be construed in various ways. We have mentioned several. But in the end recourse to public order to counteract the undesirable effects of a foreign law for various reasons is not a happy solution. Obviously, the solution runs a great risk of *not* being recognised in the parties' country of origin. Apart from that risk, the main reason why recourse to public order should be an absolutely exceptional solution, and remain so, is that its application is purely depending on the judge's conviction. The result is known: a very hesitant and divided jurisprudence with regard to this question.

1992:345–374; Alexandre, 1993:125–142; more recently: EL-Husseini, 1999, 427–468; for a chronological overview of the Belgian jurisprudence on this question, see: Foblets, 1998:295–376, particularly p. 376.

What is the appropriate connecting factor: the nationality or the domicile of the parties?

There are other legal techniques to counter the incompatibilities between foreign and local law. In countries where nationality is still widely employed as the connecting factor in matters of family law, the criterion of the domicile or that of actual residence have had a mostly secondary function, that is, they are not taken into account unless the criterion of nationality cannot be used (e.g. in the case of stateless persons) or is equivocal (e.g. in the case of a marriage between citizens with different nationalities). One way of combating effects of foreign laws considered unacceptable—such as discrimination against women—is to modify the rule of conflict. The court will replace, so to speak, the rule of conflict of laws connecting the situation of the parties to the law of their nationality with a rule of conflict connecting the situation with the law of their habitual and effective residence (domicile). The reason for this is that the law of the country in which the parties habitually reside, offers more guarantees of equal treatment of the spouses (as concerns divorce, for example). And still it is not certain that this solution, which applies according to each case—that is, depending on the judge's decision—would in fact offer more guarantees to the parties. The judge will decide one way or the other, depending on his examination of the circumstances of the case. Therefore it is difficult to predict in which case and under which conditions the *lex fori* will effectively apply.

A less arbitrary solution would be to conclude bilateral accords with the countries of origin of Muslim immigrants. This solution has been discussed at diplomatic level for several years in Belgium (as also in France).[17] The purpose of these agreements is to establish between the country of residence of the parties and their country of origin rules of international private law that guarantee reciprocal recognition of solutions worked out by courts in both countries in order to settle cross-border family disputes either between Muslim partners, or between the partners in mixed marriages [Carlier, 1994; Foblets, 1994a].

Each solution—be it public law and order or bilateral agreements—shows a *political choice*. Rules of conflict favouring the national law

---

[17] See in particular: Monéger, 1984: 29–69 and 267–288; for a critical report on the effects as far produced by this convention, Monéger, 1999:185–198.

of the parties are modified to benefit a wide application of the law of the country of habitual residence, reflect a choice for *forced integration* of Muslim families residing in Europe with the rules of family law effective in their country of habitual residence. In so doing, one does not consider the eventual complications possibly arising from that solution, for example, the fact that such an application of the law of the country of residence is generally not recognised in the country of origin [Sarhane & Lahlou-Rachdi, 1995:81–108; Elgaddawy, 1971:144–172; Deprez, 1988:42 ff.]. The solution applied in such cases is in other terms not 'exportable'. This solution thus contrasts sharply with the one in which the foreign law is upheld insofar as it is not discriminatory.[18] That solution permits a certain degree of *pluralism*, as long as the parties retain their foreign nationality, and do not seek to obtain the nationality of the country of residence and by doing so get dual nationality. Under the second solution, a Muslim may, in the context of his or her family relations, persist in claiming the application—even in the country of residence—of the law of his or her nationality, possibly Muslim family law.[19]

During the 1980s and 1990s, a number of legislative reform programmes, notably in Italy and Germany, have taken away from nationality some of its almost 'sacred' aura. In view of the growing number of immigrants from outside Europe, some authors have started pleading for a radical reduction of the role of nationality in international family issues. In French and Belgian international private law, a preference in the civil code for connection to the nationality has been tempered over the years by jurisprudence actually for various reasons relying largely on the connecting factor that is the habitual residence or domicile.[20] The few laws of conflict that so far have been worked out via legislation—and not jurisprudence—in Belgium in the realm of international family law relate to parenthood and divorce. Both laws show preference for the connecting factor that is the domicile or habitual residence of the parties.[21]

---

[18] Based on one or other criterion of discrimination prohibited under Belgian law. See among others: Watté, 1986:911–928.

[19] This would be true as long as the person remains a citizen of the country of origin, without attempting to acquire in addition citizenship of the country of residence.

[20] For an analysis of this tendency across Belgian jurisprudence, see: Meeusen, 1997.

[21] In Belgian divorce cases, by application of the law of 27 June 1960 concerning

The result of all these changes is not in doubt: over time, the scope of application of the national law of the parties in matters relating to international family law issues has been considerably reduced.

One part of the doctrine suggests restraining even more the scope of foreign law, by subjecting foreigners—in the domain of family law—to the law of the country of residence after a certain number of years of residence in that country. Distinctions related to nationality would cease to apply.[22] This suggestion is similar, directly or indirectly, to the requirement, in German doctrine and jurisprudence especially, of a minimum degree of proximity of the situation of the parties to German law. According to this viewpoint, German law applies to all situations which manifest some required degree of 'Inlands'—or 'Binnenbeziehung', and are thus 'tied' to the German legal system. The existence of such a link must be verified, case by case. The theory of 'Inlandsbeziehung' has been definitively maintained in a number of cases including those concerning Muslim family law. In cases of repudiation, for example, carried out in a foreign country, German law is held to apply—and thus the effects of repudiation are not recognised—when the woman is German or when the couple has lived in Germany for a long time. In France also, Muslim family law has been frequently set aside as soon as one of the parties, usually the one who enjoys protection under criteria of human rights or fundamental liberties, has acquired French nationality or resides in France, whether the case involves a first wife in a polygamous marriage, a woman repudiated in a foreign country, or a child seeking to establish legal paternity [Lagarde, 1993:263–282].

---

the "admissibility of divorce when one of the parties is a foreigner" ("sur l'admissibilité du divorce lorsqu'un des conjoints au moins est étranger") (*Moniteur Belge*, July 9, 1960); in adoption cases, in accordance with the law of 27 April 1987, introducing art. 344, par. 1 to the Belgian Civil Code (*Moniteur Belge*, May 27th 1987; which authorizes a legal adoption (simple adoption) of children under the age of 15 under Belgian law, even where the national law of one or both of the parties does not recognize adoption (See among others: Verwilghen, Carlier, Bedroux & de Burlet, 1991; Verwilghen, 1993:149–170.

[22] Along these lines: Monéger, 1999:374; Deprez, 1999:113 ff.

Alternative connecting factors

In the absence of unanimity for the best solution, it is not rare to see courts adopt alternative conflict of law techniques that allow for 'fair' solutions.

Let us consider the example of a marriage solemnised between Muslims in a private setting, that is, without the participation of either a public officer or a religious authority. This kind of ceremony is no longer tolerated in a number of European countries. Still, it can hardly be denied that a private ceremony—to the extent that this term is applicable—may also have, in the eyes of the parties, the effect of creating a marital bond. Some courts have not hesitated to recognise such a marriage, as long as it was valid under the laws of the place in which it had occurred, or even, in certain cases, according to the national law or the place of residence of the couple. The criterion of connection in such a case is therefore chosen according to the kind of recognition sought (*'favour matrimonii'*).[23]

The same type of reasoning can be found in the case of the recognition of a child: when litigation is about the establishment of paternity (*'favour filiationis'*, *'favour legitimitatis'*), courts tend to apply the law most favourable to that establishment. It is not rare to see a judge, through his choice of the connecting factor, attempt to avoid any application of Muslim law in cases where that law is not in harmony with the child's best interests.[24] Thus the judge does not need to invoke the exception of public law and order and the necessity to maintain it.

And despite all this, the results are not systematically against Muslim family law. It is true that rules of conflict based on the principle of *'favour filiationis'*, for example, allow to set aside rules of Muslim law hostile to extra-marital paternity [van den Eeckhout, 1994:108–115]. One must be aware, though, that alternative connecting factors can also lead to the application of Muslim law whenever this would be advantageous to the child. Such would be the case, for example, when Muslim law recognises the legitimacy of a child born well after the dissolution of a marriage, or of a child recognised under the institution of *iqrar*.[25]

---

[23] For an example of such recognition, see among others: Foblets, 1992:220–225.
[24] On this notion and the many definitions it receives throughout the world, analysed from the perspective of human rights, see: Alston, 1994.
[25] The analysis of this institution known under Muslim law shows that it involves granting legitimacy to a child whose father is unknown.

Again, examples could be multiplied. At present, it is clear that European courts one time apply the law of the country of residence, another time the law of the country of origin, depending on the technique of international private law applied, *in casu* the connecting factor. At times they may be led, by reason of the nationality of the parties, to uphold rules of Muslim family law. By seeking 'fair' solutions through the use of divergent techniques of international private law, courts over the years have contributed to what is today a very confusing jurisprudence.

As we have tried to make clear, this does create difficulties in legal terms. One way to overcome these difficulties is, more radically, the option of a blanket application of the law of the country of residence (or domicile) of the parties.

The mandatory application of the law of the country of the residence of the parties

In some cases the application of foreign law—whether this is Muslim family law or some other foreign law—does not even enter into consideration, since the law of the country of residence is applicable because its application appears just necessary (*loi de police*) and allows no exception.

In France and Belgium, for example, jurisprudence has attributed a strictly 'territorial' application to the rules on the personal effects of the marriage.[26] Another example is the obligation in a number of European countries to solemnise marriage in a form prescribed by the *lex fori*, that is, before a public officer of the state, without regard to the nationality of the parties. This is the case in Germany, France, and Belgium.[27]

The same holds as regards the adoption of minor children. In many European countries today the adoption of minors comes under the law of the country of residence. By doing so the prohibition on adoption under Muslim law is evaded. A number of courts have thus been led to acknowledge the adoption of Muslim children who

---

[26] Regarding Belgium, see especially: Watté, 1993:239–275; Watté, 1994:127–133.

[27] It is true that in Belgium an exception to this rule is made for marriage vows taken between Moroccan citizens. These couples, by virtue of an agreement between Belgium and Morocco, have the right to be married by Moroccan consular authorities officiating in Belgium. See on this subject: Verhoeven, 1980:717–722.

reside in a European country, notwithstanding their national origin.[28]

Solutions moderating the mandatory application of the law of the country of residence are more flexible, because they may bring the judge to take into account the law of the country of origin of the parties. This flexibility may prove important. It allows courts, according to the circumstances of each individual case, to take into consideration the effects of situations created or recognised under Muslim law. To do otherwise could cause harm to the litigants who thus will have to cope with the situation that their position or relationship as it is recognised under Muslim law is denied validity in the country of residence (in Europe). 'Limping' situations are difficult to live with.

The autonomy of the will of the parties

Must incompatibilities between the principles of law characteristic of western legal traditions and Muslim family laws necessarily lead to open conflict, and to the application of techniques of international private law setting aside Muslim law, sometimes in a radical way? It is true that the jurisprudence is hesitant as to which criteria should be used in order to give preference to the *lex fori*. A profoundly unfair situation is the result, in which courts are unable to offer even a minimum of security to the parties involved. Today nothing prevents two identical situations when submitted to the evaluation of a judge from being treated in completely different ways by one court or by another, despite the fact that the situations of the parties in both cases are very similar and the interests at stake practically identical. One judge will show tolerance of the way in which the status of persons and family relations are organised under Muslim law, and another judge will lay most weight on the fundamental principles European civil society is founded upon today. We have given several illustrations of this division within jurisprudence.

In order to overcome the dilemma, some authors have proposed

---

[28] See also: footnote 207 (*cfr. supra*). These acknowledgements however are submitted to the condition that only children who *legally* reside within the boundaries of the country—that is, in conformity with the immigration laws—can be adopted, so as to prevent attempts to circumvent the immigration laws. The national law (Muslim law, which prohibits adoption) still applies to children who do not habitually and legally reside in Europe.

to put more emphasis in international private law upon the autonomy of the will of the parties, and as an effect of this emphasis to allow foreigners who reside in European countries to choose between the law of the country of origin and that of the country in which they habitually reside [Carlier, 1992a].

At present, in the domain of family law, the autonomy of the will of the parties plays so to say no role, except in certain situations in which the patrimonial interests of the parties come into play. In Belgian law today for example, the choice of the matrimonial regime between spouses is admitted under certain conditions. This is also the case in e.g. France, Germany and Switzerland. The same applies in inheritance cases as well. In the domain of international private law today, only Spanish law recognises, for spouses who do not share the same nationality, the right to submit their marital relationship either to the law of the country of origin of one party, or to the law of the country of residence. In France, some jurisdictions have interpreted the fact that a marriage had been contracted under Muslim law—and with a stipulated dowry, in some cases—as an indication of the tacit will of the couple to be submitted their property to Muslim law, which acknowledges no other matrimonial regime except separation of property.

The solution based on the autonomy of the will of the parties in the area of international family law is not unanimously endorsed [Ganage, 1992:425–454]. The autonomy of the will does not provide a model for the development of international family law that also can guarantee unequivocal and thus coherent solutions and thus security.[29]

And yet this solution presents certain advantages. The option left to the parties to choose the law that applies to their relationship would permit solutions adapted to the particular circumstances of the legal relationship between the parties. It would allow overcoming the obstacle of the radical opposition between two legal systems in the name of a quest for international harmony. Traditionally, connection with the law of the country of origin is supposed to best fit the interests of parties in the context of temporary immigration; a bond with the country of origin is considered to subsist. In contrast, the solution deferring to the law of the country of habitual residence

---

[29] Along these lines, with others: Vonken, 1988:51–99.

takes its cue from a new reality, namely, that of permanent immigration. The solution involving connection with the law of the country of residence may provide a more suitable solution for foreigners who reside permanently in the host country and therefore are no longer to be considered truly 'immigrants'. They have integrated over time into the new society, and they have—whether they know it or not—reinforced their 'bond of proximity' with the country of their residence. To the extent that temporary and permanent immigration vary in time and space, and often co-exist, the *optio iuris* allows the parties to adapt the rules of conflict—national law or law of habitual residence—to the necessities of their individual situation. The choice of the legal system that applies to them thus permits the parties, under the condition that they are well informed as to the circumstances and the consequences of their choice, to (re-)gain a certain control over their family life.

It goes without saying that the flexibility conveyed to the parties by the *optio iuris* must be accompanied by clear rules of application. Strict rules will be necessary if we are to place a high value on the autonomy of the will of the parties under international private law. The option should be provided as the corrective to an excess of territoriality. How far, for example, will the autonomy of the will be carried as regards marriage and divorce? The purpose is not to grant anyone the right to do as one pleases, but to guarantee, with a view of justice regarding the parties, a right to choose to remain submitted, within limits authorised by the law, to the national law (of the parties) alone. The law of the country of residence only applies when this choice is refused. At this point, the option to choose between legal systems must be radically distinguished from the autonomy of the will in internal law. For the rest, it will be necessary to specify who is competent and in which cases, in order to formulate a choice of this kind. The future will reveal whether the solution allowing the autonomy of the will of the parties will have an effect on the long term on international private law.

What, in the domain of family law, could help stabilise the position of Muslim communities in Europe? The great number of solutions proposed over the years proves the level of interest in the question. It also indicates, perhaps, the level of misgivings that the problem gives rise to, when it provokes conflicts between different laws—all the more difficult to resolve because certain aspects of family life are conceived differently in Western and in Muslim law. But there are not only misgivings. In this as in other domains of law, complex problems call forth a variety of judicial and doctrinal solutions. A contribution such as the present article cannot review all the proposals and suggestions made in recent years across Europe giving evidence of a search for rules of conflict of laws that peacefully arrange relations between different legal systems—Muslim and Western—without changing their drift. At least, we have been able to sketch the contours of the problems, and have cited a number of concrete examples, particularly drawn from French and Belgian jurisprudence, which illustrate our account.

In general terms, our analysis has limited itself to a comprehensive review of the actual situation, proceeding by way of synthesis and abstract exposition. The stabilisation of Muslim communities in Europe is a great challenge for the mechanisms of international private law, even questioning their effectiveness. Can they make a place for institutions of foreign origin, practically unknown or sometimes even contrary to fundamental principles of law today valid for Europe? In order to go further into this observation we present in a fourth and final section the results of a study we were asked to make in collaboration with several colleagues. This study was conducted in 1997 and 1998 on the question of the matrimonial position of Muslim women of Moroccan origin in Belgium. The idea was to go beyond the level of an analysis which was necessarily quite general, in order to get hold of concrete cases. The purpose here is to confront some of the propositions made in our previous sections with fresh research of cases, coming from the lives of Muslim women who are immigrants or of immigrant stock, and who have kept their first nationality (Moroccan). At the end of the presentation of this research, we will attempt to draw some conclusions.

4. A Thorny Question: The Matrimonial Status of Muslim

A particular problem regarding the position of Muslims in Europe has to do with the matrimonial position, i.e. within marriage, of women of Muslim origin. We present here the outlines of several interviews appealing to law practitioners, and which express in their way particular aspects of the very elaborate question which occupies us here.

Too much insecurity as to the question which law applies

A comparative examination of jurisprudence allows us to make a first observation about indirect discriminatory consequences of international private law techniques. They affect in particular immigrant women who, because of their nationality, remain subjected to family laws which involve gender-based discrimination.[30] Studies of this question have found that women often resent the rules of conflict of laws that connect their matrimonial position with the law of the country of origin. They have the impression that the rule of conflict is intended merely to defend the interests of the husband.

In practice, courts override the effects of foreign law every time that law, in their opinion, violates fundamental principles esteemed basic to public order, such as the principle of equality of men and women, these violations occurring mostly in cases of marriage and divorce. They substitute as it were the law of the country of residence (Belgian or French law, etc.) in order to 'correct' the unequal treatment of women. The application of the *lex fori* by means of the public order exception does not provide a *structural* solution for these women, for two reasons: first, as mentioned above, such a solution is not exportable to the woman's country of origin; at international level, her position as a married person is no longer quite assured in a harmonious manner across the legal systems. On the other hand, the frequency with which judicial authorities in recent years have shown their disapproval of the effects of Muslim family law upon immigrant residents in Europe[31] does not generate trust between the various countries. Therefore, the legal position of Muslim women remains affected by a high level of insecurity. They can never be sure which law will apply to their case.

International private law techniques which eliminate the effects of discrimination against immigrant women[32] are being tried in several European countries, or are the subject of doctrinal discussions [Jayme,

---

[30] As we noted above: in Belgium, as in other European countries, national law normally applies to personal status and family matters as long as a person has kept the foreign nationality without possessing any other.

[31] Along these lines, for Belgium, see among others: Heyvaert, 1981–1982:425–454; by the same author: 1995:287–338; van Mensel, 1990:8–15.

[32] Seeking also to eliminate the insecurity accompanying a situation already difficult in daily life, women may decide not to claim before a court if they do not know beforehand which law is being applied.

1995; Verwilghen & De Valkeneer, 1993; Dekeeuwer-Defossez, 1993; Carlier, 1992; Meeusen, 1997].

We have enumerated these briefly. To list them again: either the judge opts for an automatic application of the *lex fori*, i.e. the law of the court hearing the case thus placing no weight upon the foreign nationality of the parties; the same law applies to everyone; or the court may leave the choice to the parties as to which legal system should apply in their case (autonomy of the will). Some have argued for a third solution relying more on legislative intervention. In this third case, it is the legislator and not the judge who determines the position of foreign law in the regulation of international family relations.[33] A fourth proposed solution, mentioned above, involves bilateral and multilateral conventional cooperation between states. A number of European countries have for several years negotiated conventions with the main countries of origin of immigrants. These conventions designate among other things the law that applies to family issues.[34]

---

[33] In Belgium, some have argued (taking reference to the Netherlands and Germany) for several years for a solution through codification of international private law. See especially: Erauw, 1989:745–763 and Meeusen, 1994:463 ff.

[34] Some years back, for several months leading up to July 1991, Belgium was also in discussions with Morocco concerning bilateral conventions. Three conventions were signed on July 15, 1991 in Rabat. One concerned *applicable law and the recognition and dissolution of marriages*. So far this convention has not been ratified. The convention would have applied to the recognition, in both countries, of divorces and marriages contracted in either. Regarding the recognition of divorces, the text of the convention indicates broadly that from the date of application of the convention, the dissolution of marriage is governed by the national law common to both parties. That means (for example) that the dissolution of the marital relationship between a Moroccan man and a Belgo-Moroccan woman (article 11) could be a case for the application of Moroccan law. One might have doubts about the effects of such a rule. The convention does establish four derogations to the rule. 1. the hypothesis of *litis pendentis*; 2. incompatibility with public order; 3. cases of judgment by default, where the defaulting party does not have enough time to contest a case, or to take advantage of due process; 4. cases of an invalid citation. These derogations have been formulated in a relatively broad fashion. Otherwise, the convention retains the possibility of a Moroccan couple divorcing in Morocco under Moroccan law, and thus for the husband to pronounce a repudiation. This possible application of Moroccan law is even available for a divorce which takes place in Belgium. The text also indicates that the reference to the common nationality of the parties remains operative even if the woman has acquired Belgian nationality since the case was pending. In practice, things would not get that far, and the Belgian judge would probably retain the option of taking into account only the Belgian nationality of the woman, thus applying the rule of effective nationality. As a result, the convention would have been without effect in Belgium. The ratification of the convention between Belgium and Morocco would have marked a step *back-*

We believe that women are offered a number of advantages by the solution that gives greater weight to the habitual residence of the parties[35] (the principle of territoriality). In the first place, a territorial application guarantees to all women in cases affecting their matrimonial position, *whatever their nationality*, an application of the law of the country of residence. From the standpoint of equality before the law, the application of the law of the country of residence is preferable. Second, courts are no longer forced, so to say, to evaluate the content or the effects of foreign law, or employ in their arguments in favour of *lex fori* any hierarchy of family law systems placed in competition with one another. The judge who applies the principle of territoriality should not give any reason(s) for this application. The *lex fori* will apply in identical fashion to citizens and to foreigners, regardless of nationality. There is hardly any need to continue to have recourse to the public order exception.

An examination of recent jurisprudence indicates that in France, Belgium, and the Netherlands, judges who have to choose between the application of Muslim family law on base of the principle of the national law and the *lex fori*, favour the latter (principle of territoriality). Muslims residing in Europe actually have been more frequently subject, in practice, to the law of the country of residence in family matters. The exception to the principle of application of the national law (of the country of origin) has thus become the rule. A recent survey we conducted among law practitioners shows the same result. Most of them favour the solution that connects the case with the rule of habitual residence of the parties. A large majority of Muslim women questioned on this point clearly seem to confirm that preference and opt for the solution that connects them with the law of the country of residence.

---

wards in the struggle to reinforce the position of Muslim women in the country. The solution proposed in the Netherlands is very different, namely they encourage the Moroccan authorities to sign the existing *multilateral* conventions on international private law (see among others: Jordens-Cotran, 1992:552–553). Doing so avoids what happens in bilateral conventions—particular categories of foreigners are created, they remain subject as regards their status to particular rules of conflict. Multilateral conventions avoid stigmatising some populations by confining them to 'special rights', and through a greater uniformity of the rules of international private law, they simplify the task of law practitioners, and thus reinforce security.

[35] The principle of territoriality or of the application of the law of (the country of) habitual residence is linked to the fact that in most cases the events which lead up to the filing of a suit (concerning, e.g., the ability of a woman to end a marriage or negotiate a division of marital property) occur within the country of residence.

Still, it is not necessarily so that women in all aspects profit from connection with the law of the habitual residence of the spouses. The principle of territoriality does carry risks for women, as we have listed. It is primarily the risk of non-recognition in the country of origin of the effects of courts' decisions or acts delivered in the country of habitual residence in conformity with the *lex fori* but considered incompatible with the national law of the parties which otherwise would have applied. This risk is quite real as regards Muslim women. Therefore more pluralistic solutions should be made possible.

In order to take account of both principles—nationality and territoriality—at the same time, some have argued in favour of an adaptation of the principle of territoriality, which would—as we have mentioned above—permit a limited autonomy of the will of the parties, taking the form of an option (in law) to choose between the national law and the law of the country of habitual residence. The principal rule of conflict of law would thus connect the matrimonial status of the woman with the law of the country of residence. A subsidiary rule of conflict of laws would still permit the parties to give preference and thus opt for their national law. Actually in most European countries, without the need of any legislative changes, it is quite possible to take into consideration, if only partially, the will of the parties (the spouses), especially as regards the effects of marriage.[36]

We therefore suggest that greater scope should be left to the free choice of the parties.[37] If there is no option available for the parties

---

[36] See among others: Casman, 1991:27 ff.

[37] In the case of Moroccan couples residing in Belgium for example, even without modifying the rule of conflict, the husband and wife can insert in their marriage contract not only clauses about possession of goods, but also clauses regarding the personal status itself. This could be accomplished now by a couple of two Moroccans or by a Belgo-Moroccan couple (*lex patriae communis*). Such clauses are authorised under Moroccan law as long as they do not undermine the basis or the purpose of marriage (see especially article 30 of the *Mudawwana*). A clause whereby the husband renounces polygamy is allowed under Moroccan law. According to one school of Moroccan doctrine (see especially: Moulay R'Chid, 1991; Lahrichi, 1985), a clause in which the husband renounces repudiation is also in conformity with the code of personal status of Morocco. These clauses have the merit of being at the forefront of discussion as soon as dissolution of the marriage is envisaged. From the standpoint of Belgian law, such clauses affecting persons, if in conformity with the personal status of the parties, are valid insofar as they contain nothing detrimental to public order. Moreover, these clauses in some cases permit institutions to be set aside on base of being declared detrimental to public order. Juridically possible now, clauses of this kind deserve, we think, more publicity among, especially, notaries.

to give preference to the national law, the law of the country of their habitual residence will apply.

Insufficient familiarity with Muslim family laws among law practitioners

A second observation relating to the status of Muslim women of immigrant origin concerns the complexity of their legal position, for being caught between (at least) two legal systems. Law practitioners often complain about the difficulty of deciding which law applies to family situations where at least one member is originating from a Muslim country. For their part, women are often ignorant of their rights and duties, apart from what they have been taught within their families or have learned through personal experience. Without a good understanding of these rights and duties, women are not capable of demanding respect under Belgian law or of appealing to it, in order to attain the protection they are looking for.

Immigrant women are thus very much in need of a competent and accessible legal assistance. Without waiting for some global reform of international private law, several means are available already to guarantee better legal services to Muslim women. We distinguish two types of means. First, a considerable improvement of the information on the eventual benefits of either foreign or local law to professionals working in the area of international administration and law practitioners.[38] Second, the further development of legal clinics for the benefit of immigrant women guaranteeing them an access to justice that is equivalent to that available to other women. And finally, and perhaps most importantly, a serious improvement of the education and training of women.[39]

---

[38] We are thinking, especially, of institutions like the Asser Institut in the Netherlands, or the Max Planck Institute in Germany—institutions which offer help: (university) centres of research; embassies which provide information on current legislation in the country they represent; expert consultations (obtaining "certificates of custom"), and, more generally, the training of practitioners who may not be familiar with foreign family law.

[39] We personally think the optimisation of existing channels of information is to be promoted, not the creation of new services.

5. Conclusion: The Bond of Proximity with the State of Residence. A Viable Criterion?

It would be an illusive idea to think that mere adaptation of a number of rules of conflict suffices to give Muslim women effective guarantees of equality of treatment or in general of emancipation. Nonetheless, few other ways are open to lawyers, as courts and administrative bodies, in handling disputes involving Muslim families, have no other instruments at hand than these rules. The responsibility of the lawyer thus is to continue to reflect diligently and to keep searching for appropriate rules of conflict.

Equality and equality of opportunity have become today the standard criteria by which we, in Europe, judge individual behaviour within a family relationship. This is true in the internal law of most European countries owing to their partnership in an impressive number of human rights treaties. Equality and equality of opportunity have become compulsory targets. We reject any infringement upon these principles, and an appeal to the public order exception must be made where necessary.

Muslim family law stems from a legal culture which in many points differs from western legal tradition. This culture still influences Muslim family laws: partners in a marriage do not enjoy equal rights as individuals. This does not mean that women have no rights, or are without protection [Moulay R'Chid, 1991 and 1994:429–446; Boumans, 1992; Carlier, 1995:698 ff.] but today in Europe we no longer accept such an unequal division of rights and duties between husband and wife. It remains within patrilinear logic that the place of the woman within the family depends on the authority of the male members of that family over her: her father, her husband, her guardian, her brother, possibly her own male children [Tillon, 1982; X, 1989].

In sum, the discussion is about the question whether solutions allowing Muslim families in Europe to live harmonious lives from a legal point of view, indeed rest on the search for appropriate rules of conflict of laws which give greater weight now to the country of residence, now to the will of the parties to choose their legal system. The risk, of course, is of breaking and subdividing the marital relationship into many different aspects, some allowing a choice, some not.

In fact, by proposing rules of conflict that so to say 'cut up' the life of Muslim families living in Europe today among various domains more or less open to the solution of the *optio iuris*, one risks accomplishing a kind of dismantling. The result may be odd. By suggesting rules of conflict that differ depending on which aspect of family life is involved, we of course 'split up', so to say, family relationships among Muslims in Europe, allowing them for some issues to connect with the law of the country of origin, i.e. Muslim family law, but prohibiting them to make use of that same technique in other domains of their family life. We force people to deviate, little by little, from the family system ingrained in these communities through their culture. We do this with the intention of giving its weaker members, especially women, the protection of the law of the country of their habitual residence. Ideally, Muslims, men and women, should be able to continue, via the technique of the *optio iuris*, to remain submitted to Muslim family law, as long as they continue to feel and to demonstrate a close tie their country of origin.[40] Even more, this preference should possibly bear on all aspects of family life, since only a free choice in favour of either one or the other law can give people the assurance of being able to continue to live within their own culture, within their own family circle.[41]

Still, experience teaches caution. The great majority of litigants concerned, women in particular, are even today not well enough informed of their rights to be able to handle negotiations by themselves with (future) spouses so that it would allow them to ignore pressure or outside influence, and control their own positions within the family circle. That is the main reason why we remain in favour of solutions allowing the law of the country of the habitual residence to be applied in principle, and not in favour of the law of the country of origin applying. The latter may apply in terms of a subsidiary rule, with a limited and conditional choice.

Do we lack tolerance with regard to Muslim family laws, i.e. with regard to the culture from which they derive? The answer is difficult. The question is to know whether, by adopting an attitude of greater

---

[40] This kind of solution, which is connected to a technique of international private law, does not apply to a native European who converts to Islam—unless this person acquires a foreign nationality which creates a bond between him and a country where Muslim law applies.

[41] Such an ideal is based on an anthropological conviction, namely that each juridical system is made up of a group of rules, which draw their coherence from society and culture, which have produced the system. Should this coherence not be respected!

openness toward rules which are not conceived according to a Western model of family life, we provide better solutions. Muslims—and Muslim women—who seek to build a future in Europe must be able to find adequate protection when problems arise.

Muslim family law comes from types of society which in social anthropology is called a kinship society, protecting women within a kingroup, either the group formed by fathers and brothers, or the group of husbands [Tillon, 1982]. The underlying logic of a kinship society is not conceived with a view to the situation of a woman who looks after herself as an individual as is the case in a western society. The time limit placed on the gift of consolation (*mut'a*) for example, that is, payments to be made to a repudiated woman, is an example of the type of limited protection which no longer meets the needs of women who in European society must take responsibility for their own livelihood after a divorce without the help of a kingroup. Our conclusion is that Muslim women on the one hand must be able to choose insofar as possible to arrange their family lives while continuing to respect their own cultural traditions, but otherwise, and most importantly, must be guaranteed the protection of the law of their country of habitual residence, should they invoke it.

Giving preponderant weight to the law of residence—the solution we suggest—seeks to multiply the applications of that law (Belgian, in our case). But we also suggest providing for a limited choice (of legal system) for the woman. The task is not easy, since it seeks to satisfy two demands: to apply the law of habitual residence of the partners in respect of international conventions on human rights and fundamental liberties, and to show a real willingness to assure Muslims—men or women—the right to individual treatment in private law. The future will reveal whether, in time, the latter alternative is a real one, offering to Muslims the opportunity to maintain (in legal terms) a harmonious family life—and whether we still respect enough the freedom they have, the freedom to belong to a civilisation rooted in Islam and its profoundest values, if they desire it so.

PART THREE

ISLAM AND SOCIETY:
PUBLIC SPACE AND INTEGRATION

There are different ways of conceiving the public space and of interpreting it culturally. The phenomenon is in itself complex to define, as it is a conceptual construction and, at the same time, a social place where the various conceptual constructions come together, confront one another and come into conflict with other conceptions of the same public space. It has various meanings: public places in the first place; the institutions that are accessible to all, in the same sense that public squares are, as they are not private and are open; the space of power referred to the public good, common to all those who are associated under the same law; the context in which public opinion is expressed through its critical function, the "indignant or informed public sphere" [Habermas, 1962].

Here we will approach it by analysing some particularly important dimensions in which Islam is the object of discussion and at the same time an interlocutor of this discussion: the world of the media, in a proper sense, the "sphere of the public that discusses", to use the words of Habermas, but also the arena of a cultural confrontation which is as articulate as it is decisive, as it has to do with symbols and the imagination; the main objects and moments of tension and friction that have seen Islam a protagonist on European soil; the context of (inter)religious relations; and, in the last place, the economic dimension, which finds a place here especially for the social value that is given to it as a subject of legitimacy or de-legitimacy of the presence of immigrants and, within it, the presence of Islam.

Here we only want to underline, by way of introduction, that today probably there is no longer *one* public sphere, but many, or rather, one public space in which the various 'public spheres' of the various possible publics meet and clash. There is no longer the public opinion, but many, and they are less stable than in the past. Not only are they of a variable geometry and different depending on the issues, but they are also of a variable duration. Structurally, the European countries have changed, and can no longer be defined through the classic elements of the definition of the nation-state (a people, a territory, a legal system, and perhaps, as a cultural implicit, a religion), at least to the extent that these elements have been overloaded with a meaning, moreover perhaps never completely corresponding to the truth, of exclusivity.

Islam shows and proves this change more explicitly than others: also because, through its many exponents, it is amongst the social subjects (not the only one: there is a tendency to forget that on the same wavelength there are other subjects, but also consistent parts of opinion in the individual churches and faiths dominant in the respective countries) which insist precisely on the religious element as constitutive of the public sphere. It is for this reason that rather than sphere it is better to talk of public space: a concept which in itself is more open, less 'round' and defined. This space includes the physical public space of the city (taking Goffman's idea of the city itself as a theatre), the *loci communes* (common places, in the double meaning, physical and metaphorical, of the term), the legal, mediatic, political and symbolic space in which cultural representations are expressed. A space that has not been defined once and for all: of which the category of change, even of the social landscape, is a constitutive element. A space, in the end, which is defined through processes of inter-connection and integration.

CHAPTER EIGHT

THE MEDIA

Stefano Allievi

The media play an important role both as the expression of a culture—in this case, Muslim cultures, in the plural—visible in the Muslim media in Europe, and as an instrument of reading and interpreting these cultures, through the news on Muslims conveyed by the general and specialised media. They also play a significant role, even if under-estimated, as a means of construction of the Muslim communities and as a way of maintaining links with the countries of origin. Lastly, the media are a place of resonance of problems and of construction of their interpretative criteria. We will put forward some considerations on these different aspects here.

1. Imaginary and the Perception of the Other

The discourse on the collective imaginary is crucial. In a certain sense, even more than on the reality of social processes under way, it is on their perception that much of the direction that they take and of their 'success' depends. This aspect is also of fundamental importance in the policies on Islam: which more than influence depend to a great extent on the perception that one has of the phenomenon. This is the reason we will make a detailed analysis of this aspect.

We will not dwell on the weight of history. We will restrict ourselves to recalling that factors come into play in the case of Islam but not in the case of other oriental religions, for example, and other cultures. We are referring in particular to the long past of confrontation with the European West and Christianity, through the periods of the Crusades, the long period of naval conflicts, but also, more recently of colonisation and the complex drifts of decolonisation; in some cases, as in Algeria, these are wounds that are still very fresh and rich in consequences. Moreover, this history is not finished and also includes the consequences of the Arab-Israeli conflict, the Gulf War, the Palestine question, and other moments of confrontation.

"L'Islam vis-à-vis de l'Occident, c'est le chat vis-à-vis du chien", wrote Braudel [quoted in Triaud, 1998]. And Delumeau, in his history of fear in the West [1978], did not forget the role played by the fear of Islam, the traces of which can still be found, not only in history but in folklore (the tournaments of the "Saracen" or of the "Moor" and many others), in town planning and landscape (the "Saracen towers" that border the Mediterranean), in language and proverbs (the Italian 'mamma li turchi'): it would be naïve to think that this legacy is not reflected in the history of today. And that weighs at least as much as the Orientalist tradition stigmatised in its defects, with some lack of generosity, by E. Said [1978]. The media are, unconsciously, the offspring of this mentality and convey it, and by conveying it they re-produce it and therefore bring it up to date, making the legacy of yesterday a problem of today.

The media are therefore fully entitled to be inserted in this complex mechanism of the construction of the cultural imaginary and they are today increasingly decisive, also because their role, following the processes of globalisation, of which they are simultaneously an effect, a cause and an accelerator, is not only that of informing but precisely of constructing our cognitive worlds, and of constructing them not only through the traditional effects of *vertical integration*, within the individual nation-states or individual societies, or of individual public spheres, to use the phrase by Habermas [1962], but also, as we will see concretely with some examples, of connecting and inter-, trans- and supra-national *horizontal integration*. These processes cannot be understood in a media-centric, so to speak, point of view, limited to the social and cultural effects of the media themselves, but it must be perceived within a view capable of reading their role in broader social processes.

2. Human Mobility and Circulation of Information

The increase of the speed and density of communications is an integral part of the processes of globalisation, for some its fundamental determinant, almost its *primum mobile*. Mobility is in fact one of the interpretative keys of the processes under way. In what has been called the 'mobiletic revolution', the mobility of information is one of the first to intervene: even before the mobility of money or goods, let alone men and women. And today it goes with these, and together they produce a further acceleration of the processes in which they are involved. The mobility of information was one of the first to be perceived: McLuhan, who before others described the global village, can only be pleased by the current diffusion of the term globalisation. Here we are interested in seeing the relationship between these forms of mobility (of information and people) in the relations they produce between them and, in the case of Islam in Europe, with respect to the host societies and those of origin. In examining it, we must have the awareness that it is a process that is still in its beginnings, but that in some of its aspects it is already showing, as we will see, a consistent maturity, and of which it is possible to outline the trends.

This is not precisely a new form or new ways of the public spheres of the individual national states, in the sense according to Habermas, nor the simple 'connection' between public spheres differentiated in the past, 'via' the Muslim immigrants and their relational and media networks. Nor is it even—not yet—the construction of a new articulation of the European public sphere, for and among those who are already European citizens and feel part of Europe by history and culture. After all, for reasons which are first but not only linguistic, there do not yet exist real European media (we can recall the case of the newspaper *The European*, perhaps born ahead of its time and which disappeared prematurely), and there are few, if there are any, public debates that can be configured as really transnational. In this sense, Europe does not exist yet, or more precisely, it exists as an 'attribute' and if we want an expansion and appendix of the individual national public spheres.

Amongst many other factors, the presence of Islam, with the openings and connections that it implies with other national public spheres and with other cultural worlds, is a not secondary element of construction and making complex this original form of public sphere, interrelated and by the force of things, even beyond the will of its players, open and rich in consequences, often unexpected. In fact, a progressive process of co-inclusion of Islam in the public sphere is under way [Dassetto, 1996]. Lastly, the world of media visibility is also the world *in which* Islam too is seen, as well as that *through which* it is seen. What Muslims do in Europe is seen [Metcalf, 1996].

And at the same time they are indirectly the means through which Islam is discovered; some Muslims seem to be aware of this to a certain extent: as one Muslim woman I interviewed said to me, about her wearing the *hijab*, even for the simple fact of walking down the street, "I am a walking symbol" [Allievi, 1998]. When this symbol is brought into the limelight through the visibility of the media, its positive and negative force becomes more important and sensational. When entire channels of communication meet, even reluctantly and without being fully aware of it, the process becomes even more complex. We intend to analyse the main articulations of this process below.

3. THE REFLECTION OF THE EXCEPTIONAL CASE

One of the ways in which Islam becomes visible is through exceptional cases, which we can interpret as hermeneutic accidents, blockages, in a certain sense, of interpretative codes and their representations. For example, the Rushdie affair, the question of the *foulard* in France and elsewhere and other more localised cases. We will analyse some examples in detail in the next chapter regarding the tensions that Islam has triggered off in Europe. Here we limit ourselves to observe the basic logic, which contributes to giving a certain image of Islam (of conflict, for example) which is also reflected on the perception of the phenomenon as a whole, and on the reception reserved for the social actors embodying it. Moreover, there is also the example of the fate of concepts such as that of *jihad*, which has entered the Western imagination as a decisive aspect, of its perception of Islam and therefore of the Muslims, and therefore also of Muslims in Europe; an interesting example of the generalisation of a local concept to a level of global importance and through this its assimilation into a now transnational discourse [Albrow, Eade, Dürrschmidt & Washbourne, 1997].

Moreover, the importance of these exceptional cases, examples of *Kulturkampf* which also become media events, must also be noted on the general level in producing a collective imagination. The theory of communication has noted how the importance of media events is such that they also become the collective memory of these cultural encounters/conflicts, becoming in some way the equivalent of historical monuments, through which these processes can be subsequently reconstructed and remembered [Dayan & Katz, 1992]. Some cases, concerning European Islam, have also been analysed in their specific instance: that it dealt with a manifestation, Muslim in this particular case, concerning international dynamics but in actual fact the sign of an internal social evolution [Dassetto & Bastenier, 1987], or of a war. We have in fact had to re-learn recently, with regard to a conflict, the Gulf War, that the conflict itself exists only if and to the extent that it is possible to document it: and therefore, if it cannot be documented, following the provocation by Baudrillard [1991], it simply "has not taken place". However, and this is the point that interests us, perhaps for the first time in recent European history, we have had to consider that, in Europe, there was a different public opinion, involved in another way: namely, the Muslim minorities in European countries, who experienced the same event, but with a significantly different way of feeling it, so different that perhaps it really was not the same event [Allievi, Bastenier, Battegay & Boubeker, 1992].

4. Muslim Press and Media

What we could call, problematising and further complicating what Toffler has called the 'infosphere', the Muslim mediasphere, is extremely articulated. It is not made up only of what we call mass media, up to today's virtual media, but also of an articulated inter-weaving of old and new forms of communication which also include relatively traditional channels of communication (letters, telephone, today the mobile phone), and periodic journeys or trips for special occasions back to the country of origin: for holidays, Ramadan, for family occasions such as weddings, births, circumcisions, for religious celebrations such as the 'Id or for periodic reunions of confraternities, but also for marriage, that is, to find a wife, marry her and bring her back to Europe. This set of traditional and non-traditional communications, this network of links, represents a world of communication, a mediasphere, which is qualified or can be qualified religiously, almost a sort of de-territorialised *Umma*. The concept of *Umma* is moreover often understood, in Muslim language, both as a localised community and as a meta-community of a symbolic order. We will analyse the public aspects of this world, those that let us speak of a new form of public sphere.

Written production

We will discuss books later on, with regard to the production of new Muslim discourses in Europe. Here we will mention the production of periodicals, which deserves an articulated consideration. It is not certain, and we do not know (it could be a subject for research) if this is what 'weighs' most in the formation of the Muslim media-sphere. Other media have a comparable or greater weight, and every speculation on the prevalence or higher status and influence of the written word, as we are in a paradigm which has made the written word—the holy word—its centre, does not appear sufficiently demonstrative. However, these speculations do not take into account that the status of the holy word is, if anything, linked to the word transmitted orally, 'recited' (after all, this is the meaning of *qur'an*: recitation).

However, we can note that, if on the one hand, in the situation of European Islam, its weight is still the object of evaluation, on the other, in its perception, its weight is absolutely decisive. We often *read* Islam, through the literature it produces, magazines in particular, and we deduce Muslims from them; using a procedure that appears 'natural' to us or which we are nevertheless used to, whilst it is only 'cultural', that is the offspring of a certain way of understanding cultural transmission and its means, and the importance of its vehicles. Thus doing, we probably also tend to overestimate this form of communication—proper, especially in an initial phase, only to a part of the Muslim communities present in Europe, and precisely some of its leaders, deducing or unduly extending our conclusions to the whole of these communities; this is an aspect of absolute importance, especially on the political level.

First of all, we have some journals which move at a trans-national level, even if most of them are based in Great Britain, aware of European opinion, especially academics, at which they are largely addressed. We are thinking of journals such as *The Journal of Muslim Minority Affairs, Islamic Studies, The Islamic Quarterly* and others.

Others take on a European dimension (in broad terms, including Eastern Europe), but in Arabic, almost as if to symbolise this new dual dimension: this is the case of *Al-Ūrubiyya*, for example, the organ of the Federation of Islamic Organisations in Europe (FIOE), linked to the world of students and Muslim Brotherhood, with its base in Great Britain, in Markfield, but with its leadership partially in France and an Internet address in Germany.

Then there are the journals of various countries, of which a general survey has not yet been made [a pioneering attempt, now superseded, is to be found in Dassetto & Bastenier, 1988].

The **British** case is particularly advanced. The publications include the fortnightly (now monthly) *Q-News*, probably the European Muslim magazine with the largest circulation and to which we will return below, *Muslim News*, which is also on the Internet, as well as magazines oriented towards dialogue with non-Muslims, such as *Encounters* and *Dialogue*. There are very many newsletters of the individual organisations, movements, local groups, political-religious associations and Sufi groups.

It is interesting to note that for a certain period of time, amongst the newsletters, on the initiative of an ad hoc group set up at the Islamic Foundation, *Muslims in Europe* (magazine) was attempted, with about ten numbers coming out, some of which were also in a French edition; probably the first attempt to create a unitary nucleus of European Muslims, in this case converts, and to create a network [GB File].

The case of *Q-News* was that of a first attempt at a 'real' magazine, with the idea of approaching religious issues without forgetting the problems of current affairs, reading through the point of view of others and even more frequently the contrary, with the ambition of being not a 'Muslim paper', but a 'paper for Muslims', and with special attention to the young generations. The experiment, which is over a decade old, shows a magazine with a conspicuous percentage, not far from half, of non-Muslim readers, once again a sign that Islam is attentively observed by various social, religious, cultural and other interlocutors. It claims to have a circulation of about fifteen thousand copies, about half of which are subscriptions. And it is interesting to note that it is a Muslim magazine sold mainly outside and, from some points of view even despite, religious circles, starting with the mosques [Fuad Nahdi, personal interview, May 2000].

The Islamic Centre of Dublin also produces a newsletter and this is the only publication we know of in the **Republic of Ireland** [IR File].

There is no shortage of magazines in **France** either. The most important experiments are however fairly recent and from some points of view surprisingly late, as this is the country with the largest presence of Muslims in Europe and so it is not possible to make considerations on their solidity. In particular, there is the magazine

La Médina (6 issues a year), which began activity in 1999, the quarterly magazine of research and study *Islam de France*, published since 1998, and the new *Islâm*, a review of Muslim history and theology that started in 2002. There is also *Hawwa Magazine*, a women's magazine, which is also of recent conception. *Le Musulman*, the magazine of the *Association des Etudiants Islamiques de France* (AEIF), however, has existed since 1970, the *Cahiers de l'Institut des Hautes Etudes Islamiques*, is a quarterly magazine that was started in 1995 by a group of Sufis based in Italy and *Le Monde Musulman* has been published since 1996. The bulletins of the different organisations and national federations, often fairly irregular in their publication, must also be added to these [FR File].

The **German** case sees, more than others, a strong presence of the ethnic, or rather national, press, Turkish in particular. About 350,000 copies of newspapers are sold daily [de Tapia, 1998], in a classification that does not, however, see the publications with a religious tendency in the best positions. Apart from Turkish dailies, Germany has a history of Muslim magazines that started between the two World Wars with the *Moslemische Revue*. Within the main currents of Turkish Islam, we can mention *Haber Bülteni* of the DITIB, the monthly *Milli Görüs & Perspektive*, *Ümmet-i Muhammed* of the ICCB, which is more militant. The many other attempts include the *Rundbrief der Deutschen Muslime*, again published by the DITIB, *Al-Muhaddschirun* by an association of German Muslims and *Al-Huda*. Some converts have created *Islamische Frauenzeitschrift*, the first attempt at a Muslim women's magazine. Then we have the *Islamische Zeitung*, which is also on-line and various other Sufi magazines, such as *Sufi*, *Zeitschrift für Islam und Sufitum*, *Al-Sufi*, *Zeitschrift für Islamische Mystik*, and other organs of the various confraternities present in Germany. The Shiites have their magazines, such as *Al-Fadschr: Die Morgendämmerung*, published by the *Islamisches Zentrum Hamburg*, which also publishes a magazine for children, *Salam Kinder!*. There are also the various magazines of the Alawis and the magazines of Muslim centres of local importance, in Munich (*Al-Islâm*, *Al-Islam Aktuell*), in Berlin and elsewhere [Spuler-Stegemann, 1998; DE File].

In **the Netherlands** there was a very well known magazine, with a good distribution, *Qiblah*, which ceased publication in 1993. The organisation of Dutch Muslim women has its bulletin, *Al Nisa*. There is also an Internet magazine, available on-line (www.omroep.nl/nmo/index.htm). As elsewhere, the Muslim bodies of local importance publish their own bulletins [NL File]. Many magazines have been attempted, publishing only a few issues before ceasing publication.

Much literature produced in France circulates in the Islamic book-shops in **Belgium**. And, in the Turkish community, several of the publications in Turkish come from Germany. In addition to the publications by the publisher *Al-Iman*, we can quote at least one bi-monthly bulletin of *Présence Musulmane* [BE File]. A magazine also exists in **Luxembourg**, *Al-Qalam*, founded in 1990, which after years of silence, resurfaced in 1997 for the Muslims in the Grand Duchy [LU File].

In **Denmark**, *Aktiv Islam* is published by the Ahmadi mosque and *Muslim i Norden*, edited by a group of converts, whilst in the second half of the 1990s, a magazine was published that was edited by a group of converts and second-generation immigrants, *Muslim i Danmark* [DK File].

In **Finland**, mention can be made in particular of *Mahalle Haberleri*, the magazine of the Tatars in Finland and the women's magazine, published by a group of converts, *An-Nur*, as well as the magazine of the Somalis *Al Furqan* [FI File]. In **Sweden**, we have *Salaam— Islamisk tidskrift* [Otterbeck, 2000].

In **Italy**, the *Centro Islamico di Milano* and Lombardy has published *Il messaggero dell'islam*, the most widespread Muslim publication, since 1982. A more ambitious attempt at a 'real' magazine, in various languages, *Il musulmano*, edited by a national federation, the UCOII, has been suspended. On the other hand, the Shiite magazine *Il puro islam*, edited by a group of Naples-based Shiites, connected with the Iranian authorities, has been published since 1992. An attempt at an on-line magazine, *Islamica*, edited by the Italian section of the Muslim World League, came to an end after only two issues. Then there are publications of local groups and confraternities with variable periodicity, such as *'Ayn al-Hayat*, of the Naqshbandis, published since 1995, and other bulletins with a smaller circulation, by Islamic centres of local interest [Allievi and Dassetto, 1993; Siggillino, 2001].

In **Spain**, the most interesting examples seem to be those of *Verde Islam*, a quarterly published in Cordoba since 1995, *Insha Allah*, the quarterly of the Association of Muslim Women, published since 1994 in Barcelona, in a rather rudimentary form, and *Al-Quibla* (since 1999), published every two months in Melilla, *Islam* (again since 1999), a monthly published in Valencia, and *Kauzar*, a quarterly of Shiite inspiration, since 1993. *País islámico* (1983–1985), the quarterly published by the Murabitun organisation of Grenada, and one of the first Spanish Muslim magazines, is no longer published, nor is *Al-Yama'a* (1994–1997), a monthly published in Melilla, of which *Al-Quibla* aims to be the continuation. Irregular newsletters and magazines (such as *Iqra*, *Islam* and *Al-'Urwa al-Uzqa*) are published by various Muslim centres and federations of associations [Carnicero, 1997; ES File].

In **Portugal**, particular mention can be made of *Al-Furqan*, since 1981, which comes out three or four times a year and is also present on-line (www.alfurqan.pt) [PT File]. **Greek** Islam, as we have seen, is mainly made up of the Turkish minority in western Thrace, which as well as following the Turkish press, produces the weeklies *Trakya'nin Sesi* (The voice of Thrace), *Ileri* (Ahead), *Trakya* (Thrace), *Gündem* (The agenda) and *Balkan* [GR File].

Bulgarian Islam is also made up of minorities and magazines can be found such as *Müslumanlar*, published by the department of the Mufti of Bulgaria, *Imit*, since 1995, from a Turkish publication and *Zaman* [BG File], which republishes articles from the magazine of the same name in Turkey, as well as *Dvizenie na Prava I Svobodi*, the organ of the party of the Turkish minority Movement for Rights and Freedoms (DPS) [Ragaru, 2001]. *Güven—Doverie* is also a publication of the Turkish minority but is bilingual [Zhelyazkova, Kepel & Nielsen, 1995].

In **Poland** there is the *Rocznik Tatarow Polskich*, the directory published by the Union of Polish Tartars, which also publishes the monthly *Swiat islamu* (The world of Islam); whilst the Union of Muslim Students publishes *Al-Hikmah* in Polish and *Al-Hadara* in Arabic. There is also the directory *Al-Islam* [PL File], and the magazines *Zycie Muzulmanskie* and *Ruch Muzulmanski*, published by a Mahdist group.

In **Romania** *Hakses*, a bilingual monthly of the Turkish community, is published together with two bilingual newsletters published by the Tatar community: *Karadeniz*, and *Cas* for young people, which are organs of the parties of the respective communities. The Albanian community also produces a bilingual magazine, *Shqiptari*, together with the annual publication *Anuarul Albanezul* [RO File].

It is important to underline that, in various countries, and in particular where the presence of Muslim minorities also represents a stake of political importance, a significant part of the readers of Muslim magazines is made up of persons and institutions that are interested in Islam but are not part of it: universities, individual observers and experts, social actors in voluntary work and NGOs, ecclesiastical and inter-religious circles, specialised journalists, security services and the police. As already observed, it is often to a great extent through this channel that they try to interpret European Islam. This may cause interpretations of it that are excessively partial and politicised (above all it is, obviously, organised groups that have and are interested in proposing written material of self-promotion and possibly of *da'wa*), with at times an excessive importance given to the world and thought of recently converted intellectuals. In countries such as Italy and Spain, for example, 'written' Islam is essentially if not completely the work of converts; elsewhere they still have a significant importance in the promotion and writing of Muslim publications [Allievi, 1998].

Muslims themselves are not yet aware of this attention, except in the more mature cases, where this is starting to be taken into consideration, and the feedback effect on the host society is beginning to be observed, inciting a consequent assumption of responsibility. Much of the written material is still conceived, in actual fact, as totally within the Muslim communities.

Audio and videocassettes

The circulation and distribution of cassettes of a religious nature is extremely wide and affects even the smallest Islamic centres; including those which do not have religious literature, apart from the Qur'an, some small collections of hadith and the usual booklets on the pillars of Islam or on how to pray or do the ablutions. The phenomenon came into being in the countries of origin, with the extraordinary diffusion of cassettes with the Friday sermons of the most famous preachers, which ended up in some cases by creating a parallel and alternative public sphere to that of the 'government' imams. The importance of the clandestine circulation of cassettes, in some specific cases, such as that of the speeches of Khomeini in the Iran of the Shah, is well known. But the diffusion of cassettes is a phenomenon in itself, even in Arab countries which have not gone through or are not in a 'revolutionary' situation, which has not been sufficiently observed and which has led some to say that cassettes in Islam today play the role of the invention of printing in the Protestant

Reformation, allowing the diffusion of the Bible and, with it, the upheavals that European history went through on that occasion on the political and religious level [Etienne, 1987].

Many of the cassettes that circulate in Arab and Muslim countries can also be found on the European market, especially for first-generation immigrants. However, it is also now possible to find, in Muslim bookshops, especially in the French-speaking world, cassettes with recordings of speeches, comments and lectures given and produced by new intellectuals trained in Europe, both of the second generation (Tareq and Hani Ramadan, Tarek Oubrou, Hassan Iquioussen, for example) and converts (Yahya Michot): these documents are in the respective European languages, mainly aimed at a public of the second generation, the same as the audiences of the lectures which are then recorded.

Whilst the production of cassettes is essentially and explicitly of a religious nature (Qur'an, sermons and lectures, Sufi music—which has a market niche outside the Muslim world, for example in new age shops), the video market is more articulate: it includes lectures by crowd-pulling leaders (for example, the conspicuous turnover of the videos of Ahmed Deedat, a sort of Muslim 'entertainer', produced by *Islamic Vision* and which can also be found outside the Anglo-Saxon world to which they are primarily addressed), but also documentaries and some famous apologetic fiction films.

Naturally we are referring here only to religious circles, which does not include the large business of imported videos in the language of origin, of pure entertainment and fiction which, as for the music cassettes, is present in its own market, in great expansion and at times even conflicting, implicitly and at times explicitly, with the religious one. The VCR has in this sense filled a need for connection with the world of origin: it is no coincidence that in the 1980s, when the VCR first started to be diffused, it was present, for example, in 75% of Turkish families, against a penetration at that time of only 30% in German families [de Tapia, 1998].

This aspect of 'competition' between the two spheres is shown by the remark of one of our English interlocutors, in front of an Asian video-shop window: those who get excited saying that there are a thousand mosques in our country should bear in mind that there are ten thousand video shops. Beyond the accuracy of the figures, it is interesting to note how this form of competition is explicitly brought up.

The ways of diffusion of Muslim (and non-Muslim) videos are many and at times significantly contorted, with off-shoots that are incomprehensible in the light of geography alone: for example, Turkish videos from Germany are widely diffused in Greece, within the Turkish-speaking minority in Thrace [Dalègre, 2001].

Radio

The radio also plays an important role, also on the religious level. It is no coincidence that in the different countries it is precisely at a time of strong religious intensification, the month of Ramadan, that ad hoc radio programmes, or even temporary radio stations are activated.

This is the case in Great Britain, where more than a dozen *Radio Fast FM* broadcast 24 hours a day, in different cities, in this period of the year, playing a role of communication but also of organisation, for example through the radio collection of the *zakat*. The forerunner of this project was the decision of the Independent Radio Authority, in 1989, to give Bradford City Radio the franchise for a commercial radio with ethnic services, directed by a Muslim which passed subsequently under the control of a Hindu. There have also been cases of internal controversy, through the attempt by the radical movement *Hizb al-Tahrir*, in one case, to block the radio's switchboards. There are however also permanent radio stations, the explicitly religious contents of which are however limited to specific broadcasts, such as in the *East* circuit. The 'Islamic' commitment of the general radios, in the first place the BBC, is obviously limited and regarding which the idea is getting ahead, according to the English multicultural approach, that the modest 'ethnic' representation of its employees is the reason and their increase will be the solution. Lastly, there are some Muslim pirate radios, again on the FM band.

The **Netherlands** shows an example of direct public intervention: a special board for Muslim broadcasting, funded by the state, produces thirty minutes of programmes a week for TV and ninety for radio and this should be doubled as from September 2000. As there are different Muslim ethnic groups in the Netherlands, the programmes are produced in three languages: Turkish, Arabic and Dutch, the last named with an audience that includes non-Muslims. The mere fact that the broadcast has existed since 1986, however, beyond the controversies on who and how it should be run, represented an important step in the process of institutionalising Islam in the country [Landman, 1997b].

Public support can also be talked of in **Denmark** but it is less direct than in the Netherlands. There are in fact several Danish local radios run by Muslims on a linguistic-national basis. There are Turkish, Pakistani, Somali and other radios. The majority are sponsored financially by the Ministry for Culture, but some also receive contributions from the Ministries for Internal Affairs or Social Affairs [DK File].

There are only local radios in **Sweden** too, the most important of which, in the Stockholm area, is Radio Islam, which has been condemned on a couple of occasions for its anti-Semitic remarks [SE File].

There are no national radio frequencies in **Belgium**. However, in Brussels there are some Arab radio stations that share the same frequency known as the *fréquence arabe*: these are Radio Al Manar (Radio Médi Inter), Radio As Salaam, Radio El Watan and Radio Médi 1 [Lambert, 2000]. Two of the three radios that merged into Radio Al Manar, and specifically Radio Culture 3 and Radio El Wafa, are trying to regain their independence through legal action. The management of the *fréquence arabe* is problematic as a whole and subject to internal clashes. Radio Al Manar also has a programme in Turkish. Initiatives similar to those of Brussels also exist in other cities, such as Liège and Antwerp [BE File].

In **Germany**, where, as almost everywhere else, there are no national Muslim radios, the main initiative is Multikulti—SFB 4 in Berlin, which regularly broadcasts Muslim religious programmes [DE File]. There are also local radios in Turkish, such as Köln Radyosu, and others.

In **France**, there are 27 radio stations that can be defined as Arab-Muslim [Naba, 1998], which sometimes also have programmes of an explicitly religious interest. There are three main networks: Radio Beur FM and Radio-Orient, the first community radio in Europe and the first Arabic-speaking radio in Europe, whilst the third French-speaking network, Radio Soleil, also has a station in Turkish.

In countries of more recent immigration, such as **Italy** and **Spain**, there are no radio stations, but during Ramadan, in some cities, specific programmes are broadcast [IT File; ES File].

In **Greece** there is nothing with a specifically religious character for the national minorities. A news bulletin of five minutes in Turkish is broadcast by the radio of Komotini, the municipality of which also retransmits a private Turkish radio. There are at least six other local radios in Turkish, some religious in nature [GR File].

Regular broadcasts in Turkish also exist in **Bulgaria**, produced both by Turks and by Bulgarians [BG File], whilst in **Poland**, a broadcasting authorisation is believed to have been granted recently to the Union of Muslim Students of Wroclaw [PL File], and in **Romania** Radio Constanta has had a weekly programme since 1990 [RO File].

Broadcasting on the air is, however, by definition, transnational, and radio waves can travel from the countries of origin to their respective communities, and a similar thing can be said for the national minorities, as in the case of the Turkish-speaking minorities in Eastern Europe. The cultural and, in this case, religious, connection is also assured this way. An interpretation of this fact and its implications will be seen below, after having discussed television, in the conclusion of the chapter.

The television market

In the strong expansion of this sector, different factors come into play: linguistic, structural (due to the development of technologies), cultural and, naturally, commercial. The presence of 'other' communities is the starting point that explains and determines these developments.

The linguistic aspect is evident in the desire to maintain a link with the country and language of origin, very evident amongst the Turkish and Arabic communities in Europe, especially but not only for the first generation. This is an aspect which moreover works in the two directions, at least for these populations: it is clear that the penetration of the CNN or of Superchannel, like the diffusion of France 2 or the BBC, is their respective former colonial areas and is a crucial factor in learning the language of the future country of immigration. Furthermore, the factor also comes into play in non-traditional places of diffusion, and is not the result of previous history. The simple opening of transmitters to the south for Rai Uno, for example, coincided with strong visibility in Tunisia and a conspicuous increase in the number of people capable at least of understanding, if not speaking, Italian: a factor which is certainly connected with the increase of Tunisian immigration to Italy. We can also note incidentally that this factor does not seem to act in the opposite direction: it is not possible to attribute for the time being an increase of the knowledge of Arabic or Turkish by Europeans following the diffusion in Europe of television channels in these languages.

The technological aspect is clear in the revolution brought about by the diffusion of satellite or 'paradiabolic' dishes as they have been rebaptised in Arabic Islamist circles, where the potential corrupting effect is feared. It has not only encouraged the diffusion of programmes, but above all the birth of new specific broadcasters, as well as the immediate reduction of the importance of local producers and within the communities resident in Europe, such as those represented by cable TV, which can be considered to have taken root probably only in Great Britain, through networks such as Asianet [Ismond, 1999], or the Turkish ones in Germany and in particular local situations, as in Berlin (there are 4 Turkish-speaking TVs in Berlin, one of which, *Türkisches Fernsehen in Deutschland* (TFD), is of a religious nature and linked with the AMGT, but there is also one in London, and Migrante TV is present in the Netherlands in the four main cities).

Satellite dishes began to flourish especially after the Gulf War. This fact, also due to the initial process of the reduction of their cost, has often been interpreted as a sort of self-segregated form of identity, the desire to be connected with Algeria or Morocco and hear their voices. The implicit presupposition of this interpretation is that if an Arabic family installs a satellite dish, it is to watch Arab TV stations and consequently be exposed to Islamic propaganda. Neither of these presuppositions are true, at least not explicitly. The Arab TVs arrive as a priority through these dishes but they are not the only ones: it is possible to receive other Western TVs, the newscasts of which may be judged more objective than the country of residence but also of origin, in cases, for example, of direct conflict (for example between France and Algeria), but above all other types of channels and programmes ranging from sport to music.

Furthermore, in many Arab countries, as the television stations are state-owned and therefore in the hands of the political power, everything will be shown except Islamic propaganda, as the Islamist movements are banned, reduced to clandestine activities or silenced or confined to the margins but in any case without or with very reduced access to the national channels of public communication. And, moreover, anyone who is familiar with the programmes of Arab

TV knows that, like others, the space devoted to religious programmes is a minimum. Various observers have however noted the 'blossoming' of satellite dishes on the houses of immigrants in Europe, to the extent that it would be possible to recognise from this simple fact the council estates or their equivalents where the inhabitants are prevailingly immigrants. The fact has already been noted that they are often commoner amongst immigrants than amongst the autochthonous population.

The Turkish case is probably the most obvious and paradoxical, as this country went in a brief period of time from a legal monopoly, with television run by the local post offices to a jungle of over five hundred TV stations and more than one thousand private radios: indeed it was the brother of the then prime minister who founded the first private chain, perfectly illegal at the time, which broadcast its signal from Europe [Aksoi & Avci, 1992]. The televisions then almost immediately went—the ones that could—on to the satellite (in the meantime the state acquired its own telecommunications satellite, Türksat), where more than fifteen are available today, of which only one has a marked Islamic character, Mesaj, whilst others are being prepared. We can note incidentally that this wide offer also serves the Turkish minorities in other European countries, tuned through the satellite to Turkish channels, in Greece, Bulgaria and wherever there are Turkish-speaking minorities.

It is interesting to note the reactions to this blossoming of international satellite links. The fear of 'fundamentalist propaganda' present in some local French reports, also echoed in some political positions on the subject in Belgium, has produced the surprising attempt by some local authorities governed both by the right and by the left (for example Saint-Cloud and Courcouronnes in France [Hargreaves & Mahdjoub, 1997]) to prohibit them—as in Iran and in some Arab countries! Amongst the justifications used was the appearance of the environment, which, when thinking of the low-rent housing would seem the least of the problems. Surveys on consumption however seem to play down these fears of Islamist contagion. The difference in the way the satellite is used by parents and children has also been noted (the former are more oriented towards the country of origin—but Eurosport is also watched—and are also greater consumers of religious programmes; the latter are also interested in international channels outside the country of residence but also of origin, for films and music above all). The satellite has also been able to foster curiosity regarding the country of origin. Regret has been shown by some mothers who underlined that before the satellite, at least, they could learn the language of the country of residence from TV. Some have observed that watching Arab TV allowed all the generations to watch TV together, as the images are more chaste and 'controlled'. The effect noted by some interviewees, according to whom the satellite has improved their approach to their country of origin and, in the case of Algeria in 1995, for example, played a role in motivating them to vote, is of interest [Hargreaves & Mahdjoub, 1997]. In general, a reduction in the 'feeling of guilt' regarding the culture of the country of origin has been seen, as this is no longer perceived as 'abandoned' and they are able to feel more comfortable in the country of residence, precisely due to the possibility of still being in contact with the country of origin [Ouali, 1997].

Apart from the satellite, there are some experiences in Europe of local TVs with a Muslim character. In Berlin, there is the experiment of a multicultural 'open channel', *Offene Kanal Berlin* (OKB), with programmes produced by diversified Muslim players (Arabs, Turks, Kurds and Sufi groups) for a total of 60 programmes a month, about half of which are sermons [Jonker, 2000; Kosnick & Bentzin, 2001]. In Germany, there exist at least three other experiments of a certain importance which broadcast programmes of interest for Muslims living in the country: these are Turkish television in Germany, linked to the IGMG, based in Berlin, Kanal 7, a Turkish channel that sometimes broadcasts religious programmes, and the private channel of the Ahmadis in Frankfurt [DE File]. In Denmark there are experiments of local TVs run by Muslims [DK File].

Different cases of public intervention are the Dutch one, already mentioned with reference to the radio, with a broadcast of some programmes on Islam funded by the state [NL File], and the Austrian one where, as Islam is one of the recognised religions, TV programmes are broadcast on the national television, ORF, called *The voice of Islam* [AT File]. In Bulgaria there were occasionally programmes in Turkish on national television, where greetings of the imam of the Bulgarian community is usually broadcast on the main Muslim holidays, after the news [BG File]. In 2000, television programmes in Turkish were introduced into the Bulgarian public television channels [Bougarel & Clayer, 2001]. In Romania too, the national channel, Romania 1, broadcasts a weekly programme dedicated to minorities, which also covers religious topics. They are also occasionally present in some local TVs, such as MTC and TV Neptun [RO File].

In Spain the official television network, Televisión Española, broadcasts a monthly programme of one hour, on Sunday mornings (*Tiempo de creer*) dedicated to the Muslim community. At a local level, Muslim representatives have tried to negotiate with local TV for the possibility of having Muslim religious programmes, so far to no avail [ES File].

In Portugal the public television channel RTP 2 broadcasts a daily programme of 30 minutes, from Mondays to Fridays, entitled *O Fé dos Homens*. The Portuguese Muslim community is entitled to participate and occasionally produces programmes inside this slot, in the same way as the other organised religious communities in the country [PT File].

The French case deserves closer examination. In France there is a Sunday slot, first broadcast on TF1 and today on France 2, which has religious programmes of the various confessions present in the country. Since 1983, a Muslim programme has existed, at the time called *Connaître l'islam* [Reeber, 1995], and which recently became *Vivre l'islam*, under new control. It is a programme that lasts half an hour, from 8.45 a.m. to 9.15 a.m., coming after the Buddhist programme and before the Jewish and Christian ones. Given the time and the slot itself, it can only have a limited audience share, estimated in the past at a tenth of the Catholic programme, which goes on the air in the late morning and which is certainly not the height of the weekly schedule. However, the case is interesting because it places the programme in a multi-religious context. Some of the viewers are not Muslims and therefore it becomes a sort of cognitive window. In addition, although to a limited extent, its audience also extends to French-speaking TV audiences in the neighbouring countries: Belgium, Switzerland but also Italy and elsewhere. And especially the intellectual leadership of these countries follow it with a certain continuity, as it is one of the few programmes, obviously in a European language, written by and concerning European Muslims themselves, as we have ascertained from feedback collected personally. In addition, the programme is also accessible on the other side of the Mediterranean via satellite.

Lastly, there are various TV stations based in European countries that are addressed outside, to the diasporas of the various countries: for example, there are the extremely different cases of the *Muslim*

TV of the Ahmadis, which broadcasts via satellite from Great Britain, the Kurdish *Med-TV* which makes its programmes in Danderleeuw, in Belgium, even if its head office is in London. Following Turkish pressure it has changed its name (today it is called *Medya TV*) and is subject to a certain control by the British authorities [Lambert, 2000].

The Internet and cyber-Muslims

The impact of the Internet is such that national borders no longer have much meaning. Indeed, also with reference to Islam, and moreover by definition, the means does not discriminate on the basis of the origin of its contents. After all, the search engines are not 'national': they look for sites by key word or chains of words. However there is at least a mode of 'preference' and selection that plays a decisive role: that based on language.

English is the hegemonic language of the Internet and therefore, above all, material and sites are in English. This cultural predominance is also valid with regard to Islam, and is not without consequences. One of these, which we could call of a geo-religious character (in the same way that we talk of geopolitics), is the clear prevalence that the instrumental means offers, at least at this stage, not only to Western Muslims or those located in the West, but also to Asians, to more frequently know and use English, compared for example to Arab Muslims, less literate in this sense, in some cases with French as their second language or at least as their first Western language. This reshuffles the cards not only by inverting the polarity between the centre and the periphery, but also by balancing differently the specific weights of the various peripheries and the equilibrium between them. Islam on the Internet, for example, is not only mainly not in Arabic, but is not culturally Arabic, and this is already very significant. In this sense, the Internet ideology finds confirmation: the web does not have a centre and its virtual centres are located differently from the real ones. O. Roy [2002a:165–183] speaks about 'virtual Oumma' and found a confirmation of a general deculturation and individualisation of contemporary Islamic movements.

This phenomenon, made even more incisive by the fact that in North America and in Europe, but also in Asia, not only are there more people connected to the web, but also more literate people technologically, with respect to many Arab countries, is not devoid

of consequences on the presence of Islam—and of which Islam—on
the Net, as there is no centre and this is important also for those
who restrict themselves to interrogating and 'consuming' the Internet,
and Muslim sites in this particular case (it is however a pity that
research, when it exists, as almost always with reference to the
Internet, is centred only on the producers, that is, on the sites, and
not on the consumers and the ways they use it, of which we know
very little). The fact that the largest 'springboard' for navigating in
the Internet is the site of the MSA, the Muslim Students' Association,
obviously American, is not devoid of consequences and this is regardless of whether the user is in the West or in the Arab world.

If it is true, as has been noted by internal observers, that after all
the Internet presupposes the return to a founding characteristic of
Muslim civilisation, the centrality of the written text [Azzi, 1999], it
is indicative that it is rather in the language of the greatest power
on the planet than in that of the Qur'an. Also indicative is the resistance shown, at least in an early phase, by Muslim scholars to the
new medium, possibly with the excuse of the fear of access to pornog-
raphy which is also on the Net, or due to the fact that control and
therefore censorship is not possible: a criticism, as it were, in the
'old style' basically no different from that of the Wahhabis 'ulama'
regarding radio and then television—supplanted in a progressive sense
by the king who had defeated them by reading passages from the
Qur'an on the new media [Della Ratta, 2000]—which nevertheless
effectively expresses the fear of being by-passed by what is new, even
conceptually. Nevertheless, some traditional scholars have already
adapted perfectly to the new means, as shown by the sites of jurists
such as al-Qaradawi and similar. Not knowing what to do, the fear
almost of a new form of civil society (however far from being a reality, as the bards of the Internet proclaims—it is still virtual) is also
visible in the diversity of policies on the matter, which go from
absolute freedom to a ban on access. Thus Algeria places no restrictions on television reception but controls the Internet, whilst Malaysia
supervises access to TV channels but encourages independent access
to the Internet.

In the Muslim context, the discourse on the Internet concerns
only an elite, but things are rapidly evolving. And today we find on
the Net not only the Qur'an recited and chanted and hadith in hypertext or the official sites of Muslim organisations and movements, but
also sites for 'private' use (from fatwa-on-line—such as those that

can be consulted in the *fatwa bank* at www.islamonline.net or that can be requested at the same address—to marriage announcements, such as those at www.matrimonials.com, and they also exist on a local and national basis in different countries), to the personal home pages. And the Internet, above all, has been explicitly identified as a new territory of *da'wa*.

To return to the European context, it appears clear from what has been said so far, in particular with regard to language, that it ends up by privileging in the first place the English sites, as well as those in English. They can be first approached through www.muslimdirectory.co.uk. The site of the British unitary representative body, the Muslim Council of Britain (MCB: www.mcb.org.uk) represents somewhat the "official" image of British Islam: it proposes a link to the web page of the government with the speech of the Prime Minister Blair at a meeting of the MCB, but also to Sala@m (www.Sala@am. co.uk), a site that acts as a link for the organisations of Muslim students, Sufi sites or the Islamic Foundation. Another fundamental on-line platform is Islamic Gateway (IG: www.ummah.org), larger and more militant, that includes access to the various sites, of which several have British addresses, of Islamic movements such as *Hizb al-Tahrir, Al Muhajiroun*, to the Taliban, up to an 'Action Zone' which have had as its flags the United States' public enemy number one, Osama bin Laden, the Saudi millionaire currently a refugee in Afghanistan, and the former public enemy number one Saddam Hussein [Bunt, 1999]. It is interesting to note that the sociological profile of the young British Islamic militants, as ascertained in personal observations, includes students of computer science and engineering and, in general, are 'modern', in the sense also found in the past for other militant groups in the country of origin. An important web address, especially because it is in a strongly minority context, and perhaps for this reason relatively successful, is www.iol.ie/~afifi, the site of the Belfast Islamic Centre, which has been operative since 1995 [Bunt, 2000].

In **France**, a site for an approach to Islam on the web can be www.allahouakbar.com, of the magazine *Islam de France*, but also www.uoif-online.org, the site of UOIF, one of the French Muslim federations. The site mosquee.free.fr reviews the mosques in the Ile de France (whilst the *Institut Musulman de la Mosquée de Paris* (IMMP) has its own site, www.mosquee-de paris.com). We can also mention www.scout-mf.com (the official site of the Muslim Scouts of France) and www.islamfrance.free.fr [FR File].

In **Belgium**, we can mention the site of the official organisation representing Muslim communities towards the state, the *Exécutif des Musulmans de Belgique* (EMB): www.embnet.be. Two other major sources of informations for a Muslim agenda: www.assabyle.com (managed by the CIB, Centre Islamique Belge) and www.Islam-Belgique.com presenting itself as "le site des musulmans de Belgique". Besides, we can mention the Shiites' http://users.skynet.be/yassine and http://club.euronet.be/mous.bar/plm.html, as well as the hotly debated personal site of Dr. Imam Sayyed Muhammad Saghir, http://club.euronet.be/mous.bar/Jamais/finale.html, which contains the detailed chronicle of a divorce in emigration, from the Muslim point of view of the husband-imam. An example of the site of a youth organisation is http://users.pandora.be/rzoezie [BE File].

In the **Netherlands** the main sites are those coming under the organisation of Muslim broadcasting, *Nederlandse Moslim Oproep* (NMO), to be found at the address www.omroep.nl/nmo/index.htm. Other useful addresses are www.salaam.nl, of the association of the same name in Rotterdam, and www.alwaqf.org. We can also mention the Ahmadi site, www.gironet.nl/home/imaks/faaiin.htm, which can be used as a link for the other European addresses of the movement on the periphery of Islam [NL File]. Luxembourg has the site of the *Centre Culturel Islamique du Grand-Duché de Luxembourg*, http://surf.to/cci [LU File].

In **Germany**, the main directory is www.Islam.de. Through www.islam-pure.de it is possible to enter into contact with Shiites in Europe: the Shiite world has its European centre in Germany. Other sites of a certain importance include www.islamische-foederation.de, with the related links, and the site of the *Islamisches Zentrum Hamburg*, www.islamische-bildung.de. The radical movement of the Murabitun, promoted by converts, has a site that boasts the Muslimness of Goethe and of other representatives of German romanticism (www.weimarinstitut.net). Access is also possible through www.web.de/suchen/muslime/deutschland, www.bellnet.com/suchen/religion/islam.htm, and www.nmia.islam-today.com. www.muslim-markt.de is interesting and indicative [DE File].

For **Austria** the compulsory entrance is www.islam.at [AT File]. For **Switzerland**, on the other hand, it is possible to pass through the detailed www.islam.ch/links.htm [CH File].

The fundamental address in **Sweden** is http://hem.passagen.se/sfcm/ [SE File].

In **Finland** it is possible to go through www.rabita.fi [FI File].

In **Italy** there are several starting points, referring to the main federation, the UCOII (www.islam-ucoii.it), the mosque of Rome, which is under the Muslim League (www.lega-musulmana.it), Sufi groups (such as the Naqshbandis site, www.sufi.it of the group of Sheikh Nazim), or more general sites such as www.arab.it, are of local importance such as www.fondaco.it in Milan or www.rcm. napoli.it/zayd in Napoli. The links, as in other situations, are repeated, and allow navigation from one to the other. The most recent and complete portal is www.islam-online.it. A women's site, created by the European Women's Muslim League can be found at www.life-hayat.net, as well as the Young Muslim's site, www.giovanimusul-mani.it [IT File].

In **Spain**, we find www.webislam.com, linked with www.verdeislam.com/index.htm, of the magazine of the same name; www.feeri.es comes under the *Federación Española de Entidades Religiosas Islámicas*, www.cie.es is under the *Comisión Islámica de España*, www.terra.es/personal/ame1972/portada1.htm is under the *Asociación Musulmana de España—Unión de Comunidades Islámicas en España*, and, under the various structures and groupings of Spanish Islam, www.islam-shia.org, www.cislamica.org, perso.wanadoo.es/murabitun/murabitun.htm of the Murabitun, as well as www.zawiya.org/index-2.htm of the *Yama'a Islámica de Al-Andalus*, and www.arrakis.es/~margarit/sufismo, a Naqshbandi site, which is certainly the Sufi organisation with the greatest presence on the Internet; and members.es.tripod.de/cima_org/present.htm of the *Comunidad Islámica Morisca-Andalusí*, and www.ahlulqi-blah.8k.com, coming under the *Association Catalana de Estudios Islámicos* [ES File].

In **Portugal**, a good starting point is www.aliasoft.com/forum-islam [PT File], which shows an example of a forum on Islamic topics. See also www.alfurqan.pt.

In **Greece**, the Turkish-speaking minority has www.trakyanins-esi.com and www.armory.com/~thrace/thrace_list.html, but it is also possible to go through the official Turkish site http://inter.mfa.gov.tr/grupa/ac/acd/default.htm, in English [GR File].

In **Bulgaria**, the department of the Mufti is on line at http://mufti-bg.tripod.com [BG File]. In Poland, a start can be made at www.islam.pl, but also at www.islam.px.pl or www.muslimonline.com/poland [PL File]. In Romania, on the other hand, only the site of the Romanian Islamic League is registered http://www.islam.ro. [RO File].

Apart from the list of starting points to enter the various Muslim sites in Europe, through the game of links, it is possible to develop some further considerations, in addition to those already put forward.

So far we have referred to collective sites. But it may be interesting to look at the personal sites of European Muslims, which open an interesting window on to the cultural mix of reference of many young people. Bunt [1999] quotes the example of the home page of a certain Afzal Merali who presents information of his main interests: 'Islam, Football, Liverpool FC, Movies'. This could be the start of further examination.

Another reflection can be offered by the links, through which interesting evolutions are produced in the image of European Islam, in terms of 'internal' opening to various contributions. Not only are the sites 'de-territorialised' but a certain cultural opening to different influences can be identified, as shown by the game of the links: organisations of strict Sunni obedience with links to Sufi sites, in their turn open to forms of alternative medicine and therefore to new age links, to international official bodies, to orientalist or academic and independent documentation centres (which often have more documentation on Islam and Muslims than those found in many specialised institutions in the Islamic world) and even to Christian sites of documentation on Islam. We are not saying that this is the rule, and that there are not exceptions, but it is clear that in a certain sense it opens up a world, especially to those who have remained closed to their original Muslim contribution, or in their country.

Opening means above all connection with one's own country of origin or with the official organisations, whether it is the Turkish Diyanet (www.diyanet.gov.tr) or the Arab Muslim World League (www.arab.net/mwl). Naturally there are also the sites of the high places of Muslim culture: the university of Al-Azhar has a great deal of material in English as well and a lot can be found on the sites of Asian universities. It is also possible to link to political groups and organisations, from the moderates such as the Muslim Brotherhood to the more radical *Hamas* or *Hizbullah*, and to the armed groups operating in various parts of the world.

On looking closely, obviously, one can find everything on the Internet, including anti-Semitic and revisionist sites, proposed by some Muslim web pages, to a *masjid* for homosexual Muslims [very strongly stigmatised in a Muslim magazine: Azzi, 1999] and various types of sites such as QueerJihad and QueerMuslims, as well as lesbian and transgender sites or sites of movements on the sidelines of Islam, such as the Baha'is and the Ahmadis, and their enemies [Lohlker, 1998]. Lastly, there are sites of dialogue, especially Muslim-Christian, which we will come back to regarding inter-religious relations. Here again the linguistic factor must be underlined which impacts on their possible penetration: the vast majority are in English, only 2.5% are in Arabic [Gaudeul, 1999]. It is evident that in the proliferation of these 'atypical' sites (another question is their effective use or the identification with them by the users) the extraordinary freedom due to the anonymity offered by the Internet comes into play, which allows going on show without really being 'seen': something even more sensational if coming from circles or countries that are perhaps 'closed' from this point of view. There also had to be Muslim hackers, under the name of MHC (Muslim Hackers' Club) [Bunt, 2000].

The intrinsic opening to the medium allows, as well as the game of links mentioned, the appearance on the virtual scene of new types of theologians and scholars. The traditional *alim* knew, in the first place, the Qur'an off by heart, as well as the *tafsir*, the commentaries and collections of hadith. Today, thanks to technological development, this memory no longer has to be individual: it can be registered and interrogated on the Net and in an extremely simple way, through the mechanisms of research by word and hypertext. In a word, issuing a fatwa, that is, delivering an opinion on the basis of past thought and jurisprudence becomes a profession within reach of far more people. and no longer makes a certain *cursus studiorum* compulsory. As a Muslim scholar, Anis Ahmad, of the Da'wa Academy at the International Islamic University of Islamabad, has said the Internet "makes the *ijtihâd* much easier for people" [quoted in Bunt, 2000]. The form of traditional knowledge cannot be by-passed, obviously; however, this technological development 'opens up' to a new type of potential Muslim leader [Mandaville, 2000]. In the 'digital Umma' [Bunt, 2000] it is not only a new type of consumption of information on Islam that is appearing but also a new form of cognitive power and consequently of leadership.

5. THE PRODUCTION OF THE ISLAMIC DISCOURSE

What has just been said about the Internet allows us to introduce another topic. So far we have discussed the media, the means of communication to be precise. But what effect does this have on its purposes? How are the contents affected? Is there a relationship between the medium and the message? Are there any changes in the latter? The answer apparently is not unequivocal. On the one hand we have new leaders who use the old media making them (books, for example) their form of legitimacy and on the other hand we have traditional leaders using the new media (television and the Internet).

But apart from the means, can we say that new, specifically European, contents are appearing? The answer does not lie in this paragraph, or even in this chapter but in this report as a whole, which clearly says yes, there is a European specificity of Islam. It also appears in the evolution of old discourses, but also in the production of new ones, a production of meaning influenced by the context, for certain aspects in the construction of a new rhetoric [Dassetto, 2000]. Its signs are, however, contrasting and less visible in the medium par excellence of cultural transmission, the book, than elsewhere.

Let us take the books available on the market. The situation is different in the various countries, according to the type of immigration.

In Islamic bookshops in **Great Britain**, the absolute predominance of works in English and the very small number in Urdu or other Asian languages and in Arabic (practically only the Qur'an and some collections of hadith) is striking. However, the literature available is not English but the great majority is only *in* English. It is made up mostly of translations of dogmatic, traditionalist and moralistic literature, simplistic and repetitive, focused on the form and on 'how' (how to pray, how to do the ablutions, how a good Muslim woman should dress, etc.) and with an almost absolute non-existence of interrogative, of 'why'. As a whole this literature gives the idea of being available only because it is translated and sent free of charge, or almost, by *da'wa* organisations, especially Saudi Arabian. There is nothing or almost nothing on current affairs, nothing or almost nothing on the new and original situation in which Muslims are and which certainly Wahhabis literature does not contemplate (starting from the fact that they are a minority in a lay and pluralist context), nothing or almost nothing that concerns the second generation and their doubts or problems, very little that is strictly religious, not linked with morals (often understood in a very external way), almost nothing spiritual or mystic.

In the **French-speaking world** the situation is different in part, with a larger quantity of works in Arabic (there is not the absolute prevalence of the language of the country of residence noted in the UK) and perhaps for this reason greater availability of differentiated sources. In **Germany** attempts are made to produce innovative material, also for the transmission of the religion to children, apart from Turkish literature and the first Islamic *Buchmessen* are opening.

However, the impression of poor production remains, of not reflecting the composition of the Muslim communities, of delay with respect to reality, unlike the case of other media. This could explain, together with the fact that the fundamental literature, not very different, is available in all Muslim centres or almost, the small number of Islamic bookshops. After all, the best of the production on the Muslim world is available in non-Muslim bookshops and in libraries, and for the remainder there are the other media, from the Friday *Khutba* in the mosques [Reeber, 2000], to magazines and the Internet. The reintellectualisation of the European Islamic discourse is therefore still to come and does not act all round. But it is true that the new public sphere produced by the media has nevertheless inserted Islam into a wider game, a system in a world of systems [Eickelmann & Anderson, 1999], in forced interrelation with them.

Perhaps something else should be noted. The new intellectuals are also starting to be formed in relation with the 'canonical' European places of intellectual production: universities, cultural associations and journalism. Not 'apart', no longer only 'elsewhere'. And this is already new and an important indication. If anything, there is still a problem of comprehension of their role in Europe, where the tendency is still often to prefer, in the academic and political worlds, as interlocutors and cognitive 'instruments', non-religious intellectuals of 'ethnically' Muslim origin, rather than the religious intellectuals. At conferences and in research too, but even only as subjects to be interviewed, there is a tendency to prefer interlocutors with an 'ethnically characterised' surname but who are culturally assimilated, underestimating, often deliberately, the religious affiliation, almost as if an explicitly religious subject is necessarily deviant in his comprehension of social reality, whereas a non-religious subject necessarily would not be. This is a questionable approach, the manifestation of a debate that has already been present for a long time amongst sociologists of religion, which the presence of Islam in Europe healthily brings back to the surface.

6. THE MEDIA ON MUSLIMS

The presence of Islam in the limelight of the media has 'globalised' the use of terms such as jihad, ayatollah, fatwa, chador, used more or less pertinently, now in common use in journalistic language, not only in the West. Naturally noting the very type of words that have become popular does not predict anything good about the image of Islam in the West. But there are also other realities, and there can be no doubt that the level of knowledge of Islam, including European Islam, after the period of the first pioneering research, is spreading and increasing. In some countries there are already periodic instruments of observation and monitoring. This is the case of the *British Muslims Monthly Survey*, begun in 1993 by the CSIC (Centre for the Study of Islam and Christian-Muslim Relations) which abstracts articles on Muslims and Islam from the national and local newspapers, other press and Muslim magazines (suspended publication in 2002).

Another source and place of observation are the journals on immigration or ethnic studies: from *New community* in Great Britain to *Migrantenstudies* or *Contrast* in the Netherlands, from *Studi emigrazione* in Italy to *Hommes & Migrations, Migrants Formation* or *Migrations et Societé* in France. Those also include, with a transnational ambition, the *Revue Européenne des Migrations Internationales*.

Amongst the more classic instruments are the academic journals on Islam, mostly of an Orientalist layout, present in almost all countries: they are the most traditional and authoritative, and usually the oldest cognitive instruments on Islam in their respective countries, but usually they also pay little attention, by definition, to European Islam, to which they sometimes devote articles or single publications, only occasionally with empirical attention and sociological sensitivity. A recent creation is also a directory of the sociology of Islam, but not specifically concerned with Europe. There are also recent instruments, which devote a certain attention to European Islam, such as the *ISIM newsletter*, from the Institute for the Study of Islam in the Modern World of Leiden, which started publication in October

1998. And lastly, there are the journals of interreligious dialogue, which we will discuss in the chapter on this subject.

7. THE ATTITUDE OF THE MEDIA TOWARDS ISLAM: ISLAMOPHOBIA?

According to some, there is allegedly, and more present than Muslim fundamentalism, a culturalist and differentialist fundamentalism, to use a term popularised by Taguieff, of Western, European, modern and lay background, different from the religious one expressed over the centuries, which does not replace it but is in addition, linked to the individual or the free market, at times also to democracy and human rights: they do not only produce the Fukuyamas or the Huntingtons but find daily expression in cultural and popular discourse and in the press.

One of its expressions is what one text which has been fairly widely diffused [Runnymede Trust, 1997] has called 'Islamophobia', popularising the expression in all European countries where the Muslim question is important, amongst specialists and especially amongst the social players, especially obviously the Muslims themselves. This highlights that peculiar form of 'semiotic pollution' [the expression was coined by the semiologist U. Volli, cf. Allievi, Bastenier, Battegay and Boubeker, 1992] which affects Islam and produces serious consequences for Muslims in Europe as well.

In Great Britain, where normally more emphasis is placed on the diversity linked with race and ethnic group, there is often a tendency to say that Islamophobia is more a question of racism than of religious intolerance: a racism with marked cultural aspects, like anti-Semitism and anti-Judaism, to which is added the fact of not being white and European [Modood in Modood & Werbner, 1999]. There is however a religious specificity of racism, which is pointed out in *Islamophobia: A challenge for us all*, a report by the Runnymede Trust [1997], also known as the "Islamophobia Report", which applies the classic "prejudice + power = discrimination" to the Muslim case, analysing its implications. In Great Britain the report received significant media coverage and succeeded in creating a certain debate on the subject, to a great extent also due to the direct impact already present in the title, which the authors of the report did not invent but have greatly contributed to popularising. Today it has now become part of the European vocabulary: articles and essays which refer to

Islamophobia in the title have appeared in almost all European countries, written both by Muslims and researchers.

Islamophobia does not only relate to the media, which are almost more an effect than a cause, even if in their turn they act as a multiplier and as a driving force. However, it appears that one of the elements of the success of the report amongst Muslim communities and the "politically correct" circles close to them was that of laying the communicative responsibility for Islamophobia wholly on non-Muslims. Now, if the mass media often have an 'exaggerated' perception of Muslim positions, it is also because the Muslim leaders frequently express them precisely in this way, due to inexperience in relating with the mass media (an element which should therefore diminish once experience is acquired). At times this may be due to linguistic weakness (which is not alien to the perception of Islam as something external—despite what is said in the report, the comparison with the authority of Jewish leadership, whilst Muslims do not have as much experience, evidently is not credible), but also because the positions are sometimes effectively 'strong' and perhaps the vicinity of a microphone or of a camera push some to add more; and lastly because often, at least in a first phase, whatever was said, and whatever exaggeration or statement that does not agreed with what Muslim leaders have said, the explicit protests within the community have often been few and far between, and people preferred to disassociate themselves privately and in whispers, even if things are now changing. Thanks also to the debate which followed the publication of the report, however, some incomprehension on the social level, of coexistence in situations such as schools, hospitals etc., but also some serious exaggerations in the media, were reduced: in Great Britain itself for the first time, following protests by representatives of the Muslim communities, the popular *Daily Mail* apologised for the headline 'plastering' the front page which, following an anti-terrorist operation, predicted a generalised threat of attacks by 'Muslims' without further specification [Lord Ahmed of Rotherham, interview, May 2000].

Going back to the question of Islamophobia, that there is a specificity of the religious reasoning and of its force can be measured with greater evidence precisely where the institutional context is not particularly favourable to its expression. It is known for example, to remain in Great Britain, how the category of cultural difference 'sponsored' by the state is the racial one (and so we have the Race

Relations Act and bodies such as the Commission for Racial Equality).
Nevertheless, some research [Statham, 1999], based on factors of
collective mobilisation measured through their form of appearance
in the media (in the specific case, an analysis of the contents of a
newspaper, *The Guardian*, between 1990 and 1996), shows that if the
active groups quoted in the articles were more often of a racial character (36.7%, against 24.5% of religious groups and 23.1% of ethnic or national groups) where organisations were specifically mentioned,
about half of these (47.9%) were Muslim organisations. This in the
context where Great Britain does not recognise equality of treatment, in its anti-discrimination policies, on the religious level, whilst
it recognises them on the ethnic-racial level (if there is discrimination on religious grounds on the labour market or housing market
for example, this cannot be prosecuted, whereas it can be if it is on
ethnic or racial grounds).

However, it is not possible to infer too much from this kind of
research. There is in fact a distortion regarding the media which
must be taken into consideration, due to the fact that the press is
more attentive to Muslim organisations than to others, especially if
antagonistic, precisely because Islam makes more news. It becomes
all the more interesting to note that Muslim religious groups have
not been involved in forms of violent action more than those of ethnic and racial grounds, less if anything.

In the same way, it is not possible to omit the importance of other
social variables: associations, media and public opinion, the role of
experts, the position and practices of other religious faiths and in
particular, the majority faiths in the respective countries, as far as
internal factors are concerned; and the existence and role played by
any Muslim organisations, of a national or supranational character,
and by the countries of origin of the immigrants, as far as external
factors are concerned.

At the same time, the diversity of the national frameworks implies
an apparent diversity in the behaviour of the press. A comparison
of the previous research shows this relativising completely and, so to
speak, 'localising' its results [Koopmans & Statham, 1999]. In Germany,
the identification with ethnic and national groups appears in the
media more frequently than in Great Britain (83% against 19%),
but, to make up for this, religious identification is practically non-
existent: only 0.4% of the cases come from Muslim religious groups.

But naturally this may mean that the religious argument is not used by the social players because they already know from the start that it would not be acknowledged (by the institutions) or perceived (by the media). Even if everything may also have to do with the diversity of the groups in question, and in particular with Turkish ethnicity, which, for example, does not have a language in common with the coloniser, because Germany was not this in Turkey. The complexity of the factors at play, in particular of those not observed, thus induces us to a certain caution in proposing generalisations on this matter.

We shall restrict ourselves to observing the signs of progressive normalisation, even ordinariness, of the Muslim presence, which more than others perhaps may be indicative of a 'long trend' which has now been acquired in the direction of a pluralisation that 'normally' also includes Muslim diversity: from the publication of the times of prayer during Ramadan in some newspapers in various European countries, to the addresses of mosques under the places of worship in the 'Yellow Pages', to the habit acquired in some media circles to ask for the opinion of Muslim representatives of subjects that are not strictly religious, but which may concern them, to the attempt currently under way in the United Kingdom of creating a *Who's Who* of Islam in the country.

To remain with the perception by the general and not Muslim press, however, the main difference and the real turning-point will probably only take place when it can count on a significant number of Muslim readers: when it will also be, therefore, at least in part, *also* Muslim. Although without any illusions as to the regulating virtues of the market, it is in fact unquestionable that if this variable were to take on an important weight, it could not be without consequences on the ways of influencing the newsvalue of Islam. In countries with a strong localised Muslim presence, some early signs of the weight of the Muslim market can already be felt today, for example on the world of advertising.

Today, some observers, such as the group of the CSIC which produced the BMMS (*British Muslims Monthly Survey*, which has already been mentioned), already note how the local press is often more careful than the national one about speaking 'badly' of Muslims, precisely because it has a quota of Muslim readers and it could lose them. To quote a concrete case, the *Birmingham Post* is believed to be 'rougher' in handling questions linked to Islam, than the *Birmingham Evening Mail*, precisely because the latter has a significant share of Muslim readers and advertisers.

However, there remains the problem of the press and above all of national general television, which rarely have this feedback and can continue to propose a stereotyped image of Islam—even if the level of information progressively deepens. This may take place in several ways, not only through the inaccuracy of information. The dissociation between images and text in the television news, for example, is a subtler way to convey an image that is not only stereotyped but 'externalised' of Islam, putting images from Muslim countries (of headscarfed women or men in prayer, for example) as the background to a news item on European Islam [Marletti, 1995]. More generally there is the problem of the lack of specific expertise on European Islam among the majority of journalists and operators of information, with few exceptions. It is not enough to assign to the special correspondent, expert on the Middle East or Iran, when they exist, the coverage of facts regarding European Muslims. This may be just as serious a mistake as asking orientalists for their opinion on an Islam unknown to them, European Islam, and who tend to interpret it as though it were the one they know: Arabic, African or Asian. The category of Islam risks becoming as worthless when it is not misleading, in these cases, as Said said [1981], as the expression 'negro-mentality' to understand the populations of colour.

8. The Opinion of the Native Population

Public opinion is not formed only through reading the press. In structuring what is first of all a 'private' opinion, even if constructed relationally, it is not only the mass media which contribute, but also the educational institutions and the cultural agencies, including those on the same religious level, such as the churches, and also researchers in the area of Muslim immigration: if they do not directly influence the final consumer, they do so indirectly, with the mediation of the mass media, which often quote, more or less correctly, the results. If it is impossible to give an idea of this complex system, it is possible at least to analyse its possible consequences, very imperfectly measured by opinion polls. In actual fact, the sources are too few and too specific (and too methodologically unchecked) in order to be able to draw reliable considerations. We will restrict ourselves to naming them, more for the use that is made of them in creating, sometimes in 'inventing' social debate, than for their intrinsic content. The majority of research and opinion polls do not concern Islam specifically, but more generally the perception of immigration: a fairly vast field but of little use for our purposes and which therefore we will not deal with.

Specific opinion polls, no longer very recent, include the two IFOP/*Le Monde* and others carried out respectively in November 1989, immediately following the *affaire* of the *foulards*, and, five years later, in 1994, on the subject of Islam in France, which are interesting as they questioned non-Muslim French and Muslim French separately. From the first [IFOP/Le Monde/RTL/La Vie, 1989] it appears that two French people out of three had a very negative image of Islam, whilst nine Muslims out of ten deemed their religion compatible with integration in French society. Obviously the two samples questioned have diametrically opposed perceptions of Islam. The former associate it with fanaticism and a return to the submission of women (however, Catholics judge it with less severity), whilst the latter consider it synonymous with tolerance and progress in the protection of women (even if the Muslims who define themselves as unbelievers and assimilated believe the contrary). The perception of mosques, meals without pork in schools, Muslim holidays and voting in elections obviously are perceived in opposite ways: desirable for the Muslims, whilst the mosques are objected to by one-third of the French, two out of three object to the right of Muslims to open private schools, 56% are even hostile to meals without pork and 75% categorically refuse the headscarf. Moreover, Muslims seem to desire an integration without conflicts: two out of three refuse any idea of derogatory personal status, 36% do not even want private schools and very few want Muslim political parties or trade unions. In addition, three out of four state they are ready to accept the choice of a spouse who abandons the mosque and more than half would refuse the call to prayer outside the mosques.

The second opinion poll, by Le Monde/IFOP RTL/Fr 3 in 1994 [*Le Monde*, 1994], in a period marked by the violent events in Algeria, the arrest of some Algerian Islamist militants and the Bayrou circular against the headscarf can perhaps be summarised thus: the image of Islam remains very negative amongst the French, whilst the Muslims increasingly want integration. However, the emotion aroused by symbols such as the headscarf and others is less incisive, a sign that if Islam is not liked, the Muslims, in daily life, seem to be less a cause of concern. This is so even if from the poll there would appear to be greater religious consciousness in the younger age group (25–34 years old): only 24% say they do not fast, against 38% in the previous poll, 64% do not drink (against 50%), 65% would like to make the pilgrimage to Mecca (against 50%), and 21% would like a specific status for Islam (against 12% in 1989).

Surveys elsewhere also show a negative idea of Islam. A study carried out in Spain in 1991, but methodologically not reliable [Martin-Muñoz, 1996], associated Islam with violence (35%), a form of regression (59%) and fanaticism (67%). An opinion poll in 1981 in Sweden showed that 45% of Swedes said they had a positive idea regarding the prospect of a mosque in their town, whilst 35% were opposed to it and 20% uncertain. Another survey, but not comparable, carried out in 1990, showed that 65% of Swedes had a negative idea of Islam and 88% considered that it was not compatible with the democratic system. Intervening in this there is the Iranian revolution, the Rushdie affair but also, and by no means of secondary importance, the publication of the bestseller by Betty Mahmoody *Not without my daughter*, also made into a film, which in Sweden alone sold between 700,000 and 800,000 copies in 1990 [Alwall, 1998]. Incidentally, we can also recall that this book was a bestseller in many European countries, to the extent that it can be said to be one of the most powerful anti-Islamic arguments that has circulated to date.

The perception of Islam in the negative has to be considered as obvious where it is associated with geopolitical arguments and historical and unsolved conflicts. It is not surprising then that in Greece 83% of the population said Turkey in response to the question in a survey in 1993 on which country is considered a threat [Dalègre, 2001]. An extensive sociological study in Bulgaria in 1992 showed how an important minority of Bulgarians consider that changing Turkish names and 'Bulgarising' them, a campaign launched by the premier Zhivkov, was necessary to obtain the unity of the nation (35.2%), and 56.2% consider that the descendants of 'Turkified' Bulgarians have to be helped to rediscover their Bulgarian origins. The majority of Orthodox Bulgarians continue to consider Islam 'a real threat for national unity' (51.1%), and almost all consider the Turks 'religious fanatics' (83.8%), even if they say they are open to friendly relations with them (56.7%), but are absolutely against mixed marriages (only 14% take this possibility into consideration) [Ragaru,

2001]. However, more recent surveys show that in the past five years the weight of these reciprocal stereotypes has been significantly reduced [BG File]. In the meanwhile, the campaign had been reversed by the Communist collapse.

9. Reciprocal Feedback between Europe and Islam

The least well known and understood of the effects of the media in the Muslim immigrant world is that of the reciprocal feedback they induce, similar to that of billiard balls: thanks to which, for example (but many other examples could be given), Algerians were able to hear the reasons of the Islamist opposition on French TV, as the latter could not express themselves in the same way in the official media of their own country. But another example, subtler from the cultural point of view, can be given. It is not without impact that a Muslim and Islamist leader such as Rached al-Ghannouchi has chosen a European country (in this case Great Britain, like France for Khomeini) as a place of exile and not another Muslim country. And it is no small consequence that here, coming into contact with a greater complexity and articulation of the Muslim situation, and probably also a different and direct image of the West, he has elaborated new reflection on relations between Islam and the West, and on Islam as such, and he also directs it towards his interlocutors still in Muslim countries in their language of origin. The examples provided so far mainly concern the countries of origin. However, there are in fact communication dynamics that go through and include in the first place another interlocutor in the communication chain, namely the Muslim minorities in Europe. We can see how a sort of triangulation is developed, distinguishing its aspects and directions, limiting ourselves to the television sector.

In the first place, we have media which start off from 'here' to go 'there', namely from Europe to the countries of origin, more properly transnational, and communication products that are therefore made by Muslims for the Muslims in their countries of origin. In the countries of the Maghreb, for example, there are about 2 million satellite dishes in Algeria, 1.2 million in Morocco and about 50,000 in Tunisia, but only because the ban on them has recently been lifted, and their number is rapidly increasing [Dalla Ratta, 2000]. The first Arab satellite, Arabsat, was launched in 1985 and nicknamed by *Libération* at the time as the highest muezzin in the world (more recent examples include Nilesat 1, the first Egyptian satellite for telecommunications, inaugurated in June 1998). To overcome the resistance of the traditionalist *'ulama'*, in the period when the radio was introduced in the 1920s, King Ibn Saud had sent some to Mecca, and from the capital he had personally read some passages from the Qur'an. More recently, the 'demonic' perception of the new media has renamed the television aerials 'para-diabolic' and some similar reactions have been noted regarding the Internet.

However, the situation from the point of view of Arab television production and broadcasting is extremely dynamic and modern, even if with accents of paradox. There is for example the ban on satellite dishes introduced by Saudi Arabia in 1994, which however is the most powerful Arab producer of programmes via satellite through the three networks of ART, ORBIT and MBC, all linked in some way to various branches of the royal family and which all broadcast from Europe: MBC from London, ART from Avezzano, near Rome, and ORBIT also from Rome [Dalla Ratta, 2000]. These are commercial channels, of which we will underline only the cultural-religious aspects of most interest from our point of view, such as the very popular *Dialogue with the West*, which has been shown by MBC since 1996. MBC, which also owns the UPI agency, the English community radio Spectrum, and other information activities, is the most important Arab multimedia holding company [Naba, 1998]. In a certain sense the 'ecological' operations of ORBIT, are also in a certain sense of a religious character: this channel, founded in 1994 as a result of an agreement with the BBC, then subsequently denounced after the airing of coverage judged too 'benevolent' to the Saudi opposition, like the others mentioned, are not used to diffuse the Sunni word, not even in the Wahhabis version; here it is not a question of diffusing but on the contrary of importing, only in an Islamically correct way. Here images are received and interpreted, shorn of the scenes of sex and violence and retransmitted to an audience of 170 million Arab consumers, in 23 different countries via 28 satellite channels, thirsty for images produced in the West but devoid of the excesses which in the West are the daily bread of television.

Other examples of this channel of communication and of this direction of the flow of information are the Turkish channels which have already been mentioned and which, from Germany, broadcast to Turkey.

There is also another aspect of these flows of communication, which go in the same direction, from 'here' to 'there' but are produced by 'us' rather than by 'them'. These flows began in the 1930s with Radio Bari, which made Italy the first European country to broadcast radio programmes in Arabic (1934) and with the BBC Arabic Service (1938), which is still the largest European producer of programmes in Arabic. Both produced and the BBC still produces programmes specifically for the Arab world and not just mere translations of home programmes.

Today, these flows appear in the pure and simple reception of European programmes, at times preferred also from the information point of view, for greater reliability or at any rate independence from local government control. This reception, however, can take on differentiated forms, as for example the retransmission, actually recorded broadcasts, of Rai Uno or France 2, for example, in Tunisia which allows control and censorship of the news broadcast, especially if it concerns the country in question.

A recent and for the time being little more than experimental flow of information is that which goes through the national European satellite channels, for other populations and other countries. An example is that of RaiMed, the 'Mediterranean' channel of Italy's Rai, which since April 2001 has produced three hours daily of programmes, one in Italian and two in Arabic, mainly for the countries of origin of the migratory flows towards Italy. The European and American channels are very popular in the Maghreb and elsewhere, especially with the young, with extremely high rates of penetration, which also favours the knowledge of European languages: incidentally, an important pre-requisite for emigration.

Information on the Muslim world itself passes to a great extent through these channels. An example is knowledge of the situation in Bosnia and the development of far-reaching inter-Muslim solidarity around it which is due to a great extent to the role of Western information and, incidentally, of the many reporters, also Western, who went to document the crimes and atrocities, at times paying for their commitment with their lives [Ahmed & Donnan, 1994].

An example rather of an attempt at co-operation on the level of the management of the information flows mentioned here is that linked to the project of Euromed TV, which is a follow-up and a direct effect of the 1995 conference of Barcelona, which saw the participation of eight television corporations—France with two broadcasters, Spain, Italy, Malta, Tunisia, Egypt and Jordan—in the project.

The last aspect which we want to underline, the most important within our analysis, is that of the channels of communication and information flows from 'there' to 'here' in the direction of the Muslim, and in particular Arab, communities in Europe.

Arabic is the most broadcast language in the world, after English. And to mention some specific cases, national televisions such as Morocco's RTM or Tunisia's TV7 have a greater 'satellite' audience outside the countries, than nationally. Apart from the national televisions there are also important inter-Arab transnational networks, such as the Lebanese LBC, the Egyptian ESC and ADTV in Dubai, Abu Dhabi TV or the important Al-Jazira, based in Qatar, which have religious programmes, increased at the week-end and during the month of Ramadan. These televisions usually present a mainstream Islam and 'average' programmes acceptable in various national contexts, such as the very popular Ramadan soap operas which have provoked remarks underlining the contrast between the fast from food and the increase in the consumption of images, even in Europe.

Important in particular, but more from the political than the religious point of view, is the role currently played by Al-Jazira, which owing to its information, which is more independent than others, together with the respect won for its coverage of the second Palestinian Intifada, has received criticism and weighty political interference from various governments, including the Tunisian, Libyan, Iraqi, Egyptian and Jordanian governments as well as the Palestinian National Authority, with a total of over 400 official complaints. Its staff also includes journalists and presenters from the former BBC Arabic TV news [Tagliaferri, 2001].

The religious programmes, however, are also important, in particular those on certain talk shows or more accurately live advice, a sort of live *fatwa*, with answers given by authoritative jurists like Yusuf al-Qaradawi and others, to answers sought over the telephone, often from European countries and concerning the ways of life and problems peculiar to European Islam. It is interesting to note that the more peripheral Muslim countries apparently follow more the religious programmes and also have a greater need of them: in proportion, for example, many telephone calls come from Scandinavian countries, where Muslims are, to a great extent, isolated from relations with their countries of origin [Roald, 2001]. New relations between the centre and the periphery are thus created but also new relations between peripheries, and between peripheries and centres that have nothing to do with the countries of origin.

10. Conclusions

The panorama presented above shows the complexity of an aspect of the Muslim presence in Europe that to date has been relatively neglected. It touches on aspects of the media as the possibility of embracing a different 'satellite nationality' [Dalla Ratta, 2000] which, together with others, nevertheless have considerable political and geopolitical implications. Contrasting dynamics are revealed: on the one hand Arabic is the most broadcast language after English, on the other London is probably home to the largest part of the Arab-Muslim press and media located outside an Arab-Muslim context, acting as an important centre of news. Lastly, English is actually the second language of Islam and in many regards even the first, if we think of communication between Muslims outside the Arab world, which after all contains a minority in Islam.

The British Muslim press, furthermore, enjoys this linguistic advantage (even if it is only beginning) of being read by other Muslim minorities but also in some Muslim countries (similar processes but on a lesser scale take place in the Francophone context and on other less well known ones): and the various problems experienced, beginning with that of living in a religiously plural context not dominated by Islam, with a secularistic approach and a dominant secular mentality, their different perception, often greater freedom and open-mindedness, can, with the future in mind, play a role and have an effect also in the countries of origin.

This aspect begins to make the interpretation of Islam within Europe more complex, in the past, in particular on the occasion of external conflicts that could become internal, seen especially in terms of a threatening potential fifth column of foreign forces, as was the case during the Gulf War in various situations [Allievi, Bastenier, Battegay & Boubeker, 1992]. And at the same time it leads towards essential differentiations but which were less known in the past, to the extent that during the Gulf War some Asians dressed in traditional garb were told to go home to Iraq and anti-Muslim graffiti was found on the walls of the Sikh gurudwaras and on mosque walls

[Runnymede Trust, 1997]. Today we believe that the level of information is no longer so low.

However, reflections within the world of journalism can also be
of use on the professional ethics applied to the question of possible
improvements and any recommendations or forms of self-discipline
relative to the way Islam and perhaps other cultural and religious
minorities are treated, to the co-operation and support between journalists of various countries and protection of the freedom of the press
where this is trampled upon. The press and the media remain important, if not decisive, means for the development of civil society and
of inter-relations between the various components of society, the
image of which passes through, and to a great extent is constructed
on, the stage of the media.

CHAPTER NINE

RELATIONS AND NEGOTIATIONS: ISSUES AND DEBATES ON ISLAM

Stefano Allievi

Introduction: The Debate in the Public Space

The presence of Islam in the European public space cannot go unobserved, either socially or culturally. It is too visible and 'cumbersome' not to induce debates as well as tensions: a sign that it is indeed an event that strikes 'sensitive' chords or that is perceived as such, to the extent that by measuring its effects one has at times the impression of a confrontation that is open all around. Islam is questioned in itself, often through essentialist and simplistic interpretations of the relations between religion and politics that it presents. Islam is also questioned in some of its aspects, for how these appear in particular in Muslim countries. Of these aspects, the most visible in the media are certainly the female condition and fundamentalism. Lastly, it produces and induces debate on the fundamentals of society, on the limits of its possibility of openness, on its limits and on various interpretations of possible thresholds of tolerance. All this takes place without, usually, there being a direct confrontation with Muslims; mostly these debates are within the receiving societies, about Muslims and Islam.

We will only deal with these debates *on* Islam—the nature of which is extremely wide even if the causes provoking them and their recurrence in time can be traced back to a limited number of issues— for some of the more general aspects, at the end of this chapter. In the rest of the chapter we intend to examine more closely some concrete examples of social and cultural confrontation (between sub-societies and cultures, therefore or, to put it better, between representatives of them) which have appeared in Europe and have directly involved Muslim social actors (but not necessarily the Muslim communities as a whole, as is too often easily said, even if these debates influence their perception and self-perception), and have caused tension, discussion, manifestations of hostility, forms of refusal or reconsideration. We are talking here of specifically anti-Muslim tension on the part of Europeans, or 'anti' some aspect of their lives in Europe, let us say culturally anti-Western, by Muslims. We are not dealing here with forms of xenophobia or 'ordinary' racism, even if this often also shows a preference for objectives, which in some way can be traced back to ethnic Muslim groups or Muslim symbols or of Muslim origin, which in some way can embody a greater diversity or foreignness.

There have been examples of ordinary racism against Muslims almost everywhere in Europe. Each country has its symbolic places and times in this sense, for example the facts of Mölln (1992) and Solingen (May 1993), in Germany, where the victims were Turks, or the *ratonnades* against the Moroccans in Terrassa (Barcelona) and El Ejido (Malaga), in Spain in 1999. But there have been 'ordinarily' racist beatings up or threats everywhere and the victims have often been, even if not only, of presumed or presumable Muslim origin.

Official social control itself, offered by the police, can be more specific in this direction: for example the controversies in France on the consequences that are not only vaguely xenophobic but sometimes, more specifically anti-Arab, of the Vigipirate operation established following the wave of attacks of Algerian origin in France, but also of repressive operations with respect to immigrant labour, especially illegal, in various countries. This is indeed one of the elements of the 'institutional production' of racism or, as in various cases, of fuelling anti-Arab feelings (but Turks, Asians or Africans can also be concerned), which does not necessarily mean anti-Muslim, even if at times the two aspects overlap. In Muslim communities in Europe, the complaint is frequent that, significantly similar to what happens in the countries of origin, a person who can be 'by appearance' defined as Muslim, and therefore in the collective imagination is also politically an Islamist (beard, djellaba, head covering etc.), is alleged to be stopped more often than other immigrants, even only to check papers.

More often, however, the targets of xenophobia and racism have been and are Muslim by chance and are affected as Arabs, Turks, Indo-Pakistanis, in short, representatives of the local typical image of foreigners. It is also possible that the Muslim characterisation is in some cases only an additional and not the primary objective: another element of otherness and extraneousness in addition to a pre-existing one.

The problem is however the 'extension' and the elasticity of the concepts: consequently the garb of a pious traditionalist Muslim can be taken for a militant Islamist uniform, and the desire to build a mosque, as a place of prayer and assembly for the community, is, so to speak, semantically overcharged with meanings that it does not have, linked with fundamentalism and terrorism, or more often to the generic fear of a cultural invasion and the introduction of foreign and potentially 'enemy' elements. As European Muslims [for example, with some irony, a former German ambassador and convert to Islam; Hofmann, 1996] note even more easily, for certain aspects, in some European countries a mosque is enough to create a suspicion of the presence of forms of Islamic radicalism. With this, a counter-deductive effect is also obtained: the Islamophobia Report quotes the editorial of a Muslim periodical according to which, amongst the 'ironic' effects of this situation is that which, by 'demonising' Muslims, the mass media also set up the romantic notion of Islam as the opposition par excellence to mainstream culture [Runnymede Trust, 1997].

Without going into them in depth here, as it lies outside our objective, we can underline that in the social context there also exist forms and places of inter-Muslim tension, which are not usually seen in the arena of social representation, by the media and others. From the difficulties of life in hostels, amongst North Africans, often greater individualists and other Africans, often also of Muslim origin, more inclined to collective living [Diop & Michalak, 1996], to the clashes between Turks and Kurds in Germany and the disputes with the Alawis in Germany but also in Bulgaria [Ragaru, 2001], to the dialectics, common everywhere, at times in tones that can be harsh, between Sunnites, represented by the leaders of mosques and Sufis, to the political clashes linked to individual issues (Palestine, Algeria, Kurdistan, Kashmir, the Gulf, Iran, etc.).

However, there is the feeling that the debate that emerges from these forms of tension, in the end, is on what integration is and how it can be achieved: whether it is a case of Muslim schools or the *hijab*, of mosques or associations, and in general of everything that raises debate and causes tension around Muslim issues. It can be of use to see some of the main examples of this tension. We will dwell in particular on an example of conflict based on fundamental principles (the Rushdie case), one based on individual human rights and the possibility of expressing them in public, in particular in places under public control (the question of the *hijab* in state schools), and one based on the presence of places and symbols considered extraneous to the territory (mosques and cemeteries). We will also mention some other examples of cultural and religious confrontation/conflict. Lastly, we will mention a theoretical debate which has immediate concrete implications, which not only concerns Islam, nor was this its origin but of which European Islam represents one, the most important exemplification, namely the issue of multiculturalism. We will then conclude with some reflections on a concrete example of a cultural relationship considered difficult and problematic if not impossible: the relationship with Muslim fundamentalism.

2. The Rushdie Affair: The Clash on Ideas

September 26th, 1988: the publishers Viking/Penguin published the book *The Satanic Verses* by the Anglo-Indian writer Salman Rushdie. October 1988: the start of the campaign against the book, first against the publishers and then all embracing [Lewis P., 1997 and 1997a]. This is what we can consider the first and to date still open case of a cultural clash on the foundations of civil coexistence brought about by Islam in Europe.

The campaign on the book and the movements it produced can be placed on a worldwide scale. And for the first time the whole of western Europe was involved in a conflict which has as its object a set of common values threatened, in the common perception, by Islam, and not 'from outside', but from within Europe. The campaign against the book and its author began in India, the country which was the first to ban the book, as early as October 5th, as its author is of Indian origin; Bangladesh, Sudan and South Africa (the first non-Muslim country to place an official ban on it, in reply to the protests of its Muslim minority) followed, and then many others, as well as the position of the Organisation of the Islamic Conference, of Al-Azhar, and of many other Muslim bodies, the official protests of ambassadors of Muslim countries to the British government and so on.

The demonstrations against a work accused of offending Islam were to provoke the first ten deaths in Pakistan, killed by the police in front of the American embassy in Islamabad (which had little to do with the situation). Another twenty deaths soon followed in various demonstrations in India. But the question was to take on a global dimension. In Great Britain, some Muslim leaders immediately supported the campaign with great determination, as this is where the largest Indo-Pakistani community in Europe is to be found, as well as being the country that published the book in its original edition, with copies of Rushdie's book being burnt in Bradford during a demonstration on 14th January 1989, which was to resurrect the worst phantoms associated with the repression of free cultural activity. The question gradually spread to the rest of the world, especially following the *fatwa* delivered by the Ayatollah Khomeini on 14th February, who accused Rushdie of apostasy and for this reason asked that he be put to death. It was in the wake of this initiative that the question was transformed into a global clash between Islam and the West. From this moment the shockwaves re-echoed throughout Europe and the West, with countries being dragged into the arena in defence of a fundamental and inalienable principle of freedom, threatened very concretely on the announcement of each translation of the book (the Japanese translator was killed, the Italian one seriously wounded, others threatened), and was to provoke unprecedented diplomatic consequences with respect to the original motivation, as well as changing the personal destiny of the book's author who for years was forced to live under police protection.

In Great Britain the case took on peculiar characteristics, as the mobilisation of the Muslim communities, not shared by all, was real, starting with the book burning episode in Bradford by demonstrators, the majority of whom were Asians. The reaction of Arab countries and their citizens was to be more subdued and diplomatic. Even the Organisation of the Islamic Conference, unable not to declare itself but limited to a verbal reprimand, was to have only mild effects, which surprised British Muslims themselves, engaged in the frontline of the clash [Ahsan, 1994].

One of its secondary effects was precisely the incentive towards a greater unity of action, through the creation of the UKACIA (UK Action Committee on Islamic Affairs), a co-ordinating organisation set up in October 1988 and which was to survive for a long time, with a significant activist commitment by second-generation Muslims [according to the internal point of view of Ahsan & Kidwai, 1991]. The tension was therefore to emerge at a moment of self-organisation and awareness but also when contact was made at an administrative level and of connection with the institutions, as is often the case.

The aspect which we are interested in emphasising here is that this was the first and very bitter clash with Islam—and a clash within Europe's frontiers—in recent times, on symbols and fundamentals of Western liberties (the book, freedom of opinion, the limit of religious interference etc.). An in-depth study of the outcome and not a mere factual reconstruction of the case, despite the thousands of pages and statements by both sides, has yet to be written. A partial but little known precedent can be found, which took place not in Europe but where the British were involved and without lasting consequences (as is inevitably the case of a fact that is not present in the historical collective memory). In 1924 in Lahore, a Hindu published a book that was deemed to insult the Prophet and he was killed by two Muslims who in turn were put to death by the British and considered martyrs of Islam at the time [Lewis P., 1997b].

In the theory of social action, mobilisation, at a symbolic level or not, also has the function of allowing social actors to measure the limits they can reach: the extent to which they can make particularistic claims, in this case for religious motives. It has certainly also had this function on this occasion.

Moreover, the Muslim communities were divided internally: if not on the principle, i.e. on the fact that Rushdie's book was offensive and blasphemous, difficult to deny from the Muslim point of view (even if few admitted having read it), certainly on the actions to take, and if it was necessary to take any. If explicit disagreement with the positions of condemnation were rare and above all limited to the intellectual classes who intended to distance themselves from the religious leadership, the silence and non-participation in the mobilisation by the majority of Muslims in Europe is already an interesting indicator.

A good number of Muslims maintained, besides, especially on the continent, that a bad book has to be answered by a good book, not by the suppression of the book and its author. However, it is certain that the Rushdie affair marked a phase of reflection and further meditation, for the Muslim communities, public opinion and the European political authorities, unwilling to let themselves be dragged on to this battleground, deemed, due to the values it contained, impossible to give up and unquestionable. If they attack you with the sword, you reply with the sword, if they attack you with a book, you reply with a book, recalled some of the interviewees in the middle of the controversy. And others emphasised how it was a scandal produced by the Muslims themselves [Diop & Kastoryano, 1991].

It has occasionally been underlined that, after all, the demonstrations at Hyde Park in London did not involve the majority of the local Muslim communities and that the politicisation in Bradford was rather the offspring of the conflict of many years for internal reasons of a different kind, like the Honeyford affair [from the name of the headmaster of a Bradford school who rose to national prominence for his articles which were strongly against the anti-racist and multicultural policies, and who exasperated feelings; Samad, 1992]. But the search for these other reasons did not impair the fact that, for the first time, as already stated, an explicit cultural problem had been brought up—and that it is still open. In 1993, in Poland, when the book was published, as it had not previously been published in that country due to a decision 'from above', a Muslim association started legal proceedings against its Warsaw publishers [PL File].

Anybody who listens to the Muslim and especially British leaders, moreover, can still perceive their sense, that they continue to convey with conviction, that they have suffered a serious injustice and insults [several of our interviews in the UK, May 2000]. It is no coincidence that the request to broaden the present anti-blasphemy law to 'protect' Islam as well, and which has hardly been applied since 1922 for the Christians of the church of England, still remains on the agenda of their demands. The anti-libel laws are moreover a double-edged sword: they can be invoked in defence of the community but also used to control the diffusion of blasphemy and apostasy within a religious community, as has been underlined by a theoretician openly favourable to the rights of communities [Kymlicka, 1995].

On the other hand, Salman Rushdie is still under the protection of the security services: the Iranian *fatwa* is still formally in force, confirmed by the successor of Khomeini, Ali Khamenei, and supported by a reward freely offered by a private individual, an aspect which certainly does not help the acceptability and the comprehension of the decision by the West.

The question then brought back into the limelight the question of respective limits between state and religious communities, a problem that not only concerns the Muslim communities. Not fortuitously there have also been, in various countries, examples of lukewarm and at times explicit support for the Muslim claims, in particular from Catholics [the film directed by Martin Scorsese *The last temp-tation of Christ*, deemed blasphemous by some, was released almost at the same time; de Galembert, 1997], but also from the Jewish and other communities [Runnymede Trust, 1997], against the insults to religious sensitivity, which led to mild solidarity against rampant blasphemy, in a sort of religious reaction to the secular attack, per-ceived as a common enemy.

3. The Question of the *Hijab*: a Public Manifestation of Individual Rights

We will now go from an essentially British question to an essentially French one in its formulation. However, both have taken on more universal connotations: the former especially in terms of principle and of reminding the natives of the foundations of their society, the latter also through concrete controversies but which were solved differently, and which have led to much less unequivocal conclusions regarding its significance.

Everyone who has had the opportunity to hold courses, seminars or lectures on Islam knows to what extent the question of the *hijab* is a sensitive and popular issue: almost a touchstone for reflection on the presence of Islam in the public space.

This is a surprising fact, if examined in terms of principle, as the principle of liberty in the way of dressing should not even be raised in the West, except possibly in the limit of the respect of the com-mon sense of decency and its juridical equivalents. In a certain sense, the question of the *hijab* is a non-issue: the analysis of the debate produced around the *hijab* shows that it was not a problem in itself but it has become a problem only if and to the extent to which some social and institutional situations, and some countries, have made it one.

The debate, as is well known, came from the decision not to let three pupils wearing the *hijab* into a *lycée* in Creil, following the intro-duction of a new school rule, in autumn 1989, at the beginning of the new school year. This was also the year when France celebrated the bicentenary of the French Revolution and of its principles, which was probably not extraneous to the sensitivity shown. This led to a major debate all over France and elsewhere and which had two main phases. The first in 1989 and 1990, when the events of Creil took place and then again in 1994–1995, when following this long discussion, the Bayrou circular of September 1994 condemned 'ostentatious signs' of religious affiliation, but accepted 'discreet' signs instead. In between, a long process of official and unofficial positions, up to the highest authorities of the state, administrative decisions at all levels, up to the Council of State, consultations, debates in the media, political controversy and electoral interests can be recorded.

The discussion also had aspects of an ideological battle, making some observers speak of secular fundamentalism [some examples from the many possible ones, representative of the strong secularistic positions, although they were written 'in cold blood' when the controversy had already boiled over, in Gokalp, 1997 and Weber, 1997]. Most of the magistrates involved ruled that the girls and their reasons were in the right. In some situations, contorted and at times surprising compromises were sought, requested by some headmasters as gestures of goodwill, such as the suggestion to tie the *hijab* at the back instead of the front, seriously made by a headmaster in Colmar, whilst elsewhere the *hijab* was forbidden during lessons but allowed on the school premises [Straßburger, 2000]. In the middle was the role of the often secularised cultural mediators, by-passed in both directions and the unexpressed but palpable fear that the rulings of the magistrates, almost always favourable to the Muslim side in deference to the fundamental principles of European societies, and of French society in particular, would end up by favouring radical Islamist opinion.

Moreover, it is interesting to note that whilst French *laïcité* declared war on the *hijab*, French Catholics accepted some of the girls who had been excluded from state education into their schools, so that, with an interesting reversal of positions, religious figures of different faiths accused *laïcité* in its French model of sectarianism. As the highest authorities of the French Catholic church emphasised, if the problem had really been linked with Islamism, it should have been confronted by the Ministry of Internal Affairs only [Cardinal Lustiger, quoted in de Galembert, 1997] and certainly not by that of Education. And if the question was of a different kind, it should not even have been confronted.

It is interesting to note the influence of the case, which also made itself felt in Canada or, rather, in Quebec, the Francophone state that was also the only one in Canada where, at the same time as the second French affair, there was a controversy concerning the *hijab*. Here, ironically, the expulsion of some Muslim girls from a school because the *hijab* violated the school dress code and could 'incite violence', had produced as a deliberately provocative response, a few days later, its compulsory introduction for non-Muslim teachers in the Muslim school of Montreal, publicly funded like the others. A positive solution was reached for the case, devoid of ambiguity, and much more rapidly than by their French cousins, showing blatantly how crucial not the fact but the interpretations given to it and the context are, in terms of civic culture and plurality [Wayland, 1997].

Moreover, the weight of this aspect is even more visible by comparing not only the attitude of France and Quebec, like the Dutch and German attitudes, which will be discussed below, but that of Quebec with the rest of Canada. As the rest of Canada is English-speaking and more influenced by the Anglo-Saxon multicultural debate than subject to French cultural influences, not only has the problem of the *hijab* never been raised here, but after a strenuous legal debate Sikhs were even allowed to carry in schools the *kirpan*, a sort of short sword or small dagger which is one of the five obligations of testimony, the 'five kakkas', that a *khalsa* or 'baptised' Sikh must respect (the best known of which is the prohibition of cutting the hair and the beard).

As we have mentioned the Sikhs, we can recall that the same comparison can be made in Europe, on both sides of the English Channel: in Great Britain the Sikhs cannot only wear their turbans, which are considerably more 'ostentatious' than a *hijab*, but even ride a motorbike without a helmet, making an exception to national laws, for the same reason.

However, the question of the *hijab* has also been raised elsewhere. As early as 1985, in the Netherlands, in Alphen aan den Rijn, the *hijab* was banned in local schools. An expert from the University of Leiden, consulted on the matter, endorsed this conduct by maintaining that the *hijab* was not essential to the observance of Islam, causing the protests of Muslims, and moreover giving visibility to the ethically important problem of the limits of the role of advisor and expert, especially if from the outside. In this case, however, it was the Christian-Democrat Minister for Education [following a question in Parliament by a Socialist MP, a Catholic priest; Jansen J.G., 1992], who maintained that forbidding the *hijab* was not compatible with modern society and that the ban should be lifted, following protests by the Muslims [Rath, Penninx, Groenendijk & Meyer, 1999]. Only in one case in the Netherlands did the appeal of a school win, limited to the gymnastics classes, maintaining that looser clothing other than that contemplated could be dangerous in some physical education activities [Lange, 2000].

In Belgium, at the same time as the events of Creil, in a middle school in Molenbeek-Saint-Jean, about twenty girls demonstrated to obtain permission to wear the headscarf at school. Temporary solutions began to be found, such as that of authorising the headscarf only in the presence of male teachers, whilst the debate extended, as a precautionary measure, to other municipalities, until the reviewing court found a compromise solution. It is interesting to note that in the question, connected to the previous one both factually and by a debate triggered off in the press, of the exemption from lessons of physical education, the real cases were very few, and not such as to justify social alarm as was the case. In a study carried out between the end of 1989 and the beginning of 1990, out of 91,583 pupils enrolled in Belgian secondary schools, 3,740 were exempted from physical education lessons (3.74%), consisting of 104 girls and 40 boys with Moroccan nationality, and 39 girls and 9 boys with Turkish nationality, against 2,929 exemptions requested by Belgian pupils [quoted in Panafit, 1999]. In Belgium too, as in France and elsewhere, it was not the legal conflict that was at the basis of the political-cultural debate but the opposite: the 'problematic' perception of Islam was already in circulation, and the Islamic headscarf became its symbol, almost the objectification of what was considered the difficulty of integrating Muslims and the problems, including political ones, raised by Islam [Panafit, 1999].

Germany also experienced strong controversy on the subject but to the contrary, as it were: when in July 1998 the Ministry for Education of Baden-Würtemberg did not grant a German teacher of Afghan origin, supported by the teachers' union, the right to teach wearing the headscarf. However, the regional government refused to forbid the headscarf in schools in a generalised way, including amongst pupils, as the political right wing and not only the extreme right, was asking. The *Zentralrat der Muslime in Deutschland* protested, more than against the decision, against the fact that it had been motivated by an 'Islamic' interpretation according to which the obligation is not really imposed by the Qur'an. Support for the Muslim positions came from neighbouring Bavaria, from some Christian-Socialists [Gabert, 1999], after a ruling of the federal constitutional court in 1995 declared the legal obligation of putting crucifixes in classrooms anti-constitutional; this ruling had caused very strong reactions in Bavarian public opinion [de Galembert, 2000].

A similar case took place in Geneva in Switzerland, regarding a teacher who had converted to Islam, with a ruling in 1996, confirmed in an appeal the following year, and who had been forbidden from teaching with the *hijab* [Haenni, 1994]. And here too some Catholic representatives showed solidarity with the teacher in question. Today all the cantons accept girls wearing the *hijab* at school [Mahnig, 2000b].

Outside the world of the school the question was again raised in Switzerland in Bienne, where there was a show of strength between about twenty Muslim women and the head of police who refused to renew the residence permits of women presenting photos in which they were wearing the *hijab* [Haenni, 1994]. More recently, in 1999, three students of medicine at the University of Geneva were prohibited from wearing the *hijab*. The students took the case to court but the final decision has not yet been delivered [Mahnig, 2002].

There was a similar case to that mentioned by Haenni in Italy, in Turin, in 1999, when there was a protest demonstration by Muslims on the Police Headquarters, with extensive media coverage. It was perhaps the first case of organised Muslim protest that had such coverage, even if its real motivations involved a certain dialectic of internal power within the Muslim community. In Italy, however, as far as schools are concerned, repeated statements by the Minister for Education in 2000 showed the perception of the question as a non-issue: no significant controversy or protests were recorded on the statements made, which opened schools to the *hijab*.

These events too, like others, shown that the 'cultural' conflict serves to favour the surfacing of latent tensions, to discuss them and bring out interlocutors and leaders and also solve problems. The dimension of the conflict is thus revealed as a dimension which cannot be expunged and indeed is physiological. It is also due to the media coverage of the conflict itself, which encourages ambitions of leadership and desires for visibility. But it also serves as a way of repositioning and discussing in public problems that do not emerge elsewhere, to measure the forces at play, on both sides, to experiment with communication strategies and, to test the limits, including the limits of the flexibility of the laws and rules of the public space.

It is to be noted that the *hijab* in some evident cases can, thanks to 'tranquil' media coverage, become an element of normalisation and we could even say of pacification with Islam. We feel that this is the case of Nabila Benaïssa, the sister of Loubna, a little girl murdered by a paedophile in Belgium. The popular mobilisation around the case and the protests against the shortcomings and the covering-up in the conduct of the investigations, were enormous, leading to the immense 'Marche Blanche' in Brussels in 1997. The figure of the young Nabila, who displayed her Muslim identity with simplicity and discretion (she always appeared wearing the *hijab*), and showing her perfect social integration (perfect French speaking and her calm reasoning) made a strong contribution towards creating a less offensive and threatening, 'polite' so to speak, perception of Islam [Ouali, 2000]. The drama contributed to triggering off a process which on that occasion we called "assimilation through grief".

As a conclusion to this section we can recall that the question of the *hijab* is only one example—the main and symbolically significant but not only example—concerning the discussion and media coverage of the female condition in Islam and its consequences in Europe. We can at least mention the other issues on which there has been discussion in various countries and on which there is repeated discussion when specific cases explode: Muslim marriage, polygamy, mixed marriages, forced marriages, excision and clitoridectomy (and the submission of minors to practices of genital mutilation), repudiation, how children are brought up and their custody in the case of separation. All these issues show the extent to which the female question, and that of the related family models, have an absolutely central place in the perception of Islam also in Europe, and is symbolically sensitive, in its contents and how they are discussed.

4. Mosques and Cemeteries: Symbolic Places

From a controversy discussed in the public space, as was the previous one, we will now move on to a controversy about public space. This point seems even more crucial to us, implying the perception of control over territory and its symbolic imprinting. An aspect which, even with all due caution, could be studied not only with the tools

of the sociology of culture, but also with categories proper to ethnology and sociobiology. After all, control of and over the territory is
not only a cultural and symbolic fact; it is also (and remains, in spite
of everything) a very concrete and material sign of dominion and
power.

We are thinking in particular of the construction of mosques, but
also of the visibility of prayer halls, in European cities: questions to
which we can relate that of the possibility of diffusing the *adhan*, the
call to prayer, outside the mosques, and cemeteries or granting specific
areas in cemeteries. The question is important for various reasons.
On the one hand, the presence of foreign communities would seem
to presuppose as a very obvious consequence that they also wish to
have their own meeting places according to their religions of affiliation,
as the 'domestic' or national minorities have. On the other hand,
conflicts have arisen around this question that are surprising sign of
a malaise and of a deeper rejection of its occasional target. These
conflicts indicate that it is not the fact in itself that is in question
(almost none of those opposing the question would say that they
want to prevent anyone from praying, the reason given is always
another), but something deeper, linked to the symbolic appropriation of the territory, which has to do with history and its reconstruction but also with deep social dynamics.

Mosques are not only religious centres, but also community centres on the local level, with interferences of ethnic, national (linked
to the countries of origin) and transnational networks [on the functions of the mosques, Waardenburg, 1988; on social practices in
Europe, Dassetto, 1996]. They therefore have, as well as a concrete
function, a representative and highly symbolic function for Islam.
They are the strong sign of its presence. It is no coincidence that
there is so much interest in and so much insistence on establishing
important Islamic centres in the various European capitals, or the
extensive coverage in Muslim countries of an event such as the inauguration of the Islamic *Centro Islamico di Roma* in 1995, perceived as
the sign of the Muslim presence in what is often considered the 'capital' of Christianity or at least of its strongest and most authoritative articulation, Catholicism. And, to mention a sign of a different
nature, the first issue of the Francophone Muslim journal *La médina*
(therefore the city in its Islamic perception, but in this case the
European *medina*), promoted by and for European Muslims, opened
with an extensive dossier on "La Mosquée dans la Cité".

We can point out in this regard that the mosques, or at least the major Islamic centres of the capital cities, have always also been used as an element of 'political symbolics' and have been the instrument of a foreign policy which also involved the respective churches dominant in the various countries. If the creation of the Muslim cemetery in Berlin is due to internal reasons, and in particular to the presence of Muslim soldiers in the Prussian cavalry, the patronage of its mosque (1866) was to be assumed directly by the Sultan, in parallel with the commercial relations between the Ottoman Empire and the Hanseatic cities [Nielsen, 1992]. In France, the country with the largest Muslim presence in Europe, the first mosque, that of Paris, inaugurated in 1926, was a sort of gift, thanks and reward for the Muslims who died in the French army during the First World War [Kepel, 1987]. It can also be remembered that the appointment of the rectors of the mosque has always been the object of diplomatic consultation and strategies, in particular with Algeria, where the secular power willingly interfered with questions which moreover were not purely religious. The piece of land on which the mosque stands in Regent's Park in London, lastly, was donated by the British government in 1944, in exchange for a similar donation made by the Egyptian government to the Anglican community in Cairo [Runnymede Trust, 1997].

The phenomenon of the diplomatic management of Islam also became more evident with the oil shock in 1973. From this date many European countries began to play the card of the mosque in their capital in order to flatter and ingratiate themselves with the Saudi Islamic oil power, with the illusion of yielding only a little religious symbolism in exchange for what was considered a more precious guarantee of energy. It was thus that Belgium hastily recognised Islam as one of the state religions in 1974 [Dassetto & Bastenier, 1984; Dassetto, 1987] (so hastily that the agreement signed is still unapplied in substance [Panafit, 1999]), whilst the lease for 99 years of the symbolic oriental pavilion in the *Parc du Cinquantenaire* in Brussels dates back to 1969. And the local authorities in Rome too, on solicitation of the Italian government, in 1974, after having discreetly consulted the Vatican authorities and received their consent, gave an area of thirty thousand square metres to build what had the ambition of being the largest Islamic centre in Europe. At the same time the government recognised the *Centro Islamico Culturale d'Italia* and its board of directors, the members of which are the ambassadors of the Muslim countries under the aegis of the Saudis, as a 'moral body', the first and for the time being the only acknowledged Muslim religious subject having obtained this recognition [Allievi & Dassetto, 1993; Allievi, 2001]. More generally, the *Rabitat al-ʿAlam al-Islami*, the Muslim World League (Saudi-based) has become an interlocutor for many European governments, and a sort of religious partner, although not being able to count, unlike other Muslim countries, on its own emigration to Europe.

Mosques, as mentioned, are also at the origin of cultural confrontations and conflicts of a certain importance, and are not to be underestimated, either as individual concrete cases or as signs of a wider problem. The construction of a mosque or the adaptation of a prayer hall is hardly ever only an architectural and town-planning problem; it produces in-depth social and cultural discussions and reactions. The conflicts also appear semantically over-determined, if we think of the numerical dimension of which we are talking.

In **France** for example, the country with the largest Muslim presence in Europe, there are only eight purpose-built mosques, out of over an estimated thousand places of Muslim worship, almost as if Islam had to make itself invisible or as little visible as possible, to be accepted in the French public space. However, there does not exist a national framework or policy: in this country, the ideology of reference of which is deeply secular and republican, and where almost half the population (46%) according to the IFOP opinion poll of 1994 opposed the fact that minarets could be higher than the church bell towers [*Le Monde*, 1994], almost all the possible options on the subject have been experimented with.

A distinct institutional stamp marked, for example, the genesis of the project of the *Mosquée de Lyon*, inaugurated in 1994 in the presence of the Minister for Internal Affairs and of Worship, Charles Pasqua, the mayor, ambassadors of Muslim countries and representatives of other religious faiths [Battegay, 1995]. It is no coincidence that all the players involved intervened, as the idea of the mosque had been suggested at the end of the 1970s to the mayor by the then cardinal and was debated on national TV; presidents took up positions and there was also opposition by the residents of the neighbourhood and by the political forces. On the other hand, not very far away, there were examples of mosques destroyed by bulldozers on the order of the mayor, as at Charvieu, about thirty kilometres from Lyon [Cesari, 1997].

Although there are many existing places of prayer, there is still no 'real' mosque in Marseilles, the historic place of French Islam, although one has been promised since the 1920s, as a gesture of gratitude for the Muslim soldiers who died in the First World War [Galizera, 2000], and although the question of the mosque has been used since the period between the wars as an element of electoral seduction for the Muslim population [Renard, 1999]. On the other hand, there have also been situations such as Evry, where the mosque was built in the 1980s with public funding, in a highly visible place. But in parallel, almost to compensate for this decision, the Catholics were encouraged to build a cathedral in the centre, with large amounts of public funding [de Galembert, 1997]. There was also municipal support for the project of a mosque in Strasbourg where, however, the regime of relations between the political and religious authorities differs from that applied in the rest of France [Frégosi, 1997]. Then there are intermediate situations, as in Montpellier, where the local administration financed a building which remains its property, but which was given to a Muslim association for use as a mosque [Renard, 1999]. And even where there has been opposition, as at Montreuil-sous-Bois, where the mayor maintained that he would never have opened to the fundamentalists, the situation was taken in hand by a group of French Muslims in defence of their rights as citizens and now the mosque is there [Imarraïne, 1999].

The contradiction between various local situations can also be seen in other situations. In **Great Britain**, apparently the visibility of the mosques, especially in the 'ethnic' neighbourhoods, is not a fact that is challenged, and there are mosques in strategic places and perhaps even with purposes of ostentation. For example, the new very visible mosques in Bradford or Birmingham are built deliberately to be seen, even by non-Muslims. It is not infrequent in Britain to find places of worship (for example, Anglican churches) transformed generally into places of worship of other religions, although seldom into mosques, a sign of a relatively less apparent although rather significant sensitivity to symbolic questions. But here too there have been forms of opposition on the territory, as for example in Chichester in 1996, where there was a popular mobilisation based on traditional more than Christian values, as the bishops of Chichester and Portsmouth had expressed their favourable opinion on the mosque and had dissociated themselves from the positions expressed in the name of Christianity by a part of their base [Runnymede Trust, 1997].

Elsewhere the justification of architectural preservation may be used, as in the case of the Brick Lane Mosque, an old Huguenot chapel and then a synagogue, in a historic building in London [Eade, 1996]. In other cases the problems were of parking, traffic and access at the busy times on Fridays. And lastly there have occasionally been, as in other European countries, initiatives and leafleting by extreme right-wing parties against the announcement of the building of a mosque. However, the United Kingdom seems an extremely open country from this point of view.

The differences in the perception of the 'gravity' of the presence of a mosque in the urban space are appreciable in a comparison between France and Germany, where the lesser degree of disputes produced in the latter case is evident [de Galembert, 1994]. However, in **Germany** too, the mosques have to make do with a secondary status compared to that of churches, or have recourse to forms of 'religious camouflage'. In Munich, for example, the mosque was built on the model of a Catholic place of worship in order not to make its 'Islam-ness' too visible. In Pforzheim (and the case is frequent in Europe, a sign that we are not wrong in pointing out the power at stake, in the 'ethological' sense mentioned, but also with 'infantile' aspects of spite), the minaret had to be lower than the bell tower of the nearby church [de Galembert, 1998]. In Berlin alone, however, there are today about seventy mosques, with various linguistic origins: in 58 mosques the language spoken is Turkish, in 2 Kurdish, in 6 Arabic, 2 are Pakistani, 1 Bosnian and 1 Albanian, whilst in 3 the dominant language is German. In the city, 4 of the mosques are recognisable as such. At a national level, there are about 2200 associations of mosques. Of these, according to the respective internal sources, about 740 are linked with the DITIB, the Turkish government religious body, with 'imported' imams, whilst another thousand have their origin in other movements in Turkish circles: almost 300 are linked with the Suleimanci, about 275 with the *Islamische Gemeinschaft Milli Görüs* (IGMG—the Turkish Islamic movement linked to the former *Refah Partisi*), about 180 come under the organisation of the Grey Wolves, about a hundred are Alawis and so on. To these must be added the independent mosques. For Germany, as for Great Britain, we can talk of a substantial openness of the public space to the Muslim presence: there are 66 mosques that have a minaret and other explicit features (purpose-built) and about thirty are currently being built [Goldberg, 2000]. However, there have also been some local initiatives in Germany against the building of mosques or linked to the height of the minarets or to the possibility of broadcasting the *adhan*.

The **Netherlands** is another country where there has been relative freedom of worship, with cases of public support being offered even by other religious communities, Catholics and Protestants, for a mosque to be built or for the right to have one [Landman, 1992]. As public space is by definition open, it becomes interesting to note the possible examples of conflict between minorities with different objectives. An interesting example is offered by an episode which took place in Zwolle in 1986: a mosque attended by Surinamese Muslims was housed in a building (a public school property that was no longer used) where the local council had also offered space to a homosexual association for their centre. The Muslims asked for the expulsion of the latter, opening a debate in the public opinion on the possible forms of discrimination between minorities. For practical reasons the affair was to come to a conclusion with the two groups being given two different premises [Jansen J.G., 1992].

Conflicts on the establishment of mosques have also taken place elsewhere. In **Switzerland**, the inhabitants of a Basel neighbourhood initially protested against a multinational Islamic centre promoted by the Turkish community in Friedensgasse, although a more modest project was then accepted. Another project financed by Saudi Arabia failed in Bern, following the politicisation of the question by a xenophobic party [Mahnig, 2000a].

In **Austria**, a country where the Muslim minority is 'historical', even if it has increased substantially following the more recent waves of immigration, the question opened in 1997, due also to mobilisation of the 'liberal' party, the representatives of which stated that there were already too many mosques in the country and that most of them were in the hands of Muslim fanatics. Discussion has also begun on whether they ought to be funded with the contribution of 'Austrian' taxes. In cities such as Graz and Salzburg, the Muslim request to build real mosques, with a dome and a minaret, has been rejected by the local populations and politicians, with severe interventions in the local media as well [AT File].

In **Sweden**, there are five purpose-built mosques today: three Sunnite, one Shiite and one Ahmadi. The Islamic centre of Malmö was inaugurated in 1984, and the *khutba* is in three languages: Bosnian, Arabic and Swedish [Stenberg, 2000]. However, there have been conflicts in this country too [Sander, 1991]. In 1993 the assault on the Shiite mosque of Trollhättan in Sweden was provoked or at least stirred up by members of the radical movement *Ny Demokrati*, which sprang up in Sweden in 1991. Significantly however, this event led to greater sympathy by public opinion for the Muslims, under attack in Bosnia: when it was re-opened in August 1994, speeches were also made by Jewish and Christian representatives, as well as by the civic authorities [Alwell, 1998].

At times a subterranean impediment can appear indirectly in 'raising the price', even in a literal sense, of consent. In Västerås, the premises—originally a Pentecostal church which had then been transformed into a theatre (the first case in Sweden of a church transformed into a mosque)—was offered by the local authorities, practically without any political opposition: but the equivalent of about $200,000 was paid in 1994, whilst according to some estimates a realistic price for the rather rundown premises would have been nearer half that figure [Alwell, 1998]. The case of Malmö is also interesting. Conceived as the project of the largest Islamic centre in Europe in the 1970s, it was reduced to more modest proportions after having asked initially for funding both from Saudi Arabia's *Rabitat al-ʿAlam al-Islami* and from the Libyan *Al-Daʾwa al-Islamiyya*, without having reciprocally informed the two—rival—organisations, so that part of the funding and support was withdrawn [Alwell, 1998].

Some European countries with a more recent Muslim and numerically more limited presence, like those in southern Europe, seemed to have fewer problems, and in any case, less public debate, on this and on other topics concerning the Muslim presence becoming more visible. However, if this was true at the beginning of the Muslim presence, it is perhaps no longer thus today.

In **Italy**, despite some controversy over the height of the minaret, lowered several times compared to the original project, and some fears over the size of the dome, which some feared would be larger than that of St. Peter's, which is simply nonsense, the Islamic *Centro Islamico di Roma* was built with the approval of the government, the donation of a vast piece of land by the city council, the blessing of the Vatican and the basic indifference, or at least the non-opposition, of public opinion [Allievi & Dassetto, 1993]. At the inauguration in 1995, the President of the Republic and other civil and religious authorities were present. The only, and numerically insignificant, protest was that of the then Speaker of the Chamber of Deputies, Irene Pivetti, a traditionalist Catholic and representative of the Northern League, who took part in a "rosary of atonement" together with some representatives of Rome's 'black nobility' for the "offence" to the Eternal City [Allievi, 2000b].

There are not many other examples, as there are only three architecturally recognisable mosques for the time being (in order of building, Catania, Milan and Rome) [Allievi & Dassetto, 1993], and they did not have to suffer significant opposition locally. However, we have entered a phase of a different perception of the Muslim presence and the situation is no longer thus. In a couple of cases (Varese and Alessandria), in cities with a Northern League council, the only Italian party that displays explicit and strong xenophobic and anti-Muslim positions, there have been forms of political instrumentalisation constructed around prayer halls and their organisation. There has also been evidence of this campaign in smaller towns, as in the Veneto region, in the case of the mosque of Col San Martino, which comes under the municipality of Farra di Soligo, in the province of Treviso, where the League and the independentist movements are strong and have deep roots. The mayor of Farra, at the head of a civic list—supported, according to the Muslim leaders, by the parish priest—in the name of the Catholic identity of the village, decided to close the local mosque in January 1999 in the middle of Ramadan. The municipal ruling, as in the past in the larger towns of Alessandria and Varese, under the League, referred to the violation of town-planning and security or hygiene rules. But as was the case in many other European countries, the real motivation was another. Amongst the Muslim players to intervene was the UCOII, the main Muslim federation in Italy and the embassy of Morocco, representing the main Muslim presence in the country. A compromise, under the auspices of the Catholic association of aid for immigrants, Migrantes, was to lead to a temporary suspension of the ruling [Guolo, 1999].

A more sensational case took place in September 2000, when in Lodi, near Milan, the Popular Party mayor's decision to give a piece of city land, with a symbolic rent, so that a mosque could be built, caused the fiercest and most controversial anti-Muslim campaign, again led by the League, that had ever been seen in Italy until then [Allievi, 2000b], with extremely serious episodes: demonstrations with offensive slogans and the invitation to sprinkle the piece of land in question with the "urine of 'Padanian' pigs", the celebration of a mass of 'atonement', the launch of an all-round anti-Muslim campaign with demonstrations in other towns as well, and which in another town with a League council (Rovato in the province of Brescia) went so far as to make the mayor issue an obviously illegal ruling which warned non-Christians not to approach the walls of the local churches within 15 metres, in response to the impossibility of non-Muslims to enter mosques in some Muslim countries. This controversy had a wider echo than it would have had if it had only been an extreme position of the Northern League because at the same period, on the secular and Catholic sides there arose authoritative voices against the 'Muslim cultural invasion' (see below). League activists also had printed and put up at the entrance to some towns adhesives with the words 'de-Islamised municipality', imitating the official sign present in some places, following the environmentalist and anti-nuclear positions of past years, which says 'denuclearised municipality' [Guolo, 2000].

There have not been any significant problems in **Spain**, the country with the longest and most important Muslim history in Europe and with rich vestiges of its past especially in Andalucia. The first 'Spanish' mosques were in fact those established by the administration of the Spanish protectorate in the enclaves in Moroccan territory of Ceuta and Melilla. Amongst the recent ones, the first mosque on the mainland was that of Marbella (Malaga), built in 1981 in the Costa del Sol town in the city centre and between the most exclusive hotels of the resort. The Abu Bakr Mosque in Madrid, the seat of the Muslim Association of Spain and of the UCIDE, one of the two main Spanish Muslim federations was also founded in the 1980s, financed by the Saudis and inaugurated in the presence of the monarchs of both countries. There are also mosques in Valencia and Cordoba (Ahmadis), and other projects are under examination in Barcelona, Oviedo, Malaga and La Palma, in the Canary Islands. The only real case of conflict arose around the plan for the Mosque of Albaicín, an old neighbourhood in Granada [ES File], but this was more due to suspicions on its promoters, belonging to the controversial movement of converts, Murabitun, and in part due to the historical nature of the place, which almost seemed to evoke a *reconquista* to the contrary, than due to real conflicts with the population and public opinion.

In **Portugal**, despite the small dimensions of the Muslim community, there are four mosques with minarets (Lisbon, Laranjeiro, Odivelas and Coimbra), and fourteen prayer halls, but no type of conflict has been reported in this regard: for example, to give an idea of the attitude, before there were any mosques, in 1979, the government offered a part of the Royal Palace for temporary use as a mosque. On just one occasion, some young people violently protested against the mosque in Odivelas, in 1983. The invitation by the Muslims to go into the mosque for a discussion, however, solved the problem without any further incidents [PT File]. One figure alone provides a good indicator of the satisfactory level of integration of the Muslim community, which moreover is of recent settlement, and although comparisons are not always significant, nor is it possible to absolutise this specific indicator, the comparison between the 30–38,000 Muslims and four mosques in Portugal immediately comes to our attention, the sign of acceptance devoid of substantial obstacles, even on the level of religious visibility, against the 4–5 million people of Muslim origin and only eight real mosques in France.

The building of mosques is however, an acquired fact, including as part of the architectural heritage and common historical memory in countries where Muslims are a national minority and the presence of Islam is not due to recent immigration, but to several centuries of settlement, as in **Eastern Europe and Greece**, in western Thrace, where there are almost 300 mosques, with over 400 preachers and imams [Akgönül, 1999]. However, some problems are present here as well. In 1996, in Kimmeria near Xanthi, in an area with a large Muslim population, the Greek Metropolitan Damaskinos organised a demonstration and succeeded in having the permission to repair a mosque withdrawn, because the minaret, 18 metres high, would have been higher than the neighbouring church bell tower. As the work had already begun, 17 labourers were arrested and sentenced for illegal work. In January 1997 the same metropolitan produced a similar uprising in the town of Pelekiti [Dalègre, 2001].

More recently, on 21 June 2000, the Greek Socialist government approved the construction of the first major Islamic centre and mosque in Athens since the nineteenth century, when the Ottomans ruled the territory that includes present-day Greece. The project, in part with the 'excuse' of the Olympic Games in 2004 in Athens, for which a Muslim place of worship is allegedly necessary, it was supported by Parliament with 55 MPs in favour and 40 against, and should be built in Peania, about 20 kilometres from the centre of Athens. The statute was drawn up by the Ministry of Foreign Affairs in collaboration with that of Culture and the ambassadors of Morocco,

Jordan and Palestine. However, it has aroused strong reactions, although approval has been given by the Orthodox church (but not by the local Metropolitan). The New Democracy party, as well as the Orthodox bishops close to the area in question, reacted harshly: Bishop Agathonikos of Mesogaia and Lavreotiki even wrote in his message to the Christians of the area that "our Holy Metropolitan in collaboration with the local authorities and the population will react with force to the attempt to adulterate the religious, cultural, social and tradition structure and the life of the citizens of Mesogeia [a name which is a symbol in itself: according to the editor's note, it means Mediterranean]. I call on each one of you to struggle in order to prevent the establishment of foreign, dangerous and heretic elements in our region" [Antoniou, 2000].

Despite occasional opposition, the renewed presence and visibility of Islam since the fall of the communist regimes is a process that has crossed the whole area of Ottoman settlement, from the Balkans eastwards. A symbol of this, despite the conflict and at the same time as a consequence of it—as it is a symbol of Muslim interest in its European part—is the impressive mosque dedicated to King Fahd ibn Abdul-Aziz, inaugurated in October 2000 in Sarajevo by the Saudi Arabians [Bougarel & Clayer, 2001].

Returning to the situation in Western Europe, it must be noted how mosques represent a way for Islam to leave the private sphere and make its official entry, so to speak, into the public sphere, and also its qualification as an interlocutor of society and institutions. In addition, mosques and prayer halls together attest to specific dynamics, linked to migratory dynamics, which have many facets. In the first place, they are often the only form of associations of reference present in the area. Sometimes they are evidence of a higher level of practice in a situation of emigration [Metcalf, 1996]. They are also a good thermometer of the level of organisation and of the ethnic threshold of the various communities, to the extent that it is possible to ascertain, as is often the case, that the organisation depending on the mosque is first of all inter-community, as a response to a common religious need, and then gradually as there are sufficient resources, it becomes communitarian on a national basis [Shadid & van Koningsveld, 1995; Sunier, 1999] (but we still have to measure the further modifications due to the second and third generations and the gradual loss of the significance of the national, and in the first place linguistic, factor which means that occasionally 'double' mosques can be found, with two prayer halls and relative imams, for example Moroccan and Turkish, as in the Netherlands). In addition, they are an element of the maturity in conflict between Muslim leaders, or a demonstration of their immaturity: the conflicts between rival leaders, which have often impeded the creation of mosques, despite the occasional good will of some local authorities, are in fact endemic; and sometimes the request for a mosque ends up by essentially having the aim of giving visibility to those who make the request, as shown, for example, by the triple request in the case of Marseilles [Bariki, 2000]. Lastly, the mosques represent an element of measuring the 'grip' of Islam, of its capacity of 'appropriation' and to transform the countries of emigration into *dar al-islam*, as according to many '*ulama*' the presence of mosques is the central element of this transformation [Siggillino, 2000].

It is interesting to note that there are the first signs that the presence of mosques is thought of as a sign of cultural open-mindedness and globalisation even by some local authorities, obviously not Muslim. In Barcelona, the chairman of the board of tourism declared in 1994 that the city needed a casino and a mosque to attract more visitors [Moreras, 2000]. In Athens the question of the mosque has been related to the Olympic Games [Antoniou, 2000]. And in Milan, it was the mayor, at a conference in the spring of 2000, who stated that the city had to have a large mosque to show that it was on an equal footing with and measured up to the other large European cities (although this declaration of principle has not been followed by any concrete gesture).

Linked to the problem of minarets is that of the *adhan*, the call to prayer, which beyond space also touches on another important symbolic aspect, that of 'acoustic space', a symbolic and communicative language that also has its traditions. Only in the Netherlands has the *adhan* explicitly been given official recognition, by law (in 1987, voted against only by three small Calvinist parties) equal to that of the sound of bells, even if how it is made, its volume and the number of times allowed (usually not for all the five daily prayers) is referred to the regulations of local authorities. In Amsterdam, for example, imitated by many other places, it is allowed only on Fridays [Rath, Penninx, Groenendijk & Meyer, 1999]. The prohibition of the *adhan* is common to many countries [de Galembert, 1998], even if the reasons are not always clear and, as for the construction of mosques, often appear more 'ethological' or legitimately cultural than social and legal, as they are tentatively defined.

In Great Britain the broadcasting of the *adhan* is often possible but subject to restrictions and occasionally extension with the local population, as in the case of the East London Mosque, situated in a very busy road and in a very ethnically characterised area: the decision to let the call to prayer be heard caused protests, including the foreseeable but not easily sustainable one, in the midst of other more or less disturbing noises, of acoustic pollution. However, with the support of the local Anglican church, two calls to prayer a day are allowed [Eade, 1996].

Elsewhere, as reported with regard to a Belgian situation, due to a surprising sense of solidarity and equality of conditions, it was even decided by the local Catholic authorities, asked for and supported by the mosque representatives, not to ring their bells any more! The subject is however still the object of discussion and negotiation in many countries and in individual local situations. It represents a change in the 'landscape' and which from certain points of view is more sensitive and 'invasive' (symbolically, not necessarily due to the noise produced) than building the mosque itself.

It is worthwhile referring to the question of Muslim cemeteries as well, or specific areas in cemeteries, as this touches on the symbolic aspects linked to the territory which we mentioned with regard to mosques in an even deeper way. Probably for this reason the question has occasionally aroused deep-rooted forms of hostility, irritation or at least opposition: all the more surprising because, in terms of principle, this is a right, the negation of which from the moral point of view, is particularly 'unpleasant', also because in religious traditions and more in general in traditional cultures there is the custom that puts the right to bury the dead amongst the pious activities and elementary duties of hospitality (for example, the Biblical story of Sarah, who died whilst Abraham was away from his land, and who was offered the best tomb available). We do not find it a coincidence that a question raised in Belgium in the early 1970s— the right to have specific areas for the burial of the dead—to which for a long time the answer was negative, with the excuse of wanting to avoid other communities putting forward similar proposals, received a strong impetus from particularly dramatic human cases and where 'no' would have been an insult, as when two children were murdered in the Brussels area (a Turkish boy in 1996 and a Moroccan girl in 1997)—cases highly exposed to the media—and the families had expressed their regret for having to send the bodies back to their home countries [Lambert, 2000].

The opening of cemeteries gives rise to different positions, at times in the different countries, for example in Switzerland, a country with a federal structure. In Zurich, which also has the oldest mosque in the country (Ahmadi, since 1963, which was also the European centre for the organisation), the request for a Muslim cemetery was rejected due to the opposition and mobilisation of a right-wing party that involved the people in the area, but also due to the difficulties of the Muslim community to find the necessary funding, as in this case it was a private cemetery [Mahnig, 2002], whilst in 1999 an allocation of funds was approved for the Muslim sector of the cemetery of Bremgarten. There are cantons where the cemetery or the specific spaces are not a problem, but mosques are, and others where on the contrary the mosques are not a problem but the cemeteries pose a problem. The question is so sensitive that in 1996 some converts felt the need to set up an ad hoc body, the FCIS (*Fédération des Cimetières islamiques de Suisse*). However, it is worth noting that it was precisely with regard to a cemetery, or rather a separate area in a pre-existing cemetery, a simple *carré islamique*, in Petit-Saconnex, that the first public debate on the relations between Islam and state started [Burkhalter, 1998; Mahnig, 2002].

Beyond the far-reaching implications that the question has on both Muslim and natives sides, and beyond the desire to continue to bury the dead in their country of origin (a practice that is commoner in some communities, such as with the Turks in Germany, for whom there is a Muslim cemetery in Berlin and 18 Muslim sectors in the same number of cities, two of which accept burial in a shroud and without a coffin [Gabert, 1999]). The question remains highly symbolic and more for reasons of marking limits of identity than for strictly religious reasons. This would also appear to be the case for Muslims, who if in some circumstances calmly accept the existing rules and adjust to them (for example, burial in a coffin), in others they raise problems and specific conditions for burial which at time make the acceptance of practices difficult, in terms of mortuary policy and local traditions [Burkhalter, 1998]. However, these conditions are not always rigidly applied in the countries of origin and differ according to origin, which cannot fail to create contrasts and clashes (even of power, and of symbolic power: the power to say how things must be) between the various elements making up the Muslim presence. In the Balkans, the members of some zealous Wahhabi organisations, who had gone to help their brothers in Bosnia or Kosovo, did not hesitate to raze to the ground cemeteries that were not, in their opinion, compliant with Muslim rules or their vision of these [Bougarel & Clayer, 2001].

No particular conflicts on this subject are recorded in other countries, such as Spain, where apart from the cemeteries of Ceuta and Melilla, run by the respective religious communities, or the historic one of Seville built on the orders of General Franco in 1936 to bury the Moroccans who had died in his ranks during the Civil War, or those under the control of the embassies of the Muslim countries, such as the Griñon cemetery in Madrid, owned by Morocco and already full, various communities have asked for land to be used as private cemeteries [ES File]. The Acuerdo of 1992 compels local authorities to reserve areas for Muslims in the municipal cemeteries but this point, like others, is often not applied. In Madrid talks are under way, whilst in Barcelona an agreement has already been reached [Moreras, 1999].

As always, there are no problems or discussions when the Muslim minorities are domestic and not immigrants. We can mention the case, lesser known than that of East European countries, of the Tatars in Finland, which makes the difference very clear indeed: they have their own cemetery in Helsinki, whilst for Muslim immigrants areas have been assigned in the Lutheran cemeteries in Helsinki, Espoo, Oulu and elsewhere [FI File].

5. OTHER DEBATES ON ISLAM

Apart from the three cases discussed above (the Rushdie affair, the *hijab*, mosques and cemeteries), which are also representative of specific areas of debate, various other questions have formed the object of discussion, some at a local or national level and others, more transversally, in various situations. These include, in addition to the cyclical debates on fundamentalism and the condition of women, the question, in countries where it is mature, due to evident reasons of generational 'mass', of the right to create Muslim schools or to receive funding for these, on an equal footing with other majority or minority religious communities.

As remarked on other occasions, often the tension and discussions do not concern a real fact, for example the right mentioned above, which if it is granted to other minorities should, in principle, also be granted to the Muslim minority. Rather, it regards, even if not explicitly, other facts, at times imaginary or only presumed: for example the contents of the education, its presumed 'fundamentalism' and incompatibility with the syllabi adopted, or even with the fundamentals of civil society. There has also often been discussion on the possible external interference from the countries of origin and if this does not always exist, then the fear of it has always existed [Rath, Penninx, Groenendijk & Meyer, 1999]. Moreover, the fear of this external interference can produce two different effects: the refusal of initiatives for which international support is suspected (and consequently of any initiative, because they can all be the object of suspicion in this sense) or, on the other hand, the support for local Muslim initiatives, which generally speaking, outlines the different choices of Utrecht and of Rotterdam.

Discussions also imply the preference of various Muslim communities and of many Muslim parents for the model of the single-sex school. In Great Britain, in the mid-1980s, when the debate started, both the Swann Committee appointed to reflect on the issue and the National Union of Teachers said they were against it [Nielsen, 1999]. And this is one of the countries which in more recent times has reopened the debate on them for the natives too, re-proposing the traditional model as educationally more efficient and advantageous, in particular for girls.

It is however indicative that, even in the presence of differing legislative and political contexts, such as the Dutch and British ones, even if both are basically favourable, at least until a short while ago, to multicultural policies in support of the communities and minorities, religious in the former case and only ethnic and racial in the latter, there are nevertheless debates and reactions [Dwyer & Meyer, 1995], and differentiated actions can be reached: today the Netherlands is the country with the greatest number of Muslim schools, Great Britain accepted funding only two from the 1999–2000 school year. Merely to give an idea of the time that this has taken, one of these, the Islamiah Primary School in Brent, near London, famous for having been supported by Yusuf Islam, better known as the former pop singer Cat Stevens, applied, in compliance with the law, for financial support for the first time in 1986. This was a mixed school (on the problem of school and education, see the chapter on this issue).

A common debate in many European countries is also that of ritual slaughter, where the animal's throat is cut and it is bled to death, both the 'ordinary' type, prohibited only in some countries such as Sweden, which nevertheless allows the import of *halal* meat, and the 'extraordinary' type on the occasion of the *'Id al-kabir*, that commemorates the sacrifice of Abraham [Brisebarre, 1998]. This is also the occasion for what, in various countries, in the wake of ecological campaigns and relying on a testimonial capable of attracting a great deal of attention (this is the case of Brigitte Bardot in France), is considered unacceptable and barbarian slaughter, even assimilating the image of the father slaughtering the animal for the celebration with that of the terrorists of the Algerian *Groupes Islamiques Armés* (GIA) with a bloody knife clenched in his teeth slaughtering innocent people! More soberly, the question is nevertheless discussed in various countries regardless of how it is organised. The legislation on protecting animals, including from suffering, and its diffusion is a sensitive cultural element in evolution.

Specific debates can be considered, for example that on forced marriages in Great Britain, also due to the specificity of its Muslim population. This is a widespread custom amongst some Asian peoples, not only Muslims, of rural origin and with little education. The question is perceived mainly as Muslim, even if, as mentioned, it is not exclusively so, and some Muslim representatives have also been brought into the debate on the request of the British government [Baroness Uddin of Bethnal Green, personal interview, May 2000]. Forced marriage is also a way of bringing new immigrants, relatives and members of the same 'clan' to the country and each year causes discussion, cases of running away from home (some Muslim representatives talk of thousands of girls a year, but often the episode is solved by returning home and is necessary to start up discussion with the parents which otherwise would be impossible) and sometimes more dramatic facts [Fuad Nahdi, interview, May 2000].

The Netherlands is perhaps the country where at present there is the greatest discussion on the fundamentals, more than on the individual epiphenomena: on the consequences of immigration, on what 'integration' should mean and on what a multicultural society should mean. School, but also the education of imams and immigrants in general, are amongst the questions currently under discussion.

In countries with a less 'mature' presence the debate is less frequent and visible and often imported from abroad, as with regard to the veil. In Italy, moreover, it is always called *chador*, with an implicitly and perhaps not completely unconsciously more 'restrictive' meaning. Here the debate is occasionally on the possible agreement with the state, but above all controversies of ecclesiastical origin are given extensive media coverage, such as the anti-Muslim position of individual bishops. Some originated in statements by the Bishop of Como, Maggiolini, who had already intervened in the past on questions of immigration. With greater impact and great media coverage, in September 2000, the Bishop of Bologna, Cardinal Biffi also had his word, proposing 'selective' forms of immigration according to religion: in a pastoral letter to the city, but with a wider intention, he even asked the Italian government to encourage the entry only of Christians, or at least Asians, but not of Muslims, opening an extensive debate within the Catholic and secular worlds (at the same time a book by the secular political commentator Giovanni Sartori was published and highly publicised in articles and interviews, with harsher and more explicit positions).

In Spain, as in Italy from many points of view, save the examples mentioned, the presence of Muslims is closely linked with the debate on immigration and therefore concerns problems other than religious ones, or also interprets these as a consequence of this more than as the fact that a new minority faith is emerging. Questions linked with the condition of women, the family, marriage and the educational success or failure of the second generation are recurring questions [ES File].

In Switzerland, the ephemeral case of a 'Voltaire affair' can be mentioned, which is indicative of a certain type of mentality: in 1993, a French director requested the local authorities in Geneva for funding to stage "Muhammed le Prophète, ou le fanatisme" on the third centenary of the birth of the philosopher of the Enlightenment. The refusal by the local authorities, which was also motivated by the desire not to offend the sensitivity of the Muslim community, opened the debate, conducted with a certain virulence by its protagonist: it also showed the difficulties and incapacity or the lack of interest of Muslim leaders of the first generation, to handle this type of debate, taken on by the second generation leaders, including the two brothers, Tareq and Hani Ramadan. The virulence of the 'secular' attack in the end brought Muslims and authorities to positions that were very close to one another [Haenni, 1994].

In Greece, the debate concerns more the ethnic recognition of the community than the religious recognition: the minority elites insist more on being recognised as Turks rather than as Muslims. An example of this debate can be the affair of schoolbooks, triggered off in 1991 by the Greek government's decision to replace the books that traditionally arrived from Turkey for the school year, by a text in Turkish written by a Greek academic, known for his studies on Pomaks and gypsies, distributing it in 1992 without having received the approval of the Turkish educational authorities. This provoked campaigns to return the book to the Greek authorities, with arrests and the next year school boycotts, until the arrival of new books from Turkey and their distribution, and in the end the acceptance of the book by the Greek teacher. However, the question, as can easily be understood, was not so much on the contents, and specifically the religious contents, but precisely on the language and on the dignity of the group: being compelled to learn Turkish from a Greek inevitably wounded popular pride [Akgönül, 1999]. Turkish and Tatar ethnic minorities are also preset in Romania, but the problems, although important, linked to this, concern the past above all. The problem today, paradoxical and unusual if interpreted with the standards of Western Europe, is with the recent Arab immigrants and Turkish businessmen, often richer in relation to Romanian standards. The xenophobia against them, partly anti-Muslim, also uses 'cultural' arguments linked to the Orthodox culture and identity of the country [RO File].

In Bulgaria the Muslim minority is the object of discussion due also to its presence with its own party and its representatives in Parliament. But apart from the emergence of public discussions linked to the wars in Bosnia and Kosovo, local sociological studies measure extremely low negative stereotypes on Muslims and therefore the absence of significant tension. They remain strong regarding nomads and gypsies, but not for religious reasons [BG File].

A case which strikes us as particularly interesting for a conclusion is that of Portugal, apparently a privileged situation. The Muslim community is recent, but still fairly small, and very well integrated. No tension can be measured around the building of mosques, the *hijab* or any other issue. Portugal also has a historical Arab heritage to be found in the architecture and language, although unlike Spain it did not have a significant Arab presence. The explanation of this fundamentally positive panorama, in addition to the small number (38,000 Muslims in the highest estimate), lies in the peculiar composition of the community. The majority is of Indian origin, but from the former African colonies such as Mozambique and Guinea Bissau and others in East Africa. Some 8,000 are Ismailis, followers of the Aga Khan, with an impressive Islamic centre in Lisbon, excellent internal networks, which were already in place when they lived in Mozambique, where they came from in a sort of collective migration. These communities are well inserted socially, on average perhaps they are better educated than elsewhere in Europe, probably with more capable leaderships, both of internal organisation and political and media relations with society: these elements represent other ingredients of this positive cocktail, together with the fact that they already knew Portuguese as they mainly come from former colonies. For the same reason, the system granted them the rights of citizenship, there was already an elite of students and intellectuals present in the country, with good relations in the political system, that helped in building up a religious infrastructure and, in addition, the Muslims were already used to living as a minority in the former colonies [PT File; Tiesler, 2000]. These conditions are rarely found in other countries but can help us reflect on the possibilities and conditions of successful integration: and which show the extent to which the religious factor, in the strict sense, is not necessarily as primary as it appears in the media when it is a case of confronting and debating tensions such as those analysed in this chapter.

6. THE DEBATE ON MULTICULTURALISM

In the previous section we have spoken of national questions and debates, even if many are to be found in various countries, as being of consequence for a common set of problems. On the other hand, some debates are fully transversal and present everywhere because they form the theoretical debate at the basis, even if often only implicitly, of all the others. The first of these is the debate on multiculturalism.

The presence of Islam has not created a multicultural situation in Europe. However, it has certainly contributed to a great extent to creating an awareness of it and making it more visible and topical, more than other 'othernesses' which are less visible or less symbolically charged, including historically, and we refer to the history of relations with Europe even if not to actual European history; or perceived as less conflicting—less 'other', in a word. Multiculturalism, which we mean here not as adhesion to a specific political philosophy, but as the mere recognition of a plurality of competing cultural options present in the same territory and of competing cultural universes, linked in particular with the arrival of populations which have these as their own heritage of reference, is now part of the European agenda. Naturally this does not mean that before there were not differences of opinion and of references. However, it is licit to hypothesise that with the arrival of the new migrations, cultural and religious plurality has not only increased in terms of potential references, but has found new collectively shared forms of presence and has triggered off dynamics that were at least partially new in the Old Continent.

At least, this is how it appears in the countries and in the traditions, including intellectual ones, and amongst academics who recognise it as such. A recognition which, if it is often frequent and even banal amongst academics of the Anglo-Saxon school (the statement by Roy Jenkins is often repeated: "equal opportunity and cultural diversity, in an atmosphere of mutual tolerance"), is far less common in other European interpretative traditions, but which everywhere is undergoing or triggering off transformations, even in the way of interpreting the phenomenon and in the policies to deal with it. In Europe the introduction of the use of the term 'multiculturalism' marked the passage from an immigration perceived only as economic and temporary to a permanent presence of populations. The "multicultural affairs" department created by the local authorities of Frankfurt with Daniel Cohn-Bendit at its head was to be one of the signs of its visibility [Kastoryano, 1998b].

In Great Britain, it still appears as a fact that multiculturalism is giving a new form (trans-forming) to the public spheres and civil societies of the new Europe [Modood & Werbner, 1997]. However, discussion is sporadically starting on the side from which it should be approached, and in particular if the emphasis on race, on the use of categories such as black, and white for the natives, still prevalent, but also 'general' ethnic categories such as Asians—categories which ignore the religious factor, as well as overestimating the importance of others—still has sufficient heuristic validity in interpreting phenomena of incomprehension or even of inter-comprehension, which have precisely a cultural character.

It also appears politically significant to approach the spectacular reversal of positions on the Netherlands, which has gone from an advanced multiculturalism, precisely on the sense of encouraging 'policies of recognition' [Taylor, 1992], to policies that would seem more markedly assimilationist, in the form of a liberalism aiming essentially at the individual, where equality before the law is accompanied by active policies not so much of cultural valorisation but of the promotion of equal chances for the individual [Entzinger, 2000]. Thus the traditional system of 'pillars' is abandoned, apparently without excessive regret, in favour of initiatives targeted only at single disadvantaged individuals, but understood precisely as such and not as a category (neither religious nor ethnic, nor the more general one of immigrants, is maintained as such). It is worthwhile underlining however, the active and almost voluntaristic role of politics of this approach which is not limited to leaving the field to the free and autonomous forces of the market: evidence of this is the law on the civic integration of new arrivals (*Wet inburgering nieuwkomers*), passed in 1998, which includes the allocation of Euro 100 million only for the training of recent immigrants [Entzinger, 2000].

The repeated attempts of regulating French Islam 'from above' seem to point in an opposite direction: opposite also with respect to the 'republican' philosophy of reference which is still dominant in French interpretative paradigms. However, the picture outlined in the early 1990s by one of the first comparative analyses of the Muslim presence in Europe still seems reliable and it can be summarised in three elements: a liberal myth of a multicultural Europe, which is indeed still a myth; the social reality of a multicultural Europe which can be found in the field; the unreality of a real cultural encounter in Europe [Nielsen, 1992]. On the one hand, therefore, the identification, which is also implicit in the interpretations of religious phenomena, handed down by classic sociology of religions, between the elements of the state (a people, a territory and a legal system) and a religion, has been superseded in and by the facts [Allievi, 2000b]. On the other hand, the ethnic, ethnic-religious and religious movements become social actors in the public space, appear in the public sphere asking not only for acceptance or mere tolerance, but visibility, public recognition, a share of resources and, lastly, social and political representation.

It is no coincidence that the debate on the communities, on their existence and persistence and on their bond with identities—including religious—once again becomes topical. Taylor [1992] put forward the well-known theory that our identity "is moulded, in part by the recognition or non-recognition or, often, by a misunderstanding by others", opening the multicultural debate with his book, or at least making a significant contribution to its diffusion. Kymlicka [1995] underlined that the subject is not capable of exercising his own individual freedom anywhere except in a context that makes personal choice possible and gives it meaning, with the invitation to respect the rights of minorities to widen the sphere of individual rights. The passage from the term of minorities to that of community is frequent and imperceptible: in the common debate they are very often equivalent. A further difficulty comes from the fact that the term community tends to be polysemic and lend itself to each interpretation; above all, its use is very different in the 'high' academic-scientific register and in the 'low' register of common speech but also of policies: "as a scientific concept, community has no value; as a tool for the creation of the social imagination, it occupies a fundamental place and is destined to last" [Busino, quoted in Bagnasco, 1999].

The language of the social actors is even more explicit, strongly insisting on the concept of community. The Muslim community in our case, even if the 'communitarian temptation' is present everywhere, in the majority religions as well as in the historical minorities: Jewish representatives have also willingly talked of "community of communities" [Jonathan Sachs, Chief Rabbi of the congregations of the Commonwealth, quoted in Fitzgerald, 1998]. Some important Muslim exponents theorise that integration can work better if it comes through the community and not individuals [Rached al-Ghannouchi, interview, May 2000]. Even if, perhaps, aware of the mistrust that weighs on the idea of community, some European Muslim intellectuals propose a version that is conceptually on the defensive, talking of "community against communitarianism" [Ramadan, 1999]. Moreover, the term has often been used, with a certain unawareness, which betrays deep-rooted processes of thought, by the language of the media and of social and political operators.

The discourse on the community, both by the civil authorities and by minority groups has become a notion "as vague as it is comfortable" which both invoke without defining, as has been noted: a fundamental resource of ethnic (but also religious) mobilisation which has led to the emerging 'politics of religion and community' [Vertovec & Peach, 1997].

And thus a category such as that of community has come back into fashion, but accompanied by an overload of ideological elements, both on the part of its supporters and by its detractors, which makes a semantically 'serene' use of it difficult. In the case of Islam, the conceptual ambiguity comes from the fact that the term, including when used by the social players involved, can refer both to social relations that involve the individual is his totality and to communities territorially limited even by religious characteristics (the neighbourhoods with a majority of Muslims for example), and lastly the meta-community of the Muslim *Umma*.

It is of little importance that religious communities too, as national ones, can be 'imagined communities' [Anderson, 1991]. It is a fact that reference to them is concrete and not at all virtual, in the lives of those who refer to them. And in the case of Islam in Europe, communities seem to form a sort of third, hybrid, space, between insiders and outsiders [Eade, 1999]. This space however, should be analysed, beyond the discourse establishing norms on it. It should be noted that this attempt of 'community objectification' takes place in a space which is, in its turn, being de-communitised. I am referring to the European space itself which, starting off from a self-definition in terms of 'common market' then called itself "European economic (only) community", and today calls itself the 'European Union': a less committed term and also emotionally less inclusive. The term 'union', unlike 'community', does not evoke a shared culture [Abélès, 1998].

A reflection of community self-organisation however seems indispensable for an understanding of the processes of insertion and integration. The Muslims who have immigrated to Europe are not only this: they are also groups, associations, communities—in a word collective social actors (also collective). As such, they are organised and make their voices heard, and as such they are or are begun to be perceived, by professional observers and, more in general, by public opinion. On the other hand, it is not possible to concentrate only on the above specificities, with the risk of hypostatising them: cultural communities are not static or rigid they come into being and are constructed socially, but individuals act in them and through them [see Dassetto, Mirdal, Roy, Amiraux, and Allievi in Dassetto, 2000]. In communities, as in the individuals that cross them, the dynamics of change and the modifications under way must be highlighted and which are not less important than the forms of cultural continuity and 'inertia', and the links with the parallel processes of individualisation are no less important than elements of communitarianism, and no less significant than for the self-definition of these identities, both from the individual and collective point of view.

The European Muslim world is living through a process of extremely rapid transformation. It will be of strategic interest to see how the processes of structuring of Muslim communities continues in this crucial phase, where they are no longer ethnic communities arriving from somewhere else, as with the generational passage they are losing at least in part and progressively the ethnic characterisation and identification with the countries of origin, but are not yet purely and simply autochthonous communities, for reasons linked both to culture and customs as well as to citizenship (nor, above all, are they perceived as such). In this perspective, the very notion of Muslim 'community' ends up by losing that idea of contraposition to 'individual' which it maintains implicitly, and often explicitly, in many interpretations of the Muslim phenomenon in Europe and which show here their excessively simplifying characteristic. In the panorama that is being formed, community and individual are not alternative ways of being Muslims, but on the contrary are concomitant and are even mutually reinforcing. It is therefore not correct to formulate the debate in terms of communitarianism or individual integration (or simply individual paths), which represents a false alternative and is not confirmed by empirical analyses of the Muslim phenomenon: rather, we have to speak of communitarianism (or more simply, and also more correctly, of community, although with a large mesh and fraying at many points) and individual integration.

CHAPTER TEN

RELATIONS BETWEEN RELIGIONS

Stefano Allievi

The fact that the definition of Europe, or rather the European specificity, can be understood in a religious interpretation, perhaps more than through any other defining criterion, although religious practice is in strong decline throughout the continent, is a possibility that, although taken with all due caution, deserves close examination [Ballard, 1996].

The extent to which religion, and in particular the relationship of conflict between Christianity—or perhaps we ought to say Christendom—and Islam has been important in the cultural self-definition of Europe is a frequent statement amongst historians and the 'classic' orientalists [cf. from the many possible references, Lewis B., 1982; Daniel, 1993; Cardini, 1999, and the references they contain], and is naturally present among the apologists and polemicists of both religions. These statements have been critically challenged by contemporary history and social sciences, and in part by modern orientalism: however, it is difficult to deny that this perception of conflict exists [Djaït, 1978; Said, 1978; and the essays in Allievi 1996b].

This is true for the origins of the conflict between Europe, at the time still a non-existent concept, and dawning Islam: "without Muhammad, Charlemagne is inconceivable" to take up the well known and debated thesis by Pirenne [1937], who, moreover, gave more importance to the economic than the cultural aspects. But the subject has been re-proposed in more recent times as well, when the modern state, and its religious identification, was taking shape. For Europe, the relationship between religious self-definition and state has its origin at least from the Treaty of Westphalia (1648), after which the state was identified with a particular religion. It was thus that Bavaria and Cologne became Catholic, whilst Hanover and Brandenburg were Protestant, Denmark and Sweden Lutheran and France Catholic [Nielsen, 1999b]. To reach the present, there is a long story in between where, quoted at random, we find the Enlightenment, the Industrial Revolution, capitalism, scientific and technological development, secularisation, and the progressive separation between the political-legal sphere and the religious one. Europe today is therefore not that of Westphalia; and it is not, simply, 'post-Westphalian'. In the first place, the widespread institutional 'incrustations' of the old majority religions suggest that this identification has not disappeared culturally from the cultural horizons of Europe. Even if these religions cannot always be defined as 'churches of state', they are nevertheless deeply engraved in the legal-political but also economic and social heritage of the respective countries (the Queen as the head of the Church of England, the Lutheran churches of state in Scandinavian countries, the concordats in Italy and Spain, the link between Orthodoxy and nation in Greece, etc.). However, it is not only this, namely a 'cultural heritage', which may be in the process of being abandoned: a fact of tradition, without evident consequences or with decreasing importance, with regard to the present. Even a certain return of the religious dimension in the definition of the nation and even in Europe, by cultural and political forces that in some countries are government forces, seems to show that this identification is anything but a vestige of the past. This return probably also owes something, in addition to internal dynamics, to the new presence of traditions considered foreign, including, in the first place, Islam.

The demand by Christian faiths dominant in their respective countries for strong forms of recognition and institutionalisation is not necessarily in decline, as a naive interpretation of the theory of secularisation may seem to assume. From the funding of religious schools to the debate on bioethics, from certain political positions to the recovery of a public symbolism which we could consider a form of re-traditionalising from above, the signs of religion becoming institutionally visible, sometimes of reinvention of forms of civil religion, are not lacking.

In Western Europe, the problem of the separation between church and state was believed to have been solved thanks to secularisation, but some internal dynamics, and the presence of immigrant minorities, create some problems for this clear-cut image. In Eastern Europe, on the other hand, it was believed to have been solved by eliminating it at the roots, and yet today its return can be noted, from Poland to Serbia, via Russia. These differences are in part due to the different conception of the relations between church and state in the Catholic world, in the Protestant world and in Orthodoxy, and in part to historical contingencies (everything, however, should be read historically: today's Protestantism is by no means that of Luther and Calvin and the same applies to Catholics and Orthodox).

However, we cannot deduce too many facile trends: *The decline of the sacred in industrial society* nor *The revenge of God* are on course, to quote two very successful books of sociology of religion, published thirty years apart and which support opposing theories [Acquaviva, 1961 and Kepel, 1991, respectively]. Or, perhaps, they are both under way. As has been noted for the case of Norway, but the fact can be transferred to a wider European scale, paradoxically, exactly while the religious subjects are committed to reciprocal dialogue and co-operation, the popular and political discourses are increasingly marked by a growing trend to reassert the so-called cultural Christian heritage of the Norwegian nation. In parallel with these communitarian trends, the Norwegian state is also marked by universal concerns in the religious field, for example regarding women's rights or in proposing a culture of dialogue and tolerance [Leirvik, 2001]. Therefore we are witnessing both forms of privatisation of the religious and, in particular in the institutional and legal dimension, forms of politicisation of religion.

These different interpretative modes can also be considered forms of a struggle of power under way, within Europe, of which Islam is only a pawn, a secondary actor or the unleashing element, the external cause of a chemical reaction that would have taken place in any case. This can be seen in the struggle between religious worlds and non-believers' opinion and between religions and secularism. But it can also be seen in relations between religions. In this triangular battle (*laïcité*, more or less supported by the state; dominant religions; religious minorities), Islam may be, for the churches, at one and the same time, "the ally and the rival, poor and competitive". In a period of secularisation and religious indifference, Islam becomes a precious ally whilst remaining a rival [de Galembert, 1994]. This may show ambiguities which are little emphasised in inter-religious relations. They depend to a great extent on the legal-institutional framework and on how this incorporates or relates to religions (see in this regard the chapter on this issue by S. Ferrari for this report). But they do not necessarily weaken the most important interlocutor, as is the prevailing interpretation amongst the 'apocalyptics' in the various religious faiths, who interpret dialogue as giving way (literature on the subject, and in relation to Islam, is vast and popular although not very present in the educated register of the dialogue—it exists, but it is not quoted). On the contrary, at times dialogue can reinforce the majority communities and religions in general: as has been seen in the French case, encouraging the insertion of Islam allows bringing the religious question back on to the agenda, and ends up by actually favouring the Catholic church, in a role of concrete and symbolic mediation with regard to the state [de Galembert, 1994]. This role is sometimes boosted by research, by local or national governments, of forms of semi-institutional inter-religious collaboration, of which we have very many examples: in these cases the 'advice' of the local dominant church becomes the required and necessary link for a possible 'inclusion' of Islam. Sometimes for this purpose bodies of inter-religious dialogue are used, often promoted on the initiative of the majority Christian interlocutor. In Berne, to give a concrete example, after a discussion without a result on the construction of a Muslim cemetery, in the end, an institution of dialogue, the *Gemeinschaft Christen und Muslime in der Schweiz*, was used as a base, perceived as legitimate by both parties, which was able to play a role of liaison [Mahnig, 2000a]. It is clear that these types of structures offer a form of legitimisation and recognition to the interlocutors and allow forms of negotiation which otherwise would be difficult. However, it is or should be a substitutive and temporary role, which cannot become a generalised and stable practice, if only because it cannot be accepted that there cannot be direct negotiation solely for Muslims. On the level of principle, it may perhaps be considered ironic, with respect to the secular principles of the state and separations of the spheres, that the Muslim interlocutors are taken more seriously by the states or by public authorities when they are in one way or another 'introduced' by churches: but it should be noted that this process is fairly widespread.

There is little research on concrete inter-religious relations that could be of use to interpret the landscape that we are trying to define: the fundamental texts are mainly of a religious and historical formulation and restrict themselves to defining the general principles of dialogue [cf. Waardenburg, 1998, with the relative bibliography]. Here we will try to describe the aspects of greatest social pertinence.

1. THE BACKGROUND LANDSCAPE: A PLURAL EUROPE

The transformations that Europe has experienced on the religious level are one of its formative and strongly characterising elements. Without wishing here to reassume complex processes and around which scientific, cultural and political debate is fierce and conclusions controversial, it is nevertheless an acquired fact that the objective effects of the processes of secularisation, with its corollary of the progressive separation between the political sphere and the religious one (at least as a tendency and aspiration, if not always as the rigorously respected reality) of privatisation of the religious, of the pluralisation of religious subjects through the gradual increase of the 'offer' available, have created a situation which is new from many points of view [cf. at least Berger, 1967; Luckmann, 1967; Wilson, 1982; Gauchet, 1985].

The religious effects, unforeseen even if not unforeseeable, of what has been called the 'mobiletic revolution', and in particular migration representing one of its decisive elements, have been grafted on to this process, already extensive and articulate in itself. In extreme synthesis, its consequences include: the gradual decline of the significance of the identification, hardly ever real and however often implicit in our way of thinking, between people, territory, legal system (the constitutive elements of the state) and religion.

However little this implicit is irrelevant is revealed to us by the religious neo-chauvinism which is often demonstrated by xenophobic movements: although they refer more willingly, from the ideological point of view, to Celtic and neo-pagan references (as it is the case for the Northern League in Italy and other groups all over Europe), they do not hesitate to use the religious argument, in its Christian expression, in an anti-Muslim function. The popularity of this 'cultural' argument is there to show us the extent to which the religious problem, often underestimated in excessively technocratic and economic analyses of the processes of development, including in Europe, is, on the other hand, of crucial importance.

The religious landscape of Europe is becoming increasingly articulated. On the one hand we have the usual religious presences, which represent the constants: very more present, if only for reasons of 'inertia', both in terms of social and cultural roots and an institutional basis, than the emphasis on the change and new religious modes can succeed in understanding. On the other, however, there is precisely the change and dynamics that, more than upsetting the status quo, modify its composition. Here we find, together with the traditional religions of old Europe—the various Christian families, the Jewish presence, some survivals which once would have been called pagan—many other actors: the new religious movements that in Europe come into being or are imported from other flourishing producers (the United States but also quite a few Asian countries: from India to Japan and Korea); an extensive production of new age spirituality; religious sects that are connected to a greater or lesser extent, possibly only by opposition, to the old Christian stock; traditions from elsewhere imported into Europe on the initiative of westerners and in their fashion (this is the case of Buddhism) and lastly, an increasingly marked presence of old and new religious traditions which have arrived with immigrants. The panorama of these is variegated: ranging from various forms and special declinations of Christianity, to Hinduism, some 'ethnic' religions (Shintoism and Sikhism) to animism and syncretistic forms such as the so-called African 'new churches' and, naturally, Islam.

It is above all with the last-named of these, the 'other' religious traditions brought by immigrants, that the problem of encounter, inter-relations and inter-religious dialogue is raised. A dialogue that does not come into being only from these presences (the need, on the global level, is also raised in relations between countries and respective majority religions, and in those characterised by a national religious plurality): but that, since the immigrant communities have begun to become visible on the religious level as well, has become an increasingly experienced and present need both for the European Christian conscience (whichever the form in which it appears) and the secular one, aware that a good relationship between religions is an inevitable element for good social co-existence.

It is evident that this dialogue is different from the ecumenism of Christian churches. Not only, as is obvious, because it concerns subjects that are more 'dissimilar', with fewer common bases for reference, at times without even a common language (even a symbolic one), which obviously creates a series of greater complications and difficulties, but because it is situated in a context of differences, including social differences, that have a considerable weight. Let us recall the main ones:

a) except in some cases, it is a question mainly of immigrants and not of nationals. The interlocutors, therefore, do not enjoy the

same rights and the same access to the social and cultural as well
as political resources that nationals have at their disposal;

b) these people have languages, cultures and traditions (at all levels;
   in addition to religious, family, juridical, customs, forms of education, of 'protection' of decency, of weight of community logics,
   etc.) that at times may be very different;

c) they are people with a degree of social insertion and integration
   which in general can be defined as 'lower' compared to the natives
   population (in many aspects 'poorer', in a word), and who have
   arrived relatively recently, which may have made their possibility of thoroughly knowing the context of insertion, understanding
   its logics and finding the language to relate to them more difficult
   or at least slower;

d) lastly, these are groups or religious communities that are not yet
   structured and are at times relatively small, where the "social division of work" and internal structuring is still at an initial stage
   and which has not yet, in the majority of cases, allowed forming
   the 'managers' necessary, with the minimum indispensable time
   and resources, and in some aspects the need for relations has not
   yet completely manifested itself. However, it must be remembered
   that in some European countries, where this Muslim presence is
   already in its second or even third generation and the dimensions
   of which are larger and the level of insertion greater, things are
   being modified with significantly rapid processes.

Therefore, this is a dialogue, if we want to speak of dialogue, which
starts off from unequal social conditions.

2. Elements of the Relationship with Islam

Whatever Islam may also be, it is in the very first place, a religion.
It is therefore decisive to see how it relates to the other majority
and minority religions present in Europe and how these relate to Islam.

In this sense, analysing the inter-religious dialogue, when and if
it exists, becomes crucial for the role that religions continue to play
in informing and forming public opinion. This is an aspect which
in particular is not very well studied by sociological analysis: inter-
religious dialogue is usually analysed on the theological level, and
by religious social actors—for the scientific community it appears a
marginal aspect. The respective literatures are separate and often

impermeable and non-communicating. On the other hand, the aspect
of religious pluralisation and its consequences are sociologically
important.

With this, we do not want to overlook what is not religious. The
institutional, legal, political, historical and social framework in which
religions are inserted, does not include only them and on the level
of principles, it is not only determined as a priority by them: there
is an autonomy, in particular of the political-legal-institutional sphere,
even *from* religions, which is now acquired heritage, an autonomy in
the framework of which Islam too is inserted and from which it
benefits.

It is worthwhile underlining, however, how often amongst the
Muslim interlocutors the opinion is common, perhaps ungenerous
but nevertheless significant, that, despite the historical and theological weight of the conflicts on religious grounds of the past (not completely finished, even if they have abandoned their more virulent
and bloody forms), on the level of the declarations of principle and
also of the social-religious practices that concern them, they often
find themselves in greater opposition with secularistic opinion than
with religious opinion: in the intellectual world, in the media and at
times in relations with states and administrations. We have also noted
some elements of these conflicts, in the chapter concerning tension
in the public space caused by the presence of Islam. We limit ourselves here to observing that there is in this perception a weighty
element of underestimation, or of selective perception: however, it is
an interpretative aspect of importance, which risks putting others, of
equal importance, into the shade. To mention the best known example, the question of the *hijab* in France and the way it was treated
wounded Muslim sensitivity, in the country and outside it, far more
than the observers habitually perceive and as it is still alive in the
European Muslim memory, also because of certain republican hyper-
sensitivity at times resentful in its interfering, assessing and limiting
some rights of religious freedom (of some). Symbolically it therefore
risks putting into the background the fact that France is the European
country with the largest number of Muslims, many of whom in that
country have found possibilities of living and liberties, including religious freedom, which they would have been unlikely to find elsewhere, starting from the own countries of origin.

Religiously motivated operators, precisely because they share the elements and needs of religious expression even if not the ways, can 'recognise' with relative facility the religious needs of others and are capable of accepting them and interpreting them as such, without having recourse to answers on other levels, from the social to the political. It is no coincidence that, in various countries, the reception of immigrants is, to a great extent, run by non-governmental organisations and associations linked to religious circles or are, at any rate, moved by religious motivations.

A group of residents praying in a hostel, an employee in a factory or a patient in hospital asking for *halal* food and a religious community asking for a place where they can celebrate the *'Id* are, in the first place, expressions of a religious faith, which all too often the secular world, including academia, tends to interpret only as social acts, demonstrations of power, desire for recognition. Identity needs, the result of malaise and of the lack of integration, the effect of uncontrolled migratory dynamics. This attitude often provokes the irritation, and absolute incomprehension of how this short-circuit of communication can be developed, of Muslims, who feel 'interpreted' with interpretative categories which they do not recognise and in which they do not recognise themselves.

It is clear that this is also a strategy and an attempt to keep their own field under control, but it is a lengthy step from here not to recognise and possibly refuse accepting that religious behaviour can, at least, be interpreted also as religious and too much research does this without even being aware of it.

It is not so much a question of underlining, with satisfaction on the part of religious representatives, and perhaps with concern by non-religious representatives, that "religion is coming back to the agenda", as we were told by a representative of the Interfaith Network [personal interview, May 2000]. But it is necessary to stress that the religious element is an important element of social analysis in itself, and as such it must be approached.

Its effects are, moreover, significant. In the specific instance of the case of Islam, it is by no means superfluous, for example, to mention the role of the majority religious institutions in facilitating or not the processes of acceptance and integration of Muslims [de Galembert, 1997], or at least their presumption of playing this role, which is nevertheless translated into concrete acts and behaviour internally and with the institutions. Internally, through conveying a 'non-demonic' image of the other, the recognition of its right to exist as a religious entity as well, and therefore implicitly as a potentially competitive religious entity (which already is not a neutral exercise and is revealed to be complex and even painful on the theological level): an educational and vocational task that, although passed in silence with respect to external activity, is probably even more important. And externally, in favouring policies of inclusion, on the institutional level for example, and also forms of symbolic recognitions which are equally anything but neutral in their effects. Numerous examples of this intervention have been seen, for example with regard to the right by Muslims to respect their customs in diet and dress, of favouring the religious education of their children, of seeing their beliefs respected and not offended, but also, more concretely, of building their own places of worship (in some cases symbolically more sensitive and favourable ecclesiastical positions are even a *conditio sine qua non*: for example, the construction of the Islamic *Centro Islamico di Roma* is inconceivable without an explicit even if 'unofficial' consent by the Vatican to the project, which there in fact was).

There is not only dialogue, of course, even if the religious subjects are readier to place emphasis on it (slightly less, logically, the mass media, more interested in rendering visible the elements of conflict and clashes). There are also the forms of indifference, refusal and competition: the pluralisation of the religious market and the substantial de-monopolisation of the various national contexts inevitably also produce this.

And there are also differences in the perception of its usefulness by, respectively, the top ranks of the religious institutions and their bases, and of those who practise and those who do not. Despite the commitment of the active minorities, the religious 'people', perhaps less committed, seem less open than their top ranks and than the non-religious: this seems to contradict at least partially the perception of a sort of greater secular 'fundamentalism' by many Muslim leaders. The French IFOP survey in 1994 noted, for example, conspicuous differences on some sensitive subjects, between those who practise and those who do not: 33% of the former were in favour of the building of mosques against 41.6% of the latter. Thirty-seven percent of church-goers are not in favour of mixed marriages, whilst 58% of non church-goers are not, for whom clearly religious *mixité* means less, with a difference of over twenty percent [*Le Monde*, 1994]. In Great Britain however, recent research shows that *committed*

Christians have fewer prejudices against Muslims compared to nom-
inal Christians, atheists and agnostics [Modood, 1997].

One aspect that has not yet been sufficiently analysed is that of
the different degree of acceptance and 'collaboration' with Muslim
diversity by the religious majorities and minorities in the respective
countries. On the one hand, a certain degree of solidarity between
minorities can be observed; on the other, the task of the majorities
is perhaps easier as they can rely on greater institutional weight and
support.

It is moreover significant to note that the minorities have, in themselves, due to this fact alone, a specific role that is also theological,
to play. It is no coincidence that the statements with the greatest
inter-religious openness and prospects of dialogue, for example in
the Catholic field, do not come from Rome, and in general from
the religious centres of the respective faiths, but from countries that
are geographically much further away and marginal from the geo-
religious point of view (from India, for example), with declarations,
even of the respective bishops' conferences, and not only of individual theologians, that are much more unbalanced and open. From
the sociological point of view, the explanation appears simple and
immediate: they can only come from there, because it was there that
the Christian churches have for some time been in interaction with
other religions, and above all, they are, in their regard, in a minority or even subordinate position and in any case a relatively recent
presence compared to the religious traditions of those lands. In these
situations, it is impossible not to realise that other religious traditions exist, knowing them is compulsory and by getting to know
them one ends up perhaps by recognising them in a certain way, a
certain value of truth that 'they' may have.

Those in the majority are often unlikely to be sensitive to the
presence of others: whilst the minorities are compelled to know the
majority that can crush them, and that in any case is too awkward
a neighbour not to be observed with care, if not concern. It is no
coincidence, on the contrary, that this is the very situation Islam is
experiencing: it is in Europe, where it is in the minority and subordinate with respect to Christian faiths and with little hope of revers-
ing the situation, that it is forced to elaborate, first in practice and
then in theory, its own theology of minority and plurality and, if
not an orthodoxy, at least an orthopraxis that contemplates it.
Moreover, this has also taken place in other situations, where Islam

is in a minority position: it was an Indian Muslim, resident in Saudi Arabia, who founded the Institute of Muslim Minority Affairs [Fitzgerald, 1998].

The underestimation of the substantial difference that the fact of being the majority or the minority implies is one of the concrete motives for a widespread incomprehension of Islam transplanted into Europe: we interpret it with the categories of the Islam in the countries of origin (one entity with the state and society, strong, in the majority, theologically solid and without comparisons and internal religious challenges), whilst in Europe it is presented through minorities that are unconnected to society and not protected by the state (on the contrary, at times even stigmatised), with weak social roots, without traditional references and confronted with other religious communities that are in the majority, powerful and, despite an official lay status of the state, strongly interwoven with the state institutions of the respective countries.

Last but not least in importance, we cannot ignore an aspect which is not strictly religious at all, but says a lot about why the aspect of the organisation and rendering visible, in religious terms as well, is crucial in European countries, also for minorities. This is the desire of Muslims to take part in the various existing national systems of 'religious welfare' [Dassetto, 2000], from which the other religions already benefit. This is one aspect on which there is less inclination to dwell, compared to the ideal aspects, but it has a fundamental strategic importance, in the orientation of the contents of action in the public space, and not only in its forms.

3. ENCOUNTER AS DIALOGUE

The simultaneous presence of religious subjects is not made of juxtaposed identities, which are impermeable to one another. This can happen and may be the case, especially for some religious groups of the 'sect' type, or which are highly characterised ethnically and/or linguistically, which end up by choosing to be 'encapsulated' in society, at the limit of eschewing it. However, this is not usually the common fate. On the contrary, and all the more so if we refer to religions with a universal vocation or which are characterised by a social presence and visibility, increasingly often moments and situations of contact, encounter and possibly even friction and conflict are created, at times not painlessly: with society, with minority religious subjects and with the majority religions in the respective societies.

This encounter and dialogue cannot be considered as the intellectual hobby of an aware elite; it increasingly appears as a real experience and social practice. The places where dialogue 'happens' are multiplied and come into being 'at the grassroots', in the various dimensions of daily life, to then be reflected 'higher up' as well. Contrary to a common perception, dialogue does not start 'up above' as a first reading of highly media-covered phenomena, such as the prayer meetings of Assisi or those organised by the community of Sant'Egidio, may suggest. On the contrary, these, at the most, symbolise something that imposes itself for reflection because it already exists in reality.

In this regard, it is necessary to introduce at least the distinction between 'localised' social dialogue, anchored in concrete experience, often coming into being from problems and difficulties of co-existence, as well as from the desire for personal knowledge, and fundamental dialogue, which is placed on the level of the fundamentals and principles with regard to the highest systems and the respective 'religious world views', the Weltanschauungen, which tend to be universal and universalising, with in addition a certain dimension of 'religious diplomacy'. Between the two, as between 'local' and 'global' there is continuous tension and interaction: they refer to one another or ought to refer to one another in a virtuous circle (the 'think globally, act locally' of the ecologists applied to religious dynamics). But although interconnected, these two forms of dialogue are not to be confused, because they have different objectives and pass through different procedures.

In both cases, contrary to common use, the word dialogue is often revealed to be more of an aspiration that a reality, and is used in an excessively 'premature' fashion. It is perhaps more honest only to speak of inter-religious meetings, and more generally of inter-religious relations or, as a certain theology of inter-religious relations is beginning to do, of conversations between religions [Dupuis, 1997]. Moreover, even in the Vatican documents (e.g. a fundamental document of inter-religious relations such as the conciliar declaration *Nostra Aetate*) the word 'dialogue' translates the Latin *colloquium*, which evokes a humbler and more daily dimension. And the dimension of dialogue that we can see appearing in the social relations between believers of different religious affiliations is, in the first place, relational and social.

We want to insist on the fact that it is the modifications under way in social reality, which nevertheless have deep consequences on the religious level, that are producing these forms of encounter and confrontation. It is sufficient to think of what the arrival of Islam in Europe, in the wake of the immigrants who have brought it, means: until yesterday, not only was it different, but it was an enemy which was elsewhere; whilst today, with most, including Muslims, being unaware of this, it has become the second religion, or better the principal religious minority in the majority of European countries. A fact of historical importance, of which we are still far from really measuring the consequences: on the social, political and cultural, but also religious and spiritual levels—for Europe, Christianity and even for Islam itself, the 'transplanted' one as well as the Islam of origin. Pluralisation is thus accompanied by a process of redefinition of the 'geo-religious' configuration of Europe.

Moreover, the question does not only concern the Islamic and Christian interlocutor, both plural in their own contexts, that we have mentioned so far. There is also the third of the so-called Abrahamic faiths: Judaism, with which relations are the most difficult and therefore collaboration in the field and amicable positions, to be found here and there in Europe, from Portugal to Great Britain [PT File and UK File], are all the more important. But according to the local situations, it can also involve other interlocutors, as in Great Britain where there are inter-Asian, inter-religious relations, especially between Muslims, Hindus and Sikhs. We will not approach here an analysis of the extensive literature on inter-religious dialogue, probably one of the 'heaviest' from the quantitative point of view, as far as literature on Islam is concerned, despite the fact that real experiences in the field are still relatively few and far between. We will restrict ourselves to noting that it is, by the mere fact of existing, a need that is felt, or at least stated, at least in some circles, and by some religious subjects.

4. Encounter as Repositioning and Conflict

There exists a need to know the other, to relate with the other, without this meaning the desire to really know them, and let alone relating with the other as the other really is. In the religious field, the space occupied by this trend of thought, which is also a very concrete social dynamic, is that of polemics and apologetics. They do not intend intervening with the other, but, so to speak, passing through the other to return to the (collective) subject from which they started, with the objective of reinforcing it, supporting the foundations, shaken by the perception that there is, precisely, the other and therefore there is another different possibility.

As far as this approach can be analysed in terms of identity weakness and often naïve in its formulations, this approach to otherness is nevertheless socially influential and obviously meets a widespread need. There are many examples of this and they are excessively overlooked as far as their importance is concerned: they appear more at the level of popular language than educated language and are perhaps for this reason better measured at the level of oral culture, the medium par excellence, than other media. It is probably for this reason that it is easier to find a trace of them in the qualitative work, by interviews and participatory observation, and possibly in opinion surveys, this in the 'texts' canonically considered as such. And, with regard to the religious specificity, more in Sunday sermons and in the Friday *khutba*, than in the diocesan press and journals or religious bookshops.

However, there is no shortage of examples in these either. A well known example on the Muslim side are the videos and publications by Ahmed Deedat—a prolific populariser of coarse and folksy but, for his public, effective apologetics—very widespread in the English-speaking world but present almost everywhere in Europe. Equally widespread is a discourse, which has deep roots in the founding fathers of Islamic radicalism, which systematically confuses the levels of confrontation, and in particular the wrongdoings of modernity and what are considered its consequences (materialism, moral disorder etc.) which are projected on to Christianity [Lewis P., 2001], and also the naïve or artful use of 'sources' which are not recognised by the other being spoken of, such as the so-called Gospel of Barnabas, which go in an opposite direction to the ABC of inter-religious dialogue, where the aim is for the other to be described as

it would describe itself, or at least so that it can recognise itself in
the descriptions that are given of it [Borrmans, 1981].

The problem is also raised on the Christian side, perhaps more
in the form of confusion of levels as above and in particular in not
recognising the difference between the cognitive level of Islam and
the real situation experienced by Muslims: deducing from a certain
reading of the basics of Islam the behaviour of Muslims, in short.
Moreover, this problem is also raised in the media visibility and academic research. Another classic misunderstanding is that which confronts high and intellectual European thought on Islam, that of the
specialists, and the positions of some European Muslim leaders, almost
never professional intellectuals, but simple activists, on Christianity.
Probably if there were a confrontation between equals, for example
between 'standard' faithful of each religion, regarding their knowledge of one another, things would be interpreted differently.

But a level of explicit polemics is also present. It can be seen in
the recent emergence, in some countries, of more or less official
strongly anti-Muslim positions. This is what has been seen recently
for example in Italy: the Bishop of Como, Maggiolini, has spoken
several times against the invasion of immigrants and the threats they
represent to Italian identity; the words of the Archbishop of Smyrna,
Bernardini, were given wide coverage in the media when, at a synod
in Rome, he maintained that the "Muslim domination in Europe
has already begun", and he is fond of recalling the words of someone he claims was an important Muslim figure, for whom "thanks
to your democratic laws we shall invade you, and thanks to our religious laws, we shall dominate you"; Don Gelmini, a popular 'anti-
drugs priest', at the congress of the National Alliance party (which
represents the right-wing of the Parliamentary political alignment,
today in the government) warned against Muslims who "marry Catholic women to convert them to Islam"; up to the well known positions
of the Cardinal of Bologna, Biffi (already mentioned in the previous
chapter, with reference to the tensions in the public space in Italy)
[Guolo, 2000].

A good example of 'non-dialoguing dialogue' (or anti-dialoguing)
can be found on the Internet, a typical 'non-place' that offers space
to all positions. In the Christian field, there are obviously explanations of the contents of the Christian faith, but also the germs of
debate with Islam and answers to professional Muslim polemicists,
such as the already mentioned A. Deedat, who in turn has his own

site with audio recordings of his lectures, on sites with names such as www.debate.org., www.islamreview.com, www.ApologeticsPress or debate.domini.org, which is also in Arabic. They are all extensively listed in a large site called appropriately http://answering-islam.org. In the Muslim field, we find various sites that are often camouflaged by references to compared religions, in actual fact very polemical and equally apologetic. The calmer ones are often characterised by a certain repetitiveness and uniformity of content.

The general harshness of tones, on both sides, is perhaps fostered by the typical anonymity of the Internet, which in itself removes responsibility and, in the absence of a real flesh and blood interlocutor allows saying what is felt or weighs on the heart, almost like an escape valve where what many think but only a few dare to say is revealed [Gaudeul, 1999].

The web is also terrain for explicit polemical conflict, with direct attacks and forms of boycotting, such as that of the site SuraLikeIt, which reported false Suras constructed, however, credibly, on the Qur'anic model (in 'reply' and challenging the Qur'anic statement and Muslim tradition according to which the Qur'an is also linguistically inimitable). The boycott of AOL (America On Line), the site provider, launched by some Muslim organisations, led to the closure of the site, which however can be found at another address and at another provider, together with a description and examples of the boycott campaign [Bunt, 1999 and 2000; Gaudeul, 1999].

It is interesting to note that 'air battles' are also fought over the radio waves, involving both sides of the Mediterranean. Apart from the non-religious Voice of America, BBC, Radio Méditerranée Internationale (Medi 1), Deutsche Welle and others such as the commercial station Radio Montecarlo-Moyen Orient (RMC-MO), many explicitly religious radios broadcast to Muslim countries, both for the Christian minorities and for missionary purposes. The main ones include the American TWR (Trans World Radio), the most powerful religious radio network in existence (it broadcasts in 100 languages, more than twice those of the BBC or Voice of America) with a base in Connecticut, which thanks to an agreement with RMC-France is broadcasted with considerable power to Muslim countries, AWR (Adventist World Radio), FEBA (Far East Broadcasting Association), which broadcasts from Great Britain to the Middle East as well, the Swedish IBRA and others, all Protestant; in addition naturally to Vatican Radio, a historical presence of the Catholic world in the 'cathodic world' [Naba, 1998]. On the other hand, there are very many Muslim radios that broadcast in Europe. The fundamental difference is that while the Christian radios broadcast in local languages for the Christian minorities, but also with a strong and explicitly missionary purpose, in particular by the Protestant radios, the Muslim radios broadcast in the language of the respective populations who have emigrated to Europe, more with the aim of 'preserving' them from Western contamination and without any missionary attitude. Both have the aim however of consolidating the links between dispersed minorities and the majorities in the respective religious universes; the latter however have a greater concern to maintain transnational community bonds, despite the migration of their populations. Moreover, as they are often, in the case of the Muslim radios, networks connected with governments and reigning families, who fear Islamist contagion on the political level, this further function, which obviously plays into the hands of Western countries as well, must not be overlooked.

5. 'Official' Dialogue

It is necessary to distinguish two different dimensions: that of official dialogue and that of grassroots dialogue, respectively dialogue from above and from below, as it were.

On official dialogue, there is a fairly wide literature, with a self-fuelling tendency, as for the level of media coverage. This is the institutional and symbolic dimension of interreligious dialogue: that of the meeting between official representatives of the religions themselves, as in the paradigmatic example of Assisi since 1986 and the later episodes of meeting and prayer, on the one hand; and on the other that of conferences between specialists and theologians, consisting of official talks with the related papers, articles connecting the intellectuals and we could say professionals, specialised journals and therefore an extensive presence in the debate of ideas.

We can recall some stages of these, beginning from the pre-conditions. In the Catholic church, the fundamental pre-condition was the opening, to the world and to a certain extent to other religions as well, of the Second Vatican Council (1962–1965); during the Council, in 1964, the Secretariat for non-Christians was also created, transformed in 1989 into the Pontifical Council for Interreligious

Dialogue. In the rest of the Christian world, the pre-condition is the foundation of the World Council of Churches (1948), which was to be extended in 1961 to the Orthodox churches; since 1971 a unit for dialogue with the members of other faiths and 'ideologies', which has organised many meetings, including in developing countries, has been active. Following these events of a 'geo-religious' nature, there have been attempts at dialogue at the grassroots, first in Europe which at the time was not yet acquainted with the significant Muslim immigration which was to determine a new 'dialogue reawakening', in the Middle East and in various 'mixed' situations, from Lebanon to Egypt.

The dialogues 'at the summit' follow a rhythm of appointments that are familiar at least to the specialists, which we can summarise briefly [on the pattern of Waardenburg, 1998]. The author under-lines the singular parallel with the need for dialogue that has been felt in politics since the Cold War (which also represented an impe-tus to intensify relations with Muslim countries, from an anti-com-munist point of view), and then, after the 1973 war when, threatened with the oil embargo, Europe activated the 'Euro-Arab dialogue'.

Perhaps the most prestigious 'event' of Muslim-Christian dialogue took place in Tripoli in February 1976, strongly desired by Colonel Khadafi, promoted by *Al-Da'wa al-Islamiyya* and by the Secretariat for non-Christians of the Holy See, and financed by Libya with over one hundred guests. Before this there had already been the meet-ings in Spain, the place of the principal and 'richest' historical encounter of Europe with Islam, in the Arabic *al-Andalus*: three meet-ings, from 1974, in Cordoba, organised by the group Amistad, then the meetings of the Group of Islamic-Christian Study (CRISLAM), the foundation of the *Universidad Islamica Averroes* (Ibn Rushd) in Cordoba and of the Mediterranean University in Granada.

Again in 1974 a Muslim-Christian meeting was held in Tunis, promoted by CERES. Four other meetings were to follow, again organised by CERES and to a great extent financed by the Adenauer Foundation, in 1979, 1982, 1986 and 1991.

Various meetings were also promoted by the Royal Academy of Jordan, from 1984, in Amman, then in Istanbul and elsewhere in Europe: two with the Anglicans, four with the Orthodox and sev-eral others with the Catholic church.

From the 1980s, the number of appointments for dialogue, at least as they had been conceived until then, sharply decreased: due to a lack of financial resources, but also for 'demoralisation' or at least the lack of motivation of many participants [for a reflection from many sides, see for example CRISLAM, 1990]. In addition to reciprocal incomprehension, and the lack of a real desire for dialogue by some of the interlocutors, they were forced to acknowledge, on the one hand, how great the weight of the structures of origin is cumbersome and, on the other, the modest efficacy of these attempts of encounter in fighting 'real' crises in the field: the Israeli-Palestinian conflict, the civil war in Lebanon, the second Gulf War, the conflict between Armenians and Azeris and recently Bosnia, Sudan, Chechnya and many others. To these many problems must be added the growth of fundamentalist movements and intransigent and anti-dialogue forces, in particular in the Muslim world, but also of a widespread anti-Islam-ism at the level of public opinion in Europe and North America [Waardenburg, 1998].

6. Forms of Dialogue: Bodies, Conferences and Journals

The best known forms of this type of dialogue are characterised by a significant degree of an official character and formality: this is what passes through the conferences, the meetings and journals. In the words of those who take part, these forms of encounter have at times the tendency to be self-defining and become *the* dialogue; if not to the exclusion of the others, at least with some form of underestimation of them. To the extent that the others, in the lists of occasions of interreligious dialogue, simply do not exist: the majority of books and articles on interreligious dialogue only mention and comment upon conferences and are reproduced in turn in specialised journals, which in turn quote other articles, conferences and journals, in a production of paper via paper which is, moreover, not exclusive to interreligious dialogue but is typical precisely of the 'academic' approach to the problem.

The interreligious question is also raised in different ways. At European level, the activities of reflection on the presence of Muslim have also been raised, at a certain stage, as reflections starting from the spiritual needs of immigrants, even if not yet with a Muslim specificity. In 1964, for example, the Churches' Committee for Migrant Workers in Europe was founded in Brussels and various other similar bodies in a national context, beginning obviously in countries with a larger immigrant population. Often, in a first stage, these were ecumenical bodies (therefore Christian) which also took on an interreligious dimension and later of real interreligious collaboration [Johnstone & Slomp, 1998].

A not indifferent investment was made in the preparation for Islam-Christian dialogue, with ad hoc initiatives and specific journals, which often are of an importance that extends beyond national borders.

Despite what the word presupposes, many of the 'places' of dialogue are in fact journals, which meet the need for a non-occasional foundation of encounter, of in-depth study of its possible cultural and religious bases, with a longer term vision and not limited to the contingencies of an everyday nature. Amongst the principal ones, we can recall, with a 'transnational' vision, on the Catholic side, the annual journal *Islamochristiana*, of the Pisai of Rome, which has come out since 1975 (the White Fathers, at the origin of the Pisai, also publish the monthly journals *Se Comprendre*, in France, and *Encounter*, in Italy). In the Protestant area, we can find *The Muslim World*, which has been published since 1910 with its editorial office in Hartford, Connecticut, and since 1990 *Islam and Christian-Muslim Relations* published by the CSIC of Birmingham. On the Muslim side, we can mention in particular *Encounters. A journal of intercultural perspectives*, produced by the Islamic Foundation of Leicester, and for certain aspects the *Journal of the Institute of Muslim Minorities Affairs*, which however does not have a specificity of dialogue.

Several countries have their own journals devoted specifically to the Muslim-Christian dialogue. *Begrip Moslims-Christenen* is published in the Netherlands, also penetrating Belgium [NL File and BE File]. The experiment got under way in the mid-1970s on the initiative of a White Father, who was joined in 1979 by two representatives of the main Dutch Reformed faiths. In Germany *Cibedo* (Christlich-islamische Begegnung und Dokumentationsleitstelle) is published by the eponymous German documentation centre, which is the body on the subject of the German Bishops' Conference [DE File]. In France, the *Bulletin* of the SRI (Secretariat for relations with Islam) is published, again the relevant body of the French Bishops' Conference [FR File]. In Spain, the most important journal is *Encuentro Islamo-Cristiano*, directed by the White Father Emilio Galindo, and published in Madrid since 1973 under the patronage of the Episcopal Commission for Interfaith Relations [ES File]. Newsletters on the subject, with a variable periodicity, are published by various local and diocesan bodies involved in dialogue or, more frequently, in the formation for dialogue or at least knowledge of the other. These are bodies which are not a direct and 'official' emanation of the respective churches, at national level, but at times which have a more extensive function of connection than the local one. This is the case of, for example, of *Il dialogo/Al-Hiwar*, from the Peirone Centre of Turin [IT File].

Apart from journals, there are important training and documentation centres which are also stable bodies of confrontation, encounter and cultural activities. We can mention at least the Pontifical Institute for Arabic and Islamic Studies, a body with a certain official character (almost all the experts and delegates for Islam on the Pontifical Council for Interreligious Dialogue come from its ranks) and the Centre for the Study of Islam and Christian-Muslim Relations in Birmingham, founded in 1975. Some of these bodies (as also for example, the Centre for Muslim-Christian Understanding of Washington's Georgetown University), as well as various academic centres, in particular orientalist ones (from Oxford to Bologna), receive conspicuous funding from foundations or bodies in Arab Muslim countries and Saudi Arabia in particular in support of the centres or their individual initiatives. A fact that, after all, is in itself a way of forming relations and producing cultural influence: incidentally, this influence does not necessarily go only in the same direction as the funding, but, on the contrary, often goes in the opposite direction.

Amongst the *ad hoc* transnational groups we can mention that of the *Journées d'Arras*, from the place where these meetings were held for the first time in 1979. These meetings have the important characteristics, as they do not have to produce and do not want to produce documents or conference proceedings, of allowing non-stop discussion amongst the participants, which can allow the frankness of the debate to make considerable progress [Nielsen, 1995]. The GRIC, Islamic-Christian Research Group is a group of specialists that meets to examine in depth issues of common interest, from the theological and spiritual point of view. Created in 1977, with four working groups based in Paris, Brussels, Tunis and Rabat, its publications so far include four volumes translated into various languages: *Ces Ecritures qui nous questionnent*, 1987, *Foi et Justice*, 1993, *Pluralisme et laïcité. Chrétiens et musulmans proposent*, 1996, and *Péché et responsabilité éthique dans le monde contemporain*, 2000 [for a Catholic analysis of these initiatives, Teissier, 2000].

Both the Catholic church and the World Council of Churches have created their own instruments of relations with Islam and also at European level both Catholics and the WCC have their own specific committees. An Islam in Europe Committee was established jointly by the Council of European Bishops' Conferences (CCEE), a European body of the Catholic church and by the Conference of European churches (CEC).

7. Aspects of the 'Grassroots' Dialogue: Experiences in the Field

After having dwelt on the 'official' and intellectual dimension of dialogue, it is interesting for us to look at the second dimension in greater depth, which receives less attention from the media and is less intellectualised, but more practised in the field. The actors of this type of religious interrelation, at times, are not qualified explicitly or primarily as religious players, or at least their interest is not aimed at an interrelation between religions or a dialogue between these—a concept that has in itself a high degree of abstraction—but a more concrete interrelation, and dialogue between men and women who are also religious: an activity where the religious dimension is not necessarily the centre or the focus of attention. They certainly have behind them less theological reflection than the actors analysed in the previous paragraph, but they have a greater inclination towards concrete action.

It is clear that these two dimensions do not exclude each other, but on the contrary they are mutually supporting. An effective desire for dialogue by the top ranks can foster grassroots initiatives, starting off from minor practical problems which are those on which the relational level is played, for example in work with immigrants. Inversely, if there is some 'stop' that comes from above on the general criteria of dialogue (especially in the more hierarchical bodies, such as the Catholic church, perhaps from an authoritative bishop), it is reasonable to hypothesise that some grassroots initiatives will have to adjust or they will come up against greater obstacles and misunderstandings (consequences have been seen in Italy after the declarations of Cardinal Biffi quoted above).

Even before the specific initiatives aimed at promoting interreligious relations, there are social dynamics that move by themselves and that are not and do not want to be interreligious, let alone forms of dialogue but which simply imply a position and a use of religious plurality and therefore, from the sociological point of view, its acceptance. The case of the kosher restaurants in Belleville comes to mind, which employ Muslims so that they can stay open for the Sabbath [Simon, 1995], a practice which is common in many other countries with a marked religious plurality: a good example of accommodation to interreligious reality, purely instrumental and not at all rooted in a 'finalising' will, let alone eschatological, and yet not devoid of significant consequences, even in the long term.

To remain on the subject, collaboration may even be strictly religious, although still instrumental, that is, related to a concrete problem. This is the fairly common case of *halal* food and ritual slaughtering which was provided for, in many places before Muslims could provide for themselves, by Jews. At times the relationship consisted simply of using kosher butchers for their own needs, as did Roman Muslims who bought their meat in the shops in the Jewish ghetto [Allievi & Dassetto, 1993], as has happened in several European cities. On other occasions, thanks also to the personal friendship between the leaders of the respective communities, as in the Portuguese case, it was able to become concrete when the Jews offered their facilities to the Muslims or the rabbi of Lisbon arranged directly for slaughtering on behalf of the Muslims [Tiesler, 2000]. The example of food can be extended to many different examples, including the fact that *halal* butchers are also frequented by non-Muslims, natives, who, for reasons that are not religious, nevertheless prefer meat from animals that have been slaughtered in the Muslim way. The same can be said of some restaurants run by Muslims who, implicitly, by using *halal* food and refusing to serve alcohol, actually also offer a religious view, sometimes made explicit by the availability of religious material, for consultation or on sale: books, journals, music and religious objects.

'Structural' factors linked to immigration can have importance in the dialogic attitude of religious subjects. The fact, for example, that in Great Britain the churches themselves are multiethnic probably fosters greater openness and a certain habit towards otherness [Lewis P., personal interview, May 2000]. In this case, moreover, the presence of a minority Catholic world has played in favour of its greater openness towards Islam: by means of concrete practices such as the acceptance of Muslim girls in Catholic schools, preferred by Muslim parents because they are single sex (a practice which we also find in other countries such as France and Belgium, etc.), but also fostering the desire by Muslims to open their own schools with declarations expressing their openness, with the motivation that for Catholics too separate schools are the forerunners of integration and not of divisiveness [Lewis P., 1997].

Another level is that related to the places of worship, on which there have been several experiences and also polemics of making available, for the religious needs of Muslims, their own premises appointed for Christian worship and discussion within the various religious faiths has at times been heated. There has been less analysis of the reciprocal imagination on these facts, as in the case of the churches sold to other religious faiths, in the Netherlands and in Great Britain and elsewhere, and the symbolic implications that these facts may have, for example, on the Muslim perception of them and on the opinions matured on religious subjects involved.

Below we will dedicate some space to some examples of social relational, if not dialogic, practice. We give these examples without any presumption of completeness, but as signs and indicators of the most widespread trends and social practices.

A relatively interventionist role of the state can be found in different situations. The institutions can also play an active role, if only on a symbolic level. In the British case, for example, an invitation for collaboration and a sign of interest came from the Royal Family, which also plays an 'educational' role of the religious type, as the Queen is the Head of the Church of England. If the declarations by Prince Charles, saying that he wanted to be known as the Defender of Faiths and not of the Faith (one of the monarch's titles is precisely that of *fidei defensor*), in the event of his ascent to the throne, caused an outcry, his interventions at two conferences, in Oxford in 1993 and in Wilton Park in 1996, where he invited "building bridges between Islam and the West" are known and used in the circles referring to interreligious collaboration. What also caused greater surprise, giving rise to lively dialogue and wide criticism was his invitation to learn from Islam that 'sense of the sacred' that it has maintained to a greater extent, possible through a greater presence of Muslim teachers in schools [HRH Prince of Wales, 1998]. Prince Charles has also visited, giving it implicit recognition, the Islamiyya School of London, founded and directed by Yusuf Islam, the former Cat Stevens, in a period of discussion on the opportunity to finance Muslim schools in the same way as other religious schools in the country. The forms of collaboration of religious exponents at a political-representative level are also an expression of this essentially positive climate, as Muslim Lords and Bishop Lords can meet in the same *political* institution: the House of Lords.

Experiences such as that of the Interfaith Network, are of a different nature and characterised by action, which in Great Britain exist on both national and local bases [UK File]. This national body, independent and not financed by state authorities, was established in 1987 and includes the nine main religions of the country (Baha'is, Buddhists, Christians in the various denominations, Hindus, Jains, Jews, Muslims, Sikhs and Zoroastrians, for a total of more than 80 bodies, who have signed the common document *Building Good Relations with People of Different Faiths and Beliefs*). It has a leadership by rotation with a dual presence which always includes a Christian and a member of a non-Christian religion. It promotes studies, in-depth research and meetings and tries to collaborate in solving concrete problems that can be common to various faiths (for example, the availability of prayer halls or documents such as *Religions in the UK. A Multi-Faith Directory* [Inter Faith Network, 1997], in collaboration with the University of Derby, and a *Local Inter-faith Guide* in 1999: instruments which in themselves attest to a climate and a potentiality, if not a habit of interreligious collaboration (see www.multifaithnetorg.net). The Interfaith Network is also part of various commissions at government and local council level. The main government instrument of involvement of the religious communities on the social level is the Inner Cities Religious Council, chaired by the Minister for the Environment, Transport and Regions, with the presence of the five main religious faiths (Hindus, Jews, Muslims, Sikhs and Christians, including a large presence of black Christians). It also promotes the project *Involving Communities in Urban and Rural Regeneration* [from The Local Interfaith Guide, 1999].

It is interesting to underline the practical effect of this type of network, present in less structured forms in other countries as well, not only for the habit of plurality and acceptance of other points of view, but also for the role that they offer to minority groups, putting them psychologically on the same level as the majority groups, and basically offering minorities opportunities of confrontation between themselves, which they perhaps do not find elsewhere. They also represent the means to access relational resources with regard to the media and policy makers, normally more easily accessible only to groups that have greater relational capital. And lastly, they represent, ordinarily but significantly, the means to create in each participant a capital of references, names, telephone numbers to use at a time of need and possibly of confrontation or conflict between a single religious community and the state or other sectors of the population. Especially at local level, these networks can allow a sufficient level of social and institutional trust to be maintained and make a concrete contribution to relieving the more serious tensions at times of social confrontation. An example of this function was in the meeting of a group of women of the Interfaith Network on the occasion of the problems in Bradford in 1995 [Runnymede Trust, 1997].

Examples of relations of collaboration between members of different religions and, an element that precedes or accompanies these, of reflection in the religions on the presence of other religious communities, can be found in earlier years. The British Council of Churches, for example, created an advisory group of the presence of Islam in Great Britain back in the early 1970s, under the guidance of the Bishop of Guildford. In 1976, the group published *A New Threshold: Guidelines for the churches in their Relations with Muslim Communities.* The Standing Conference of Jews, Christians and Muslims in Europe was founded in 1976. The Calamus Foundation, established by a group of Muslims in 1989, promotes dialogue amongst the followers of the three Abrahamic faiths. The Maimonides Foundation is attentive to Jewish-Muslim relations, with special attention to the consequences of the Israeli-Palestinian conflict on these relations [Runnymede Trust, 1997]. The Runnymede Trust itself, although not having explicit religious aims, can be considered an example of this collaboration: the foundation that promoted the *Islamophobia Report* has in fact behind it capital from liberal Jewish circles [K. Amin, personal interview, May 2000].

We can also recall that each year the Islam Awareness Week takes place on Muslim initiative [Lewis P., 2001] and which in a similar form also takes place in Germany. On this occasion, the mosques are open to the non-Muslim public, with initiatives involving the population, especially on a local level.

In France, Muslim-Christian dialogue is in fact mainly Muslim-Catholic, even if the Federation of French Protestants created a church-Islam Commission some years ago, under the organisational lead of a pastor of Algerian origin [Bencheikh, 1998]. In France the SRI (Secretariat for Relations with Islam) was established in 1973 and the first secretary was a White Father (similarly the White Fathers were the promoters of initiatives of dialogue in other countries, from Belgium to Spain and from Italy to the Netherlands [Nielsen, 1995]. In addition to some local groups, at least three national associations are to be mentioned which have a specific dialogical perspective: the *Association de Dialogue Islamo-Chrétien* (ADIC), which brings together diplomats and eminent religious leaders; the *Groupe d'Amitié Islamo-Chrétienne* (GAIC), which has its origin in a scission of the previous one and regularly organises conferences and publishes various types of material: and the *Fraternité d'Abraham*, a more discreet group that has the important characteristic of involving members of all three Abrahamic monotheistic faiths [FR File].

We can also recall the experience of the programme *Vivre l'islam* on France 2. Or rather, we can quote its container as an example, although 'passive', of dialogue as all the religious programmes are on a Sunday morning, one after the other and there are people who watch more than one, and not only 'their own'. In addition, once a year there is an 'interreligious' programme, almost a form of television dialogue from above.

As elsewhere, there is not a single 'line' in relations with Islam, and it is possible to find diversified positions within the Christian world. Thus, whilst in the French region of Bretagne some Catholics celebrate the feast of the seven sleepers (a common episode, with some variations, to the Bible and the Qur'an) together with Muslims in Vieux-Marché, in Versailles the pastoral council of the parish of St. Elizabeth, against the opinion of the local priest, became mobilised against the project of a Muslim prayer hall [de Galembert, 1998]. In France, moreover, at least in the past—unlike in Germany, for example—there has been a certain Catholic mobilisation in favour of places of worship for Muslims, even if this drive seems to have lost its intensity today [de Galembert, 1994]. Some groups also involve an initiative by the local authorities, as in the case of the association Marseille Espérance, created on the initiative of the local council, which groups together representatives of the city and religious leaders from the various communities in the area, and sometimes secular members, producing thematic debates and an interreligious calendar [FR File]. Sometimes the promotion of forms of dialogue from above comes about at critical times: an example of this was the decision of the council of Maubeuge to establish a council of faiths, with Catholic, Protestant and Muslim representatives following the Gulf War [de Galembert, 1998]. Forms of dialogue with Islam on a government scale are discussed in another chapter of this report.

In Belgium there exist both Catholic and Protestant bodies for relations and dialogue with Islam, with debates that only exceptionally affect the 'grassroots'. A more structured example is that of the *El Kalima* Centre in Brussels, which can claim about twenty years of activity, with groups of reflection on topics ranging from circumcision to Ramadan or the respective forms of prayer. An example of local encounter is that of Cheratte, in the region of Liège, where there have been meetings both at the mosque and at Banneux, where the Virgin Mary is believed to have appeared, for about twelve years now [BE File].

In the Netherlands, a country where the churches, both Protestant and Catholic, were amongst the first to take ecumenism and interreligious dialogue seriously, the examples of collaboration, even on a local scale, are not lacking and often the grassroots dialogue is implicit in the social and cultural processes, through various forms of sharing. We can mention as a more atypical and in a certain sense 'extreme' example the attempt, in order to overcome the ambiguity of the Muslim presence in Christian schools (where sometimes it was compulsory for the pupils to attend the religious education lesson on Christianity or in other schools there were courses on Islam but perhaps held by Christian teachers), to form 'schools of encounter', involving Muslim and Hindu parents, where some imams were authorised to give lessons on Islam. These schools were later expelled from the Union of Christian Schools and many Christian parents took their children out of them [Shadid & van Koningsveld, 1994]. Both the main denominations present in the country, namely the Catholic church and the Netherlands Reformed church, have their own departments for dialogue with Muslims [NL File].

In Luxembourg the International Association for Dialogue between Christians, Jews and Muslims was founded in 1993 and from this a foundation with the same name which has amongst its sponsors the rector of the Muslim Institute of Paris, the Chief Rabbi of the Grand Duchy and the former President of the Chamber of Deputies. In 1992 a body called *Agir* (from *Action Groupe Inter-religions*) was set up, on the initiative of the Christian organisations ACAT, Pax Christi and Sesopi (Service Socio-pastoral Intercommunautaire), which involves the various Christian communities (Catholic, Greek Orthodox,

Protestant, Anglican and Adventist) as well as the Muslim, Jewish, Baha'is and Buddhist communities, in annual meetings of prayer and reflection [LU File].

In Germany, in 1974, the same year that at a national level, for the first time, a body was established for relations with non-Christians (*Ökumenische Kontaktstelle für Nichtchristen*), the archdiocese of Cologne founded the Cibedo (*Christlich-islamische Begegnung und Dokumentations-leitstelle*), which was then moved to Frankfurt and became a department of the German Bishops' Conference in the early 1990s. Here, there is relatively less mobilisation, compared to France for example, in favour of Muslim places of worship, by Christian exponents, and rarely have churches been granted for this purpose, even if as early as 1965 the then Archbishop of Cologne lent the cathedral to local Muslims to celebrate the end of Ramadan, explicitly as a sign of reconciliation of the memory, precisely where eight centuries earlier Bernard of Clairvaux had preached the Crusades [de Galembert, 1994]. However, it has to be said that in this country there seems to be less need, as on the one hand, the Muslims are better organised and on the other the public authorities are more open: with the result that Germany is the country with the largest number of 'visible' mosques in Europe (see the chapter on relations and negotiations in the public space).

We can mention one particularly demanding initiative, promoted in Rheinland Pfalz and Nordrhein-Westfalen: here, at the Protestant Pastoral-Kolleg, about 30–40 imams (mostly members of the Turkish and official DITIB, the organisation with the greatest presence in the country) meet with a group of pastors to discuss theological questions for a whole week. The majority of Muslim organisations have activated interreligious meetings and conferences. One of the first was Imam Mehdi Razvi, at the Hamburg-based Shiite organisation (we can recall that Germany is the main Shiite organisational centre in Europe). The majority of the Protestant churches has a delegate for relations with Islam (Islambeauftragte/r). Amongst the initiatives, the following can be mentioned: the CIG (*Christlich-Islamische Gesellschaft*), the GCIB (*Gesellschaft für Christliche Islamische Begegnung*), and the 'trilateral' JCM (*Ständige Europäische Konferenz der Juden, Christen und Muslime*) [DE File]. However, we can also find contradictory opinions and actions within the Christian world, as in the Muslim one, with respect to relations with other religions. Thus, whilst in Pforzheim Catholics and Protestants jointly collected DM 4000 to offer an Ottoman-style lamp to the newly-built mosque, a fundamentalist Protestant group derided the initiative distributing defamatory leaflets on Islam [de Galembert, 1998].

In Austria an official initiative of interreligious dialogue is that represented by the Africa-Asian Institute (AAI), promoted by the Catholic church in Vienna in 1959 and today also present in Graz and Salzburg. In 1990 the Austrian Bishops' Conference promoted the *Kontaktstelle für Weltreligionen* (KWR), with branches in various towns, where material on Islam is at the disposal of priests, teachers and students and lectures, meetings and training are organised as well as aid for refugees, intercultural parties etc. The institute of Religionstheologie of the St. Gabriel Theological School of Mödling, near Vienna, organised an international Muslim-Christian conference in 1993 [AT File].

Switzerland would appear to be at an advantage in interreligious relations aiming at uprooting minorities, due to the fact that it does not have a colonial history and is not built on a strong centralised base [Haenni, 1994]. In actual fact, as we have seen in the chapter on tension in the public space, the situation is no different from that in other countries. On a federal level there exists the IRAS (*Interreligiöse Arbeitsgemeinschaft in der Schweiz* or *Communauté de travail interreligieuse en Suisse*), which deals with the criteria of admittance to the country of religious personnel, now limited by a new law which effectively prevents many religious communities from having support [CH File]. Another type of semi-institutional interreligious collaboration can be exemplified with the case already mentioned of Berne, where a discussion with no outcome on the construction of a Muslim cemetery, looked in the end for support from an institution for dialogue, the Gemeinschaft von Christen und Muslime in der Schweiz. A body for dialogue also exists in Zurich, the *Zürcher Forum der Religionen* [Mahnig, 2000a].

In Northern Europe we can find various examples of confrontation and dialogue. In the Danish capital of Copenhagen, there is the *Islamisk-Kristen Studiecentre* [DK File]. In Sweden, the most important forum is the Dialoggruppen, in Stockholm, but there have been meetings in various other minor towns as well [SE File]. In Finland there has been a body of the Lutheran church for dialogue with Islam since 1996 and there is a semi-official working group that involves Lutherans and Muslims from the Tatar minority as well as immigrants and converts. The work by the Lutheran church with immigrants also includes organising summer camps for young Muslims [FI File]. In 1996, a representative structure of the various religious communities was also set up in Norway, the Coordination Committee for Faith and Life Stance Communities, which includes the Lutheran statly church, other churches, Muslims, Jews, Buddhists, Ba'hais and Hindus as well as the humanist federation and a so-called Alternative Network (which includes, roughly speaking, the world of new age). In 2000 dialogue work on a large scale was carried out throughout the country under its aegis. The initiatives for dialogue are often funded by the state [Leirvik, 2001].

In Italy there has been a sort of de facto superimposition between the bodies of the Italian Bishops' Conference and those of the Vatican, in this specific case the Pontifical Council for Interreligious Dialogue. This means that in fact, above all in the early years of the Muslim presence, it was the PISAI, the Pontifical Institute for Arabic and Islamic Studies, the think tank founded by the White Fathers, and the aforementioned Vatican Pontifical Council, that carried out the training role of the Italian Catholic church [Allievi & Dassetto, 1993; Schmidt di Friedberg & Borrmans, 1993]. Therefore, to date the Italian Bishops' Conference has not been very active, although it has appointed a person with responsibility for Islam. The PISAI represents the main documentation centre on the Muslim world in the country and also publishes the multilingual annual journal *Islamochristiana*, which in 2000 reached its twentieth issue; however, this has a supranational dimension and does not have a particular interest in the Italian situation. There are some diocesan centres (Milan with the CADR, Centro ambrosiano di documentazione sulle religioni, and Turin with the Centro Peirone) of local importance, and the initiatives by some dioceses for knowledge of Islam (for example Venice, with a major conference in 2000). It is therefore amongst the religious movements, rather than in the 'institutional church' (which, besides, through some of its exponents, has recently more frequently taken positions 'against' rather than in favour of Islam; cf. the chapter on relations and negotiations in the public space), that the greatest activity is to be found, in particular by Caritas, the most active organisation in the reception of immigrants. The Community of Sant'Egidio also has activities of relations with Islam, as does the movement of the Focolari, and the SAE (Secretariat for ecumenical activities) has also made an attempt to include it in its horizons. The Waldensian church, despite its small dimensions, has organised meetings and political initiatives, linked to the Italian specificity which sees minority religions (and only some of these: Islam not yet) enjoy a specific legal status, that of agreements with the state, whilst the Catholic church enjoys a privileged treatment guaranteed by the Concordat [IT File]. The most important and continuative experience of Muslim-Christian dialogue existing today is that represented by the Christian-Muslim Encounters of Modena, which have taken place since 1995 and which have the significant characteristic of being promoted by secular figures from both worlds (and, as far as the Christian world is concerned, a very rare event in Italy, not only Catholics), released from 'obediences' which would have made the work very difficult, due to the impulse of a Christian but secularly oriented organisation (ACLI, Association of Italian Christian Workers), which allows a very close dialogue, devoted each year to a specific social issue [the places of dialogue, the school, children, the religious presence in cities, the mass media, women etc.; cf. at least Siggillino 1999; 2000a and 2000b], with a deliberate exclusion of specifically theological topics.

In Spain, there is a past, that of *al-Andalus*, to be re-read and to which reference can be made, which at one and the same time is a reason of glory for the Muslims and an important part of the history of all Spaniards and perhaps this has led to greater attention to this aspect [Galindo & Alonso, 1996]. This also causes the interest of the Arab world, for which this past is also a reason for pride and therefore it is more interested here than elsewhere in intervening and 'investing', despite the currently relatively contained Muslim presence. The Spanish Bishops' Conference created a Commission of Interfaith Relations in 1966 and in 1968 some Muslim and Christian personalities founded the Association for Muslim-Christian Friendship in Madrid which organised two major meetings in Cordoba in 1974 and 1977, whilst the Darek-Nyumba association has existed, again in Madrid, since 1973 and publishes the journal *Encuentro*. The *Bait al-Thaqafa Association* has operated in Catalonia since 1974 whilst more recent initiatives have promoted the Joan Maragall Foundation and the Ecumenical Centre of Catalonia [ES File]. On the twelfth centenary of the mosque of Cordoba, in 1986, an Encuentro Islamo-Cristiano was organised by the Episcopal Commission, in collaboration with the Islamic Centre of Spain.

The Portuguese example of dialogue between minorities is also interesting, represented by the Alliance of non-Christian faiths and

promoted by the Jewish and Muslim communities, with their own
platform of requests concerning weekly holidays and their possible
observance (Saturday for the former, Friday for the latter), the formal acceptance of ritual slaughtering which in practice already exists,
as we have seen, religious food in schools, hospitals etc. In 1996, on
the occasion of the debate on a new law of religious freedom, the
government invited the minorities, including the Muslims, to give
their opinion on the matter [PT File].

In countries where the Muslim presence is considered more an
'ethnic' than a religious problem, the situation is different: on the
one hand, the relations with state bodies is more frequent; on the
other, perhaps, those with the majority religious faiths are less frequent and in a certain sense less necessary, also given the fact that
these majorities are sometimes not very interested in closer relations.

In Greece, there are forms of debate, but informal, between the
Orthodox and Muslims (Turks): but nothing that involves, for example, the Muslim Albanian immigrants [GR File]. There are however
moments of tension, due to the opposition, by members of the
Orthodox church, to the building of the Islamic Centre of Athens
but also, occasionally, the building of new mosques in the Muslim
areas of Thrace [Antoniou, 2000; cf. the paragraph on mosques in
the chapter on the relations and negotiations in the public space].

In Bulgaria some forms of encounter have been organised but
above all at the academic and scientific level [BG File]. In actual
fact, here as in other countries where there are Muslim minorities
in a Christian context (in this case Orthodox), interreligious relations
are measured above all at an everyday level, in the experience of
the family, the neighbourhood and community, as in the reciprocal
invitations and exchanges on the religious festivals of the two communities, and the reciprocal participation, with the physical presence
and the exchange of gifts, for example, of rites of passage [Zhelyazkova,
Kepel & Nielsen, 1995]. However, this country is still paying, at
least in part, for the effects of the policy of forced de-Turkification
conducted in the last period of communist rule: in 1989 more than
369,000 people had to leave Bulgaria for Turkey, in the largest population shift in such a short time from one Socialist country to a
non-Socialist one [Küçükcan, 1999]. Of these, less than half (about
154,000) were to return after the fall of the communist regime.
Incidentally, we can recall that due to this exodus, Bulgaria was to
lose more than 10% of its active population, which was to repre-

sent a fatal blow for the country's economy: many firms closed, the countryside found itself deserted and the government was forced to launch a civil mobilisation in times of peace, sending the population to the country for forced labour. When President Zhivkov was deposed, in November 1989, one of the first decisions taken by the new government was to revoke the laws on assimilation [Ragaru, 2001]. On the political level the process of 'pacification' can be considered confirmed by the entry of the main party of the Turkish-speaking minority into the coalition supporting the former King Simeon II, in 2001: a fact that can also represent a sign of the improvement in relations between the respective religious communities.

There are no particular activities of dialogue in Romania either, or of interreligious relations, apart from the contacts, but at state level, with the Secretary of State for Faiths and the Department for Minorities [RO File]. However, there is also a political presence in Parliament of Muslim minorities [cf. the chapter on Islam and politics]. The absence of significant actions of dialogue and interreligious collaboration in the East European countries, whilst bearing in mind that these are communities of a different ethnic group and language, may appear paradoxical, given their presence dating back several centuries. And this leads us to put forward the cautious reflection that in a certain sense it is replaced by a political presence and visibility, on the one hand, and by daily contact, at a literally anthropological level, on the other. In a certain sense, if there are both, as in Bulgaria and Romania, the explicit interreligious relationship becomes less necessary and urgent. It is however possible and probable that this trend also has to do with the general policy of the Orthodox churches, and with their strict self-identification with the state and the nation, which could lead to not wanting and not soliciting relations with a minority such as that of the Muslims, perceived as extraneous to the nation, if not to the state (as we have seen, the Muslims can relate to the state thanks to their political presence as a minority). We can also note that the arrival of new immigrants can upset the inter-Muslim ethnic balance: in Bucharest, for example, the recent Muslim immigrants are considerably more numerous than the original ethnic components [Lederer, 1996], and have little in common with these populations, creating problems of intra-Muslim comprehension on very different ways of being Muslims but also dynamics that can affect the interreligious and political balances achieved.

In Hungary, where the Muslim presence is far smaller compared to countries such as Bulgaria and Romania, the initiatives for dialogue have increased in recent years but are still modest in number [HU File]. In Poland, some encounters have been organised since the 1980s [Sakowicz, 1997], but without any notable consequences. There is however a Common Council of Catholics and Muslims (*Rada Wspolna Katolikow i Muzulmanow*), which was established in 1997, with only the presence of Tatar Muslims [PL File].

In addition to the situation in these countries there is that of the Balkans, where the current state of interreligious relations is heavily marked by the past and current conflicts in Bosnia, Kosovo and Macedonia. The level of support and complicity that the respective majority religious representations in a specific area have given and continue to give to the respective governments inevitably plays an important role as does the level of intellectual and religious legitimisation that they have provided and provide to nationalist policies. In these countries some modest but symbolically significant sign of practical collaboration, is given through those organisms and NGOs of religious inspiration, especially from Western Europe, which promote forms of reconstruction and training that involve the various the majority and minority religious communities present in a given area.

For these religious subjects, as for others moreover, the city of Sarajevo has become a symbol of the necessity to resume a real process of interrelation and collaboration between religions. It is no coincidence that it was chosen to host the conference on the topic *"Christians and Muslims in Europe: responsibility and religious commitment in the pluralist society"*, in September 2001, organised jointly by the Council of Episcopal Conferences of Europe (CCEE) and the Conference of European churches (CEC), where Christian and Muslim representatives were present.

8. The Push from Above: The Role of the European Commission

After having analysed the situation of interreligious relations in the various countries, it is of use to analyse an example of dialogue from above, which in a certain sense is atypical and not promoted by religious requests, but with declared purposes of fostering intercommunication between the religions present in Europe.

The treaties that established the European Community and the European Union do not refer to churches or to religions [Jansen T., 2000]. A Europe created, by force of circumstances and political farsightedness, on bases of another kind, above all economic, could not be founded on an element that had, besides, been at the origin of a long sequence of conflicts within and outside Europe; and Europe, as it was then imagined and as a survivor of a world war that had lacerated it and destroyed it, wanted, on the other hand, to help quell such conflict. In addition, the Union does not have an explicit mandate to deal with religious questions. However, Europe was also trying to give itself or rediscover a soul as it has been said when launching initiatives in this direction: *giving Europe a soul* was precisely one part of the cultural project that has been launched in recent years.

More than this, as already noted, churches and religious communities are becoming important partners at various levels of the Union. Owing to the influence they have on civil society, non-governmental organisations and voluntary work, which to a significant extent control or contribute to orienting, and which has such a large part, or at least it is said to have, in the construction of a Europe that can also be social and 'civil'. And because they try to give a soul to Europe which, if it has one, risks losing it if it remains—the paradox here is only verbal—a consortium of interests in conflict and an arena for the conflict between state and economic lobbies.

For this reason, the European Commission, especially under the impetus of the Delors and then Santer presidencies, started up relations with the Christian churches and other religious communities. As early as 1991, President Delors invited church representatives to an informal meeting in Brussels. And in December 1994 for the first time these meetings were also attended by Muslims. The Forward Studies Unit (or Cellule de prospective), depending directly on the Presidency, was the agency appointed for this dialogue, meeting ecclesiastical and religious representatives, organising meetings and seminars of dialogue, promoting initiatives of reciprocal knowledge and financing, atypically with respect to the common European dynamics, projects on a religious and spiritual basis, including the Conference of Toledo [European Commission, 1998], which was also attended by Muslim academics, all from outside Europe. President Santer, through the activity of the Forward Studies Unit, then promoted some meetings of reflection on Islam with experts and social actors in 1999, from which the need emerged for greater knowledge of the problem (and of which this research is one of the results). This is one item on the budget, of course, which is not funded like others; with a symbolic importance that is not only greater than in the past, but also subject to discussion.

One of the reasons of European interest, however, more than a general return of religion to the social, symbolic and media and perhaps political scene, on the situation of which the debate is still open, is due to the increasing presence of religions 'other' than those traditionally present in Europe, as we have already highlighted. In addition, these religions are, in some cases, linked to geopolitical worlds that are outside the borders of the European Union but which have important relations with it.

These presences are increasingly making their effects seen in an increasing number of contexts that are anything but religious, as we have seen in this report: the family, welfare, the school, politics, the economy and more in general the role and above all the 'weight' of the religious variable in the public space, where they seem to reintroduce visibility and, at times, conflict. This is, therefore, something that absolutely has to do with the process of European unification and its cohesion, all the more so in a phase of enlargement which will see the European religious landscape change again and in a significant way with the massive entry of Orthodoxy into the western European religious field, less similar to the other Christian 'cousins' that to date have formed the majority, and also, of Islam: both through incorporation, through the Muslim minorities which are anything but new in those countries, from which there could be something to learn in terms of coping with religious plurality and of the Muslim component in particular, and through further immigration and an increase of the Muslim component, which is taking root through the passage from the situation of the first immigrants to that of second, third and now in some cases even fourth generations. *Giving Europe a soul* today also means looking after its Muslim soul.

9. INTRA-MUSLIM DYNAMICS

The plural Muslim presence in Europe also has effects on the Muslim communities themselves. After all, here in Europe, far more than in the countries of origin which is far more 'monocultural', the Muslim *Umma* can recognise itself as such: in its great plurality of contributions, customs, languages, behaviour and ways of living and experiencing religion; in its desire and also in its celebration of its unity (probably only in Mecca, on the occasion of the *hajj*—but there it is a question of an extraordinary and temporary event, not of everyday living—can a Muslim recognise both these aspects of unity and multiplicity in such a visible way); and in its internal division, in its fragility and in its partiality.

There are no studies that specifically examine these aspects in depth. Attention to date has been turned essentially to relations between Muslim minorities and the countries of insertion and they have still not addressed the intra-Muslim dynamics that this plural presence entails and to an even lesser extent the existence of mechanisms of dialogue between these varied and differentiated contributions. We will therefore restrict ourselves to raising some aspects.

A first problem is that of the internal relations between the various 'faiths' of Islam: for example, to mention the best known, between Sunnites and Shiites. In some cases, collaboration exists but mainly reciprocal indifference is sovereign. And the Christian bodies of dialogue are mainly interested only in the majority Sunnite group.

Equally, the divisions of political and ideological formulation can influence the dialogic attitude of the various groups. In France, for instance, whereas one of the Muslim organisations, the FNMF, is not interested in relations with churches, the UOIF has relations with the SRI and, an example which is still fairly rare in Europe, hosts courses on Christianity held by a Benedictine monk in one of its training centres [Delorme, 1995]. And of a different formulation, according to the positions of origin but also depending on the context, is Muslim political writing marked by dialogue: we can quote, for example, the names of Muhammed Salim Abdullah in Germany, Ataullah Siddiqui in the United Kingdom and Tareq Ramadan in the French-speaking world.

A rather interesting dynamic to observe will be that of the relation between the national 'historical' Muslim minorities of the countries that have one, especially in Eastern Europe (and also of the more recent ones but with citizenship), and the new immigrants. On the one hand we have 'European' minorities, nationals of their respective countries, with a tradition of centuries-old co-existence, with little or nothing to request in terms of rights, which they enjoy on an equal footing with other citizens, and of integration without substantial problems (even if ghosts from the past can always arise again, as the tragic case of Bosnia has taught us). On the other hand, we have foreign newcomers, with cultural conflicts and problems of legal, economic and social inequality. In between, the former immigrants who have acquired citizenship, who have more guarantees and the European nationals who have converted to Islam, who do not have and do not experience any real conflict. And with the passing of time, the second and third generations.

Some dynamics have already been seen in various countries, for example, by groups of converts in wanting to be distinguished from immigrants, from the point of view of organisation and institutional recognition as well—or on the contrary, in their commitment to a common form of religious association [Allievi, 1998]. Elsewhere the risks are different. For example, countries like Romania, where the newly arrived immigrants are surpassing in number the original Turkish minorities, upsetting the ethnic but also cultural balance within the Muslim group: in Bucharest, the recent Muslim immigrants are probably twenty times as many as the original Tatars or Turks, who are mainly resident in other parts of the country, and they certainly have little understanding of the ethnic Dobrudja Islam [Lederer, 1996]. But similar problems are also posed in other Eastern European countries and in Greece, with the recently arrived Albanian component. In these countries there are also the relations between the Sunnite Islam 'of the mosques', sometimes supported by external requests, and the confraternities and religious orders (for example, the Bektashis in the Albanian and Kosovar area) which can be difficult.

But more generally problems are posed throughout Europe between Arab, Turkish and Asian components, who still do not speak, in both a literal and figurative sense, a common language. Other divisions are seen in the juridical sector, with the different interpretative schools or due to the taking root of a 'Sunni' Islam and of a 'Sufi' Islam and the existence of many different histories and pasts, including of internal conflict which have to share a common space and time. Not to mention the traditional ethnic, political and also religious differences.

The variant of the 'dilemma of the prisoner' that has been used for the engagement of immigrants on the political level [Cadat & Fennema, 1998] also risks being valid for Muslims: the collaboration of the Muslim populations of different origins would be advantageous for all, but a specific alliance with the natives can give a greater advantage to one or other of the communities. This fact also has consequences on the relations with the religious faiths: it is not infrequent to see the attempts by some Muslim leader, especially if in a minority and aware of being so in the Muslim world, of becoming 'accredited' as the dialogic interlocutor with the dominant Christian church in order to gain visibility within the Muslim community itself but above all in the eyes of the non-Muslim world and in particular of the institutions. This occurs to an extent that some Muslims believe that dialogue is an instrument in the hands of the church (and, in relation to some specific cases, the Catholic church), capable of modifying balances in the Muslim community [Bencheikh, 1998]. If this is probably excessive, it is not mistaken to note that the churches also use Islam for purposes of internal repositioning, even if this may take place in various directions: encouraging Islam and the expression of its rights—as we have highlighted in the forms of 'mediation' promoted by churches in various situations—or, on the contrary, contrasting it, even harshly [as some ecclesiastical positions, for example, in the Italian and Greek cases, show; cf. the chapter on relations and negotiations in the public space].

As has been noted, not recognising an interlocutor, the church is not responsible for the division between Muslims: it can however contribute to maintaining it [Bencheikh, 1998]. At the same time the attempts, including those visible in various countries, made by Christian interlocutors to invite, when there are meetings, seminars and conferences, Muslims of different trends, contributing effectively to the creation of a Muslim-Muslim dialogue, should be underlined [*ibid.*]. On more than one occasion we have observed empirically how encounters of this type are the only opportunities when the various tendencies of Islam, including those which do not reciprocally recognise their legitimacy, confront one another, due to the simple fact that they are forced to do so.

In this regard, it should be noted that the policies of the different governments can also have an extremely concrete and direct effect, with respect to inter-Muslim dynamics, and the directions these take. In Sweden, for example, the centralised structures of the various religions (not only Islam) receive financial contributions, whilst in Norway the individual local congregations receive them: this difference in arrangement can make a considerable difference, producing in the second case a pluralising effect which some do not hesitate to define beneficial, within the individual religious communities [Leirvik, 2001].

Even more than this, with the passing of time the context, which seems to have a significant influence on the Muslim world, takes on more weight with processes that can, in a certain sense, be defined as 'Christianisation' of Islam: naturally on the social level and not in the theological sense of the term. For example, the insertion of Muslim exponents in institutionalised forms of 'religious welfare' (for example, Muslim 'chaplains' in prisons and hospitals) or the fairly widespread habit of celebrating Muslim marriages in mosques, in imitation of Christian marriages in church, which is also alien to practices in the countries of origin.

These are aspects of research which have still to be done, on a situation which should nevertheless be observed with care, in their particular effects as well as in their more general consequences which could reveal themselves as being more significant than what we today know and think.

10. Some Considerations on Prospects and 'Hot' Issues

What are the possible evolutions of interreligious dialogue and what have its results been so far?

We do not profess to outline the situation here: those who have done so have already noted that now, after the subsequent periods of reflection, exploration and explanation, Muslim-Christian dialogue is in a period of introspection [Siddiqui, 2001] and reconsideration of its fundamentals and results. We will restrict ourselves to some general considerations.

In the first place, a consideration of the absentees: the non-religious. Certainly, the dialogue outlined here is not their competence. However, the picture is also offered by them, and their voice, the voice of those who are not moved in their lives and in their commitment in society and in politics by religious considerations, is a not indifferent aspect; in addition, evolutions in the relationship between religions, their possible common objectives and the 'quantity' of their weight in society, also has an effect on them. Some ways of confrontation must therefore be found, which is not that of claims and militancy of certain secularistic groups, a phenomenon which is moreover to be found mainly in the Francophone area and which is now dated, but which is on the other hand the ground for an open and all-round confrontation.

Some reflections must also be made on the effects of dialogue, at least of that from above, as conceived so far. It has been conducted, not infrequently, by a class of professionals, still excessively linked to their respective religious (and political) hierarchies, with a modest generational changeover and an absolutely undersized involvement of non-religious personnel, and for these reasons quite far from the social dynamics under way. The parties to the dialogue, as noted, belong to the self-defined group of the same rather than to their respective communities: what, in the French case, a Muslim interlocutor has called "le Tout-Paris islamo-chrétien" [Bencheikh, 1998].

The emphasis on written material, on the form of the conference and on some figures who are a certain way historic but as such irremovable, has made of this form of dialogue a sort of self-selected class, which has classified everything but which considers as a form of dialogue only what can be classified, that is, journals and conferences, and not their results and their social consequences, when and if they exist [cf. many of the results of the dialogue in various countries which have appeared in the 'official' publications of the respective churches or in *Islamochristiana* and other reviews].

The same comprehensible centrality of theological and doctrinal subjects in this type of dialogue, as well as exposing it to the abundantly run risks of monologues, which is not the least of paradoxes, also makes it extraneous to the reality experienced and to the interests of the individual and social actors; this is not because these subjects are not in themselves important, but because, paradoxically, they do not presuppose, in a technical sense, only a dialogue between two sides but as a concomitant condition or even subject to a dialogue within the various communities on and starting off from the other. The prevalence of theological topics also contributes to excluding from the status of interlocutors all those who, and they are the majority, are not capable of intervening on the theological level on an equal footing with the professionals of the branch: the problem is all the greater for the Muslim interlocutor who does not have, except to a reduced degree and insufficient for the need, actors equal to the task (to the extent that the countries of origin have to be turned to), but which deeply concerns Christian interlocutors and even more, the 'non-robed' members of churches.

It is clear that these are different levels and all are necessary: those of theological, spiritual and social dialogue. The problem is that often the last-named is not yet considered such, and the first two are the almost exclusive dominion of their promoters: in short, there is a lack, more than of interreligious communication, of the intra-communication of experience. This is also a limit which concerns dialogue promoted through the institutions, even at governmental or European level.

On the other hand, the trends under way in the field must be observed. In the first place, to see which effects are produced by interreligious bodies in religious self-comprehension, both by themselves and of the other. In the second place to measure the dynamics present outside them, on the individual members of the various communities. On their interest in religion, in the first place, too often postulated and too seldom verified in its contents and modalities. And on the changes under way in the way of experiencing it, for example, following a generational passage. Lastly, on the dynamics of syncretism in the facts induced by the context; already known to the sociology of religions but which should be observed more carefully in this specific sector, where the self-definitions of a normative order prevail, but measuring real behaviour is accurately avoided, in particular by the religious interlocutors.

Lastly, it would be opportune to begin to reflect on the 'non-dialoguers' [Waardenburg, 1997], and on the effects of growing internal distance in the various communities between dialoguers, open and comprehensive of the reasons of the other, and non-dialoguers, closed and religiously chauvinistic. This divergence would seem to outline a landscape where the progressive deepening of the level of interlocution *ad extra* leads to a progressive and increasingly marked incommunicability *ad intra*, as shown by the diametrically opposed positions which can be found in the same religious communities. This is an aspect in which perhaps a difference between the 'high clergy' and the 'low clergy' comes into play, or, quite simply, between the clergy and the laity, which can also be ascertained in the field, but in very different directions according to the situations (it is not always clear who is the most open and who is the most closed, for example).

An important role is also played by the context and the overall religious landscape, characterized by secularisation and pluralisation. Summarising these processes under the general name of postmodernity, it has been defined as the 'silent third partner' of Muslim-Christian dialogue [Nasr, 1998]. Nor is it possible to elude, and this is a further element of interrogation for religious subjects, the role that secularisation and laicity and, specifically, the overall conception of human rights that has been constructed along this path, have had and have in guaranteeing the rights of majority and minority religious subjects, as they represent the 'legal secular standard' [Bielefeldt, 1996] to which both refer. As a Muslim interlocutor has noted: "I prefer being a Muslim in France than a Muslim in a Muslim country. Here my religion is not the object of political manipulation or of social pressure" [Bencheikh, 1999; more widely, see, on this aspect, the theoretical elaboration in Ramadan, 1999].

What seems certain is that we can consider closed the season of the usual reference to values common to the three religions of Abrahamic origin or to a common Mediterranean culture, a mask of real differences which are also 'common' and shared as such. And so today we have to aim less at general conferences on dialogue, the gymnasium of a generic humanism, facile and proposing an irenic theology, or the exclusive pasture of what Weber called social entrepreneurs of the sacred, who have, so to speak, too many things to defend (and some of which cannot be defended) and much more on projects that are concretely dialogic, in the way of conducting them as well as in their intentions (promoted, for example, by several real partners), based on effective and effectively committed human resources, in this sense secular. Therefore, nor must the role of local groups be forgotten, who have an effect that is slightly underestimated, of 'transformation' of the persons that belong to them due to the simple fact that these groups 'exist' and the persons that go to them are in reciprocal relationships [Babès, 1997].

A potential context of investment in these dynamics may be that of the main controversial issues, within religions and between religions, but which imply important areas of institutional intervention, in this sense not motivated religiously (even if rarely *super partes*), which here we will only mention. In the first place, the problem of conversions, in the various directions, the freedom or obligation of changing religion, postulated in different ways by the two religious worlds and the respective consequences.

In the second place, the questions linked to mixed marriages, with the related legal but also religious implications: a question over which there is also great concern in public opinion, linked to difficult and sometimes dramatic cases, which accentuate the emotional approach, but also few concrete studies on the effective points of arrival of these marriages and their success. We can also mention the protection of minors from the religious obligations imposed by the family and by the religious communities, their freedom to choose and to avoid them.

The questions related to the respective perceptions of women and the family are also fundamental, also due to the more general cultural implications: where the necessary confrontation is not only between the present customs and prevailing (or at least 'declared') Western sensitivity and Islam but also concerns the conception of women in other religious communities, and in general the confrontation between different cultural models which does not necessarily see the dominant religion in Europe and Islam, let alone the whole of Islam, on two different fronts. Then there is all the vast range of moral behaviour linked to the use of the body, sexuality and the acceptance of behaviour and models that are different from those proposed by the different religions (homosexuality, for example) and so on.

And lastly the question, of an 'international' character but which also has domestic consequences, of reciprocity: a question that is raised too often in regard to religion, especially by those who are diffident of it, to remove it from the space of reflection.

These are some of the questions, not the only ones, but probably the main ones, which we must expect that the confrontation between religions, and as we have seen not only between them, must approach.

CHAPTER ELEVEN

THE ECONOMIC DIMENSION

Brigitte Maréchal

In this chapter we present the diverse aspects of a presence whose economic impact is far from reaching its complete extent. First, the resources of Muslim communities in Europe, in relation to financial support received from abroad. Second, the Muslim presence in the job market. Third, ethnic and religious business, involving several sectors, especially the market for halal meat. Fourth, Islamic banks and insurance. Finally, we examine recent events, concentrating on the development of wider professional opportunities, the emergence of Muslim entrepreneurs, and the transformation of economic relations with countries of origin.

1. Some Limitations

Before exploring the aspects of the Muslim economic presence in Europe, we should make several remarks concerning the state of research, in order to make clear the limits of the synthesis presented here.

First, a remark which has to do with the generally somewhat neglected state of this area of study. Many causes can be cited for the lack of relevant information. Recent series of events of an economic, ethnic, or religious nature have had many more consequences than they did in the past.[1] It was once a commonplace, even among European researchers, to believe that 'immigrants' and 'Muslims' were simply in a marginal category of society. Many were slow to realize, for whatever reason, the real impact of the establishment of

---

[1] Cf. Ma Mung E. (1992), who reminds us how much more 'sensitive' the presence of foreigners in independent activities was, at least in France, even before the Second World War.

permanent Muslim communities on all sectors of society. There was a lack of interest, insight, and knowledge regarding changes within the Muslim community on the part of people who studied economic processes. Perhaps changes in the behaviour of many Muslims have occurred; where once they had more of a need or desire to express their religious preferences, now they may find it easier to express such preferences in regard to more ordinary actions such as economic behaviour.

Another caveat has to do with the great disparities in the amount of attention paid to different areas of research. Most analyses deal with two areas: the economic and/or occupational situation of certain national, ethnic, or sector-related groups, and the area of commercial networks, even within underground economies, sometimes as related to particular ethnic or religious membership. There are two limitations of these studies which should be borne in mind: first, most studies are case studies of an extremely limited nature, as regards time period and distribution. As for the groups themselves, the criterion which allows them to be picked out is more ethnic than religious; the first type of analyses mentioned above never takes religion into account. There are some good analyses of the commercial networks of a few Muslim associations, notably the Naqshbandis or the Murids.

In addition, as concerns financial flows and a banking system which operates according to Islamic rules, almost no research is available. Theoretical discussions are plentiful, especially those published during a period of increased interest in the subject in the 1980s. These concern types of organisations involving partnerships in business in an environment where loan interest is not permitted. In such organisations, the accent is placed on solidarity and ethical rules for investments. However, these writings are lacking various kinds of socio-anthropological data, which no subsequent study has provided.

As for Eastern Europe, no depth study in an EU language has been located. Perhaps such exist. But for the moment we can say little; a few notes collected here and there, such as information about the perceptible influx of Turkish businessmen, especially bakers, opening businesses in Sofia and Bucharest [de Tapia, 1995:38]. This example proves again how hard it is to set up categories for ethnic and religious behaviour as regards economic activity and consumer behaviour.

2. Resources in Religious Communities: Self-Financing, Types of Aid, and Influences

Many studies or commentaries have spoken of the shadowy influence of Gulf states, following many cases in which these states have agreed to finance projects in Muslim communities within European territory. It is time to set this record straight, and to realise that such insinuations are exaggerated and fantastic, and today out of date.

Locally financed projects

Looking at the whole group of currently operating prayer rooms, it must be said that most are quite modest. Their support within Muslim communities is mostly gathered from among religious people, sometimes regularly and sometimes only on certain occasions.[2]

Members are fairly generous, and the names of donors and their amounts are displayed at the entrance to mosques. The dues pay for rental or purchase of space to worship in, for building upkeep, and for certain events such as free evening Ramadan meals, or for help for people in the community who experience crises. The amounts collected are a measure of the importance of the *zakat* (general and ritual duty of charity), the *zakat al-fitr* (charity on the occasion of the end of the Ramadan fast), usually faithfully observed, and even of the *sadaqa* (charity which is voluntary and supererogatory or meritorious). A Muslim is responsible for his or her actions, and the Qur'an sets great store upon actions for which rewards are promised in the afterlife. As it is written in sura 13, verses 22–23: "Those who seek constantly the face of their Lord, those who accomplish their duty of prayer, those who give alms secretly or publicly, from the goods which we have given them, those who reject evil in favour of the good, they will possess a final resting place in the gardens of Eden".

---

[2] For example: all members of the Millî Görüs organisation pay dues of between 10 and 20 DM (approx. 5 and 10 €) per month, depending on their income. Active male members are also encouraged to give as much as a month's salary per year to the organisation, and women are asked to make further gifts [Manço, 1997].

Subsidies from European societies

In various ways, states pay for part of the cost of worship facilities. This happens most often indirectly, when the state provides rent-free space, grants tax exemptions on buildings, and/or makes donations for this purpose. Some possibility of this kind of support exists in all the countries of Western Europe [Shadid & van Koningsveld, 1995:28], even if it appears clear that not all communities benefit from it, especially the smallest communities, which are more likely to be forced to depend entirely on their own resources.[3]

Sometimes state assistance does come in the form of direct financing. The number of states in this category is small: Spain, Belgium, Greece and (in certain respects) the Netherlands. However, procedures for obtaining direct aid which exist in theory are not always applied. For example, though an *Exécutif des Musulmans de Belgique* was established as the partial result of an electoral process organized in December 1998, funding is still being negotiated. Discussions between the Ministry of Justice, which is responsible for the administrative oversight of religion, and this representative body are now in their final phase, determining the procedures which would establish the financing of Muslim places of worship on an equal footing with that of other recognised religions. As for Eastern countries, no real state assistance is given in Poland or Hungary. In Bulgaria, though, a system of aid exists under the department of ecclesiastical affairs within the Bulgarian Council of Ministers, which regulates the relations between various faiths and state institutions. When the state budget is voted each year, there is funding for the abovementioned department. The funds are distributed by the department to various religious groups, with a part being reserved for the Grand Mufti, who distributes it as he sees fit [BG File]. In Romania, a very similar system prevails, though it acts a bit more directly: the state finances the Office of the Mufti pays imams' salaries, pays the administrative and maintenance costs of mosques, and gives logistical support to the effort to preserve the cultural heritage [RO File].

---

[3] Concerning some of the forms of such state subsidy, see the chapter by S. Ferrari.

Outside assistance

External aid comes from both public and private sources within Muslim countries. Two types occur. First, in countries which have citizens or ex-citizens in Europe, it sometimes happens that in a non-systematic way these foreign states will pay for expenses connected with the operation of certain mosques, or the salary of certain imams (see chapter on Mosques, organisations and leadership). Second, Muslim countries, especially Arab Gulf states, provide support out of public and private funds, the latter from foundations and wealthy persons, or from the Muslim World League, which is headquartered in Mecca.

These contributions are occasional for the most part, in the sense that they are arranged to cover budget deficits and/or to cover short-falls in the construction budgets of prestigious mosques and buildings, for example the Regent's Park mosque in London, the mosque situated in the *Parc du Cinquantenaire* in Brussels, the Centro Islamico Culturale d'Italia in Rome, the Grand Islamic Cultural Centre in Madrid, the *Islamisches Zentrum Wien*, or the *Fondation culturelle Islamique de Genève*. Support is made available for these highly visible and imposing structures in a way which seldom occurs with other places of Muslim worship in Europe [Dassetto, 1996:170].

Contrary to what is believed, and despite the probable existence of certain conditions on the funding, these forms of assistance are not automatically accompanied by ideological or political obedience to the donors. This is proven by the diversity of the sources of funding, which comes from many persons, agencies, and countries [Cesari, 1997:76].

It is necessary to admit that while oil money is a reality, it has become harder to come by and less accessible for various groups. This is partly due to increased competition between Islamic organisations in Europe, more numerous every day, which engage in running rivalries. But reductions in the availability of funds are also due to two major changes in the general context: first, there is increased need on the part of the underprivileged populations in Gulf countries, at a time when Muslim populations in Europe are prospering and becoming more able to pay for their own mosques and for the activities connected with them. In concrete terms, in 1997: "Hassan Iquioussen, founder and first president of the association of *Jeunes Musulmans de France* (JMF), says that despite the support of the *Union*

des Organisations Islamiques de France (UOIF), itself heavily supported
by Gulf philanthropists, his association has only been able to count
on about 50,000 FF per year" (around 7,400 €) [Bourg, 1998:77].

Funding in Eastern Europe

Here Muslim communities are much weaker and poorer than those
elsewhere in Europe and lack their own resources. Help for Muslim
institutions in the region has been proposed, and aid from Islamic
humanitarian organisations is the primary source. Some Turkish and
Arab foundations, which are sometimes active in Western Europe,
have their activities coordinated by the Muslim World League, though
some may be merely associated with it [Lederer, 1994:74]

Some countries get more attention than others. Albania, Croatia,
Bosnia and Kosovo have been favoured, but Bulgaria and Romania
are more resistant to what is seen as interference, and contacts are
more limited. Arab proselytisers have shown a fair degree of ignorance regarding Eastern European socialism, despite the basically
good relations of these countries with 'progressive' Arab regimes,
which over quite some time now have led a certain number of Arabs
to move to the region [Lederer, 1996:364].

3. Presence in the Job Market

Studies of the question of the entry of immigrant populations into
the job market are numerous. We will only take those into account
which make reference to data concerning the Islamic religion.

Theoretical foundations

According to the precepts of Islamic doctrine, success in work or
career can be said to have a high value. Economic activity can be
taken as meaningful from a religious point of view to the extent that
it is an affirmation of the community. This brings honour and social
prestige to the Muslim who does succeed, which these examples
amply show. Beyond the many individual and private initiatives which
have been carried out, and which appear later in this chapter, the
Arab community of London is noteworthy for having acquired large
holdings in real estate, commerce, and media outlets [UK File]. Most

Muslims in Ireland work in the tertiary sector. In Italy, those who arrived with the first wave of immigration have become well integrated in Italian society, and a high percentage of them are self-employed or are professionals, e.g., doctors [Allievi, 2001]. The Ismaili community of Portugal counts many merchants, and persons working as administrators, and a quite significant elite in the banking sector, in e-commerce, and in academia [PL File].

The actual situation

In general, however, the situation of populations from Muslim countries in the social hierarchy of Europe is rather poor.

First observation: in comparison with rates for the nation as a whole, their unemployment rate is higher. In France, statistical research sponsored by the National Institute of Demographic Studies, with a sample of 13,000 persons in 1995, showed that for people with the same educational levels, young Muslims' rate of unemployment was twice that for young non-Muslims [Tribalat, 1995]. In Great Britain, the 1991 census showed 25% unemployment for Asians and 8.8% for whites; the same difference was observed for professional people like doctors and teachers [Anwar, 1998:54 ff.]. In the Netherlands, Moroccans and Turks have rates of 31% and 24%, respectively, which is quite worrying [Kloosterman, van der Leun & Rath, 1999:253]. The Turkish population of Germany also has high unemployment rates, but Turks as a group are the most willing to accept any kind of work, and so find work more quickly.

Second observation: most Muslims find work in primary or secondary sectors, jobs which require few qualifications, in which pay is low and turnover high, although a gradual movement toward service jobs can be observed. In Great Britain, two-thirds of Pakistani and Bengali men do some form of manual labour, while only 50% of whites do [Modood & al., 1997]. Only 9.7% of Turks in Austria have any form of qualification [Rasuly-Paleczek, 1995:177 ff.] and average monthly income for Turks and ex-Yugoslavs is 15% under that of Austrians [Strobl, 1997:67 ff.]. The majority of the working Turkish population in Europe is thus over-represented in occupations such as metalworking, industrial cleaning services, automobile manufacturing, public works, textiles, confectioners, and mine labour [Manço, 1997:97 ff.]. They move easily into temporary work, day or night, and are adapted to a fast pace, as in sales. In most cases it has been observed that children continue the trades of their parents [Manço, 1997]. A different pattern is followed sometimes by Asian families in Great Britain, as when Pakistani children refuse to work in the family restaurant, forcing their parents to advertise for help, and then they hire the British people who answer the ad.

But most of the studies over the last 15 years about the integration of immigrants "show a fairly radical change in the process of job choice and choice of profession" for Muslims in Western job markets [Peraldi, 1999:51]. In fact, "even if the highest concentration of these populations are still found in economic sectors which are heavily dependent on the business cycle, there has been some progress in professional qualification, and much entrepreneurial activity" [Amiraux, 1995:67], and this is no longer limited to Turkish people. These visible changes through development of 'small artisanal or commercial businesses' are not only underway; we see their effects. And even if "these better jobs are far from erasing the massive unemployment among those of the second generation, they are nonetheless meaningful enough not to be considered as statistically insignificant flukes any longer" [Peraldi, 1999:51].

Similar scenarios occur in most parts of Western Europe, especially in the countries with immigrant communities of longer date: to start one's own business is felt to be "a much-desired transition to an economic category which is seen as advantageous in both host country and home country alike." Most often this occurs within a community of "immigration that has been stabilized, or is about to be", and of people who have enough money and have made careful market studies. Success in business depends on a good understanding of one's area, and its needs in the given sector [Weibel, 1992]. This is not really an antidote for unemployment, but demonstrates people's desire to make use of their abilities [Weibel, 1992] and to emerge from a marginalised situation [Jones & McEvoy, 1992].

Women's position in the job market

Women's position in the job market is not enviable. They are often the least qualified and more women than men are illiterate. But this situation is changing completely with the more recent waves of immigration, made up of better educated and more urbanised people.

Early on in the process, women were placed in even more difficult situations. They had not expected to emigrate; often they have no choice but to follow and/or join their husbands in the host country. The situation was all the more delicate when their right to stay there depended on their continuing to live with those husbands, so that divorce meant in most cases a probable forced return to the country of origin.

Once they arrived in the host country, they were often very dependent on their husbands, and did not speak the language of the host country. They lost their extended family support, and could no longer count on the solidarity of a group. They often became isolated, behind closed doors in their homes, limited to household labour. They were discouraged or even forbidden to work outside the home the case with many Asian [Rafiq, 1992] and Turkish women. If extra money was needed, they took on extra work which could also be done at home, which allowed them to care for their children at the same time [Anwar, 1998:70]. Turkish women did sometimes accept domestic work. But at the level of the second and third generations, things are changing. These women will not accept being cooped up at home, and want to realise their potential, even in ways other than those offered by the family. Women from the Maghreb have an easier time getting acceptance for their outside work and some differences appear in the occupations they enter: Algerian women tend to enter secondary or tertiary-level jobs; Tunisian and Moroccan women are much more numerous in the primary sector [Santelli, 1999]. For the rest, the work women do, when they find work, can become a source of conflict within families, especially if they are the actual breadwinners, the only ones bringing money in, a role which is supposed to go the husband, the protector and leader of the family.

Very few single women immigrate, but again things are in flux. In Spain, for example, there is a "colony of Moroccan women who are part of the first generation to immigrate, the only group like it in Europe", and whose large numbers have been apparent since 1991. They work mostly in the domestic service sector and are contributing to a "major change in the mentality of the Moroccan community". From this point on the category of 'working woman' and the idea of work which can confer dignity upon the human person has entered into *gender ideology* such as this is perceived in Morocco". Immigrant women are no longer seeing their work as a simple means of 'support'. They send money back to the home country and now they can represent a 'key to the future' because they have the power to decide who the next candidate for immigration will be [Ramirez, 1999]. This radically different way of looking at things may change some minds.

Discrimination

Alongside the lack of training and qualifications mentioned in the chapter on education, many forms of discrimination operate, which accentuate low income stratification, and endanger the success of integration. They affect immigrants as individuals, as members of a race, as persons of a certain ethnic origin, and as adherents to the Muslim religion;[4] structural and institutional discriminations are also at work.

The consequences are noticeable in regard to availability of rental apartments and purchase of homes or apartments. We note for example that some landlords put obstacles in the path of Muslim tenants in neighbourhoods where foreigners were not wanted. This led to the formation of small 'ghettos' as in Great Britain, where during the 1960s Pakistani workers had no option but to "go into partnership to buy low priced and dilapidated houses in run-down neighbourhoods" [Kepel, 1994:161]. Even if many Asians own homes (77% in the 1991 census, and 79% of Pakistanis in a national survey in 1994), these houses must be considered as usually of poor quality [Anwar, 1998:73 ff.]. In Austria, even if there has been some improvement since the 1980s, only 74% of Turks and 68% of Yugoslavs have apartments with heating and a bathtub, as opposed to 98% of Austrians [Strobl, 1997:73]. It has been shown that even if "a German Turk could pay a high rent, neither his name nor his passport allow him free access to the housing market" [A. Caglar cited by Amiraux, 1999:48]. Similar situations occur everywhere in Europe, to one degree or another.

The area in which the worst discrimination occurs is the job market, despite the daily denial of this fact in European society, based on the usual lack of tangible proof. But there is global discrimina-

---

[4] We should underline the symbolic importance of Article 13 of the Maastricht Treaty, which closes a former gap in legal protection: formerly, only race and ethnic group membership qualified as categories of discrimination for the purposes of filing lawsuits, but Article 13 adds religion as an equal ground for claims of illegal discrimination.

tion in legal manoeuvres carried out by the state, avoidance of immigrant workers by employers, and, still occasionally, racism in the conduct of business.

Legal practices

Among legal forms of discrimination, we may mention first the prohibition on immigrants working for the government and its agencies. This restriction is quite different from country to country; it occurs more frequently in countries in which naturalisation is slow or avoided altogether as in Germany. In Great Britain, on the other hand, the systematic acquisition of British nationality by persons coming from former colonies has significantly reduced this kind of discrimination.

Over and above this kind of prohibition, the difficulties immigrants have in getting jobs in the public sector relate to the lack of confidence in government and administration which, it is supposed, might be caused by immigrant employees dealing with the general public in this sector. Under these conditions, an equal right to employment is subordinated to the necessity of preserving the public's belief that bureaucrats administer their duties in a completely equitable and, so to speak, neutral manner [Panafit, 1999:349 ff.]. Where such prejudices are really taken seriously, they can cause problems.

In Bulgaria and Greece, discrimination through legal practices occurs in another way. In Bulgaria in 1999 it was noted that the unemployment rate for Turks and Pomaks was 34%, while the national rate was between 18 and 20%. Part of this was due to lack of education or training, but a great deal was due to restructuring moves in the public sector, especially in the Rhodopi region, the most disadvantaged from an economic point of view, although this region had traditionally furnished jobs for Muslims in agriculture, mining, or tobacco production [BG File]. In this case we cannot say whether this is a conscious strategy directed against Muslims, but the unemployment rate remains a fact.

In Greece, by contrast, the procedures are clearer and more direct, and based on rearrangements of territorial property. During the 1970s, in the name of the public interest, the extent of Turkish possessions in Western Thrace fell by somewhere between 30 and 60%. This was carried out through expropriations in the public interest and redistributions of land, which led to Muslims being given inferior land and increased litigation over Muslim property titles, at a time when it was made more difficult for them to make new acquisitions [Christidis, 1996:154 ff.; Akgönül, 1999:137 ff.]. Added to the deficiencies in education already noted, these developments tend to confirm that discrimination is alive and well as regards the Turkish minority in Western Thrace, the majority of whom still work in agriculture, mainly in growing wheat and tobacco [Akgönül, 1999].

Discrimination in hiring by businesses

Some cases of discrimination in business occur in relation to the creation of businesses by immigrants. Such practices have been noted in Great Britain: bankers, insurance companies, suppliers, employees working in urbanism, and even entrepreneurs have been guilty [Rafiq, 1985; Jones & al., 1989 cited by Jones & McEvoy, 1992].

Employers manage to derail immigrant workers at different stages in the employment process. Sometimes discrimination occurs as soon as the candidate gives his or her name, even though no qualifications have been mentioned. It may occur at the moment the necessary qualifications relative to the given job are given out, or at the time when hiring decisions are actually made. Such discrimination has been proven in Great Britain in regard to South Asian people [Anwar, 1998:54 ff.], and in all three regions of Belgium in relation to Moroccan immigrants [Services fédéraux des Affaires Scientifiques, Techniques et Culturelles, 1997:129]. The impact of this discrimination has also been verified at the personal level, in the expectations of young people concerning their own opportunities. Discrimination causes them to lower these expectations; they no longer try to decide "in which sector of activity or at what salary level they will be employed, but only to know whether they will be able to get a first job and whether they will be able to stabilize themselves within the job market" [Rea & Bortolini, 1999].

Discrimination and religion

Though the respectful observance of religious precepts would seem to promise honest effort and good work habits, with regard to the Muslim religion, employers continue to practice a number of avoidance strategies. The obstacles to hiring most often cited are: not wanting to arrange for time for daily prayers, possible fatigue related to Ramadan fasting, and/or possible prolonged absences during religious holidays.

In general as concerns getting time off for religious holidays, most countries have no regulations in the matter and leave decisions up to individual employers. Some countries do notify administrators of the dates of these holidays. Some recommend that their agencies give time off to Muslims who ask for it, as in Denmark. Some allow time off in a conditional way, as in Great Britain where such time off is usually deducted from the number of legal days off or sick days available to the employee [UK File]. In France, permission to participate in those holidays which are not legal holidays on the calendar depends on whether the absence of the employee would disturb the smooth functioning of the agency [FR File]. But in some public administrations these holidays are officially recognized, as in Spain, Bulgaria [BG File] and in Romania, where two days off are granted for each of the two major Muslim holidays [RO File].

In private enterprise, decisions about days off for religious holidays are made case by case. In the Netherlands, for example, the pattern seems to be that Muslims have the right to take unpaid days off during religious vacations as long as their absence does not cause any major economic harm to the employer [NL File]. In Spain, where the Muslim holy days are recognised, and where employees are allowed to stop working to pray between 1:30 and 4:30 p.m. on Friday, or to end work an hour early during Ramadan, these specific times have to be negotiated with employers too [ES File].

And then there is the problem of the headscarf for women who have decided not to give it up under any circumstances. In the Qur'an, sura 24, verses 31 and 33–59, it is written (especially in the second passage): "Prophet, tell your wives, tell your daughters, tell the women of believers to cover their heads: a sure way of being recognised (as women) and to escape any offense". Obedience to this injunction, which is left to the decision of the individual, is probably the hardest to maintain in daily life because of the many limits it causes for women looking for a job. Lack of understanding and prejudices are still common: many unthinking employers refuse to hire a headscarfed woman for fear of damaging the image of their business, or for fear of negative reactions from clients. In this regard, it is common to find many young women who wear headscarves who are forced to accept jobs, such as telemarketing, where they are in contact with the clientele without being seen. A few of them no doubt appreciate this, since it allows avoidance of situations that violate rules about modesty or the separation of the sexes.

This observation brings up some others, linked to the fact that reluctance, complications, and other difficulties can also come from the Muslim person who decides not to work in certain jobs because he or she believes the work contradicts certain prohibitions, or goes against a sincere attempt to follow the prescriptions of faith. Jobs in which alcoholic drinks or certain kinds of meat are served, snack bars, restaurants, hotels or even chemical laboratories may be involved. Any job which seems to allow trangressions of rules about modesty or the separation of men and women may be involved. Among South Asian populations, first and second generation members cite the importance of their religious convictions, according to which men and women should not be mixed together at work [Anwar, 1998:69]. This attitude also figures in the choice of jobs in the medical sector, in health care professions, or in jobs connected to sports (gym teacher, swimming instructor, etc.). Even some positions in the film industry, journalism, public relations, or photography may be involved.

Clashes between on-the-job demands and religious practices also may arise as concerns rights to unemployment compensation, since refusal of a job may violate the unemployed person's duty to accept any 'suitable job'. When "religious obligations can be treated as an obstacle to this 'availability for work', a Muslim who respects certain precepts may lose his or her right to minimum compensation". In Belgium, for example, the decisive criterion for Public Centres for Social Assistance "is not a study of the conditions of each worker's willingness to work, but the setting-up of a general framework which establishes rules for not working for certain reasons". Because the "notion of a suitable job is not defined in abstract and limiting terms, the judge opined that "such a conviction must stem from an objective and absolute precept" [Panafit, 1999:349 ff.]. This decision led to a number of different solutions in practice.

All these religious considerations affect only a small minority of people who belong to Muslim culture. Such extreme situations are rare, since people can also decide to practice certain occupations within certain limits which make the work acceptable in religious terms, such as working only with children or those of the same gender as oneself.

4. Ethnic Business and Religion

Ethnic commerce is defined as a "practical activity by persons who use and draw support from ethnic networks as regards financing, supply, worker recruitment and even clientele, and when the business primarily seeks to draw its customers from the community in which the businessperson is a member" [Ma Mung, 1996:214]. The latter situation is illustrated by Turkish people in Germany. It has been said that 24% of them buy only from Turkish businesses [Amiraux, 1995:69]. Based on this explanation, it is easy to understand how the community dimension can trump the religious, since there are many non-Islamic practices in these businesses. Still, Islamic practice affects the feeling of belonging to Muslim communities, and their organisation. And we can see a social usage of Islam when the Muslim person attempts to "prove his or her conformity to Islam as a sign of honesty and fairness" in commercial and professional transactions [Manço, 2000:271]. The exact boundary between these two aspects, religious and community-based, is impossible to fix, and so we consider them together, while keeping in mind these remarks about the separation between them.

First impressions

Ethnic commerce in Eastern Europe, including Bulgaria and Romania [RO File] is less important at first glance than in Western Europe, where it is growing rapidly. Certainly there are differences in the West from one country to another, but in general the first images which surface are those of small local groceries and snack bars selling pita sandwiches and döner kebab. Then we encounter Islamic butcher shops (see next section), or even the carrying out of this work in mosques, which is sometimes a significant source of income for them. This business concerns mostly small or recent communities, in order to satisfy certain religious needs, notably the need for halal meat, and in order to provide a range of products not available in local markets in the host country.

In the Netherlands, many such stores belonging to Muslim organisations are connected to various mosques and also sell religious items, including books, and imported items from the country of origin [Shadid & van Koningsveld, 1995:25]. Such establishments exist also in Great Britain. These stores are small community businesses located in run-down neighbourhoods where many immigrants live. They are often looked down on, although they may prove to occupy "very favourable economic niches". In fact, host country natives often have left these neighbourhoods, together with their store operators, and Muslim businesspersons take advantage of the opportunity to set up shop, benefiting from the fact that they speak the language of most of the current residents of the neighbourhood, that they offer products from the country of origin, and that they are willing to extend credit to their clients. There is also the fact that family members are available to work in the store [Manço A. & Manço, 1995:121].

But over and above these typical and cliché situations, other realities exist. Some important businesses are in operation, representing large potential. They may be the result of individual initiatives, or set up as cooperatives. Since 1985, the Al Halal Supermarket in Bradford has catered exclusively to the needs of Muslim clients. One of its principal investors was a representative of the Deobandi movement, and the store was set up on the basis of "contributions coming from severance pay packages of Muslims who went on unemployment during the 1970s"; its employees wear uniforms and headscarves [Kepel, 1994:163]. Similarly in Germany, a new supermarket with 2000 square meters of floor space has opened in Stuttgart, behind the central train station. The range of products sold there is quite impressive, most of which are directly imported from Turkey, such as ritually slaughtered meat, fruits, vegetables, spices, cheeses, and teas. The store also sells Islamic clothing, cloth, non-alcohol based perfume, religious objects such as rosaries or Muslim calendars, posters, religious greeting cards, audio cassettes, videos, software, and small items of furniture, etc. [Spuler-Stegemann, 1998:277 ff.]. Bulletin boards offer live animals for sale, for slaughter on the occasion of religious feasts, or halls for hire where marriages can take place. In France, where Islamic commerce does not seem as developed as in Germany (if only in Turkish communities), a facility for cheese production has been purchased in Normandy, named Hegire Sarl. This facility produces white cheese, guaranteed strictly halal, which is made out of vegetable rennets [Kepel, 1987]. Despite great differences from country to country, it appears that, in Germany at least, the needs of Muslims are being met. The absence of these products, community and religious needs, from the host country market, is being remedied in some areas where it had been lacking for a long time.

Historical forms and importance

The development of businesses belonging to Turkish immigrants "really began in the mid 1970s in Great Britain, France, Germany and the Netherlands" [Akagül, 1995:47]. In Great Britain, Asian businesses also probably emerged during this period. The census of 1991 showed that the percentage of Asians who started their own businesses grew more rapidly than it did for indigenous people, 21% versus 13% [Anwar, 1998:54 ff.]. In 1992, 61,000 businesses were created in Great Britain: grocery stores, news stands, clothing stores, restaurants, take-out and eat-in, wholesale grocery and food suppliers and early efforts in textile production. Still, in relation to other Asians, businesses run by Muslims remained heavily ethnic, small, and located in low-profit areas [Rafiq, 1992:43 ff.]. In France, alongside some 3,300 Turkish entrepreneurs in 1995 [Manco, 1997], 17% of recent immigrants from the Maghreb were working as artisans, businesspeople, or business owners [Tribalat, 1995]. In Germany in 1996 there were about 40,500 Turkish businesses, whose total annual gross was close to 34 billion DM. From this point families began to sell their possessions in Turkey in order to invest in their children's education, preferably in medicine, dentistry, language services (interpretation) or law, or in order to amass sufficient capital to start businesses [Spuler-Stegemann, 1998:269]. Their favourite sectors are grocery stores, the many kebab shops which are popular among German consumers [Caglar, 1995], travel agencies, transport companies, music stores, video shops, and video game parlours, and they are branching out now into service companies, and companies which do manual labour [Amiraux, 1995:68]. In the Netherlands and Austria, mention has been made of 2,600 and 2,000 (respectively) Turkish entrepreneurs in 1995 [Manco, 1997], while in Belgium, the National Institute of Social Insurance for Independents listed 1,870 Turkish and 2,064 Moroccan independent businesspeople as of January 1, 1998, especially in the areas of building and construction, which had been starved of labour. As for Turkish businesses, these were listed in a publication distributed in Gent [Manco, 1995:121], which speaks for the effectiveness of their community organisation. Such coordination goes even further: since 1990, several Turkish Chambers of Commerce have opened in Germany, the Netherlands, Belgium and Switzerland, and there is now a German Federation of Turkish Enterprises (TIDAF). The Association of

Turkish Entrepreneurs in Europe (ATIAD) has also for several years worked to group together such businesses [Manco, 1997:97 ff.].[5]

One characteristic common to all these businesses is that they are more and more attuned to customers from the host country. The business owners realise that if their customers are drawn only from the immigrant community, their business is "doomed to stay small, if not struggling to survive" [Palidda, 1992], despite the success of 'community' supermarkets which have opened recently, operating at a new level altogether. These businesses have also begun, more and more, to rely on employees outside family circles. This tendency is most pronounced among larger businesses; it means not only that the business is expanding beyond the family, but that indigenous persons from outside the Muslim community are finding work there. For example, in Germany, out of 150,000 employees working for Turkish entrepreneurs, 25,000 are German [Amiraux, 1995:69]. These populations do not contribute in a merely 'passive' fashion to the social security system through their own payments, but actually invest in it more and more actively. Here are some figures relating to the 1.9 million Turks and Kurds living in Germany, which show that they are a "non-negligible economic force: they pay 3.4 billion DM per year in taxes and 3.4 billion in state pension insurance, and thus have paid about a half billion toward the cost of German reunification with East Germany. As consumers, they spend 10 billion DM per year, representing the total business generated by German retail commerce" [Spuler-Stegemann, 1998:268].

Over and above "commerce in community goods (groceries, services) and the setting up of businesses, trades and specialty shops in sectors where immigrants once provided only labour, in building construction and public works", real "commercial networks at the international level have been created" [Peraldi, 1999]. The Belsunce quarter of Marseilles has been described as a 'trading post' [Tarrius, 1995], and some have taken note of its "inventories which bring together many foodstuffs unavailable in European markets, and a range of manufactured products unavailable in the countries of ori-

---

[5] Looking long term, and from a religious point of view only, one might wonder whether it is not likely that Europe will see people trying to imitate Chambers of Commerce and the American Islamic Industries group, which popularised the slogan, 'Remember—Buy from your Muslim brother' on the Internet, where it received worldwide exposure [Spuler-Stegemann, 1998:277 ff.].

gin". Belsunce is also a "place to get products which have been dis-counted (discontinued items, unsold products, counterfeit luxury brands) or have been subject to political embargo"; its commercial networks are present both locally (as with the Sephardic Jews from Morocco or Algeria who specialise in wholesale confectionery prod-ucts) and in numerous foreign countries: Belgium for carpets, Germany for new cars and used cars which are then shipped to Libya, Italy for leather and shoes, and as a shipping destination for Asian house-hold appliances, Turkey for jewelry, including unregulated gold, Syria for confectionery products, etc. Sales efforts are handled by the busi-nesspeople themselves, thanks to numerous 'relationship arrange-ments' and to the 'individual prowess' of 'traveling salesmen' and door-to-door people, like the members of the Murid brotherhood.

Diversity of sectors which have a connection to Islamic practices

Sometimes entire service sectors are set up. Islamic bookstores are especially numerous in Great Britain and France, with a few in Belgium, the Netherlands, and Denmark, while in Spain the small number of bookstores is offset by their high level of publishing activ-ity. We note also the presence of two publishing companies, the Islamic Foundation of Leicester, and *Al-Tawhid* company in Marseilles. Bookstores usually sell books in several languages, including that of the host country and Arabic. The quality of publications varies widely, depending on individual stores, different countries, and whether or not the store is independent. In Melilla, a new Islamic bookstore offering delivery service to the home across all of Spain, has been open since 1999 [ES File].

Other areas of activity include the hotel and restaurant sector (some Muslim hotels have opened in Germany, in Hamburg, Kall-Sötenich, Schopfheim and Trebbus, and there is also one in London) and travel agencies. Besides the usual services, these agencies offer especially trips to Mecca, not only at times of pilgrimage but year-round, and voyages to other Muslim holy sites, such as in Iran or Iraq. Some agencies have relationships with mosques, or pay a per-centage to them in order to generate the minimum number of pas-sengers for a pilgrimage. An example of this practice is the *Institut Musulman de la Mosquée de Paris* (IMMP), which runs radio adver-tisements on Radio-Orient recommending the El Djazaïr agency [Islam de France, n° 2, 1998:147].

Media outlets are another sector showing activity in Europe which is likely to increase even more (see the chapter on the media). We note here just a few effects on the daily life of Muslims, starting with the same Radio Orient in France, which from a modern studio broadcasts the call to prayer five times a day. This programme has put an end, de facto, to the many quarrels which had continued over the exact time for prayers [Kepel, 1987].

From anecdotal evidence in a quite new sector (though it will probably grow rapidly), we see activity in the area of sports which goes beyond the simple motive of rules of conduct such as those mandating the separation of the sexes, and respect for the innocence of children. In Denmark, since the late 1990s, there have been several specialty agencies offering training in gymnastics and other sports to Muslims, or arranged specifically for Muslims [DK File].

Another area of growth over the last few years is the funeral business. This may involve providing either funeral accessories in the Muslim manner or in the European style, and the handling of burial according to Islamic precepts by either Muslim funeral directors or local ones who have learned how to offer such services effectively. Burial in the country of origin is expensive (between 2000 and 3000 Euros), and the rise of a new and younger generation has changed the characteristics of Muslim populations, such that behaviours have changed, and burial in Europe seems less objectionable. In most European countries discussions are going on concerning the establishment of Islamic sections in existing cemeteries, while the indigenous population is beginning to prefer cremation. These tendencies suggest that in future, a higher proportion of Muslims will be interred in European cemeteries. In countries like Great Britain, measures have long since been made to accommodate this trend, so that for example tombs can be oriented so as to allow the body to face toward Mecca.

Still another growth sector for Muslim populations in Europe is the matrimonial business, especially busy for British Asians, while in other European countries this sector remains one of non-commercialized matchmaking, making arrangements through families or Muslim ideological movements. There is an Asha Marriage Bureau, a Suman Marriage Bureau, the Asian Marriage Lines, and, more specifically Islamic, The Muslim Matrimonial, which claims to charge no fee for registering or for finding a spouse. But the use of such agencies, or even just putting a personal ad in magazines or Asian newspapers, is still normally a last resort [Anwar, 1998:110].

Finally under this heading, we may mention the humanitarian organisations. Besides the World Assembly of Muslim Youth, one of the most important is the international organisation Islamic Relief, created in 1984 and now recognized as a consulting member of UNESCO. Its international headquarters is in Birmingham, and it has offices in other British cities, France, Germany, Belgium, the Netherlands, Italy, Sweden, Switzerland, Finland, Bulgaria, and Hungary. The work of this charitable organisation focuses on education for the poorest children, involving setting up centres and giving away book-bags; preventive medicine, agricultural development (digging wells, setting up fishing operations), support for orphans, and gifts of clothing and food, most notably cans of licit meat for the 'Id al-Fitr (end of Ramadan) which are distributed in suffering regions. This organisation operates almost everywhere, from Bangladesh and the Sudan to Palestine and Chechenya, perhaps favouring Bosnia and Albania to some extent. Collections have been taken up to renovate mosques in these countries, and to produce copies of the Qur'an in their languages. At the European level, for example in Belgium, the Secours Islamique (Islamic Relief) helps students and persons in financial difficulty, and provides funerals for uninsured persons. We note that these tasks are also performed by certain movements such as the Milli Görüs, which though working on a smaller scale with humanitarian problems, has provided help as well in certain crisis situations, and also grants a number of student scholarships. At the annual European meeting of the Milli Görüs in Köln in June 2000, it was announced that 245 students would receive these scholarships. Another Muslim organisation working in this sector in Europe, and acting as fund-raiser for various causes located mostly in Algeria, Palestine, Iraq, Egypt, and Bosnia: the notable *Al-Muntada al-Islami*, linked to the Salafi tendency. Despite the high profile of this phenomenon in newspapers, and apart from a certain consciousness-raising effect, the impact of all these movements appears to be very limited [Vertovec & Peach, 1997:29].

Variety of establishments and reactions to them

Sometimes these commercial activities are scattered around in the public space, especially in cities. But in some great urban centres, they are found together in 'ethnic enclaves' where through competition with each other, they eventually become more visible as a group. This phenomenon is even more important in countries where the immigrant community is more recent, as in Italy and Spain.

The reactions of European societies to this presence in the street are of different kinds. In France, despite heavy concentration in some neighbourhoods, it is felt that this is not the important thing, and that "relations with the country of origin are just another part of the process of integration in the host country" [Cesari, 1999:15]. In Germany, however, such concentration of businesses is seen as an attempt to establish territory and operate in parallel to the German economy. This feeling seems all the more significant, because all the religious structures organise themselves in a much more direct way, and carry on their own business, usually in relation with mosques [Spuler-Stegemann, 1998:277 ff.]. As for the arrangements in Great Britain, they seem to occupy a median position. There are heavy ethnic concentrations of people here and there, which sometimes create the impression of an exclusive space, and of the power and influence of certain religious currents, but these do not seem to be as focused as the Turkish populations are on the idea of a central-ised economic area which must be defended against competition from outside. In contrast to the German case, the advantage seems to go to individual businesses, always in relation to the amount of capital the immigrant begins with.

Here are some instructive examples regarding the situation in Germany (not necessarily in order of importance): the Süleymancis movement (*Verband Islamischer Kulturzentren*—VIKZ) owns houses and companies in a number of cities; the Kaplan group (ICCB) owns the *Kar-Bir Lebensmittel und Textil GmbH*, which deals in foodstuffs and textiles, and whose shares are sold to members for 1000 DM each. Other movements have similar holdings. The *Avrupa Türk Islam Birligi* (ATIB, a movement which promotes pan-Turk ideas) owns large fruit and vegetable import companies, and it has been said that the Milli Görüs movement controls a sixth of the food business in Germany. They own about fifteen commercial companies, with combined annual sales estimated at 10 billion dollars [Spuler-Stegemann, 1998:277 ff.],[6] and their real estate holdings in Germany are worth 130 million

---

[6] Businesses in sectors such as: travel agencies, halal food (Selâm), clothing (Büsra Giyim) and Islamic cosmetics, audio and video cassettes (Es-Selâm Video), pub-lishing houses (Hicret Yayinevi), bookstores, gift shops, lending agencies and insur-ance agents (Finans Kredi Pazarlama) and Islamic funeral arrangements (Cinar Cenaze Nakliyat) [Manço, 1997].

DM. Most of these properties came to them as gifts or bequests [Manço, 1997]. As for the four biggest stores connected to mosques in Germany, they belong to the Turkish-Islamic organisation Yimpaça Holding; its 4,500 stockholders, including representatives of *Refah Partisi*, want to see an enlargement of the retail market in Central Europe [Spuler-Stegemann, 1998:277 ff.].

Official Islamic commerce and labour

Returning to the European level, it is important to realise that all these manoeuvres must be seen as related to the tendency toward a progressive affirmation of the religious dimension of several ethnic commercial sectors. Since the 1980s, we have seen in fact a development of the "formally Islamic commercial sector, still functioning in a quite consumer-oriented manner". Today, it is possible to speak about 'Islamic fashions' and 'Muslim brand names', although such fashions and brands were until recently considered by Muslims as imitations of the immoral West perpetrated by Westernized (and thus alienated) Turks [Arslan, cited by Manço, 2000:269 ff.].

In Germany, there is a chain of 35 Tekbir stores distributed throughout the country, which sell a collection of clothing called the Tesettür Mode Collection, including robes and scarves of all sizes and all colors. As for pilgrims' gear, consisting of a white sheet, a prayer rug and perhaps essential oils or perfumes, all this is now available in every major German city [Spuler-Stegemann, 1998: 280 ff.].

Beyond these purely commercial aspects, another appears, that of 'professional Islamic workers', full-time, whose role is quite essential in the process of establishing and spreading Islamic culture in Europe [Allievi, 1998:203]. These positions are still rather rare, but the phenomenon merits attention because of its symbolic importance, and because its general importance is likely to increase. At present, this category includes missionaries, preachers who are usually benevolent, and especially activists, directors, organisers, intellectuals, and (in increasing numbers) chaplains and counsellors who work in the army, in hospitals, and in prisons. In the framework of this kind of 'Islam business', converted Muslims play a critical role, more often in the areas of politics and academia than the financial sector. They accomplish their work in the areas of editing and publishing and university teaching, where they profit from their knowledge of languages and cultures while advancing themselves along their own paths. They may even become local spokespersons in communities, dialoguing with politicians and the media [Allievi, 1998:205 ff.].

Resources for funding this kind of position are rare, except for the chaplain's service, whose value is beginning to be recognised and even funded in some European states, especially in prisons and in the army, as in Belgium where twelve regular Muslim chaplains are employed, and in France, the Netherlands, Great Britain, and Spain. At the European level, there are only a few centres which can undertake this work, and then only because they operate for profit, or receive funds from countries or from organisations that can afford the cost.

5. The Special Case of Halal Meat

This business has a direct relation to Islamic prescriptions according to which Muslims must not eat pork, or the flesh of any animal that has not been slaughtered according to Islamic requirements. This has given rise to several practices. First, Islamic slaughterhouses for beef, mutton, and poultry have been opened, or else existing slaughterhouse capacity has been converted to Islamic slaughter. Then these businesses have established retail outlets. Following that, they attempt to obtain the right to use the halal label for products. In general, methods of Islamic slaughtering run counter to some European legislation concerning the well-being of animals. The whole trick, then, is to harmonise respect for ritual prescriptions, similar to those for Jewish kosher food, and European recommendations and norms.

Special features and importance of this business

This sector of activity needs a separate section for two reasons: it has been the quickest to appear, sometimes even before a place of worship [ES File], and it also appears to be the most important and most burgeoning sector. An indication of this in France: where professional butchers say that halal business represents 300,000 tons of meat a year, and nearly six hundred ritual slaughterers are working for a network of more than 3,000 butcher shops in the country, with large clients in the Gulf states, who import quantities of halal meat [Cesari, 1997:149 ff.]. There have been additions to the sheep flocks in the Cevennes region, for the purpose of supplying Muslims, especially for the feast of the ʿId al-Kabir [Brisebarre, 1998]. In Germany, a number of large companies have been established in this sector: Gel-Tat (wholesaler), Helal Gida, and Misir Bazaar [Amiraux, 1995:69], not to mention the quite unexpected success of the döner kebab business, which supports its own factory [Caglar, 1995]. Danish exports of chicken and fowl to Muslim countries have increased greatly since the mid-1970s, and it is generally agreed that close to 90% of that production is halal, regardless of its destination [Nielsen, 1992:78]. There are a number of important halal butcher shops in Belgium, and 360 Islamic butcher shops were listed in the Netherlands in 1998; the latter figure may actually be 500, if clandestine sellers and slaughterhouses which furnish customers directly are counted [Kloostermann, van der Leun & Rath, 1999:260]. In Spain, it is estimated that 400 or 500 butcher shops and grocery stores sell halal products [ES File].

All these figures should not make us forget that important variations in these trends can be observed. A study conducted in the Netherlands argued that even a large number of such butcher shops still made up a small part of the market because few of them made substantial profits or stayed in operation for a long time. In fact the survival of many of them depends on such factors as being able to use more parts of the animals than Western butchers usually do, less money spent on the appearance of stores, and acceptance of lower profits than Western butchers make. These small businesspeople sometimes manage to reduce their fixed costs by selling meat without declaring the sale for tax purposes, employing their relatives only when there is a rush of customers and paying these relatives in food. Such shortcuts are made necessary by the level of competition, sharpened even more by the fact that large food stores are now beginning to sell packaged halal meat [Kloostermann, van der Leun & Rath, 1999:260 ff.].

In some countries ritual slaughter raises no particular debates, but in others, there is a major objection: it's illegal. In Norway, Sweden, and Switzerland this is the case, but they can import halal meat from neighbouring countries, from France, Denmark, Germany, or even Australia. Some butchers travel to other countries regularly to purchase stocks of meat for sale in stores, personally assuring the quality of the meat they buy [Shadid & van Koningsveld, 1995:84].

There are also some countries with very few halal butchers: there is one in Finland [FI File], one in Luxembourg [LU File], three in

Portugal [PT File], one in Austria [AT File], and none in Italy. Halal meat there is handled only through mosques [IT File].

Various strategies and stages

The size of this market supports many different business models. There are small scale slaughterhouses which produce for mosques and private customers, and there are cooperatives located in urban centres, usually connected in one way or another with Islamic centres, which establish networks of distribution. And then there are multinational-sized businesses worth fortunes, which have occasionally generated scandals [Allievi, 1998:167].

The amount of money to be made is so large that this market can fall into the hands of unscrupulous dealers, who care less about religious prescriptions than about money [Cesari, 1997:149 ff.]. Cases of fraud are numerous: some firms may have failed to keep halal through the incompetence of a ritual butcher [Cesari, 1997:149 ff.], and in some cases there may have been questions about the criteria for ritual guarantees (the definition of halal) in relation to various Muslim tendencies [Panafit, 1999:149 ff.], or there may have been real cheating linked to the resale of certificates from Islamic centres without any real inspection or certification being performed by these centres [Allievi, 1998:167]. At present, according to the director of the *Centre Islamique et Culturel—Parc du Cinquantenaire* in Brussels, the "majority of butchers who claim to sell halal meat do so without any ritual guarantee" [Panafit, 1999:375]. Suspicions about the Islamic authenticity of meat are sometimes such that they have pushed certain "dealers to use various tricks in order to be able to claim legitimacy, such as filming the ritual slaughter, or putting a well-known imam on camera in a slaughterhouse" [Cesari, 1997: 149 ff.].

These large financial stakes thus depend on the legal authorisation to slaughter in the ritual manner, which depends on the laws in force in European countries. They depend too on the issuance of certificates proving the licit character of ritual slaughter, the definition of which depends further on criteria established by authorities within the Muslim community. It is sometimes said that an official label should be set up, for the benefit of purists who want to have proof of the quality of their merchandise, if only in regard to products destined for export to Muslim countries [Shadid & van Koningsveld,

1992:12]. Few things appear to have been decided at the European level in this matter.

There have been a variety of attempts, however. The *Institut Musulman de la Mosquée de Paris* (IMMP) made an official request to the French Ministry of Agriculture in 1998 for the right to establish a label, Halal France, modelled after the Jewish label Beth Din. In Spain, nothing has been put in practice despite the Agreement on Cooperation of 1992, which in its 14th article states that only the *Comisión Islámica de España* has the authority to guarantee a halal label on foodstuffs. Since 2000, though, the *Federación Española de Entidades Religiosas Islámicas* (FEERI) has endorsed standards related to a sticker guaranteeing 'Halal Quality', these standards being checked by the Spanish Institute of Halal Quality in Cordova, in cooperation with the Diputacion Provincial of Cordoba [ES File].

Political and symbolic contention

These halting steps and delays are actually to be explained in general by the great interest in and size of the halal meat business, which in some ways goes far beyond the simple economic aspect of the business. The question of the control of halal brings political authority into play. From a symbolic point of view, political power can determine who will be able to declare foodstuffs licit or illicit. More pragmatically, the financial advantage which can be obtained in this way raises a question about the need to strengthen certain organisational structures or associations, and even about the need for representation at the national level.

Trends of this sort have been observed especially in France and Germany, where competition in the ethnic commerce sector is increasing, each side getting support from various groups "whose ideologies, objectives, and sources of community support or even international support are different" [Boubakri, 1999:88]. The situation remains one of freewheeling competition; in this struggle, things get sorted out at the local level, perhaps according to some local religious authority, while each organisation keeps gathering strength and jockeying for position. Many protests were raised when the French Ministry of Agriculture decided, in December 1994, to "accredit the *Institut Musulman de la Mosquée de Paris* (IMMP) as the only religious organism with the legal power to license ritual slaughterers within the Hexagon, and the right to collect dues of one French franc

(= 0.15 €) per kilo of meat sold which is slaughtered ritually". The
protests against this monopoly came from those who did not recognize the leadership of the *Institut Musulman de la Mosquée de Paris*
(IMMP), and from certain governments, notably Morocco, who
entered the debate on behalf of its citizens in France. The monopoly was eventually rescinded; since June 1996 the *Mosquée de Lyon*
and Evry's have been empowered to "license halal slaughterers".
While waiting for further formalisation, many organisations continue
to struggle for advantage, like the *Union des Organisations Islamiques de
France* (UOIF), which after creating an office of inspection and religious authentication for foodstuffs, won the support of Kuwait, the
United Arab Emirates, and Yemen, giving it financial sources of
great importance [Cesari, 1997:149 ff.].

6. Islamic Banks, Licit Insurance, and Money Transfers

The Islamic economic phenomenon emerged from the necessity of
reconciling money and business with Qur'anic prescriptions, at the
same time that petrodollars were beginning to weigh in on financial
markets. There was a necessity to get around the traditional Islamic
prohibition on loan interest and usury (*riba*). Bank interest counts as
usury, though "the interpretation of the word *riba* has always been
the subject of arguments. For some, it refers to any form of 'fixed
(rate) interest', but for others it means only excessive interest". From
that point, "although some religious authorities have proclaimed
the licit character of certain types of interest, many 'ulamâ' continue
to follow a strict interpretation" [Warde, 2001]. In reality, "without
arguing against the principle of the repayment of the money lent,
the Islamic tradition is opposed to the 'fixed and predetermined'
character of an interest rate, and to what that principle implies as
regards fairness and the potential for exploitation of the borrower".
[Warde, 2001]. Out of respect for these prohibitions, Islamic associative financing "recommends instead an equitable sharing of risks
and benefits". This type of financing is intended to give opportunities to dynamic entrepreneurs who lack capital, and to help Muslims
gain borrowing power; it is also thought that banks have a duty to
combat poverty and discrimination because of their role as managers
of the *zakat* funds, charitable contributions commanded by Islam
[Warde, 2001]. The prohibitions are tempered by the licit charac-

ter of certain forms of usury, such as unsecured loans when concluded outside the territory of Islam and if they are made to non-practicing Muslims or to non-Muslims [Parigi, 1989].

Principles and special provisions regarding contracts

The principles of operation of an Islamic bank concentrate on short and long term investments of venture capital and start-up capital through purchase of partial ownership or other means of participation in the start-up expenses of companies. Two methods of associative financing are found: the first is that of the *mudaraba* (limited partnership). This is a silent partnership in which the entrepreneur manages the business, and shares profits with the bank at a fixed percentage, but is not liable for debts incurred in the event of failure as long as normal management standards are maintained. There is also a form called *musharaka* (association), in which the bank and its client take over the management of an existing business which has operating capital, and bank and client are each liable for debts incurred depending on the percentage of ownership of each. There are other types of contract, involving short-term financing (*ijara*), insurance, or the purchase of merchandise for sale, in which the bank makes the purchase for the client, who may take possession of the goods immediately but delay payment [Parigi, 1989:73 ff.]. Long term goals of such investment include profit for all, but also the promotion of socially and/or economically beneficial projects in the Third World [Obeidi, 1988].

History and present extent

In 1975, in the "wake of a fourfold increase in the price of oil", the Islamic Development Bank (IDB) was created at Jeddah as the result of a decision by the Organisation of the Islamic Conference (OIC) to "put Islamic economic principles back on the agenda" [Warde, 2001]. This was the first large-scale Islamic economic project to be supported by Islamic deposit banks from most Muslim countries. This inter-governmental financial institution is intended to 'awaken' Islam by financing religious construction projects throughout the world, as well as 'cultural' projects and a number of economic rescue projects. Islamic Centres of economic research were created and their number grew in Europe, with one of the most important located in Leicester. In 1978 the company, Islamic Bank System International Holding, operating according to Islamic principles, became the first of its kind to establish itself in Europe. In 1985 it became the Islamic Finance House Universal Holding (IFHUH), and this institution has given birth to most others of its type in Europe today, with the possible exception of the one in Geneva. [Parigi, 1989].

Islamic banks have been set up in all major regions of the world: Africa, Europe, America, the Gulf Cooperation Council (GCC), the Middle East, South Asia and Southeast Asia. Europe and America have only four, less than 3% of the total [Shaikh, 1997:117 ff.]. In 1981, the Arab bank *Dar al-Maal al-Islami* (DMI) opened in Geneva. This is the most important investment company. It has financed economic and cultural projects designed to support Islam in Africa. Since 1982, the Islamic Bank International has operated in Copenhagen. In London there is the famous Kuwait Investment Office, which manages capital funds estimated at 80 billion dollars. And the European branch of the Islamic Takaful Company has headquarters in Luxembourg and offices in Köln, though it is not registered with the Chamber of Commerce and Industry [Spuler-Stegemann, 1998:273 ff.].

Commercial success

The small number of Islamic banks operating in Europe is not indicative of their financial muscle, and they have been quite successful. The Geneva bank is said to have doubled its original capital of a billion dollars between 1981 and 1988 [Spuler-Stegemann, 1998:273 ff.]. And if we take into consideration Islamic capital handled by conventional banks, indicators of importance at the regional level would probably change a great deal. In fact, some institutions which serve minority populations in the West register themselves under non-Islamic names, to comply with conventional banking laws. But they may still operate according to Islamic banking principles [Shaikh, 1997:117 ff.].

On one hand, many banks and insurance companies based in Muslim countries have established offices in Europe since the 1980s. One example is the Morocco Assistance Internationale, subscribed through the Chaabi Bank, or the Mondial Assistance group subscribed via the Wafa Bank or the Banque du Commerce Exterieur. Agencies of these banks in Belgium sell repatriation insurance (for return to the country of origin); 13 Euros a month are automatically deducted from the insured's account. A majority of Turks are affiliated with the Diyanet in this regard, and the Tunisian government covers all burial expenses for its nationals abroad [Panafit, 1999:409]. On another hand, a number of European banks are practicing the Islamic system. In 1985, the Union of Swiss Banks (UBS) responded to demands from Arab clients by opening an Islamic department in its home city of Zurich [Parigi, 1989:12]. Other banks, like the Bank of England, the Banco di Roma, and Banque Bruxelles Lambert in Brussels followed suit across Europe. Like Citibank, which "opened an Islamic branch in 1996 in Bahrain, most large Western financial institutions have entered this type of business, by opening branches, offering 'Islamic tellers', or providing Islamic-type financial instruments for Muslim clients" [Warde, 2001]. Clients can get guarantees about the 'disinterested' character of various investments, or of their non-involvement in activities prohibited by Islamic doctrine, e.g., alcohol, the arms trade, gambling, etc. [Parigi, 1989:161].

As for true Islamic banks, their uniqueness goes beyond the (already unprecedented) fact that they cater exclusively to a religious community, even if their services are usually aimed at a business clientele. However, the Islamic Takaful Company does offer a number of services for individuals, including insurance of all types, except civil liability. This company operates almost like an Islamic solidarity fund, whose participants agree to make payments proportional to their level of investment, in order to make up for missed payments following the anticipated death of other members. Beyond regular investment operations, which benefit many Muslim projects in Europe, this company has progressively established life insurance and pension insurance systems. It also offers savings programmes for brides' trousseaux, and for people nearing the end of military service, plus instalment plans for funeral expenses or burial in the country of origin.

Although insurance may seem suspect as such to pious or conservative Muslims, who believe it shows a lack of confidence in God, or seems to go against the Muslim model of family solidarity in periods of difficulty, it is likely that this sector will grow in the future. This is partly because of an increasing sense of individualism [Super-Stegemann, 1998:273 ff.], but is also the growing importance of the second and third generations in the European societies in which they have taken root. Instead of sending money back to the country of

origin, these younger people increasingly rely on the banking system
in order to advance their commercial affairs, to provide education
for their children, or to save for retirement.

These goals are becoming more practical because Islamic banks
are becoming 'very pragmatic'. They are prepared to balance practical business principles with traditional Islamic principles; *riba* is still
considered interest, but Islamic bankers are proving "creative in their
approach to the development of their institutional operations" [Saeed,
1999:7]. In fact, according to I. Warde, after the low point at the
end of the 1980s, when partnership financing came to be seen as
disappointing because it was imitative of conventional banking, there
has been a revitalisation of the sector. One reason for this was "revolutions in international finance (technological changes and deregu-
lation) and socio-political changes such as the impact of the Iranian
revolution, the Gulf War, the emergence of new Islamic states, the
rise of a religious Muslim bourgeoisie, etc." Another reason was that
the practice of 'moral economics' had increased, beginning with the
return to "principles which had for a long time allowed Islam to
adapt to the most diverse cultures: *'urf* (acceptance of local customs),
darura (necessity) and *maslaha* (the public interest)." But while "the
attractions of Islamic finance are explained above all by the excesses
of international finance", the functioning of the former gives rise to
its own paradoxes. Debates about the nature of *riba* have been got-
ten around by systems which generate profits through commissions
and fees for services (not by charging interest on deposits); however,
"the financial instruments whose markets are growing the fastest are
often those which, during the 1970s, were considered illicit (insurance) or were rarely used" [Warde, 2001]. During 2000, a certain
number of online Islamic financial services became available in Great
Britain. A variety of services, from insurance and pension contracts
to information about companies which adhere to ethical standards
of production, from the establishment of a list of charitable foundations to investment counselling regarding businesses which are
acceptable under Islamic criteria [The Times Higher Education
Supplement, 13/04/01, mentioned in British Muslims Monthly Survey,
vol. 9, n° 5, CSIC-The University of Birmingham, May 2001:5].
Aside from guarantees regarding an ethical system of finance sanc-
tioned by religion, such options allowed bank clients "to invest in
halal products", a trend which "will certainly be accentuated in the
future" [Saeed, 1999:7].

Changes in the flow of remittances to the country of origin

Payments for support of families continue, even to countries of origin, but less often now in the form of sending money home, or offering to pay for family members to come to Europe. Gifts of money are still important: it has been estimated that money transfers to Morocco, Tunisia, and Algeria "exceed the amount of direct foreign investment and the net amount of public aid for development" [Cesari, 1997b]. A quarter of Pakistani and Bengali households in Great Britain still send money home, often to elderly parents [Beishon, Modood & Virdee, 1998:54]. In Germany, money transfers from Turkish workers reached 1.5 billion dollars in 1992 [Manço, 1997]. Still, the amount of these transfers is diminishing over the duration of implantation, the time families have lived in Europe. Taking again the example of Turks in Germany: the 1992 figure fell forty percent in relation to its level of 1984, when the highest yearly total, 2.4 billion, was sent [Manço, 1997]. This series of events was also influenced by economic recession in Europe; by the completion of a process of family regrouping in Europe, leaving only a few in the country of origin; by the gradual abandonment of the idea of a return; by the desire to participate more fully in the host country, etc.

Several successful project types are appearing. One example is that of the Algerian community of France, which is the largest source of foreign currencies through parallel markets [Benbouzid, 1999]. Another, more Islamic, has been developing for some time: the *Refah Partisi* and its successors, the Muslim Brotherhood, and the Murids among others have established fund-raising organs for specific causes, such as construction or restoration of mosques, especially in Tunisia. There has also been a move toward reinvestment of profits made in Europe for the purpose of creating jobs in the country of origin, as in Algeria with the establishment of import-export houses and taxicab concessions [Santelli, 1999], or in Tunisia, where 5,629 businesses were started by emigrants between 1975 and 1990 [Boubakri, 1999:79].

Such activities can be carried on by private businesspersons, intellectuals, or teachers without their having to return for long periods to the country of origin [Santelli, 1999]: "permanent mobility has replaced traditional forms of migration" [Cesari, 1999]. For these persons, the potential profits are not as important as the fact of 'doing something together'. These economic and/or professional investments "testify to the debts that emigration contracted, as well as to ties of loyalty" between family members and their community of origin. It is interesting to note that some justify their actions with reference to the national economy, and others cite the desire to participate in the creation of a common economic space that includes Europe and the Maghreb [Santelli, 1999]; an ensemble of attitudes which already raises the question, whether "some of these actors are not already part of a kind of *transnational civil society*" [Cesari, 1999:22].

CHAPTER TWELVE

THE INTERNATIONAL DIMENSION

Stefano Allievi

1. GLOBALISATION, EUROPE AND ISLAM

The process of globalisation implies consequences that concern us directly, including with regard to relations between Europe and Islam. The emphasis, in the analysis of these processes, has often been on the economic and technological aspects and possibly on the political ones: today, we know that its cultural consequences, its consequences on society and on individuals, including their beliefs, are at least equally crucial.

The processes of globalisation imply a reconsideration of our way of interpreting the traditional relations between the centre and the periphery. Not only, as is often said, because in the era of the Internet there is no longer a centre, which is much truer in the virtual world than in the real one, but because these relations are no longer unidirectional. And it is precisely the cultural flows, more visibly for example than the economic ones and those of political and military power, that show that they are always multidirectional and may even be between peripheries, without the mediation of a centre.

If it is true, as has been said, that modernity is inherently globalising [Giddens, 1991], now that it has been, so to speak, boosted and radicalised, the mechanisms, systems, modalities and nodes of connection have been multiplied, in a process of intensification of links which is starting to cover all the interrelations on a global scale. The phases of this process are sufficiently well known: amongst its effects, we can recall the development of global movements and institutions, the acceleration and the boosting of global means of communication or which allow global access, the accentuated multiculturality of its practices and contents, the growth of interest for a world conceived as 'one', etc. All these phenomena also imply traditional cultures and systems of belief which find themselves playing a role of de-re-territorialisation, repositioning the traditional relations between local and global, and fostering processes of universalisation of the particularities and of particularisation of universalisms [Robertson, 1992].

A more anthropological vision can help us to understand better the cultural effects of this process: there is a tendency towards the creation of a global ecumene, but it has to be understood as a region of persistent interaction and cultural exchange [Hannerz, 1989]. The cultural aspect, which substantially mediates the ways of appropriation of the process of globalisation, assumes in this interpretation a priority characterisation. And it also helps us to understand how the cultural production of the peripheries is in some way also the response to the political and economic domination of the centre. We can add that the traffic and cultural exchange is in any case transnational more than international: it subverts, devaluates or is at any rate capable of overlooking national borders—and travels in all directions. In the case of Islam, with regard to the relations between Islam and the West, it has been described as a flow that can now be assimilated to a "multi-lane super highway with two-way traffic" [Esposito, 2001]; but the discourse is also valid within the Muslim *Umma* as a whole.

European Islam is a good demonstration of this. On the one hand it can be interpreted, in the relations between former colonial powers and former colonised countries, where the flows often come from, as a centre-periphery relationship. On the other hand, in the Muslim world in general, and in the European part of the *Umma* in particular, it produces interconnections between peripheries. It is no coincidence, besides, that its borders, if it has any, do not correspond with those of the EU or even with those of present-day Western Europe: they also start from the Atlantic and not only do they end beyond the Urals, but include the countries bordering the Mediterranean, on both the south and eastern shores, as well. And they also include the countries of origin of the Muslim communities residing in Europe who may be very far from Europe, as the British case, for example, shows.

Having said this, the processes mentioned are not founded on a 'static' base: they presuppose, imply and produce mobility—of information, money, goods but also of men and women. There is therefore a mobility of cultures, which 'exports' their products, including symbolic and intangible ones, but there is also a concrete mobility of people who are their bearers, which clearly increases the efficacy and the stability of the effects: one thing is the diffusion of a fashion or a cultural or even religious trend, another thing is that consistent groups of individuals who share a common belief move to another place, taking with them this same culture and/or religion, transplanting it elsewhere, so to speak. In the case of Buddhism, for example, the first way of penetration mentioned has, for the time being, been more significant, even if the second, with the relative interactions is beginning to assume a certain importance; in the case of Islam the second is certainly the most significant, even if in this case too there is a cultural component that is extraneous to migratory flows and there are important interactions between the two [Allievi, 2000].

2. ISLAM, A EUROPEAN FACT

The introductory chapter to this report outlines a history and picture of the presence of Islam in Europe today. This is sufficient not only to recall that Islam also has a European history, or that there has been an important history of reciprocal cultural influences, but that Islam is now to be definitively considered a domestic European fact: in a word, Islam is *inlandisch* and with dimensions, on the quantitative as well as qualitative levels, that are anything but negligible. But this is an internal fact, that can be analysed as such in its dynamics and which nevertheless comes into relation with states, societies, movements and centres of cultural elaboration that are elsewhere: and it is in this dual dynamic that it is to be interpreted. An internal social actor, then, but also an externalised element, and in any case perceived as such by observers and public opinion, at times even beyond empirical evidence. Much of our relationship with Islam and our capacities to understand it, both within and outside Europe, comes into play in the weave of these two dynamics, internal and external, national and international.

However, external influences can be measured through many indicators which are not only those of international relations: in social dynamics, in the first place from phenomena of mobility (in the two directions: migratory flows, including on a temporary basis, travel but also remittance of funds, forms of import-export etc.), from the cultural, political and, not least, religious point of view and, in the last place, on international politics. And these are, we underline, influences in both directions, although the emphasis of research and reflection is above all on external influences, from the Muslim world to Europe and in particular to Muslims resident here.

Some observers have wanted to underline that the current process of construction of Europe, and not only the long term historical process, essentially took place against Islam and as an alternative to it. Beyond the debated and debatable theory of the clash of civilisations [Huntington, 1996], we can recall one of its well known 'translations', such as that of Willy Claes, former Secretary General of the NATO who, in a television interview in February 1995 stated that Muslim fundamentalism was "at least as dangerous as communism once was" [quoted in Runnymede Trust, 1997], referring to a conflicting vision of relations with it. Expressions of this kind have been repeated infinitely by political leaders and commentators in different countries and at various levels: without considering that often, at a level of popularising work, the expression 'Muslim fundamentalism', in *realpolitik* and in the world of the media, and more in general in the cultural perception of the phenomenon, stands for Islam *tout court*.

Beyond the theories mentioned and their foundations, which do not interest us here, the question of the problem of the self-definition of Europe returns, understood as a process and project of construction of a European union, the bases of which today appear in need of urgent redefinition, in a situation of greater complexity and increasingly less homogenity of the countries involved (and of those that will be involved). The problem is precisely how to do it, on the grounds of which criteria. There are some who note that, in the current state, the construction of Europe, in the absence of a civic European identity, risks leading to a definition of a European 'us' based on a social order as a common asset defined in terms of prosperity (welfare) and security, more prone to exclusion than to inclusion [Kastoryano, 1998b]. Europe, in the opinion of some, today asserts itself more for a defensive refusal than a desire for conquest and domination [Leveau, 1998]. The problem remains of having to define what really is being defended and if this includes a founding nucleus of cultural and possibly religious values: and if so, which ones are in question. This poses a problem of identity and of definition of the same: political, economic, social, cultural and, lastly, religious.

The events in former Yugoslavia, relations with Albania and the discussion on the candidature of Turkey are recent elements that confirm the 'conflicting' theory and its definition in terms that are essentially of confrontation/conflict with Islam to the extent that various voices have been raised, in both the political and intellectual worlds (as well as in the religious sphere) to repeat that Europe ends where Orthodoxy and Islam begin. The process of enlargement eastwards of the European Union, however, begins to include precisely countries with an Orthodox majority and, as far as Islam is concerned, as we have seen, it is already an internal element that cannot be overlooked, which could develop further, including identities with an ethnic-religious character that, although already present, for example in Greece, are nevertheless even more highly visible in East European countries, Cyprus and, naturally, Turkey. Beyond what happens within Europe, it therefore becomes necessary to examine the relations between Europe and what lies outside; relations that are international but, from certain points of view, as we shall see, also intra-Muslim.

3. European Public Space and Muslim Countries: Trans-Mediterranean Dynamics

There are important connections between the European space (public and not) and Islam, the majority of which we shall only mention without being able to examine them in depth here. In the first place, important trans-Mediterranean (and transnational, including beyond the Mediterranean basin) dynamics of the structural type are at play: how the evolutions of demographic processes, which see in the Mediterranean one of the acutest areas of fracture in the world, with a remarkable divergence of trends [Livi Bacci & Martuzzi Veronesi, 1990], on the one hand, but on the other, just as remarkable and rapid phenomena of adjustment, often beyond expectations [Courbage, 1999]. Amongst the elements that it is important to underline, in addition to the current numbers and projections, there is also the effect of feedback on the countries of origin through the immigrant communities, whilst at the beginning of the migratory process it is mainly the contrary that takes place. To what extent this is the effect of cultural and also religious changes is naturally a hypothesis to be verified, also because the dynamics are anything but harmonious: the fertility rate of Turks, for example, is increasing in Germany and the Netherlands and decreasing in Turkey [Courbage, 1999], which calls for caution in projecting and defining trends. Nor do Muslim populations necessarily have similar demographic behaviour, as the differences between the Moroccan and Turkish communities in the same country of immigration show, both in relation to the rates of reproduction and to the rates of exogamy, measured in different studies. These differences tell us of the discordance of data and the difficulties to find unequivocal trends: in short, we can hypothesise that there are cultural influences that weigh on the definition of these trends, but it is much less clear through which factors, in which circumstances and with which evidence to the contrary.

But beyond the structural (demographic and economic) trends, it is clear that an important role in outlining and limiting the relations between European public space and Islam is obviously played by the role of international politics, both of the European countries and of the Muslim countries, in particular those of origin of the Muslim immigrants resident in Europe. The possibility of an in-depth analysis of international politics on this subject, which would necessarily have to produce a detailed case by case analysis, lies outside our competence. However, we feel that it would not be wrong to make at least some mention of the problem in this context.

On the European side, both as individual countries and, more weakly, as the Union, there exist political, strategic, diplomatic and military (both of 'attack' or at least of intervention in the various forms of humanitarian interference to a greater or lesser degree—for example, the Gulf War, or more recently Bosnia, Kosovo and Macedonia—and of defence, for example from possible terrorist infiltration) and economic (in particular relating to energy) interests that concern Muslim countries. Now, how unrealistic it may be to think that these factors exclude religious arguments is shown for example, by the events subsequent to the 1973 oil crisis, after which, at various latitudes, from Rome to Brussels, various European countries vied with each other in offering some type of formal recognition of Islam as a religion, as we have seen in the chapter on the tensions in the public space: from granting building permits for an Islamic centre in the capital to a more substantial and symbolically significant legal recognition, as occurred in 1974 in Belgium, the first European country to have recognised Islam as one of its own 'national' religions, in exchange for hypothetical benefits on the energy level, as Islam, in these situations, almost always means Saudi Arabia.

On the other hand, this legitimised an influence in the inverse meaning of Saudi Arabia itself, through the *Rabitat al-ʿAlam al-Islami* (Muslim World League), as the *de facto* 'external' representative of Islam, although at times with some ambitions of 'internal' representation. It is no coincidence today that almost all the major Islamic centres in the capitals of Europe depend, at least financially, on the *Rabita*, which takes it on itself, through the same channels, to distribute religious literature (and a particular literature: that which is reconciled with rigorous and formalist Wahhabi interpretation), Qur'ans, fund associations, educational structures, extemporaneous initiatives and publications, which do not depend directly on it but in some way end up by responding to it, even if perhaps less directly than may be thought (for example, the capacity that Saudi Arabia seems to have shown at international level as the real great almsgiver of the Muslim world, in financing even its own enemies). This role finds real competition perhaps only in the action of the DITIB (*Diyanet Isleri Türk Islam Birligi*) as far as the Turkish world is concerned whilst the action of the Libyan *Al-Daʿwa al-Islamiyya* is today more flexible, even if it was active and more incisive in the past, at least in some European countries. However, apart from the official transnational organisations, political-religious organisations, national movements and confraternities have a wide sphere of influence, as has been documented in another part of this report.

Saudi investment in Europe is, however, limited, if limits can be talked of, to the top ranks of the Islamic institutions in the capital cities (and not always) and, if anything, its weight is felt elsewhere, in the economic and financial world, with the obvious political-diplomatic consequences. However, it is lacking a decisive ingredient in order to be able to exercise greater influence in the European Muslim world: what we could call, paraphrasing the English writer Graham Greene, the 'human factor'. In other words, there are no Saudis amongst the Muslim immigrants in Europe, except the few ambassadors, economic operators and officials, with their respective families. This is a problem that also affects Libya, with a scarce presence in its former coloniser, Italy, although where in a recent period in history, it had a presence of conspicuous investments and showed a certain activism, including in cultural production and in the activation of Muslim initiatives, especially in nearby Sicily [Allievi & Dassetto, 1993].

On the other hand, other countries are present, in terms of real and often substantial 'human capital'; a presence that comes from the Arab world, in particular from Morocco, Tunisia, Algeria, Egypt as well as from other Middle Eastern countries; from sub-Saharan Africa, with the presence of Senegalese 'black Islam' and that of the Horn of Africa; from Iran and other Shiite minorities; from the Indian sub-continent in the case of the British 'exception', in part of the Netherlands and to a lesser extent in other countries and above all from Turkey, which has not been sufficiently studied, but which today has become the main Muslim component in Europe. According to a 1995 estimate, there were 2 million Turks in Germany, 350,000 in France, 182,000 in the Netherlands, 88,000 in Belgium, 78,000 in Switzerland, 36,000 in Denmark, 29,000 in Great Britain, 20,000 in Sweden etc. [Elmas, 1998]. Other estimates give the even more significant and perhaps excessive figure of around 4.5 million Turks in Europe, 3 million of whom representing the quota of the active population [Insel, 1999]: this would now clearly show that immigration is no longer (only) for work, but has a population widely represented in the female component and in the second and third generations.

The Turkish presence is greatly concentrated in Germany and in other countries in the 'median' section of Europe, from Switzerland and Austria to Sweden. These are countries which, from the point of view of the presence of Muslims (with the exception perhaps of Belgium and the Netherlands) are on average less studied than the others, or less 'seen' outside, compared to Great Britain and France; or at least they are countries, the scientific elaboration of which, also due to linguistic factors, is known to a lesser extent elsewhere. This has meant that in other countries, less directly concerned, for example Great Britain and France (which have done the most to form opinions, so far, on the study of Islam), but also the Mediterranean countries of new immigration, where the Turkish presence is more contained on a percentage basis, it has been substantially underestimated for several years. And this is despite the fact that the bibliography on the subject is anything but modest: more than 4,000 titles were listed in the early 1990s [de Tapia, 1995]. Even France, which after all has a Turkish presence of a certain importance, has discussed it less: the main emphasis, in the debate on Islam and in the attention given to it by the media, for reasons linked to the colonial heritage, to the Francophone projection and to recent events of post-colonisation, as in the case of Algeria, and obviously the weight of numbers, has always been on the Arab world and their relationship—and only in relatively recent times has a part of the attention been shifted to the Turkish component of immigration. Evidence of this more recent attention is, for example, special issues of journals (such as *Les Annales de l'autre islam* [1995] and *Hommes & Migrations* [1998]), an increasing number of books and various conferences on the subject.

Today, the aggregate data compel us to review the angle of our perception of the phenomenon of Islam in Europe, even in countries where this presence is lesser or even non-existent. However, we will deal with the Turkish case more specifically below. For the time being, it will be sufficient here to underline that these multiple presences are enough to create original trans-Mediterranean and transnational dynamics; and to bring distant questions to Europe, with a sense of topicality and 'vividness' that was unthinkable in the past, except perhaps at the time of the colonial empires but restricted to the individual imperial dominions of each country. The most varied questions can thus bounce into Europe, so to speak, as on the cushions of a billiard table, through migration and in Muslim communities and other segments of society. Therefore, the destruction in India of the Babri Mosque in Ayodhya, in 1992, by Hindus, generated a response in Great Britain, with Hindu temples and property becoming the target of attacks in Bradford [Lewis P., 1997]; more generally, the effects of events in Kashmir are heard of periodically; France undergoes the internal repercussions of the fratricidal war in Algeria; the Kurdish case becomes for many a European question and a German one in the first place (but also, with the Ocalan case, Italian and Greek [Antoniou, 2000]: countries that were directly involved, for various reasons, in the capture of the Kurdish leader), and takes on an unthinkable visibility in Turkey or in other Muslim countries; lastly, the external effects of conflicts that have developed elsewhere, at times at the doors of Europe or even within the continent are felt: from the Iran-Iraq war to the Israeli-Palestinian conflict to the Gulf War and the various conflicts triggered off following the break-up of former Yugoslavia (Bosnia and Kosovo, as well as the tensions in Albania, Macedonia and elsewhere). The trans-Mediterranean and transnational dynamics do not lend themselves however only to a political interpretation, related to the evolution of the international scene. A perhaps less obvious aspect but which is at least as important is of a social type and we will approach this below.

4. The Role of Networks

Does a transnational Muslim space exist? The question is legitimate and is clearly raised [Roy, 2002a]. Muslims, like other immigrants, are now used to crossing frontiers, including those of Europe, the valency of which is, in a certain sense, played down. Moreover, all things considered, they have been seen to be and are still much less impassable and much more permeable than the states would wish, even for some irregular components of migration. This is naturally easier for those who are not irregular, either because they enjoy full rights, as is the case of Muslims who have acquired a European citizenship or because they have 'limited' rights but which nevertheless allow extensive mobility, as residents.

Basically, immigrants are, from some points of view, the vanguard of the process of globalisation; not only is it their trade, as for market operators: it is their very lives. The 'coming and going' through frontiers has become (relatively) possible and real transnational spaces and circuits are created usually, but not exclusively, based on a primary bi-national link: typically the country of origin and that of settlement of the immigrant. In this process, of which only the economic implications have been analysed in the past, although in relation to the cultural capital and social and relational dynamics [Portes, 1995], the intervening variables, fundamental in the world of associations, politics and religion, which can act in isolation or together, play a decisive role. Often the relationship with the country of origin and participation and activism in the ethnic movements with a bipolar rooting (in the country of origin and in that of emigration) ends up by coming a chicken-and-egg situation, where it is not always clear who represents the base and who is the active subject in a process which can nevertheless be defined as integration: perhaps an original form of 'transnational integration' (for example, political—but also economic, not infrequently interwoven with the former—careers straddling both the country of origin and associations in the country of immigration). These processes, of decisive interest, have been studied above all, with illustrious precedents in the classics of sociology (including by Simmel, Sombart and Park) starting from ethnic entrepreneurship and the bonds that it creates between the countries of origin and countries of settlement. But their importance is neither only nor perhaps primarily economic.

Islam can be considered one of these original transnational social spaces and probably one that is eminently explicative of their functioning. All the elements necessary for the definition of these spaces [which we describe here following Faist, 1998] contribute to its development: a combination of social and symbolic bonds, the existence of positions between them in networks, the presence of organisations and networks of organisation that can be found in at least two geographically and internationally distinct places. More in detail, we also find at the same time capital of an economic type, both the resources in terms of human capital (skills and know-how) and, lastly, that fundamental resource which is social capital, made up in its turn of social bonds (a continuous series of interpersonal transactions involving shared interests, obligations, expectations and rules) and symbolic bonds (a continuous series of both face to face and indirect transactions, to which participants attribute and where they find shared meanings, memories, future expectations and symbols).

As can be seen, although the theoretical picture is conceived from the importance of social capital in the economic exchange between countries, it lends itself very well to an application to that transnational space that is the 'migratory Umma'. Not, that is, the Umma in its static meaning of all Muslims (this is a mere juxtaposition, devoid of the consequences that we are trying to outline here), but in a dynamic meaning of Muslims who 'move' and as such come into relation with one another and in their turn, bring into relation the countries and communities through which they transit or where they settle, to a greater or lesser degree of stability. This is the qualitative difference that must be underlined. And it is also this that makes these transnational spaces self-feeding processes which, once they have triggered off, are self-fuelling, producing their own dynamics. Some examples can give us a better appreciation of the consequences. An example of transnational economy that has been studied fairly well is that of Turkish entrepreneurship in Germany. As it can rely on solid bases in the country of origin but also on a consistent 'community market', it is one example of the many of ethnic business, which can be opened up, as often happens, outside the community, thus entering the global market and then becoming simply business. Now, it can be observed that, in addition to Turkish entrepreneurs, the Turkish Islamists have also followed the same model: and in particular the bi-national careers that have emerged through Islamic militancy in the *Milli Görüs* in Germany and in the *Refah Partisi* in Turkey can be outlined fairly well [Amiraux, 2001]. Concretely, this is translated into various aspects.

The first is what appears in consistent financial flows in the two directions, but in particular from Germany to Turkey: flows that show us that now 'Islamodollars' are also beginning to take the opposite direction to that to which attention is normally turned. The funds collected in Germany and that went to support the electoral campaign of the *Refah Partisi* in 1991 are estimated at DM 6 million. And the Turkish military seems to have fully understood the importance of the transnational enjeu which this example makes clear, to the extent of imposing, through the National Security Council, on the Islamists of Erbakan, once these acceded to power with the Refah-Yol coalition, amongst the other restrictive clauses, that of prohibiting funding from abroad for Turkish political parties, and specifically that from 'organisations established in Europe', with an explicit reference to *Milli Görüs* [Amiraux, 1999a]. To mention another case, Lewis P. [1998] quotes Muslim sources that complain that 90% of the funds collected in the United Kingdom for charity goes to the countries of origin, seriously underestimating local needs and, in short, causing damage to the Muslim presence in the country. And the same can be said of the funds collected by the Senegalese Murids which go to enrich Touba, the spiritual—but also political—capital of this confraternity [Schmidt di Friedberg, 1994].

But the aspect of financial flows is not the only or even the main one: it is in fact, the most obvious one, from certain points of view. On the other hand, it becomes more interesting to follow other manifestations of these new transnationalities: we are referring for example to the political careers that, emerging from neighbourhood religious work in Berlin or Frankfurt, can be translated into a parliamentary seat in Ankara. We have already mentioned the best known cases of members of parliament and mayors elected in the *Refah Partisi*. A more extreme case of attempted internationalisation is that of Cemalettin Kaplan, who in 1985 founded his Union of Islamic Societies and Communities (*Islami Camiler ve Cemaatler Birligi*—ICCB) in Germany, with the aim of establishing an Islamic state in Turkey, proclaiming himself caliph in 1992 and then naming his son Metin successor to the caliphate (a counter-caliph was also proclaimed in Berlin, following a scission under the leadership of Ibrahim Sofu, who was then killed after the proclamation of a fatwa that sentenced him to death) [Schiffauer, 2000]. It is interesting to note that the movement, with a minority presence in the Turkish communities in Germany, the Netherlands, Belgium, France and Denmark, was even smaller in Turkey, where its members were mainly relatives of emigrants [Ataçan, 1999].

There are also those who 'spend' their social capital, acquired again through links with associations with the countries of origin, on both markets, trying to gain credit and legitimacy in the receiving country as both an economic subject and as a social or political subject. But apart from the 'ethnic' examples, which could be multiplied, with reference to the main communities present in the various countries (these strategies can be identified, to a greater or lesser extent, amongst the Indians and Pakistanis in Great Britain and amongst the Algerians in France), the functioning of this mechanism can also be shown in other contexts. For example, in the confraternities: moreover, some *turuq* operate on the double register of confraternity and ethnic group, thus accummulating the strength of the various links [for example, the very clear and already quoted example of the Senegalese Murids; on them, as far as their operation in Europe is concerned, Schmidt di Friedberg, 1994]. But also, even more visibly, in missionary movements such as the *Jama'at al-Tabligh* [on these, see, amongst others, Dassetto, 1988; Kepel, 1987 and 1994; Masud, 2000], where the progressive exit and expansion of the market of reference outside the narrow bi-national context also appears evident (the movement, created in India, has had its greatest development in Europe, amongst North African immigrants in the urban suburbs), in the direction of a wider and more 'circular' presence: which we could define, coining a neologism which we feel is pertinent, 'ummic'.

This example is also valid for other minority religious groups in the Muslim world. For example, the Ahmadis, or the Shiite groups under the World Federation of Khojas Shia Ithna-Asheri Muslim Communities, to which some Muslim communities in Northern European countries refer and which has its head office in London [Alwell, 1998]. In the future, we could get used to finding an increasing number of Muslim organisations having their head office or important independent branches in the West.

We feel that the reasoning is less valid for political movements such as the *Ikhwan Muslimun*, who do adopt a transnational organisational form and strategies of intervention, but keep the centre of their interest and of their activities in the countries of origin and for whom Europe is as yet only a piece, although important, of a set of dominoes which is being created and is to continue elsewhere. Europe is, in short, in their case, a function of the traditional centres of interest of the movement: behind the lines, rather than the battlefield. This is at least so for the time being, even if we feel we can intuit some element of modification of the strategy, as the stay of the leaders of this and other associations in Europe is increasingly oriented towards 'here and now' rather than an increasingly distant and remote 'there' (and also in this case, as a consequence only of a slow generational changeover) [on Islamic movements and organisations in Europe, see the chapter on them].

The social networks developed in the Muslim (and non-Muslim) immigration have the important characteristic of being, according to classic formulations of network analysis, multistratum [Mitchell, 1969; Scidà, 2000]: that is, they are multiple social networks, with multiple contents (family, ethnic, economic, cultural and lastly religious) which cross national borders, those of physical and political geography (slightly less linguistic barriers, which are more complex to overcome than those due to the configuration of the territory). Therefore, amongst other factors, relations of kinship, friendship, marriage (perhaps, as in the case of Islam, induced and boosted by the—partial—bond of religious endogamy) but also interdependence, come into play on various levels and, not last, what we can define 'imaginary relations' [Cesari, 1997].

The networks are an important social innovation within European Islam and help to 'produce community' allowing at the same time contacts to be maintained with the country (or countries) of origin. Their effect increases thanks to the more important numerical weight of immigrant communities and thanks to the progressively increasing facility and declining cost of communications and mobility (of information, goods and persons: at least for those with a relatively stable status in Europe), which allow an increasing presence of the media from the countries of origin (satellite TV, radio and video) and with the countries of origin (e-mail and the Internet), more frequent personal contacts at the level of basic relations (telephone and mobile phone), and more frequent travel and contacts with the country of origin (for family and religious holidays, occasions linked to rites of passage, holidays, visits etc.) [on all this see the chapter on the media elsewhere in the report]. They contribute to producing loyalties, especially from the second generations onwards, which are at one and the same time internal and transnational: an aspect not without influence but amongst the least thematised of what contemporary sociology has become used to calling reflexivity, which is the affair of individuals but also of their groups of reference [on this subject see, amongst others, Giddens, 1991 and Beck, Giddens & Lash, 1994, the last-named author in particular on the implications related to the role of the community].

In conclusion, a sort of 'median space' is produced through these networks and bonds that does not correspond to a territory [Cesari, 1999b], and in the case of religions is also a sort of 'reference space of the soul' [from some points of view it would be suggestive to take Park's terminology, who spoke of 'moral regions'—Peraldi, 1999— even if by these he referred to a concrete and territorially definable element of 'urban ecology']. It can be measured in very concrete social practices and channels of communication, through which, in the name of religion, men and women, goods, customs and ways of dressing or eating (and the relative products), ideals, political and cultural values pass, in a process of uninterrupted mobility: no longer the classic migratory chain [Reyneri, 1979], characterised by a single direction and subjected to the primacy of the economy, but a third space, characterised by (not only) bi-directional flows, where cultural values play a decisive role.

To interpret this situation, which is still waiting for an objectively difficult defining arrangement, recourse has recently been made to varying concepts, including that of the diaspora. Taken from the classic Jewish example, it nevertheless appears more pertinent and functional, perhaps, for some individual ethnic-religious groups, where the linguistic factor also plays a decisive importance (perhaps, for example, we can speak of a Murid diaspora or a Turkish diaspora) or possibly for individual national groups but not for Muslims as a whole, who are lacking many elements of a diaspora. For example, there is no common territorial origin as point of reference (both of the symbolic or 'memorial' type, as is historical Israel and concretely 'state' as in present-day Israel), with which to maintain relations, even if only imaginary. There is also the absence of the awareness of a shared ethnic-cultural identity (there are various ones, in the same religious framework in Islam), and the existence of religious and community organisations of reference for all Muslims. There is not even a linguistic common denominator: not even, on close examination, when we restrict ourselves to the Arabic-speaking communities. In addition the historical example of the diaspora to which reference is made was a forced event, caused by circumstances; this cannot be said, or certainly not in the same way, of today's 'dispersions'. Lastly, as has been noted [Soysal, 2000], the category of a diaspora is an extension of the concept of nation-state which assumes, rather than demonstrates, a congruence between territorial state and national community, and as a consequence (with a *consecutio* that should not be considered automatic) a congruency between territory, culture and identity. In short, it presumptively accepts the existence of close community bonds of solidarity, on the basis of common ethnic and cultural references, between the place of arrival and the country of arrival. In a word, the diaspora is nothing but the extension of the place that has been left behind, of 'home' [*ibid.*].

The less characterised concept of networks allows a 'broader' perception of the dynamics in progress and those who have concretely analysed these dynamics prefer to insist with definitions that have to do with the concept of transnationality, talking of 'transnational ethnic networks' or possibly mentioning a possible 'sleeping—or potential—diaspora' that has not yet developed as such [Cesari, 1997]; or more simply of transversal solidarity [again Soysal, 2000] and of relative transnational loyalties, or again of transnational communities, characterising a situation where those who move and those who stay are still connected by thick and strong social and symbolic bonds through time and space (a concept where not only the idea but also the 'practice' of the Muslim *Umma* can be placed), in the conviction that other interpretative modalities do not add anything on the scientific level or risk being misleading [Faist, 1998].

The same concept of a relation of a transnational type is perhaps no longer sufficient: amongst the other reasons precisely for the emphasis, although negative, that is placed on the concept of nation, which partially conceals the cultural and 'cult-ual' specificity (we must also remember that the two terms share the same etymology and therefore an original connection which is often lost in the division of scientific work and its subsequent specialisations, which tend to analyse one or the other, separately). However, concepts borrowed from 'geographical' categories can be of some heuristic use and give an idea of the processes under way: Muslim spaces are certainly spaces of social practice [Amiraux, 1999a] crossed by symbols, an imagination and at times, utopias—in short, if the figure does not seem too complex, spaces without a place [which is something different from the non-places analysed by Augé, 1992] or frontier spaces [Faist, 1998], situated simultaneously in and between states, but also beyond them. It is no coincidence, with regard, for example to Sufi groups, that it has been possible to refer to a new 'global sacred geography' [Werbner, 1996]. Besides, the very definition of confraternity, *tariqa*, translates the concept of 'way' which in present-day and not only European reality, precisely following a further process of trans-nationalisation, which for the *turuq* is not a historical innovation but it has certainly undergone, in connection with migratory flows, unsuspected acceleration and globalisation, not only has a metaphysical meaning and one of a path and of religious initiation, but also takes on an extremely factual and concrete significance [for a general picture on confraternities today Popovic & Veinstein, 1996]. More in general, these modifications in the transnational collocation of the religious, with the typical alternation of majority and minority situations, according to latitudes, compels us to reason in terms of a different 'geo-religion' [Allievi, 1998], as we do when we talk of geopolitics.

That we are not talking about abstract principles but of extremely operative dynamics in progress, is shown to us by the apparently 'non-religious' consequences of a shared Muslim reference. The reference to ethnic and religious businesses is easy [on which we refer the reader for the Muslim effects of these to the chapter devoted to this subject]. After all, it has to be noted that the commercial networks, including those linked to very material things such as food (*halal* slaughtering but also ethnic restaurants, *doner kebab* stands etc.) often accompany the association and religious networks, especially in the context of some communities, even if in a strict sense they do not depend on one another: almost as if to ensure an adequate correspondence between terrestrial and spiritual nourishment [Petek-Salom, 1998], which may, moreover, take on aspects of a certain 'reality'. Beyond the intrinsic connections between the religious and economic sphere, we have *halal* entrepreneurs who finance community radio stations and neighbourhood mosques, specialised bodies in the production of Islamic radio and TV programmes or in the sale of religious literature and videos. But the commercial and religious spheres can also be intertwined within the economic activities, as in the case of Muslim-run restaurants which, even if they are for a non-community and indeed mainly native clientele, nevertheless mark the religious nature of their activity by the absence of alcohol and obviously of pork but the presence of *halal* meat and the contextual sale of Islamic literature and even gadgets. More specifically religious are the businesses linked to an Islamically correct way of dressing, all the activities connected with Muslim death (respect of specific rules on the corpse and burial, or repatriation of bodies to the countries of origin), but also the organisation of travel and so forth on the occasion of the *hajj* or of significant religious holidays such as the *magall* of the Senegalese Murids [all subjects on which we refer the reader to the relevant chapter].

In all this, religion has such a role and the networks it influences such a weight that it can even occur that criminal economies and networks refer to them; these criminal economies and networks, aware of the religious disapproval that weighs on their activity, can be tempted, as was the case in a large Italian city, to distribute to immigrants a leaflet in Arabic, therefore not addressed to the natives, in which an attempt was made at self-legitimacy of the religious type, maintaining the rash theory that selling drugs to infidels was not a sin. The leaflet in question was immediately stigmatised and condemned, naturally, by the religious leadership of the place, in a process of internal self-regulation of the Muslim community network which did not have any effect outside the religious world or on the city in question, which remained unaware of the incident.

Moreover, we can point out that the dynamics of religious legitimisation are transnational by definition, in particular in the first generations, who in the case of interpretative doubt regarding the lawfulness of certain behaviour often turn to the respective authorities in the country of origin, including in the modern form of interactive television programmes (with telephone calls from the public) and on-line *fatwas*: whilst for the later generations the discourse becomes more complex and a reduction in the references with respect to the country of origin (of their parents) does not necessarily mean retreating to the national sphere but it may mean, as was the case precisely in this field, an activation of European resources, for example, which incorporate in their turn the countries of origin in some form, as in the recent attempts of the council of fatwa which has already been mentioned elsewhere.

Some apparently unsuspected affinities can be produced, for example, from linguistic and cultural affinities, and they show very well the network dynamics to which we are referring and the nature of these complex community spaces, continuously crossed in both directions. It is interesting to note in this regard the recent relationships of collaboration between Portuguese and Brazilian Muslims (consisting of exchanges of visits by imams and by chat lines), that have nothing common from the point of view of origin (the former come from Mozambique or other African countries, although previously of Indian origin, the latter are mainly of Middle Eastern origin) and whose only common bond, in addition to their religion is precisely language (and not the sacred language of the Qur'an but a language that is certainly a minority in Islam, Portuguese). At the same time, the members of the elite of this Portuguese Muslim component send their children to study in England, also because they share with the Muslims in that country common Indian-Pakistani origins [Tiesler, 2000].

For other communities it is sufficient to recall that these 'spaces of crossing' by men and ideas also have an effect on the countries of origin. We want to underline in this regard the interesting feedback that this phenomenon of transnationalisation produces and the consequences that it can have and already has in the perception and interpretation of Islam, initially above all as orthopraxis but subsequently also as theorisation and therefore as orthodoxy. And this is a simple consequence of movement and continuous personal interaction, facilitated by the presence of a fluid transnational space, easy to travel through and equally as permeable: in brief, those who come and go bring with them opinions, behaviour, organisational methods, family choices, etc., and even if only implicitly they compare them with what they encounter in their interactions in the space of reference (for example in the countries of origin but also with and between third countries compared to the bilateral relationship country of origin/country of residence), which in turn is compared, in their opinions and in their behaviour, which are differentiated, although starting off from the same religious reference.

5. The Presence of Islam and EU Foreign Policy

We do not intend here to propose an analysis of the foreign policy of the European Union with respect to Muslim countries, which lies far outside our task and competence. We are concerned only with remarking the weight that the Muslim presence in the individual member states, but also the Union as a whole, can have on its foreign policy, that it can influence and in fact already influences. These are therefore the 'external effects' of this internal presence (even if coming from outside, in what is not a play on words but, here again, of reciprocal feedback of a certain complexity). The separation between internal and external politics, in this case, is moreover, more useful for heuristic purposes than real.

In general, the presence of minorities from Muslim countries can influence the policies of European countries in relation to the countries of origin of these minorities, and all the more so if these are also former colonies or belong to spheres of influence clearly connoted as such. We can therefore talk of a clear influence on bilateral and also multilateral relations, in which are interwoven migratory policies, labour policies, mutual economic interests and social problems, as well as strategic or diplomatic considerations. So far we are in the field of the obvious and it does not seem necessary to go into any further depth: each European country has its specific circumstances. Some are more active in the field of cultural policies, of which they have perceived the crucial importance. For example, the network of institutions that have to do with Islam and Muslim countries set up over the years by France: from the IMA (*Institut du Monde Arabe*) in Paris, to the various centres of the IRMC in the countries of North Africa, to the *Centre d'Etudes et de Documentation Economique, Juridique et Sociale* (CEDEJ) in Cairo, the *Institut Français d'Etudes Arabes de Damas* (IFEAD), etc.—in which different disciplinary competences converge (Islamic studies, social sciences, economics and law), but also an explicit link with foreign and domestic policy relative to the Muslim minorities in the country, in a network that has no parallel in Europe.

A classic and, in a certain way, extreme case of the link between foreign policy and the presence of Muslims, as it implied the involvement in a military confrontation, was that of the Gulf War when, at the start of France's participation in it, President Mitterand felt obliged to address, as his first act, that part of French public opinion represented by the Arabs and Muslims resident in the country [Battegay & Boubeker, 1992]; and he addressed them again on its conclusion, thanking together the Muslim and Jewish communities. The wars in Bosnia have showed these links from other points of view, considering the feelings of solidarity of Muslim communities in Europe with Bosnian Muslims.

In other cases, it may be the European Union as such which can be characterised as a place of elaborating policies which may even diverge from those of the individual member states, and to a certain extent, also as a place of 'recourse' or 'appeal'. This is the case, for example of initiatives of debate and solidarity, but also missions in respect to human rights in individual countries, organised at the level of the European Parliament. The Muslim minorities in Europe can also play a role of solicitation and pressure (for example, the missions by Euro-MPs to Tunisia and Algeria). However, at this stage, we cannot speak of an organic European Muslim policy, which perhaps cannot even be hypothesised, due also to the specificity of the various histories (colonial or otherwise) of the various European countries and the various populations involved and/or present in the various countries. There are however signs of 'communitarisation' of some policies, following the 1995 Barcelona agreements, and also some signs of interest, although contradictory, by the European Commission in religion, in this specific case, Islam.

An example of the supposed bond between foreign policy and the domestic situation was also seen on the occasion of the report to the European Parliament on fundamentalism [European Parliament, 1997]: the text was subsequently rejected but it showed a certain and fairly widespread possible interpretation of the links between these two factors. The report, starting off from the apparently justifying premises, we could say 'conciliating' as well as questionable ("whereas no religion contains in itself the seeds of hatred and only a false interpretation of religions leads to intolerance, genocide and holy wars", and "whereas very violent groups are active within the EU, but these are not of a fundamentalist character", as well as the fact that "in terms of scale violent religious fundamentalism is a relatively small problem in the Union at present"), added in the paragraph following immediately afterwards that "as far as violent religious fundamentalism is concerned, it is Islamic fundamentalism which is on the increase internationally, rendering it possible that in future pressure on Muslims in Europe to confirm to a more fundamentalist line will grow". This consideration expresses a widespread essentialist conception of Islam which naturally makes it one and the same thing in contrast with the European political and legal system. The document, however, insists on the register of integration precisely in order to avoid Islamist contagion and then puts forward an egalitarian concern, suggesting granting Islam "rights similar to those granted to the religions already recognised in the EU countries". It also asks for a common policy on immigration, with a positive invitation to "draw the attention of foreign regimes which concern themselves intensively with their former nationals to the right of these people to achieve the highest degree of integration in the society in which they live" (we can add that, of the requests put forward, one finds an echo in the present report which recommends to the Commission "a comparative study of the position of Islam and Muslim organisations in the various Member states").

A more interesting and more 'strategic' interpretation of the phenomenon comes to us from the moderate Muslim leaders in Europe, often as exiles and political refugees. They warn Western countries of the neo-colonialist policies expressed in support of the worst regimes in the Arab (and not only Arab) world which, in their opinion, is "the main obstacle between Islam and the West" and which end up by producing negative effects, with respect to the minorities from these countries residing in Europe, also because this policy gives the possibility to extremist movements to try and monopolise Islamic policy in Europe [Rached al-Ghannouchi, personal interview, London, May 2000]. At the same time, they insist that the new generations must invest politically in the country of residence rather than the country of their origin or of their parents' origin, developing a conception of Islam interpreted through Western paradigms, capable of influencing the countries of origin on the political and cultural and, in the future, political level. "In time we will be independent of the countries of origin. Here, moreover, many Muslims are richer than in their countries of origin. It will soon be that money will go from Europe to the Arab countries and not the other way round. The associations supported from outside will die. And one day we will see mosques in Morocco built with contributions from European Muslims" [Rached al-Ghannouchi, ibid.]. Moreover, periodically, what is advocated has already begun happening and we have already noted the flows of financing from Germany to Turkey, for example.

These leaders are almost formulating an invitation, at times explicitly, to "save Muslims from their own origins", in the long term unproductive in creating roots in the country of residence, and to develop their capacity of integration.

The weight of the European context, from the point of view of cultural and religious elaboration, is systematically underestimated or not even noted, but it is crucial. Many Muslim leaders, forced into exile by their respective countries, have chosen Europe and not other Muslim countries as a place of residence and activity: and from Europe they feel more protected also as Muslims. Their choice is not only instrumental: they are also beginning to reflect on it, to say it, to put it in writing, to discuss it passionately and not without internal controversy and to act consequently. And it is a singular self-underestimation, of the mechanisms that it has invented and also of the values it bears that makes Europe so 'distracted' in this regard. They are perhaps embryonic but sufficiently explicit to be visible, but the signs of this reflection are beginning to make their weight felt in the dynamics of internal feedback to the Islamic networks and to relations with the countries of origin [Saad Eddin Ibrahim and Dia Rashwan, personal interviews, Cairo, May 2000]. After all, an influential intellectual such as al-Ghannouchi (and with him many others, more or less well known), an exile from Tunisia and living in London, addresses British Muslim communities, including through the Islamic press to which he contributes, but writing in Arabic he also addresses, with similar contents, the Muslims in Cairo and Tunis, playing a role of 'cultural bridge' of which we do not feel that the interest and importance has been felt yet; similar and in a certain way parallel to what we have already noted with regard to the media.

Phenomena of European influence and 'visibility' (or at least of some countries, more strategically attentive to these aspects) have also been seen in forms that would have been unthinkable until a few years ago. Evidence of this was the participation, for the first time, in 2000 in the pilgrimage to Mecca of an official British delegation led by Lord Ahmed of Rotherham. The delegation was objected to by some marginal fringes but it certainly marked a symbolic significant step in showing, both the European (in the future) and Muslim countries (that on this occasion had a sample), that there is now an indigenous European Islam and they must now reckon with it. At the same time it can rely on it in a role of interface between the two worlds and is not to be underestimated—nor by European foreign policy [Lord Ahmed of Rotherham, personal interview, London, May 2000]. Moreover, it is no coincidence that some European countries consult, even only informally, representatives of importance of some Muslim communities on the eve of visits of state or other times when the countries of origin of the respective communities are involved or that authoritative Muslims take part in commercial delegations or similar to other Muslim countries, for whom those European Muslims who can boast of a success which is also political in the countries where they live, are both a surprise and an enigma, but in any case can enjoy an influence and credibility that is probably higher than that of a leading politician or minister of another Muslim country.

It would also appear, from some rumours heard in various circles, that some European countries intend appointing Muslim ambassadors to some Muslim countries and requests in this direction have been made by some Muslim communities in Europe (moreover some already exist: former ambassadors who have converted to Islam are amongst the leading figures with important roles—intellectual and political—in the Muslim communities in Italy and Germany, for instance).

However, understandably there are also forms of influence in the inverse direction: from the countries of origin to Europe. A first element is that of the import, amongst immigrant communities, of topics from the countries of origin: we have already seen, for example, the facts of the Ayodhya mosque or of Kashmir. But there have also been examples with the clashes between Turks and Kurds in Germany or between Iranians who were respectively for and against Khomeini's revolution, etc. Then there is a traditional influence, made of the (attempted) control of the associations, and at times espionage, by some countries of origin of their nationals, to the extent of seeing strong positions being taken by leaders of the second generation asking for the end of the influence of foreign states on Islam in Europe [Ramadan, 2000 for example]. This influence is often encouraged and even solicited, at times, by the European countries, with a seesaw attitude between policies of integration and hopes of 'returning their immigrants to the sender'.

The fact remains that European Muslims form an important part and have a specific weight (political, economic and cultural) that is far superior to their numerical weight, of that minority Islam which, according to some, today represents 42% of Muslims in the world [Ataullah Siddiqui, personal interview, Leicester, May 2000], and which is about to become increasingly decisive with respect to the central countries of Islam too, starting with the Arab countries. Not only are new 'Muslim geopolitics' [Lord Ahmed of Rotherham, cit.], being developed but the question of the role of these Muslims is raised: internally, in Europe and externally, in what were their countries of origin. More generally, in fact, their role and their interest is with regard to the entire Muslim *Umma*: in which they are considered 'brothers'—brothers who today represent a numerical minority which nevertheless comes from one of the centres of the developed world, to which the Muslim countries themselves make specific reference on the economic and often political level and at times even on the religious level. A serious analysis is required of the opinions of the Muslims in the countries of origin and of immigrant Muslims on European religious freedom, always much greater than in the countries of origin even for Muslims themselves! This is something the Muslim intellectuals of the first and second generation do not fail to observe but also, on a more day to day basis, many 'ordinary' Muslims. Some of them, and many of our interlocutors in the first place (we have quoted al-Ghannouchi and Ataullah Siddiqui, from different geographical areas and with very different origins and political positions; we could add Tareq Ramadan and many of the lesser known figures: the 'second row' which rarely obtains space in the media and is not very familiar to academics either), are beginning to raise the problem of the original contribution that they can make to the development of the West, with a discourse of almost a Kennedyan flavour: we are not wondering what Europe can do for us, but how we can contribute to build a different Europe—and however we are committed to fostering knowledge and the reciprocal exchange of information between the two worlds, also knowing how to "listen to the criticism of the West" [Siddiqui again, cit.].

6. The Case of Turkey

The 'Turkish problem' deserves a brief separate discussion, owing to the complexity of the factors at stake. A close examination is necessary for many reasons, two of which are in themselves sufficient to justify European interest and ours here. In the first place, it is the only country with a Muslim majority that has applied to enter the European Union; a similar request made in 1986, but perhaps without much conviction, by Morocco was rejected for evident lack of grounds, as Morocco is geographically outside Europe, and unable to boast a European history that is comparable to that of the Ottoman empire, for example. In the second place, as we have seen, the Turkish component represents the main Muslim presence in the Old Continent.

The first argument weighs on the cultural reflections: those that consider Europe a continent of Christian, or at the most Judeo-Christian civilisation and therefore (but this therefore should be explained and articulated) incompatible with Islam, or at least finding it difficult to accept a country with a Muslim majority. This argument, as is well known, is not on the official agenda of the Union, but is certainly part of the hidden (and at time subconscious) agenda of many of those who have spoken on the subject, or who are 'instinctively', at times viscerally, against the entry of Turkey into Europe. This is an argument, moreover, used in Turkey as well, as the reactions of the Islamist party, *Refah Partisi*, have shown, which is fairly lukewarm to this process, and more generally of the Turkish political-intellectual world after the Luxembourg summit of 1998 (where Europe was accused of being a 'Christian club', etc.); an argument that is also useful domestically to hide the weight of reasons such as the Kurdish question, the respect of human rights, the role of the military, doubts as to the real democracy and the Cypriot question (Turkey militarily occupies a part of a country that is a candidate for entry into the Union before it was).

The second argument, that of being the principal Muslim component in Europe, is also a significant topic but one which is infrequently rendered explicit, also because public opinion is less aware of it, in particular in countries where this presence is smaller and the more visible Muslim components are others.

This is not the place to put forward proposals or express intentions: besides, the Union has already outlined its policy, not devoid of uncertainties and ambiguities, on the subject. We shall limit ourselves to mentioning some of the factors that make the candidature of Turkey a request that is 'not like the others' and on which discussion is more heated. First of all, let us recapitulate some chronological stages. Turkey has been associated with the European Community since 1963 and then promised to start the procedures for membership in 25 years. A request for full membership, presented in 1987, was rejected in 1989. Since 1996 it has been part of the Custom Union. Lastly, it is a member of the Council of Europe. In addition, during the Helsinki summit meeting in December 1999, the Greek veto against the Turkish candidature for entry into the EU fell, so that the formal and simultaneous applications of Turkey, Bulgaria and Romania were accepted at the same summit meeting [Bougarel & Clayer, 2001]. Basically, Turkey is the only country applying for membership to which Europe had, at least for a time, closed the door [Buzan & Diez, 1999]. Where does the difficulty lie then?

We have already seen two reasons: let us look at some others. Turkey has a consistent demographic weight, of about 64 million people, mostly in continental Asia and Muslim: the equivalent, alone, of all the other 11 candidate countries put together. In addition, it is a young population, half of which is under 20 and probably more mobile or willing to move than others, as shown by the high rates of urbanisation [Insel, 1998]. On a political level, Turkey is, according to the political commentator Cengiz Candar, an illiberal, military, imperfect, minimalist and pseudo-democratic, or at the most electoral, democracy. In particular, the role of the army is decisive: 639,000 men, of whom 528,000 are conscripts, 1/3 of the national budget spent for the war in Kurdistan, a body like the National Security Council, introduced with the constitution of 1961, also present in the legal system through military judges in the security courts, economic power of its own (the health insurance scheme for career soldiers represents the third largest economic group in the country): another political commentator, U.C. Sakialloglu, has said that the main contradiction of Turkish democracy is the proven inability of civil politics to control the military [Amiraux, in press].

On the economic level, the situation is fairly complex. The Turkish economy has certainly fewer problems and fewer structural difficulties than those of other candidate countries from Eastern Europe and has an acceptable and even 'interesting' profile for the Union: the country is growing rapidly if chaotically, the society is extremely dynamic, it has a large domestic market, but a high level of inflation and an extremely unequal distribution of income. However, it needs extensive structural programmes, such as those always drawn up for new countries with a less developed economy entering the Union and, given the size of the country, these would be 'tough' [Insel, 1998]. And then there is the problem that full entry would allow free circulation for 64 million more people and, more than citizens of other countries, perhaps motivated to leave their own: this is a palpable fear, especially in countries such as Germany, where the Turkish communities are already considerable and would undergo a greater impact in this sense.

On the other hand, Turkey, unlike other Muslim countries the minorities of which are in Europe, is not a former colony (and therefore does not have problems of relations with a former mother country) and can boast of its own Ottoman past, when it was a coloniser itself and dominated vast areas of Europe, especially in the East: it therefore has no complexes of inferiority with respect to European countries and can claim its own specificity in terms of language, history, culture and power. The European space is therefore not marked negatively (even when there have been historical defeats, they were defeats between two powers) but in this sense, is indifferent [Kastoryano, 1999]. In addition, Turkey has its own policies and strategic interests in the Turkish-speaking world of Central Asia (which makes it interesting, for example, for NATO, of which it is a member); and, as mentioned, it militarily occupies Cyprus and is in open territorial conflict not only with Cyprus but with another European country, Greece. This is a cultural conflict which also involves the Turkish minorities in Thrace, for whom the following self-definition is often valid: "First of all I am Turkish, then I'm a Muslim and lastly I am a Greek citizen" [quoted in Akgönül, 1999]. This is not all: the relationship between the two populations, in the present conflicts, is significantly changing in favour of the Turks; and it has been seen how the weight of changed demographic differentials can come into play and has also come into play elsewhere [Livi Bacci & Martuzzi Veronesi, 1990]. Then account has to be taken of its cultural influence on the Muslim minorities in some other countries in Eastern Europe, which are also candidates for entry into the Union. For Turkey, this influence can also be a problem. In 1984–85, when the Bulgarian leader Zhivkov launched the campaign of Bulgarisation of the Turks, inviting them to leave the country, 320,000 people left Bulgaria in three months and the flow was to continue until 21st August 1989 when Turkey was forced to close its borders [Ragaru, 2001].

Turkish identity also has a force, which has also been shown in Europe and here we are referring to Western Europe, where communities which in some cases are very well inserted often have higher rates than others of endogamy, a linguistic specificity with respect to other Muslims, some ethnic-religious specificities (Alawis, Kurds) and the Turkish flag, behind which they can find one another through the consolidation of the discourse on identity, as for example after the events of Solingen in 1993 [Kastoryano, 1998, who in a study on Turks in France notes how 77.8% see their future in France, but 19.2% associate only with people from the same village of origin in their neighbourhood and 12.9% of young people want a spouse from the same region and of the same language and religion].

On the other hand, the problem does not seem to be Islamism. The experience in government of the *Refah Partisi*, although brief and in a coalition, and politically more hostile to entry in the Union, was not particularly problematic for Europe either in the accents or in the practice, and gave, if anything, in the opinion of many observers, good proof of itself in the government of the city, from the electoral victory in Istanbul and Ankara in 1994. At the most, on an international level, it led to the promotion of a fragile union of Muslim countries in contraposition to the G7, the so-called D8: eight Muslim countries which met in Turkey in 1997 on the initiative of the leader of the *Refah Partisi*, Necmettin Erbakan, but did not become a stable and important organisation. Moreover, it is interesting to note how the leadership of the *Refah Partisi* (Party of welfare, banned by the military in 1997 and which subsequently became Fazilet, Party of Virtue, and then after having been banned a second time, was refounded as Saadet, Party of Happiness—and banned for the nth time by the Turkish Constitutional Court for having carried out activity contrary to the secular nature of the state on 22nd June 2001, at the time of writing) appealed against the decisions of the Turkish Constitutional Court to the European Court of Human Rights which, with a ruling on 31st July 2001 rejected the appeal, with a controversial and in certain aspects surprising position. The seven judges in Strasbourg, 4 against 3, rejected the appeal, with the motivation that a European state founded on the Sharia, such as that advocated by the plaintiffs, was in contrast with the values of the Convention on Human Rights (*La Republica*, 1st August 2001). This decision can certainly not have increased the European vocation of the party, whilst it was certainly well received by military and governmental circles. The full Court has since upheld the decision.

Very clear to Europe but much less so to Turkey is the weight of the Kurdish problem, which is not one for the Turkish state as it refuses to consider that it exists, prohibiting even naming it, although investing a large part of its military budget in it. It is interesting to note that the Kurdish community [if such, in the singular, it is licit to define it, in view of its internal fragmentation on the level of the national origins and also on the religious level, due also to the role of the confraternities; Bozarslan, 1998a] was formed as such, in a certain sense, in Europe, and it is organised on a European scale, as it remains divided in the different countries of origin (in particular Turkey, Syria, Iraq and Iran), even opening Kurdish Institutes in Paris in 1983, in Brussels in 1989, in Berlin in 1993 and then in Washington in 1997 [Bozarslan, 1998b]. To give an example, Nawroz, the Kurdish New Year, was 'invented' in Europe and only later recovered by Turkey: another example to be added to the many analysed by Anderson to prove his theory of nationalisms as 'imagined communities' [Anderson, 1991].

Today, the Kurds are conservatively estimated to number some 500,000 in Germany, 60,000 in France, 30,000 in the Netherlands, 25,000 in Austria and Switzerland, 15,000 in Sweden, 12,000 in Denmark and Belgium and 9,000 in Great Britain. And the repercussions in Europe of their presence has been seen, more than in some waves of attacks, especially in Germany, in the ban on the activities of the PKK which was introduced in Germany and in France in 1993 due to Turkish pressure, in the pressure on the Netherlands in 1995 at the time of the creation of the Kurdish Parliament in exile, in sending ships full of Kurds to Italy in 1997 and 1998 to stop aid to Kurds and these ships were sent again when Italy decided not to extradite Abdullah Ocalan, in the looting of the Kurdish centres in Brussels by the Grey Wolves when APO arrived in Italy [Rigoni, 1998]. All these elements make the Kurdish problem a problem within the Turkish problem for Europe, which cannot be eliminated, despite obvious Turkish annoyance in mentioning it.

Much of what Europe thinks often remains in what is 'unsaid' in diplomacy; however much has been said and even rendered explicit officially [see the *Regular Report from the Commission on Progress towards Accession Turkey*—13th October, 1999, European Commission, 1999]. However, we have the sense that the weight of the cultural argument remains important, rendered explicit especially in Christian-Democrat circles but also present elsewhere, as well as in Turkey (not necessarily only in Islamic or Islamist circles, moreover): an argument which, it has to be said, was not such and was not perceived as such 25 years ago on the first request by Turkey for membership.

Indicating a solution, as mentioned, is not the job of the writer: a possible itinerary has already been suggested by the Commission and by the European Council of Helsinki (see the final statement of the European Council held in Helsinki on 10th and 11th December 1999). We can also recall the insistent pressing by the United States on Europe for Turkey to be accepted in the Union at last: in this case the argument sustained is simply that of the obsession with security and United States' policy in the area (to which moreover the role of the defence industry is not irrelevant). Other intermediate solutions have been proposed by those who, for example, consider Turkey not a Western but a 'Westernist' country, in the same way as Japan, Russia or Israel are. This would evoke a mechanism of concentric circles of membership of the EU on the basis of common interests (strategic, economic and political), in the respect of the specificity and history, as this concept is not alien to Turkish and Ottoman history [Buzan & Diez, 1999].

In any case, Turkey's request for membership remains an open problem for Europe, from the point of view of identity as well: it is no coincidence that it has again brought up a question (on what Europe is, on what it wants to be and what its borders are) that other more recent 'enlargements', including those announced in the east, at least officially, have not raised. We believe that these are healthy questions; after all it is not without benefit if some form of debate is opened in European public opinion—even regardless of the Turkish problem.

7. The Role of the EU and Euro-Mediterranean Co-operation

It is again our intention to mention only some reflections that are relevant for our subject on this topic, which is extremely broad and on which there is abundant literature, although often repetitive and consisting more of rhetoric than of contents (or mainly economic contents). In this area there is a long history of relations including institutional ones: global Mediterranean policy in the 1970s and 1980s; the bilateral agreements with countries of the Maghreb (North Africa) and the Mashreq (Middle East) and also of the east; the membership of Greece in 1981 and of Spain and Portugal in 1986; the fall of the Wall in 1989 which, by shifting European priorities eastwards caused a partial disengagement in the south.

The recent stages of the policy of Euro-Mediterranean dialogue are well known. In March 1992 Spain, very much a coastal country, proposed an area of free commercial exchange between the European Union and the countries of the Maghreb. In June of the same year, the European Council at Lisbon declared that "the

Maghreb represents the southern frontier of the Union". This was the start of the 'discovery' that partnership cannot only be economic and the Med programmes were promoted, including, more openly cultural ones, Med-Campus and Med-Media—then suspended by the European Court of Auditors in 1995 and resumed in 1998.

The Conference of Barcelona in November 1995 (incongruously, exactly 900 years previously on the same date of 27th November, in 1095 Pope Urban II preached the first Crusade . . .) was a truly symbolic and practical turning point, which saw the fifteen countries of the Union meeting with twelve countries of the southern and eastern Mediterranean: the North African countries of Morocco, Algeria and Tunisia (not Libya due to its links with international terrorism), Middle Eastern countries such as Egypt, Lebanon, Syria, Jordan (a country which strictly speaking, does not border the Mediterranean), Israel, the Palestinian Authority until it becomes a real state, the islands of Cyprus and Malta as well as Turkey [Balta, 1997]. The declaration of Barcelona was made here and is now not only a formal point of reference of this new stage in the collaboration between two geographical entities, Europe and the Mediterranean, with countries which are geo-culturally and politically part of both acting as a hinge.

As is known, it consider three aspects: a political and security aspect, an economic and financial aspect and for the first time one concerning socio-cultural aspects as well. Around the Barcelona Conference there were inter-government forums and Euro-Mediterranean civil forums, with the explicit purpose of involving civil society: university, research, media, NGOs, trade unions and business. The Mediterranean is a crucial hinge and there is no need to recall Braudel or Matvejevic to realise this. A sort of Mediterranean 'Rio Grande' has been formed [Papadopoulou, 1997]—the *green line*, as the Americans call the territory that separates Mexico from the United States and symbolically the Third World from the First World, poverty from wealth—going from Istanbul to Gibraltar, with on the one side, as starting points, the ports of Turkey, Albania, Tunisia and Morocco, possibly via Cyprus and the enclaves of Ceuta and Melilla and on the other, the coasts of Greece, Italy, Spain, and partly also France. Knowing that on both sides, in actual fact, penetration is much deeper: the magnet attracts people from China, the Indian sub-continent or Anatolia and projects them as far as Germany, the Netherlands and Great Britain.

On the economic level, the links are close but more crucial for the Mediterranean countries than for Europe: the Med12 (Algeria, Morocco, Tunisia, Jordan, Lebanon, Syria, Egypt, Cyprus, Malta, Turkey, Palestine and Israel) are the main trading partners of the EU15, of all developing countries. For all except Jordan, the Union is the dominant partner [Giovannetti, 1999]. However on other levels things become more complicated. In the area there are major imbalances of development, demography and democracy (the '3 Ds' in English and French) [Khader, 1999]. And the demographic differential, incidentally, is of population but also of religion, considering the weight in it of the Muslim component. Now, if it is true that the Mediterranean could in the near future be one of the main, if not the main, area of economic expansion in Europe, it also becomes important politically to understand who and what this involves. The countries with relations with the EU (the MED12) are, in the majority, Muslim countries or with consistent Muslim minorities: even a historic 'enemy' of Islam such as Israel includes, after all, Palestinian minorities, with Muslims. But they are also in conflict with one another: a conflict where the religious aspects are of major importance (in Israel, obviously, and with regard to the Palestinian Authority, but that is not the only example: there is also Cyprus).

In international politics, there has been in the past a tendency by European countries to encourage or even foment division between Arab countries. This has not been, however, the official EU policy. However, the divisions within the Arab side have contributed towards making the EU position more critical with regard to the past attempts to dialogue with the Arab world as a whole (the Euro-Arab dialogue) [Niblock, 1998]. Once again, with respect to this problem, the religious dimension is not indifferent: in the first place in the individual Arab countries, with respect to their Islamist components (Egypt, Tunisia, Algeria etc.) but also in relation to the policies that the European countries—individually or, less probably, as the Union— will assume with regard to these components, and their activities in their own territory (reception or otherwise of political-religious leaders fighting against their respective governments as political exiles, tolerance or intolerance of legal Islamist political activity in their territories, co-operation or otherwise with the countries of origin in the control and repression of this opposition, even when it moves exclusively on a legal level). And again, with respect to the present policies with regard to these countries: it is not realistic and it is not of any use to pretend not to see that economic support to the countries in question is also support for their governments and their leadership and their positions, which are often harsh and at times unacceptable, according to 'Western European' criteria, regarding their Islamist oppositions.

Today policies are often differentiated: France has the Francophone world and its colonial past, the United Kingdom the Commonwealth and its former colonies, Spain the relationship with its enclaves etc. But in addition, there are also differentiated policies with respect to the internal opposition in the various countries: therefore an Islamist leader forced into exile may find asylum in one European country but not in another. There is no common European policy on the situation in the Middle East, where margins seem to be limited by the engagement of the United States, but also by the differentiated relations with Israel and the Palestinian Authority: after the declaration of Venice in 1980, after all, nothing further than development projects in Palestinian territory has been done. What we are anxious to note, beyond the single questions, is that the Muslim minorities in Europe are not indifferent to the policies implemented by Europe and by the individual European countries in this area.

A serious problem of knowledge and construction of the reciprocal image is also raised (conveyed in the media, in school books, on television, among popular stereotypes) which is also valid in its political effects. We shall restrict ourselves to mentioning the issue, which is so serious as to hypothesise that, after the many Med programmes activated (Campus, Urbs, Media, Invest, etc.), perhaps it would also be necessary to launch an extensive Med-Culture [Khader, 1999], capable of incorporating religious aspects as well. At stake is the knowledge and therefore the relationship between Europe and the Arab world, Europe and Arabness: *Urupa* and *Uruba*, to repeat the terms of confrontation used by Laroui [1986].

8. ENLARGEMENT EASTWARDS

Apart from the specific Turkish situation, which we have already discussed and the very particular one, linked to the previous one, of Cyprus, which would also deserve some reflection (what effect will the probable entry of Cyprus into the Union before Turkey have, including on its relations with Turkey?), a further aspect, which concerns the immediate future of the European Union, deserves analysis. Several of the East European countries that are candidates for entry to the Union have significant Muslim minorities: over 1 million in Bulgaria, out of a population of less than 8.5 million, about 400,000 in Romania with some smaller presences elsewhere. There is also the situation of the Balkans, which have links with the presence of Muslim minorities in European countries and, more in general with their 'Islamic' policies. We will not discuss here the situation in the individual countries, but we will restrict ourselves to some general considerations, of greater importance for the consequences they will have in our relation with Islam, including internally.

When we talk of Muslim minorities in Eastern European countries (and also in the Balkans, where they are not always minorities), we are referring to historical and deep-rooted presences, in some cases or periods oppressed as well (in particular, until the fall of the communist regimes) but nevertheless recognised, stable, stabilised, with citizenship and with nothing or almost nothing to request in terms of rights and integration (except with requests for recognition of their specificity), with traditions of centuries of co-existence, although at times tumultuous and with peaks of drama, very different from the Muslim immigration familiar to us in Western Europe (there is a similar situation only in Greece, relative to the Turkish minority in Thrace).

They are, almost always, nationals who enjoy full rights, at times taking advantage of specific legislation, as minorities also from the linguistic point of view (many groups are Turkish-speaking), at times with an effective political representation and institutional presence (for example, the former King Simeon II, who triumphed in the Bulgarian elections in June 2001, opened the doors of the government, for the first time, to the Turkish minority, represented by the Movement for Rights and Freedoms), and control of the territory in the areas where they form the majority. To give one example, for them the right to have a mosque or a cemetery or to dress as they believe is by no means a problem. The problems may be in the form of cultural and economic exclusion.

Much of what has been written in this report is not applicable, however, or is applied very differently, to these populations. There are problems but they are not those common in Western European countries: where Muslim immigrants represent the newcomers, in many cases they do not enjoy full rights, they are not considered a national minority (linguistic or religious), their religion is not recognised on an equal footing with others, they are the object of interrogation, concern, control and occasionally of cultural conflict. What has been said does not mean that the situation of Muslims in the Eastern European countries is ideal—it is not—or that the situation of Muslims in the Western countries is worse—it is not, economically it is often better—at times the process of insertion is very successful, both at individual and community level. We simply want to show that these situations are very different, which means, amongst other things, that they do not presuppose the same interventions and that to approach them different policies are required.

A European 'Muslim' policy, as far as it can exist and as far as it can be hoped for, of which we are not certain, must however take this diversity into account. At the same time, it is reasonable to hypothesise that the entry of these countries and greater knowledge of these situations will lead to new intra-Muslim dynamics in Europe. On the one hand it is clear that the complexity of the picture will increase. On the other it is possible that forms of reciprocal knowledge and confrontation will be sparked off. The communities in Eastern Europe are often moderate having acquired pluralism and using a secular terminology. It is true that these are minorities where religious diversity 'accompanies' ethnic-linguistic diversity, but probably it does not prevail over the latter: this is so in relations with the institutions, but even before that in community self-comprehension and self-definition (an observer has noted how one of his informers, a Romanian Muslim, said of himself that he 'spoke Muslim' [Lederer, 1996]). They are, in short, very similar to what Europe discovered, during the conflict in the Balkans, was the diversity of 'Bosnian' Islam: without Sarajevo, however—more rural, less educated and with fewer relations with the centres of European culture but not different, at least from this point of view. In this sense, it will be interesting to see which forms the confrontation takes with the prevalently Arab, Turkish, Indo-Pakistani and African Muslim communities in Western Europe. In addition, the relation with Turkey has not fostered phenomena of closure or of detachment from mainstream European culture: also because, after all, in the socialist period, Turkey represented a more 'European' reality and was more open than many countries in the East.

Enlargement eastwards is therefore also a geopolitical problem in terms of relations with Islam and in the specific case with Turkey.

It appears reasonable to hypothesise, for example, that these minorities will implement forms of lobbying, with their governments and with Europe to encourage entry into the Union of Turkey, the country of which they are natural allies and with which relations, at all levels—culture, media, political and economic, for reasons linked to the shifting of populations and, in the past decades, family—are intense. And in any case, from their entry, they will shift decisively and further the balance of the Muslim presence in Europe towards the Turkish side. If the main Muslim component in the West today is represented by those of Turkish origin, tomorrow they will be a more visible and politically 'weighty' component, of which scholars and observers of the Muslim phenomenon in Europe, especially in countries where the Turkish component is not so important, still have no perception. On the other hand, the Arabs of the 'central' countries of Islam often show a strongly anti-Turkish cultural attitude which could also appear in Europe (in the east, the effect of the traditional anti-Turk tendency of the Arab world appears for the time being in its relative absence, unlike the situation in the Balkans). It is premature to think of a sort of pan-Turkish phenomenon in Europe, let alone a 'Turkification' of European Islam (although we can note that as early as 1993 in Davos, a conference was held, on the initiative of a federation of Turks in Germany, with the title 'Towards Muslim unity in Europe'); but with all probability the model of Islam that the Turkish state tries to propose to European rulers (secular, but controlled centrally by the state, according to the well known Turkish paradox) will have, or will try to have (a great deal will depend on the answers of the European states) a greater weight than today.

We restrict ourselves to underlining that the differences, for example, between Arabic Islam and Turkish Islam are destined to become more visible; this does not necessarily mean become deeper (it will be interesting to see the internal effects of this development, of this greater and more visible plurality, including theological developments for example). That difference of presences, of cultural inspiration, of schools of jurisprudence and of institutions of reference, which is already today a characteristic of European Islam, will thus become even more apparent in the continent. The division or, if preferred, the plurality is already internal, with the presence of Turks, Tatars and new Arab immigrants: each year, for example, the office of the Grand Mufti of Bulgaria sends several dozen students who have completed their studies at Islamic Institute in Sofia for specialisation abroad, to become familiar with forms of Islam that are not 'Ottoman' and they have led to the appearance of two currents: one pro-Turkish, as is obvious, and one pro-Arab [Ragaru, 2001]. The governments of these countries can play the card of division, in the most classic *divide et impera*: using the new Arab immigrants in an anti-Turkish function (in Poland, for example, in Wroclaw, it was an Arab organisation that received permission to open a Muslim radio) [PL File].

The question of the Balkans, although the countries in question are not candidates for entry into the Union, is no less important, although for very different reasons: due to the military presence and the European political engagements in the region and owing to the strong presence of Muslims from these countries, today, within the European frontiers, and the respective Muslim communities, to which they bring their diversity. It has been noted that the decade between 1990 and 2000 which, for the people of Central Europe represented the period of regained freedom, was one of the most tragic of the post-Ottoman period for the Muslims of the Balkans [Bougarel & Clayer, 2001]. And nevertheless, it was also that of its 'opening' to the world or the discovery by the 'world' of its existence. The dynamics in progress are significant, also because the Balkans are involved in a dual process of globalisation, which integrates them at the same time into the West and into the Muslim world, but without losing their own distinctive identity [van Bruinessen, 2001b]. Once again, inter-Muslim dynamics come into play. It is sufficient to think that the encounter between the Islam of the Balkans and supranational trends has often had the effect of a cultural clash rather than that of a fraternal reunion in the *Umma*. The effort of some zealous preachers from the Arab world, with the 'deviated' brothers of the Balkans has often been received with intolerance and irritation, leading to cases of substantial reciprocal incomprehension [Bougarel & Clayer, 2001].

However, due to the impact that the Bosnian *jihad* had on the Muslim communities in Europe that supported it economically, logistically and above all with great emotional investment, the weight of which has probably not been sufficiently estimated, Sarajevo has become a sort of 'capital' of European Islam. This is in the first place a perception of the Bosnians themselves: according to the press of the SDA party, the Bosnian Muslims were the "first European

Muslims to be defended militarily and to have remained in the European country thanks to their army". But this was also a perception from the outside: not by chance, it was in Sarajevo that the European Council for Fatwas and Research (CEFR) symbolically met in 1998 [*ibidem*].

In the whole area, moreover, there has been a strong presence, by Iran, Saudi Arabia, especially through the Rabita, NGOs of radical movements and trends, linked to the Muslim Brotherhood and other supranational trends, Turkey and others, the sign of effective interest.

There is not only Bosnia in the area. There is also Albania, the only European country, apart from Turkey, to have a Muslim majority, or at least in 1945: today its real Muslimness, following the processes of imposition of state atheism by the regime of Enver Hoxha, remains to be measured. But above all, it is the first European country to have requested and obtained, in 1992, entry to the Organisation of the Islamic Conference, perhaps for strategic location, perhaps for money, considering that this implied a significant investment by the Arab world in its presence in the country. If we look even further east, lastly, we can see that the weight of the Muslim 'card' can be played on several levels. A pan-Slavism, with an anti-Muslim function is probably present in Moscow's plans (or of some in Moscow). And there is, more in general, a problem of relations between Orthodoxy and Islam, which has yet to be defined. It is probably more difficult, despite certain resemblances 'of principle' (for example, the relationship between religion and political power) than that between Islam and Western Catholicism and Protantism.

One last aspect deserves note. The Muslim communities in the area have tried in the past few years to have relations with Europe and its institutions, intending Europe as a recourse, defence and guarantee from the action or opposition of their governments; this may create interesting dynamics. It is not only a cultural relationship, although this is important. For example, they decided to appeal to the European Court of Strasbourg and other European institutions. This happened with the condemnation of Greece for having punished the muftis elected by the Turkish minority, considered illegal by the state which had appointed its own (December 1999); and with that of Bulgaria for having interfered in the appointment of the Grand Mufti of Bulgaria in 1995 (the ruling was delivered in October

2000) [Bougarel & Clayer, 2001]. It is not important in this sense that one was a member state of the Union and the other one not. What is important is that these minorities, of common origin, and that conceive themselves and are considered by their respective governments as minorities have found the way of 'using' Europe against the majorities and the governments that represent them, which in their opinion reserved a different treatment for them. A question that is not only juridical but opens up to political and cultural considerations of some interest.

CHAPTER THIRTEEN

AFTER SEPTEMBER 11TH: RADICAL ISLAMIC POLITICS AND EUROPEAN ISLAM

Felice Dassetto

The attacks carried out by al-Qaeda on September 11, 2001 on the World Trade Centre and the Pentagon have given rise to a plethora of articles and analyses, some 200 in English and about 80 in French as of the end of 2002. The greater part of this material has been written by male authors. Some are eyewitness accounts, some present documentary evidence, and they approach the event in various terms—geopolitical analysis, analysis of terrorism, of Islam, and attempts to understand in philosophical terms this world-shattering event at the beginning of 21st century. European Muslims have been affected in symbolic terms, since the attacks were carried out in the name of Islam, and in social terms, to the extent that characters in the drama had been part of European-based groups, or were themselves Europeans, or had attended certain mosques in Europe. The question arises of how far Muslims are 'integrated' into European society. Certainly, the distinction between terrorism and Islam is widely observed, and Muslim authorities make declarations condemning terrorism. But what is at issue is the real relation between European Muslims living ordinary lives and radical movements and associations, which may accept violence. Moreover to the extent that the perpetrators of these attacks acted through worldwide linkage and to the extent too that the response takes on a global dimension [Encel, 2002; Adler, 2002], European Islam, as that elsewhere, is implicated in the globalising process or, more precisely, in a tension between local realities—those of European towns and countries—and global issues.[1]

Political action involving Islam was often undertaken by Europeans during the colonial period. As those countries became independent,

---

[1] In the expression coined by R. Robertson (1992), *Globalization. Social Theory and Global Culture*, London, Sage.

the level of this involvement decreased. Then it emerged again during the 1970s. The new emergence was due to political events in Muslim states, of course, but the associated social movements rapidly appeared among Muslims living in Europe. In 1968 Khaddafi's 'Green Book' appeared. The Saudi hegemony emerged, and 'Islamist' movements appeared in North Africa and Lebanon. Islamic and Islamic nationalist parties appeared in 1960 and 1970 in Turkey, and in 1976 General Zia came to power in Pakistan. Things came to a head with the overthrow of the Shah of Iran, and Ayatollah Khomeini's return to Tehran in 1979.

The 1980s saw a perceptible increase in the number of Islamic names associated with political action by means of arms or terrorism: Afghanistan, Bosnia, Lebanon, Palestine, North Africa, the Philippines, Nigeria. A. Merad [1981] has spoken of the 'ideological use' of Islam in the Muslim world. 'Religious revivalism' and Islamic politics made their appearance.[2] In the daily life of Muslim countries, the signs of 'Islamity' multiplied. The governments of the Muslim countries were increasingly obliged to justify their actions with regard to Islam, in internal affairs (family law, religious leaders' authority), in foreign relations, and in international action (especially through the Muslim World League, founded in 1964, the Organisation of the Islamic Conference, founded in 1968, the Islamic Development Bank, founded in 1975, and the Society for the Islamic Call founded in 1972). The international sphere had been secularised for centuries, but now became redefined in religious terms [George, 1996].

Even if the Islamic Revolution preached by Khomeini was never exported as such before getting side-tracked by war with Iraq, its effects did spread in symbolic and cultural ways. Gradually but visibly, Islam becomes more and more visible in the public sphere [Meddeb, 2002]. This is why certain otherwise brilliantly formulated diagnoses which conclude that the Jihad has run out of gas [Kepel, 2000], or that we have reached the 'end of political Islam' [Roy, 1992] since no more states have been overthrown, leave us wondering.

---

[2] See among others Ibrahim S.E., 1980; Ibrahim I., 1981; Danner, 1981; Ayubi Nazih, 1981; Rochot, 1981; Toprak, 1981; Etienne & Tozy, 1981. The political involvement of Islam no longer appeared to be associated with traditional structures [Geertz, 1968] or historical reality [Mitchell, 1969], or to function as the ideological 'foundation' for an Arab Renaissance [Khader, 1974].

In Europe during the 1980s Islam became more visible as well, and with it emerged certain groups associated with Islamism [Abdullah, 1980; Dassetto & Bastenier, 1984]. But the groups' visibility led to problems; public opinion and media coverage became more hostile, and since the various groups usually lacked leaders or spokespersons able to defend them in public, they retreated from view to some extent. But the situation was quickly developing. Beginning at the end of the 80s, among the second and third generation Muslims in Europe, a certain pan-European leadership emerged. In addition, another increase in the visibility of Islam was associated with the arrival in Europe of a number of Islamic leaders forced to seek political asylum. Germany received Turkish leaders, Britain received Arab and persons of the Indian subcontinent, and other European countries, such as Italy, Sweden, Belgium, or the Netherlands—countries with large Muslim populations—were also affected. Another important arrival: a new generation of immigrants, gaining entry via marriage or family members already in Europe. This new wave of immigrants were better educated than former groups, but they had been educated in the context of rising Islamisation in their native countries.

The exchange of ideas continued to grow. Audio and video cassettes added to the effect of books and magazines. Also the Internet, once this scientific and military communication system was opened to the public in 1992, became a popular means of communication among Muslims as computer use became widespread.

Then certain public (and media) events indicated a new turn in the public and political expression of European Islam. Both were media circuses: the Rushdie affair and the battle over Muslim girls not being allowed to wear headscarves in public school (1989). These mark an entry of Islam into post-modern society [Ahmed & Donnan, 1994]; that is, Islam had assumed a certain importance in the general cultural dynamic of society, and in its presentation by the media, at the point where these co-operate to constitute social reality. The September 11 attacks and subsequent events strongly confirm Islam's new, post-modern dimension. During the Soviet war in Afghanistan the papers would from time to time publish the announcement that some young people had signed up to fight there, and though that war itself seemed far away, it appeared to be a legitimate struggle. At the beginning of the 1990s reports began to appear concerning the movement of Muslim warriors to less distant places, such as

Bosnia or Algeria. A few years later, terrorist attacks in France focused attention on the fact that violent action in the name of Islam was penetrating Europe. Thus a new and startling reading of the transformations within political Islam in world and in European terms became necessary [Roy, 1995; see below].

To sum up: upon the threshold still of a new millennium, we can make the following observations [Dassetto, 2000]. First, the public presence of Islam has come back even stronger than before. Muslims are leaving a traditional life and are searching for new practices, rules, and meanings. This social reality is as striking in Europe as in the Muslim countries, or elsewhere. Its understanding must be sought in an analysis of the relation between religion and post-modernity, for it energises the question of religion in the contemporary world. Second: looking back over the last twenty years, we see a great deal of success for political Islam in the Muslim countries. It appears in the acts of organisations and movements, and also through the fact that no Muslim country can really afford to be called anything but a Muslim state, or to refuse privileged status for Islam, even to the detriment of other religions (or various kinds of non-belief). In legislation (family law), in teaching, etc., it is the same. In some cases only political rhetoric is in play, but we should underline the fact that the adoption of such rhetoric is a sort of obligatory passage toward legitimisation conferred upon the powers that be. In the European zone we are still seeing actions carried out by Islamic political groups whose actions are intended to affect the country of origin. Other Muslims are active in trying to generate spirituality, perhaps in the context of various associations. When this action is political, it concerns above all the 'religious and institutional policies' which European states are encouraged to put in place, in order for Muslims' rights to be respected as much as the rights of those who belong to other religions.[3] European states are led more and more to intervene in the Islamic question, in order to manage and regulate the Islamic presence, transgressing in a way the limits which those states had placed around the distinction between church and state. In France, Islam has succeeded over time in calling into question the very notion of a lay state (laïcité), which is not its small-

---

[3] See in this volume the writings of S. Ferrari (chapter 6) and S. Allievi (chapter 5).

est victory. Third: political terror groups and those which claim a right to armed resistance continue to be active in Muslim regions, whether in Asia or in the Arab world, not forgetting Europe. They have been and remain a minority; they have had and have still quite ambivalent relations with Muslim populations in general, as well as with the system of reciprocal instrumental relationships between states. But they are not just expressions of a lunatic fringe. They believe themselves to have a political future. Following O. Roy [1995], we should note the ways in which these groups pursue the new logic of their actions. Fourth: certainly, this dynamic could fall apart. Everything depends on the social and individual function which is performed by politico-ideological mobilisation, beginning with the repertoires of meaning furnished by Islam.

The attacks on September 11 focused the world's attention on violent action, upon its underlying political causes, and more generally on the future of European and world Islam, the question being to know if this political involvement by Muslims in the name of Islam—at the level of actors and of organisations as well as of states— is a key question or the only question, for an understanding of the future of Islam and Muslims, and their relationship with the rest of the world.

The purpose of this chapter is to analyse the manner in which the view on the future of European Islam has been changed, after September 11, in its relations with Islam in general and in terms of world geopolitics. But first we will briefly review analyses made before that date in order to show how the view of scientific observers on European Islam has been altered.

1. ANALYSES OF RADICAL ISLAMIC POLITICS WITH REGARD TO MUSLIMS IN EUROPE BEFORE SEPTEMBER 11

In general, the question of the presence of groups who support radical political action in the name of Islam in Europe, or who plan violent actions, has been played up by the media, and has been co-opted by politicians and certain political parties. Thus public opinion has been made highly sensitive to this question; people are better informed and also more agitated by it. Terrorist-type action which claims justification from Islam, as this has occurred in Muslim countries such as Egypt, Algeria, the Middle East, Pakistan or Turkey, has shaped the nature of the questioning regarding European Islam. Would Europe be subjected to spill-over from these areas?

Scientific researchers have approached the question with a good deal of caution. All have pointed to the existence of Islamic organisations with political agendas.[4] Analyses made between 1980 and 1990 allowed researchers to sketch out a general picture of the organisational status of such groups and their Muslim membership.[5] Therefore in-depth analyses exist, which give us in general terms the information necessary for an understanding of the operations of political Islam.

But most researchers had remained curiously silent as regards the phenomena of political radicalisation, even though journalists and the media in general were bearing in on just that point. There are probably several reason why this was so. First, social science, in respect of its methods and its deontological principles, cannot conduct research in areas which almost by definition remain opaque to the questioning of a scientist. Second, a relative poverty of means, and thus time available for investigation in this particular area is also scarce. The visible Islam, which allowed itself to be investigated, was more accessible. But above all, probably, researchers were guided by the desire to focus their analyses on 'normal' Islam, the majority case, the Islam that appeared to be in the process of integration, and which appeared to be able to integrate itself into European society. They were all the more willing to avoid studying phenomena of political radicalisation, since some feared that their work might be grist to the mill of public opinion or to policy positions hostile to immigration, which might use Islamophobia to support xenophobia.

More specific work concerned more radicalised groups and associations.[6] Such work has begun to bring to light the way in which the general movement toward Islamisation, which can be observed among Muslim populations, can serve as an incubator for the emergence of types of reference which are more politicised and more radicalised [for instance Kepel, 1987; Masud, 2000]. A porous boundary

---

[4] See for example: Nielsen, 1992; Kepel, 1987; Dassetto & Bastenier, 1988; Landman, 1992; Lewis, 1994; Dassetto, 1996.

[5] See B. Maréchal's chapter in this volume (chapter 3).

[6] See for example: Kepel, 1991, 1994; Lemmen, 1998; Ataçan, 1999; Seufert, 1999; Schiffauer, 2000; Taji-Farouki, 1996.

is thus seen to exist between the action of re-Islamisation, the process of politicisation, and the move to a politically radical Islam—an important subject of analysis in these terms for French researchers,[7] and (with a bit more circumspection) by those from other countries.

Events leading to armed action in Algeria have been the subject of specific analyses. The terrorist actions which occurred in the 1990s in France, the work of the 'Kelkal network' (the name of a young resident of Lyon), gave rise to commentaries only after the fact, and French researchers had to face the dishonourable fact that the only interview which was obtained with Khaled Kelkal before police killed him, was the work of a German researcher[8] who had conducted a study some years before concerning young people in the Lyon suburbs. Work has been done to lift a corner of the veil concealing the presence of a network linked to the *Groupes Islamiques Armés* (GIA), which uses Europe and a number of sites in Islamic countries as safe bases for their action or propaganda [Grignard, 1997].

In addition, another form of politicisation is pointed up by the study of conversions to Islam, in which we observe certain extreme-right political figures converting to Islam as an act of anti-Semitism, and in line with a vision of Islam based on symbolic criticisms of Western modernity [Allievi, 1998].

2. On the Use of Words and their Evolution: How to Describe 'Political Islam'

The entry onto the political scene of actors who make reference to Islam and who legitimise or justify their actions with reference to Islam, doing so through means of action and arguments which are relatively new in form, has raised the question of their legitimacy. This question had already arisen during the 1980s. It becomes a problem again in the wake of September 11, to the extent that attempts are made to reinterpret the meaning of actions on the part

---

[7] The question had already arisen in France at the time of the Islamic-inspired strikes at Renault factories [Barou, 1985; Wihtol de Wenden, 1985]. It returned insistently in following years [Kepel, 1994; Aziz, 1996; Cesari, 1998a].

[8] D. Loch of the University of Bielefeld. The interview was published in French in the newspaper *Le Monde*, October 7, 1995.

of groups such as al-Qaeda in terms of their relation to political Islam in general.

The scientific description of groups and actors poses an epistemological problem, to the extent that scientists have at their disposition several frameworks with which to begin the work of description. One such is intra-Islamic: one translates into scientific language the self-references made by various groups. Thus one speaks of Salafis, Wahhabis, or (in a more general way) of Islamists and Jihadists. Another framework comes from the history of religions in the Christian West, linked at times to political questions. In this connection one speaks of fundamentalism or in a more politically pointed way of integralism ("*intégrisme*"). A third descriptive framework comes from sociology and political science. This is paradoxically the least used by social science researchers. Thus the sociology of religion has developed an analysis of different variations of sectarian movements, but no one makes use of it.[9] Political sociology is also not used to categorise various political ideologies, nor is the sociology of movements employed to distinguish modes of political action.[10]

The reason for this hesitation can be sought in several directions. On one hand, there is the context of the various disciplines studying Islam, some of which are operating without familiarity with these conceptions. Also, there is a link between scientific research and mediatised representation. This link is shown in the fact that scientists have to operate with concepts first elaborated by journalists, and by the fact that these scientists have to produce concepts which can fit themselves into the media context. It is clear also that terminological developments are linked to ideological ones and to the practices of these groups. And finally, the hesitation of researchers is also due to the fact that, besides groups and movements, there are also nation-states to describe, who support these groups. How should we characterise the Libyan or the Moroccan state? How should we characterise in this context General Zia's Pakistan, or the Saudi state [Gause, 2001]? The question of the exact relation between certain groups and actions within the civil society of states which endorse

---

[9] Among others, B. Wilson, *The Social Dimension of Sectarianism*, Oxford, Oxford Univ. Press, 1990.

[10] Examples: A. Touraine (1973), *La production de la société*, Paris, Seuil; A. Oberschall (1973), *Social conflict and Social Movements*, Englewood Cliffs, Prentice Hall; Ch. Tilly (1978), *From Mobilization to Revolution*, Addison-Wesley.

the groups or sympathise with them also raises a conceptual problem, one which is often ignored by analysts. How, indeed, should we characterise the relations between Saudis, the Saudi state, and al-Qaeda?

In general the concepts which are employed are essentially descriptive and remain quite close to actual practices. They pay little attention to a theoretical apparatus which would afford them a considerable gain in analytic power.

Between 1950 and the beginning of the 70s one generally used terms referring to "Salafiyyah" or "reformism" or "canonical reformism",[11] but also to "fundamentalism", "radical fundamentalism", "neo-orthodoxy", undergirded by "scripturalism" (as opposed to the animistic practices of marabouts) [Geertz, 1968], all in reference to positions held by Jamal al-Din al-Afghani, Muhammad 'Abduh, or the Muslim Brotherhood.[12] One also heard people refer to "political Islam" [Kramer, 1980], though this term rapidly appeared unable to really distinguish the movements under consideration. The analysis we are talking about [in for example Geertz] consists in questions posed about developments in religion, under pressure from secularisation and from ideologisation via reform movements.

As of the end of the 1970s, multiple terms were available to designate political groups, and a certain semantic debate was carried on as to how these were to be characterised. The need to invent new terms went along with researchers' discovery of a renewal of the return to Islam, still then described in older terms as "revolutionary pan-Islamism", or the associated "official pan-Islamism" [Lewis B., 1976]. The Egyptian scholar H. Hanafi spoke in 1979 in terms

---

[11] Following the terms already proposed in 1932 by H. Laoust. The last chapter of the article entitled 'The Salafiyyah and Europe', in which Laoust analyses the position of periodicals such as Al-Manar or the Revue des Jeunes Musulmans, shows to what extent the contemporary terms of debate regarding a future of Islam and its relations with the West are already well in evidence. There is no longer a colonial presence, but the relations between Muslims and the West are still framed in terms of that period, with a cultural dominating force considered as destructive of Islam's values. The situation is the same as regards observations on the subject of the 'deep and measured minds of the Salafiyyah', who have spiritualised the notion of jihad, who prefer the da'wa to any violent action (p. 215 ff.). And this da'wa is conceived by Rashid Rida as an "intelligently thought out imitation of Christian institutions" (p. 216). A view of the terminology of the period is found in Charnay, 1966.

[12] The Brotherhood (term still used by O. Roy in 1995) is also referred to as a simple 'society' [Mitchell, 1969].

of revolutions (text published in 1982): he observed that religious conservatism, secular progressivism, national liberalism, and military coups had all failed. Revolutionary Islam was the last hope in this line, which had gained victory in Iran, realising the hopes of Jamal al-Din al-Afghani and Hasan al-Banna, something presenting itself as an "agent of transformation of the world". New actors carried the new dynamic forward. In the words of the Tunisian sociologist A. Zghal [1981:43]: "The recent phenomenon of return to Islam does not mobilise the social forces of the past, but involves urban social categories created in the process of integration of economies into the international economic market. (. . .) The most disturbing thing for positivist and neo-positivist intellectuals is that the cutting edge of this return to what is sacred in the Muslim world is not drawn, as one might think, from students in the theology department who cannot find a job, but from students in sciences and in technology schools. They are mostly children of urban or semi-urban middle class families".[13] The observation about Tunisia seems of general application. Once the initial surprise wore off, scientists tried to find an explanation.

A term from the new Muslim context was introduced at the beginning of the 1980s. This was *islamiyyun*, introduced into French by B. Etienne and M. Tozy [1981], and popularised further in B. Etienne [1987] and F. Burgat [1988] [see *Cahiers de l'Orient*, 2000]. B. Etienne added the adjective 'radical' in order to describe "contemporary Islamic discourse" which is described as "a sort of ideological framework, extremely strong, constituted not with reference to any exact theological teaching, nor by a return of moderns to foundational classic texts . . . but with the purpose of giving ideological support to the struggle against colonialism and imperialism" [Arkoun, 1984].

At this point terminology loses focus. In the context of Romance languages, particularly in France, the media adopted the term 'intégrisme' making reference to a period of Catholic integration, and to the action of Ch. Maurras, between the turn of the century and 1930, action opposed in the name of Catholicism to modernisation movements in the Church and in society at large—not without a certain nostalgia for political regimes which operated with the Church's

---

[13] J. Berque in his work *L'islam au défi*, published in 1980, did not yet perceive this new dynamic.

blessing against modernising liberal or socialist ideas.[14] In the English and German spheres the concept of 'fundamentalism' has been used most often [already during the 1960s; Lawrence 1989] (to refer to the appearance of this type of thinking among certain Protestant sects). The pertinence of the concept was questioned by Esposito [1992:8], and has been considered by some as more of a label than a concept [Sidhamed & Ehteshami, 1996:2–5]. Attention is focused more on cognitive style (a search for 'fundaments') and internal policies (a return to the foundation of religion, in spite of the apparent course of history), and this notion rejoins that of 'scripturalism' as in Geertz. The comparative (principally descriptive) analysis of 'fundamentalism' in the three major monotheistic religions sees this variant growing and developing [Lawrence, 1989; Kepel, 1991; Gehl, 1996], and this has given rise to a large research programme into fundamentalism [Marty & Appleby, 1991–95]. More conceptual work appeared at the end of the 1990s [Eisenstadt, 1999; Pace & Guolo, 1998; Bruce, 2000].

Less often used is the category of 'revivalism', also developed in Protestantism.[15] This concept was implicit in the idea of an awakening of Islam [Lewis B., 1976]. Little emerges from the supposed function of social protest attached to religious revivalism.[16] The use of the 'awakening' metaphor reveals the difficulty in conceptualising that which political science and sociology have described as social movements.

The terms 'Islamic extremism' or 'radicalism' also appear [Etienne, 1987; Lemmen, 1998; Amanat, 2001].[17] A voluminous literature on

---

[14] See regarding this matter, among others: E. Poulat (1987), *Liberté laïcité. La guerre des deux France et le principe de la modernité*, Paris, Cerf/Cujas; also the special number of the journal *Social Compass*, 1984, n° 4.

[15] Religious revivalism was conceptualised by A.F.C. Wallace in "Revitalization Movements", *American Anthropologist*, 1956, 58:264–81, mentioned by J.G. Jansen, 1997:15.

[16] As did a Marxist-inspired interpretation of the religious movements of oppressed peoples. See for example: G. Althabe (1968), *Oppression et libération dans l'imaginaire. Les communautés villageoises de la côte orientale de Madagascar*, Paris, Maspero. Some authors interpret Islamism as a theology of liberation.

[17] See for example the title of the American translation of G. Kepel's book, *Muslim Extremism in Egypt: The Prophet and the Pharaoh*, Berkeley, University of California Press, 1989; also the report of the Committee on Foreign Affairs, U.S. House of Representatives on *Islamic Fundamentalism and Islamic Radicalism* (U.S. Government Printing Office, Washington D.C., 1986, cited in Esposito) In political science, the extremist category applies in general to movements which see political and social

the subject concerning Muslim countries began to appear in the early 1980s. This literature systematised a certain amount of information, but was often repetitive, seldom provoking real advances in conceptualisation and interpretation. Most of it is simply descriptive and interpretations remain quite close to the phenomena.

In sum, the categories generated in order to understand political Islam during the period 1980–1990, still in use today, can be arranged in the following table. The category of islamiyyun/Islamism is constructed on the basis of self-identification by groups which cut across the spectrum of categories.

Vocabulary used to characterise movements in political Islam, 1970–1990

General criterion	Categories from Western religious context	Categories from political ideology	Categories from Arab-Islamic context	Corresponding Arab-Islamic categories
Overall attitude	Revivalism	( )	( )	Ijtihad Tajdîd
Cognitive style	Fundamentalism	( )	Salafiyyah or Reform movement	Islah
Political/ Governmental aims	Integralism	Integralism		Din wa Dawla wa Dunya
Type of action:				
Political	Religious war	Extremism/ Radicalism	Jihadism	Jihad
Religious	Proselytising/ Preaching/ Religious mission	Militant attitude	Da'wa	( )

relations in alternative terms, which refuse gradual processes and partial attainment of goals, which refuse negotiations and do not tolerate middle and long term agendas well. In Great Britain such positions are exemplified by the 'radical' reformism (which was inspired by the Methodist revival of John Wesley), founded upon utilitarian individualism of J. Bentham during the 19th century, which developed into radical movements in other European countries.

On the basis of this conceptual background, from the mid-90s on, within the French context there arose a necessity for generating new terminology, which would take account of and respond to analyses which had been made of the transformations undergone by political movements associated with Islam. This transformation appeared even more important after September 11, in the effort to give specific characterisations of groups such as al-Qaeda, considered as having revealed a transformation or turning point in political Islam.

One may thus speak of 'post-Islamism' [Carré, 1991, and the term was used by Haenni, 1999], associated with the fact that this author produced a diagnosis of the "end of political Islam" [Roy, 1995], which was echoed in references to the "decline of the jihad" [Kepel, 2000].[18] For Roy, the Islamist project which had unified the political field and the religious field has given way to a new arrangement. For Roy these two fields today tend to operate separately, insofar as the intensity of religious people (due especially to individualisation) makes it impossible to co-ordinate religion and any political area, since the former cannot be confined or limited to politics, The 'end of politics' as described by Roy refers to something which happens to Islamic nation-states, namely that they are dominated by religious forces.

At the same time, it has been important to identify and give descriptive names to the various groups which practice a new form of political action in the name of Islam.

Thus, a certain terminological slippage has occurred: the older 'Islamist' movements which concerned themselves mostly with actions within home countries are now called by Roy 'national-Islamist'. The new groups are called 'neo-fundamentalist', of which there are two varieties, one oriented toward the propagation of Islam through preaching, and one toward armed action [also called 'jihadists' by Roy, 1995].[19] These tendencies have different methods. They both accept, however, the same ideological framework (which prefers to use the term 'Salafiyyah' according to its more traditional meaning,

---

[18] The introduction of the concept of post-Islamism generated a polemic debate among French pundits writing in the journal *Esprit*, August-September 2001. The underlying question regarding these large-scale theses is whether their validity can be grounded in factual material.

[19] As Paz [2002] remembers, the concept of jihadism had been theorised in 1994 by the Palestinian, exiled in London, Omar Abu Omar Qutadah.

associated with Wahhabism and with Ibn Taymiyya), and the same internationalist or transnational ambitions. At present terminology is drawn from an Islamic vocabulary, with the exception of Fuku-yama [2002] who uses a Western political vocabulary to speak of "Islamo-fascism".

Since 1990, and even more since September 11, attention has been focused on movements which are considered to be in conti-nuity with Hanbalism, Ibn Taymiyya, and Wahhabism. If we take up the distinction proposed by J.G. Jansen [1997], it is a matter of two natures of fundamentalism. It should also be a question of the development of the other 'nature of Islamism', that which is related to Jamal al-Din al-Afghani, in order to know if this tendency has been definitively outdistanced by dogmatic universalist neo-funda-mentalism [Ramadan, 1998, 2003:47–60].

3. AFTER SEPTEMBER 11: ISLAM IN GENERAL AND EUROPEAN MUSLIMS

The events of September 11 have led to the observation of two facts, insofar as Europe is concerned. On one hand, the persons who were implicated in the attack from Muslim countries had passed through Europe, and had been in contact with associations in those coun-tries. On another hand young European Muslims have gone to Afghanistan, Bosnia, and other places in order to receive military training and to participate in jihad actions. It may be that various national security services knew these things before September 11. The attacks have forced these services to co-operate more than they used to, which has had the effect of bringing to light (perhaps overem-phasising to some degree) the international dimension of the events of September 11, and their relative coherence.

On the basis of such information, relayed by the press or obtained in confidence, researchers have begun to ask themselves certain ques-tions: What does this Islamic radicalisation mean, and how can we situate it in the history of Islamism? To what extent have Muslim populations in general, in Europe, or in the West been radicalised in this way? What is the relation between Islamic radicalisation and the more general phenomena of Islamisation? And how do things stand with the future of European Islam.

The event

How has it been seen and interpreted? It has been the subject of innumerable publications, eyewitness accounts, timelines, and images.

The act was described as a 'terrorist' act, and a certain hyperbole employed to express the importance of the event. The term 'hyper-terrorism' was used [Heisbourg, 2002], and the attacks have also been referred to as an "ultimate stage of terrorism" directed against a global world, a model of society which because of its worldwide nature is less able to respond [Bergen, 2002].

These observations have often been accompanied by affirmations to the effect that the 'nature' of Islam is not terrorist, all while others searched for sources and models of 'terrorism' in Muslim history [Lewis B., 2001].[20] In general, the applicability of the term 'terrorist' is rarely discussed by researchers, and is considered self-evident. It is much less so in the sources and documents pointed out by Muslim authors [MCB, 2002]. This raises a question about the use of the category of terrorism by Western authors [Scraton, 2002]. Some authors have asked in turn about the 'terrorism' practised by the United States at various times in recent history [Chomsky, 2002].

In fact it seems to go without saying that the acts themselves can be called terrorist acts since they are violent, involve the indiscriminate killing of civilians, and aim at 'terrorising' a population in general (the word has its origins, fittingly enough, in the period after the French Revolution known as the Terror). The problem with this description is that it gives up trying to analyse in political terms the acts and the logic of action of the actors. The resort to large-scale and murderous means is difficult to situate from a historical perspective that would permit us to understand the use of violent and murderous action. At any rate, such acts are attributed, via the 'terrorist deviation' of Islamism, to its relations with the extreme left [Roy, 2002], or by drawing similar parallels [Khosrokhavar, 2002], though it has been proven, at least as concerns terrorism between 1960 and 1980 in Europe (understood as a strategic use of mass attacks), that this was the work of the extreme right.

---

[20] More in-depth information from this perspective can be found in the work of J.P. Charnay (1986), *L'islam et la guerre. De la guerre juste à la révolution sainte*, Paris, Fayard. On terrorism in general in contemporary societies, see M. Wieviorka (1988), *Sociétés et terrorisme*, Paris, Fayard.

The event cannot be separated from its mediatised representation. Khosrokhavar [2002:292] considers the hypothesis of a connection between a capacity for manipulation, transformation and reduction of the real through the use of computerised equipment, and the possibility of rendering cognitively thinkable a terrorist action which normally would belong to the order of the unthinkable. Moreover, the existence of the event is partly due to its media coverage. The collective and worldwide experience of the event was constructed through images, front pages and media narration [Dayan, 2002; Barber, 2002].

We do not yet have clear analyses about the way in which these events were experienced by Muslims and non-Muslims, whether in Western countries or in the other parts of the world. Few analyses have attempted to compare the different points of view. The attempt made by Muslim theologians and by representatives of various Christian denominations engaged in a Muslim-Christian dialogue [Markham & Abu-Rabi', 2002] show the complexity of interpretations and the importance, in our globalised world, of continuing to elaborate what Markham [2002:224] has called a "science of dialogue" which would be capable of relating reciprocal narration's. This is also noted by G. Kepel [2002:86] after contacts with Muslim intellectuals in the wake of September 11: "in our globalised world, the West exists in Muslim lands, and Muslims live in the West. There is no war between civilisations, but a complex conflict within civilisations which are mutually intertwined, and there is no avoiding the permanent dialogue between their cultures, whatever the Islamists on one side and the extreme right on the other may say".

Descriptions: radical Islamic political action in Europe and in the world

Radical political action carried out in the name of Islam was far from unknown before, but September 11 has called forth a new effort of description and synthesis. This effort attempts to come to grips with a social reality and with the actors and ideologies involved.

Groups and networks

What is the composition of groups which endorse violent political action in Europe? Several works have described terrorist networks, al-Qaeda in chief, sometimes basing their analysis on original and documented information [Brisard & Dasquié, 2001; Bergen, 2001;

Jacquard, 2002]. In general these are syntheses, carried out by specialised journalists or scientists, of information which appeared in the press or on the Internet, including information from web sites of investigating agencies [Laïdi, 2002; Jacquard, 2002; Roy, 2002b]. Attention has been paid also to other networks acting in other countries, such as Pakistan or central Asia [Abou Zahab & Roy, 2002; Rashid, 2002]. Some of these works were hastily written, and resemble police or investigative dossiers. These exposés stick closely to the style of police work, concentrating on names, facts, contacts and connections.

Islamic associations for the purpose of humanitarian aid have also been targeted by investigation agencies because of the possibility that some might have given financial support to terrorist networks. These humanitarian NGOs emerged during the wars in Afghanistan and Lebanon at the beginning of the 1980s, following an older tradition of responsive action, one which was associated earlier with the work of the Muslim Brotherhood. These associations add religious fervour to humanitarian work, and even try to rival Christian associations in this respect. Their work is seen as a new version of the jihad, a "humanitarian jihad" [Ghandour, 2002].

The term 'network' is often used in spontaneous fashion to characterise these groups. This concept, employed as often by the media as by essayists or researchers, is used in a fairly intuitive manner. By its use, two aspects appear to be indicated. First, the fact that the organisation under consideration operates in a clandestine fashion to some degree. The term network indicates thus a social reality more or less hidden, as opposed to associations which operate in the light, declaring their purposes. Second, the idea of a network involves the fact that this particular reality is difficult to define and determine, that it remains to be revealed to some extent, and thus that it may still be some sort of menace. Notions such as flexibility, decentralised structure, and elusiveness[21] are used to characterise such groups [Khosrokhavar, 2002] without being backed up by specific data. The same author, referring to the world of sects in order to indicate its separation from and hostility to the ordinary world,

---

[21] With contemporary references to the analysis of far-flung computerised or mediated networks, such as this appears for example in the work by M. Castells (1996), *The Rise of Network Society*, Oxford, Blackwell.

employs the hyperbolic term "hypersects" [p. 262]. An implicit analogy is here made between the general sociology of humans as connected by electronic or computerised networks (with the contemporary ideology which goes with them) and human networks in general.

These descriptions also refer frequently to Internet use, to the use of encryption, and in general to the circulation of ideas. This may be interpreted as directed toward the constitution of the public sphere [Eickelmann & Anderson, 1999; Bunt, 2000; Mandaville, 2001].

Due to lack of data, it is not easy to characterise or interpret sociologically these social realities and the various logic of their functioning. The information which can be gleaned from these writings is largely known already: there are these associations, certain individuals, cells which have been in contact with the al-Qaeda terrorist network or other groups. They have served either as support groups or have assisted the movement of terrorists, or have actually contributed men and means to the carrying out of such actions.

The individuals involved are in fact all men, even though Islamism in general is also supported by women [Göle, 1993]. This masculine aspect of radical Islamism appears evident to the authors we are studying, but they do not explain it. A 'gender analysis' of radical Islamism has not yet been carried out.[22] The process of joining these 'networks' for European Muslims, almost always young men, and their eventual travel to Afghanistan, Bosnia, or Algeria before returning to Europe—all this is attributed on one hand to sociological factors (which we will examine in more detail) and on another to the influence of certain leaders. Some of these appear to have played a major role within the hard core of al-Qaeda, the role of actual professional actors and organisers. One typical figure fitting this profile would be (for example) Fateh Kamel, arrested in Jordan in April 1999 and extradited to France. This individual appears to have played a large part in the setting up of al-Qaeda cells in France, Italy, and Canada [Laïdi, 2002:225 ff.]. The works we have cited[23] provide numerous lists, sometimes with photos, of key persons who have been incriminated.

---

[22] Khosrokhavar [2002] analyses the gender difference with reference to the role of 'martyr', a role which is supposed to be prohibited for women. But episodes of women terrorists during 2002 have begun to give the lie to this supposed prohibition.
[23] See also Jacquard, 2002; Laïdi, 2002; Roy, 2002; Abou Zahab & Roy, 2002b.

But these analyses leave large gaps, areas of obscurity: we can see that for a generation of male actors, born between 1970 and 1980, coming from the Muslim world, whether from Muslim countries or from Europe, there has been a process of socialisation toward radical Islamism. What role has this socialisation played among peer groups? Is it significant that their adolescence occurred during the Gulf War? What role did certain 'heroic' models play in their imagination, which exceeded that of 'Islamic' models? What does it mean for the future that a generation of Muslim adolescents in Europe and elsewhere may imagine someone like Osama bin Laden to be a heroic figure? Finally, these analyses [sometimes accompanied by chronologies: Laïdi, 2002; Brisard & Dasquié, 2002] show the continuities and constructions during the period of radical militant activity, extending across complex processes of socialisation, and they contradict analyses which attribute the willingness of young people to join radical groups to the almost magical power of certain leaders, or to illusions of financial gain.

The scale of these phenomena is also difficult to determine. Some sources assert that as many as 14,000 men have passed through Afghan training camps. It is possible that security services have their own figures in this regard. Magdi Allam [2002] conducted one of the rare studies published[24] which was based on interviews with persons actually connected to the Islamist movement in Italy and in Britain after September 11. Her inquiry did not limit itself to 'terrorists', but also involved persons who consider themselves to be 'mujahidin' of one kind or another, who consider battle on behalf of the Islamic faith to be the sixth pillar of Islam. The study concentrates on various groups, the most significant from that point of view. This author was struck by the number of persons who had been trained in camps in Afghanistan and who claimed to be ready to take up arms (which is not the same thing as becoming a terrorist). The number, which the author considers quite significant as concerns Italy (she speaks of some 2,000 persons, without revealing the basis for this estimate), is probably due to the fact that Italy served as a feeder for persons intending to fight in the war in Bosnia. The author thus sees several new factors at work. The terrorist networks, such as al-Qaeda, have been as it were 'privatised', and thus

---

[24] As of the end of November 2002.

disconnected from any normal social base. The networks are connected to Palestinian terrorism, which has been 'Islamised'. And finally, the terrorist dynamic could intensify in response to the war on terrorism declared by the United States. Because of this, Allam thinks that the truce which existed between secret intelligence agencies and terrorism, which kept Italy safe from terrorism between 1980 and 1990, has been broken. This analysis, fairly comprehensively argued [like that of Brisard & Dasquié, 2001], returns us to a level of analysis which social scientists hesitate to occupy, since they lack the analytical tools to understand it: that of underground action in relation to spheres of power.

The actors

Can we give a sociological profile of the actors implicated in radical Islamism? The question is important, and is linked to the search for explanations concerning the act of joining groups which endorse violent action. Observations in this matter have been made over a long period of time. During the 1970s important observations were made concerning the modern form of intellectual training among militant members of Islamist groups [Ibrahim S.E., 1980; Kepel, 1984], both men and women [Göle, 1993]. Later, connections were noted to disadvantaged populations and to the 'pious' among the middle class, in order to show that there were circles of support which considered a plan for the Islamisation of whole societies to be legitimate.

The militants of al-Qaeda have been said to have five types of origin [Khosrokavar, 2002]. First there are professional men who are the 'bosses' of al-Qaeda. Second, there are members of the new Arab diaspora, men from the Gulf States, from Palestine, or other countries, who are critical of their own countries and their governments. Third, there are Arabs who have studied in the West and who have been disturbed by their experiences there, to the point of conceiving a hatred of the West. Fourth, there are young European Muslims (and to a lesser extent American Muslims) who for reasons which vary from country to country have also conceived a hatred for the West, and who identify strongly with Islam. Finally there are European converts (and again a lesser number of Americans). But it remains for us to try to understand the various circles of membership, and the reciprocal relations between various actors.

The ideologies

One common trait emerges in the attempt to describe radical Islamic ideologies, given the available sources:[25] hostility to the West and to the United States in particular, because of that country's supposed total domination of the world, the cultural alienation it causes, and the oppression of Muslims in general—and also because of the decline and degradation of the West itself due to pollution, AIDS, and a decline in family values. This hostility is above all oppositional and negative, apparently based on repeated arguments present in radical Islamic preaching.[26]

The political ideology involved seems to have two main aspects: there is a desire to see Islam triumph in the world at large, fed by nostalgic imaginings about past greatness—which are themselves stoked higher by an image of the universal Umma to be realised. There is also a desire to see society governed according to Islamic principles in the areas of education, relations between the sexes, economic life, and eventually international relations. F. Benslama [2002] thinks that this ideology is based on religion, on an idea about nation-states and the sacralisation of state power, and on the idea of modern science, which has given rise to new myths of modernism which are according to him quite new in the history of Islam. He calls this complex of ideas and myths "nationalistic theo-scientism" [p. 74].

As concerns political activism, Khosrokhavar [1995, 2002] sees its source particularly in the Shiite model which places a martyr's death at the highest level.

A search for explanations: the question of political action carried out in the name of Islam

September 11 has forced researchers to focus on 'radical and terrorist' political action, and to inquire as to its reasons and causes.

These analyses can be brought together according to one or another key explanation: the absolutisation of the event, an internal analysis

---

[25] Surveys based on limited samples [Khosrokhavar, 2002; Allam, 2002] or from the Internet. Empirical data are still lacking for the most part.

[26] Inspired especially by S. Qutb and Abu'l-A'la Mawdudi. Regarding their expression in Muslim countries, see (among others) Kepel, 1984. For an analysis of one of these sermons (in the Italian monthly "Il messaggero dell'islam") from Europe, see Dassetto & Bastenier, 1988:175–191.

of Islamic dynamics, socio-cultural causal explanations and socio-historical contexts. We shall see in what follows attempts at interpretations based on a comprehensive sociology.

The absolute event
Some early explanations focus on the terrorist acts almost exclusively. This approach mentions psychological explanations, up to the level of murderous insanity. The absurdity, the unthinkable character of the event has been thought so great that it is practically impossible to fit the actions and those who carried them out into an ordinary logical social context. From this perspective analyses with a philosophical bent appear which speak of nihilism [Glucksman, 2002], evil and excess [Maffesoli, 2002; Dupuy, 2002; Baudrillard, 2002], or of violence and horror in more general terms [Sofski, 2002]. These analyses may pacify troubled minds, but do not help us to understand the logics of action involved or the political aspects of the actions committed.

Intra-Islamic dynamics
Another type of explanation looks at internal logics and at the interests of various persons and groups. In this connection the idea of recruitment occupies an important place (and remains a little mysterious), as well as the desire to explain how the acts were actually financed, something which is seen as an important cause over and above the mere providing of means. In more pyscho-sociological terms, analyses have focused on the internal dynamics of various networks, on their lack of connection to the ordinary world, and on pyscho-sociological processes of the orthodox regulation of language and its relationships of belonging.[27]

Other internal dynamics are also taken into account, in particular those having to do with leadership, a theme which has been studied before in connection with Muslim countries [Etienne, 1987; Kepel & Richard, 1990] or Muslims in Europe [Dassetto, 1996, 1999]. The system of education in Muslim countries and Islamic institutions are seen as responsible. A dichotomy has been instituted in these countries between modern scientific education and theological

---

[27] Cf. J.P. Deconchy (1971), *L'orthodoxie religieuse. Essai de logique psycho-sociale*, Paris, Les éditions ouvrières.

training. The former is promoted by faceless institutions, while the masses, reacting against secularisation, turn to religion [Abu-Rabi', 2002]. Whence the appearance of new intellectuals, who have "an education but no culture" [Meddeb, 2002:61], "lumpen-intellectuals" [Roy, 2002] wielding Qur'an and Kalashnikov [Esposito, 2002] who in reality contribute to a fragmentation of authority [Moaddel, following Eickelman & Piscatori, 1996]. These analyses can be rendered more complex if one links the internal trends within groups and associations, the actions of Islamic organisations and states, and the concrete institutional processes set in motion since 1970–80 for the production of intellectuals. This is a matter of analysing mechanisms of development and production of 'sectarian' intra-Islamic forms, equally connected to classic forms of sectarianism as to contemporary expressions; according to Khosrokhavar [1995] this is at one and the same time autonomy and individualism and insertion into a milieu of solidarity and identification of selves as members of a group or organisation. An increased marginality as concerns actors who live on the world transnational circuit, passing through France, Britain, Afghanistan, the United States, etc.

From similar internalist perspectives, analyses simply multiply as concerns intellectual relationships between contemporary Islam and Wahhabism, with Ibn Taymiyya more than with Jamal al-Din al-Afghani and the reformers [J.G. Jansen, 1997].

Radical Islam in the light of contemporary transformations
The event and the action of Islamic groups can be read, not from a purely internalist perspective, but as the result or expression of large scale tendencies in contemporary society. The validity of the analysis relative to Islamism should be related to the validity of the analysis of social change or the future development of society.

Most often, such interpretations only have media images to serve as their empirical data. Still, their interest consists in their situating Islamic radicalism and Islamic terrorism as a phenomenon which is part and parcel of contemporary social dynamics, not some reality which would be completely unconnected to them. The importance accorded to religious identity is typical of the importance given to culture in post-modernity [Levine, 2002].

J. Urry [2002] and Z. Bauman [2002] see in this event a confirmation of the analysis of the contemporary world in terms of fluidity and circulation. Urry [2002:60] writes: "the 'criss-crossing societies' are many systems in complex interconnections with their environments, there are many chaotic effects which are time-space distanciated from where they originate, there are positive as well as negative feedback mechanisms that mean that order and chaos are always intertwined, there are selforganising global networks and global fluid moving systems far from equilibrium, and there is never a social order accounted for by purified social processes".

For U. Beck [2002] this event confirms that we live in a risk-based society, subject already to ecological and financial risks, to which terrorism is now added. This new type of risk is typically unforeseeable, global, and non-egalitarian, and its solution can only come in a global manner by pushing forward toward some type of world regulation.

Another approach consists in linking the future of modernity to a process of increasing individualisation and terrorist action. O. Roy develops this hypothesis.[28] His work *L'islam mondialisé* [2002] is one of the few to analyse at one and the same time the logics of world Islam and those of the development of European Islam.

The contemporary phase is thought to be the result of a process of increasing individualisation in people's conduct, characteristic of the general development of world society. This individualisation makes the question of a choice of religiosity, quite important. Since it is an 'individual' choice, it leads to a de-acculturation of Islamic references. Otherwise, this individualisation goes along with globalisation processes which bring about a de-nationalisation of behaviour. The Internet is the prime expression of this de-nationalisation and de-territorialisation of actors (a question which once again calls into question the very notion of a public sphere). While 'classic' Islamism focused on national issues and actions with national references, this framework is today outmoded. One arrives at a vision of the virtual universal Umma. O. Roy has been quite impressed in this connection by the actors implicated in Islamic networks of the al-Qaeda type, often perceived through the filter of the media, but also by the way in which these actors have taken advantage of the capabilities of the Internet.

This analysis points up a dynamic which is certainly in process, at least in Europe, but also in Muslim countries, though to a perhaps

---

[28] See also Saghieh, 2000, 2002.

lesser degree. O. Roy, following current analytic trends, interprets this as a type of individualisation. Khosrokhavar [1995] had attempted to analyse in subtle fashion the specific type of person (whom he calls a 'quasi-individual') who emerges within the militant Muslim world. One should probably correct this by thinking in terms of a new vision of the self on one hand, and new articulations between the individual and the collective on the other.[29]

Speaking of a new vision of the self is at first to reason in terms of an individualist ideology more than in terms of objective individualisation (as Roy appears to do). This ideology brings on a self-perception based on psychological categories such as self-satisfaction, well-being, etc. The question, otherwise, is to know which one pertains to the self-understanding of one's own individuality in the case of Islamic radicals. And besides, contrary to the hypothesis of objective individualism, it is not a matter of postulating the emergence of a monadic individual, someone de-socialised, but rather that of an individual who relates in a new way to collective entities. The bond, for example, to an extended family, to traditionally legitimate authority, or to new utopias. Ignoring these aspects condemns us to failing to see them, to attribute too little importance to them, or to end up with a truncated analysis.

Socio-cultural and political causes
Radical Islamism may also be explained on the basis of various paradigms which attempt to explain the emergence of an attitude, an ideology, various practices, etc., with reference to factors external to the actors. These are macro-explanations, or (most often) meso-sociological explanations of the Durkheimian type.

The explanations identify several types of causes [some were identified in Moaddel, 2002].

Theories of marginality
These attribute the origin of Islamism to marginality and social and economic deprivation, whether this is in Europe or in Muslim countries [Khosrokhavar, 2002]. The analyses can be actualised in connection with developments in large cities of today, related to worldwide population flows, but to the fact that some cities are places in which

---

[29] For more information regarding this debate, see Dassetto, 2000b.

large numbers of people are marginalised. Identity-grounding references to religion become a functional substitute for precarious and
marginal situations, and an ideological instrument. The economic
crisis of the marginal life is greater than the hope of acceding to
the world of increased consumption, egged on by advertising techniques [the McWorld of B. Barber, 1995]. The economic situation
does not allow these hopes to be realised [Khosrokhavar, 1995]. In
a general way these analyses refer to a failure of modernism, to the
fact that Muslim societies remain on the sidelines, sometimes consuming the products of modernism but rarely producing in a modern way themselves. Thus they constitute a new sort of Third World
[Roy, 2002].

   This explanation has some truth to it, and it is not contradicted
by the fairly curt affirmation which consists in observing that the
persons who carried out the terrorist attacks did not come from particularly disadvantaged segments of the population. There are in fact
sociological processes of identification at work, identification with
those disadvantaged people, leading to a sort of moral obligation
which would seem to lead toward an eventual uprising of those disadvantaged people. This is not really a new phenomenon, and is
rather common among political and religious actors.

Political theories
These underline the political gridlock which seems to prevent structural problems from being addressed, the appropriation of power by
an elite, marginalisation, and political repression of a population
which has only violence as last resort [Heisbourg, 2001; Ali, 2002].
This would explain the fact that so many of the September 11 actors
were Saudis. This political theory would also take into consideration
a loss of world regulation due to the end of the two-superpower
world, as well as a conversion of the Muslim world into a sort of
global minority. F. Benslama [2002] argues in a political vein that
Arab leaders, especially those of the Gulf States, are responsible for
a degradation of political life in their countries, which is at the origin of much radicalisation. This author rails against explanations
drawn from what he calls "elementary moral psychology (humilia-
tion, resentment, etc.)", often put forward in reference to the West,
though the root of the problem is to be found in the absence of
possibilities for political expression, even that which is expressed in
religious language.

These two types of explanation may appear to be holistic or macro-sociological, thus falling foul of critiques applied to paradigms which are inspired by methodological individualism (among other things).[30] In fact they establish a causal link between a macro-reality, economic crises, and political gridlock and radical or terrorist political behaviour. These are functionalist explanations: religious belonging appears in such a conception as the functional substitute for social and political integration. Research at other levels may take other paths.

Psychosociological theories

In an implicit fashion these employ the idea that the economic crisis and political gridlock are at the root of frustrations which are more or less related to actors' expectations.[31] Some theories would allow us to account for individual consequences, as for example the classic theory of R.K. Merton[32] concerning the gap between cultural and societal objectives, and the institutional means of achieving them. This concept and its later elaboration's would allow us to understand the mobilisation of the middle class (among other things) in relation to relatively high expectations.

Theories of social movement

What has been said up to now does not take into account the passage from collective mobilisation which theories of social movement and collective mobilisations would explain. This could be understood either by taking account of the actors' logic and the role of 'belief' among the resources of actions which give rise to mobilisation.[33] The sociology of social movements also allows us to consider Islamism, at least hypothetically, as something other than the result of a crisis or a piece of pathology [Göle, 1995]. It has been produced at the heart of contemporary societies (not only as an unwanted excrescence), and is productive of values which are considered central in

---

[30] For example (among others) J.S. Coleman (1990), *Foundations of Social Theory*, Cambridge (Mass) & London, The Belknap Press of Harvard Univ. Press.

[31] Worked out after the classic work of N.E. Miller & J. Dollard (1941), *Social Learning and Imitation*, New Haven, Yale Univ. Press.

[32] R.K. Merton (1957), *Social Theory and Social Structure*, Glencoe, The Free Press.

[33] In (for example) T. Gurr (1970), *Why men Rebel*, Princeton, Princeton Univ. Press. A summary of all these questions is given in F. Chazel (1992), "Mouvements sociaux", and in R. Boudon (ed.) (1992), *Traité de sociologie*, Paris, PUF.

certain societies. But then it will be necessary to explain the passage from Islam to radical Islamism and thence to terrorist action [Khosrokhavar, 2002].

4. From External Causes to Subjective Meaning

Very few analyses focus on the meaning which actors give to their own action, or on the interpretations one might give in order to understand the meaning of a militant commitment which can become total. In this connection there are several axes of understanding.

Research should be oriented toward an in-depth study of masculine anthropological structures. This approach would emphasise self-understanding of men in at least three categories: honour, patriarchalism, and the view of one's body as a 'temple of the spirit'. This approach would be classified as culturalist (and would for example postulate an Arab-Muslim personality). In order to do this, it would be necessary to construct an analysis of the process of the constitution of personalities.[34]

Another axis of comprehension would take its starting point from the question of identity, beyond general observations concerning the Islamisation of identities [Levine, 2002]. A reference to Islamic categories would allow a restructuration of personality, either on the level of morality or on the level of recovery of pride and honour seen as lost or disrespected, or in connection with a search for recognition.[35] This interpretation should also be complemented by a study of family socialisation of young people in early infancy in order to capture the eventual contradictions between a personality expected by society and that which is created within families. The analysis of the case of the young Khaled Kelkal, who committed a series of attacks, allows us to see the pertinence of such an interpretation [Dassetto, 1996:132–135]. Or, the analysis of the quest for identity through Islam might look at the role of tension, studying situations in which a 'double bind'[36] occurs between loyalty to certain ways of

---

[34] In for example C. Lacoste-Dujardin (1985), *Des mères contre des femmes*, Paris, La Découverte.

[35] cf. A. Honneth (1996), *The struggle for Recognition. The Moral Grammar of Social Conflicts*, Cambridge, Mass, The MIT Press.

[36] In the meaning of G. Bateson.

life or values from the West and the refusal of these values, or the tension between affective involvement and taking one's distance. We end up with the figure of a "quasi-individual" [Khosrokhavar, 1995] who is neither a post-modern ego nor a subject capable of expressing universal values. Others have spoken of a "fragmented" individual [Saghieh, 2002]. In other words, theories of identity would allow us to explain the reasons and the motivations for a militant Islamic stance.

A third focus might consist in establishing cognitive, symbolic, or narrative categories employed by militants, which form part of their assumptions or 'common knowledge'. Thus Khosrokhavar [2002] focuses his analysis on the reference to the category of martyr which is important in Muslim culture and history, particularly for Shiites. Certainly, understanding on the basis of repertoires of meaning available to actors which are part of their common assumptions is important. But unless we are willing to remain at the level of the description furnished by the anthropologist or sociologist, this approach cannot satisfy us, since it does not allow us to understand the subjective reasons for the attachment to these categories, or the actions which follow.

5. The Muslim World and the World at Large

Since September 11, the question of the relationship between the Muslim world and the rest of the world has been raised anew. More particularly, the question of the relation between the Muslim world and the West has been raised in terms of the political agenda to which September 11 gave rise.

The main cognitive framework available for the analysis of a world-shaking event such as the September 11 attacks is undoubtedly that furnished by the writings of Samuel P. Huntington [1993, 1996]. Whether one accepts his analyses or rejects them, it has become obligatory to refer to the title of his book, *The Clash of Civilizations*, though not necessarily to its specific contents. This author's complex thesis is in fact most often reduced to a simple view of the future of world history in terms of an inevitable clash or war between civilisations, specifically, between Islam and the West. The September 11 attacks seem to provide the proof of the validity of this theory, proof that there is a fundamental conflict which underlies the relations between these two civilisations. It should be noted at the outset that Huntington does not analyse intercultural relations between Muslims and non-Muslims in general, but assumes the viewpoint of American geopolitics, asking what strategy best suits the post-Cold War period. In addition, his discussions are not conducted in dichotomous terms (West vs. Islam), but in terms of the whole set of relations between various civilisations.

In view of the importance which Huntington's terms of argument have assumed, we too are obliged to present it in its essential features. Modifying to some extent the words of D. Skidmore [1998], we may sum up Huntington's theses in this way:

- In the post-Cold War period the main divisions no longer run between ideologies or nation-states, but between 'civilisations'. Huntington defines this term as the most inclusive level based on culture (not on political or legal systems), where culture itself is understood as a sum of material and spiritual reality. Understanding the contemporary world in terms of civilisations which extend over various parts of it is for Huntington more realistic than understanding it in terms of a unification of the world (Fukuyama), or in dichotomous form (East/West, rich/poor, etc.),[37] or according to classical (realist) theories of international relations based on the interest of various states, or theories which view this situation as partly chaotic. One should note that for Huntington the main spontaneous tendency followed by relations between groups of humans is a violent one, and this violence takes on specific dynamic forms in the case of conflicts between civilisations. Political action must attempt to channel and control violence.
- For Huntington—and this notion has given rise to the most important ideological critiques—Islam is the civilisation which has the largest zones of conflict along its borders. Islam is a provocative civilisation, at least in recent decades, and it will be at the centre of future conflicts between civilisations, mainly because of its contention with the West, which will in time confront an alliance between Islam and the 'Confucian' civilisation.

---

[37] Fukuyama [2002] envisions both a convergence toward modernisation in the world (especially as an effect of science and technology) and a persistence of cultural differences, which for him are and must remain aspects of private life.

- States remain central, but their actions occur within a context of alliances and oppositions of cultures and civilisations. Huntington, like Toynbee, Eisenstadt, Braudel and others before him, sees a limited number of world civilisations (in this case seven or eight) which have a global reach: Chinese, Japanese, Muslim, Hindu, Orthodox, Latin American, African (only a possible) and Western (with European and American branches). Religions, for Huntington, play a key role in the identification of different civilisations.
- Western civilisation has risen to a dominant place in the international order through the use of organised violence, through processes of modernisation which it has itself caused, and through a culture of consumption. But this universal modernisation and consumption, like the universalism "of Davos" (Huntington's reference) does not equal a universal civilisation for all that. There can be modernisation without Westernisation. Huntington maintains that claiming that the Western model has produced a universal civilisation is false, an immoral and dangerous idea which could lead to war.
- Because of the role of violence in its ascendancy, Western civilisation provokes attempts at reform, reactions in opposition, and subsequent processes of counter-identification and nativisation (these movements are largely based on religion, in a manner which tends to attenuate historical distinctions between religion and politics).[38]
- Western civilisation is now experiencing strong competition in economic and demographic terms, due to the rise of other civilisations, and has lost some of its power as a result.[39]
- From these considerations stems the geopolitical strategy favoured by Huntington: the West should not seek to export its model of civilisation (as with, e.g., human rights and democracy). It should work at consolidating its own civilisation and avoid falling into multiculturalism. Here Huntington is not attacking the existence of many cultures, but the post-modern cultural relativism which in North America is associated with the term multiculturalism. Huntington also recommends an economic integration of the West, and keeping up its technological superiority.

---

[38] In this sense Huntington's thesis appears close to that of B. Barber [1995], despite what Turner [2002] appears to think.

[39] This theme in Huntington is thought by some to associate him with the position of O. Spengler concerning a decline of the West. See also Farrenkopf, 2000.

– Thus, in a world of multiple civilisations, the constructive option
  is to renounce universalism, accept diversity, and look for common ground.

It is hard to evaluate Huntington's complex arguments, mainly because
they are bound up with his analysis of the role of cultures and civilisations in the world of today, and because this analysis itself is closely
tied to a vision of American geopolitical strategy which is based on
a pragmatic theory of relations between civilisations. Certainly, his
efforts cannot be reduced to a simple opposition, to the idea of some
inevitable war between Islam and the West, symbolised by the image
of the aeroplanes slamming into the Twin Towers followed by a
'payback' response. Still, it appears inarguable that such a dichotomy
has become a paradigm of reference for interpretations of the future
of relations between the Muslim world and the West in the wake
of September 11. The book's highly coloured images and its com-
mercially inspired title appear to lend themselves to 'us vs. them'
interpretations. Whether one agrees or disagrees with Huntington,
most of those who have commented on his book have interpreted
it in black-and-white terms. In this regard it would appear that the
terrorists of September 11 have succeeded in defining the terms in
which the event is to be interpreted, by polarising the way in which
relations between Islam and the West are viewed [George, 1996].

The concept of civilisation

Huntington's central concept is that of 'civilisation'. The content of
this notion is the source of great perplexity within social science.
First, the concept has a variety of connotations according to the
different languages in which it occurs. In Germany, the term desig-
nates external or material aspects of 'Kultur', the name for the soul
or essence of a people.[40] In English and in Romance languages the
term 'civilisation' was often used in an evolutionary sense, to refer
to a highly advanced culture (ordinarily Western culture is meant).
This view of things was once used to justify colonialism, then considered the pioneering bearer of civilisation.

---

[40] On this point see the introduction by N. Elias to *Über den Prozess des Zivilisation*,
1939, or M. Horkheimer & T. Adorno (1966), "Kultur und Zivilisation" in *Soziologiske
Exkurse* (Italian trans.: *Lezioni di sociologia*, Torino, Einaudi, 1966).

Perhaps the time has come to use 'civilisation' in a new way,[41] one connected to a certain return to historical macro-sociology, especially if by this we mean an attempt to understand the function of ideas and cognitive and normative references in the contemporary formation of political groupings, even deeper than the level of the nation-state. From this point of view the neutral term 'culture' borrowed from ethnology seems insufficient, and references to ethnicity or nationalism seem too narrow. The concept of civilisation appears to be regaining some of its former broad scope in social science, as in the definition given by Eisenstadt [2000:2]: "The central core of civilisations is the symbolic and institutional interrelation between the formulation, promulgation, articulation, and continuous reinterpretation of the basic ontological visions prevalent in a society, its basic ideological premises and core symbols on the one hand, and on the other the definition, structuration, and regulation of the major arenas of institutional life (including the political arena, authority and its accountability, the economy, family life, social stratification, and the construction of collective identity)".

This quite inclusive concept should probably be modified. For one thing, if we admit a certain trend toward convergence between civilisations, it becomes important to give an account of internal variations within civilisations.[42] We would also need to account for connections between globalisation and these convergences. At all events one may say in the manner of Huntington and with Melleuish [2000:110] that "civilisation should be seen as a particular way of understanding the people and societies who compose it".

A closely allied variant, less historical and more anthropological, is that of 'moral communities' [proposed by P. Werbner, 2002], which focuses on the feeling of belonging which affects populations at a deeper level than that of their association with ideological tendencies (e.g. as in the idea of an Umma, or a nation).

Thus the analytical interest in a concept of civilisation (or some other closely related concept) is quite evident. But we must tailor it

---

[41] See for example the special number of *Thesis Eleven* (August 2000, n° 62), edited by J.P. Arnason, including a contribution by S.N. Eisenstadt. Also: S. Sanderson (ed.) (1995), *Civilization and World Systems. Studying World-Historical Change*, London, Sage/Altamira Press.

[42] As many of Huntington's critics do. See for example Skidmore, 1998; Brown, 2002.

in a constructivist sense, avoiding the substantialist or ontological traps that have plagued analyses of national identities and of the sense of belonging to such an identity. This is probably the biggest mistake made by Huntington, and by some of his critics as well: civilisations are taken as given, as relative invariants which issue from history. What is more, in conformity with 'realism' or pragmatism in political science, civilisations are thought of as larger versions of states, things with defined boundaries, like billiard balls which smack against each other. But the past is not some sort of fixed grammar. It is a dynamic reality which can be modified through many encounters and connections, especially in the context of processes of globalisation which speed up the development of these encounters, often leading to people thinking of themselves as belonging to things which extend across formerly recognised boundaries between civilisations.

The destiny of such encounters remains open, despite the fact that certain civilisations remain closed (the hypothesis of Huntington). In certain cases there is a progressive inter-penetration, leading toward relations which have a novel aspect (such as those which may occur between Islam and the West in Europe) or even toward the formation of a 'world culture'.

Islam and the West

How should we conceive of the present and future relationship between Islam and the West, upon which the attacks of September 11 have cast a long shadow?

In social science, relations between large-scale groups of humans having different cultures or ethnic identification or identities based on membership in a particular civilisation (terminology varies) have been conceptualised either in terms of political science (on the model of relations between nation-states), or in terms of inter-cultural communication (on the model of interpersonal relations) and the educational activities which stem from this. In broad general terms social science has remained dependent on concepts created by American cultural anthropology, or on concepts issuing from the sociology of race relations and colonialism. Despite the residual pertinence of certain theories and concepts worked out in these contexts,[43] the fact

---

[43] E.g., concepts of acculturation, categorisation, and stereotype, stratification of

remains that they relate to nation-states in a context of domination,[44] and were created prior not only to current processes leading toward the globalisation of exchanges, but also prior to the crucial role of television in these processes (and in the collective constitution of shared consciousness). In addition, contemporary dynamics of the construction of the individual and of the construction of the relationship between individuals and groups are not taken into account by these concepts, nor are the dynamics of the affirmation of the self and the quest for self-recognition, which have resulted from a diffusion of psychological categories of self-understanding and of the ideology of human rights. An analysis of these relations must include an historical and constructivist dimension which attempts to determine the historical and generational aspect of their development [Dassetto, 1996].

The lack of adequate conceptual tools makes existing analyses of relations between Muslim and non-Muslim culture and civilisation little better than mere descriptions. Let us re-examine the essential elements of these analyses.

When we speak of Islam, who are we talking about? Most often, in the wake of September 11, Western commentators refer to radical Islamist groups or to terrorists. But what about the other actors in Islamic society? They are not often referred to. Everything happens as if the other Muslims, not terrorists, not radical Islamists, had no role to play in the new situation which September 11 brought about. Certainly, there are references to Islam in general, or to 'Muslim moderates' or to 'moderate Islamists' (a new category used after the Turkish elections in November 2002). But these do not appear to be considered as important parts of the contemporary encounter between Islam and the West, apart from their contribution to a rhetoric of consensus—a consensus which is only possible as long as they do not question the Western model of development and the resulting power structure as radical Islamists and terrorists do.

Such a consensus sometimes is formulated in hesitant terms, and the position of 'moderate' Muslims may seem too timid. As G.E.

---

the concept of culture in terms of center and periphery, or concepts of identity, representation, and imaginary construction.

[44] Whether or not colonial domination is referred to directly, we think of the application of the analyses of American investigators of culture to Native Americans, these investigators' principal area of research.

Fuller writes [2002:57]: "Today most moderate Islamists, as well as the few Muslim liberals around, maintain a discouragingly low profile. Although they have condemned the September 11 attacks, they have been reluctant to scrutinise the conditions of their own societies which contribute to these problems".

The tendency to concentrate on religious figures, in particular on radicals and terrorists who claim to be religious, has been called in question by G. Corm [2002], who has spoken of certain regrets and also demands which are likely to come in the future. On one hand, he thinks the West should stop concentrating exclusively on the Islamist part of the Muslim world, and pay some attention to the more liberal current of what may be called lay Muslims. On the other hand, Corm thinks that the encounter between civilisations, under the sign of a search for common values over and above simple religious allegiances, should have a democratic and secular character. Corm counters a number of Huntington's theses, refusing especially to characterise the identities which go with particular civilisations primarily in terms of religious orientation.

It is worthy of note that most analyses also present the West as a monolith, in which government officials stand in for the entire society. Other expressions coming from that civil society are mostly ignored.

In sum, in the aftermath of September 11, the relation between Islam and the West has been presented as a relation between Western governments (The United States and Europe) and radical Islamists or terrorists. The war on terrorism as of the end of 2002 continues thus to monopolise not only the military and political scene, but also to draw the bulk of analysts' attention.

How should we conceive of the relations between Islam and the West? Evidently if the opposite term of the relation involves only actors identified as terrorists, the only possible relation is one of self-defence and war. Accordingly, a number of American intellectuals of considerable renown have publicly made reference to the concept of a 'just war', complete with unambiguous religious references.[45] This just war is to be followed by a grand effort at reconciliation—after "our country" wins. But which just war is this, exactly? Certainly

---

[45] The following names (among others) have endorsed positions of this nature in the press: A. Etzioni, F. Fukuyama, S. Huntington, P.D. Moyniham, M. Novack, R. Putnam, M. Walzer. Cf. *Le Monde* for Feb. 15, 2002.

there is a war against the members of the al-Qaeda network. But one statement suggests that the just war might go a little further. "This group (al-Qaeda) is only one arm of a vast radical Islamist movement which has been growing for decades under the benign neglect of certain governments, or even with their support, and which openly proclaims its willingness to resort to assassination to accomplish its objectives, by showing us that it has the means to do so."

Even apart from questions of war and terrorism, and apart from conciliatory statements made by Muslims and non-Muslims, analyses of ordinary relations with the Muslim world in the current context are also dominated by the category of conflict, which is part of Huntington's basic political philosophy. The attempt by radical Islamists to set a violent agenda seems to have succeeded all too well, even beyond their networks.

September 11 has also generated self-criticism from the Muslim side [for example Abu-Rabi', 2002; An-Naim Abdullahi, 2002] as well as from the Western or more precisely the American side [see for example the book edited by Phil Scraton, 2002 as well as Cardini, 2002]. The attacks gave rise to a new round of reflections on the philosophical foundations of relations between different civilisations in the context of globalisation, insofar as they are confronted with a resurgence of various kinds of barbarism [Mattéi & Rosenfield, 2002]. Another example, dealing with new issues which complicate the dialogue between different religions, is provided by Markham and Abu-Rabi' [2002, a publication in which most of the contributions are from non-Muslims].

The future of relations between civilisations must be thought out not only in terms of one party's position, even if one is inclined to criticise one's own party. In analysing radical Islamism and all forms of religious or ethnic fundamentalism, Barber [1995] referred to the complementarity of certain consumerist forms ('McWorld') with fundamentalism ("Jihad"), and Kilani [2002] wrote of American messianic fundamentalism and Islamic radicalism as 'twins'.

6. The Future of European Islam

As we begin 2003, serious analyses of the consequences of September 11 for the future of European Islam and its relation to the immediate context are still difficult to find.

The position of Muslims within European societies is seen in terms of vulnerability [Werbner, 2002] because of stigmatisation (in the sense of suspicion and prejudicial assumptions) resulting for Werbner from a sort of 'moral panic'—but perhaps also because of the difficulty Muslims have in bearing up under such widespread suspicion. In such a situation, we see emerging (in Britain and probably elsewhere) a sort of challenge to Muslims, implicit and sometimes explicit, to demonstrate their loyalty to the countries in which they reside. Some commentators will see this as Islamophobia. One might nonetheless remember that such a phenomenon is far from new in the history of the process of integration which immigrants go through, and that it can be analysed in general sociological terms. For example, during the First World War German immigrants in America were required to recite pledges of allegiance to the American flag in group patriotic ceremonies. In fact, this is the origin of the concept of 'Americanisation'.[46]

In emphasising the aspect of vulnerability, analysts and commentators put forward an Islamophobia which Muslims are supposed to be subjected to. It is not the case of some Muslim leaders such as Tareq Ramadan. Nevertheless it is strange that his last book [2003], concerning European Muslims contains only marginal references to terrorism and to the aftermath of September 11. A report commissioned by the European Monitoring Centre on Racism and Xenophobia [Allen & Nielsen, 2002] draws moderate conclusions in this regard. It recognises the presence of isolated acts of verbal prejudice against Muslims (or those taken to be Muslim), and an increase in the activities of extreme right or neo-Nazi groups. On the other hand, the report notes progress in the development of a dialogue, and a general emphasis on conciliation and solidarity by politicians and in the media. Overall, this report takes note of various groups and persons who have shown hostility to Muslims, but does not draw the conclusion that anything like Islamophobia is widespread, as the usage of the term itself might lead some to conclude.[47]

---

[46] See for example C. Aronovici, "Americanization: its meaning and function" in *American Journal of Sociology*, 1920. Cf. F. Dassetto (1993), "L'immigré (et le Noir) dans la ville et la nation au cours de l'entre-deux-guerres. Une société et des personnalités à découvrir" in A. Bastenier & F. Dassetto, *Immigration et espace public. La controverse de l'intégration*, Paris, L'Harmattan, 71 ff.

[47] A question about the analytical usefulness of this concept may be raised, since

The situation of Muslims in Europe after September 11 has also been examined in a book published by the Muslim Council of Britain [2002] on the first anniversary of the attacks. This collection of contributions from Muslim authors takes Islamophobia as its theme,[48] suggesting that the media bear the greatest responsibility for its spread. The book does not analyse the fact of terrorism, nor the fact that radical Islamist movements and terrorist groups have based themselves in Britain, nor the fact that some young British Muslims have chosen to align themselves with radical movements in preference to more traditional religious groups. The book focuses on the victim status of Muslims.

An analogous position is taken in an anthology [Bousetta, 2002] of texts by Arab Muslim authors. These authors also portray themselves as victims of accusing stares, as well as victims of discrimination and marginalisation within Belgian and European society. This book also fails to provide any analysis of radical Islamism or its terrorist connections, or of the place this radical current occupies among Arab Muslim populations. The fact of September 11 is discussed only in terms of the event's effect on the authors' lives, and on the lives of other individuals around them. The authors, from the Maghrib region (Morocco and North Africa more generally), do not emphasise any religious affiliations they may have. That they should have felt moved to defend themselves in print once the fact of being Muslim became the subject of discussion shows at least two things. First, the agenda has been set by the radical Islamists, who have thus succeeded in drawing even people whose primary focus is not religion into the discussion on their terms. Second, the analytical pertinence of the categories 'moral community' or 'civilisation' (as one of several) is demonstrated.

In these publications which mention Islamophobia, we see divergences as regards the interpretation of certain facts. This divergence has been noticed before [Markham, 2002]. It should be the object of in-depth studies with regard to the process of the construction of

---

it is primarily a political concept, and since it confines analysis to love/hate relationships. It is unsuitable for analysing reciprocal representations and practices which in effect connect Muslims and non-Muslims, and these representations and practices can only be commented on usefully in a comparative manner.

[48] This book continues analyses carried out by the Runnymede Trust; see also (in the present volume) chapter 9, by S. Allievi. The analysis in terms of Islamophobia is that of Modood, 2002.

varying points of view. Is it merely a matter of ideological differences, or does this involve rather allegiance to different 'moral communities' [Werbner, 2002] which affect people at a deeper level than that of ideology? An answer to these questions cannot be found only through reasoning out all points of view separately; we must also examine reciprocal relations, of responses and counter-responses, which take place between parties to a conflict.

Except for the analyses of supposed Islamophobia, the categories of confrontation and conflict do not appear to have dominated the European discourse, though some analysts have focused on terrorist groups and radical Islamists. The present and future reciprocal relations in this regard remain to be analysed [Modood, 2002; Allievi, 2001a].

As concerns the future of Muslim groups, we have already given an account of the analyses which deal with Islamist or terrorist networks which exist within Muslim populations living in Europe. Some believe they are the key to an understanding of European Islam— like one American analyst, one of the few to have posed the question of the future of Muslims in Europe after September 11 [Paz, 2002; Roy, 2002b]. For Paz, immigration has allowed Islamism to create a "non-territorial Islamic state", and he considers as serious, even factual, the statements of an al-Qaeda ideologue, Abd al-Mun'im Halimah Abu Basir, for whom immigration and jihad go together.

This analysis is conducted from a perspective which is anti-terrorist, close to that of various police agencies. Obviously it does not attempt to predict the future for Islamic populations in Europe in general. Still, it will be important in the future to be able to foresee the place radical Islam may occupy within European Islam, as Werbner [2002] does for the South Asian community in Europe, which is seen as standing before two possible futures, "one positive, leading to mutual respect and toleration, the other negative, leading to spiralling estrangement".

Another facet of the analysis should deal with the awareness, attitudes, and practices of non-Muslims. Will they, in future, define themselves more and more in relation to their religious and civilisation-based attachments (as in Huntington's analysis, and as in the collection of statements from American intellectuals mentioned above)? How, in the social construction of their identities, will they define themselves in relation to others? These questions have not been fully analysed, and the polemical nature of the question of Islamophobia causes most work on this problem to go round in circles when it should be attempting to clarify larger and larger questions related to the construction of opinions, their fixation in individuals' minds, their establishment in social terms, and their construction as public problems.[49]

7. Conclusions

We do not know how to judge the implications of September 11 on the future of European Islam or its relations to its context. What people have gone through has been described, the geopolitical consequences have been speculated about, and quite a few philosophical reflections on the whole topic have appeared, but more than a year after the attacks the analysis of the future of European Islam remains a slender volume. Is this because of general unfamiliarity with European Islam? Is there a lack of interpretative tools? Is there a kind of silence regarding the visible process of circling the wagons within Muslim communities, even a radicalisation that one hopes will be temporary, or that one dares not underline for fear of uttering a self-fulfilling prophecy? Or has the field of what can be said simply been divided between the denunciation of Islamophobia on one hand and of Islamic radicalism on the other?

Certainly there is a wider awareness among Muslims and non-Muslims concerning the fragility of the relationship between the two groups. Muslim populations are seen as relatively porous, at least around the edges, to radical discourses. At the end of the day we understand clearly that the process of inclusion (which we ought really to call co-inclusion) between Islam and European society is far from finished. Reciprocal adjustments will have to take place, not only in institutional terms but also in terms of cognitive and representational categories.

At this moment nothing would force us to call into question the various models of the future of European Islam or the possible solutions to the issues presented at the end of the present book. Much will depend on the context in which world Islam develops, and on

---

[49] The point is to understand the editorial success the frankly Islamophobic and even racist book by Oriana Fallaci has had.

the character of the intellectuals and leaders who assume responsibility for these things upon the European stage.

The question will be to see how the various issues which have been raised will be handled within the unified vision of 'moral communities' or the 'civilisation' of Europe in relation to the rest of the Muslim world. Today keeping faith with simple unity seems most important (which explains the relative silence of Muslims with regard to radical groups among them). This embarrassing position for Muslims will be challenged by calls coming from the rest of the world. But how will this position develop if armed conflict continues (in Afghanistan, Palestine, or elsewhere)?

If the social sciences have a role to play, it must be to continue the empirical analysis of processes which are underway. This should be accompanied by innovative thinking to produce adequate interpretative categories, which are tested critically before being adopted. We shall also be obliged to explain clearly the process of interpenetration between Muslims and non-Muslims, and between the various cultures present, in micro-sociological and in macro-sociological terms (the latter having been the more neglected of the two). Without this effort, relations between nation-states will dominate the creation and transfer into the popular mind of representational categories, as we have seen with the spread of the notion of a 'clash of civilisations'.

This analysis of interrelations is important for social science because it brings social science to the core of socio-anthropological questions. As Kilani [2002:102] notes: the "events of September 11 have crystallised the question-set which affects the discourse on otherness at this moment. 'Who sees who', 'How does he see him', 'What stereotypes are at work', What are the underlying values, What objectives are in view'? The creation and diffusion of imaginary constructs in operation, the diverse nature of values and norms, the divergence of historical tracks which run up against each other, the great conflicts of interest, all these force us to grasp in these events the kaleidoscopic game of otherness, and the processes of its construction. Such a situation forces us to re-examine the stereotyping of the Other, no doubt, but also and perhaps even more that of our own identities and Selves. The mirror effect underlies all".

CONCLUSIONS

Felice Dassetto and Jørgen Nielsen

The extensive survey of the situation of Muslims in Europe (the Union and some of the applicant countries) in the preceding pages shows the complexity of the issues. It also serves as a warning against easy generalisations.

1. PAST

Firstly, there is the marked differences in historical background between those countries, mostly the current member states, where the Muslim presence is primarily the result of settlement during the late 19th and the 20th centuries and particularly after 1945, and the countries, mostly in central and eastern Europe where the Muslim presence is centuries old.

Second, this division is itself a generalisation. The countries of recent settlement include those with a direct historical colonial relationship with the regions of origin in whole or in part (France, Britain, the Netherlands, Portugal and Spain) and other countries without such a link. Here Germany is in a category of its own in that its relations with the late Ottoman Empire had an economic colonial character which did not develop to political empire.

Third, the main periods of settlement in Scandinavia and most of southern Europe were rather later than in Britain, France and to an extent Germany and the Netherlands. Given that the general process of settlement has gone through phases, this contributes to some noticeable differences in the experiences of various European countries. In general terms it is possible to distinguish three phases, the earliest being of migrant labourers, the second one of family reunion, and the third dominated by refugees and asylum seekers. In countries like Britain, France and Germany where the process of settlement is oldest all three phases can be recorded and have a roughly equal impact on the way in which communities, the public and the state respond. In countries where the settlement is generally more recent, the picture is predominantly coloured by the priorities associated with refugees and asylum seekers.

In eastern Europe, also, it is difficult to be too general. In some regions, especially the Balkans, the bloody collapse of Yugoslavia has determined the ways in which Muslim communities are seen and see themselves, and thence also the social, economic and organisational priorities being adopted both by the Muslims and the wider society. However, such extreme ethno-religious tensions have not been reflected in countries like Bulgaria, Romania and Poland where Muslims are a much smaller proportion of the national population— although, having said that, it is again easy to identify further differences among the three countries.

Another dimension contributing to difference across Europe is the differences among the countries and cultures of Muslim origin. There can be no doubt that the fact that the largest element of the diverse Muslim communities in Britain originate in the Indian subcontinent impacts very markedly on the character of the Muslim community in Britain, on its relations with its surroundings and on how they are perceived by those surroundings. For the same reason the character of the Muslim communities and their relationships with their national societies in France or Germany have their own very specific characteristics which differ them from each other, sometimes quite markedly. Part of what constitutes such differences are, of course, to be found deep in the long histories of the regions of origin. But it is also to be found in the more recent relationships between those regions of origin and Europe generally, and the countries of settlement in particular. Thus the colonial history of France in North Africa has helped form a set of mutual experiences and perceptions which are very different from those pertaining to Britain and south Asia or Germany and Turkey.

A further factor on the Muslim side of the equation is the various religio-political movements and the expectations they have both of relations with the political power and the public space in general and more specifically of their attitudes as minorities to these questions. Having said that, it is also clear that, on the European side, the shifting balances of power between inclusive and exclusive political movements, including the impact of racist and xenophobic tendencies, and between perceptions of the place of religion in the public space are an equally significant dimension.

2. Present

Having identified the various factors in our common histories which have contributed to the present situation it is essential to emphasise the changes which are currently taking place. These are above all characterised by two processes: a deeply significant demographic change and a growing inter-linkage between Europe and the 'other side' of the Mediterranean.

In western Europe, the Muslim presence is no longer mainly an issue of immigration—and it never was in the east European applicant countries. Increasingly, the Muslims in western Europe are native to their countries of residence. In some countries, the native-born are already a majority, and a new generation is beginning to grow as the grandchildren of the immigrant generation. To this must be added a proportionately small but numerically increasingly noticeable population of converts to Islam. In some countries, particularly France and the UK, the majority already carry the citizenship of the country of residence, while in others the trend towards becoming a citizen is accelerating. Because of the history, the Muslim communities are on average much younger than the wider society. While this creates some specific challenges it cannot be ignored that the immigrant generation is rapidly entering the ranks of the pensioners which raises new challenges to the related institutions and welfare structures.

The 'europeanisation' of the Muslim communities has a number of quite direct consequences. Firstly, the younger generation is in the process of taking over the leadership of community organisations and representative structures. So just as local and national government civil servants had begun to get used to working with the representatives of the immigrant generation, they are now faced with their children, who often have very different perceptions and priorities. In particular, the new younger leaderships have a much better understanding of how the political and administrative processes of their countries function, and they are clearly prepared to use them. On the whole their aims appear to be a much more constructive engagement with the local and national institutions. They want to participate, to be recognised and respected as native citizens, but as Muslim native citizens. It is naive to expect this to mean a process of assimilation into the existing structures, to expect an adaptation on the part of Muslims to inherited European perceptions of the place of religion in the public space. They are looking for an active Muslim presence in the public space, and their desire coincides, in any case, with a wider renewed debate concerning the place of religion in the public space generally. It is interesting to note, in this context, the extent to which cooperation between the various religious traditions in different European countries, under the broad heading of inter-religious dialogue, is growing both locally and nationally.

Another, longer term consequence of this demographic change and the associated 'europeanisation' is a process among young Muslims, especially the growing numbers of successfully educated ones moving into the professions, which involves a rethinking of traditional Islamic concepts and their expression in a specific cultural form. The Islamic expression of the immigrant generations was closely integrated with the cultural frameworks and practices of the regions of origin, usually rural rather than urban. The new generation is actively, both consciously and unconsciously, separating the culturally specific from the 'universally' Islamic in a process which is re-clothing the latter in a new cultural 'dress' which is oriented to the European environment and replacing or, at least, significantly re-interpreting the cultural dress carried over from the parents' regions of origin.

This development is already leading to a situation where the traditional categorisation, or typology, of Islamic movements is becoming unsatisfactory. The political and social priorities both of the Muslim communities themselves and of their European interlocutors are beginning to produce new types of Muslim organisation. These are weakening their reference to the regions of origin, and the agendas of the regions of origin, just as they are also becoming more 'ecumenical' in their attitudes to cooperation with Islamic religio-political movements different from their own. New organisations and alliances are coming into being with reference to agendas and priorities associated with the European environment. The centralisation of political decision-making in Britain during the 1980s and 90s has been matched by the rise of national Muslim 'umbrella' organisations, particularly notable in the success of the MCB, the Muslim Council of Britain's various issue-specific negotiations with government ministries. The pressures of central government initiatives in France have likewise influenced the nature of intra-Muslim cooperation in moving towards some degree of consensus on Muslim priorities in France. In both cases, issues related to the countries of origin (e.g. Kashmir and Algeria respectively) continue to play a role, sometimes an important one, in mobilising community political interests but these issues are now just one part of a broader range in which domestic issues are playing an increasingly important role.

A further dimension of this process is the growing identification of sectors of the younger Muslim population with issues relating to the broader Muslim world, as they increasingly identify with Islam rather than with their parents' (or grandparents') regions of origin. So, for example, younger Turkish Muslims begin to be concerned about Muslim issues in places like Palestine, the northern Caucasus, or the southern Philippines, and not just with Turkish issues. The same has been observed among Muslims of South Asian and North African origin. This has already been reflected in the growth of Islamic emergency and relief agencies working with some success in crisis situations like those of Bosnia, Kosovo and Sudan, and the ability of such agencies to mobilise many young people who have previously had little active mosque connections. (In the case of support for Bosnian Muslims this was associated with a widespread perception that their fate was somehow ominous for the fate of Muslims in Europe generally.) Such broader identification should not be regarded as sinister in itself: essentially it is no different from the tendencies of European Christians in certain situations to identify with the fate of fellow believers in areas of conflict (the southern Sudan might be cited as an example).

But these developments also appear to be part of a wider European tendency which unites east and west. Following the collapse of the Soviet system a decade ago, questions of the relationships between national, ethnic and religious identities have again become a priority after generations of suppression. In former Yugoslavia they were a major factor in the disintegration of the multi-national federation. While the conflictual extremes of Yugoslavia have been avoided in, for example, Bulgaria and Romania, ethnic politics, flavoured with a *soupçon* of religious reference, have played an active part in domestic politics, especially in Bulgaria. The wisdom and restraint of certain political and community leaders in such countries have contributed to the process remaining one of negotiation rather than conflict, but the issue remains live and its negotiation is contributing to changes in both the public discourse and political perceptions as well as in changing self-awareness of national identity. In the west, coming out of very different histories, the presence of large, relatively new ethnic and religious minorities has raised anew precisely the same issues. How do, for example, countries which have inherited a self-understanding

of a *folk* sharing a common history, culture and collective self-awareness, part of which is often, as in the case of Scandinavia or Greece,
a shared religious tradition and national church, integrate people
who do not share such a common heritage? There are here profound issues of local, regional, national and continental identities and
self-awareness which are converging across Europe, east and west.
This has implications for how the debate over a common European
identity is developed.

3. Future

Having suggested that we are dealing with a situation which is in a
high degree of flux, a corollary would seem to be that devising policy responses is likely to be extremely difficult. It would certainly
seem to be impossible to devise Europe-wide responses, given the
enormous local differences which this study has identified.

The factors of the development of Islam

However, at the same time the study has also suggested some elements
which may be common across the continent while they differ in their
local specificities. So while it is obvious that neither we nor anyone
else have anything like patented solutions to specific issues, it is possible to suggest a number of factors which impact on a national and
local situation. In that these factors differ in their detail from one
country to another they will contribute to the differences actually
playing out on the ground. But identification of the factors as such
can be helpful in understanding why a specific national situation has
become as it is. It may therefore also assist in guiding speculation
as to how a specific situation may develop in the future.

a) *Settlement*: One factor is inherent to the immigrants' dynamic of
entry into an arrival area. The circumstances in which the settlement has taken and is taking place forms part of the foundation of
local and national situations which remain active. Step by step, they
cross the gap with the host country: culture and daily sociability,
organisations and institutions, past and future. Moreover, this process
is hard, in the European context at least, and, unlike the American
context, for two or even three generations. Regarding the social situation, the question is to get to know whether and in what way,

above all for the second and third generations, Islam will be an instrument of social positioning, or even of social mobility. But the future and, above all, the form of European Islam will also be constructed in terms of reactions, positions and reciprocal images which will prevail in the years to come.

b) *Social relations*: The second factor is linked to the social situation of Muslim populations and to relations with non-Muslim Europe. It is important to note the role played by European unification on the one hand and by contemporary means of communication on the other. Many Muslims now have the nationality of a European country and can travel around Europe freely and easily. It is almost the same for those who do not have or have not yet obtained a new citizenship, despite the travel limitations due to the necessity of visas for certain categories of foreigners. Elsewhere, fax, video and audio electronic communications have sped up the circulation of information.

Among the questions connected to the relations of Muslims with the non-Muslim context we must point the following aspects:

– The image of Muslims and Islam purveyed by the media and public figures.
– The experience of discrimination and approaches to the legal and practical implementation of human rights principles.
– The nature and extent of political participation, individually and collectively.
– The purpose, nature and implementation of educational policies and their approach to accommodating young Muslims and other minorities and reflecting the changing nature of society as a whole.
– The development of social and economic policies in response to the different needs of different communities and their response to community-based differences in access to public resources and levels of unemployment.
– The attitudes of cultural policies to the cultural activities of minorities.
– The degree to which the training of public sector workers reflects the full variety of potential client groups.

c) *Muslim world*: The third factor is internal to the Muslim world. This parameter is animated by four dynamics:
A leadership dynamic: here it is a matter of knowing what the profile of future leaders of Islam will be. Until now, 'natural' leaders coming from the first generation have dominated as well as leaders imported from Muslim spaces or Europeans converted to Islam. We have said

that a new generation is beginning to emerge. What models of Islam will it be the bearer of? With what projects? Will it manage to formulate the necessarily original response to their presence as a statistical minority, unprecedented for the Muslims, in a pluralistic and secularized society? And more generally, to what extent will European Muslims be capable of producing a leadership up to the social, cultural and institutional issues European Islam is confronted with?

A second dynamic is organisational and partly linked to the preceding: the local and federative organisational capacity of European Muslims has been considerable. Will they manage or would they want to take the new steps?

A third dynamic is cultural: it is sufficiently clear that the younger generations are proceeding towards a de-culturation of the Islam they have received from their parents and towards an inculturation. The question of its content and form remains open. The challenge will be the formulation of what it means being Muslims in Europe. To that end European Muslims are proceeding to a new formulation of Muslim identity using references to the tradition as well as European discourses, for instance, of human rights, the categories of psychology, and the categories of philosophy. Doing that, European Muslims are obliged to clear a way between the general process of secularisation on one hand and, on the other hand, the process of ethnic identification (Arabs, Turks, Pakistanis, African and so on).

Finally, the fourth dynamic concerns Muslim countries. Beyond events and conjunctures, it seems sufficiently clear that in these countries, the dynamic of the collective and public attestation of Islam is not going to die out, even if it is difficult to envisage the orientations that will prevail in the years to come. But it is certain that for European Muslims these 'centres of Islam' are significant realities from the point of view of symbols, ideas and organisations

d) *Place of religion*: Finally, the last parameter concerns the situation and development relative to the place of the religious within European society. The way in which inherited church-state relations in the countries of Europe have adapted to and made space for the new Muslim communities (or have not as the case may be) influences the way in which Muslims view the public sphere: is it inclusive or exclusive?

On this subject, the various European nation-states do not take the same attitude towards religion. They differ due to their history, their past experience of religious pluralism (intra-Christian) or of religious struggles, but equally due to the role they attribute to the construction of public space and relations between the civil society and state.

In each European country, the Muslim populations are obliged to answer to specific questions of states and societies. For instance in France the main question is that of '*laïcité*' that is the French formulation of relations between state and religion. The consequence is a strong reflection among the Muslim populations on the relation between religion and state and between religion and society. In Belgium or in Britain the main question is the ability of institutional management of religion. The same in Spain, but in the framework of a peculiar vision of religion and of Islam in this country. In Germany this question is paired with the question of national identity.

Anyway the reflection does not concern only Muslim populations but also non-Muslims. It is clear that the presence of Islam has obliged European societies to reflect again on the relations between religion and the public life: for instance in France after the 'affaire des foulards' there is a new reflection on '*laïcité*'. And in other countries there is a new reflection on the privileged status of old European religions.

e) *International relations and images*: The impact of events abroad and the response of European foreign policy, both in terms of its substance and in terms of its domestic presentation

Hypotheses relating to the models of implantation of Islam

Currently various models for the implantation of active forms of Islam seem possible. They are probably not exclusive of one another.

a) *The intra-European models*

In some models the religious action is mainly oriented in relation to the European existence and to European society. We can observe four different models:

a1) *De-islamization/culturalization*: in proceeding in parallel with a movement observable in European space, Muslims progressively abandon their references to Islam as a religion, perhaps maintaining references to it as a fact of culture and civilisation.

a2) *Assimilation to western models of religion*, which signifies that Muslims draw their inspiration from the dominant model of religions in Europe and develop a privatised and spiritualised Islam, which is elaborated within a perspective of autonomisation of the religious sphere. If one considers the developments which have taken place until now, this model may appear rather improbable, but this spiritualisation of Islam, copied from the model of contemporary Christianity, does not seem to be rejected by some younger Muslims. So it can be a possible model of development for the future.

a3) *Cosmopolitan-autonomous integration*: This is a variant of the preceding model more oriented to the cultural global integration of Islam. Muslims are worried about an institutional integration of Islam and are developing a European Islamic discourse, all the while maintaining cultural and symbolic ties with worldwide Islam.

a4) *Protest implantation*: in this case Islam becomes a tool of social protest for groups which are or just perceive themselves as 'marginalised'; it draws its inspiration from and is linked with Islamic expressions of protest. It meets up with a refusal of the west and its models. The Islam of Malcolm X might seem to be a sort of paradigm of this model but more articulated and with dynamics similar to what is going on in the Muslim world.

b) *The extra-European models*

In other models the religious action continues to be mainly orientated by currents external to Europe concerning values, society references or organisation. We can observe two different models.

b1) *Dependent geopolitisation*: Muslims consider themselves and are considered as an appendix, an expression of geopolitical strategies developed on the basis of centres of Islam. From the viewpoint of its generalisation, this model seems the least probable, but it could exist and be advanced by quasi-diplomatic actors, elected by the central powers of Islam, based on their strategies of religious geopolitics.

b2) *The Diaspora Network*: Muslims above all worried about being regrouped are not in the least concerned about the question of their implantation in the context. Their primary social horizon is constituted by all the connections which link them to groups, associations and brotherhood movements.

c) *The in-between models*

In some models we can observe a tension, more or less accentuated, between religious action with European references and religious action with external references. Two models can be observed.

c1) *Externalised integration*: Muslims are worried about an institutional integration into European spaces, but retain cultural and normative references and inspirations from the whole Muslim world. This model corresponds to one deriving from the Catholic churches during modernity. A sort of tension arises here between two references, two loyalties or two interests between the strategy of insertion into European space and the maintenance of references to spaces pulsating with Islam.

c2) *Dualisation*: In this case Muslims consider that it will be impossible to have a relation with the European society and culture. They conclude that the only possibility is to separate themselves from the context and to leave in a kind of communitarian ghetto.

d) *Absorption model*

In this model we observe an effort of religious conquest of Europe. This model is just the opposite of the model of assimilation.

d1) *Islamisation*: Muslims might envisage a massive investment in European space in order to bring it into the Islamic fold. This model would thus tend to reverse the present situation.
Many of these models will probably cohabit in the future. Some of them seem less probable today (for example: model d1). But beyond this plurality of forms, it is striking to observe a relative convergence of Muslim dynamism.

From the point of view of sociological categories, it is not correct to speak of a Muslim 'community'. The notion of community is used in reference to social groups having intense face-to-face emotional relations, founded on the tradition. For the moment, the sociological categories to name this social and cultural entity, which is in the process of constituting itself in western Europe, are lacking.

Underlying such specific factors and responses lies a blunt choice for European society with regard to the presence of ethnic and religious minorities, and in particular the presence of Muslim communities: integrate or expel. There is no 'third way' in this question, least of all denial of the realities of immigration and its consequences. The economic and political choice in favour of integration has essentially been made, even if to some extent by default rather than by deliberate decision. If the option of integration is to succeed we have to be reminded of the fundamental assumptions of the European democratic traditions, namely that good government and socio-political stability rests on a foundation of the consent of the governed, a 'contract' where loyalty and consent are granted in exchange for participation and access to the social and political 'goods'.

BIBLIOGRAPHY

Abdullah M.S. (1980), *Die Präsenz des Islam in der Bundesrepublik Deutschland*, Köln, Cibedo
Abedin S.Z. & Sardar Z. (eds) (1995), *Muslim Minorities in the West*, London, Grey Seal
Abélès M. (1998), "Homo communautarius" in R. Kastoryano, *Quelle identité pour l'Europe? Le multiculturalisme à l'épreuve*, Paris, Presses de Sciences Po, pp. 43–64
Abou Zahab M. & Roy O. (2002), *Les réseaux islamiques. La connexion afghano-pakistanaise*, Paris, Autrement
Abumalham M. (ed.) (1995), *Comunidades islámicas en Europa*, Madrid, Trotta
Abu-Rabi' I.M. (2002), "A post-September 11 critical assessment of modern Islamic history" in I. Markahan & M. Abu-Rabi' (ed.), *11 September. Religious Perspectives on the Causes and Consequences*, Oxford, Oneworld, pp. 21–52
Acquaviva S. (1961), *L'eclissi del sacro nella civiltà industriale*, Milano, Edizioni di Comunità
Adler A. (2002), *J'ai vu finir le monde ancien*, Paris, Grasset
Affes H. (2000), "L'arabe dans l'enseignement public" in *La médina*, n° 2, pp. 66–67
Aguer B. (1991), "Résurgence de l'Islam en Espagne" in *Revue Européenne des Migrations Internationales*, vol. 7, n° 3, pp. 59–75
Ahmad M. (1999), "Da'wat-i Islami: an aspiring transnational movement" in *ISIM Newsletter*, n° 4, Leiden, p. 16
Ahmed A.S. (1967), *Islamic Modernism in India and Pakistan, 1857–1964*, London, Oxford University Press
——. (1992) *Postmodernism and Islam: Predicament and Promise*, London-New York, Routledge
——. (1993), *Living Islam: from Samarkand to Stornoway*, London, Penguin
——. & Donnan H. (eds) (1994), *Islam, Globalization and Postmodernity*, London-New York, Routledge
Ahsan M.M. (1994), "Islam and Muslims in Britain" in H. Mutalib & T.I. Hashmi (eds), *op. cit.*, pp. 339–361
Ahsan M.M. & Kidwai A.R. (eds) (1991), *Sacrilege versus Civility: Muslim Perspective on the Satanic Verses Affaire*, Leicester, Islamic Foundation
Akagül D. (1995), "Emigration de la main-d'œuvre turque en Europe—approche économique" in *Les Annales de l'Autre Islam*, n° 3, Paris, Inalco, pp. 45–60
Akgönül S. (1999), *Une communauté, deux Etats: la minorité turco-musulmane de Thrace occidentale*, Istanbul, Isis
——. (1999a), "L'émigration des musulmans de Thrace occidentale" in *Mésogéios*, n° 3, Hêrodotos/Kadmos, pp. 31–49
Aksoi A. & Avci N. (1992), "Spreading Turkish Identity" in *Intermedia*, vol. 20, n° 4–5, pp. 39–50
Ali T. (2002), *The Clash of Fundamentalism*, London, Verso (french translation: *Le choc des intégrismes. Croisades, djihad et modernité*, Paris, Textuel, 2002)
Al Sayyad N. & Castells M. (eds) (2002), *Muslim Europe or Euro-Islam: Politics, Culture and Citizenship in the Age of Globalization*, Lanham, Lexington Books
Albrow M., Eade J., Dürrschmidt J. & Weshbourne N. (1997), "The impact of globalization on sociological concepts: community, culture and milieu" in J. Eade (ed.), *Living the Global City, op. cit.*, pp. 20–36
Aldeeb S. & Bonomi A. (eds), Aronovitz A. & al. (1999), *Le droit musulman de la famille et des successions à l'épreuve des ordres juridiques occidentaux: étude de droit comparé sur les aspects de droit international privé liés à l'immigration des musulmans en Allemagne, en Angleterre, en France, en Espagne, en Italie et en Suisse*, Institut suisse de droit comparé, Zürich, Schulthess

Alexandre D. (1993), "La protection de l'épouse contre la répudiation" in Fr. Dekeuwer-Defossez (dir.), *Le droit de la famille, op. cit.*, pp. 125–142

Algar H. (1985), "Der Naksibendi-Orden in der republikanischen Türkei" in J. Blaschke & M. van Bruinessen (eds), *op. cit.*, pp. 167–196

Allam M. (2002), *Bin Laden in Italia. Viaggio nell'islam radicale*, Milano, Mondadori

Allen C. & Nielsen J.S. (2002, May), *Summary report on Islamophobia in the EU after 11 September 2001*, Vienna, European Monitoring Centre on Racism and Xenophobia

Allievi S. (1996a), "Muslim organisations and Islam-state Relations: The Italian Case" in W.A.R. Shadid & P.S. van Koningsveld (eds), *Muslims in the Margin, op. cit.*, pp. 182–201

——. (1996b), "Islam e occidente: lo specchio e l'immagine" in S. Allievi (ed.), *L'occidente di fronte all'islam*, Franco Angeli, Milano, pp. 11–48

——. (1996c), "The muslim community in Italy" in G. Nonneman, T. Niblock & B. Szajkowski (eds), *Muslim Communities, op. cit.*, pp. 315–329

——. (1996d), "L'Islam in Italia: profili storici e sociologici" in S. Ferrari (ed.), *L'Islam in Europa, op. cit.*, pp. 241–267

——. (1997), "Muslims minorities in Italy and their image in Italian media" in S. Vertovec & C. Peach (eds), *Islam in Europe, op. cit.*, pp. 211–223

——. (1998), *Les convertis à l'islam. Les nouveaux musulmans d'Europe*, Paris, L'Harmattan

——. (2000a), *Nouveaux protagonistes de l'islam européen. Naissance d'une culture euro-islamique? Le rôle des convertis*, European University Institute, Working Papers, n° 18

——. (2000b), "Il multiculturalismo alla prova. L'islam come attore sociale interno" in *Sociologia e politiche sociali*, n° 3, pp. 45–81

——. (2001), "Islam in Italy: sociology of a newcomer" in S. Hunter (ed.), *Islam in Europe, op. cit.*, 20 p

——. (2001a), *La tentazione della guerra*, Milano, Zelig

Allevi, S., Bastenier A., Battegay A. & Boubeker A. (1992), *Médias et minorités ethniques. Le cas de la guerre du Golfe*, Louvain-la-Neuve, Academia-Sybidi Papers n° 13

Allievi S., Bidussa D. & Naso P. (2000), *Il Libro e la spada. La sfida dei fondamentalismi*, Torino, Claudiana

Allievi S. & Castro F. (2000), "The Islamic Presence in Italy: Social Rootedness and Legal Questions" in S. Ferrari & A. Bradney (eds), *op. cit.*, pp. 155–180

Allievi S. & Dassetto F. (1993), *Il ritorno dell'islam. I musulmani in Italia*, Roma, Edizioni Lavoro/ISCOS

Almanya Alevi Birlikleri Federasyonu (2000), *Bin Yilin Türküsü—Das Epos des Jahrtausends—Saga of the Millennium*, Köln

Almond G., Appleby R.S. & Sivan E. (2002), *Strong religion: The Rise of Fundamentalism around the World*, Chicago, The University of Chicago Press

Alston Ph. (dir.) (1994), *The Best Interest of The Child. Reconciling Culture and Human Rights*, Oxford, Clarendon Press

Alwall J. (1998), *Muslim Rights and Plights. The Religious Liberty Situation of a Minority in Sweden*, Lund, Lund University Press

Amanat A. (2001), "Empowering through violence: the reinventing of Islamic extremism" in S. Talbott & N. Chanda (ed.), *The Age of Terror. American and the World after September 11*, New York, Basic Books & Yale Centre for the Study of Globalization

Amiraux V. (1995), "Turcs en Allemagne et turcs d'Allemagne—Histoire imprévue d'une co-existence" in *Les Annales de l'Autre Islam*, n° 3, Paris, Inalco, pp. 61–82

——. (1997), "Turkish islamic associations in Germany and the issue of European citizenship" in S. Vertovec & C. Peach (eds), *Islam in Europe, op. cit.*, pp. 245–259

——. (2001), *Acteurs de l'Islam entre Allemagne et Turquie: parcours militants et expériences religieuses*, Paris, L'Harmattan

——. (1999), "Les limites du transnational comme espace de mobilisation" in *Cultures & Conflits*, n° 33–34, pp. 25–50

——. (1999a), "Is Islam soluble into Germany? Sunni Muslims of Turkish Origin" in *ISIM Newsletter*, n° 4, Leiden, p. 30

——. (2000a), "Jeunes musulmanes turques d'Allemagne—Voix et voies de l'individuation" in F. Dassetto (ed.), *Paroles d'Islam, op. cit.*, pp. 101–124

——. (2001), "La Turchia: Il dilemma dell'appartenenza" in R. Ragionieri & O. Schmidt di Friedberg (dir.), *Culture e conflitti nel Mediterraneo*, Trieste, Asterios

Ancel B. (1993), "Le statut de la femme polygame" in Fr. Dekeuwer-Defossez (dir.), *Le droit de la famille, op. cit.*, pp. 105–123

Anderson B. (1991), *Imagined Communities. Reflections on the Origins and Spread of Nationalism*, London, Verso

Andezian S. (1996), "L'Algérie, le Maroc, la Tunisie" in A. Popovic & G. Veinstein (dir.), *Les Voies d'Allah, op. cit.*, pp. 389–408

Andrews A. (1993), "Sociological analysis of Jamaat-i-Islami in the United Kingdom" in R. Barot (ed.), *Religion and Ethnicity, op. cit.*, pp. 68–79

——. (1994), "Muslim women in a western European society: Gujarati Muslim women in Lecester" in J. Fulton & P. Gee (eds), *Religion in Contemporary Europe*, Lampeter, Edwin Mellen Press

——. (1996), "Muslim Attitudes Towards Political Activity in the United Kingdom: A Case Study of Leicester" in W.A.R. Shadid & P.S. van Koningsveld (eds), *Political Participation, op. cit.*, pp. 115–128

Anghelescu N. (1999), "La minorité musulmane de Roumanie" in *Islamochristiana*, n° 25, pp. 125–137

An-Na'im Abdullahi A. (2002), "Upholding International Legality Against Islamic and American Jihad" in K. Booth & T. Dunne, *World in Collision. Terror and the Future of Global Order*, New York, Plagrave—MacMillan, pp. 162–171

Antes P. & Hewer C. (1994), "Islam in Europe" in S. Gill, G. D'Costa & U. King, *Religion in Europe: contemporary perspectives*, Kampen, Kok Pharos, pp. 46–67

Antoniou D.A. (2000), "Islam in Greece", intervento al convegno *Islam in Europa*, Lisbona, Fundação Luso-Americana/Csis, 16 ottobre

Anwar M. (1998), *Between Cultures—Continuity and Change in the Lives of Young Asians*, London, Routledge

——. (1999), "Muslims in Western Europe: Responses to Integration" in T. Miyajima, T. Kajita & Yamada M. (eds), *Regionalism and Immigration in the Context of European Integration*, Osaka, Japan Centre for Area Studies, pp. 117–142

Arayici A.A. (1999), "La scolarisation des enfants turcs en Allemagne" in *Migrations Société*, vol. 11, n° 62, pp. 47–65

Arjomand, S.A. (1986), "Social change and movements of revitalization in contemporary Islam" in J.A. Beckford (ed.), *New Religious Movements and Rapid Social Change*, London, Sage-Unesco

Arkoun M. (1984), "L'Islam et les islams. Entretien avec Mohamed Arkoun" in *Hérodote*, n° 35, pp. 19–34

Arkoun M., Leveau R. & El-Jisr B. (1993), *L'islam et les musulmans dans le monde. Tome I—L'Europe Occidentale*, Beyrouth, Centre Culturel Hariri

Askeland H. (2000), *Reforming State—Reforming Church. How does New Public Management Affect reforms in the church of Norway?*, paper presented to the 15th Nordic Conference on the Sociology of Religion, Oslo 10–13 August 2000

Ataçan F. (1999), "Cemaleddin Kaplan's Union of Islamic Societies and Communities. The ICCB in Germany" in G. Seufert & G. Waardenburg (eds), *Turkish Islam and Europe, op. cit.*, pp. 241–260

Augé M. (1992), *Non-lieux. Introduction à une anthropologie de la surmodernité*, Paris, Seuil

Ayubi Nazih N.M. (1980, December), "The Political Revival of Islam: the Case of Egypt" in *International Journal of Middle Eastern Studies*, n° 12

Aziz Ph. (1996), *Le paradoxe de Roubaix*, Paris, Plon

Azzi A. (1999), "Islam in cyberspace: Muslim presence on the Internet" in *Islamic Studies*, vol. 38, n° 1, pp. 103–117

Babès B. (1997), *L'Islam positif—La religion des jeunes musulmans de France*, Paris, Editions de l'Atelier

Badie B. (1992), *L'Etat importé*, Paris, Fayard

Bagnasco A. (1999), *Tracce di comunità*, Bologna, Il Mulino

Ballard R. (1996), "Islam and the Construction of Europe" in W.A.R. Shadid & P.S. van Koningsveld (eds), *Muslims in the Margin*, *op. cit.*, pp. 15–50

Ballon F. (1989), "La pratique judiciaire et administrative et le droit maghrébin des personnes dans l'arrondissement judiciaire de Bruxelles" in *Journal des Juges de Paix et de Police*, pp. 69–94

Balta P. (1997), "Le projet culturel euro-méditerranéen: intentions et réalités" in *Dialogue interculturel. Fondement du partenariat euro-méditerranéen*, Lisbonne, Centre Nord-Sud, pp. 65–71

Barber B.J. (1995), *Jihad vs McWorld*, New York, Times Book

——. (2002), "Democracy and Terror in the Era of Jihad and McWorld" in K. Booth & T. Dunne, *World in Collision*, *op. cit.*, pp. 245–262

Bariki S. (2000), "Les imams marseillais, acteurs juridiques privés" in *Islam de France*, n° 8, pp. 85–106

Barot R. (ed.) (1993), *Religion and Ethnicity: Minorities and Social Change in the Metropolis*, Kampen, Kok Pharos

Barou J. (1985, June), "L'islam, facteur de régulation sociale" in *Esprit*, n° 6, pp. 207–215

Basdevant Gaudemet B. & Messner F. (1994), "Statut juridique des minorités religieuses en France" in European Consortium for church-State Research, *The Legal Status of Religious Minorities*, *op. cit.*, pp. 115–152

——. (eds) (1999), *Les origines historiques du statut des confessions religieuses dans les pays de l'Union européenne*, Paris, PUF

Basdevant Gaudemet B. (2000), "The legal status of Islam in France" in S. Ferrari & A. Bradney (eds), *Islam and European Legal Systems*, *op. cit.*, pp. 97–124

Basil M. (1999), "Education for integration: case study of a British Muslim high school for girls" in *Journal of Muslim Minority affairs*, vol. 19, n° 2, pp. 291–298

Basit T. (1997), *Eastern Values—Western Milieu: Identities and Aspirations of Adolescent British Muslim Girls*, Aldershot, Ashgate

Bastenier A. (1988), "Islam in Belgium: contradictions and perspectives" in T. Gerholm & Y.G. Lithman (eds), *The New Islamic Presence*, *op. cit.*, pp. 133–143

——. (1998), "L'incidence du facteur religieux dans la 'conscience ethnique' des immigrés marocains en Belgique" in *Social Compass*, vol. 45, n° 2, pp. 195–218

Bastenier A. & Dassetto F. (eds) (1990), *Immigrations et nouveaux pluralismes*, Bruxelles, De Boeck

——. (1993), *Immigration et espace public. La controverse de l'intégration*, Paris, L'Harmattan

Bastenier A. & Targosz P. (1991), *Les organisations syndicales et l'immigration en Europe*, Louvain-la-Neuve, Academia-Sybidi papers

Battegay A. (1995), "Mosquée de Lyon: la construction d'un symbole" in *Hommes & Migrations*, n° 1186, pp. 26–30

Battegay A. & Boubeker A. (1992), "Les médias, la guerre du Golfe et les figures de l'opinion arabe en France" in S. Allievi, A. Bastenier, A. Battegay & A. Boubeker, *op. cit.*, pp. 81–156

Bauberot J. (1995, October-December), "Laïcité et sécularisation dans la crise de la modernité en Europe" in *Cahiers Français (Religion et société)*, n° 273

Baudrillard J. (1991), *La guerre du Golfe n'a pas eu lieu*, Paris, Galilée

——. (2002), *Power Inferno. Requiem pour les Twin Towers. Hypothèses sur le terrorisme. La violence du mondial*, Paris, Galilée

Baumann G. (1995), "Convergence and encompassment. Two dynamics of syncretization in a multi-ethnic part of London" in G. Baumann & T. Sunier (eds), *Post-migration Ethnicity*, *op. cit.*, pp. 99–117

Baumann G. & Sunier T. (eds) (1995), *Post-migration Ethnicity, Cohesion, Commitments, Comparison*, Amsterdam, Het Spinhuis

Bauman Z. (2002), "Reconnaissance Wars of the Planetary Frontierland" in *Theory, Culture and Society*, 19(4), pp. 81–90

Beck U., Giddens A. & Lash S. (1994), *Reflexive Modernization. Politics, Tradition and Aesthetics in the Modern Social Order*, Oxford, Blackwell-Polity Press

——. (2002), "The Terrorist Threat. World Risk Society Revisited" in *Theory, Culture and Society*, 19(4), pp. 39–55

Beishon S., Modood T. & Virdee S. (1998), *Ethnic Minority Families*, Policy Studies Institute, London

Bellion-Jourdan J. (1997), "L'humanitaire et l'islamisme soudanais. Les organisations Da'wa Islamiya et Islamic African Relief Society" in *Politique Africaine*, n° 66, pp. 61–73

Benbouzid M. (1999), "Réseaux financiers et marchés parallèles de devises—des algériens dans l'économie informelle" in *Revue Européenne des Migrations Internationales*, vol. 15, n° 2, pp. 123–139

Bencheikh S. (1998), *Marianne et le Prophète. L'Islam dans la France laïque*, Paris, Grasset

——. (1999), "Une théologie des minorités" in Groupe d'amitié islamo-chrétien, *Musulmans et chrétiens, op. cit.*, pp. 133–138

Benkheira M.H. (1995), "La nourriture carnée comme frontière rituelle. Les boucheries musulmanes en France" in *Archives de sciences sociales des religions*, n° 92, pp. 67–88

Ben Mansour L. (2002), *Frères musulmans, frères féroces. Voyage dans l'enfer du discours islamiste*, Paris, Ramses

Benningsen A. & Wimbush S.E. (1985), *Muslims of the Soviet Empire*, London, C. Hurst

Bensalah N. (1994), *Familles turques et maghrébines aujourd'hui—Evolution dans les espaces d'origine et d'immigration*, Louvain-la-Neuve, Académia-Maisonneuve & Larose

Benslama F. (2002), *La psychanalyse à l'épreuve de l'islam*, Paris, Aubier

Bergen P.L. (2001), *Holy War, Inc.: Inside the Secret World of Osama bin Laden*, New York, Free Press

——. (2002, March-April), "Picking up the Pieces" in *Foreign Affairs*

Berger P. (1967), *The Sacred Canopy. Elements of a Sociological Theory of Religion*, New York, Doubleday

Berque J. (1980), *L'islam au défi*, Paris, Gallimard

Bielefeldt H. (1996), "Secular Human Rights: challenge and opportunity to Christians and Muslims" in *Islam and Christian-Muslim Relations*, n° 3 (7), pp. 311–325

Bilici F. (1997), "Le parti islamiste turc (Refah Partisi) et sa dimension internationale" in *Les Annales de l'Autre Islam*, n° 4, Paris, Inalco, pp. 35–60

Bjørgo T. (1997), "'The Invaders', 'the Traitors' and 'the Resistance Movement': The Extreme Right's Conceptualisation of Opponents and Self in Scandinavia" in T. Modood & P. Werbner (eds), *The Politics of Multiculturalism, op. cit.*, pp. 54–72

Blaschke J. & van Bruinessen M. (eds) (1985), *Jahrbuch zur Geschichte und Gesellschaft des Vorderen und Mittleren Orients*, Berlin, Express Edition

Bloul R. (1996), "Engendering Muslim identities—Deterritorializatoin and the ethnicization process in France" in B.D. Metcalf (ed.), *op. cit.*, pp. 234–50

——. (1999), "Beyond ethnic identity: resisting exclusionary identification" in *Social Identities*, vol. 5, n° 1, pp. 7–30

Bono S. (1993), *Corsari nel Mediterraneo. Cristiani e musulmani fra guerra, schiavitù e commercio*, Milano, Mondadori

Bonte P., Brisebarre A.-M. & Gokalp A. (dir.) (1999), *Sacrifice en islam*, Paris, CNRS Editions

Booth K. & Dunne T. (eds) (2002), *Worlds in Collision. Terror and the Future of Global Order*, New York, Palgrave—MacMillan

Borrmans M. (1981), *Orientations pour un dialogue entre Chrétiens et Musulmans*, Paris, Editions du Cerf

Bossuyt M. (1976), *L'interdiction de la discrimination dans le droit international des droits de l'homme*, Bruxelles, Bruylant

Botta R. (2000), "Diritto alla moschea" tra 'intesa islamica' e legislazione regionale sull'edilizia di culto" in S. Ferrari (ed.), *Musulmani in Italia, op. cit.*, pp. 109–130

Boubakri H. (1999), "Les entrepreneurs migrants d'Europe" in *Cultures & Conflits*, n° 33–34, pp. 69–88

Bougarel X. & Clayer N. (dir.) (2001), *Le nouvel Islam balkanique—Les musulmans, acteurs du post-communisme 1990–2000*, Paris, Maisonneuve & Larose

Bouhdiba A. (1975), *La sexualité en Islam*, Paris, Presses Universitaires de France

Boumans L. (1992), *Huwelijksvoorwaarden in het islamitisch huwelijksrecht van Marokko* [Clauses matrimoniales en droit du mariage marocain] (thèse de doctorat), RU Limburg (Pays-Bas)

Bourdelois B. (1993), *Mariage polygamique en droit positif français*, Paris, GLN-Joly

Bourg D. (1998), "Qu'est-ce que l' 'islam des jeunes'?" in *Islam de France*, n° 2, pp. 72–81

Bousetta H. (coord.) (2002), *Rompre le silence. 11 septembre 2001–11 septembre 2002. Une prise de position citoyenne d'intellectuels belges d'origine maghrébine sur les événements qui ont marqué l'année*, Bruxelles, Labor

Bozarslan H. (1990), "Une communauté et ses institutions: le cas des Turcs de RFA" in *Revue Européenne des Migrations Internationales*, vol. 6, n° 3, pp. 63–82

———. (1998), "Espaces immigrés et violence: Le cas français et allemand" in R. Leveau (ed.), *Islam(s) en Europe, op. cit.*, pp. 119–138

———. (1998a), "Islam, islamisme et question minoritaire: le cas kurde" in *Les Annales de l'Autre Islam*, n° 1, Paris, Inalco, pp. 333–350

———. (1998b), "Le groupe kurde" in *Hommes & Migrations*, n° 1212, pp. 24–34

Bozdémir M. (dir.) (1996), *Islam et laïcité. Approches globales et régionales*, Paris, L'Harmattan

Bradney A. (1993), *Religions, Rights and Law*, Leicester, Leicester University Press

Branca P. (2000), "Internet e globalizzazione: riflessioni da parte islamica" in *Quaderni Asiatici*, n° 52, pp. 87–95

Breuer R. (1998), *Familienleben im Islam: Traditionen; konflikte, Vorurteile*, Breiburg im Br, Herder

Brewin C. (1997), "Society as a Kind of Community: Communitarian Voting with Equal Rights in the European Union" in T. Modood & P. Werbner (eds), *The Politics of Multiculturalism, op. cit.*, pp. 223–239

Brisard J.-C. & Dasquié G. (2001), *Ben Laden. La vérité interdite*, Paris, Denoël

Brisebarre A.-M. (1998), *La fête du mouton—un sacrifice musulman dans l'espace urbain*, Paris, CNRS Editions

Brown C. (2002), "Narratives of Religion, Civilization and Modernity" in K. Booth & T. Dunne, *World in Collision, op. cit.*, pp. 293–302

Bruce S. (2000), *Fundamentalism*, Cambridge, Polity Press

Bunt G. (1998), "Decision-making concerns in British islamic environments" in *Islam and Christian-Muslim Relations*, vol. 9, n° 1, pp. 103–113

———. (1999), "islam@britain.net: British Muslim identities in Cyberspace" in *Islam and Christian-Muslim Relations*, vol. 10, n° 3, pp. 353–362

———. (2000), *Virtually Islamic—Computer-mediated, Communication and Cyber Islamic Environments*, Cardiff, University of Wales Press

Burgat F. (1988), *L'islamisme au Maghreb*, Paris, Karthala

———. (1996), *L'islamisme en face*, Paris, La Découverte

Burkhalter S. (1998), "La question du cimetière islamique en Suisse: quels enjeux pour la communauté musulmane?" in *Revue Européenne des Migrations Internationales*, vol. 14, n° 3, pp. 61–75

Buskens L. (1999), "Marokkaans familierecht in Nederland" in L. Buskens, *Islamitisch recht en familiebetrekkingen in Marokko*, Amsterdam, Bulaaq, pp. 536–560

Buzan B. & Diez T. (1999), "The European Union and Turkey" in *Survival*, vol. 41, n° 1, pp. 41–57

Cacciari M. (1994), *Geo-filosofia dell'Europa*, Milano, Adelphi

Cadat B.-Y. & Fennema M. (1998), "Les hommes politiques issus de l'immigration à Amsterdam: image de soi, image des autres" in *Revue Européenne des Migrations Internationales*, vol. 14, n° 2, pp. 97–121

Caglar A. (1995), "McDöner: Döner Kebap and the Social Positioning Struggle of German Turks" in G.J. Bamossy & J.A. Costa (eds), *Marketing in a Multicultural World. Ethnicity, Nationalism, and Cultural Identity*, London, Sage Publications, pp. 209–230

———. (1997), "Hyphenated Identities and the Limits of Culture" in T. Modood & P. Werbner (eds), *The Politics of Multiculturalism, op. cit.*, pp. 169–185

Cahiers de l'Orient (dir.) (2002), *Dictionnaire mondial de l'islamisme*, Paris, Plon

Cardini F. (1999), *Europa e Islam. Storia di un malinteso*, Bari-Roma, Laterza

———. (ed.) (2002), *La paura e l'arroganza*, Roma-Bari, Laterza

Carlier J.-Y. (1985), "La reconnaissance en Belgique de répudiations unilatérales intervenues au Maroc ou l'ordre public répudié?" in *Journal des Tribunaux*, pp. 101–108

———. (1991), "Volonté, ordre public et fraude dans la reconnaissance des divorces et répudiations intervenus à l'étranger" in *Revue trimestrielle de droit familial*, pp. 165–172

———. (1992), *Autonomie de la volonté et statut personnel. Etude prospective de droit international privé*, Bruxelles, Bruylant

———. (1994), "Les conventions entre la Belgique et le Maroc en matière de droit familial" in *Revue trimestrielle de droit familial*, n° 3, pp. 447–462

———. (1995), "Les conventions en matière matrimoniale et successorale au regard des droits marocain, algérien, tunisien et turc" in *Les relations contractuelles. Le rôle du notaire* (Fédération Royale des Notaires de Belgique), Anvers/Apeldoorn, Maklu, pp. 698 ss

———. (1996), "Le droit confronté à la présence de familles musulmanes en Europe: quelles perspectives?" in M.-C. Foblets (dir.), *op. cit.*, pp. 20–32

———. (1997), "Deux facettes des relations entre le droit et l'islam: la répudiation et le foulard" in F. Dassetto (ed.), *Facettes, op. cit.*, pp. 239–252

———. (1998), "Droit de vote et citoyenneté" in *La Revue Nouvelle*, vol. 108, n° 9, pp. 32–37

Carlier J.-Y. & Verwilghen M. (dir.) (1992a), *Le statut personnel des musulmans. Droit comparé et droit international privé*, Bruxelles, Bruylant

Carré O. & Michaud G. (1983), *Les frères musulmans*, Paris, Gallimard-Julliard

Carré O. (1991), *L'utopie islamique dans l'Orient Arabe*, Paris, Presses de Sciences-Po

Casey J. (1994), "Legal status of minority churches and religious communities in Ireland" in European Consortium for church-State Research, *The Legal Status of Religious Minorities, op. cit.*, pp. 183–202

Casman H. (1991), *Notarieel Familierecht*, Gent, Mys & Breesch, pp. 27 ss.

Cassano F. (1995), "Pensare la frontiera" in *Rassegna Italiana di Sociologia*, n° 1, pp. 27–39

Castro F. (1996), "L'Islam in Italia: profili giuridici" in S. Ferrari (ed.), *L'islam in Europa. Lo statuto giuridico delle comunità musulmane*, Bologna, Il Mulino, pp. 269–280

Cesari J. (1997), *Etre musulman en France aujourd'hui*, Paris, Hachette

———. (1997a), *Faut-il avoir peur de l'islam?*, Paris, Presses de Sciences Po

———. (1997b), "Les réseaux transnationaux entre l'Europe et le Maghreb: l'international sans territoire" in *Revue Européenne des Migrations Internationales*, vol. 13, n° 2, pp. 81–94

———. (1998), "Islam in France: social challenge or challenge of secularism?" in S. Vertovec & A. Rogers (eds), *Muslim European Youth, op. cit.*, pp. 25–38

———. (1998a), *Musulmans et républicains. Les jeunes, l'islam et la France*, Bruxelles-Paris, Editions Complexe

———. (1999), "Le multiculturalisme mondialisé: le défi de l'hétérogénéité" in *Cultures & Conflits*, n° 33–34, pp. 5–24

———. (1999a), "The Re-Islamization of Muslim Immigration in Europe" in G. Martin-Muñoz (ed.), *Islam, Modernism and the West, op. cit.*, pp. 211–223

Champion F. & Cohen M. (1999), *Sectes et démocratie*, Paris, Seuil
Charnay J.-P. (1966), "Courants réformateurs de la pensée musulmane contemporaine" in J. Berque & J.-P. Charnay, *Normes et valeurs dans l'islam contemporain*, Paris, Payot, pp. 225–246
——. (1977), *Sociologie religieuse de l'islam*, Paris, Sindbad
Chodkiewicz M. (1996), "Le soufisme au XXIème siècle" in A. Popovic & G. Veinstein (dir.), *Les Voies d'Allah*, *op. cit.*, pp. 532–543
Chomsky N. (2002), "Why are the Global terrorist?" in K. Booth & T. Dunne, *World in Collision*, *op. cit.*, pp. 128–137
Choueri Y. (1996), "The Political Discourse of Contemporary Islamist Movements" in A.S. Sidahmed & A. Ehteshami (eds), *Islamic Fundamentalism*, Oxford, Westview press, pp. 19–34
Christidis Y. (1996), "The Muslim minority in Greece" in G. Nonneman, T. Niblock & B. Szajkowski (eds), *Muslim Communities in Europe*, *op. cit.*, pp. 153–160
Clayer N. (1996), "La Bektachiyya" in A. Popovic & G. Veinstein (dir.), *op. cit.*, pp. 468–474
Clayer N. & Popovic A. (1999), "A new era for Sufi trends in the Balkans" in *ISIM Newsletter*, n° 3, Leiden, p. 32
——. (1999a), "Identités musulmanes dans les Balkans à l'époque post-ottomane" in *Mésogeios*, n° 3, Paris, pp. 7–30
Colaianni N. (2000), "Le intese con i Buddisti ed i Testimoni di Geova" in *Quaderni di diritto e politica ecclesiastica*, n° 2, pp. 475–494
——. (2000), "L'istruzione religiosa nelle scuole pubbliche" in S. Ferrari (ed.), *Musulmani in Italia*, *op. cit.*, Bologna, Mulino, pp. 157–174
Commission Européenne—Cahiers de la Cellule Prospective (1998), *Les religions méditerranéennes: islam, judaïsme et christianisme. Un dialogue en marche*, Luxembourg, Apogée
Consorzio Europeo di Ricerca sui Rapporti tra Stati e Confessioni Religiose (1992), *Stati e confessioni religiose in Europa. Modelli di finanziamento pubblico. Scuola e fattore religioso*, Milano, Giuffrè
Corm G. (2002), *Orient-Occident la fracture imaginaire*, Paris, La Découverte
Cossuto G. (1994), "I musulmani di Romania e il nuovo corso politico" in *Oriente moderno*, vol. XIII, n° 7–12, pp. 23–218
——. (1996), "Il senso d'identita dei Turco-tatari di Romania dal 1878 al oggi" in *Oriente Moderno*, vol. XV, n° 3, pp. 113–166
Courbage Y. (1999), *Aspects démographiques de la migration vers l'Europe, les convergences et les divergences dans les comportements démographiques des migrants et la méthodologie pour les études comparées des migrants*, Groupe des spécialistes sur les caractéristiques démographiques des populations immigrées, Strasbourg, Conseil de l'Europe
——. (1999a), "Enquête sur les sources statistiques relatives à la religion, la/les langue(s), le groupe national et le groupe ethnique en Europe" in W. Haug, Y. Courbage & P. Compton, *Les caractéristiques démographiques des minorités nationales dans certains États européens*, Strasbourg, Conseil de l'Europe
CRESM (1981), *Le Maghreb Musulman en 1989*, Paris, CNRS
CRISLAM (1990), *La foi en marche. Les problèmes de fond du dialogue islamo-chrétien*, Atti del Primo congresso internazionale a distanza, Roma, Pisai
Crowley J. (1999), "Some Thoughts on Theorizing European Citizenship" in *Innovation*, n° 4 (12), pp. 471–488
Crul M. (1999), "Turkish and Moroccan sibling support and school achievement levels: an optimistic view" in *The Netherlands' Journal of Social Sciences*, vol. 35, n° 2, pp. 110–127
Crul M., Lindo F. & Lin Pang C. (eds) (1999), *Culture, Structure and Beyond. Changing Identities and Social Positions of Immigrants and their Children*, Amsterdam, Het Spinhuis,
Cultures & Conflits (1999), n° 33–34, Paris, L'Harmattan, (n° spécial sur "Les anonymes de la mondialisation")

Dalègre J. (1997), *La Thrace grecque. Populations et territoire*, Paris, L'Harmattan
——. (2001), "Grèce: comment peut-on être musulman?" in X. Bougarel & N. Clayer (dir.), *Le nouvel Islam balkanique, op. cit.*, pp. 289–314
Damrel D. (1999), "A sufi Apocalypse" in *ISIM Newsletter*, n° 4, Leiden, p. 1
Daniel N. (1975), *The Arabs and Medieval Europe*, London-New York, Longman
——. (1993), *Islam and the West. The Making of an Image*, Oxford, Oneworld
Danner V. (1981), "Religious revivalism in Islam. Past and Present" in C.K. Pullapilly, *Islam in Contemporary world*, Cross Roads Books
Dassetto F. (1988a), *Le Tabligh en Belgique. Diffuser l'Islam sur les traces du Prophète*, Bruxelles-Louvain-la-Neuve, Academia, Sybidi Papers n° 2, 25 p.
——. (1990), "Visibilisation de l'Islam dans l'espace public" in A. Bastenier & F. Dassetto (eds), *Immigrations et nouveaux pluralismes*, Bruxelles, De Boeck
——. (1996), *La construction de l'islam européen. Approche socio-anthropologique*, Paris, L'Harmattan
——, (ed.) (1997), *Facettes de l'islam belge*, Louvain-la-Neuve, Academia-Bruylant
——. (1999), "Leaders and Leaderships in Islam and in Transplanted Islam in Europe" in E. Helander (ed.), *Religion and Social Transitions*, Helsinki, Publications of Department of Practical Theology, Helsinki University Press, pp. 87–103
——. (2000), *Paroles d'Islam—Individus, Sociétés et Discours dans l'Islam européen contemporain/Islamic Words—Individuals, Societies and Discourse in Contemporary European Islam*, Paris, Maisonneuve & Larose
——. (2000a), Discours, société et individus dans l'islam européen" in F. Dassetto (dir.), *Islamic Words, op. cit.*, pp. 13–34
——. (2000b), "Tablighi Jama'at in Belgium" in M.K. Masud (ed.), *Travellers in faith, op. cit.*, pp. 174–187
——. (2000c), "Quel islamisme et quel déclin? A propos de G. Kepel, Jihad, expansion et déclin de l'islamisme. Lecture critique" in *Recherches Sociologiques*, n° 3, pp. 133–138
Dassetto F. & Bastenier A. (1984), *L'Islam transplanté. Vie et organisation des minorités musulmanes de Belgique*, Antwerp-Bruxelles, EPO
——. (1987), *Médias u Akbar. Confrontations autour d'une manifestation*, Louvain-la-Neuve, Ciaco
——. (1988), *Europa: nuova frontiera dell'islam*, Roma, Edizioni Lavoro (ediz. aggiornata 1991)
Dassetto F. & Conrad Y. (eds) (1996), *Musulmans en Europe. Bibliographie commentée*, Paris, L'Harmattan
Davis D.H. (2000), "Religious Persecution in Today's Germany: Old Habits Renewed" in D.H. Davis (ed.), *Religious Liberty in Northern Europe in the Twenty-first Century*, Waco, Baylor University
Dayan D. & Katz E. (1992), *Media Events. The live broadcasting of history*, Cambridge, Harvard University Press
Dayan D. (coord.) (2002, July-August), "A chacun son 11 septembre?" in *Dossiers de l'Audiovisuel*, n° 104
de Galembert C. (1994), "Intégration des musulmans en France et en Allemagne. Le poids de l'intermédiaire catholique" in A. Dierkens (ed.), *Pluralisme Religieux et Laïcité dans l'Union Européenne, Problèmes d'Histoire des Religions*, n° 5, pp. 109–121
——. (1997), "Etat, musulmans et société en France: la médiation catholique et ses limites" in *Migrations Société*, vol. 53, n° 9
——. (1998), "Eglises chrétiennes, Etat et Islam en Europe: Entre institutionnalisation et désinstitutionnalisation" in R. Leveau (ed.), *Islam(s) en Europe, op. cit.*, pp. 69–82
——. (2000), "Etat, nation et religion dans l'Allemagne réunifiée" in *Vingtième siècle*, n° 66, pp. 37–51
de Jong F. (1986), "The Turks and Tatars in Romania" in *Turcica*, vol. 18, pp. 165–189

de Sousa e Brito J. (1994), "La situation juridique des Eglises et des communautés religieuses minoritaires au Portugal" in European Consortium for church-State Research, *The Legal Status of Religious Minorities, op. cit.*, pp. 235–250

de Sousa e Brito J. & Teles Pereira J.A. (1998), "Nouveaux droits" in European Consortium for church-State Research, *"New liberties", op. cit.*, pp. 331–366

Dekeuwer-Defossez Fr. (dir.) (1993), *Le droit de la famille à l'épreuve des migrations internationales*, Paris, L.G.D.J.

Della Ratta D. (2000), *Media Oriente. Modelli, strategie, tecnologie nelle nuove televisioni arabe*, Roma, Seam

Delorme C. (1995), "Chrétiens et musulmans en France" in *Etudes*, pp. 649–660

Delumeau J. (1978), *La peur en Occident: une cité assiégée*, Paris, Fayard

Deprez J. (1988), "Droit international privé et conflits de civilisations. Aspects méthodologiques. Les relations entre systèmes d'Europe occidentale et systèmes islamiques en matière de statut personnel" in *Recueil des Cours de l'Académie de La Haye*, vol. 211, 1988–IV, pp. 9–372

——. (1989), "Au carrefour de droit comparé et du droit international privé, quelle place pour le droit musulman?" in J.R. Henry (dir.), *L'enseignement du droit musulman en France*, CNRS (Cahier du CRESM), pp. 17–92

——. (1998), "Statut personnel et pratiques familiales des étrangers musulmans en France. Aspects de droit international privé" in M.-C. Foblets, *op. cit.*, pp. 113 ss.

de Tapia S. (1995), "L'émigration turque: des portes de l'étranger aux portes d'entrée" in *Les Annales de l'Autre Islam*, n° 3, Paris, Inalco, pp. 27–44

——. (1998), "La communication et l'intrusion satellitaire dans le champ migratoire turc" in *Hommes & Migrations*, n° 1212, pp. 102–110

Diop M. (1985), "Les associations murid en France" in *Esprit*, n° 102, pp. 197–206

Diop M. & Kastoryano R. (1991), "Le mouvement associatif islamique en Ile-de-France" in *Revue Européenne des Migrations Internationales*, vol. 7, n° 3, pp. 91–117

Diop M. & Michalak L. (1996) "Refuge and Prison: Islam, Ethnicity, and the Adaptation of Space in Workers' Housing in France" in B.D. Metcalf (ed.), *Making Muslim Space, op. cit.*, pp. 74–91

Djait H. (1978), *L'Europe et l'Islam*, Paris, Seuil

Doomernik J. (1995), "The institutionalization of Turkish Islam in Germany and the Netherlands: a comparison" in *Ethnic and Racial Studies*, vol. 18, n° 1, pp. 46–63

Dreyfus F.-G. (1993), "Le protestantisme contre l'Europe" in G. Vincent & J.-P. Willaime, *Religions et transformations de l'Europe*, Strasbourg, Presses Universitaires de Strasbourg

Driessen G. (1999), "Kwalitatieve aspecten van het functioneren van islamitische basisscholen" in *Nederlands Tijdschrift voor Opvoeding, Vorming en Onderwijs*, vol. 15, n° 3, pp. 143–158

Dupuis J. (1997), *Verso una teologia cristiana del pluralismo religioso*, Brescia, Queriniana

Dupuy J.P. (2002), *Avions-nous oublié le mal? Penser la politique après le 11 septembre*, Paris, Bayard

Duran K. (1991), "Muslim diaspora: the Sufis in Western Europe" in *Islamic Studies*, n° 30, pp. 463–483

During J. (1996), "Musique et rites: le samâ'" in A. Popovic & G. Veinstein (dir.), *op. cit.*, pp. 157–172

Dwyer C. & Meyer A. (1995), "The institutionalisation of Islam in the Netherlands and in the UK: the case of islamic schools" in *New Community*, vol. 21, n° 1, pp. 37–54

Eade J. (1992), "Quests for belonging: Bangladeshis in Tower Hamlet's" in A.X. Cambridge & S.C. Feuchtwang (eds), *Where you belong. Government and Black Culture*, Aldershot, Avebury

——. (1996), "Nationalism, Community and the Islamization of Space in London" in B.D. Metcalf (ed.), *Making Muslim Space, op. cit.*, pp. 217–233

——. (ed.) (1997), *Living the Global City. Globalization as Local Process*, London, Routledge

Ebin V. (1996), "Making room versus creating space—the construction of spatial categories by itinerant Mouride traders" in B.D. Metcalf (ed.), *op. cit.*, pp. 92–109

Eickelman D.F. & Piscatori J. (1996), *Muslims Politics*, Princeton, Princeton University Press

Eickelmann D.F. & Anderson J.W. (eds) (1999), *New Media in the Muslim World. The Emergence Public Sphere*, Bloomington, Indiana University Press

Eisenstadt S.N. (1992), *Fundamentalism, Sectarianism and Revolution. The Jacobin Dimension of Modernity*, Cambridge, Cambridge University Press

——. (2000), "The Civilizational Dimension in Sociological Analysis" in *Thesis Eleven*, n° 62, pp. 1–21

El Karouni M. (1999), "La dot: une institution contraire à l'ordre public international belge?" in M.-C. Foblets & F. Strijbosch (dir.), *op. cit.*, pp. 85–108

Elgeddawy A.K. (1971), *Relations entre systèmes confessionnel et laïque en droit international privé*, Paris, Dalloz

El-Husseini R. (1999), "Le droit international privé français et la répudiation islamique" in *Revue critique de droit international privé*, pp. 427–468

Elmas H.B. (1998), "L'intervention du facteur 'immigration' dans les relations turco-européennes" in *Revue Européenne des Migrations Internationales*, vol. 14, n° 3, pp. 77–101

Eminov A. (1997), *Turkish and Other Muslim Minorities of Bulgaria*, London, Hurst

Encel F. (2002), *Géopolitique de l'apocalypse. La démocratie à l'épreuve de l'islamisme*, Paris, Flammarion

Ennaïfer H. (1996), "Les musulmans dans la cité: contraintes et perspectives" in *Revue de Droit Canonique*, Strasbourg, vol. 46, n° 2, pp. 291–299

Entzinger H. (2000), "L'islam aux Pays-Bas. Culture ou religion?" in *Confluences Méditerranée*, n° 32, pp. 103–118

Epalza M. (1995), "Formación e investigación universitaria sobre el Islam" in M. Abumalham (ed.), *Comunidades islámicas en Europa*, *op. cit.*, pp. 213–228

Erauw J. (1989), "De nood aan codificatie van het Belgisch internationaal privaatrecht" [La nécessité de codifier le droit international privé belge] in J. Erauw (dir.), *Liber Memorialis François Laurent (1810–1887)*, Bruxelles, Story-Scientia, pp. 745–763

Esposito J.L. (1992), *The Islamic Threat. Myth or Reality?*, New York-Oxford, Oxford University Press

——. (2001), "The dynamics of Interaction Between the Muslim Diaspora and the Islamic World: Europe and America" in S. Hunter (ed.), *Islam in Europe, op. cit.*

——. (2002), *Unholy War. Terror in the Name of Islam*, Oxford, Oxford University Press

Etienne B. (1987), *L'islamisme radical*, Paris, Hachette

——. (1989), *La France et l'Islam*, Paris, Hachette

——. (ed.) (1990), *L'Islam en France*, Paris, CNRS Editions

Etienne B. & Tozy M. (1981), "Le glissement des obligations islamiques vers le phénomène associatif à Casablanca" in CRESM, *Le Maghreb Musulman en 1979*, Paris, CNRS, pp. 235–259

European Commission (1999), *Turkey: Regular Report from the Commission on Progress towards Accession*—October 13, Bruxelles

European Consortium for Church and State Research (1993), *Churches and Labour Law in the EC Countries*, Milan-Madrid, Giuffrè-Facultad de Derecho

——. (1994), *The Legal Status of Religious Minorities in the Countries of the European Union*, Thessaloniki-Milan, Sakkoulas-Giuffrè

——. (1995), *Le statut constitutionnel des cultes dans les pays de l'Union européenne*, Paris-Milan, Litec-Giuffrè

——. (1998), *"New liberties" and church and State Relationships in Europe*, Brussels-Milan-Baden-Baden, Bruylant-Giuffrè-Nomos

——. (1999), *New Religious Movements and the Law in the European Union*, Bruylant-Giuffrè-Nomos, Brussels-Milan-Baden-Baden

Evans M.D. (1997), *Religious Liberty and International Law in Europe*, Cambridge, Cambridge University Press

Faist T. (1998), "Transnational social spaces out of international migration: evolution, significance and future prospects" in *Archives Européennes de Sociologie*, vol. 39, n° 2, pp. 213–247

Farrenkopf J. (2000), "Spengler's Theory of Civilization" in *Thesis Eleven*, n° 62, August, pp. 23–38

Faust E. (2000), "Close ties and New boundaries: Tablighi Jama'at in Britain and Germany" in M.K. Masud (ed.), *Travellers in Faith, op. cit.*, pp. 139–160

Featherstone M. (1995), *Undoing Culture. Globalization, Postmodernism and Identity*, London, Sage Publications

——. (ed.) (1999), *Global culture. Nationalism, Globalization and Diversity*, London, Sage Publications

Feindt-Riggers N. & Steinbach U. (1997), *Islamische Organisationen in Deutschland—Eine aktuelle Bestandsaufnahme und Analyse*, Hamburg, Deutsches Orient-Institut

Feirabend J. & Rath J. (1996), "Making a Place for Islam in Politics. Local Authorities Dealing with Islamic Associations" in W.A.R. Shadid & P.S. van Koningsveld (eds), *Muslims in the Margin, op. cit.*, pp. 243–258

Fermin A. (1999), "Does culture makes a difference? Political discourse on minority policy in the Netherlands 1977–1998" in M. Crul, F. Lindo & C. Lin Pang (eds), *op. cit.*, pp. 196–215

Ferrari S. (1988), "Separation of church and State in Contemporary European Society" in *Journal of church and State*, n° 3, Autumn, pp. 533–547

——. (1996), *L'islam in Europa. Lo statuto giuridico delle comunità musulmane*, Bologna, Il Mulino

——. (1996), "La libertà religiosa nell'Europa occidentale" in *La libertad religiosa. Memoria del IX Congreso Internacional de Derecho Canónico*, Mexico, Universidad Nacional Autónoma de Mexico, pp. 125–129

——. (ed.) (1996), *L'islam in Europa. Lo statuto giuridico delle comunità musulmane*, Bologna, Il Mulino

——. (2000), *Musulmani in Italia. La condizione giuridica delle comunità islamiche*, Bologna, Mulino

Ferrari S. & Bradney A. (eds) (2000), *Islam and European Legal Systems*, Aldershot, Ashgate

Ferry J.-M. (1992), "Pertinence du postnational" in J. Lenoble & N. Dewandre (dir.), *op. cit.*, pp. 39–58

Fierro M. & Carnicero M.J. (1997), *Las publicaciones de los musulmanes españoles* in *Awraq*, n° 18, pp. 105–150

Finocchiaro F. (1995), *Diritto ecclesiastico*, Bologna, Zanichelli

Fitzgerald M.L. (1998), "Christian and Muslims in Europe: perspectives for dialogue" in *Encounter*, n° 247, pp. 3–13

Foblets M.-C. (1992), "La célébration du mariage devant le Consul" (note sous Civ. Liège, 28 juin 1991) in *Revue du droit des étrangers*, pp. 220–225

——. (1994), *Les familles maghrébines et la justice en Belgique. Anthropologie juridique et immigration*, Paris, Karthala.

——. (1994a), "Remaniements de quelques dispositions-clés du Code de Statut Personnel et des Successions marocain relative à la position matrimoniale de l'épouse. Des modifications génératrices d'une pacification des relations internationales privées?" in *Revue du droit des étrangers*, pp. 125–135

——. (1996), *Familles—Islam—Europe. Le droit confronté au changement*, Paris, L'Harmattan

——. (dir.) (1998), *Femmes marocaines et conflits familiaux en immigration: quelles solutions juridiques appropriées?*, Anvers/Apeldoorn, Maklu

Foblets M.-C. & Strijbosch F. (dir.) (1999), *Relations familiales interculturelles—Cross-Cultural Family Relations*, Onati papers, n° 8, I.I.S.L.

Frégosi F. (1997), "L'islam en terre concordataire" in *Hommes & Migrations*, n° 1209, pp. 29–48

——. (dir.) (1998a), *La formation des cadres religieux musulmans en France—Approches socio-juridiques*, Paris, L'Harmattan

——. (1998b), "Les filières nationales de formation des imams en France: L'Institut européen des sciences humaines et l'Institut d'études islamiques de Paris" in F. Frégosi (ed.), *La formation des cadres, op. cit.*, pp. 101–140

——. (1998c), "Les problèmes d'organisation de la religion musulmane en France" in *Esprit*, n° 1, pp. 109–134

——. (1999), "La formation des cadres religieux musulmans en France" in Groupe d'amitié islamo-chrétien, *Musulmans et chrétiens, op. cit.*, pp. 153–164

——. (1999a), "Les contours fluctuants d'une régulation étatique de l'islam" in *Hommes & Migrations*, n° 1220, pp. 14–29

——. (2000), "Les contours discursifs d'une religiosité citoyenne: laïcité et identité islamique chez Tariq Ramadan" in F. Dassetto (ed.), *Paroles d'Islam, op. cit.* pp. 205–222

——. (2000a), "Le culte musulman dans ses rapports à la République de France. Réflexions sur les contours théoriques et pratiques d'un islam républicain selon Jean Pierre Chevènement" in *Quaderni di diritto e politica ecclesiastica*, 2000/1, pp. 281–293

——. (2000b), "L'islam en Europe, entre dynamiques d'institutionnalisation, de reconnaissance et difficultés objectives d'organisation" in *Religions, droit et sociétés dans l'Europe communautaire*, Actes du XIIIème Colloque de l'Institut de Droit et d'Histoire Religieuse (IDHR), Aix-en-Provence, 19–20 mai 1999, Presses Universitaires d'Aix-Marseille-Puam, pp. 91–117

Fukuyama F. (2002), "History and September 11" in K. Booth & T. Dunne, *World in Collision. Terror and the Future of Global Order*, New York, Plagrave—MacMillan, pp. 27–36

Fuller G.E. (2002, March-April), "The Future of Political Islam" in *Foreign Affairs*, pp. 48–60

Gabert G. (1999), "L'islam dans la société allemande—un changement culturel majeur" in *Confluences Méditerranée*, n° 32, Paris, pp. 87–102

Gaboriau M. (1996), "Tarîqa et orthodoxie" in A. Popovic & G. Veinstein (dir.), *op. cit.*, pp. 195–204

——. (1999), "Transnational Islamic Movements: Tablighi Jama'at in politics?" in *ISIM Newsletter*, n° 3, Leiden, p. 21

——. (2000), "The transformation of Tablighi Jama'at into a transnational movement" in M.K. Masud (ed.), *Travellers in Faith, op. cit.*, pp. 121–138

Galindo E. & Alonso E. (1996), "Les relations entre musulmans et chrétiens en Espagne" in *Islamochristiana*, n° 22, pp. 161–191

Galizera M. (2000), "L'islam et les musulmans à Marseille" in *Islam de France*, n° 8, pp. 67–84

Ganage P. (1992), "La pénétration de la volonté dans le droit international privé de la famille" in *Revue critique de droit international privé*, pp. 425–454

García Pardo D. (2000), "El contenido de los acuerdos previstos en el artículo 7.1 de la ley orgánica de libertad religiosa" in *Anuario de derecho eclesiástico del Estado*, pp. 293–99

Garde P. (1994), "Legal status of minority churches and religious communities in the Kingdom of Denmark. Liberty without equality" in European Consortium for church-State Research, *The Legal Status of Religious Minorities, op. cit.*, pp. 81–114

Gaspard F. & Khosrokhavar F. (1995), *Le Foulard et la République*, Paris, La Découverte

Gauchet M. (1985), *Le désenchantement du monde. Une histoire politique de la religion*, Paris, Gallimard

Gaudeul J.M. (1999), "Dialogue à l'aigre-doux sur Internet" in *Se Comprendre*, n° 1, pp. 1–18

Gause G. (2001), "The Kingdom in the Middle" in J.F. Hoge, Jr. & G. Rose, *How Did This Happen? Terrorism and the New War*, New York, Public Affairs

Geertz C. (1968), *Islam Observed*, New Haven, Yale University Press

Gehl G. (ed.) (1996), *Fundamentalismus contra Weltfriede?*, Weimar, Dadder

Geisser V. (1997), *Ethnicité républicaine. Les élites d'origine maghrébine dans le système politique français*, Paris, Presses de Sciences Po

Geisser V. & Kelfaoui S. (1998), "Tabous et enjeux de l'ethnicité maghrébine dans le système politique français" in *Revue Européenne des Migrations Internationales*, vol. 14, n° 2, pp. 19–32

Geoffroy E. (1996), "La Châdhiliyya" in A. Popovic & G. Veinstein (dir.), *op. cit.*, pp. 509–520

George D. (1996), "An Alternative New World order?" in A.S. Sidahmed & A. Ehteshami (eds), *Islamic Fundamentalism*, Oxford, Westview Press, pp. 71–92

Georgieva T. (2001), "Pomaks: Muslim Bulgarian" in *Islam and Christian-Muslim Relations*, vol. 12, n° 3, pp. 303–316

Gerholm T. & Lithman Y.G. (eds) (1988), *The New Islamic Presence in Western Europe*, London-New York, Mansell

Ghandour A.-R. (2002), *Jihad humanitaire. Enquête sur les ONG islamiques*, Paris, Flammarion

Giovannetti G. (1999), *EMU and the Mediterranean Area*, Firenze, European University Institute, EUI Working Papers, n° 1

Glucksman A. (2002), *Dostoïevski à Manhattan*, Paris, Robert Laffont

Gokalp A. (1997), "Réflexions sur l'islam et la France" in *Panoramiques* (n° monographique: L'islam est-il soluble dans la République?), n° 29, pp. 95–109

———. (1998), "L'islam des Turcs" in *Hommes & Migrations*, n° 1212, pp. 35–52

Goldberg A. (2000), "Islam in Germany", intervento al convegno *Islam in Europa*, Lisbona, Fundação Luso-Americana/Csis, 16 octobre

Göle N. (1993), *Musulmanes et modernes. Voile et civilisation en Turquie*, Paris, La Découverte

———. (1995), "L'émergence du sujet islamique" in F. Dubet & M. Wieviorka (dir.), *Penser le sujet. Autour de Alain Touraine*, Paris, Fayard, pp. 221–234

Greaves R.A. (1995), "The reproduction of Jamaat-i Islami in Britain" in *Islam and Christian-Muslim Relations*, vol. 6, n° 2, pp. 187–210

Grignard A. (1997), "L'islam radical en Belgique à travers la littérature de propagande: une introduction" in F. Dassetto (ed.), *Facettes, op. cit.*, pp. 167–178

———. (1998, October-November), "L'islamisme radical en Belgique" in *Nouvelle Tribune*, n° 18, Bruxelles, pp. 82–83

Groupe d'Amitié islamo-chrétien (1999), *Musulmans et chrétiens. Politiques d'accueil dans les terres d'origine ou d'immigration*, Paris, Bayard/Centurion

Guimezanes N. (1993), "L'Eglise et le droit du travail" in European Consortium for church and State Research, *Churches and Labour Law, op. cit.*, pp. 83–104

Guntau B. (2000), "La condizione giuridica dell'Islam in Germania" in S. Ferrari (ed.), *Musulmani in Italia, op. cit.*, pp. 265–288

Guolo R. (1999), "Le tensioni latenti nell'islam italiano" in C. Saint-Blancat (ed.), *L'islam in Italia, op. cit.*, pp. 159–176

———. (2000), "I nuovi Crociati: la Lega e l'Islam" in *Il Mulino*, n° 5, pp. 890–901

Gür M. (1993), *Türkisch-islamische Vereinigungen in der Bundesrepublik Deutschland*, Frankfurt am Main, Brandes & Apsel

Habermas J. (1962), *Strukturwandel der Oeffentlichkeit*, Neuwied, Hermann Luchterhand Verlag (italian translation: *Storia e critica dell'opinione pubblica*, Bari, Laterza, 1971)

Haddad Y.Y. (1982), *Contemporary Islam and the Challenge of History*, Albany, State University of New York Press

———. (2002) (ed.), *Muslims in the West: From Sojourners to Citizens*, Oxford, Oxford University Press, to be published

Haddad Y.Y. & Qurqmaz I. (2000), "Muslims in the West: a select bibliography" in *Islam and Christian-Muslim Relations*, vol. 11, n° 1, pp. 5–49

Haenni P. (1994), "Dynamiques sociales et rapport à l'Etat. L'institutionnalisation de l'Islam en Suisse" in *Revue Européenne des Migrations Internationales*, vol. 10, n° 1, pp. 183–198

———. (1999), "Le Post-islamisme" in *Revue des Mondes Musulmans et de la Méditerranée*, n° 85–86

Hafez K. (ed.) (1997), *Der Islam und der Westen. Anstiftung zum Dialog*, Frankfurt am Main, Fischer Taschenbuch Verlag

Halliday F. (1996), *Islam and the Myth of Confrontation*, London, I.B. Tauris

Hamès C. (1996), "Confréries, sociétés et sociabilité" in A. Popovic & G. Veinstein (dir.), *op. cit.*, pp. 231–241

Hargreaves A.G. (1995), *Immigration, 'Race' and Ethnicity in Contemporary France*, London, Routledge

Hargreaves A.G. & Mahdjoub D. (1997), "Antennes paraboliques et consommation télévisuelle des immigrés" in *Hommes & Migrations*, n° 1210, pp. 111–119

Hargreaves A.G. & Stenhouse T.S. (1991), "Islamic Beliefs among youths of North African origin in France" in *Modern and Contemporary France*, n° 45, pp. 27–35

Hargreaves A.G. & Wihtol de Wenden C. (1993), "The political participation of ethnic minorities in Europe: A framework for analysis" in *New Community*, vol. 20, n° 1, pp. 1–8

Hashmi N. (2000), "Immigrant children in Europe: constructing a transnational identity" in A. Höfert & A. Salvatore (eds), *op. cit.*, pp. 163–175

Haug W., Courbage Y. & Compton P. (1999), *Les caractéristiques démographiques des minorités nationales dans certains États européens*, Strasbourg, Conseil de l'Europe

Haw K. (1995), "Why Muslim girls are more feminist in Muslim schools" in *Education*, Stoke-on-Trent, Trentham, pp. 43–60

Hawwa Magazine (2000), n° 2, Paris, (dossier: Femmes musulmanes de France et pratiques associatives), pp. 14–29

Heisbourg F. & la Fondation pour la recherche stratégique (2001), *Hyperterrorisme: la nouvelle guerre*, Paris, Odile Jacob

Heitmeyer W., Müller J. & Schröder H. (1997), *Verlockender Fundamentalismus. Türkische Jugendliche in Deutschland*, Frankfurt a. M. Suhrkamp

Hermann R. (1996), "Fetullah Gülen: eine alternative zur Refah-Partei?" in *Orient*, vol. XXXVII, n° 4, pp. 619–645

Hervieu-Leger D. (1997), "La transmission religieuse en modernité: éléments pour la construction d'un objet de recherche" in *Social Compass*, vol. 44, n° 1, Sage Publications, pp. 131–143

Heuberger V. (1999), *Der Islam in Europa*, Frankfurt a. Main, Peter Lang

Heyvaert A. (1981–1982), "De grenzen van de gezinsautonomie en de internationale openbare orde in België" [Les limites de l'autonomie du couple et l'ordre public international en Belgique] in *Rechtskundig Weekblad*, pp. 2221–2242

———. (1981–1982), "Het gelijkheidsbeginsel in het Belgisch internationaal huwelijks-, echtscheidings- en afstammingsrecht" in *Rechtskundig Weekblad*, pp. 425–454

———. (1995), "De gezinsrechtelijke situatie van Marokkanen met vast verblijf in België" [La position familiale des ressortissants marocains résidant de manière durable en Belgique] in K. de Feyter, M.-C. Foblets & B. Hubeau (red.), *Migratie- en migrantenrecht* (I), Bruges, La Charte, pp. 287–338

Hjarno J. (1996), "Muslims in Denmark" in G. Nonneman, T. Niblock & B. Szajkowski (eds), *Muslim Communities in Europe, op. cit.*, pp. 291–302

Höfert A. & Salvatore A. (eds) (1999), *Between Europe and Islam—Shaping Modernity in a Transcultural Space*, Brussels, P.I.E.-Peter Lang

Hoffer C. (2000), "Religious healing methods among Muslims in the Netherlands" in *ISIM Newsletter*, n° 6, Leiden, p. 8

Hofmann M. (1996), "The European Mentality and Islam" in *Islamic Studies*, vol. 35, n° 1, pp. 87–97

Hollerbach A. (1999), "Concordati e accordi concordatari in Germania sotto il pontificato di Giovanni Paolo II" in *Quaderni di diritto e politica ecclesiastica*, n° 1, pp. 73–79.

Hollerbach A. & de Frenne A. (1998), "New rights and new social developments in Germany" in European Consortium for church-State Research, "*New liberties*", *op. cit.*, pp. 131–140

Hommes & Migrations (1998), n° 1212, Paris (n° spécial sur les "*Immigrés de Turquie*")

Höpken W. (1992), "Türken und Pomaken in Bulgarien" in *Südosteuropa-Mitteilungen*, vol. XXXII, n° 2, pp. 141–151

———. (1997), "From religious identity to ethnic mobilization: the Turks of Bulgaria, before, under and since Communism" in H. Poulton & S. Taji-Farouki (eds), *op. cit.*, pp. 64–71

HRH Prince of Wales, "A Sense of the Sacred. Building Bridges between Islam and the West" in *European Judaism*, n° 1 (31), pp. 4–8

Hunke S. (1960) *Allahs Sonne uber dem Abendland* (french translation: *Le soleil d'Allah brille sur l'Occident*, Paris, Albin Michel, 1963)

———. (ed.) (2001), *Islam in Europe: The New Social, Cultural and Political Landscape*, Westport, Greenwood Publishing

Huntington S.P. (1993), "The clash of civilizations?" in *Foreign Affairs*, summer, pp. 22–49

———. (1996), *The Clash of Civilization and the Remaking of the World Order*, New York, Simon & Schuster

Ibrahim I. (1981), "Islamic Revival in Egypt and Greater Syria" in C.K. Pullapilly, *Islam in Contemporary world*, Cross Roads Books

Ibrahim S.E. (1980), "Anatomy of Egypt's militant Islamic groups: methodological notes and preliminary findings" in *International Journal of Middle Eastern Studies*, vol. 12, pp. 423–453

Ilchev I. & Perry D. (1996), "The Muslims of Bulgaria" in G. Nonneman, T. Niblock & B. Szajkowski (eds), *op. cit.*, pp. 115–138

Il Regno-attualità (2002), "Norvegia: Chiesa-Stato. Un nuovo ordinamento" in *Il Regno-attualità*, 15 aprile, p. 234

Imarraïne F. (1999), "La présence des mosquées en France" in Groupe d'Amitié islamo-chrétien, *Musulmans et chrétiens, op. cit.*, pp. 145–148

Insel A. (1998), "Pourquoi la candidature turque n'est pas acceptée par l'Union" in *Hommes & Migrations*, n° 1216, pp. 70–77

———. (ed.) (1999), *La Turquie et l'Europe, une coopération tumultueuse*, Paris, L'Harmattan

Inter Faith Network (1997), *Religions in the UK. A Multi-Faith Directory*, Derby, University of Derby-Inter Faith Network

Irwin Z.T. (1989), "The fate of Islam in the Balkans: a comparison of four state policies" in P. Ramet (ed.), *Religion and Nationalism, op. cit.*, pp. 207–225

Ismond P. (1999), "Ethnic Minority Broadcasting and two Cable Stations in the UK" in *European Journal of Communication Research*, n° 3 (24), pp. 351–365

Jacobson J. (1997), "Religion and Ethnicity: Dual and Alternative Sources of Identity among Young British Pakistanis" in *Ethnic and Racial Studies*, vol. 20, n° 2, pp. 238–256

———. (1998), *Islam in Transition—Religion and Identity among British Pakistani Youth*, London & New York, Routledge

Jacquard R. (2002), *Les archives secrètes d'Al Qaida. Révélations sur les héritiers de Ben Laden*, Paris, Jean Picollec

Jahel S. (1994), "La lente acculturation du droit maghrébin de la famille dans l'espace juridique français" in *Revue internationale de droit comparé*, pp. 31–58

Jansen J.G. (1992), "L'islam et les droits civiques aux Pays-Bas" in B. Lewis & D. Schnapper (eds), *Musulmans en Europe, op. cit.*, pp. 55–72

———. (1997), *The Dual Nature of Islamic Fundamentalism*, London, Hurst & Co.

Jansen T. (2000), "Europe and Religions: the Dialogue between the European Commission and churches or Religious Communities" in *Social Compass*, vol. 47, n° 1, pp. 103–112

Jayme E. (1995), "Identité culturelle et intégration: le droit international privé post-moderne" in *Recueil des Cours de l'Académie de Droit International de La Haye*, pp. 9–268

Johnstone P. & Slomp J. (1998), "Islam and churches in Europe: A Christian Perspective" in *Journal of Muslim Minority Affairs*, vol. 18, n° 2, pp. 355–363

Joly D. (1995), *Britannia's Crescent: Making a Place for Muslims in British Society*, Aldershot, Avebury

Jones T.P. & McEvoy D. (1992), "Ressources ethniques et égalités des chances: les entreprises indo-pakistanaises en Grande-Bretagne et au Canada" in *Revue Européenne des Migrations Internationales*, vol. 8, n° 1, pp. 107–126

Jonker G. (1999), *Kern und Rand. Religiöse Mindernheiten aus der Türkei in Deutschland*, Studien 11, Berlin, Verlag das Arabische Buch

——. (2000), "Islamic Television 'Made in Berlin'" in F. Dassetto (ed.), *Paroles d'Islam, op. cit.*, pp. 267–280

Jordens-Cotran L. (1992), "De wenselijkheid van een bilateraal verdrag Marokko-Nederland. Verslag van een studiedag" in *Nederlands Juristenblad*, pp. 552–553

——. (1999), "Quelle attitude à l'égard de la répudiation? Le cas des Pays-Bas" in M.-C. Foblets & F. Strijbosch (dir.), *op. cit.*, pp. 199–220

——. (2000), *Het Marokkaanse familierecht en de Nederlandse rechtspraktijk*, Utrecht, Forum

Kallscheuer O. (ed.) (1996), *Das Europa des Religionen. Eine Kontinent zwischen Säkularisierung und Fundamentalismus*, Frankfurt am Main, Fischer

Karakasoglu Y. & Nonneman G. (1996), "Muslims in Germany, with special reference to the Turkish-Islamic community" in G. Nonneman, T. Niblock & B. Szajkowski (eds), *op. cit.*, pp. 241–268

Karpat K. (1990), *The Turks of Bulgaria: the History, Culture and Political Fate of a Minority*, Istanbul, Isis

Kastoryano R. (1998a), "Les migrants de Turquie face à la France: confrontations d'identités" in *Hommes & Migrations*, n° 1212, pp. 111–119

——. (1998b), *Quelle identité pour l'Europe? Le multiculturalisme à l'épreuve*, Paris, Presses de Sciences Po

——. (1999), "Les Turcs d'Europe: une communauté transnationale" in A. Insel (ed.), *La Turquie et l'Europe, op. cit.*

Kaya A. (1997), *Constructing Diasporas: Turkish Hip-Hop Youth in Berlin*, Ph.D. Thesis, Race & Ethnic Studies, University of Warwick

Keller C.A. (1994), "Le soufisme en Europe occidentale" in J. Waardenburg (coord.), *L'islam en Europe. Aspects religieux*, Lausanne, Université de Lausanne, Cahiers du département interfacultaire d'histoire et des sciences des religions, pp. 7–31

Kelly P. (1999), "Integration and identity in Muslim schools: Britain, United states and Montreal" in *Islam and Christian-Muslim Relations*, vol. 10, n° 2, pp. 197–217

Kepel G. (1984), *Le Prophète et le Pharaon. Les mouvements islamistes dans l'Egypte contemporaine*, Paris, La Découverte

——. (1987), *Les banlieues de l'Islam: naissance d'une religion en France*, Paris, Seuil

——. (1991), *La Revanche de Dieu—Chrétiens, Juifs et Musulmans à la reconquête du monde*, Paris, Seuil

——. (1994), *A l'Ouest d'Allah*, Paris, Seuil

——. (1997), "Islamic groups in Europe: between community affirmation and social crisis" in S. Vertovec & C. Peach (eds), *Islam in Europe, op. cit.*, pp. 48–55

——. (1998), "Réislamisation et passage au terrorisme: quelques hypothèses de réflexion" in R. Leveau (ed.), *Islam(s) en Europe, op. cit.*, pp. 107–118

——. (2000), *Jihad. Expansion et déclin de l'islamisme*, Paris, Gallimard

——. (2002), *Chronique d'une guerre d'orient (automne 2001)*, suivi de *Brève chronique d'Israël et de Palestine (Avril-Mai 2001)*, Paris, Gallimard

Kepel G. & Richard Y. (1990), *Intellectuels et militants de l'islam contemporain*, Paris, Seuil

Khader B. (1974), "L'islam, soubassement idéologique de la renaissance arabe" in *Maghreb-Machrek*

——. (1994), *L'Europe et la Méditerranée—Géopolitique de la proximité*, Paris, L'Harmattan-Academia

——. (1999), "The Euro-Mediterranean Partnership: A Singular Approach to a Plural Mediterranean" in G. Martín-Muñoz (ed.), *op. cit.*, pp. 47–62

Khosrokhavar R. (1995), "Le quasi-individu: de la néo-communauté à la nécro-communauté" in F. Dubet & M. Wieviorka (dir.), *Penser le sujet. Autour de Alain Touraine*, Paris, Fayard, pp. 235–255

——. (1997), *L'islam des jeunes*, Paris, Flammarion

——. (2002), *Les nouveaux martyrs d'Allah*, Paris, Flammarion

Kilani M. (2002), *L'universalisme américain et les banlieues de l'humanité*, Lausanne, Payot

King J. (1997), "Tablighi Jamaat and the Deobandis Mosques in Britain" in S. Vertovec & C. Peach (eds), *Islam in Europe, op. cit.*, pp. 129–146

Kloosterman R., van der Leun J. & Rath J. (1999), "Mixed embeddedness: (in)formal economic activities and immigrant businesses in the Netherlands" in *International Journal of Urban and Regional Research*, vol. 23, n° 2, pp. 252–266

Knott K. & Khoker S. (1993), "Religious and ethnic identity among young Muslim women in Bradford" in *New Community*, vol. 19, n° 3, pp. 539–610

Konidaris J.M. (1994), "Legal status of minority churches and religious communities in Greece" in European Consortium for church-State Research, *op. cit.*, pp. 171–182

Koolen B. (1999), "Politique d'intégration aux Pays-Bas vis-à-vis des minorités ethniques et de leurs chef religieux" in *La religion et l'intégration des immigrés*, Strasbourg, Conseil de l'Europe

Koopmans R. & Statham P. (1999), "Challenging the Liberal Nation-state? Post-nationalism, Multiculturalism, and the Collective Claims Making of Migrants and Ethnic Minorities in Britain and Germany" in *American Journal of Sociology*, vol. 105, n° 3, pp. 652–696

Köse A. (1996), *Conversion to Islam. A Study of Native British Converts*, London, Kegan Paul

Kosnick K. & Bentzin A. (2001), "Representing Islam on Berlin's Open Channel", intervento al *Secondo convegno di studi socio-politici sul Mediterraneo*, Firenze, Istituto Universitario Europeo, 21–25 marzo (in corso di pubblicazione)

Kramer M. (1980), *Political Islam*, Beverly Hills, Sage Publications

Krasteva A. (1998) (ed.), *Communities and Identities in Bulgaria*, Ravenna, Longo Editore

Küçükcan T. (1998), "Young Turks in London" in S. Vertovec & A. Rogers (eds), *Muslim European Youth, op. cit.*, pp. 103–131

——. (1999), "Re-claiming identity: ethnicity, religion and politics among Turkish-Muslims in Bulgaria and Greece" in *Journal of Muslim Minority Affairs*, vol. 19, n° 1, pp. 49–68

Kymlicka W. (1995), *Multicultural Citizenship. A Liberal Theory of Minority Rights*, Oxford, Clarendon Press

Lacomba J. & del Olmo Vicén N. (1996), *La inmigración musulmana y su inserción. Musulmanes en Valencia*, València, Universitat de València, Papers Sud-Nord, n° 1

Lagarde P. (1993), "La théorie de l'ordre public international face à la polygamie et à la répudiation. L'expérience française" in *Nouveaux itinéraires en droit. Hommages à François Rigaux*, Bruxelles, Bruylant, pp. 263–282

Lahrichi F.S. (1985), *Vivre musulmane au Maroc. Guide de droits et obligations*, Paris, Librairie Générale de Droit et de Jurisprudence

Laïdi A. (with A. Salam) (2002), *Le Jihad en Europe. Les filières du terrorisme islamiste*, Paris, Seuil

Lambert P.-Y. (2000), "La participation politique et les médias de la population musulmane en Belgique" in U. Manço (ed.), *Voix et voies musulmanes, op. cit.*, pp. 63–82

Landman N. (1992), *Van mat tot minaret. De institutionalisering van de islam in Nederland*, Amsterdam, VU Uitgeverij

——. (1992a), "Sufi orders in the Netherlands—their role in the institutionnalization of Islam" in W.A.R. Shadid & P.S. van Koningsveld, *Islam in Dutch Society, op. cit.*, pp. 29–39

——. (1996), *Imamopleiding in Nederland: kansen en knelpunten*—Eindrapportage van een terreinverkenning in opdracht van het Ministerie van Onderwijs, Cultuur en Wetenschappen, Utrecht, OC en W

——. (1997), "The Islamic Broadcasting Foundation in the Netherlands: Platform or Arena?" in S. Vertovec & C. Peach (eds), *Islam in Europe, op. cit.*, pp. 224–244

——. (1997a), "Sustaining Turkish-islamic loyalties: the diyanet in western Europe" in H. Poulton & S. Taji-Farouki (eds), *Muslim Identity, op. cit.*, pp. 214–231

——. (1998), Report to the state Secretary for Education, Cultural Affairs and Science—"*Imamopleiding in Nederland: kansen en knelpunten—Imam training in the Netherlands: opportunities and problems*", Utrecht, OC en W, 1996–, (on the occasion of the presentation of) The Hague, February 1998, (MG-SEM III—98–4ᵉ)

——. (1999), "Imams in the Netherlands: Home-made better than import?" in *ISIM Newsletter*, n° 2, Leiden, p. 5

Lange Y. (2000), "A handshake may be refused" in *ISIM Newletter*, n° 5, Leiden, p. 29

Laoust H. (1932), "Le réformisme orthodoxe des 'Salafiya' et les caractères généraux de son orientation actuelle" in *Revue d'études islamiques*, Tome VI, pp. 175–233

——. (1965), *Les schismes dans l'islam*, Paris, Payot

Lapidus I.I. (1988), *A history of Islamic Societies*, Cambridge, Cambridge University Press

Lardinois Ph. (1996), "Réflexion critique sur la réception du statut personnel musulman en Belgique, ou de la négociabilité de l'ordre public dans une société pluriculturelle" in P. Gérard, Fr. Ost & M. van de Kerchove (dir.), *Droit négocié, droit imposé*, Bruxelles, Facultés universitaires Saint-Louis, pp. 605–629

Laroui A. (1986), *Islam et modernité*, Paris, La Découverte

Latouche S. (1989), *L'occidentalisation du monde. Essai sur la signification, la portée et les limites de l'uniformisation planétaire*, Paris, La Découverte

Lawrence B. (1989), *Defenders of God. The Fundamentalist Revolt against the Modern Age*, New York, Harper & Row

Lederer G. (1994), "Modern Islam in Eastern Europe" in *Journal of the Institute for Muslim Minority Affairs*, vol. 15, n° 1–2, pp. 74–83

——. (1996), "Islam in Romania" in *Central Asian Survey*, vol. 15, n° 3–4, pp. 349–368

Leirvik O. (2001), "Christian-Mulism Relations in a state church Situation. Politics of religion and interfaith dialogue: Lessons from Norway", intervento al convegno *Muslim Minority Societies in Europe*, Erfurt, 1–4 maggio (in corso di pubblicazione)

Leiß J. (1996), "Islam im internet" in *Al-Islam. Zeitschrift von Muslimen in Deutschland*, n° 1, pp. 14–17

Lemmen T. (2000), *Islamische Organisationen in Deutschland*, Bonn, Friedrich Ebert Stiftung

Lemmen Th. (1998), *Islamic Extremist Activities in the Federal Republic of Germany*, in www.Verfaussungsschutz.de

Lemmens P. & Alen A. (dir.) (1991), *Egalité et non-discrimination*, Anvers, Kluwer Rechtswetenschappen

Le Monde (1994), "La France et l'Islam", 13 octobre, pp. V–VIII

Lenoble J. & Dewandre N. (dir.) (1992), *L'Europe au soir du siècle—Identité et démocratie*, Paris, Editions Esprit

Les Annales de l'Autre Islam (1995), n° 3, Paris, Inalco (n° spécial sur les "Turcs d'Europe et d'ailleurs")

——. (1997), n° 4, Paris, Inalco (n° spécial sur les "Solidarités islamiques")

Lesthaeghe R. (ed.) (2000), *Communities and Generations: Turkish and Moroccan Populations in Belgium*, Bruxelles, NIDI-CBGS Publications

Lesthaeghe R. & Neels K. (2000), "Islamic communities in Belgium: religious orientations and secularisation" in R. Lesthaeghe (ed.), *op. cit.*, pp. 129–164

Levine M. (2002), "Muslim Responses to Globalization" in *ISIM Newsletter*, n° 10, Leiden, p. 139

Leveau R. (1997), "The political culture of the 'Beurs'" in S. Vertovec & C. Peach (eds), *Islam in Europe, op. cit.*, pp. 147–55

——. (ed.) (1998a), *Islam(s) en Europe. Approches d'un nouveau pluralisme culturel européen*, Travaux du Centre Marc Bloch, Cahier n° 13, Berlin, Centre Marc Bloch

——. (1998b), "Espace, culture, frontière. Projection de l'Europe à l'extérieur" in R. Kastoryano, *Quelle identité pour l'Europe?, op. cit.*, pp. 247–260

Lévy-Vroelant C. (1999), "A chacun selon son ethnie? Réflexions sur une innovation à la française" in *Les Temps Modernes*, n° 305, pp. 242–267

Lewis B. (1976, January), "The Return of Islam" in *Commentary*, pp. 39–49

——. (1982), *The Muslim Discovery of Europe*, New York, Norton & Co.

——. (2001), "The Revolt of Islam" in *The New Yorker*, 19 November (french translation in *Le débat*, n° 119, March-April 2002)

——. (2002), *What Went Wrong. Western Impact and Middle Eastern Response*, Oxford, Oxford University Press (french translation B. Lewis, *Que s'est-il passé? L'islam, l'Occident et la modernité*, Paris, Gallimard)

—— & D. Schnapper (eds) (1992), *Musulmans en Europe*, Poitiers, Actes Sud

Lewis P. (1994), *Islamic Britain—Religion, Politics and Identity among British Muslims*, London, I.B. Tauris

——. (1997), "Arenas of Ethnic Negotiation: Cooperation and Conflict in Bradford" in T. Modood & P. Werbner (eds), *op. cit.*, pp. 126–146

——. (1997a), "The Bradford Council for Mosques and the search for Muslim Unity" in S. Vertovec & C. Peach (eds), *Islam in Europe, op. cit.*, pp. 103–128

——. (1998), "Muslim communities in Britain: towards an 'Arab' contribution to religious and cultural understanding" in J.S. Nielsen & S.A. Khasawnih, *Arabs and the West, op. cit.*, pp. 43–58

——. (1999), "Muslims in Britain: entering the mainstream" in *ISIM Newsletter*, n° 4, Leiden, p. 28

——. (2001), "Depictions of 'Christianity' within British Islamic institutions" in L. Ridgeon (ed.), *Islamic Interpretations on Christianity*, London, Curzon Press

Lindo F. (1995), "Ethnic myth or ethnic might? On the divergence in educational attainment between Portuguese and Turkish youth in the Netherlands" in G. Baumann & T. Sunier (eds), *Post-migration Ethnicity, op. cit.*, pp. 144–164

Livi Bacci M. & Martuzzi Veronesi F. (eds) (1990), *Le risorse umane del Mediterraneo*, Bologna, Il Mulino

Lo Giacco M.L. (2000), "La rappresentanza unitaria dell'Islam in Belgio" in S. Ferrari (ed.), *Musulmani in Italia, op. cit.*, pp. 289–300

Lohlker R. (1997), "Cybermuslim. Islamisches und Arabisches im Internet" in *Orient*, n° 2 (38), pp. 236–244

——. (1998), "Cybermoschee. Islam und Internet" in *Orient*, n° 2 (39), pp. 205–218

López Garcia B. & del Olmo Vicén N. (1995), "Islam e inmigración: el Islam en la formación des grupos étnicos en España" in M. Abumalham (ed.), *Comunidades islámicas en Europa, op. cit.*, pp. 257–276

Lourenco E. (1991), *L'Europe introuvable—Jalons pour une mythologie européenne*, Paris, Editions A.M. Métailié

Luckmann T. (1967), *The Invisible Religion*, New York, MacMillan

Lyall F. & McClean D. (1995), "Constitutional Status of churches in Great Britain" in European Consortium for church-State Research, *op. cit.*, pp. 139–152

Maffesoli M. (2002), *La part du diable. Précis de subversion postmoderne*, Paris, Flammarion

Mahnig H. (2000a), "L'intégration institutionnelle des Musulmans en Suisse: l'exemple de Bâle-Ville, Berne, Genève, Neuchâtel et Zurich" in *Tangram. Bulletin de la Commission fédérale contre le racisme*, n° 8, pp. 102–111

——. (2000b, June), "Vers un islam suisse?" in *Choisir*, pp. 18–21

——. (2002), "Islam in Switzerland: Fragmented Accomodation in a Federal Country" in Y. Haddad (ed.), *Muslims in the West, op. cit.* (to be published)

Malik J. (1996), "Muslim identities suspended between tradition and modernity" in *Comparative Studies of South Asia, Africa and the Middle East*, vol. 16, n° 2, pp. 1–9

Ma Mung E. (1992), "L'expansion du commerce ethnique: Asiatiques et Maghrébins dans la région parisienne" in *Revue Européenne des Migrations Internationales*, vol. 8, n° 1, Paris, pp. 39–59

——. (1996), "Entreprise économique et appartenance ethnique" in *Revue Européenne des Migrations Internationales*, vol. 12, n° 2, Paris, pp. 211–233

Mancini L. (1998), *Immigrazione musulmana e cultura giuridica. Osservazioni empiriche su due comunità di egiziani*, Milano, Giuffrè

Manço U. (1997), "Des organisations socio-politiques comme solidarité islamique dans l'immigration turque en Europe" in *Les Annales de l'Autre Islam*, n° 4, Paris, Inalco, pp. 97–134

——. (2000), "L'éthique du derviche et l'esprit de la confrérie: identité et stratégie. Le discours du cheikh Nakshibendi Mehmet Es'ad Cosan" in F. Dassetto (ed.), *Paroles d'Islam, op. cit.*, pp. 223–244

——. (ed.) (2000a), *Voix et voies musulmanes de Belgique*, Bruxelles, Publications des Facultés Universitaires Saint-Louis

Manço A. & Manço U. (1995), "Les Turcs de Belgique: le repli communautaire comme dynamique d'intégration?" in *Les Annales de l'Autre Islam*, n° 3, Paris, Inalco, pp. 111–124

Mandaville P. (2000), "Information Technology and the Changing Boundaries of European Islam" in F. Dassetto (ed.), *Paroles d'Islam, op. cit.*, pp. 281–298

——. (2001), *Transnational Muslim Politics: Reimagining the Umma*, London, Routledge

Mandel R. (1996), "A Place of Their Own. Contesting Spaces and Defining Places in Berlin's Migrant Community" in B.D. Metcalf (ed.), *op. cit.*, pp. 147–166

Manitakis A. (1998), "New liberties and church-State relationships in Greece" in European Consortium for church-State Research, *op. cit.*, pp. 141–158

Manssoury F. (1989), "Muslims in Europe: the lost tribe of Islam?" in *Journal Institute of Muslim Minority Affairs*, vol. 10, n° 1, pp. 63–84

Mantecón Sancho J. (1998), "L'enseignement de la religion dans le système éducatif espagnol. Référence spéciale à l'enseignement religieux évangélique et islamique" in F. Messner & A. Vierling (eds), *L'enseignement religieux, op. cit.*, pp. 119–134

Marinos A.N. (1994), "La notion du proselytisme religieux selon la Constitution" in *Revue hellenique de droit international*, pp. 377–415

Markham I. (2002), "9.11: contrasting reactions and the challenge of dialogue" in I. Markham & M. Abu-Rabi' (eds), *11 September. Religious perspectives on the causes and consequences*, Oxford, Oneworld, pp. 206–230

Marletti C. (ed.) (1995), *Televisione e islam. Immagini e stereotipi dell'islam nella comunicazione italiana*, Torino, VQPT/Nuova Eri

Martin de Agar J.T. (2000), *Raccolta di concordati 1950–1999*, Vatican City, Libreria Editrice Vaticana

Martin-Muñoz G. (1996), "Perceptions de l'Islam en Espagne" in *Confluences Méditerranée*, n° 19, pp. 183–196

——. (1997), "Perceptions culturelles en Méditerranée. Regards croisés entre l'Islam et l'Occident" in *Dialogue interculturel. Fondement du partenariat euroméditerranéen*, Lisbonne, Centre Nord-Sud, pp. 33–42

——. (ed.) (1999), *Islam, Modernism and the West*, London-New-York, I.B. Tauris

Martínez Torrón J. (1996), "Lo statuto giuridico dell'islam in Spagna" in *Quaderni di diritto e politica ecclesiastica*, n° 1, pp. 53–80

Martiniello M. (1998a), "Les immigrés et les minorités ethniques dans les institutions politiques: ethnicisation des systèmes politiques européens ou renforcement de la démocratie?" in *Revue Européenne des Migrations Internationales*, n° 2 (14), pp. 9–17

——. (1998b), "Les élus d'origine étrangère à Bruxelles: une nouvelle étape de la participation politique des populations d'origine immigrée" in *Revue Européenne des Migrations Internationales*, vol. 14, n° 2, pp. 123–149

——. (2001), "Politique d'immigration, asile et citoyenneté en Belgique: nouveaux développements", comunicazione presentata al seminario *Les nouveaux territoires de la citoyenneté en Europe*, Paris, Ifri, 18–19 gennaio

Marty M. & Appleby R.S. (eds) (1991–1995), *The Fundamentalism Project*, 5 vol., Chicago-London, University of Chicago Press

Massart-Pierard Fr. (1993), *L'Europe en tous ses états: entre mythe et contrainte communautaire?*, Louvain-la-Neuve-Bruxelles, Academia-Bruylant

Masud M.K. (2001), "Muslim jurists' quest for the normative basis of shari'a" in *ISIM Newsletter*, n° 7, Leiden, p. 5

———. (ed.) (2000), *Travellers in Faith—Studies of the Tablighi Jama'at as a Transnational Islamic Movement for Faith Renewal*, Leiden, Brill

Mattéi J.-F. & Rosenfield D. (dir.), *Civilisation et barbarie. Réflexions sur le terrorisme contemporain*, Paris, PUF

MCB (The Muslim Council of Britain) (2002), *The Quest for Sanity. Reflections on September 11 and the Aftermath*, London, MCB, September

Meddeb A. (2002), *La maladie de l'islam*, Paris, Seuil

Meeusen J. (1997), *Nationalisme en internationalisme in het internationaal privaatrecht* [Nationalisme et internationalisme en droit international privé belge], Anvers, Intersentia

Melleuish G. (2000), "The Clash of Civilizations: A Model of Historical Development?" in *Thesis Eleven*, August, pp. 109–120

Merad A. (1981), "L'idéologisation de l'islam dans le monde musulman contemporain" in CRESM, *Le Maghreb musulman en 1979*, Paris, CNRS

Mercier P. (1972), *Conflits de civilisations et droit international privé: polygamie et répudiation*, Genève

Messner F. (ed.) (1995), *La culture religieuse à l'école*, Paris, Cerf

———. (1996), "L'organisation du culte musulman dans certains pays de l'Union européenne" in *Revue de Droit Canonique*, tome 46/2, pp. 195–213

———. (1997), "Le droit local des cultes alsacien-mosellan en 1996" in *European Journal for church and State Research*, pp. 72–77

———. (1998), "L'enseignement de la théologie à l'Université publique: l'exemple de la création d'une faculté de théologie musulmane à Strasbourg" in F. Frégosi (dir.), *op. cit.*, pp. 141–167

———. (1999), "Le droit des religions dans une Europe interculturelle" in *Hermès—La cohabitation culturelle en Europe, Regards croisés des Quinze, de l'Est et du Sud*, n° 23–24, pp. 57–64

———. (1999), "Le droit local des cultes alsacien-mosellan en 1998" in *European Journal for church and State Research*, pp. 102–03

Messner F. & A. Vierling (eds) (1998), *L'enseignement religieux à l'école publique*, Strasbourg, Oberlin

Metcalf B.D. (1982), *Islamic Revival in British India: Deoband, 1860–1900*, Princeton, Princeton University Press

———. (ed.) (1996), *Making Muslim Space in North America and Europe*, Berkeley, University of California Press

———. (2000), "Tablighi Jama'at and women" in M.K. Masud (ed.), *Travellers in Faith*, *op. cit.*, pp. 44–58

Michel T. (1996), "Post-migranti. I musulmani europei alla ricerca di una nuova sintesi" in S. Allievi (ed.), *L'occidente di fronte all'islam*, Milano, Franco Angeli, pp. 202–221

Mirdal G. (2000), "The construction of Muslim identities in contemporary Europe" in F. Dassetto (ed.), *Paroles d'Islam, op. cit.*, pp. 32–53

Mitchell J.C. (1969), "The Concept and Use of Social Networks" in *Social Networks in Urban Situations*, University of Manchester Press, pp. 1–50

Mitchell R.P. (1969), *The Society of the Muslim Brothers*, New York—Oxford, Oxford University Press

Moaddel M. (2002), "The Study of Islamic Culture and Politics: An Overview and Assessment" in *Annual Review of Sociology*, n° 28, pp. 359–86

Moatassime A. (1996), "Islam, arabisation et francophonie" in *Confluences Méditerranéennes*, n° 19, pp. 69–86

Modood T. (1994), "Political Blackness and British Asians" in *Sociology*, vol. 28, n° 3, pp. 859–876

———. (1994a), "Establishment, multiculturalism and British citizenship" in *Political Quarterly*, n° 65, pp. 53–71

———. (1997a), *Church, State and Religious Minorities*, London, Policy Studies Institute

———. (1998), "Anti-essentialism, multiculturalism and the 'recognition' of religious minorities" in *Journal of Political Philosophy*, vol. 6, n° 4, pp. 378–399

———. (2000), "La place des musulmans dans le multiculturalisme laïc en Grande-Bretagne" in *Social Compass*, vol. 47, n° 1, pp. 41–55

———. (2002), "Muslims in the West: A positive Asset" in www.srsc.org/sept11/essays.modood.htm

Modood T. & Werbner P. (eds) (1997), *The Politics of Multiculturalism in the New Europe. Racism, Identity and Community*, London-New York, Zed Books

Modood T. & al. (1997b), *Britain's Ethnic Minorities: diversity and disadvantage*, London, Policy Studies Institute

Moneger Fr. (1984), "La Convention franco-marocaine du 10 août 1981 relative au statut des personnes et de la famille et à la coopération judiciaire" in *Revue critique de droit international privé*, pp. 29–69 & 267–288

———. (1992), "Vers la fin de la reconnaissance des répudiations musulmanes par le juge français" in *Journal de droit international* (Clunet), pp. 345–374

———. (1994), "Les musulmans devant le juge français" in *Jurisclasseur Pénant*, pp. 344–374

———. (1999), "L'application de la Convention franco-marocaine du 10 août 1981 par la jurisprudence française" in M.-C. Foblets & F. Strijbosch (dir.), *op. cit.*, pp. 185–198

Morck Y. (1998), "Gender and generation: young Muslims in Copenhagen" in S. Vertovec & A. Rogers (eds), *Muslim European Youth, op. cit.*, pp. 133–144

Moreras J. (1996), "Les Accords de Coopération entre l'Etat Espagnol et la Commission Islamique d'Espagne" in *Revue Européenne des Migrations Internationales*, vol. 12, n° 1, Paris, pp. 77–90

———. (1999) *Musulmanes en Barcelona. Espacios y dinámicas comunitarias*, Barcelona, Cidob edicions

———. (2000), "Una alteridad no deseada? Las comunidades musulmanas en Barcelona" in *Barcelona, ciudad de culturas*, Barcelona, Museu d'Etnologia (in corso di pubblicazione)

Moscovici S. (1976), *Social Influence and Social Change*, London, Academic Press (italian translation: *Psicologia delle minoranze attive*, Torino, Boringhieri, 1981)

Motchane D. (2000), "L'islam de France sera t-il républicain?" in *Confluences Méditerranée*, n° 32, pp. 21–34

Motilla A. (2000), "L'accordo di cooperazione tra la Spagna e la Commissione islamica. Bilancio e prospettive" in S. Ferrari (ed.), *op. cit.*, pp. 245–63

Moulay R'Chid A. (1991), *La femme et la loi au Maroc*, Casablanca, Le Fennec

———. (1994), "La réforme du Code de statut personnel marocain: une avancée dans la codification des droits de l'homme" in *Revue trimestrielle de droit familial*, pp. 429–446

Mouriaux R. & Wihtol de Wenden C. (1987), "Syndicalisme français et islam" in *Revue Française de Science Politique*, vol. 37, n° 6, Paris, pp. 794–819

Musselli L. & Tozzi V. (2000), *La disciplina giuridica del fenomeno religioso*, Roma-Bari Laterza

Mutalib H. & Hashmi T.I. (eds) (1994), *Islam, Muslims and the Modern state*, Basingstoke, St. Martin's Press

Mutlu H. & Tschannen O. (1995), "Les Turcs de Suisse" in *Les Annales de l'Autre Islam*, n° 3, Paris, Inalco, pp. 147–167

Naba R. (1998), *Guerre des ondes . . . guerre des religions. La bataille hertzienne dans le ciel méditerranéen*, Paris, L'Harmattan

——. (1999), "L'identité française en mutation" in *Islam de France*, n° 4, pp. 7–13

Nasr S.H. (1998), "Islamic-Christian Dialogue: Problems and obstacles to be pondered and overcome" in *The Muslim World*, n° 3–4 (LXXXVIII), pp. 218–237

Niblock T. (1998), "Prospects for Cooperation between Europe and the Arab World: Creating a framework which recognises the Arab regional dimension" in J.S. Nielsen & S.A. Khasawnih (eds), *Arabs and the West, op. cit.*, pp. 99–113

Nielsen J.S. (1981), "Muslims in Europe: an overview" in *Research Paper*, n° 12, Birmingham, Centre for the study of Islam and christian-Muslim Relations

——. (1987), "Muslim in Britain: searching for an identity?" in *New Community*, vol. 13, n° 3, pp. 384–394

——. (1991), "A muslim agenda for Britain: some reflections" in *New Community*, n° 17, pp. 467–475

——. (1992), *Muslims in Western Europe*, Edinburgh, Edinburgh University Press

——. (1995), "Christian-Muslim relations in Western Europe" in *Islamochristiana*, n° 21, pp. 121–131

——. (1996), *Etude sur les aspects culturels et religieux de l'égalité des chances*, MG-S-REL (95) 3 final

——. (1998a), "Muslims in Europe or European Muslims: the Western Experience" in *Encounters*, 4:2, The Islamic Foundation, Leicester, pp. 203–216

——. (1999), *Towards a European Islam*, London, Basingstoke, MacMillan Press

——. (1999a), "Muslims and European Education Systems" in G. Martin-Muñoz (ed.), *op. cit.*, Conseil de l'Europe, pp. 224–236

——. (1999b), "Le rôle de l'Etat dans l'intégration des minorités religieuses et, notamment, celui des structures favourisant le dialogue" in *La religion et l'intégration des immigrés*, Strasbourg, Conseil de l'Europe pp. 177–185

Nielsen J.S. & Khasawnih S.A. (1998), *Arabs and the West: Mutual Images* (proceedings of a three-day seminar organised by the University of Jordan 3–5 april 1998), Amman

Nonneman G., Niblock T. & Szajkowski B. (eds) (1996), *Muslim Communities in Europe*, United Kingdom, Ithaca Press

Norris H.T. (1993), *Islam in the Balkans. Religion and Society between Europe and the Arab World*, London, Hurst

Nouvelle Tribune (1998, October-November), "Etre musulman en Belgique et en Europe", n° 18, Bruxelles

Obdeijn H. & de Ruiter J.J. (eds) (1998), *L'enseignement de la langue et culture d'origine (ELCO) aux élèves marocains dans cinq pays européens*, Tilburg, Syntax Datura

Obeidi Z. (1988), *La banque islamique—une nouvelle technique d'investissement*, Beyrouth, Dar Al-Rashad Al-Islamiya

Ockelton M. (1995), "La situation en Grande-Bretagne" in F. Messner (ed.), *La culture religieuse à l'école, op. cit.*, pp. 171–186

Oran B. (1994), "Religious and national identity among the Balkan muslims" in *Cahiers du CEMOTI*, n° 18, pp. 307–323

Otterbeck J. (1999), "'A school for all'—Muslim pupils in Sweden" in *ISIM Newsletter*, n° 3, Leiden, p. 35

——. (2000), "Local Islamic Universalism. Analyses of an Islamic Journal in Sweden" in F. Dassetto (ed.), *Paroles d'Islam, op. cit.*, pp. 247–266

Ouali N. (1997), "Télévision et immigration. Un enjeu pour l'intégration et la lutte contre le racisme?" in *Migrations Société*, n° 54, pp. 21–30

——. (2000), "Affirmation de soi et sécularisation des identités musulmanes" in U. Manço (ed.), *Voix et voies musulmanes, op. cit.*, pp. 189–194

Oubrou T. (1998), "Introduction théorique à la charî'a de minorité" in *Islam de France*, n° 2, pp. 27–34

Pace E. (1995), *Islam e Occidente*, Roma, Edizioni Lavoro

Pace E. & Guolo R. (1998), *I fondamentalismi*, Laterza, Roma-Bari

Palidda S. (1992), "Le développement des activités indépendantes des immigrés en

Europe et en France" in *Revue Européenne des Migrations Internationales*, vol. 8, n° 1, pp. 83–96

Panafit L. (1999), *Quand le droit écrit l'islam—L'intégration juridique de l'Islam en Belgique*, Bruxelles, Bruylant

——. (2000), "En Belgique, les ambiguïtés d'une représentation 'ethnique" in *Le Monde Diplomatique*, juin, pp. 12–13

Panoramiques (1997), n° 29, Paris, Arléa-Corlet (n° spécial "L'islam est-il soluble dans la République?")

Papadopoulou C. (1997), "De soi à l'autre" in *Confluences Méditerranée*, n° 24, pp. 77–83

Papastathis C.K. (1995), "State financial support for the church in Greece" in F. Messner (ed.), *La culture religieuse à l'école, op. cit.*, pp. 1–18

——. (1998), "church and State in Greece 1997" in *European Journal for church and State Research*, pp. 29–54

Parigi S. (1989), *Des banques islamiques—Argent et religion*, Paris, Ramsay

Parker-Jenkins M. (1995), *Children of Islam: a Teacher's Guide to Meeting the Needs of Muslim Pupils*, Stoke-on-Trent, Trentham Books

Parker-Jenkins M. & Haw K.F. (1998) "Educational needs of Muslim children in Britain: accommodation or neglect?" in S. Vertovec & A. Rogers (eds), *Muslim European Youth, op. cit.*, pp. 193–215

Parlement Européen (1997), *Rapport accompagné d'un projet de recommandation du Parlement européen au Conseil sur le fondamentalisme et le défi qu'il constitue pour l'ordre juridique européen*, Commission des libertés publiques et des affaires intérieures (Rapporteur Arie Oostlander)

Paz R. (2002), "Middle East Islamism in the European Arena" in *MERIA Middle East Review of International Affairs*, n° 3 (http://meria.idc.ac.il/)

Peach C. & Glebe G. (1995), "Muslim minorities in Western Europe" in *Ethnic and Racial Studies*, n° 18, pp. 26–45

Pedersen L. (1999), *Newer Islamic Movements in Western Europe*, Aldershot, Ashgate

Peev Y. (1996), "L'appartenance religieuse et l'identité ethnique des musulmans en Bulgarie" in M. Bozdémir (dir.), *Islam et laïcité, op. cit.* pp. 151–168

——. (1997), "Courants islamiques en Bulgarie" in *Les Annales de l'Autre Islam*, n° 4, Paris, Inalco, pp. 183–197

Peraldi M. (1999), "Marseille: réseaux migrants transfrontaliers, place marchande et économie de bazar" in *Cultures & Conflits*, n° 33–34, pp. 51–68

Perenditis S. (1994), "Ortodossia e Stato laico: tradizione, dottrina, ideologia" in A. Riccardi (ed.), *Il Mediterraneo nel Novecento: Religioni e Stati*, Cinisello Balsamo, San Paolo, pp. 231–246

Petek-Salom G. (1995), "Les femmes de l'immigration turque en France" in *Les Annales de l'Autre Islam—"Turcs d'Europe et d'ailleurs"*, n° 3, Paris, Inalco, pp. 365–474

——. (1998), "L'organisation communautaire, du commerce aux associations" in *Hommes & Migrations*, n° 1212, pp. 88–101

Petiti L.-E., Decaux E. & Imbert P.-H. (dir.) (1995), *La Convention européenne des droits de l'homme. Commentaire article par article*, Paris, Economica

Pickles M.E. (1995), "Muslim immigration stress in Australia" in S.Z. Abedin & Z. Sardar (eds), *op. cit.*, pp. 106–116

Pipes D. & Stillman M. (2002), "The United States Government: Patron of Islam" in *Middle East Quarterly*, (Winter) and *MERIA Journal*, vol. 9, n° 1

Pirenne H. (1937), *Mahomet et Charlemagne*, Paris, Librairie Félix Alcan

Pisci A. (2000), "L'islam tra i banchi di scuola" in *Il dialogo*, n° 4, pp. 16–19

Planet A.I. (1998), *Melilla y Ceuta: Espacios-frontera hispano-marroquíes*, Ceuta-Melilla, Universidad nacional a distancia

Poncelet M. (1994), *Une utopie post-tiers-mondiste—La dimension culturelle du développement*, Paris, L'Harmattan

Popovic A. (1986), *L'Islam balkanique. Les musulmans du sud-est européen dans la période post-ottomane*, Berlin-Wiesbaden, Otto Harrassowitz
——. (1992), "L'islam dans les Balkans depuis la chute du mur de Berlin" in P. Michel (ed.), *Les religions à l'est*, Paris, Editions du Cerf, pp. 161–181
——. (1994), *Cultures musulmanes balkaniques*, Istanbul, Isis
——. (1994a), *Les musulmans des Balkans à l'époque post-ottomane. Histoire et politique*, Istanbul, Isis
——. (1997), "The Balkan Muslim communities in the post-communist period" in S. Vertovec & C. Peach (eds), *Islam in Europe, op. cit.*, pp. 59–72
Popovic A. & Veinstein G. (dir.) (1996), *Les Voies d'Allah- Les ordres mystiques dans le monde musulman des origines à aujourd'hui*, Paris, Fayard
Portes A. (ed.) (1995), *The Economic Sociology of Immigration: Essays on Networks, Ethnicity and Entrepreneurship*, New York, Russell Sage Foundation
Poston L. (1992), *Islamic Da'wah in the West. Muslim Missionary Activity and the Dynamics of Conversion to Islam*, New York—Oxford, Oxford University Press
Potz R. (1998), "New liberties and church-State relationships in Austria" in European Consortium for church-State Research, *"New liberties", op. cit.*, pp. 311–330
——. (1999), "Church and State in Austria in 1998" in *European Journal for church and State Research*, pp. 29–54
Poulton H. (1997), "Turkey as kin-state: Turkish foreign policy towards Turkish and Muslim communities in the Balkans" in H. Poulton & S. Taji-Farouki (eds), *Muslim Identity and the Balkan State, op. cit.*, pp. 194–213
Poulton H. & Taji-Farouki S. (eds) (1997), *Muslim Identity and the Balkan State*, London, Hurst & Company in association with the Islamic council
Prelot P.H. (1999), "Droit français des religions" in *European Journal for church and State Research*, pp. 114–16
Prunier G. (1987), "L'essor des banques islamiques—entretien avec G. Prunier" in *Autrement* (Islam, Le grand malentendu), Paris
Pullapilly C.K. (1981), *Islam in Contemporary World*, Cross Roads Books
Purdam K. (1996), "Settler Political Participation: Muslim Local Councillors" in W.A.R. Shadid & P.S. van Koningsveld (eds), *Political Participation, op. cit.*, pp. 129–143
Puza R. (1998), "Les problèmes actuels de l'enseignement religieux dans l'école publique en Allemagne" in F. Messner & A. Vierling (eds), *L'enseignement religieux, op. cit.*, pp. 129–34
——. (1999), "Le droit allemand des religions en 1998" in *European Journal for church and State Research*, pp. 47–58
Al-Qaradawi Y. (1992), *Le licite et l'illicite en Islam*, Paris, al Qalam
Rafiq M. (1992), "Ethnicity and Enterprise: a comparison of Muslim and non Muslim owned Asian businesses in Britain" in *New Community*, vol. 19, n° 1, pp. 43–60
Ragaru N. (2001), "Islam et coexistence intercommunautaire en Bulgarie" in X. Bougarel & N. Clayer (dir.), *Le nouvel Islam balkanique, op. cit.*, pp. 241–288
Ramadan T. (1994), *Les musulmans dans la laïcité. Responsabilités et droits des musulmans dans les sociétés occidentales*, Lyon, Tawhid
——. (1998), *Aux sources du renouveau musulman. D'al-Afghani à Hasan al-Banna, un siècle de réformisme islamique*, Paris, Bayard
——. (1999), *Etre musulman européen—Etude des sources islamiques à la lumière du contexte européen*, Lyon, Tawhid
——. (2000), "Les musulmans d'Europe pris en tenaille" in *Le Monde Diplomatique*, juin, pp. 12–13
——. (2000a), "L'islam d'Europe sort de l'isolement" in *Le monde diplomatique*, avril 2000, p. 13
Ramet P. (ed.) (1989), *Religion and Nationalism in Soviet and East European Politics*, revised edition, Durham, NC, Duke University Press
Ramirez A. (1999), "La valeur du travail—l'insertion dans le marché du travail des

immigrées marocaines en Espagne" in *Revue Européenne des Migrations Internationales* vol. 15, n° 2, pp. 9–36

Rashid A. (2002), *The Rise of Militant Islam in Central Asia*, New Haven, Yale University Press

Rasuly-Paleczek G. (1995), "Turkish migrants in Austria" in *Les Annales de l'Autre Islam*, n° 3, Paris, Inalco, pp. 177–204

Rath J., Groenendijk K. & Penninx R. (1991), "The recognition and instiutionalization of Islam in Belgium, Great Britain and the Netherlands" in *New Community*, n° 18, pp. 101–114

Rath J., Groenendijk K. et Penninx R. & Meyer A. (1996), *Nederland en zijn islam— een ontzuilende samenleving reageert op het ontstaan an een geloofsgemeenschap*, Amsterdam, Het Spinhuis

——. (1999), "The politics of recognizing religious diversity in Europe. Social reactions to the institutionalization of islam in the Netherlands, Belgium and Great Britain" in *Journal of Social Sciences*, vol. 35, n° 1, pp. 53–68

——. (2001), *Western Europe and its Islam*, Leiden, Brill

Rea A. & Bortolini M. (1999), "L'insertion scolaire et professionnelle des jeunes issus de l'immigration en Belgique" in *Migrations société*, vol. 11, n° 62, pp. 67–75

Reeber M. (1995), "La référence au Coran dans les émissions religieuses islamiques en France" in *Archives de Sciences Sociales des Religion*, n° 92, pp. 46–95

——. (2000), "Les khutbas de la diaspora: enquête sur les tendances de la prédication dans les mosquées en France et dans plusieurs pays d'Europe occidentale" in F. Dassetto (ed.), *Paroles d'Islam, op. cit.*, pp. 185–204

Reesink P. (2000), "Islam en internet" in *Begrip Moslims-Christenen*, vol. 26, n° 2, pp. 38–46

Renaerts M. (1997), "La mort: de l'exclusion à l'intégration" in F. Dassetto (ed.), *Facettes, op. cit.*, pp. 211–226

Renaerts M. & Manço U. (2000), "Lente institutionnalisation de l'islam et persistance d'inégalités face aux autres cultes reconnus" in U. Manço (ed.), *Voix et voies musulmanes, op. cit.*, pp. 83–106

Renard M. (1999), "France, terre des mosquées?" in *Hommes & Migrations*, n° 1220, pp. 31–41

Rex J. (1994), "The political sociology of multiculturalism and the place of Muslims" in *Social Compass*, vol. 41, 79 ff.

Reyneri E. (1979), *La catena migratoria*, Bologna, Il Mulino

Rhodes R.E. (1991), *Law and Modernization in the church of England*, Notre Dame-London, The University of Notre Dame Press

Rigoni I. (1998), "Les mobilisations des Kurdes en Europe" in *Revue Européenne des Migrations Internationale*s, vol. 14, n° 3, pp. 203–223

Rimanque K. (1987), *De toepassing van het E.V.R.M. in de praktijk* [L'application en pratique de la Convention européenne des droits de l'homme et des libertés fondamentales], Anvers, Kluwer Rechtswetenschappen

Roald A.S. (2001), "The Immigrants' Extended Ear to their Homelands: the Case of Satellite-Channels" intervento al convegno *Muslim Minority Societies in Europe*, Erfurt, 1–4 maggio (in corso di pubblicazione)

Robbers G. (ed.) (1996), *State and Church in the European Union*, Baden-Baden, Nomos

Robertson R. (1992), *Globalization. Social Theory and Global Culture*, London-Newbury, Sage

Rochot J. (1981), *La grande fièvre du monde musulman*, Paris, Le Sycomore

Rodinson M. (1993), *La fascination de l'islam*, Paris, La Découverte/Presses Pocket

Rommel G. (1980), "Le statut personnel marocain" in *Journal des Juges de Paix et de Police*, pp. 193–243

——. (1986), "Over Moslimimmigranten, het sociaal beleid van de vrederechter. Van paternalisme naar bevrijding" in P. van der Vorst (dir.), *Honderd Jaar Belgisch sociaal recht*, Bruxelles, Bruylant, pp. 604–620

Rooijackers M. (1992), "Religious identity, integration and subjective well-being among young turkish muslims" in W.A.R Shadid & P.S. van Koningsveld, *Islam in Dutch society, op. cit.*, pp. 66–74

Roy O. (1992), *L'échec de l'Islam politique*, Paris, Editions du Seuil

——. (1995), *Généalogie de l'islamisme*, Paris, Hachette

——. (1999), *Vers un islam européen*, Paris, Editions Esprit

——. (2000), "L'individualisation dans l'islam européen contemporain" in F. Dassetto (ed.), *Paroles d'Islam, op. cit.*, pp. 69–84

——. (2002a), *L'islam mondialisé*, Paris, Seuil

——. (2002b), *Les illusions du 11 septembre. Le débat stratégique face au 11 septembre*, Paris, Seuil

Rozenberg D. (1997), "L'Etat et les minorités religieuses en Espagne (du national-catholicisme à la construction démocratique)" in *Archives des Sciences sociales des Religions*, n° 98 (avril-juin), pp. 9–30

Rude-Antoine E. (1990), *Le mariage maghrébin en France*, Paris, Karthala

——. (1997), *La vie des familles. Les immigrés, la loi et la coutume*, Paris, O. Jacob

Runnymede Trust (1997), *Islamophobia. A challenge for us all*, London

Rutten S. (1988), *Moslims in de Nederlandse rechtspraak*, Kampen, Kok

——. (1997), *Erven naar Marokkaans recht. Aspecten van Nederlands internationaal privaatrecht bij de toepasselijkheid van Marokkaans erfrecht*, Maastricht, Intersentie

Saad H. (1997), *Multi-cultural Birmingham in the new millennium: Implications for policy makers* in AA.VV., *Ethnic Minorities and the New Millennium*, Birmingham City Council, Equalities Division

Saeed A. (1999), "Islamic Banking: moving towards a pragmatic approach?" in *ISIM Newsletter*, n° 3, Leiden, p. 7.

Saggar S. (1998), "British South Asian Elites and Political Participation: Testing the Cultural Thesis" in *Revue Européenne des Migrations Internationales*, n° 2 (14), pp. 51–69

Saghieh H. (ed.) (2000), *The predicament of the Individual in the Middle East*, London, Saqi Books

——. (2002), "On suicide, Martyrdom and the Quest of Individuality" in *ISIM Newsletter*, n° 10, Leiden, p. 9

Said E.W. (1978), *Orientalism*, New York, Pantheon Books

——. (1981), *Covering Islam. How the media and the experts determine how we see the rest of the world*, London, Routledge & Kegan Paul

Saint-Blancat C. (1995), *L'islam della diaspora*, Roma, Edizioni Lavoro

——. (ed.) (1999), *L'islam in Italia. Una presenza plurale*, Roma, Edizioni Lavoro

Sakkouni A., "Quel rapport à la langue arabe chez les enfants d'origine marocaine?" in *Migrations Société*, vol. 55, n° 10, pp. 5–21

Sakowicz E. (1997), "Islam and Christian-Muslim Relations in Poland" in *Islamochristiana*, n° 23, pp. 139–146

Salvatore A. (1997), *Islam and the political discourse of modernity*, United Kingdom, Ithaca Press

Samad Y. (1992), "Book burning and race relations: Political mobilisation of Bradford Muslims" in *New Community*, vol. 18, n° 4, pp. 507–519

——. (1998), "Imagining a British Muslim identification" in S. Vertovec & A. Rogers, *op. cit.*, pp. 59–76

Sanchez M.I. (1992), "The financing of religious confessions in Spanish law" in Consorzio Europeo di Ricerca sui Rapporti tra Stati e Confessioni Religiose, *Stati e confessioni religiose in Europa. Modelli di finanziamento pubblico. Scuola e fattore religioso*, Milan, Giuffrè, pp. 19–40

Sander Å (1991), "The Road from Musalla to Mosque. The Process of Integration and Institutionalization of Islam in Sweden" in W.A.R. Shadid & P.S. van Koningsveld (eds), *The Integration of Islam, op. cit.*, pp. 62–88

Santelli E. (1999), "Les enfants d'immigrés algériens et leur pays d'origine—modes de relations économiques et professionnelles" in *Revue Européenne des Migrations Internationales*, vol. 15, n° 2, pp. 141–166

Sarhane F. & Lahlou-Rachdi N. (1995), "Réflexions sur quelques règles de conflit de lois à l'épreuve de la pratique" in *Le droit international privé dans les pays maghrébins. Les conflits de lois: le statut personnel* (Cahiers des droits maghrébins), n° 1, pp. 81–108

Sarolea S. (1997), "Chronique de jurisprudence. Les conflits de lois relatifs à la personne et aux relations familiales (1988–1996)" in *Revue trimestrielle de droit familial*, pp. 9–30

Sassen S. (1995), *Loosing control. Sovereignity in an Age of Globalisation*, New York, Columbia University Press

Sayyid B. (1997), *A fundamental Fear. Eurocentrism and the Emergence of Islamism*, London-New York, Zed Books

Scantlebury E. (1995), "Muslims in Manchester: the depiction of a religious community" in *New Community*, vol. 21, n° 3, pp. 425–435

Schiffauer W. (1988), "Migration and religiousness" in T. Gerholm & Y.G. Lithman (eds), *The New Islamic Presence, op. cit.*, pp. 146–158

———. (1997), "Islamic Vision and social reality: the political culture of sunni Muslims in Germany" in S. Vertovec & C. Peach (eds), *Islam in Europe, op. cit.* pp. 156–176

———. (2000), *Die Gottesmänner. Türkische Islamisten in Deutschland—Eine Studie in religiöser Evidenz*, Frankfurt am Main, Suhrkamp-Taschenbuch

Schlessmann L. (1999), "Sufi-Gemeinschaften in Deutschland" in *Cibedo—Beiträge*, vol. 13, n° 1, Frankfurt, pp. 12–22

Schmidt di Friedberg O. & Borrmans M. (1993), "Musulmans et Chrétiens en Italie" in *Islamochristiana*, n° 19, pp. 153–198

Schmidt di Friedberg O. (1994), *Islam, solidarietà e lavoro. I muridi senegalesi in Italia*, Torino, Fondazione Agnelli

Schmied M. (1999), *Familienkonflikte zwischen Scharia und Bürgerlichem Recht. Konfliktlösungsmodell im Vorfeld der Justiz am Beispiel Österreichs*, Frankfurt am Main, Peter Lang

Schreiner P. (dir.) (2000), *Religious Education in Europe—A Collection of Basic Information about RE in European countries*, Munster, Comenius Institut

Schulze R. (1990), *Islamischer Internationalismus im XX*, Jahrhundert, Leiden, Brill

Scidà G. (1990), *Globalizzazione e culture. Lo sviluppo sociale fra omogeneità e diversità*, Milano, Jaca Book

———. (2000), "Globalizzazione, mobilità spaziale e comunità transnazionali" in *Sociologia e Politiche Sociali*, n° 1, pp. 57–90

Scraton P. (ed.) (2002), *Beyond September 11. An Anthology of Dissent*, London, Pluto Press

Sellam S. (1998), "Enseigner l'Islam en France" in *Islam de France*, n° 2, pp. 17–25

Services fédéraux des Affaires Scientifiques, Techniques et Culturelles (1997), *Discrimination à l'embauche*, Bruxelles, Centre pour l'égalité des chances et la lutte contre le racisme

Seufert G. & Waardenburg J. (eds) (1999), *Turkish Islam and Europe: Europe and Christianity as reflected in Turkish Muslim discourse and Turkish Muslim life in the diaspora* (papers of the Istanbul Workshop, October 1996 "Türkischer Islam und Europa", Orient Institut), Türkische Welten, Bd. 6, Beiruter Texte und Studien, Bd. 82, Stuttgart, Steiner

Seufert G. (1999), "Die Turkisch-Islamische Union (DITIB) der Turkischen Religionsbehörde: Zwischen Integration und Isolation" in G. Seufert & J. Waardenburg (eds), *Turkish Islam and Europe, op. cit.*, pp. 261–294

Shadid W.A.R. & van Koningsveld P.S. (eds) (1991), *The Integration of Islam and Hindouism in Western Europe*, Kampen, Kok Pharos

———. (1992), *Islam in Dutch society: current developments and future prospects*, Kampen, Kok Pharos

——. (1994), "Islamic Religious Education in the Netherlands: Implications of Dutch Law and Government Policies" in *Journal of Muslim Minority Affairs*, vol. 14, n° 1–2, pp. 17–26

——, (eds) (1995), *Religious Freedom and the Position of Islam in Western Europe: Opportunities and Obstacles in the Acquisition of Equal Rights*, Kampen, Pharos

——, (eds) (1996), *Muslims in the Margin. Political Responses to the Presence of Islam in Western Europe*, Kampen, Kok Pharos

——, (eds) (1996a), *Political Participation and Identities of Muslims in non-Muslim States*, Kampen, Kok Pharos

——. (1996b), "Islam in the Netherlands: Constitutional Law and Islamic Organisations" in *Journal of Muslim Minority Affairs*, vol. 16, n° 1, pp. 111–128

——. (1996c), "Dutch Political Views on the Multicultural Societies" in W.A.R. Shadid & P.S. van Koningsveld (eds), *Muslims in the Margin, op. cit.*, pp. 93–113

——, (eds) (1997), *Moslims in Nederland—Minderheden en religie in een multiculturele samenleving*, Houten—Diegem, Bohn Stafleu van Loghum

——, (eds) (2002), *Religious Freedom and the Neutrality of the State: the Position of Islam in the European Union*, Leuven, Peeters

Shaggar S. (1998), "British South Asian Elites and Political Participation: Testing the Cultural Thesis" in *Revue Européenne des Migrations Internationales*, vol. 14, n° 2, pp. 51–69

Shaikh S.A. (1997), "Islamic banks and financial institutions: a survey" in *Journal of Muslim Minority Affairs*, vol. 17, n° 1, pp. 117–127

Siddiqui A. (2000), "Fifty years of Christian-Muslim Relations: Exploring and Engaging in a new Relationship" in *Islamochristiana*, n° 26, pp. 51–77

Sidhamed A.S. & Ehteshami A. (eds), (1996), *Islamic fundamentalism*, Oxford, Westview press

Siggillino I. (ed.) (1999), *L'islam nella scuola*, Milano, Franco Angeli

——, (ed.) (2000a), *I bambini dell'islam*, Milano, Franco Angeli

——, (ed.) (2000b), *L'islam nelle città. Dalle identità separate alla comunità plurale*, Milano, Franco Angeli

——, (ed.) (2001), *Religioni e mass media. Riflessioni a partire dal caso islam*, Bologna, Emi

Sikand Y.S. (1998), "The origins and growth of the Tablighi Jama'at in Britain" in *Islam and Christian-Muslim Relations*, vol. 9, n° 2, pp. 171–192

——. (1999), "Women and the Tablighi Jama'at" in *Islam and Christian-Muslim Relations*, vol. 10, n° 1, pp. 41–52

Simon P. (1995), "La société partagée. Relations interethniques et interclasses dans un quartier en rénovation. Belleville, Paris XX" in *Cahiers Internationaux de Sociologie*, n° 98, pp. 161–190

Simonsen J.B. (1998), "A means to change or transform images of the Other-private arab schools in Denmark" in J.S. Nielsen & S.A. Khasawnih (eds), *op. cit.*, pp. 115–128

Simonsen J.B. (2000), "From defensive silence to creative participation—Muslim discourses in Denmark" in F. Dassetto (ed.), *Paroles d'Islam, op. cit.*, pp. 145–156

Sindonino P. (1998), *Responsables associatifs musulmans en région parisienne: entre participation militante et représentation communautaire*, Paris, Thèse de doctorat de sociologie— Ecole des Hautes Etudes en Sciences Sociales

Skidmore D. (1998), "Huntington's Clash Revisited" in *Journal of World-Systems Research*, vol. 4, n° 2

Slaughter I. & McClean D. (1993), "church and Labour Law in England" in European Consortium for church and State Research, *op. cit.*, pp. 231–242

Slymovics S. (1996), "The Muslim World Day Parade and "Storefront" Mosques of New York City" in B.D. Metcalf (ed.), *Making Muslim, op. cit.*, pp. 204–216

Social Compass (1999), *Les Conversions à l'Islam en Europe*, London, Sage Publications

Sofski W. (2002), *Zeiten des Schrecken. Amok, Terror, Krieg*, Frankfurt am Main, S. Ficher Verlag

Soysal Y.N. (1994), *Limits of citizenship. Migrants and postnational membership in Europe*, Chicago, University of Chicago Press

Soysal Y. (1997), "Changing parameters of citizenship and claims-making: Organized Islam in European public spheres" in *Theory and Society*, vol. 24, n° 4, pp. 509–527

———. (2000), "Citizenship and identity: living in diasporas in post-war Europe?" in *Ethnic and Racial Studies*, vol. 23, n° 1, pp. 1–15

Speelman G., van Lin J. & Mulder D. (eds) (1995), *Muslims and Christians in Europe: Breaking New Ground*, Kampen, Kok Pharos

Spuler-Stegemann U. (1998), *Muslime in Deutschland—Nebeneinander oder Miteinander?*, Freiburg, Herder

Stahnke T. (1999), "Proselytism and the Freedom to Change Religion in International Human Rights Law" in *Brigham Young University Law Review*, n° 1, pp. 251 ff.

Statham P. (1999), "Political mobilisation by minorities in Britain: negative feedback of 'race relations'?" in *Journal of Ethnic and Migration Studies*, vol. 25, n° 4, pp. 597–626

Stenberg L. (2000), "Islam in Scandinavia", intervento al convegno *Islam in Europa*, Lisbona, Fundação Luso-Americana/Csis, 16 ottobre

Stojanov V. (1997), "Ausgrenzung und integration: die bulgarischen Türken nach dem Zweiten Weltkrieg", in *Österreichische Osthefte*, vol. XXXIX, n° 2, pp. 193–221

Straßburger G. (1999), "Er kann deutsch sein und kennt sich hier aus" in G. Jonker, *Kern und Rand, op. cit.*, pp. 147–168

———. (2000), "Fundamentalism versus Human Rights: Headscarf Discourses in an Established-Outsider-Figuration in France" in F. Dassetto (ed.), *Paroles d'Islam, op. cit.*, pp. 125–144

Streiff-Fenart J. (1989), *Les couples franco-maghrébins en France*, Paris, L'Harmattan

Strijp R. (1999), "Moroccan associations in a Dutch town" in M. Crul, F. Lindo & C.L. Pang (eds), *Culture, Structure and Beyond, op. cit.*, pp. 49–74

Strobl A. (1997), *Islam in Österreich—Eine religionssoziologische Untersuchung*, Frankfurt am Main, Peter Lang

Suhbi T. (1985), "Musulmans dans l'entreprise" in *Esprit*, n° 106, pp. 216–221

Suleiman Y. (1998), "Like a Bridge over Troubled Waters" in J.S. Nielsen & S.A. Khasawnih (eds), *Arabs and the West, op. cit.*, pp. 129–138

Sunier T. (1992), "Islam and ethnicity among Turks—the changing role of Islam and muslim organisations" in W.A.R. Shadid & P.S. van Koningsveld (eds), *Islam in Dutch society, op. cit.*, pp. 144–162

———. (1994), "Islam en etniciteit onder jonge leden van Turkse islamitische organisaties in Nederland" in *Migrantenstudies*, vol. 10, n° 1, pp. 19–32

———. (1998), "Islam and interest struggle: religious collective action among Turkish Muslims in the Netherlands" in S. Vertovec & A. Rogers (eds), *Muslim European Youth, op. cit.*, pp. 39–58

———. (1999), "Muslim migrants, Muslim citizens. Islam and Dutch Society" in *The Netherlands Journal of Social Sciences*, vol. 35, n° 1, pp. 69–82

Sunier T. & Meyer A. (1997), "Religie" in H. Vermeulen (ed.), *Immigrantenbeleid voor de multiculturele samenleving. Integratie, taal en religiebeleid voor immigranten in vijf West-Europese landen*, TWCM voorstudie n° 9, Amsterdam, Het Spinhuis, pp. 95–126

Svanberg I. (1995), "Turkish immigrants in Sweden" in *Les Annales de l'Autre Islam*, n° 3, Paris, Inalco, pp. 215–227

Swerry J.M. (1998), "L'enseignement religieux dans l'école publique en régime français de séparation" in F. Messner & A. Vierling (eds), *op. cit.*, pp. 99–104

Szajkowski B. (1988), "Muslim people in Eastern Europe: ethnicity and religion" in *Journal of the Institute of Muslim Minority Affairs*, n° 9, pp. 103–118

———. (1997), "The muslim minority in Poland" in S. Vertovec & C. Peach (eds), *Islam in Europe, op. cit.*, pp. 91–100

Tagliaferri F. (2001), "La stampa di fronte all'islam" in I. Siggillino (ed.), *Religioni e mass media. Riflessioni a partire dal caso islam*, Bologna, EMI

Taji-Farouki S. (1996), *A Fundamental Quest, Hizb al-Tahrir and the Search for the Islamic Caliphate*, Grey Seal, London

Talbott S. & Chanda N. (ed.), *The Age of Terror. American and the World after September 11*, New York, Basic Books & Yale Centre for the Study of Globalization

Talib M. (2000), "Construction and reconstruction of the world in the Tablighi ideology" in M.K. Masud (ed.), *Travellers in Faith, op. cit.*, pp. 59–78

Tamimi A.S. (2001), *Rachid Ghannouchi—A Democrat within Islamism*, New York, Oxford University Press

Tangram—Bulletin de la Commission fédérale contre le racisme (1999), *Musulmans en Suisse*, n° 7, Berne

Tarrius A. (1995), "Naissance d'une colonie: un comptoir commercial à Marseille" in *Revue Européenne des Migrations Internationales*, vol. 11, n° 1, pp. 21–52

Taverne M. (1981), *Le droit familial maghrébin (Algérie, Maroc, Tunisie) et son application en Belgique*, Bruxelles, Larcier

——. (1983), "Quelques réflexions à propos de la polygamie" in *Annales de Droit de Louvain*, pp. 237–248

Taylor C. (1992a), *Multiculturalism and the Politics of Recognition*, Princeton University Press (italian translation: Multiculturalismo. La politica del riconoscimento, Milano, Anabasi, 1993)

Teheri A. (1989), *Crescent in a Red Sky: the Future of Islam in the Soviet Union*, London, Hutchinson

Teissier H. (2000), "Chrétiens et musulmans: cinquante années pour approfondir leurs relations" in *Islamochristiana*, n° 26, pp. 33–50

Telhine M. (1998, Mars-Avril), "Une école confessionnelle musulmane?" in *Migrations Société*, vol. 10, pp. 19–32

Ternisien X. (2002), *La France des mosquées*, Paris, Editions Albin Michel

Theunis J. (1997), "Het gelijkheidsbeginsel—Juridisch interpretatiekader, met bijzondere aandacht voor 'corrigerende ongelijkheden' en doorwerking in private rechtsverhoudingen" [Le principe d'égalité—Cadre d'interprétation juridique, avec une attention particulière portée aux 'inégalités correctives' et à l'effet horizontal dans les relations privées] in *Publiekrecht. De doorwerking van het publiekrecht in het privaatrecht* [Les répercussions du droit public en droit privé], Gand, Mys & Breesch (cycle W. Delva 1996–1997), pp. 129–182

Tiesler N.C. (2001), "No bad news from the European Margin: The New Islamic Presence in Portugal" in *Islam and Christian-Muslim Relations*, vol. 12, n° 1, pp. 71–91

Tillie J. (1998), "Explaining Migrant Voting Behaviour in the Netherlands. Combining the Electoral Research and Ethnic Studies Perspective" in *Revue Européenne des Migrations Internationales*, vol. 14, n° 2, pp. 71–95

Tillion G. (1982), *Le harem et les cousins*, Paris, Seuil (1966)

Timmerman Ch. (1995), "Cultural practices and ethnicity: diversifications among Turkish young women" in *International Journal of Educational Research*, vol. 23, n° 1, pp. 23–32

——. (1999), "Islamism or the need for alternatives. The case of young Turkish women in Belgium" in M. Crul, F. Lindo & C.L. Pang (eds), *Culture, Structure and Beyond, op. cit.*, pp. 177–198

Toprack B. (1981), *Islam and Political Development in Turkey*, Leiden, Brill

Torfs R. (1994), "Le régime constitutionnel des cultes en Belgique" in European Consortium for church-State Research, *op. cit.*, pp. 47–80

——. (1998), "Nouvelles libertés et relations Eglise-Etat en Belgique" in European Consortium for church-State Research, *"New liberties", op. cit.*, pp. 39–82

——. (1998a), "European Nationalism. Coexistence in a Multi-ethnic and Multi-religious society" in G. Morán (ed.), *Nacionalismo en Europa, nacionalismo en Galicia. La religión como elemento impulsor de la ideología nacionalista*, Santiago de Compostela, Universidade da Coruña, pp. 117–147

Tozy M. (2000), "Sequences of a quest: Tablighi Jama'at in Morocco" in M.K. Masud (ed.), *Travellers in Faith, op. cit.*, pp. 161–173

Triaud J.-L. (1998), "L'Islam vu par les historiens français" in *Esprit*, n° 256, pp. 110–132

Tribalat M. (1995), *Faire France—Une enquête sur les immigrés et leurs enfants*, Paris, La Découverte

Turner B. (2002), "Sovereignty and Emergency. Political Theology, Islam and American Conservatism" in *Theory, Culture and Society*, vol. 19, n° 4, pp.103–119

Urry J. (2002), "The Global Complexities of September 11th" in *Theory, Culture and Society*, vol. 19, n° 4, pp. 57–69

Valencia R. (1995), "Acerca de las comunidades musulmanas en Andalucia occidental" in M. Abumalham (ed.), *Comunidades islámicas, op. cit.*, pp. 175–188

van Bijsterveld S.C. (1994), "Religious minorities and minority churches in the Netherlands" in European Consortium for church-State Research, *The Legal Status of Religious Minorities, op. cit.*, pp. 277–298

——. (1999), "church and State in the Netherlands in 1998" in *European Journal for church and State Research*, pp. 149–160

van Bommel A. (1992), "The history of Muslim umbrella organisations" in W.A.R. Shadid & P.S. van Koningsveld (eds), *Islam in Dutch society, op. cit.*, pp. 124–143

——. (1995), "Old and new Europeans: Muslim resistance to 'Europeanization': causes, effects and possible solutions" in G. Speelman, J. Van Lin & D. Mulder (eds), *Muslims and Christians in Europe, op. cit.*, pp. 112–124

van Bruinessen M. (2001), "Préface" in X. Bougarel & N. Clayer (dir.), *Le nouvel Islam balkanique, op. cit.*, pp. 5–6

—— (2001a), "Transformation of heterodoxy" in *ISIM Newsletter*, n° 7, Leiden, p. 5

van der Weyer R (2002), *Islam and the West*, New York, J. Hunt Publications

van de Wetering S. (1992), "The arabic language and culture teaching programme to Moroccan children" in W.A.R. Shadid & P.S. van Koningsveld, *op. cit.*, pp. 90–106

van den Eeckhout V. (1994), "Tussen vaderschapsvermoeden en biologische werkelijkheid: komen opgelegde Marokkaanse afstammingswetten gelegen voor de ontrouwe echtgenote van een Marokkaanse man?" (note sous: Civ. Bruxelles, 27 octobre 1993) in *Tijdschrift voor Vreemdelingenrecht*, pp. 108–115

——. (1996), "Voyage sur les canaux du droit international privé belge et marocain: le gouvernail de la filiation paternelle dans le mariage" in *Revue du droit des étrangers*, n° 89, pp. 317–340

van Mensel A. (1990), "De houding van de Belgische rechters t.a.v. de echtscheiding door verstoting" [L'attitude des juges belges face à la répudiation], (note sous: Justice de Paix, Gand, 30 avril 1990 et 22 mai 1989) in *Tijdschrift voor Gentse Rechtspraak*, pp. 8–15

Velu J. (1981), *Les effets directs des instruments internationaux en matière des droits de l'homme*, Bruxelles, Swinnen

Venel N. (1999), *Musulmanes françaises. Des pratiquantes voilées à l'université*, Paris, L'Harmattan

Verhoeven J. (1980), "Etat des personnes et compétences consulaires. A propos d'un accord belgo-marocain" in *Journal des Tribunaux*, pp. 717–722

Vertovec S. & Peach C. (eds) (1997), *Islam in Europe. The politics of religion and community*, London-Basingstoke, MacMillan & St. Martin's Press

Vertovec S. & Rogers A. (eds) (1998), *Muslim European Youth—Reproducing Ethnicity, Religion, Culture*, Ashgate, Aldershot

Verwilghen M., Carlier J.-Y., Bedroux C. & de Burlet J. (1991), *L'adoption internationale en droit belge*, Bruxelles, Bruylant

Verwilghen M. (1993), "Renouveau de l'adoption internationale" in M. Verwilghen & R. de Valkeneer (dir.), *op. cit.*, pp. 149–170

Verwilghen M. & de Valkeneer R. (dir.) (1993), *Relations familiales internationales*, Bruxelles, Bruylant von Bar Ch. (dir.) (1999), *Islamic Law and its Reception by the Courts in the West* (Congress, Osnabrück, 23–24 October, 1998), Köln, C. Heymanns

Vonken A.P. (1988), "Rechtsvinding in het hedendaags internationale familierecht" in *Tijdschrift voor Familie- en Jeugdrecht*, pp. 51–99

Waardenburg J. (1988), "The Institutionalization of Islam in the Netherlands, 1961–1986" in T. Gerholm & Y.G. Lithman (eds), *op. cit.*, pp. 8–31

——. (1991), "Muslim associations and official bodies in some European countries" in W.A.R. Shadid & P.S. van Koningsveld (eds), *op. cit.*, pp. 24–42

——. (1997), "Critical Issues in Muslim-Christian Relations: theoretical, practical, dialogical, scholarly" in *Islam and Christian Muslim Relations*, vol. 8, n° 1, pp. 9–26

——. (1998), *Islam et Occident face à face*, Genève, Labor et Fides

——. (2000), "Normative Islam in Europe" in F. Dassetto (ed.), *Paroles d'Islam, op cit.*, pp. 49–68

Warde I. (2000), *Islamic Finance in the Global Economy*, Edinburgh, Edinburgh University Press

——. (2001), "Les principes religieux à l'épreuve de la mondialisation—paradoxes de la finance islamique" in *Le Monde Diplomatique*, sept. 2001, p. 20

Watt M. (1972), *The Influence of Islam on Medieval Europe*, Edinburgh, Edinburgh University Press

Watte N. (1986), "Les relations familiales en droit international privé et l'incidence du principe de l'égalité entre l'homme et la femme" in *Mélanges offerts à Raymond Vander Elst (T. II)*, Bruxelles, Nemesis, pp. 911–928

——. (1993), "Les régimes matrimoniaux dans les relations internationales" in M. Verwilghen & R. de Valkeneer (dir.), *op. cit.*, pp. 239–275

——. (1994), "La loi du régime primaire de couples mixtes est-elle définitivement déterminée?" (note sous Cass., 25 mai 1992) in *Revue générale de droit civil belge*, pp. 127–133

Wayland S.V. (1997), "Religious expression in public schools: kirpans in Canada, hijab in France" in *Ethnic and Racial Studies*, vol. 20, n° 3, pp. 545–561

Weber E. (1997), "Le voile n'est que le début d'une stratégie islamiste . . ." in *Panoramiques* (L'islam est-il soluble dans la République?), n° 29, pp. 68–74

Weibel N. (1992), "Les étrangers et la création d'entreprise en Alsace" in *Revue Européenne des Migrations Internationales*, vol. 8, n° 1, pp. 73–81

——. (1996), "Islamité, égalité et complémentarité: vers une nouvelle approche de l'identité féminine" in *Archives de Sciences sociales des religions*, n° 95, pp. 133–141

——. (2000), *Par-delà le voile. Femmes d'islam en Europe*, Bruxelles, Editions Complexe

Weil P. & Hansen R. (eds) (1999), *Nationalité et citoyenneté en Europe*, Paris, La Découverte

Werbner P. (1996), "Stamping the Earth with the Name of Allah: Zikr and the Sacralizing of Space among British Muslims" in B.D. Metcalf (ed.), *Making Muslim Space in North America and Europe, op. cit.*, pp. 167–185

——. (1996a), "Fun spaces: on identity and social empowerment among British Pakistanis" in *Theory, Culture and Society*, vol. 13, n° 4, pp. 53–79

——. (2002), "The Predicament of Diaspora and Millenial Islam: Reflections in the Aftermath of September 11" in www.ssrc.org/sept 11/essays/werbner.htm

Wihtol de Wenden C. (1985), "L'émergence d'une force politique? Les conflits des immigrés musulmans dans l'entreprise" in *Esprit*, n° 6, pp. 222–231

Wilson B. (1982), *Religion in Sociological Perspective*, Oxford, Oxford University Press

Woehrling J.-M. (1998, Janvier-Mars), "Réflexions sur le principe de la neutralité de l'Etat en matière religieuse et sa mise en œuvre en droit français" in *Archives de Sciences Sociales des Religions*, n° 101, pp. 31–52

X. (1989), *Droit et environnement social au Maghreb*, Paris/Casablanca, CNRS/Fondation du Roi Abdel-Aziz Al Souad

Yalçin-Heckmann L. (1998), "Growing up as a Muslim in Germany: religious socialization among Turkish migrant families" in S. Vertovec & A. Rogers (eds), *Muslim European Youth, op. cit.*, pp. 167–192

Yavuz M.H. (1995), "The patterns of political Islamic identity: dynamics of national and transnational loyalties and identities" in *Central Asian Survey*, vol. 14, n° 3, pp. 341–372

——. (1999), "Towards an Islamic liberalism? The Nursis movement and Fetullah Gülen" in *Middle East Journal*, vol. LIII, n° 4, pp. 584–605

——. (2000), "Being Modern in the Nursis way" in *ISIM Newsletter*, n° 6, Leiden, p. 7

Yegane Arani A. (1999), "Religion als medium der integration. Die Baha'i in Deutschland" in G. Jonker, *Kern und Rand, op. cit.*, pp. 91–114

Zarcone T. (1996), "La Naqchbandiyya", "La Qâdiriyya", "La mevleviye, confrérie des derviches tourneurs" in A. Popovic & G. Veinstein (dir.), *op. cit.*, pp. 451–460, 461–467, 504–508

Zebiri K. (1995), "Relations between Muslims and non-Muslims in the thought of Western-educated Muslim intellectuals" in *Islam and Christian-Muslim Relations*, vol. 6, n° 2, pp. 255–277

——. (1997), *Muslims and Christians face to face*, Oxford, One World

Zghal A. (1981), "Le retour du sacré et la nouvelle demande idéologique" in CRESM, *Le Maghreb Musulman en 1979*, Paris, CNRS, pp. 41–64

Zhelyazkova A. (2001), "Bulgaria in transition: the Muslim minorities" in *Islam and Christian-Muslim Relations*, vol. 12, n° 3, pp. 283–301

Zhelyazkova A., Kepel G. & Nielsen J. (1995), *Relations of Compatibility and Incompatibility between Christians and Muslims in Bulgaria*, Sofia, International Centre for Minority Studies and Intercultural Relations Foundation

Ziakas G.G. (1995), "The reality of education in Greece: the picture of the muslim in school textbooks and the mass media" in *Islamochristiana*, n° 21, pp. 65–74

APPENDIX

- Austria [AU]: Anna Strobl, Karl-Franzens University, Graz
- Germany [DE]: Schirin Amir-Moazami, European University Institute, Florence
- Belgium [BE]: Brigitte Maréchal, CiMOC, Catholic University of Louvain-la-Neuve
- Bulgaria [BG]: Antonina Zhelyazkova, International Centre for Minority Studies and Intercultural Relations, Sofia
- Denmark [DK]: Jorgen Baeck Simonsen, The Carsten Niebuhr Institute for Near Eastern Studies, Copenhagen
- Spain [ES]: Jordi Moreras, CIDOB, Barcelona
- Finland [FI]: Tuula Sakaranaho, University of Helsinki
- France [FR]: Franck Frégosi, Robert Schuman University, Strasbourg
- United Kingdom [UK]: Jorgen Nielsen, Centre for the Study of Islam and Christian-Muslim Relations University of Birmingham
- Greece [GR]: Samim Akgonül (Centre de recherche sur l'Asie intérieure, le monde turc et l'espace ottoman, Strasbourg) and Gilles de Rapper (Institut d'Ethnologie méditerranéenne et comparative, Aix-en Provence)
- Hungary [HU]: Andras Mate-Toth, Documentary Centre of Denominations in Hungary, University of Szeged
- Italy [IT]: Stefano Allievi, University of Padova
- Luxembourg [LU]: Sylvain Besch, SESOPI, Luxembourg
- Poland [PL]: Stanislaw Grodz, Catholic University of Lublin
- The Netherlands [NL]: Nico Landman, University of Utrecht
- Portugal [PT]: Nina Clara Tiesler, University of Hanover
- Roumania [RO]: Zhivko Georgiev, BBSS Gallup, Bucarest
- Sweden [SE]: Jonas Otterbeeck, University of Lund
- Switzerland [CH]: Hans Mahnig, University of Neuchâtel

THE AUTHORS

Allievi Stefano, Ph.D. in sociology and social research, researcher and lecturer of sociology at the university of Padova. Specialised on sociology of migration and sociology of Islam. Among others books and publications: *La sfida dell'immigrazione*, Bologna, EMI, 1991; *Les convertis à l'islam*, Paris, L'Harmattan, 1998; *Muslim Networks and Transnational Communities in and across Europe*, Leiden, Brill, 2003 published with J. Nielsen.

Dassetto Felice, Ph.D. in sociology. Professor of sociology and socio-anthropology of Islam at the Catholic University of Louvain (UCL); in charge of the CIMOC, Centre for Interdisciplinary Research on Islam in Contemporary World. Among others books and articles: *La construction de l'islam européen*, Paris, L'Harmattan, 1996; *Islamic Words. Individuals, Societies and Discourse in Contemporary European Islam* (ed.), Paris, Maisonneuve-Larose, 2000.

Ferrari Silvio, Ph.D., professor of Law and of Canon Law at the faculty of jurisprudence, University of Milan. Specialised in the relations between States and Religions. Among other publications: S. Ferrari and A. Bradney (eds), *Islam and European Legal Status*, Aldershot, Ashgate, 2000; *Law and Religion in Post-Communist Europe*, Leuven, Peeters, 2003, edited with C.W. Durham and E. Sewell.

Foblets Marie-Claire, lawyers, Ph.D. in anthropology, professor of law and anthropology at the universities of Leuven (K.U.L.), Antwerpen (U.I.A.) and Brussels (K.U.B.). Many publications on family law. Among others: *Les familles maghrébines et la justice en Belgique: anthropologie juridique et émigration*, Paris, Karthala, 1994; *Famille, islam, Europe: le droit confronté au changement*, Paris, L'Harmattan, 1996.

Maréchal Brigitte, degrees in political science and islamology at the University of Louvain and at the *Institut Français d'Etudes Arabes* of Damascus. Research on the relations between Europe and Arabic world and on Egyptian newspaper reporting of European social behaviour. Actually preparing a thesis on the movement of Muslim

Brothers in Europe. Coordination of the book: *A Guidebook on Islam and Muslims in the Wide Contemporary Europe*, Louvain-la-Neuve, Academia/Bruylant, 2002.

Nielsen Jørgen, Ph.D., islamologist, professor at the University of Birmingham, Director of the Centre for the Study of Islam and Christian-Islam relations. Author of many books on European Islam, namely: *Muslims in Western Europe*, Edinburgh University Press, 1995 (2nd edition); *Towards a European Islam*, London, MacMillan, 1999; *Muslim Networks and Transnational Communities in and across Europe*, Leiden, Brill, 2003 (published with S. Allievi).

THEMATIC INDEX

INDEX OF AUTHORS

INDEX OF MUSLIM MEDIAS

INDEX OF MUSLIM PERSONALITIES

INDEX OF ORGANISATIONS AND
IDEOLOGICAL MOVEMENTS

MUSLIM MINORITIES

ISSN 1570-7571

1. Allievi, S. & Nielsen, J. (eds.). *Muslim Networks and Transnational Communities in and across Europe.* 2003. ISBN 90 04 12858 1
2. Maréchal, B., Allievi, S., Dassetto, F. & Nielsen, J. (eds.). *Muslims in the Enlarged Europe.* Religion and Society. 2003. ISBN 90 04 13201 5